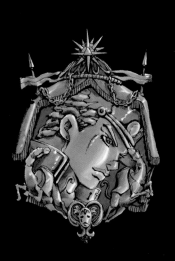

07

JOJO'S
BIZARRE ADVENTURE

PART 3
STARDUST CRUSADERS

荒 木 飛 呂 彦

HIROHIKO ARAKI

JoJo's Bizarre Adventure
PART 3 STARDUST CRUSADERS

CONTENTS

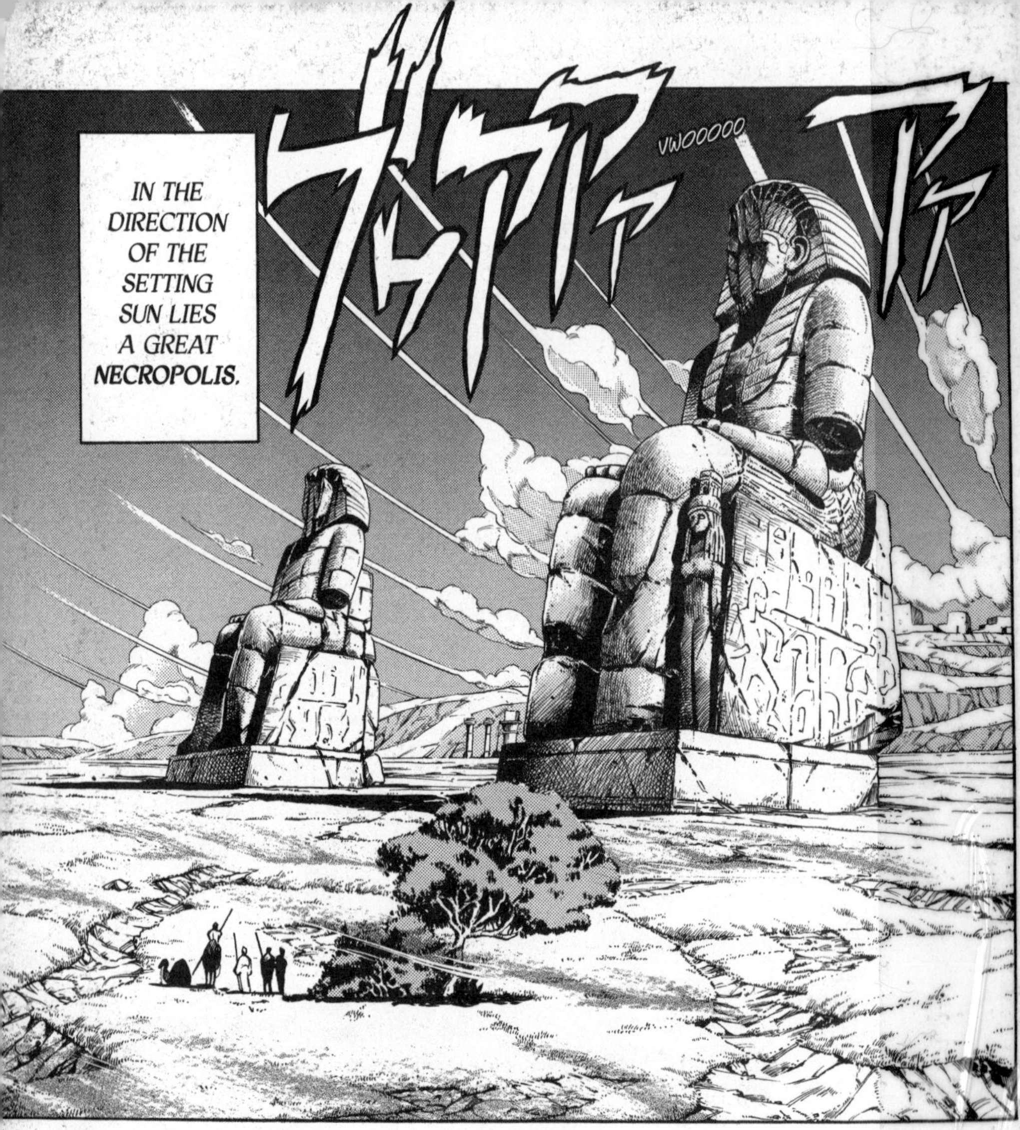
IN THE DIRECTION OF THE SETTING SUN LIES A GREAT NECROPOLIS.
VWOOOOO

CHAPTER 86: "Bast" Mariah PART 1

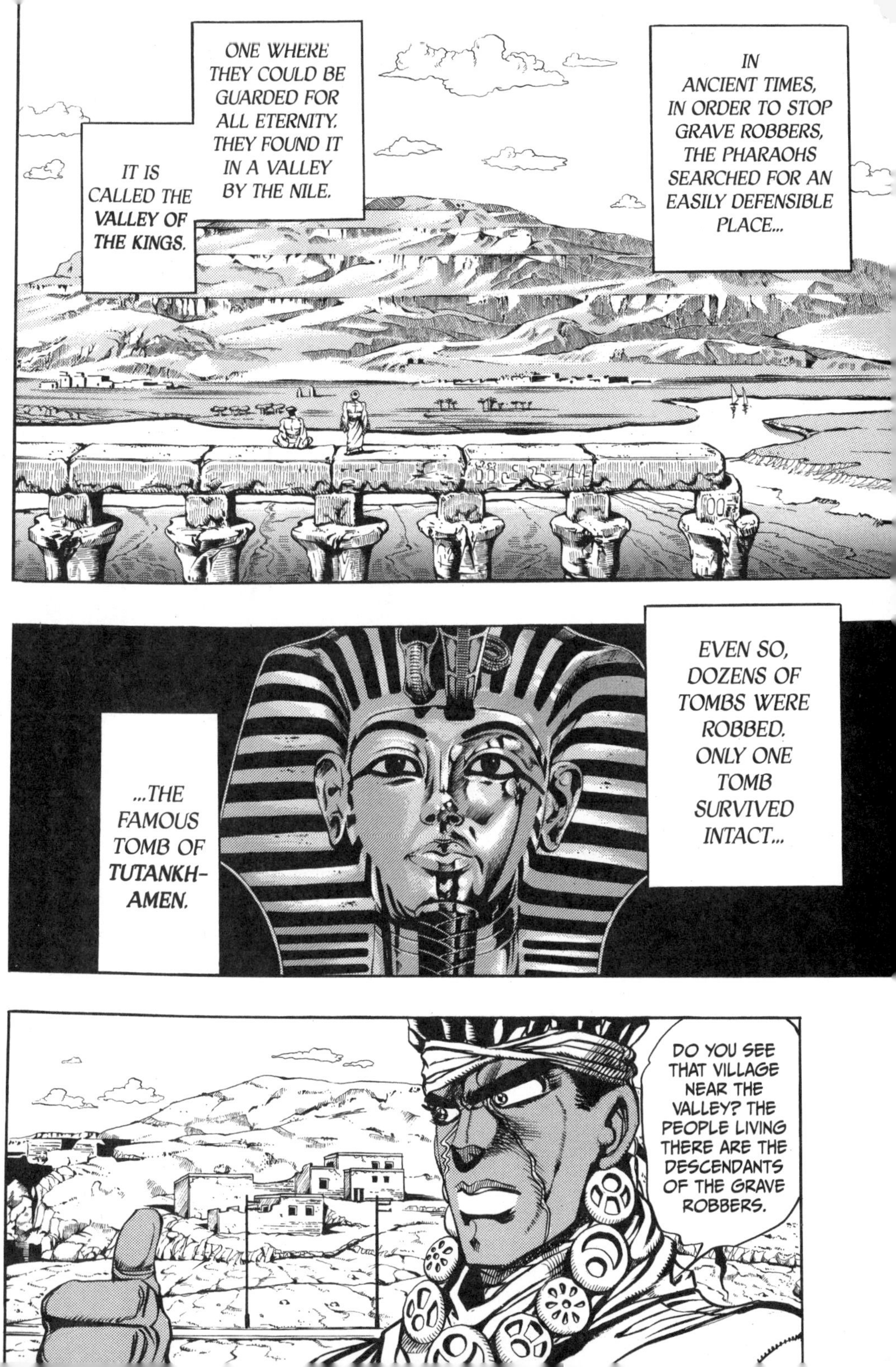
IN ANCIENT TIMES, IN ORDER TO STOP GRAVE ROBBERS, THE PHARAOHS SEARCHED FOR AN EASILY DEFENSIBLE PLACE...
ONE WHERE THEY COULD BE GUARDED FOR ALL ETERNITY. THEY FOUND IT IN A VALLEY BY THE NILE.
IT IS CALLED THE VALLEY OF THE KINGS.
EVEN SO, DOZENS OF TOMBS WERE ROBBED. ONLY ONE TOMB SURVIVED INTACT...
...THE FAMOUS TOMB OF TUTANKH-AMEN.
DO YOU SEE THAT VILLAGE NEAR THE VALLEY? THE PEOPLE LIVING THERE ARE THE DESCENDANTS OF THE GRAVE ROBBERS.

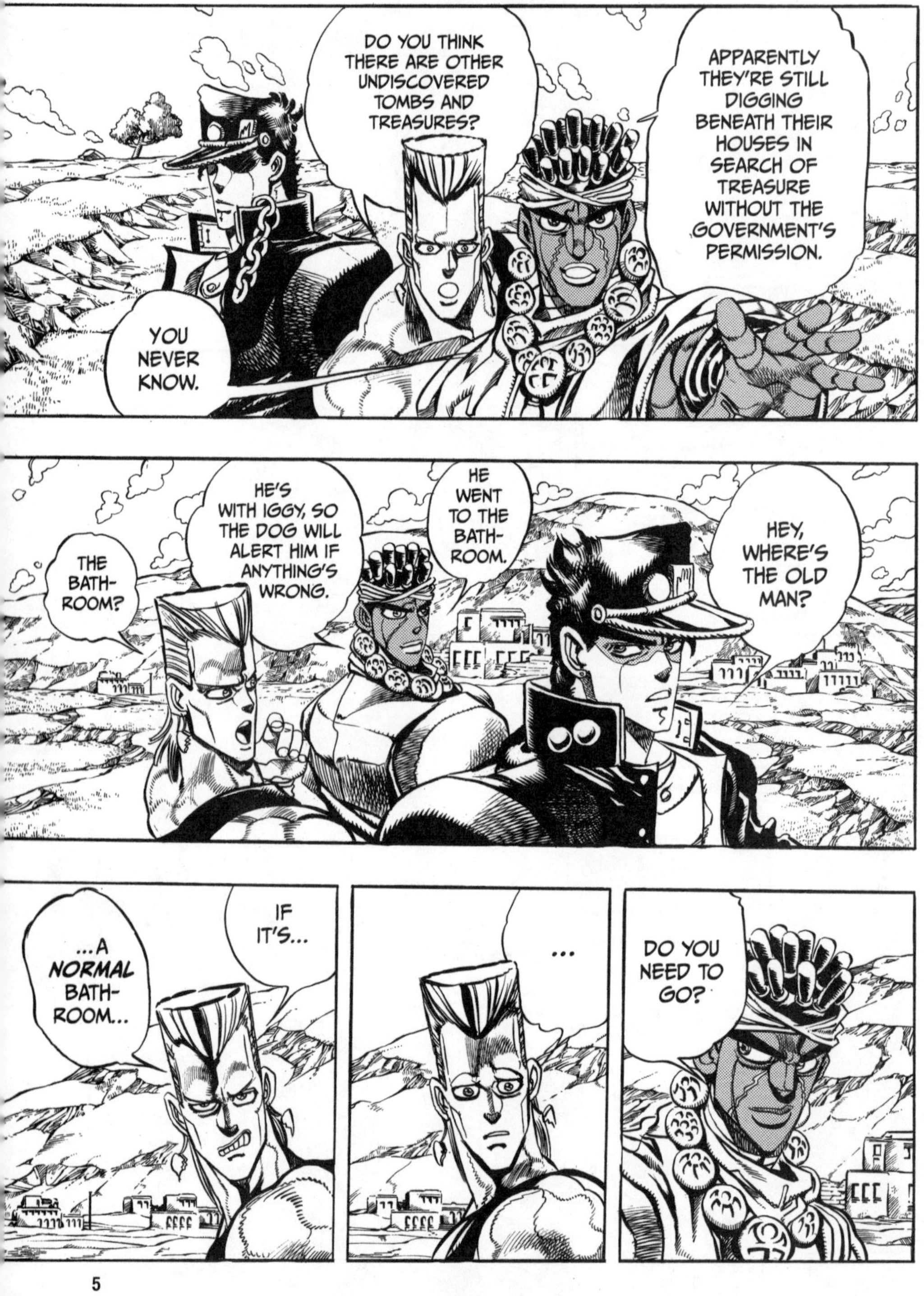
APPARENTLY THEY'RE STILL DIGGING BENEATH THEIR HOUSES IN SEARCH OF TREASURE WITHOUT THE GOVERNMENT'S PERMISSION.
DO YOU THINK THERE ARE OTHER UNDISCOVERED TOMBS AND TREASURES?
YOU NEVER KNOW.
HEY, WHERE'S THE OLD MAN?
HE WENT TO THE BATH-ROOM.
THE BATH-ROOM?
HE'S WITH IGGY, SO THE DOG WILL ALERT HIM IF ANYTHING'S WRONG.
DO YOU NEED TO GO?
...
IF IT'S...
...A **NORMAL** BATH-ROOM...

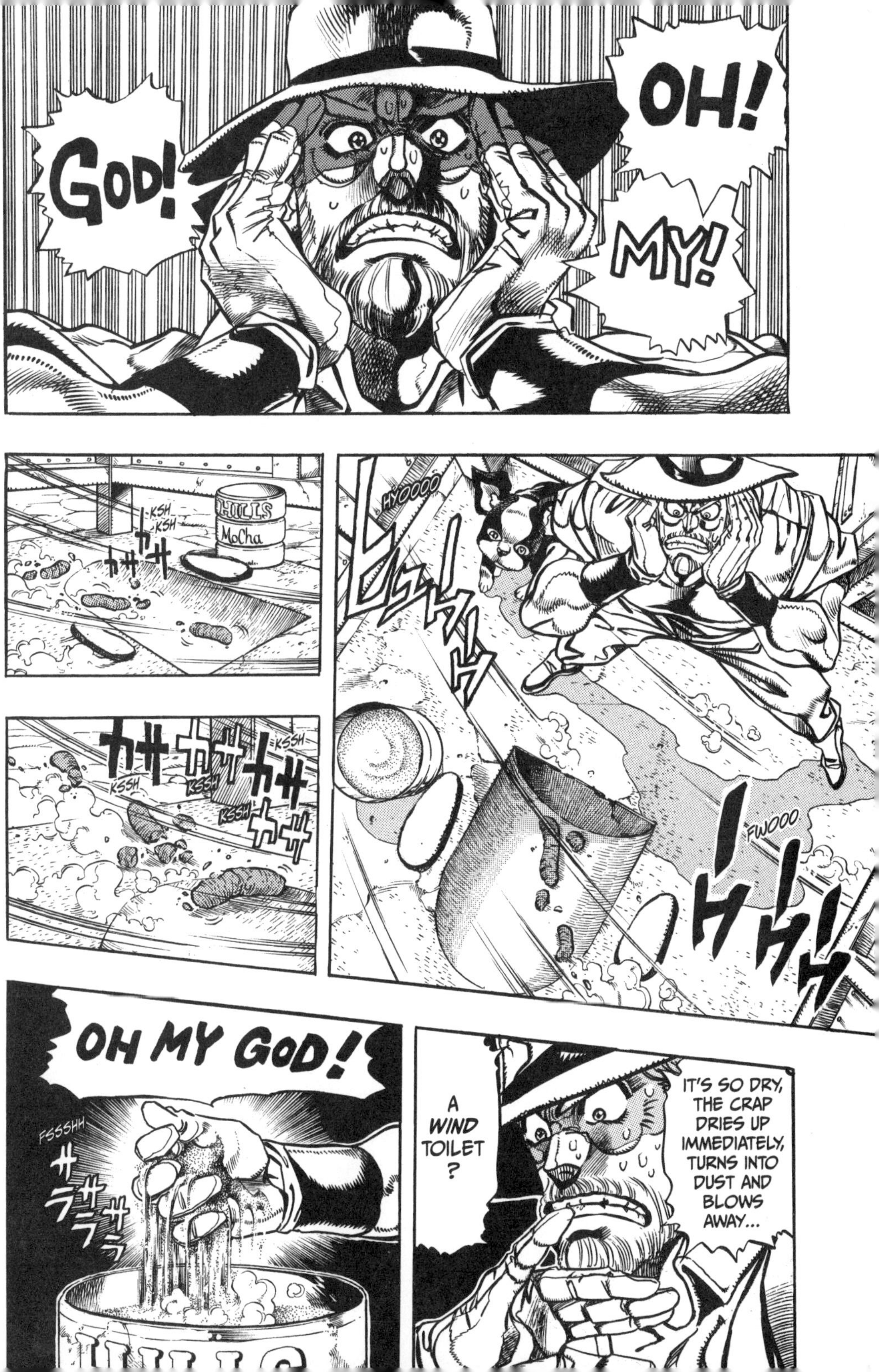
OH!
MY!
GOD!
HYOOOO
FWOOO
HILLS
MoCha
KSH
KSH
KSSH
KSSH
KSSH
KSSH
IT'S SO DRY, THE CRAP DRIES UP IMMEDIATELY, TURNS INTO DUST AND BLOWS AWAY...
A WIND TOILET ?
OH MY GOD!
FSSSHH

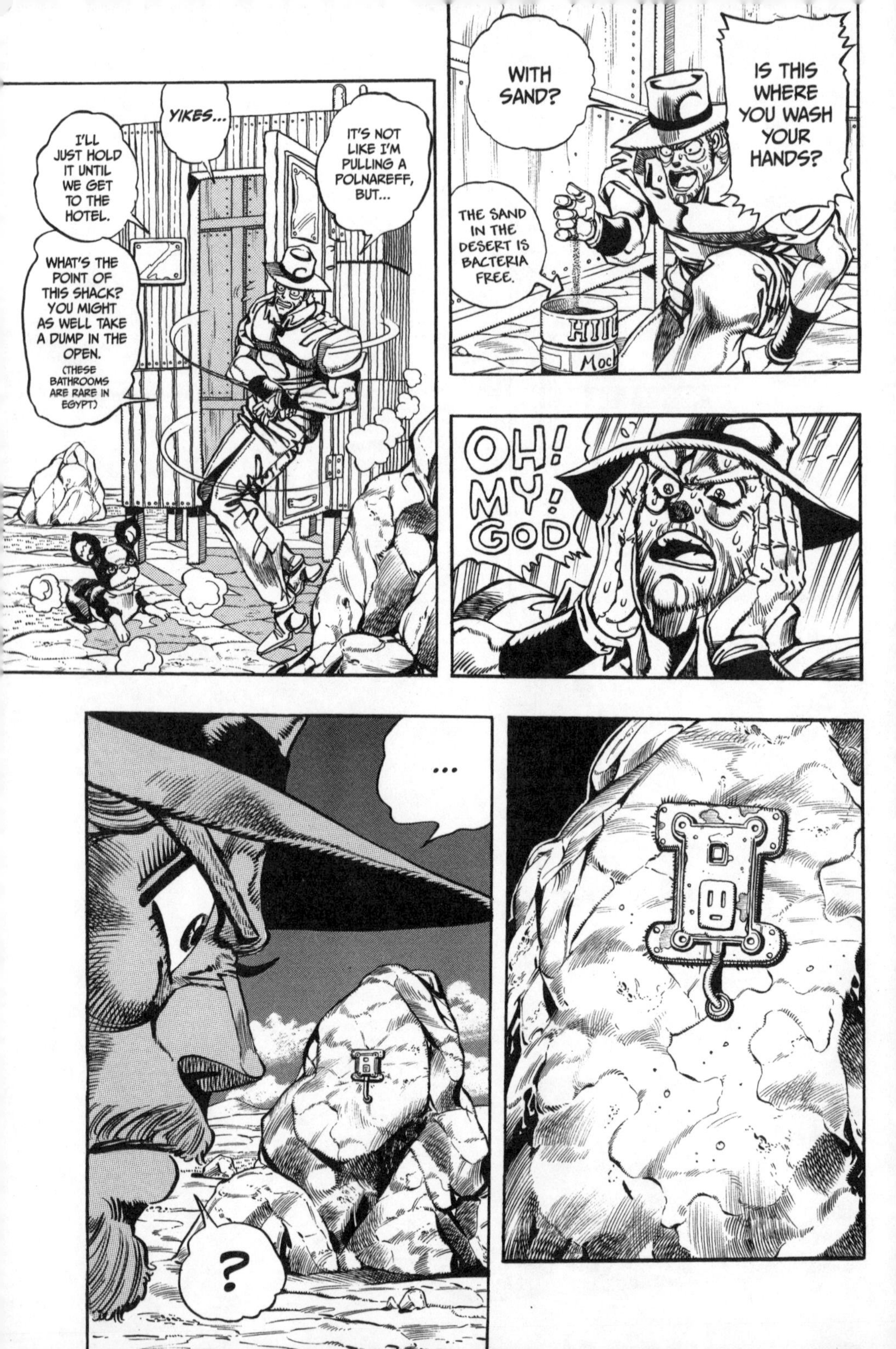
IS THIS WHERE YOU WASH YOUR HANDS?
WITH SAND?
THE SAND IN THE DESERT IS BACTERIA FREE.
HILL
Moc
OH! MY! GOD
IT'S NOT LIKE I'M PULLING A POLNAREFF, BUT...
YIKES...
I'LL JUST HOLD IT UNTIL WE GET TO THE HOTEL.
WHAT'S THE POINT OF THIS SHACK? YOU MIGHT AS WELL TAKE A DUMP IN THE OPEN.
(THESE BATHROOMS ARE RARE IN EGYPT)
...
?

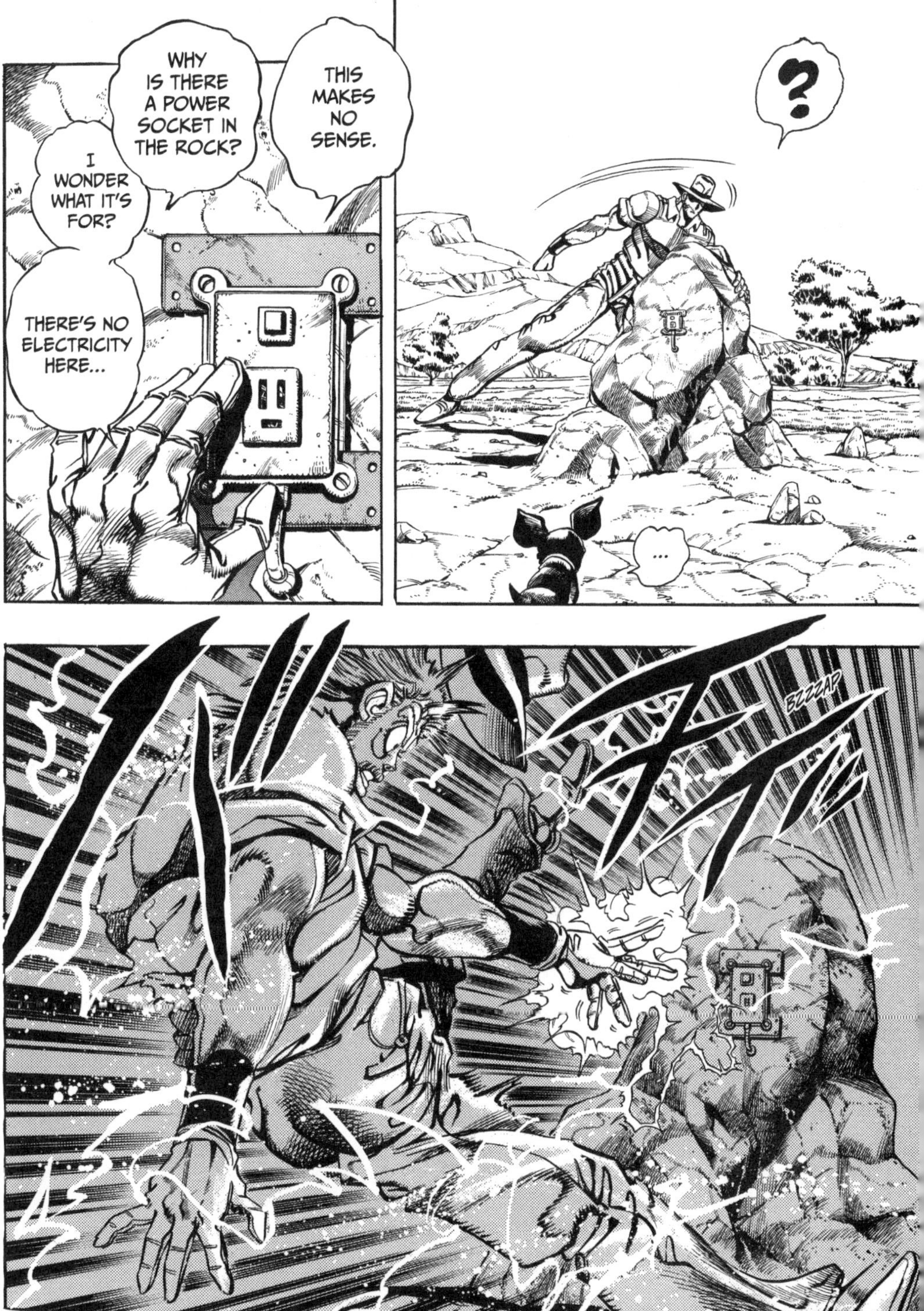
?
...
THIS MAKES NO SENSE.
WHY IS THERE A POWER SOCKET IN THE ROCK?
I WONDER WHAT IT'S FOR?
THERE'S NO ELECTRICITY HERE...
BZZZAP

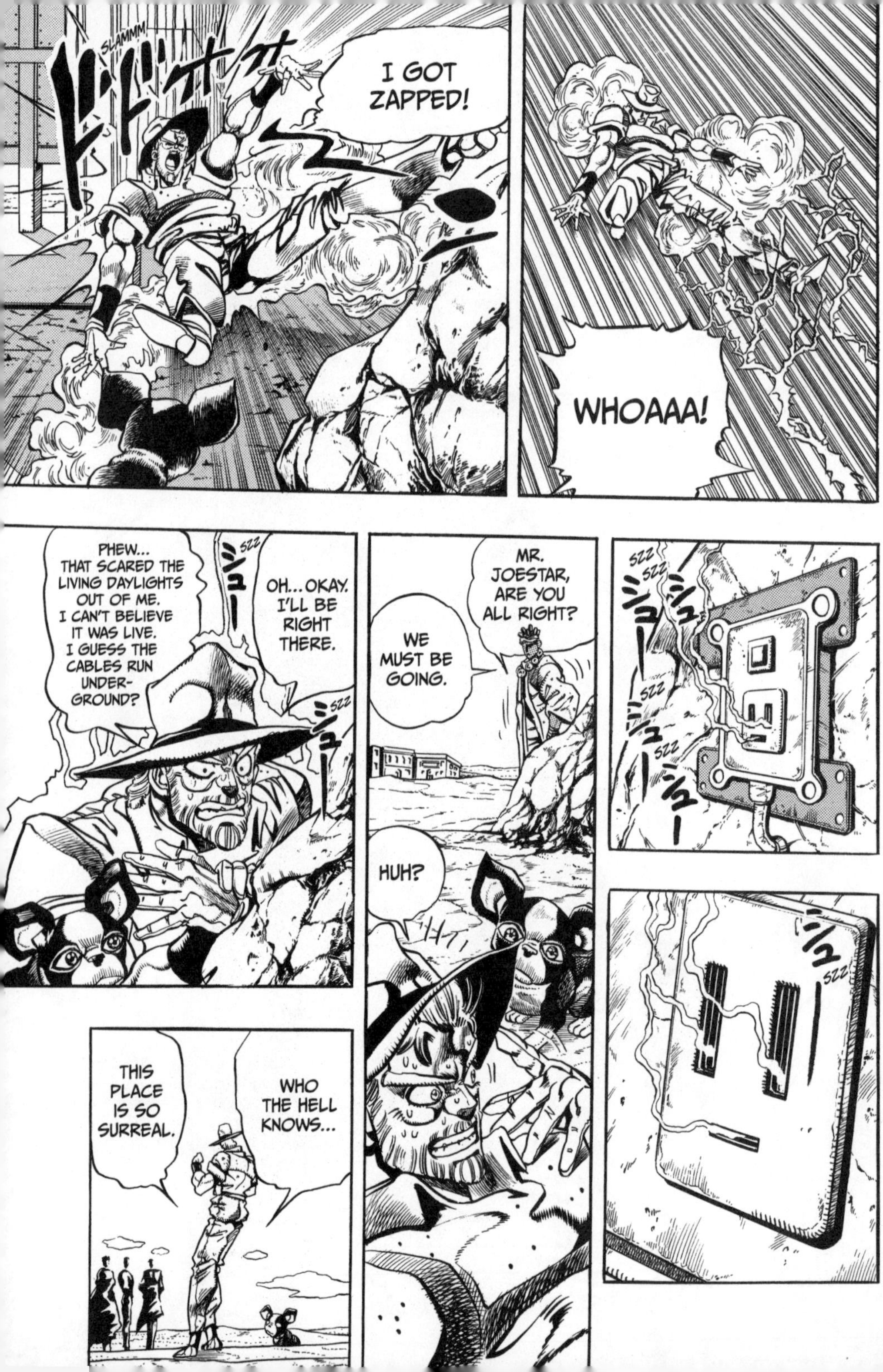
WHOAAA!
SLAMMM
I GOT ZAPPED!
SZZ SZZ
SZZ
SZZ
SZZ
MR. JOESTAR, ARE YOU ALL RIGHT?
WE MUST BE GOING.
HUH?
SZZ
OH... OKAY. I'LL BE RIGHT THERE.
PHEW... THAT SCARED THE LIVING DAYLIGHTS OUT OF ME. I CAN'T BELIEVE IT WAS LIVE. I GUESS THE CABLES RUN UNDER-GROUND?
SZZ
WHO THE HELL KNOWS...
THIS PLACE IS SO SURREAL.

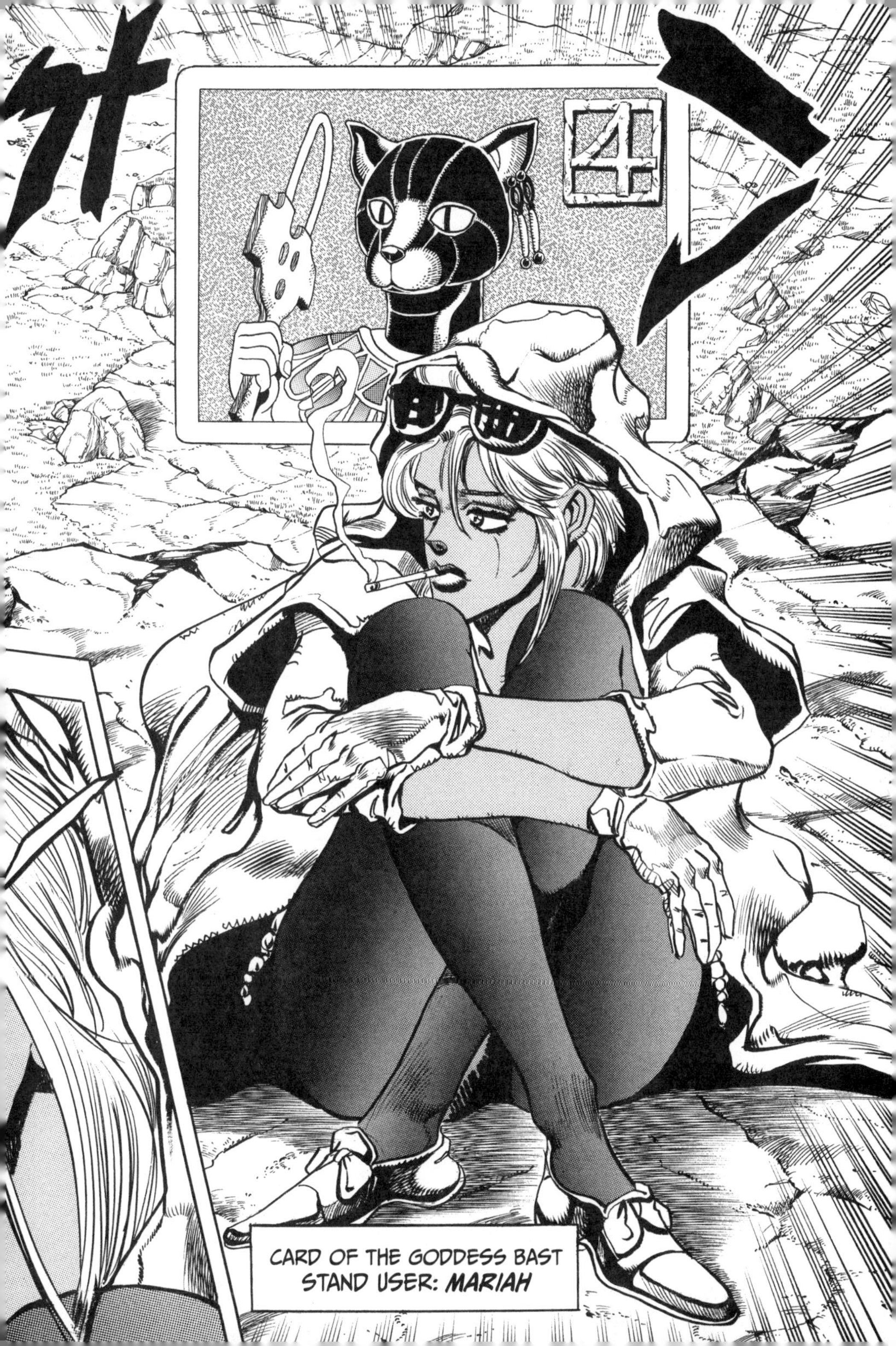
CARD OF THE GODDESS BAST
STAND USER: *MARIAH*

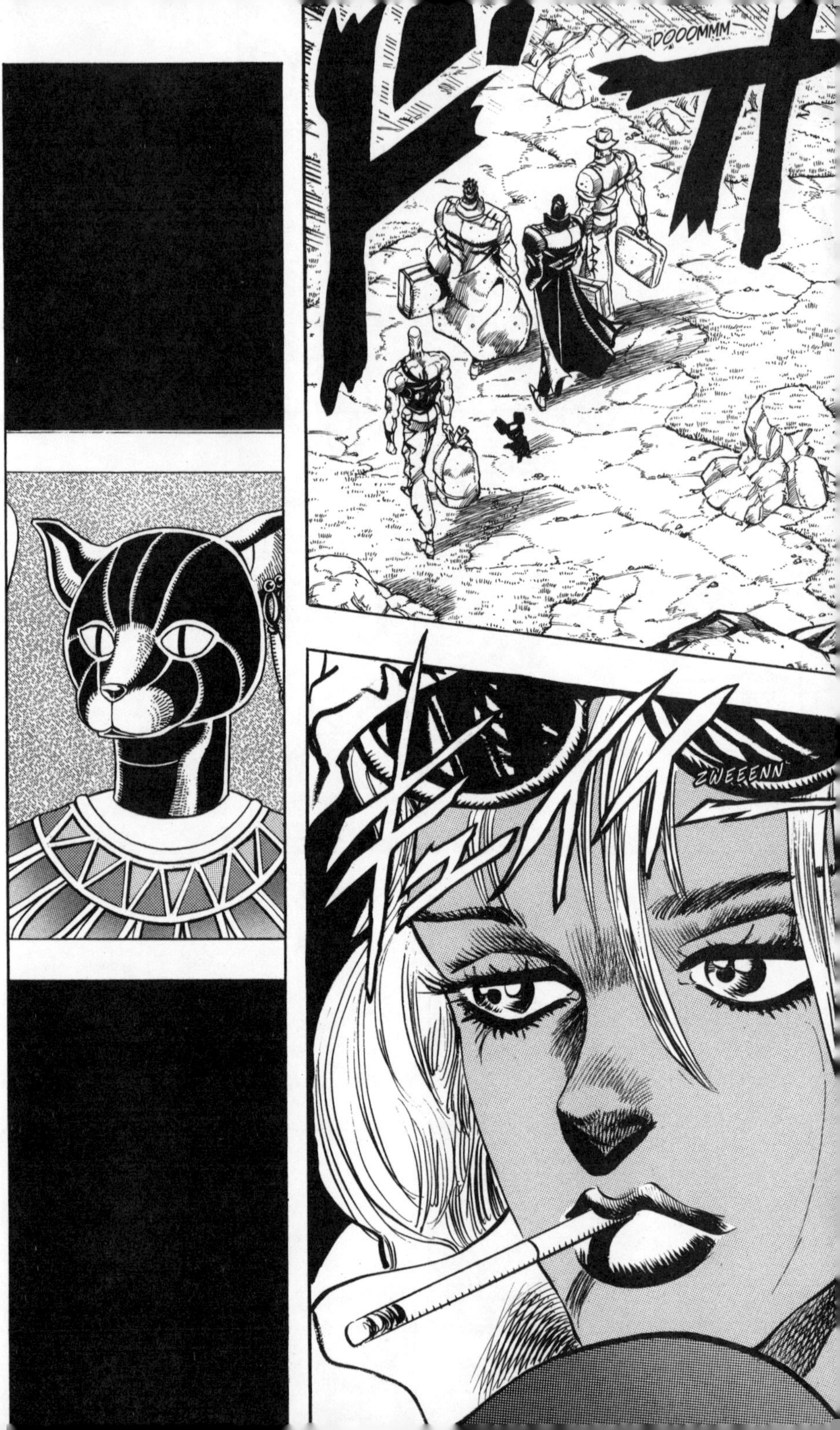
DOOOMMM
ZWEEENN

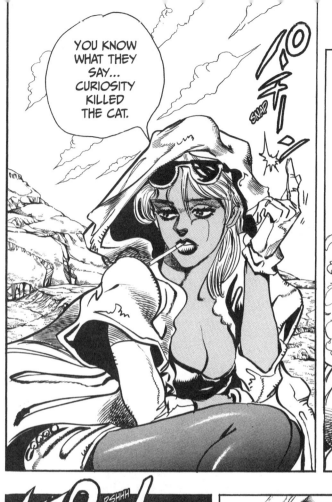

YOU KNOW WHAT THEY SAY... CURIOSITY KILLED THE CAT.

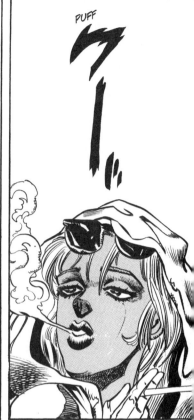

PUFF

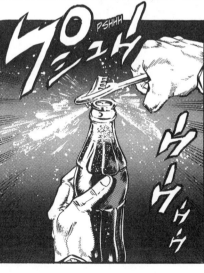

PSHHH

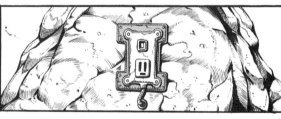

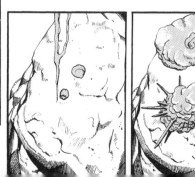

POOF

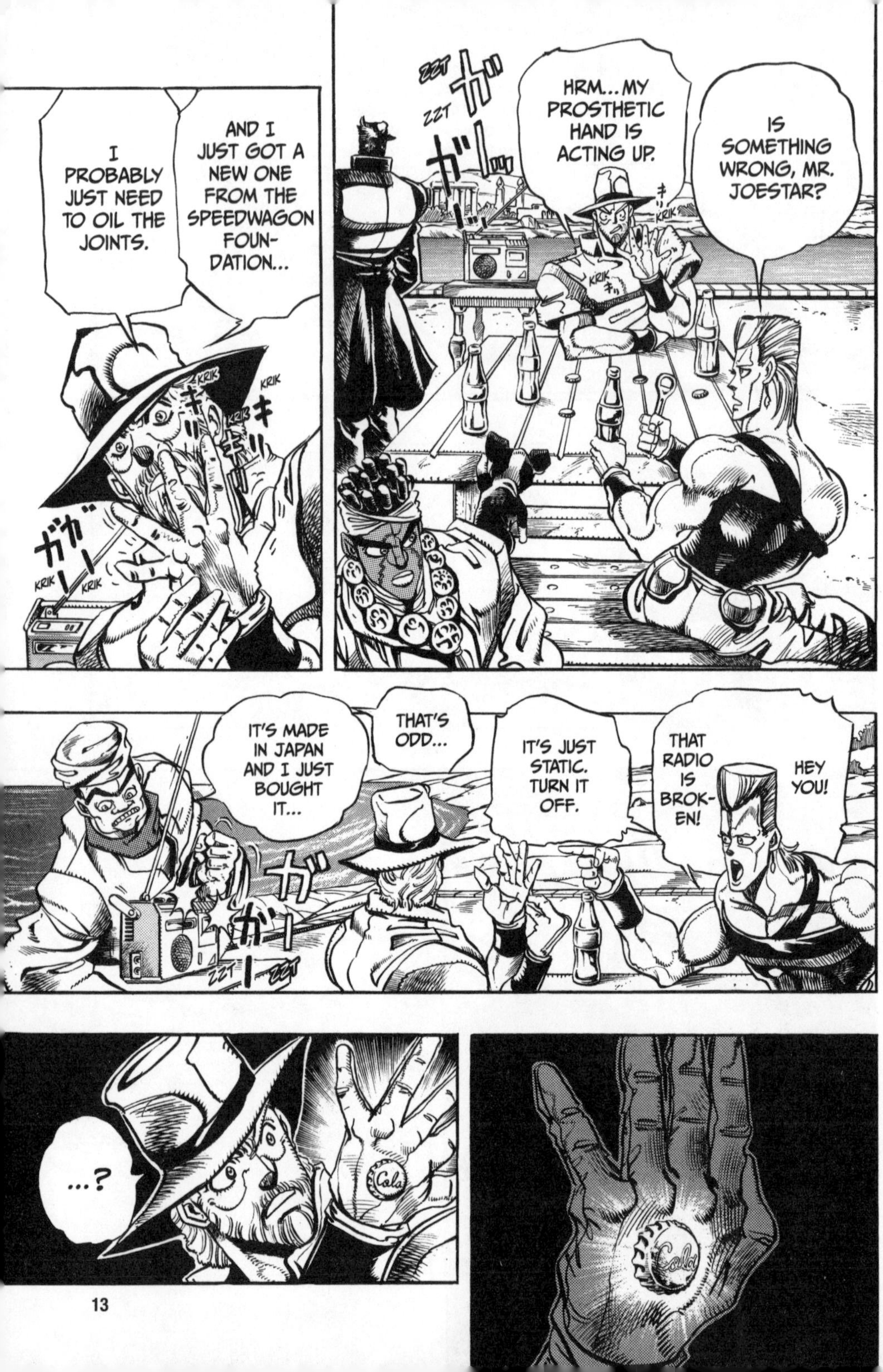
ZZT
ZZT
IS SOMETHING WRONG, MR. JOESTAR?
HRM... MY PROSTHETIC HAND IS ACTING UP.
KRIK
KRIK
AND I JUST GOT A NEW ONE FROM THE SPEEDWAGON FOUNDATION...
I PROBABLY JUST NEED TO OIL THE JOINTS.
KRIK
KRIK
KRIK
KRIK
KRIK
HEY YOU!
THAT RADIO IS BROKEN!
IT'S JUST STATIC. TURN IT OFF.
THAT'S ODD...
IT'S MADE IN JAPAN AND I JUST BOUGHT IT...
ZZT
ZZT
Cola
...?
Cola

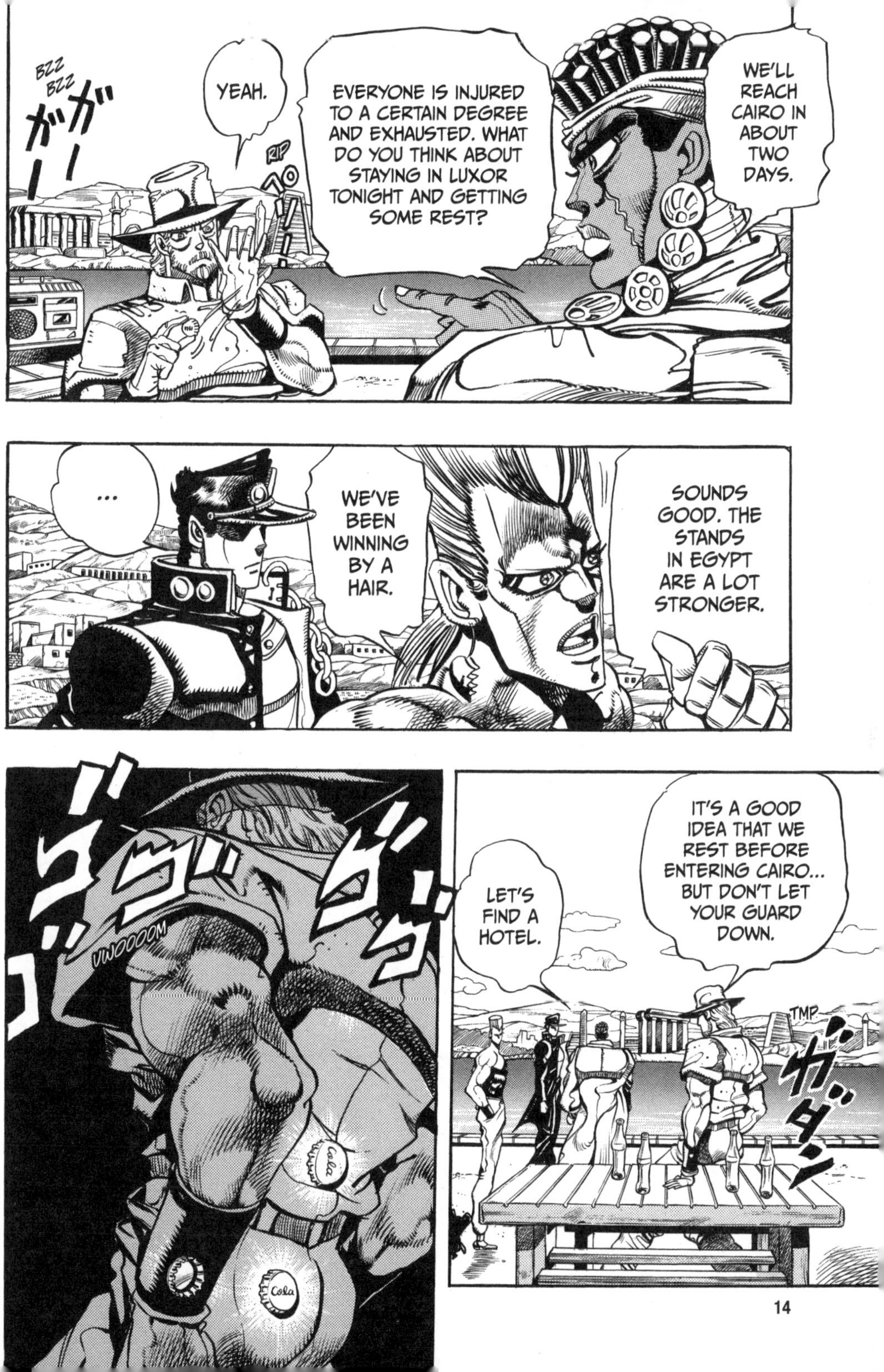

WE'LL REACH CAIRO IN ABOUT TWO DAYS.
EVERYONE IS INJURED TO A CERTAIN DEGREE AND EXHAUSTED. WHAT DO YOU THINK ABOUT STAYING IN LUXOR TONIGHT AND GETTING SOME REST?
RIP
YEAH.
BZZ BZZ
SOUNDS GOOD. THE STANDS IN EGYPT ARE A LOT STRONGER.
WE'VE BEEN WINNING BY A HAIR.
...
IT'S A GOOD IDEA THAT WE REST BEFORE ENTERING CAIRO... BUT DON'T LET YOUR GUARD DOWN.
TMP
LET'S FIND A HOTEL.
UWOOOOM

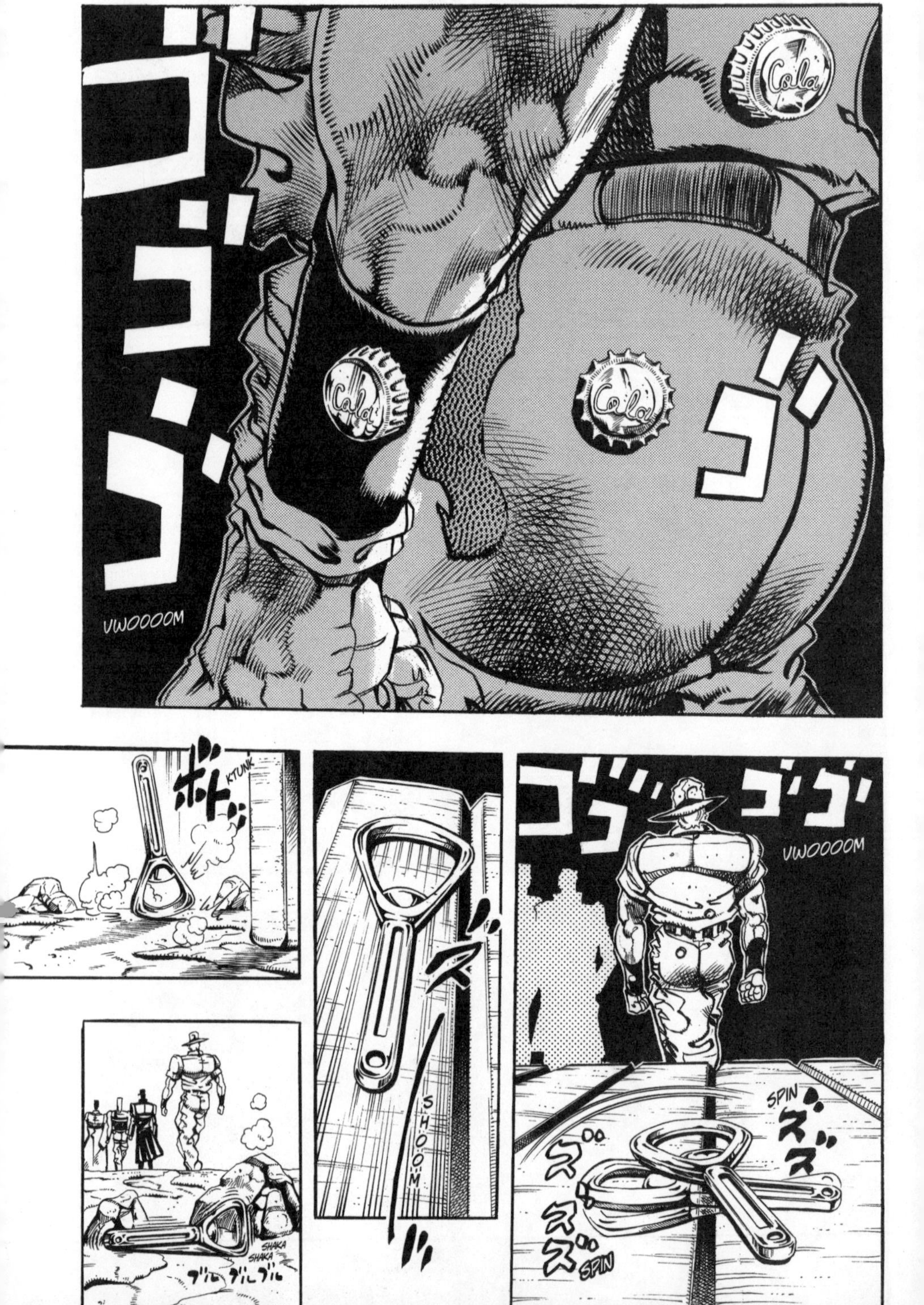
ゴ
ゴゴゴゴ
UWOOOOM
ゴゴゴゴ
UWOOOOM
SPIN
ズズズ
ズズズ
SPIN
SHOOOM
ボトッ
KTUNK
SHAKA
SHAKA
ブルブルブル

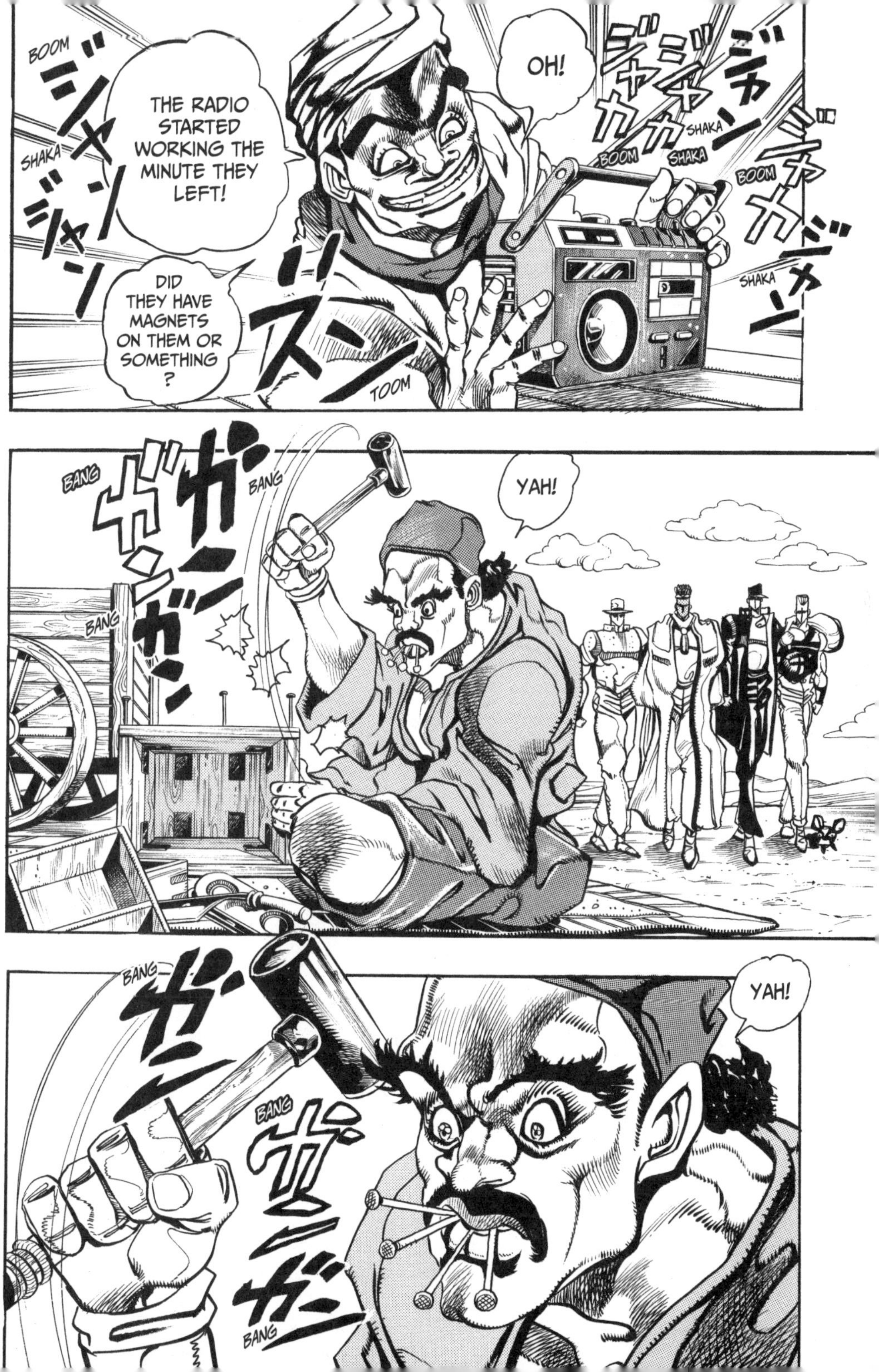

BOOM
SHAKA
BOOM
SHAKA
SHAKA
BOOM
OH!
THE RADIO STARTED WORKING THE MINUTE THEY LEFT!
BOOM
SHAKA
DID THEY HAVE MAGNETS ON THEM OR SOMETHING?
TOOM
YAH!
BANG
BANG
BANG
YAH!
BANG
BANG
BANG

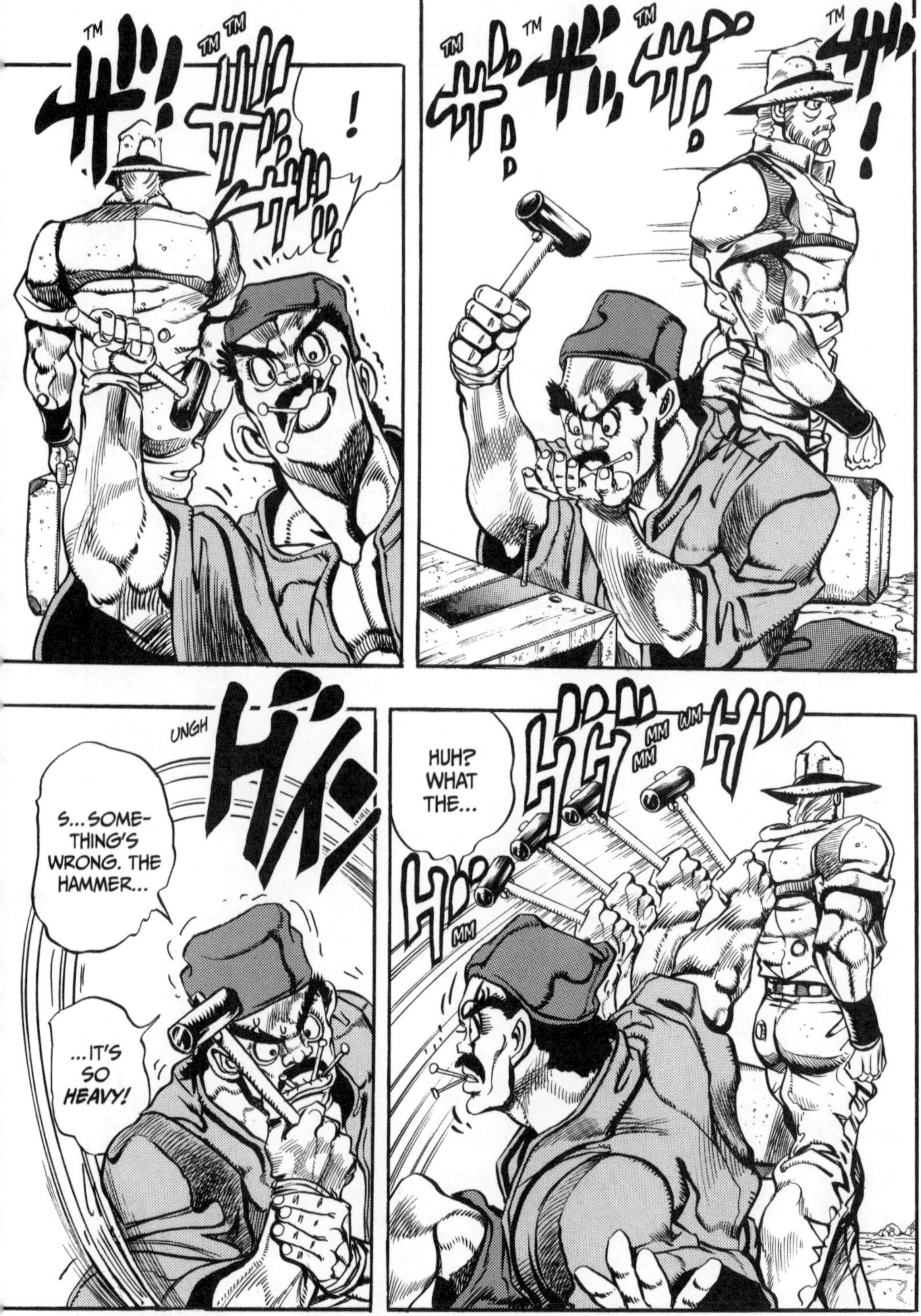
TM
TM
TM
TM
TM
TM
TM
TM
!
!
HUH? WHAT THE...
MM
WM
MM
MM
MM
UNGH
S...SOME-THING'S WRONG. THE HAMMER...
...IT'S SO *HEAVY!*

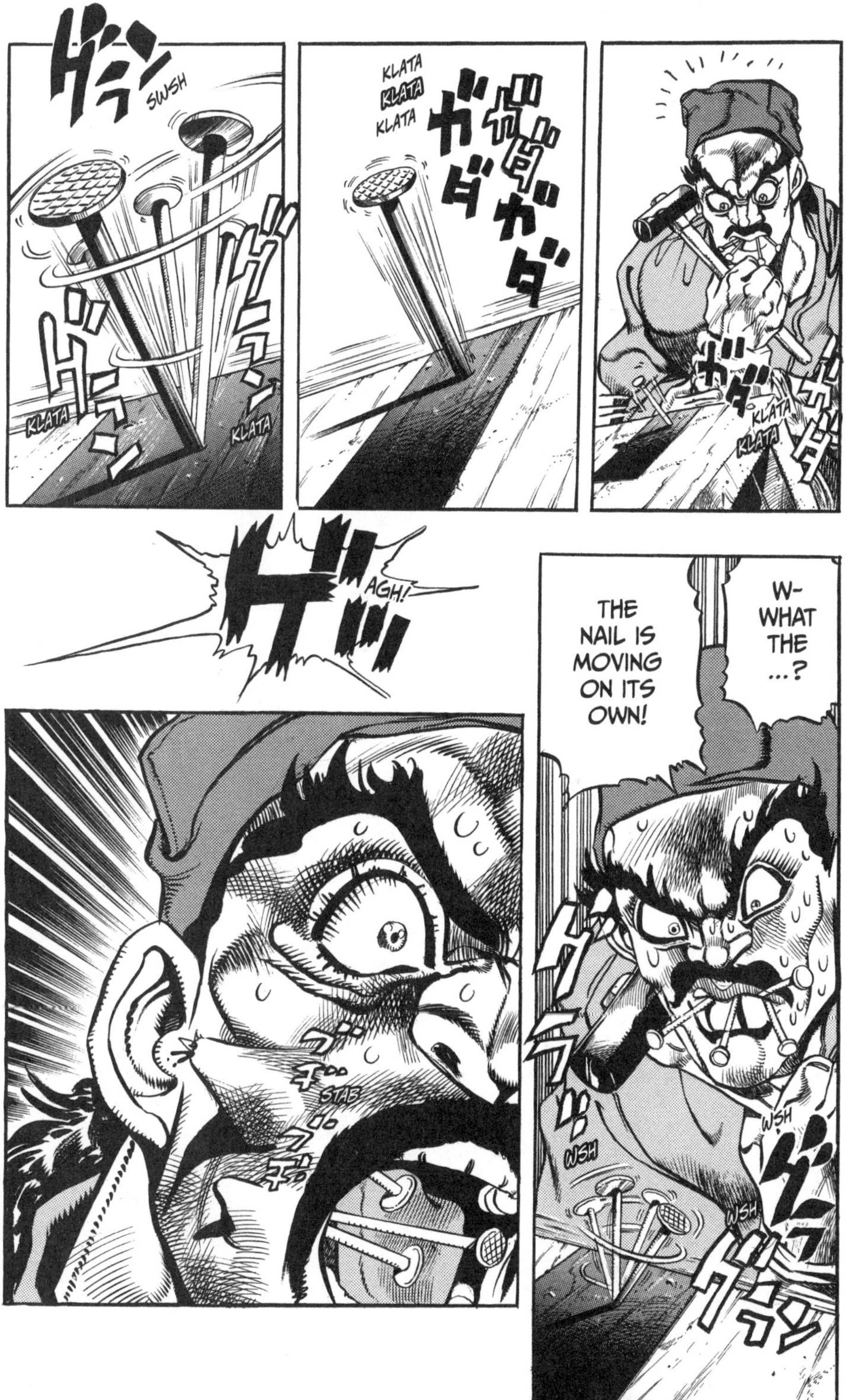
KLATA
KLATA
KLATA
KLATA
KLATA
SWSH
KLATA
KLATA
W- WHAT THE ...?
THE NAIL IS MOVING ON ITS OWN!
WSH
WSH
WSH
AGH!
STAB

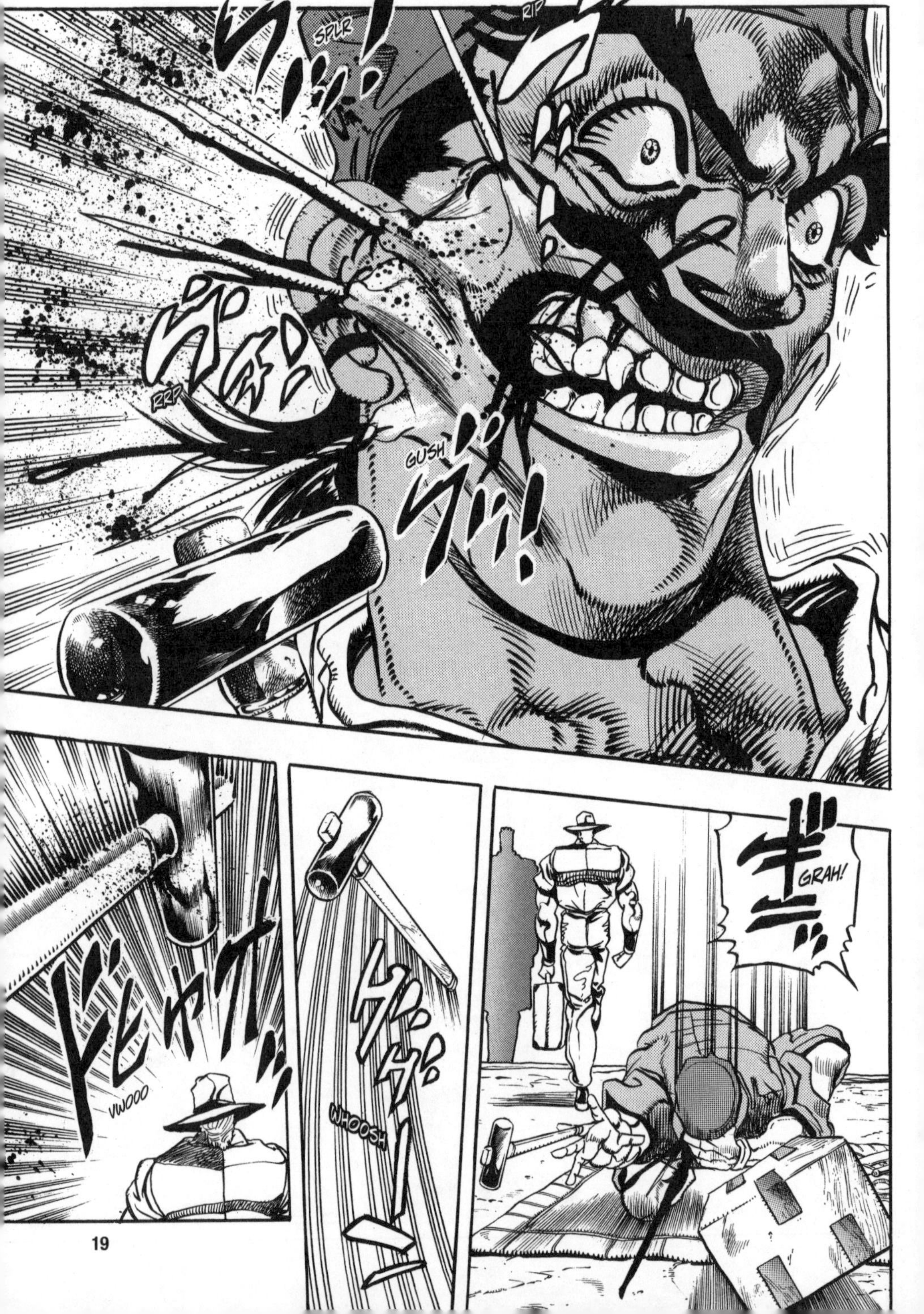
RIP
SPLR
RRP
GUSH
GRAH!
WHOOSH
VWOOO

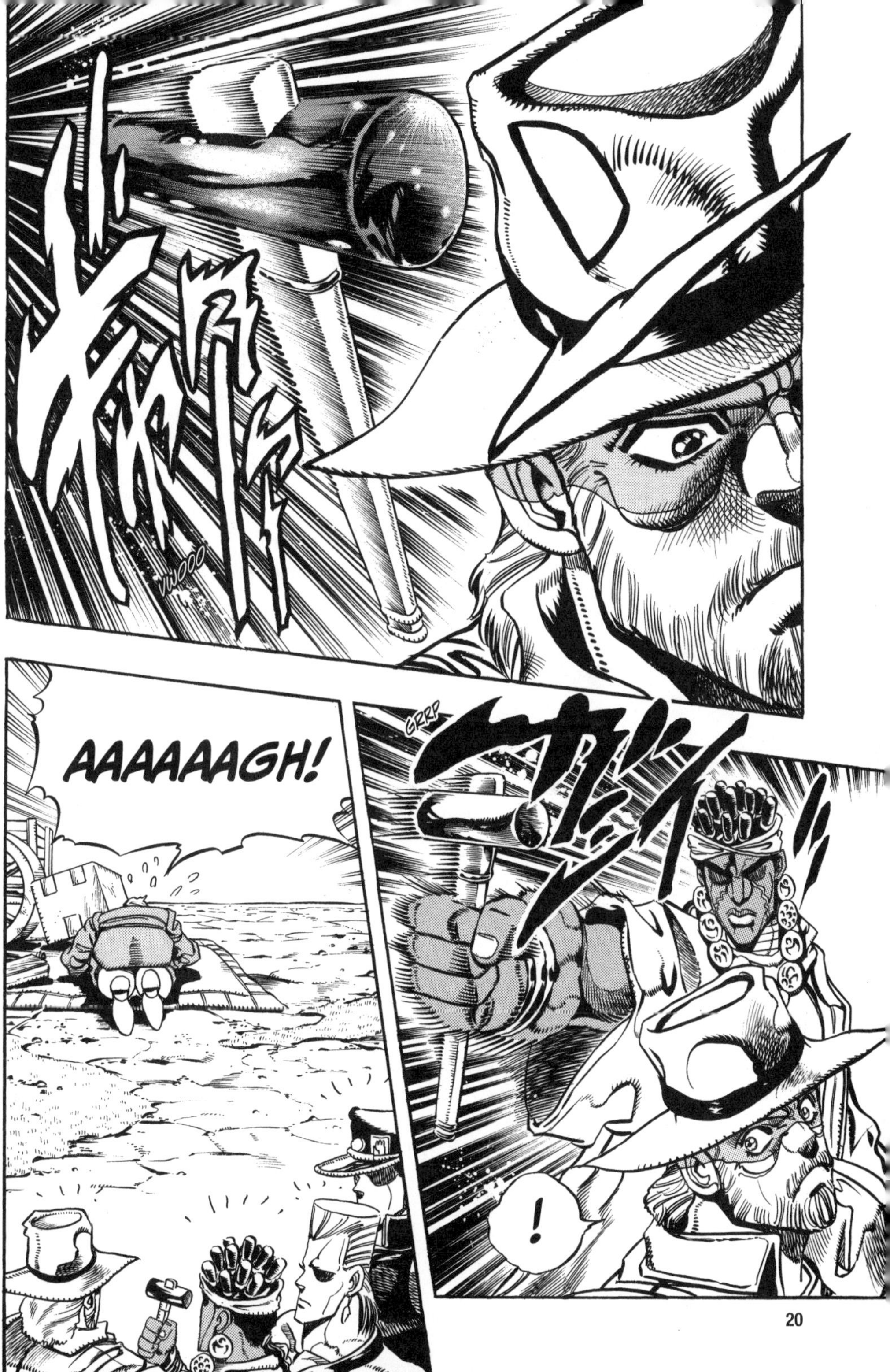
VWOOO
GRRP
!
AAAAAAGH!

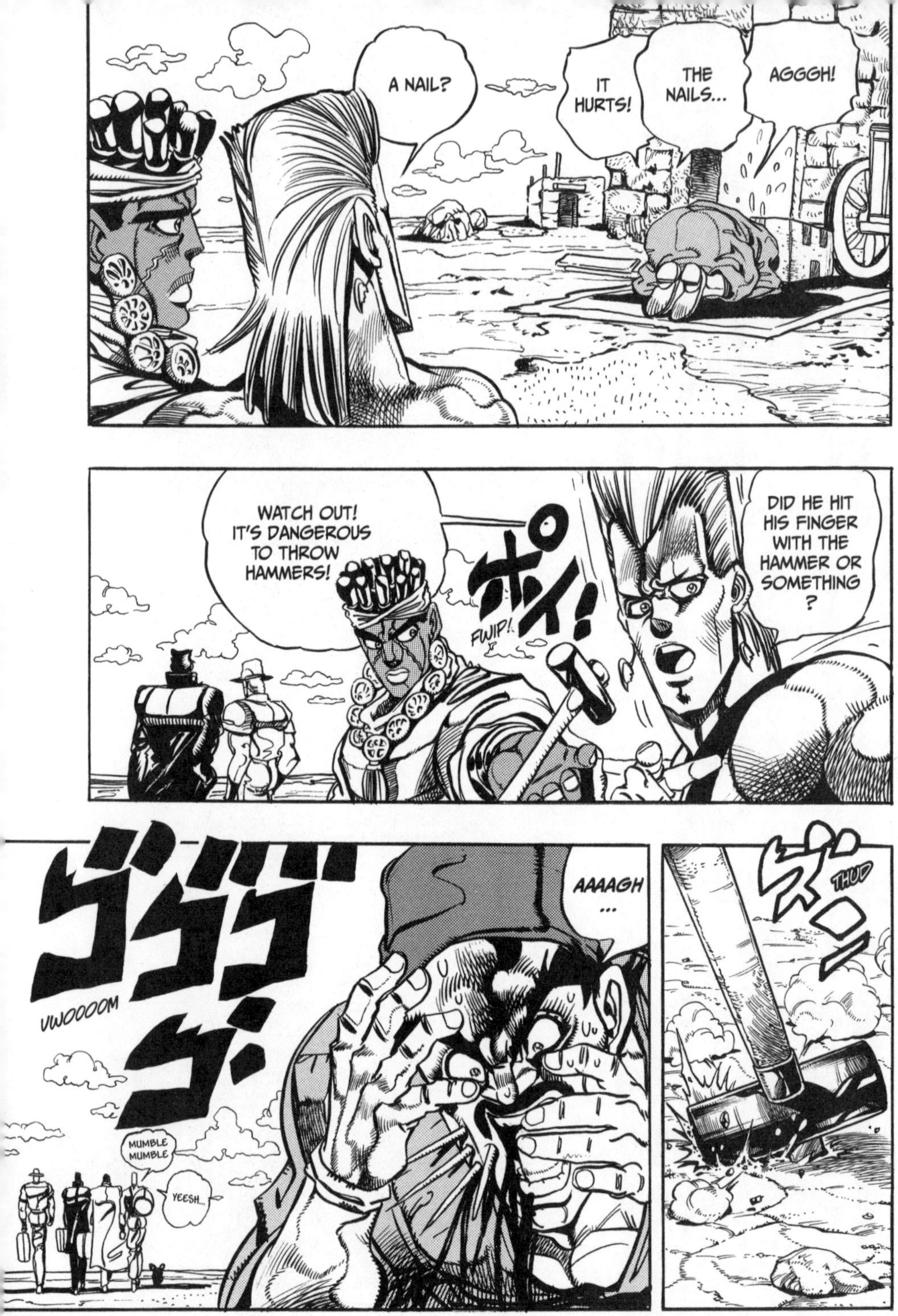
AGGGH!
THE NAILS...
IT HURTS!
A NAIL?
DID HE HIT HIS FINGER WITH THE HAMMER OR SOMETHING?
ポイ!
FWIP!
WATCH OUT! IT'S DANGEROUS TO THROW HAMMERS!
ズン
THUD
AAAAGH...
ゴゴゴゴ
VWOOOOM
MUMBLE MUMBLE
YEESH...

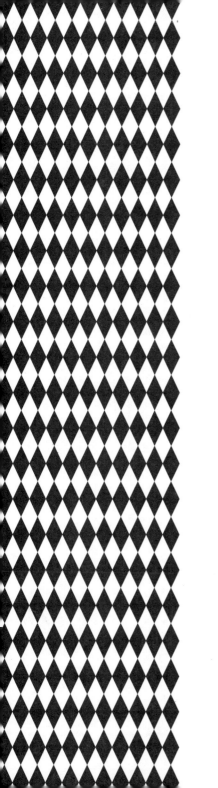

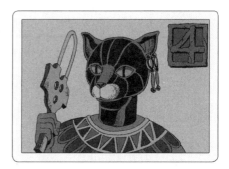

CHAPTER 87: "Bast" Mariah PART 2

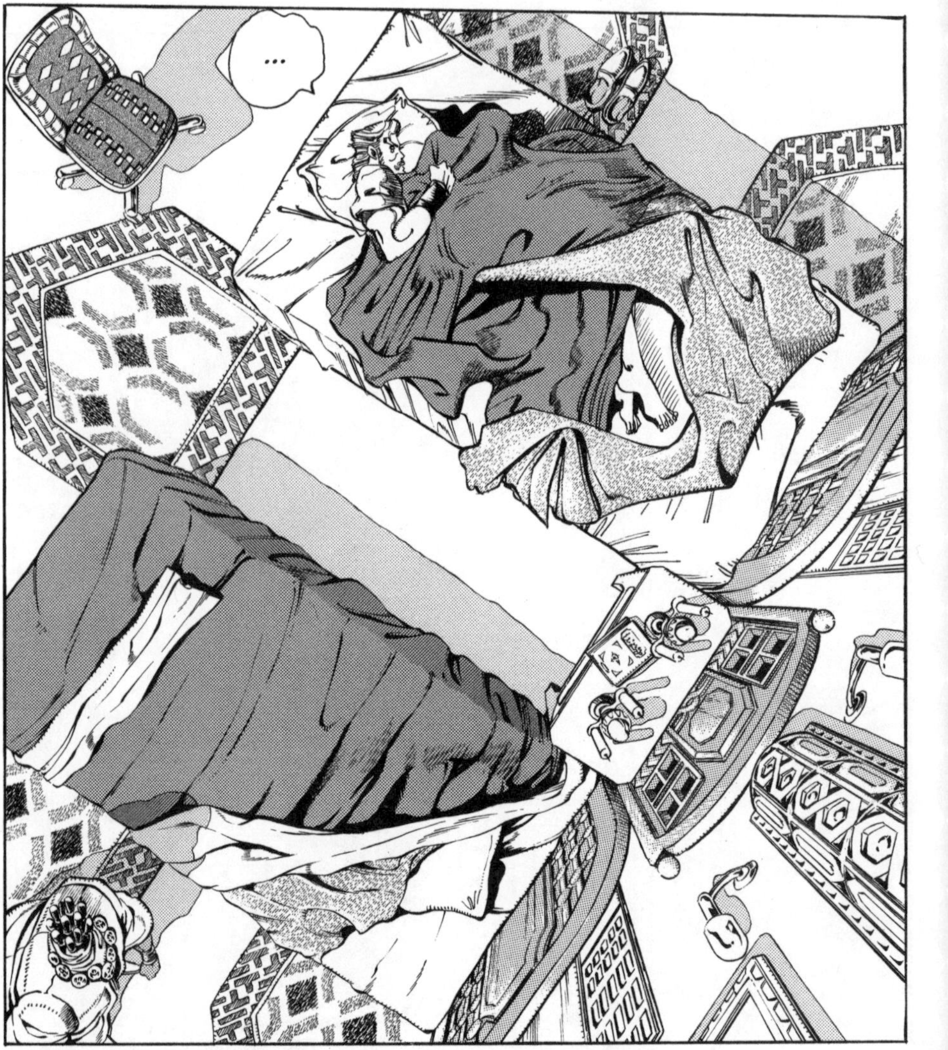
...

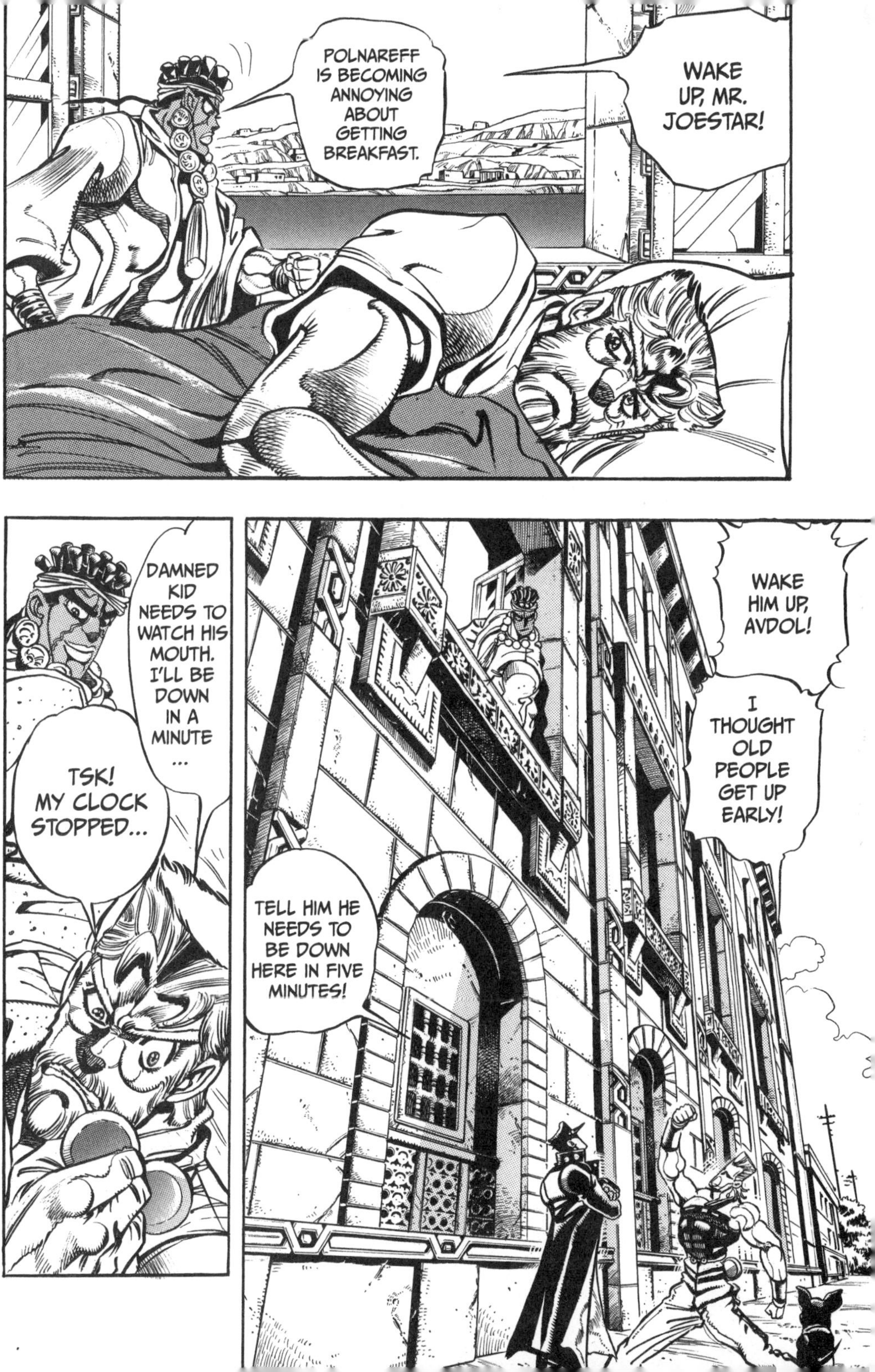
WAKE UP, MR. JOESTAR!
POLNAREFF IS BECOMING ANNOYING ABOUT GETTING BREAKFAST.
WAKE HIM UP, AVDOL!
I THOUGHT OLD PEOPLE GET UP EARLY!
TELL HIM HE NEEDS TO BE DOWN HERE IN FIVE MINUTES!
DAMNED KID NEEDS TO WATCH HIS MOUTH. I'LL BE DOWN IN A MINUTE ...
TSK! MY CLOCK STOPPED...

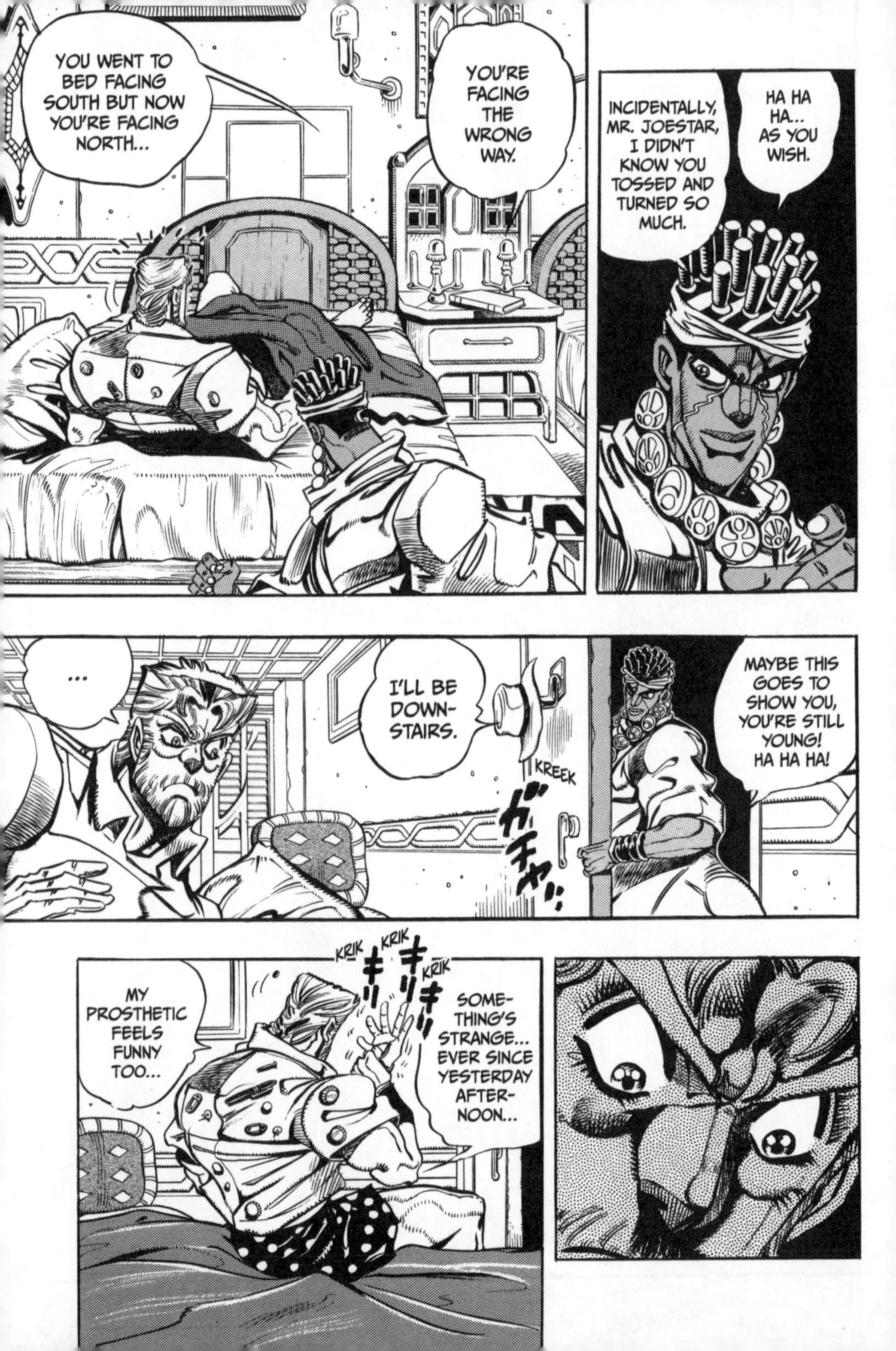
HA HA HA... AS YOU WISH.
INCIDENTALLY, MR. JOESTAR, I DIDN'T KNOW YOU TOSSED AND TURNED SO MUCH.
YOU'RE FACING THE WRONG WAY.
YOU WENT TO BED FACING SOUTH BUT NOW YOU'RE FACING NORTH...
MAYBE THIS GOES TO SHOW YOU, YOU'RE STILL YOUNG! HA HA HA!
KREEK
ガチャッ
I'LL BE DOWN-STAIRS.
...
KRIK KRIK KRIK
SOME-THING'S STRANGE... EVER SINCE YESTERDAY AFTER-NOON...
MY PROSTHETIC FEELS FUNNY TOO...

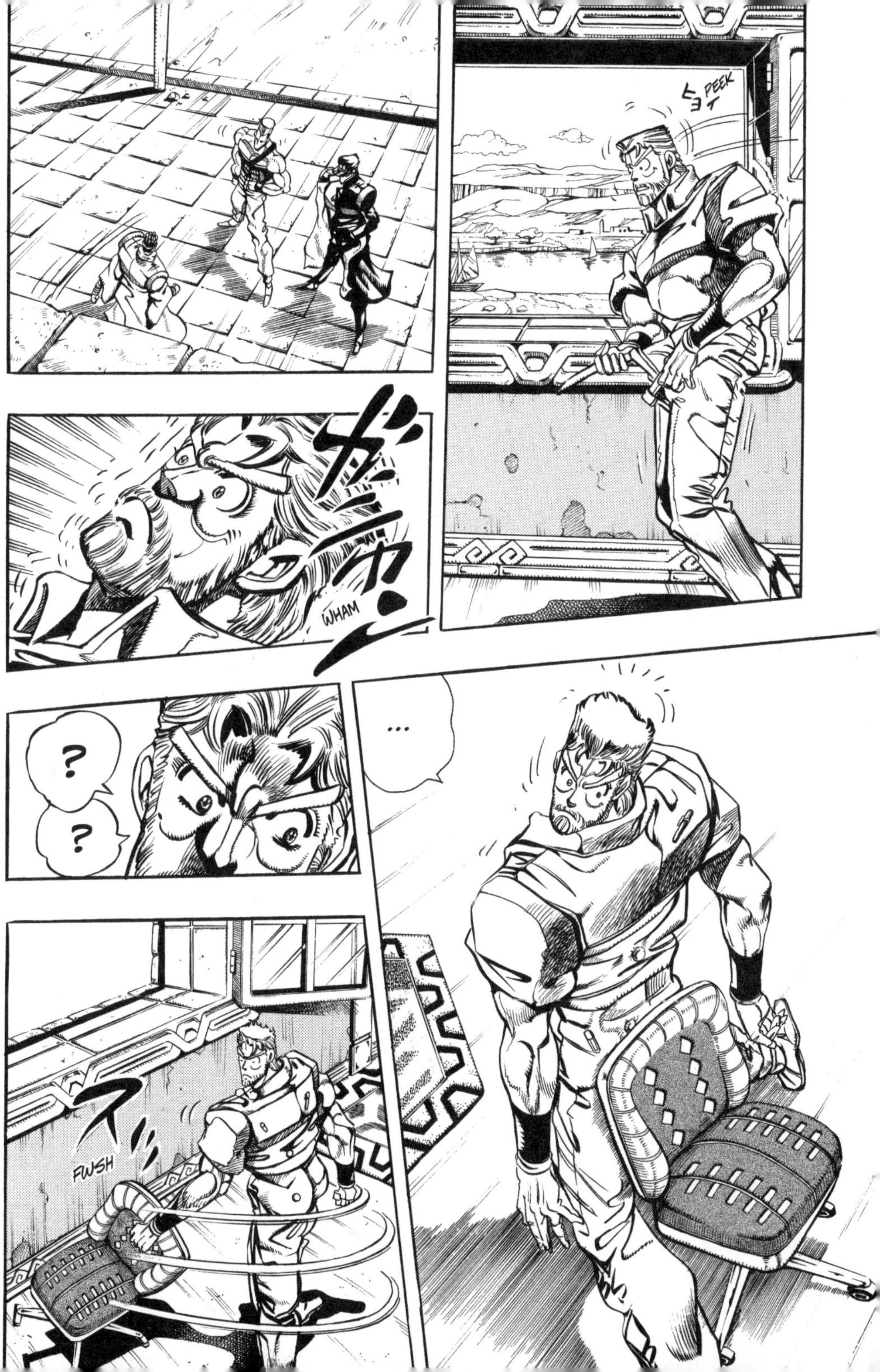
ヒョイ
PEEK
WHAM
...
?
?
FWSH

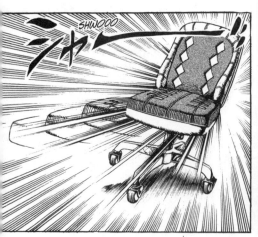

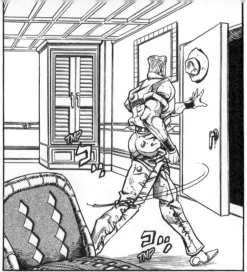

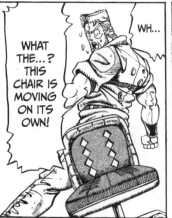

WH...

WHAT THE...? THIS CHAIR IS MOVING ON ITS OWN!

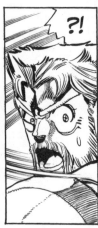

?!

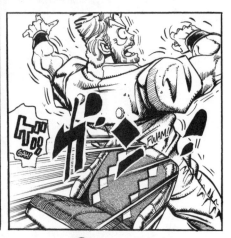

GAH!

FWAM!!

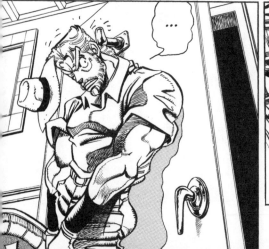

...

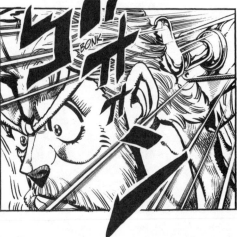

BONK

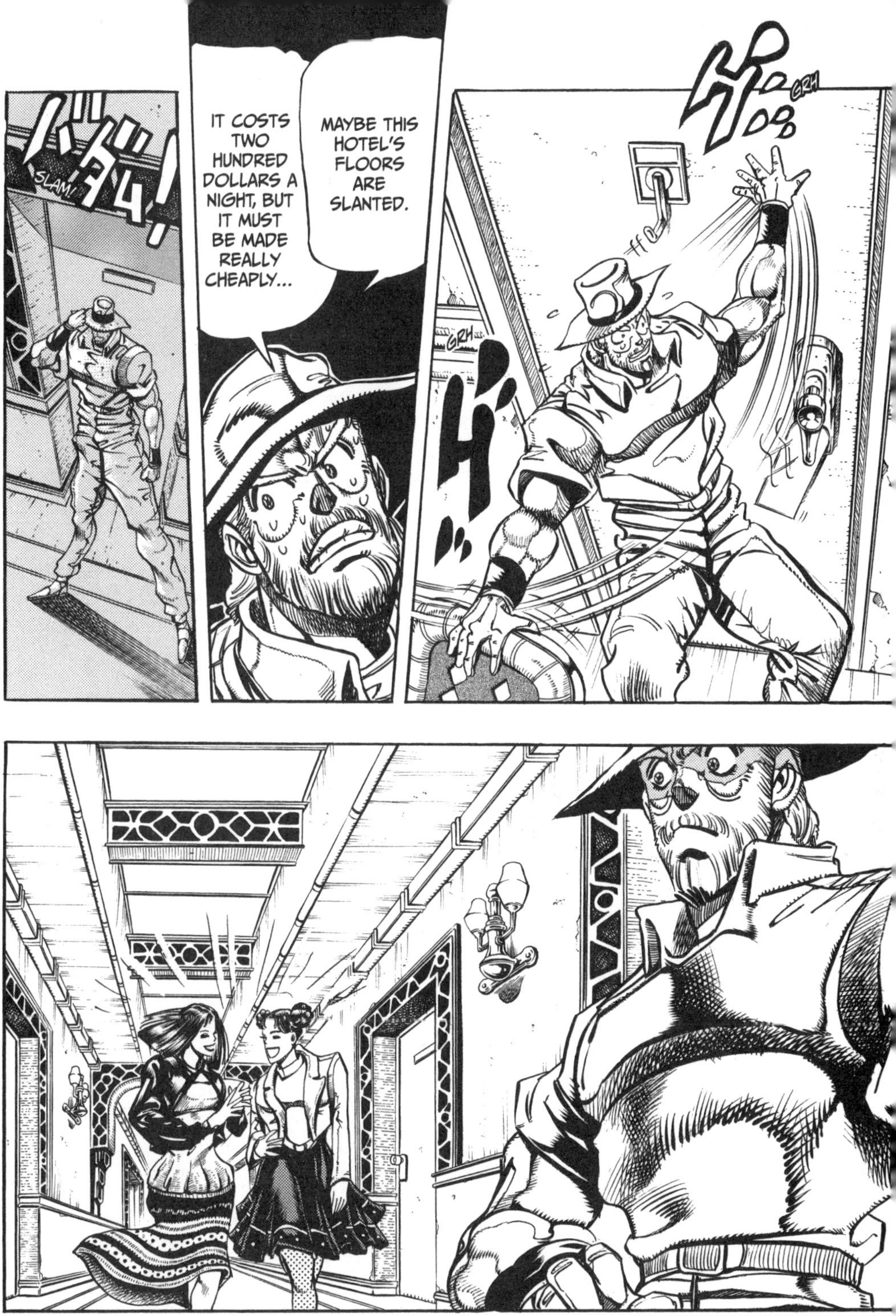
GRH
GRH
MAYBE THIS HOTEL'S FLOORS ARE SLANTED.
IT COSTS TWO HUNDRED DOLLARS A NIGHT, BUT IT MUST BE MADE REALLY CHEAPLY...
バダム!
SLAM!

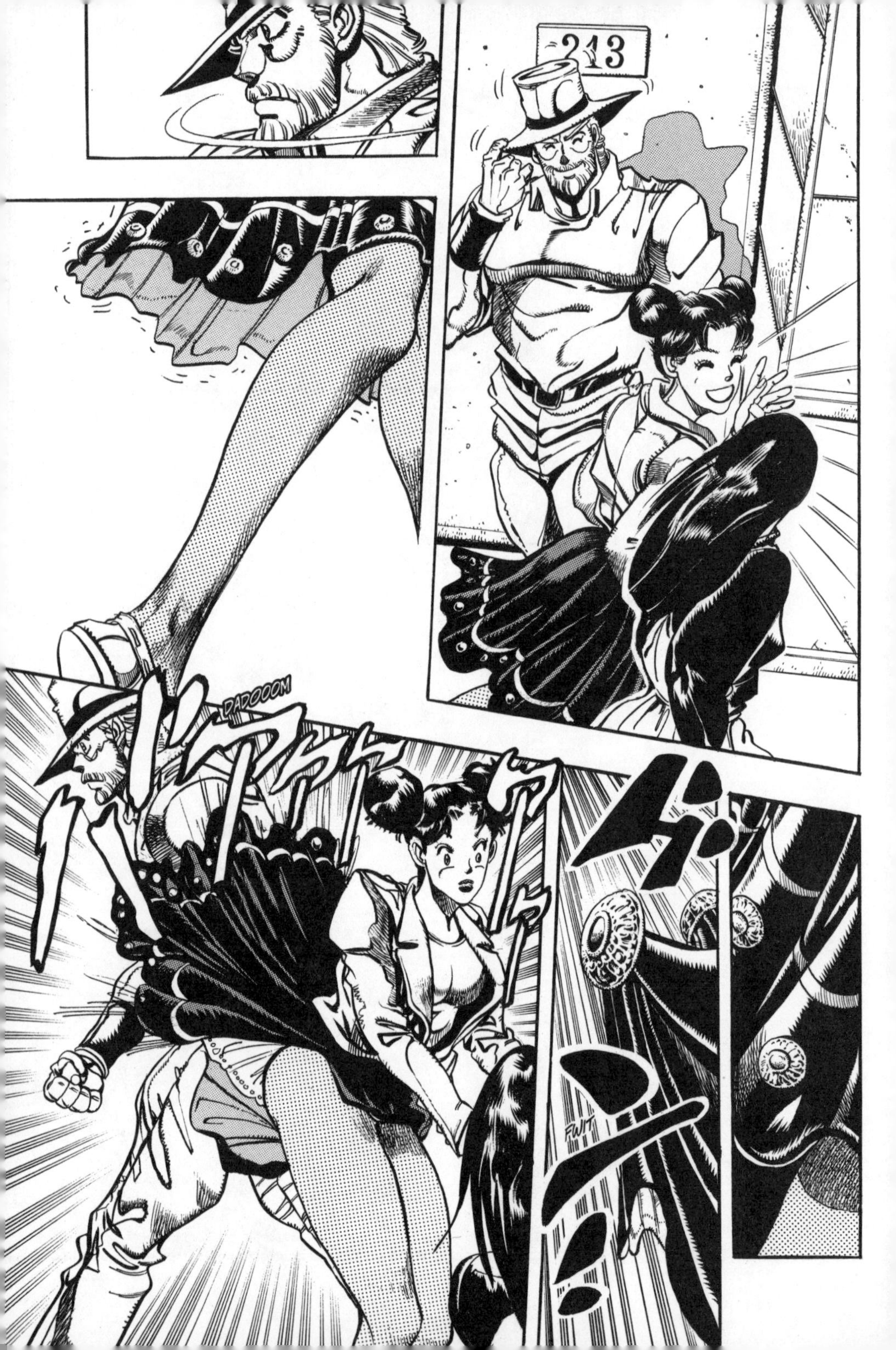
213
FWIT
DADOOOM

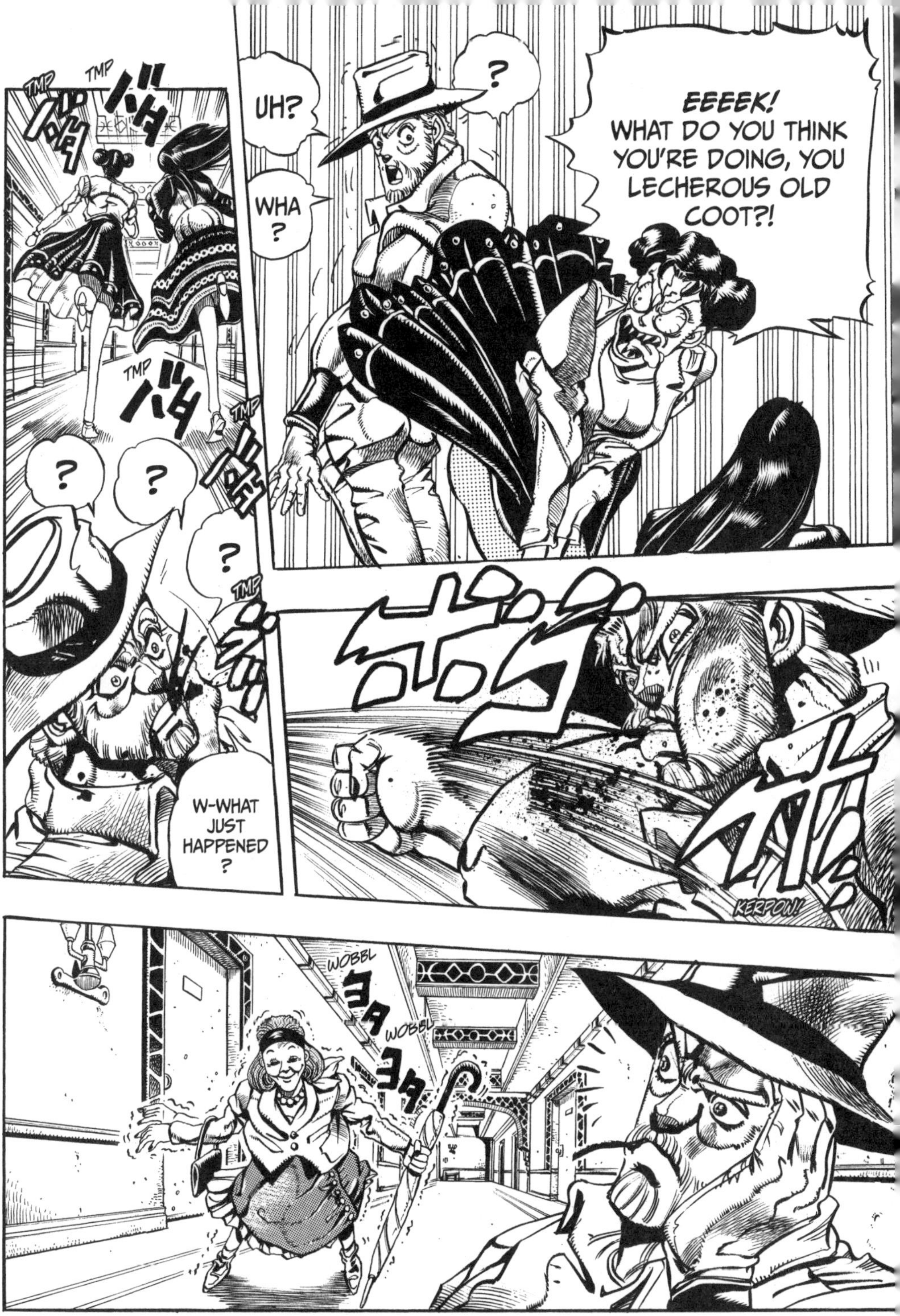
EEEEK!
WHAT DO YOU THINK YOU'RE DOING, YOU LECHEROUS OLD COOT?!
?
UH?
WHA ?
KERPOW!
TMP
TMP
TMP
TMP
?
?
?
TMP
W-WHAT JUST HAPPENED ?
WOBBL
WOBBL

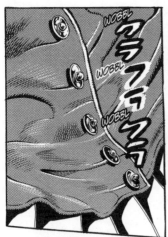

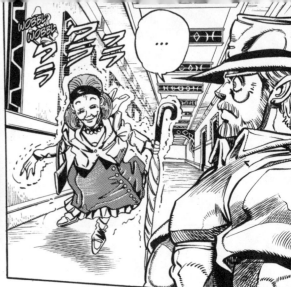

WOBBLY
WOBBLY

WOBEL

WOBEL

WOBEL

...

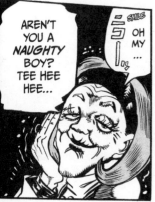

AREN'T YOU A *NAUGHTY BOY?* TEE HEE HEE...

SMILE

OH MY ...

OH MY ...

WOBEL

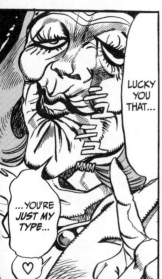

LUCKY YOU THAT...

...YOU'RE JUST MY TYPE...

MMM

♥

...

HUH ?!

?

?

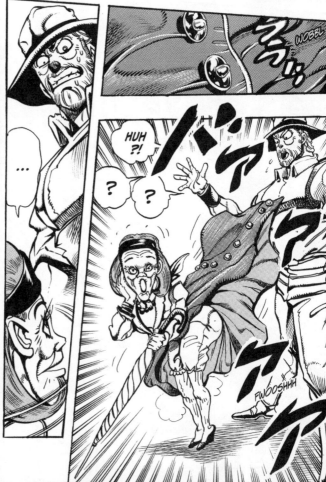

FWOOSHHH

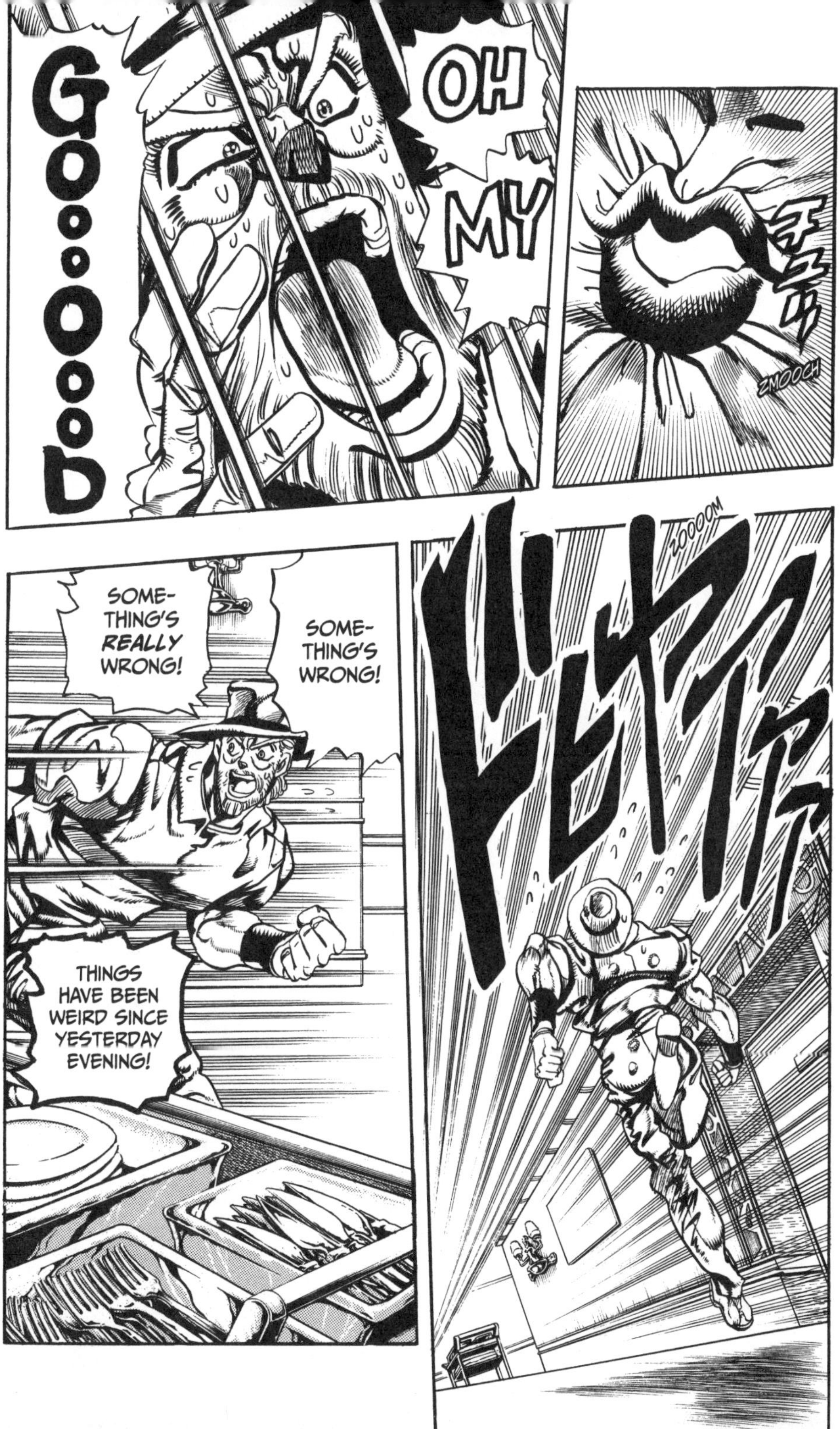
ZMOOCH
OH MY
GOOOOOOD
ZOOOOM
SOME-THING'S WRONG!
SOME-THING'S *REALLY* WRONG!
THINGS HAVE BEEN WEIRD SINCE YESTERDAY EVENING!

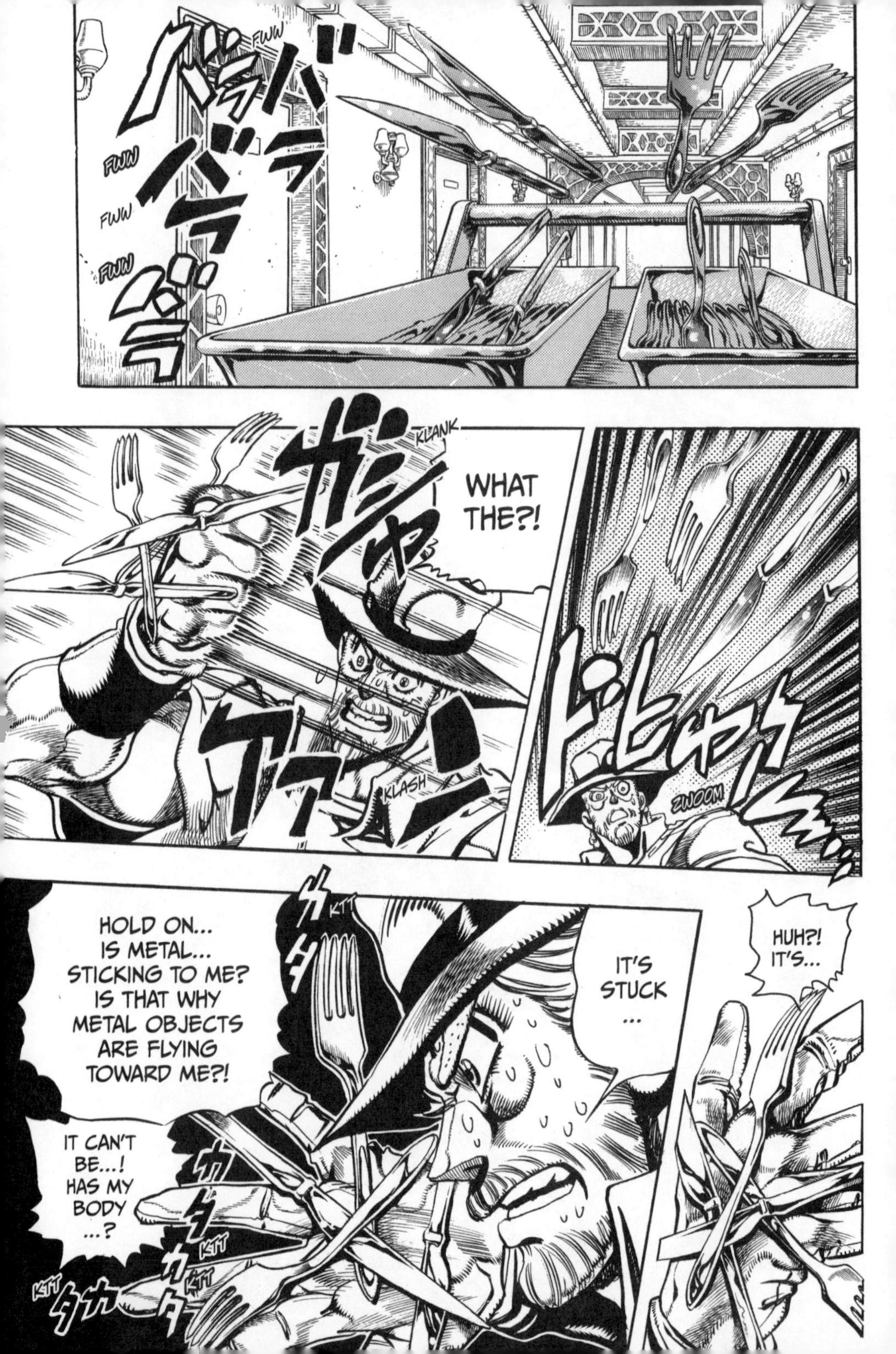
FWW
FWW
FWW
FWW
ZWOOM
KLANK
WHAT THE?!
KLASH
HUH?! IT'S...
IT'S STUCK ...
HOLD ON... IS METAL... STICKING TO ME? IS THAT WHY METAL OBJECTS ARE FLYING TOWARD ME?!
KTT
IT CAN'T BE...! HAS MY BODY ...?
KTT
KTT
KTT

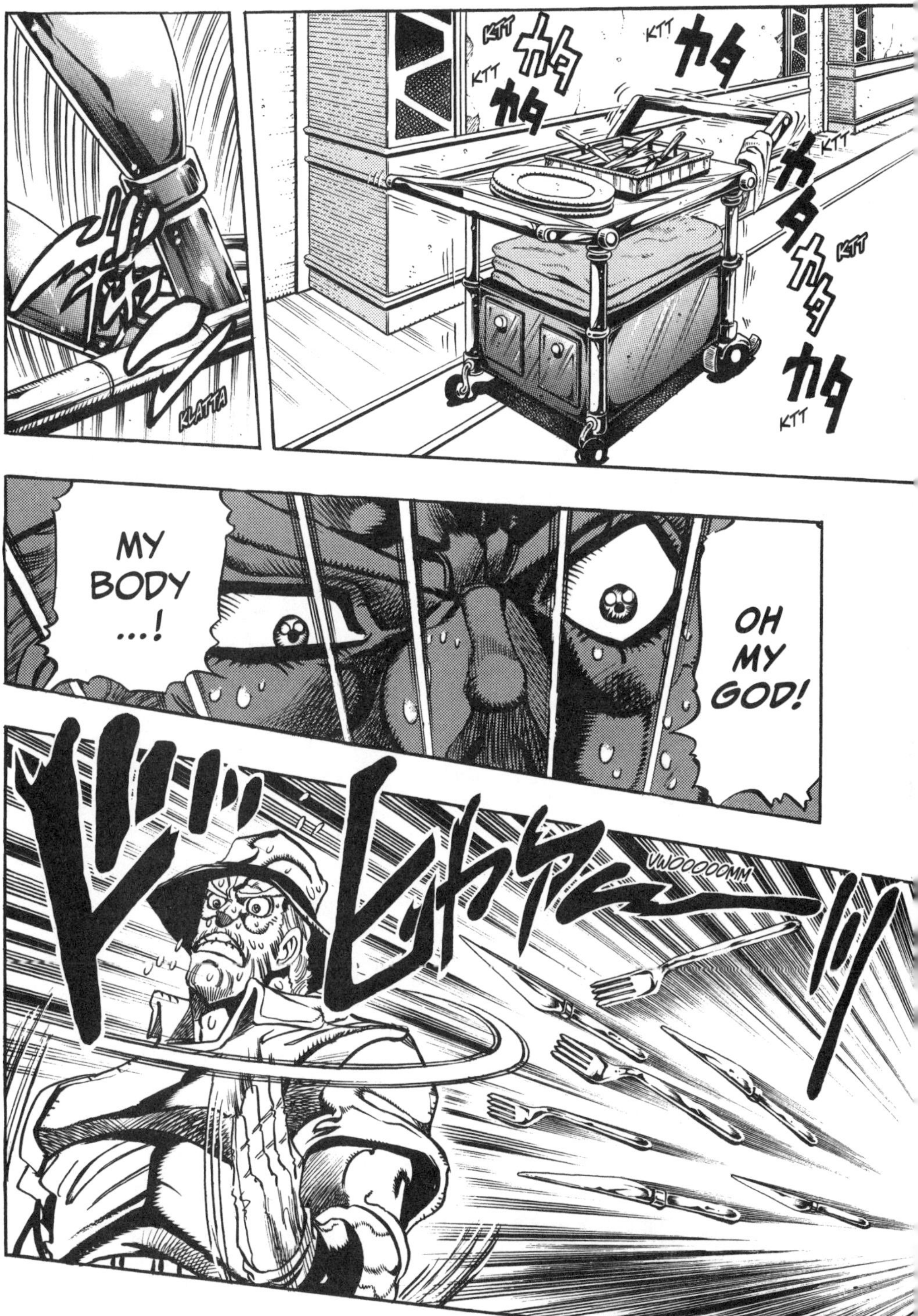
KTT
カタ
KTT
カタ
KTT
カタ
KTT
カタ
KTT
カタ
KTT
KLATTA
OH MY GOD!
MY BODY ...!
VWOOOOOMM

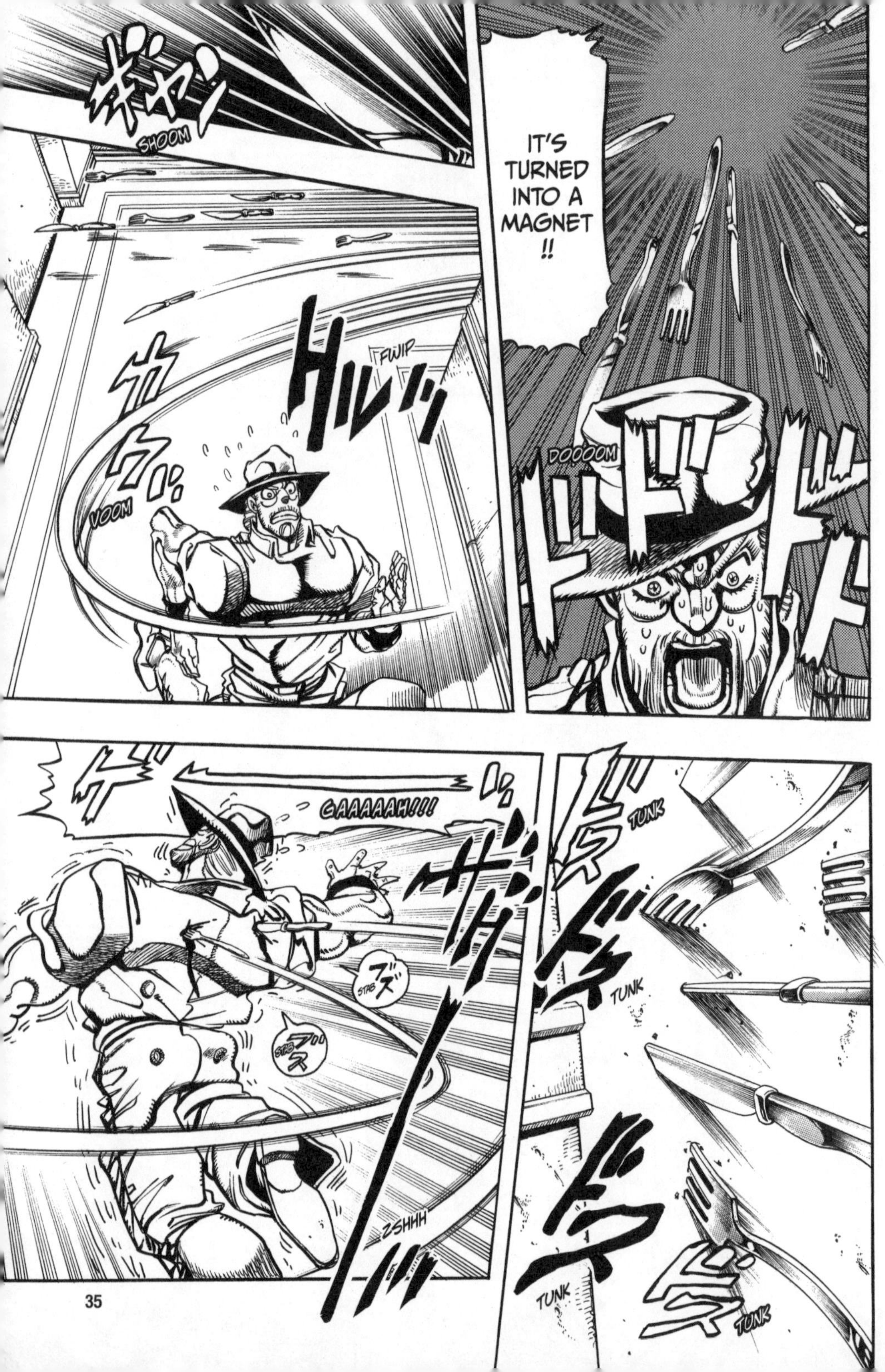
IT'S TURNED INTO A MAGNET !!
DOOOOM
SHOOM
FWIP
VOOM
TUNK
TUNK
TUNK
TUNK
GAAAAAH!!!
STAB
STAB
ZSHHH

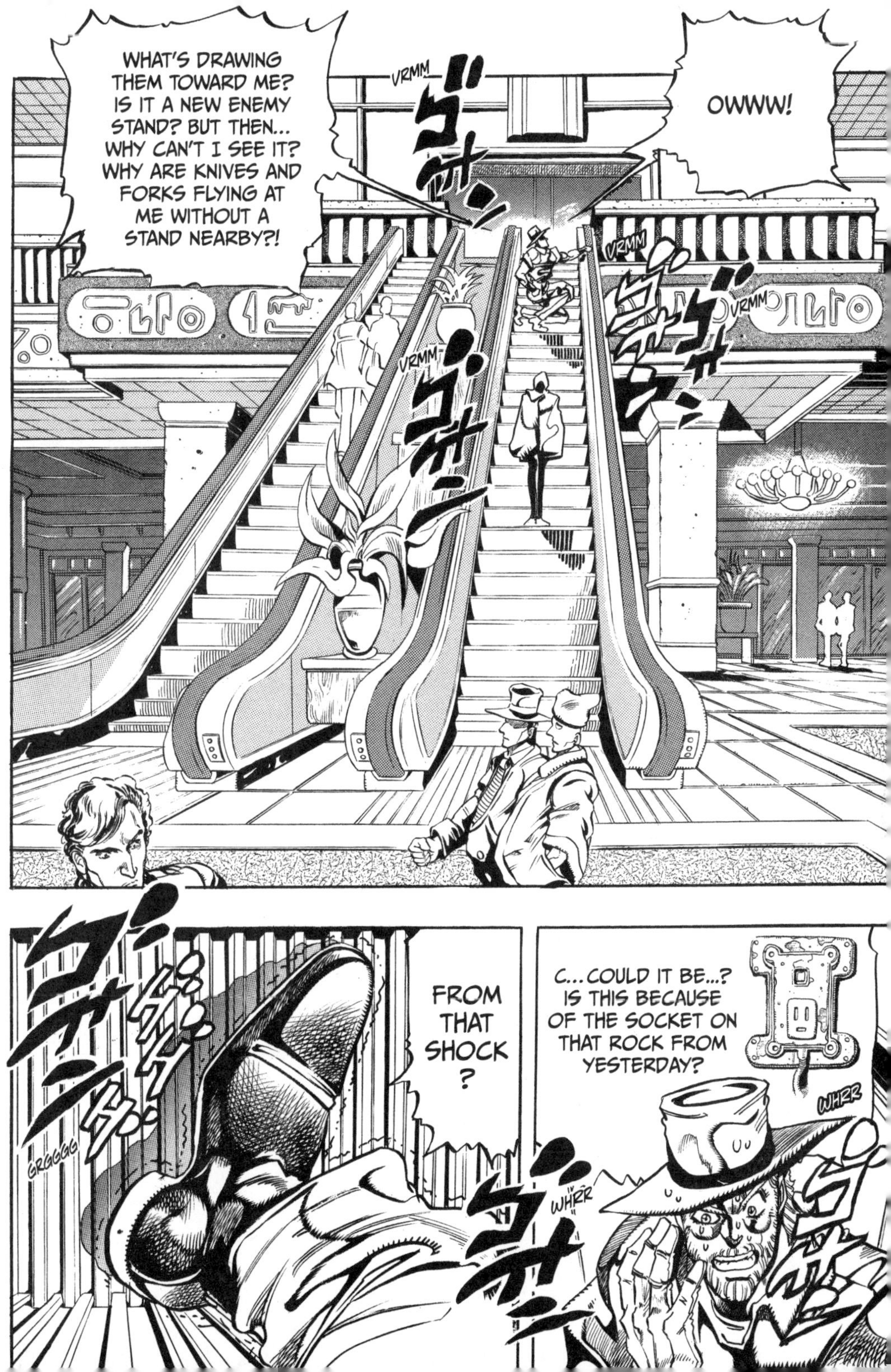
OWWW!
VRMM
WHAT'S DRAWING THEM TOWARD ME? IS IT A NEW ENEMY STAND? BUT THEN... WHY CAN'T I SEE IT? WHY ARE KNIVES AND FORKS FLYING AT ME WITHOUT A STAND NEARBY?!
VRMM
VRMM
VRMM
WHRR
C...COULD IT BE...? IS THIS BECAUSE OF THE SOCKET ON THAT ROCK FROM YESTERDAY?
WHRR
FROM THAT SHOCK ?
GRGGGG

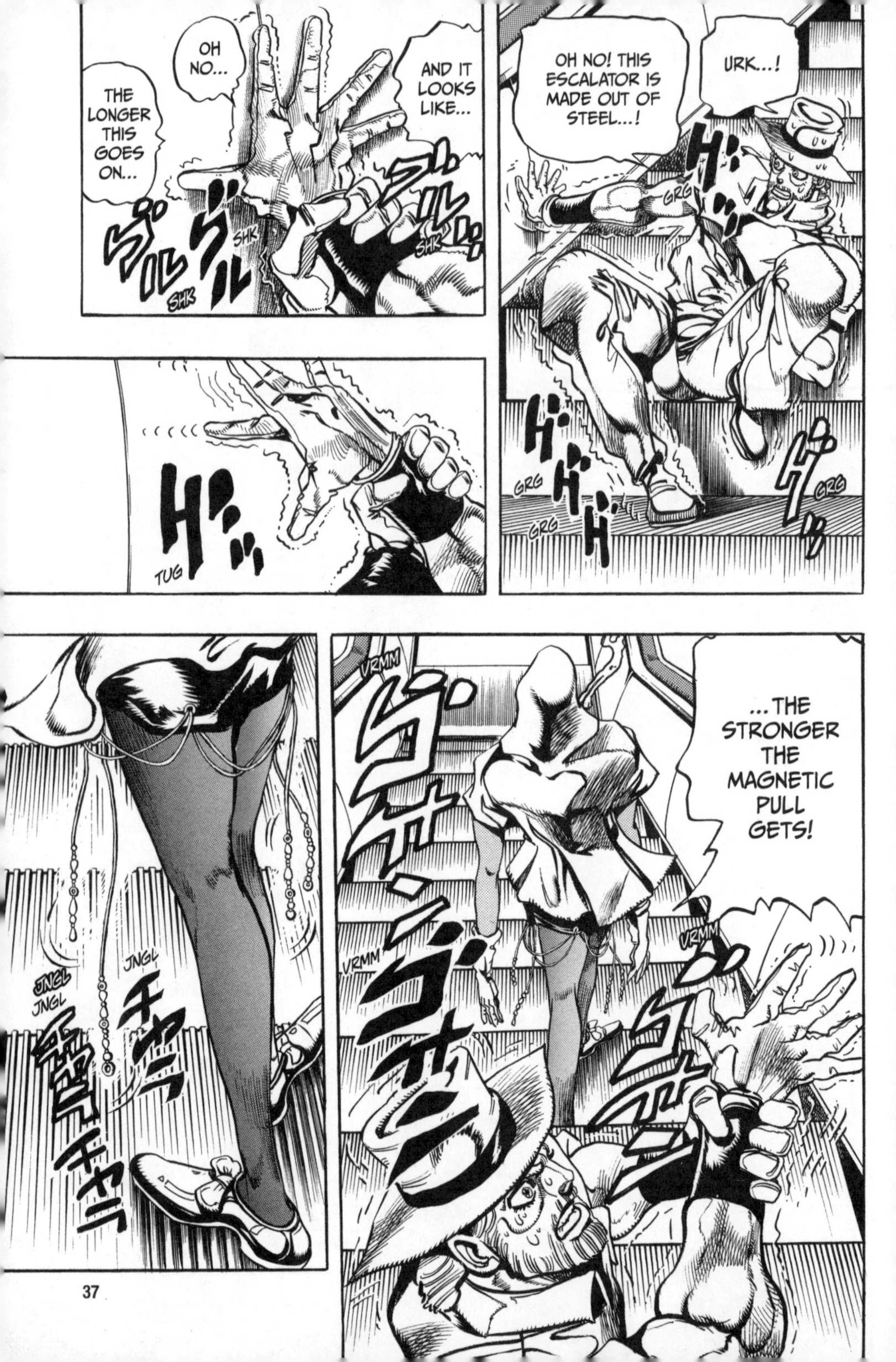
URK...!
OH NO! THIS ESCALATOR IS MADE OUT OF STEEL...!
GRG
GRG
GRG
GRG
AND IT LOOKS LIKE...
OH NO...
THE LONGER THIS GOES ON...
SHK
SHK
SHK
TUG
...THE STRONGER THE MAGNETIC PULL GETS!
VRMM
VRMM
VRMM
JNGL
JNGL
JNGL

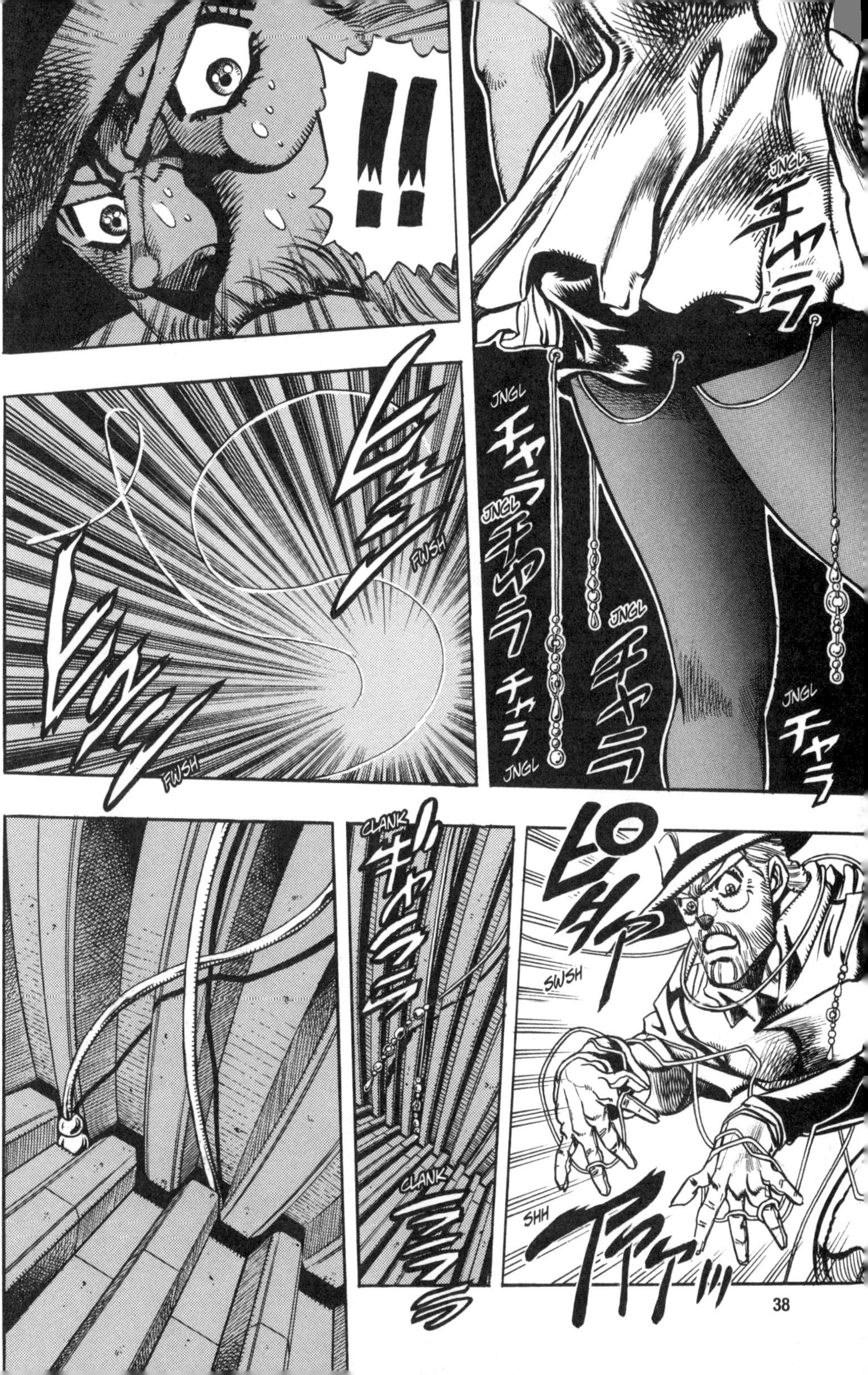
JNGL
チャラ
JNGL
チャラ
JNGL
チャラ
JNGL
チャラ
チャラ
JNGL
JNGL
チャラ
!!
FWSH
FWSH
SWSH
SHH
CLANK
CLANK

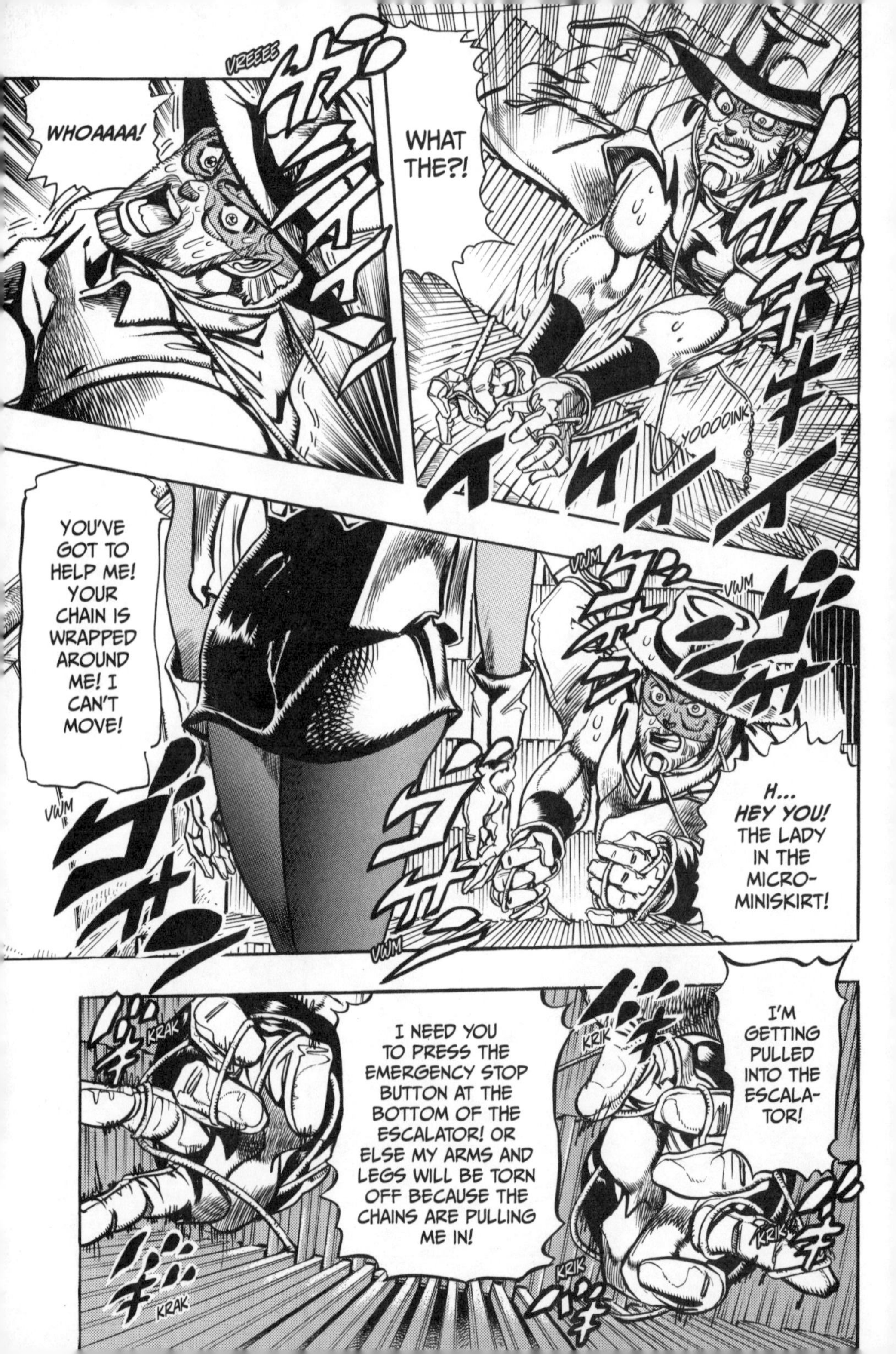
WHAT THE?!
YOOOOINK
VREEEE
WHOAAAA!
VWM
VWM
H... HEY YOU! THE LADY IN THE MICRO-MINISKIRT!
YOU'VE GOT TO HELP ME! YOUR CHAIN IS WRAPPED AROUND ME! I CAN'T MOVE!
VWM
VWM
I'M GETTING PULLED INTO THE ESCALATOR!
KRIK
KRIK
KRIK
I NEED YOU TO PRESS THE EMERGENCY STOP BUTTON AT THE BOTTOM OF THE ESCALATOR! OR ELSE MY ARMS AND LEGS WILL BE TORN OFF BECAUSE THE CHAINS ARE PULLING ME IN!
KRAK
KRAK

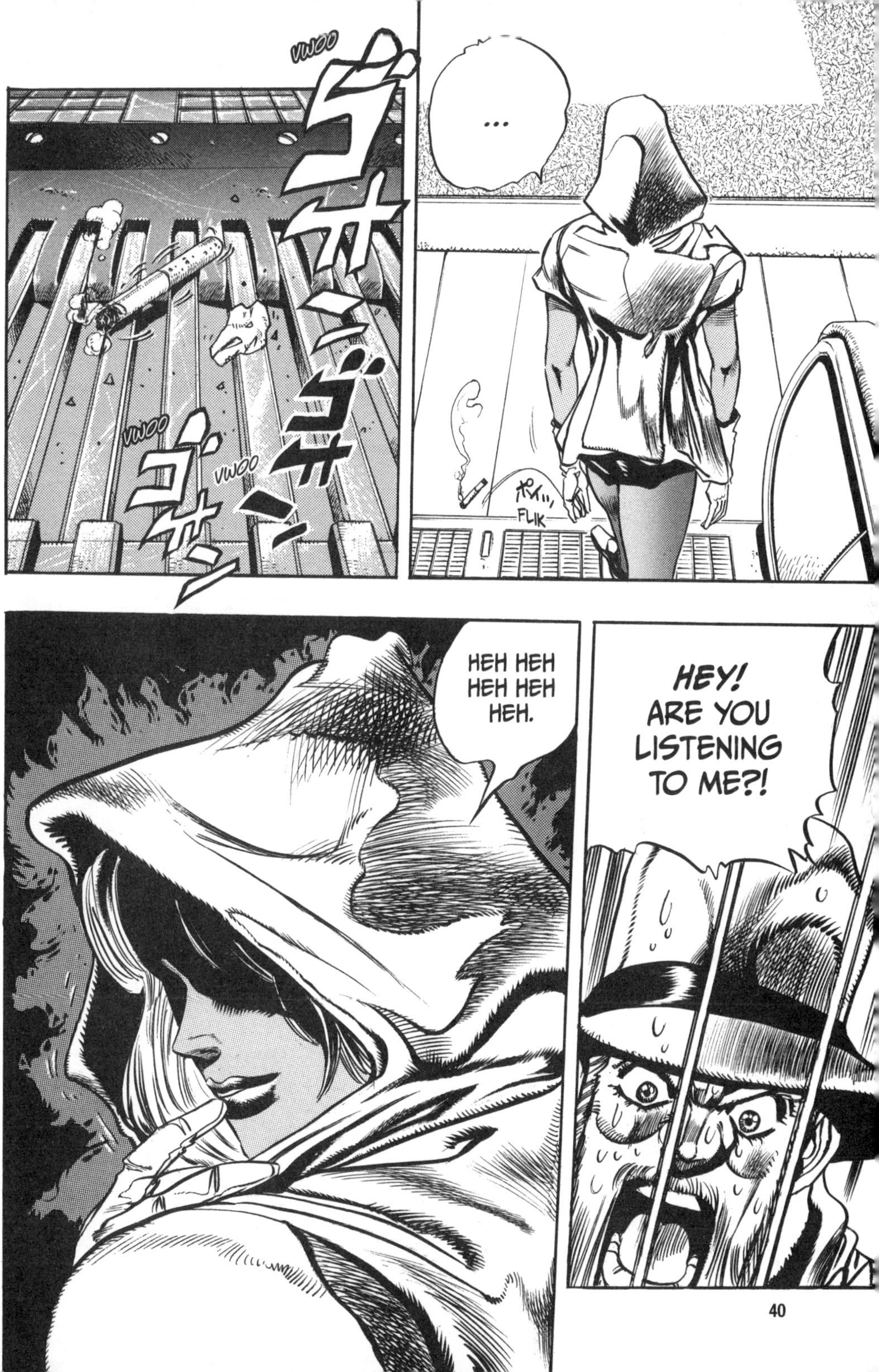
...
ポイッ
FLIK
VWOO
VWOO
VWOO
HEY!
ARE YOU LISTENING TO ME?!
HEH HEH HEH HEH HEH.

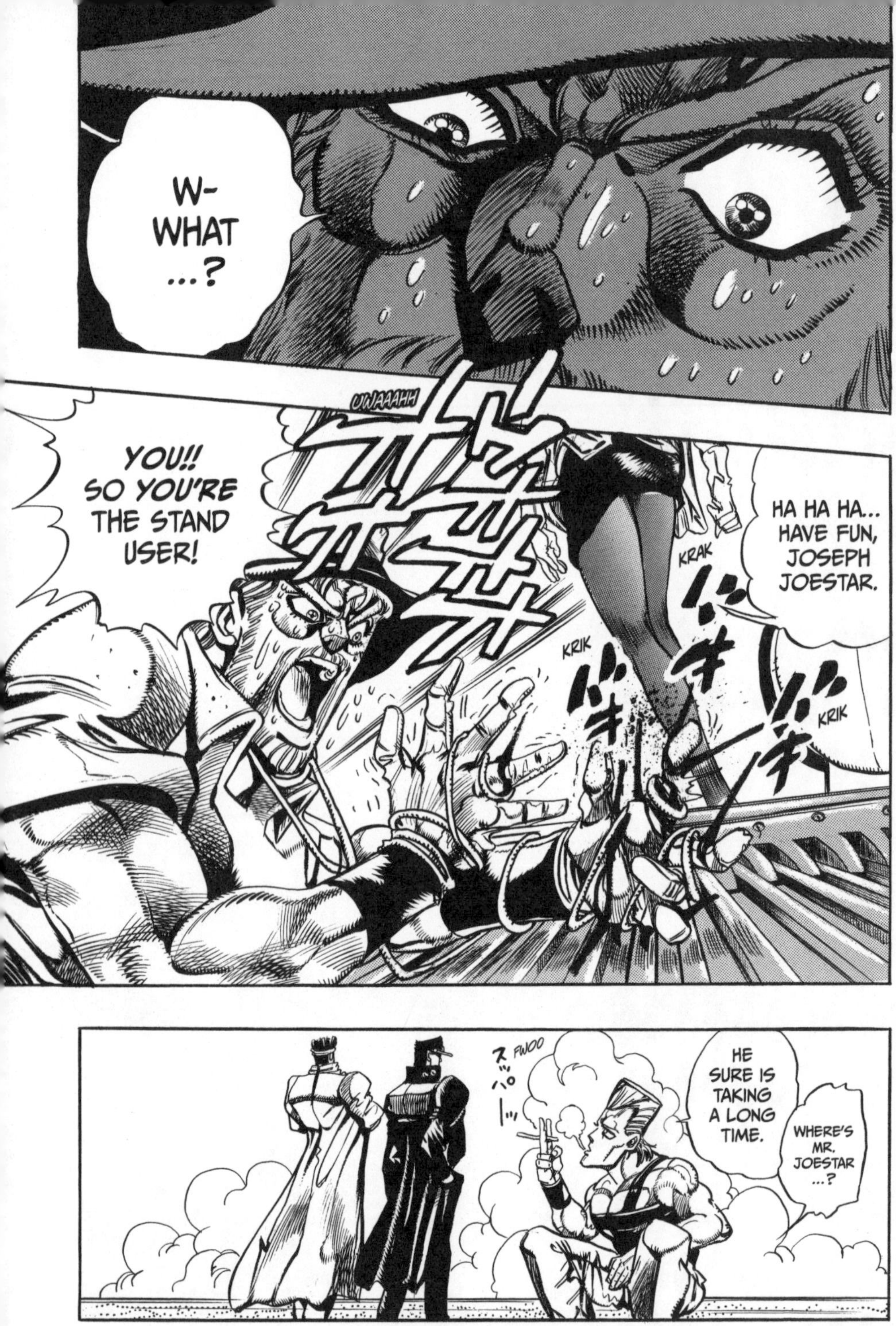
W-WHAT ...?
HA HA HA... HAVE FUN, JOSEPH JOESTAR.
KRAK
KRIK
KRIK
UWAAAHH
YOU!! SO YOU'RE THE STAND USER!
WHERE'S MR. JOESTAR ...?
HE SURE IS TAKING A LONG TIME.
FWOO

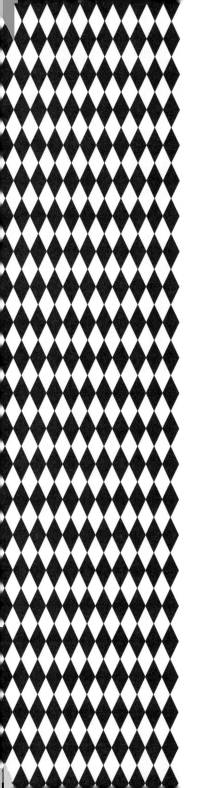

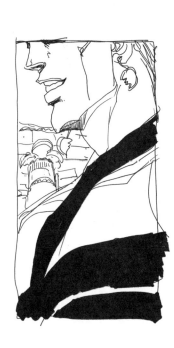

CHAPTER 88: "Bast" Mariah PART 3

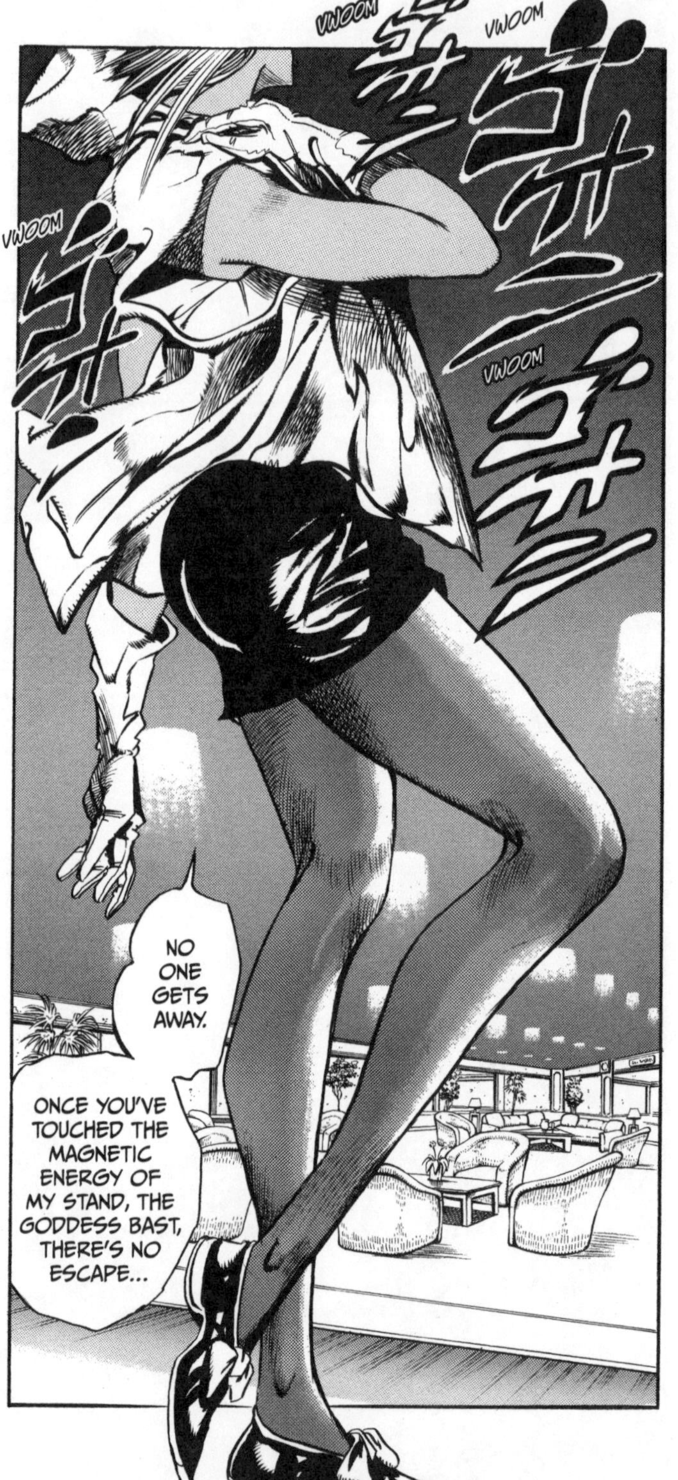
VWOOM
VWOOM
VWOOM
VWOOM
NO ONE GETS AWAY.
ONCE YOU'VE TOUCHED THE MAGNETIC ENERGY OF MY STAND, THE GODDESS BAST, THERE'S NO ESCAPE...

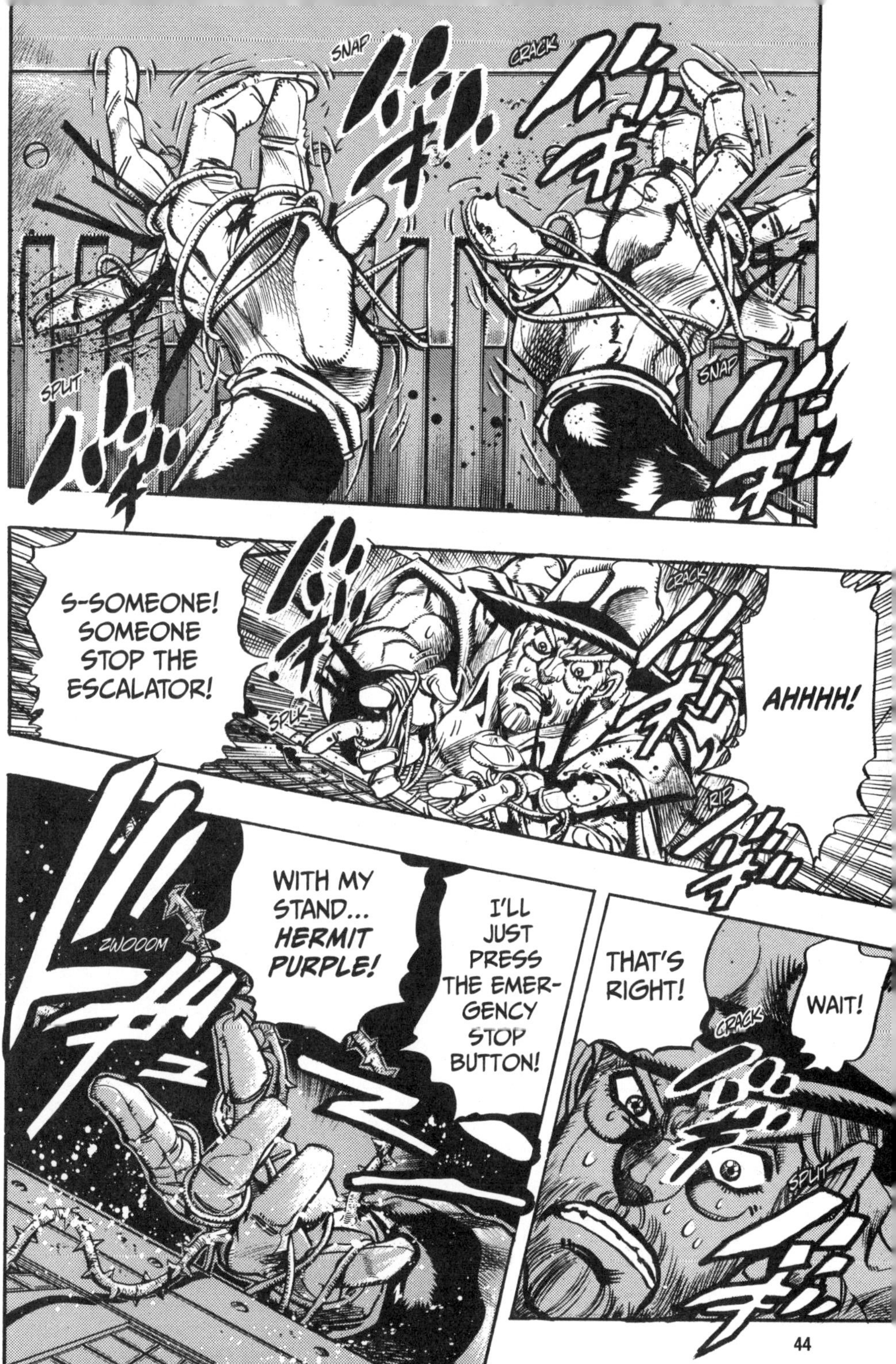
CRACK
SNAP
SNAP
SPLIT
CRACK
AHHHH!
RIP
SPLK
S-SOMEONE! SOMEONE STOP THE ESCALATOR!
WAIT!
THAT'S RIGHT!
CRACK
SPLIT
I'LL JUST PRESS THE EMER-GENCY STOP BUTTON!
WITH MY STAND... HERMIT PURPLE!
ZWOOOM

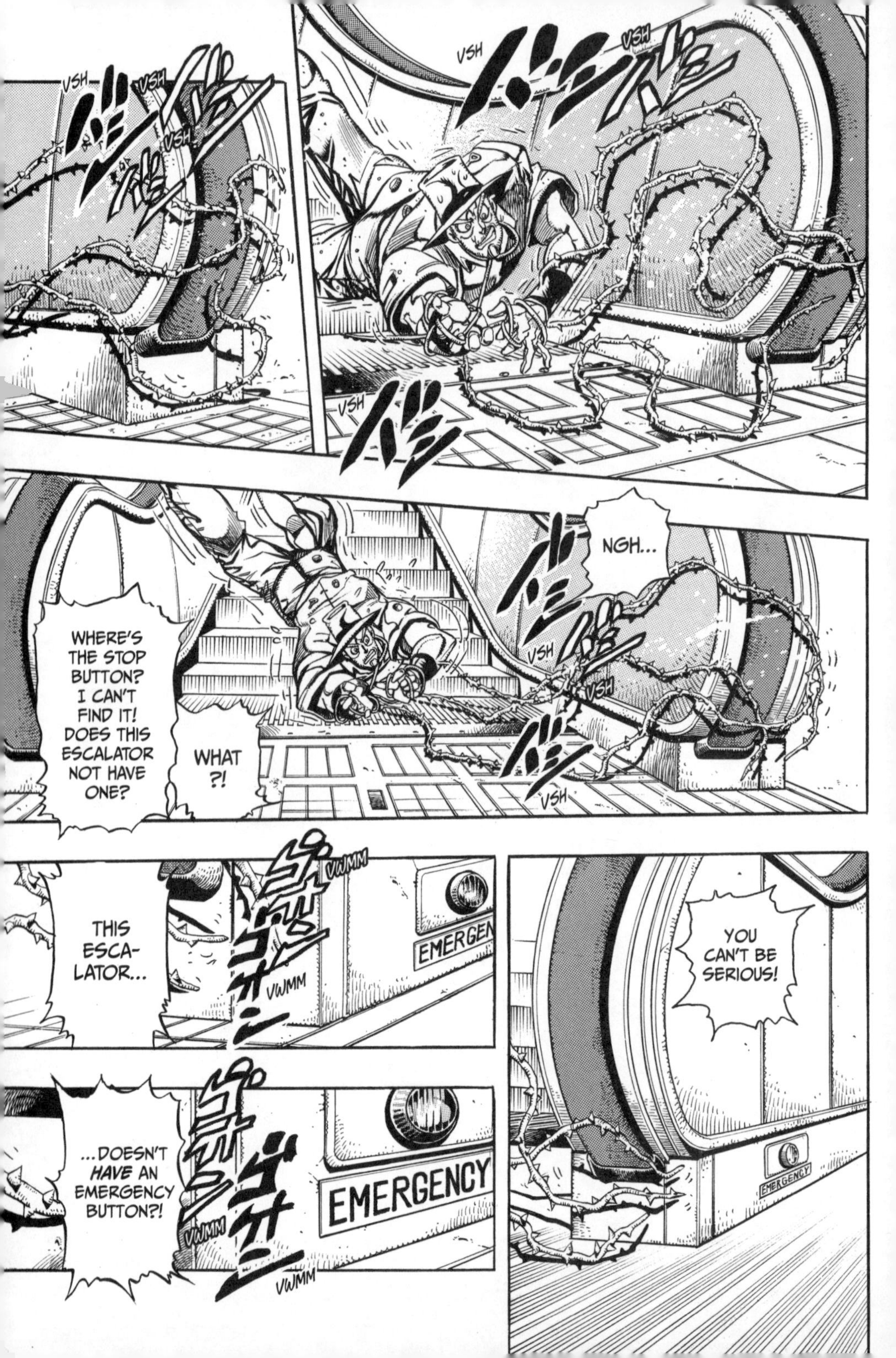
VSH
VSH
VSH
VSH
VSH
VSH
NGH...
VSH
VSH
VSH
WHAT ?!
WHERE'S THE STOP BUTTON? I CAN'T FIND IT! DOES THIS ESCALATOR NOT HAVE ONE?
YOU CAN'T BE SERIOUS!
EMERGENCY
VWMM
EMERGEN
VWMM
THIS ESCA-LATOR...
EMERGENCY
...DOESN'T *HAVE* AN EMERGENCY BUTTON?!
VWMM
VWMM

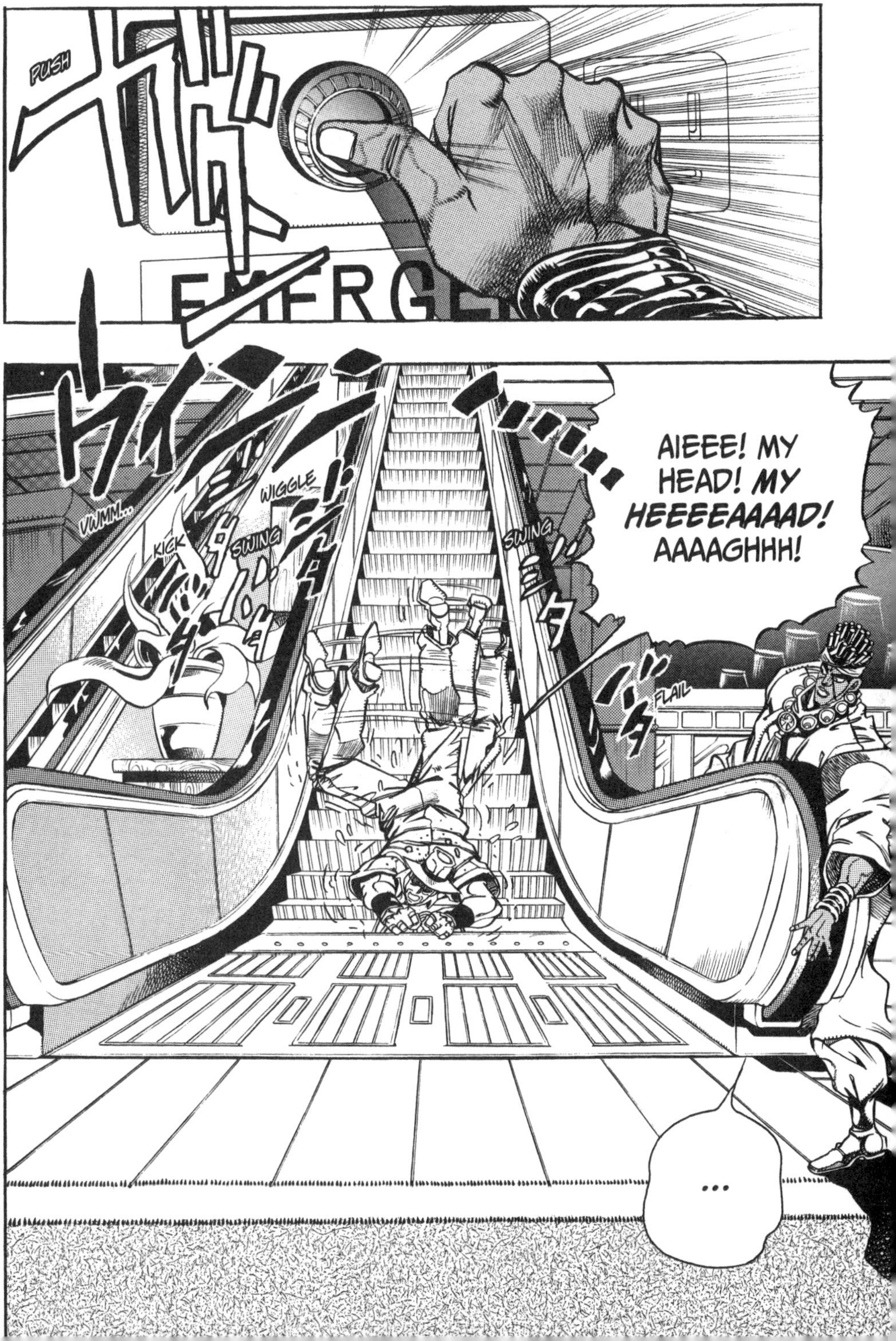
PUSH
EMERG
AIEEE! MY HEAD! *MY HEEEEAAAAD!* AAAAGHHH!
FLAIL
SWING
WIGGLE
SWING
KICK
VWMM...
...

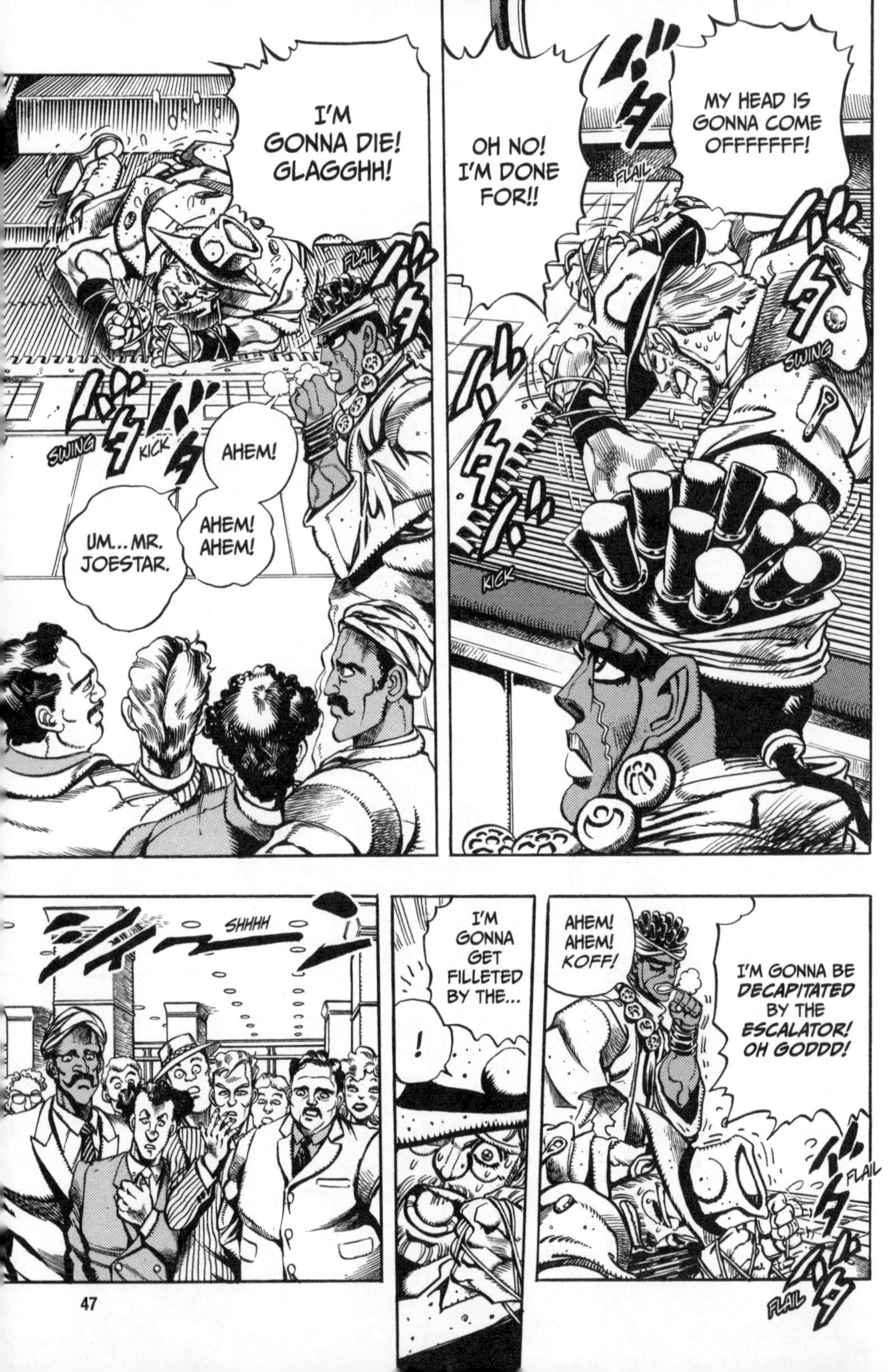
MY HEAD IS GONNA COME OFFFFFFF!
OH NO! I'M DONE FOR!!
FLAIL
SWING
KICK
I'M GONNA DIE! GLAGGHH!
FLAIL
SWING
KICK
AHEM!
AHEM! AHEM!
UM... MR. JOESTAR.
AHEM! AHEM! KOFF!
I'M GONNA BE *DECAPITATED* BY THE *ESCALATOR!* *OH GODDD!*
FLAIL
FLAIL
I'M GONNA GET FILLETED BY THE...
!
SHHHH

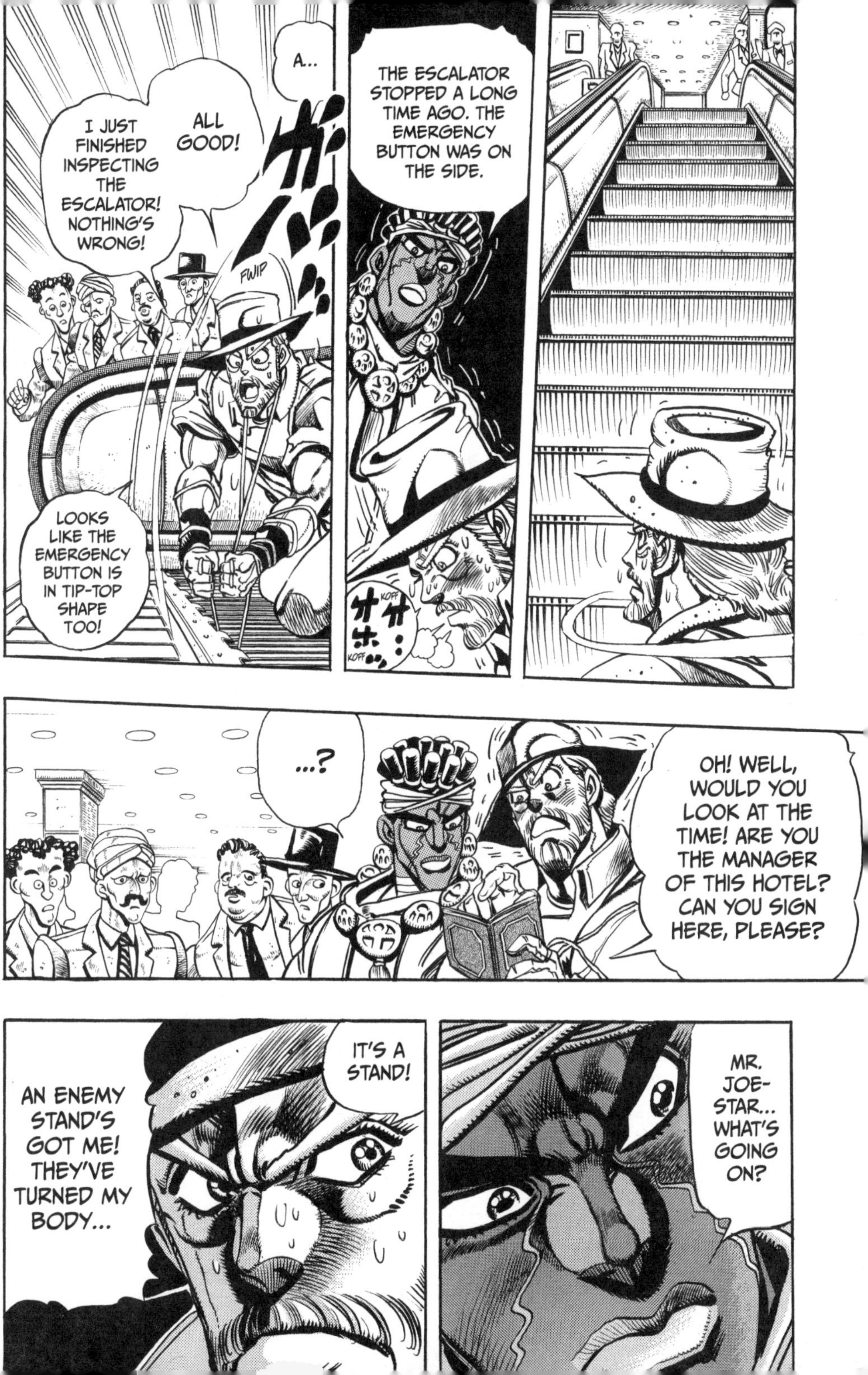
THE ESCALATOR STOPPED A LONG TIME AGO. THE EMERGENCY BUTTON WAS ON THE SIDE.
KOFF
KOFF
A...
ALL GOOD!
I JUST FINISHED INSPECTING THE ESCALATOR! NOTHING'S WRONG!
FWIP
LOOKS LIKE THE EMERGENCY BUTTON IS IN TIP-TOP SHAPE TOO!
OH! WELL, WOULD YOU LOOK AT THE TIME! ARE YOU THE MANAGER OF THIS HOTEL? CAN YOU SIGN HERE, PLEASE?
...?
MR. JOE-STAR... WHAT'S GOING ON?
IT'S A STAND!
AN ENEMY STAND'S GOT ME! THEY'VE TURNED MY BODY...

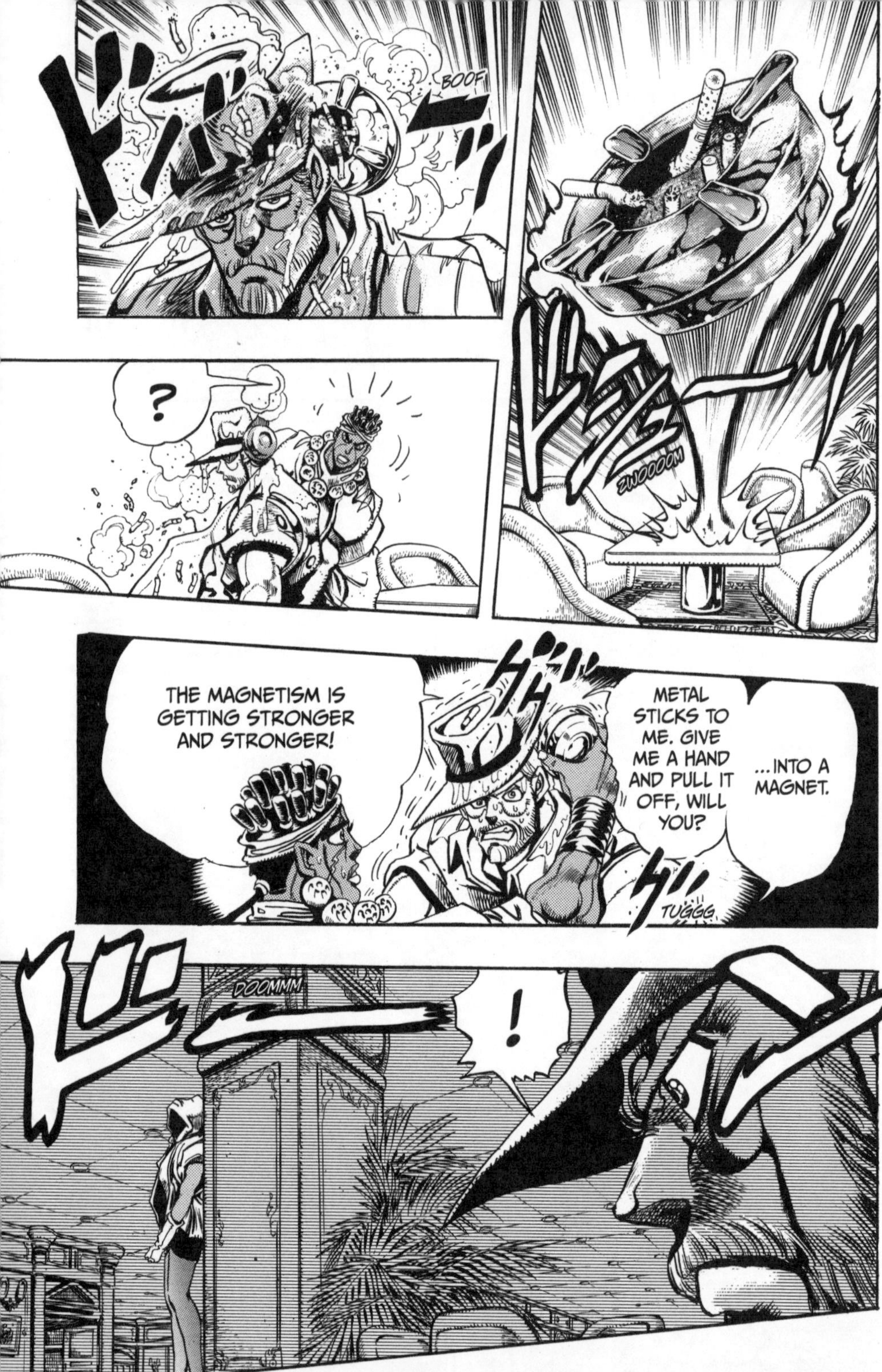
ZWOOOOM
BOOF
?
...INTO A MAGNET.
METAL STICKS TO ME. GIVE ME A HAND AND PULL IT OFF, WILL YOU?
TUGGG
THE MAGNETISM IS GETTING STRONGER AND STRONGER!
!
DOOMMM

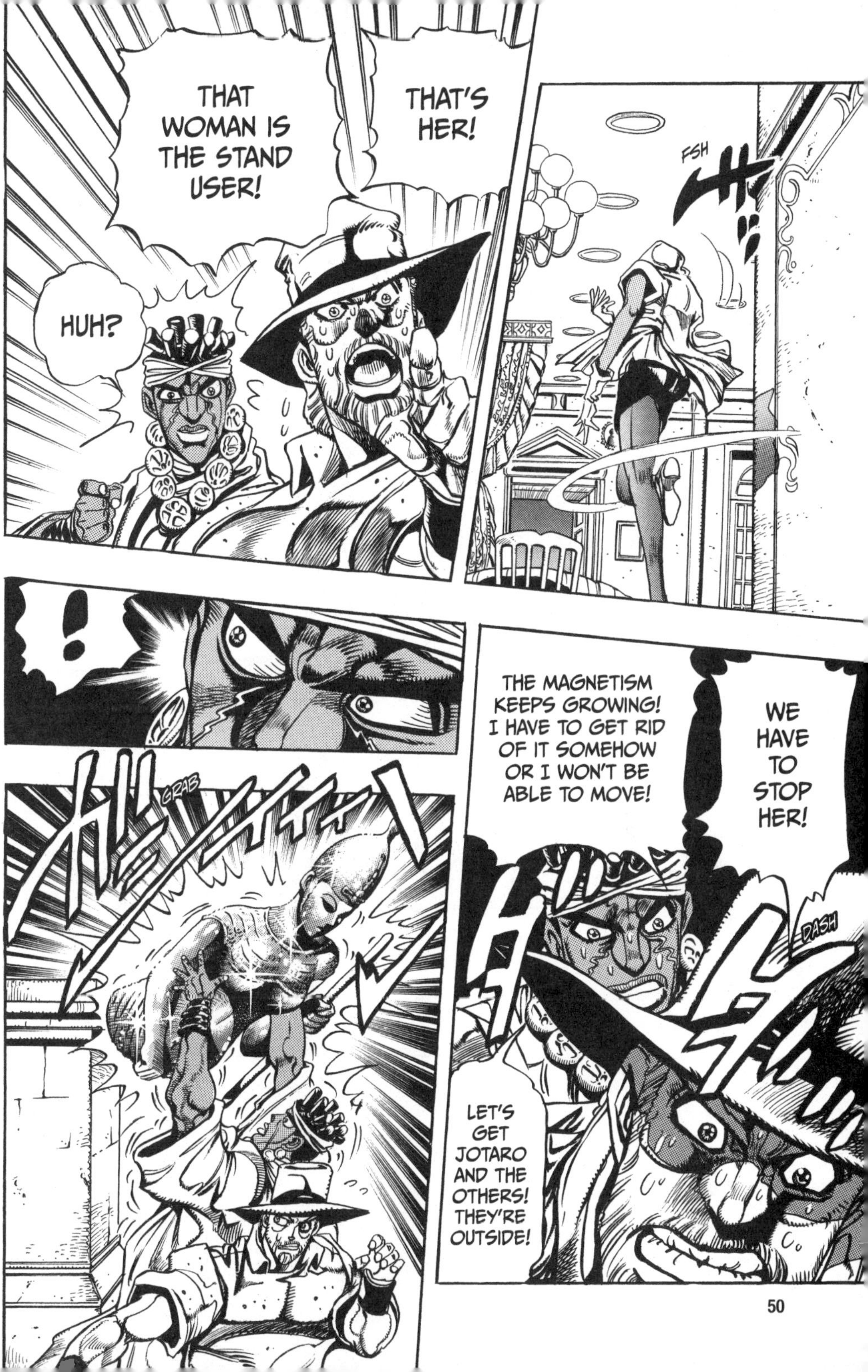
FSH
THAT'S HER!
THAT WOMAN IS THE STAND USER!
HUH?
WE HAVE TO STOP HER!
THE MAGNETISM KEEPS GROWING! I HAVE TO GET RID OF IT SOMEHOW OR I WON'T BE ABLE TO MOVE!
DASH
LET'S GET JOTARO AND THE OTHERS! THEY'RE OUTSIDE!
!
GRAB

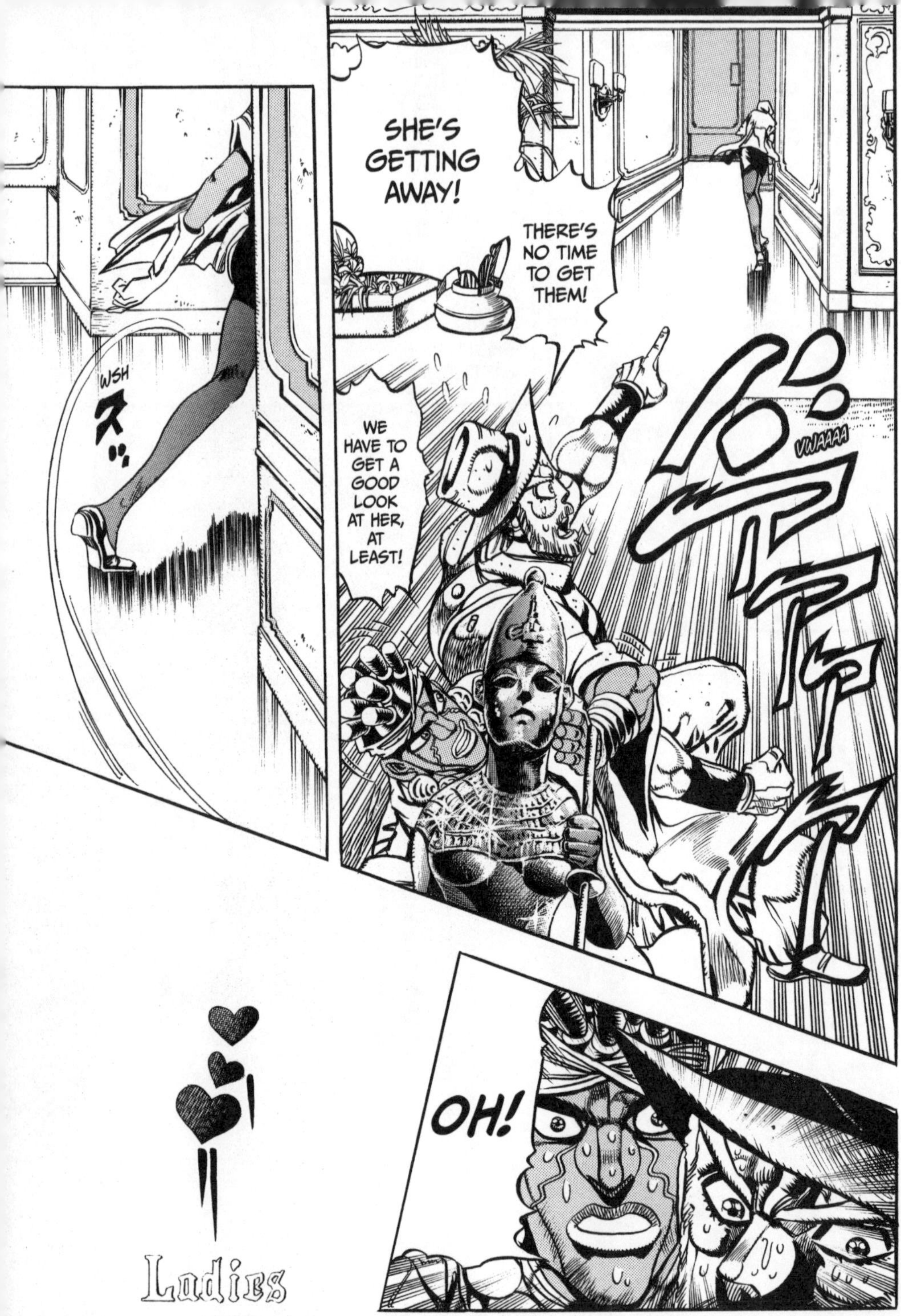
SHE'S GETTING AWAY!
THERE'S NO TIME TO GET THEM!
WE HAVE TO GET A GOOD LOOK AT HER, AT LEAST!
VWAAAA
WSH
ス
OH!
Ladies

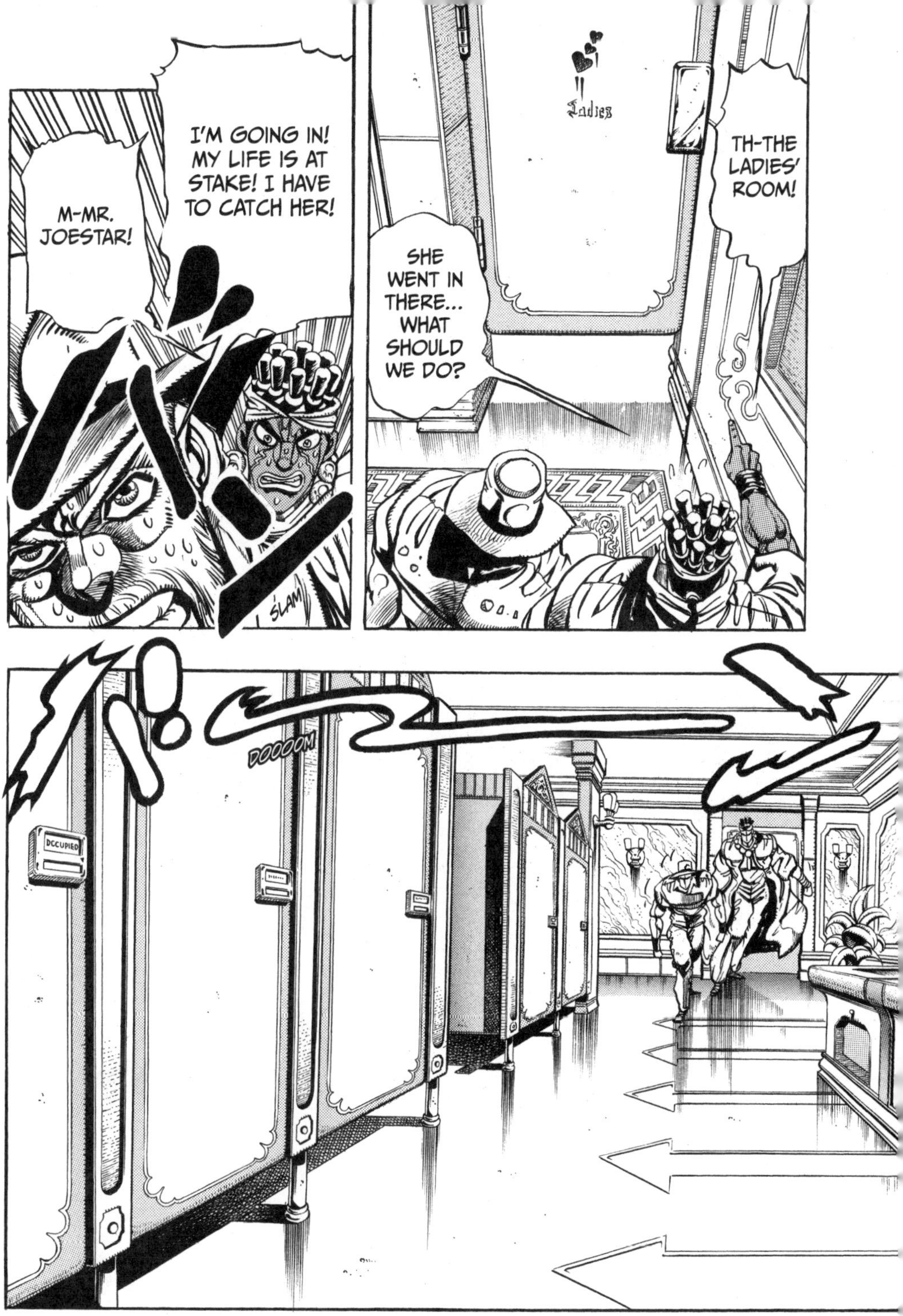
Ladies
TH-THE LADIES' ROOM!
SHE WENT IN THERE... WHAT SHOULD WE DO?
I'M GOING IN! MY LIFE IS AT STAKE! I HAVE TO CATCH HER!
M-MR. JOESTAR!
SLAM
DOOOOM
OCCUPIED

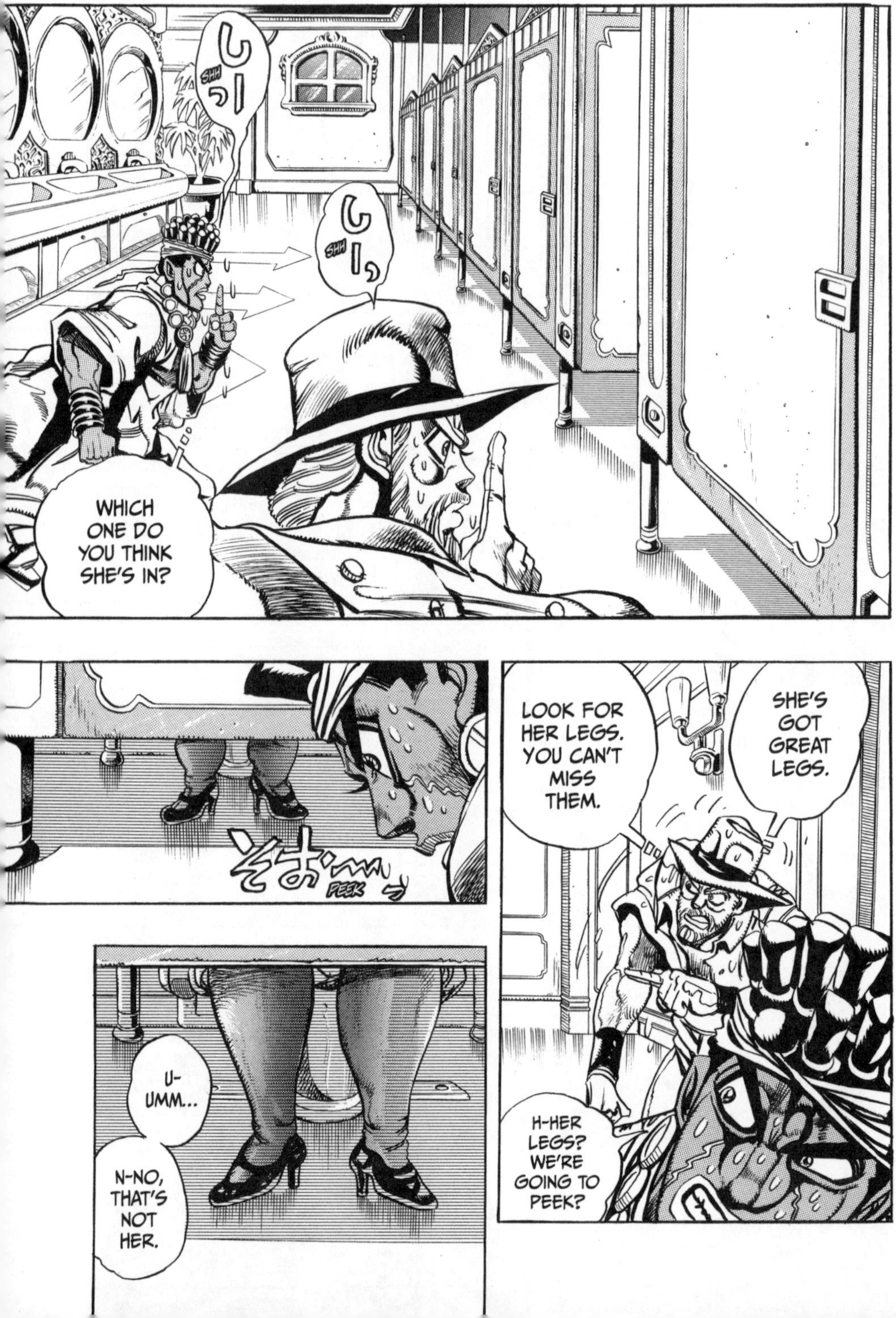

SHH
SHH
WHICH ONE DO YOU THINK SHE'S IN?
SHE'S GOT GREAT LEGS.
LOOK FOR HER LEGS. YOU CAN'T MISS THEM.
H-HER LEGS? WE'RE GOING TO PEEK?
PEEK
U-UMM...
N-NO, THAT'S NOT HER.

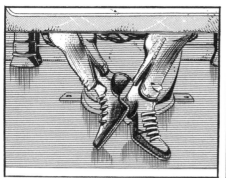
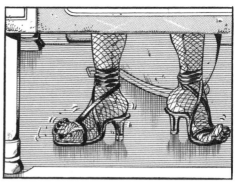
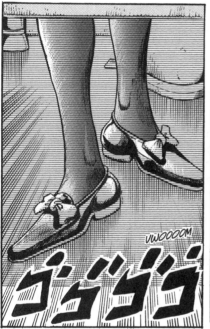
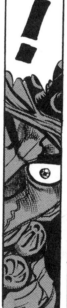
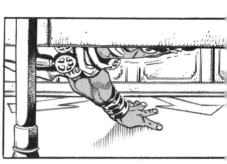
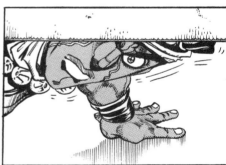
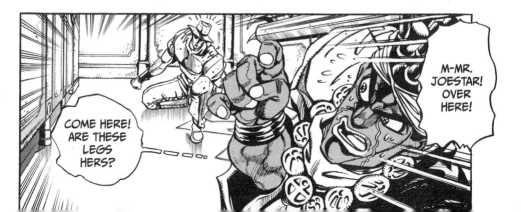

M—MR. JOESTAR! OVER HERE!

COME HERE! ARE THESE LEGS HERS?

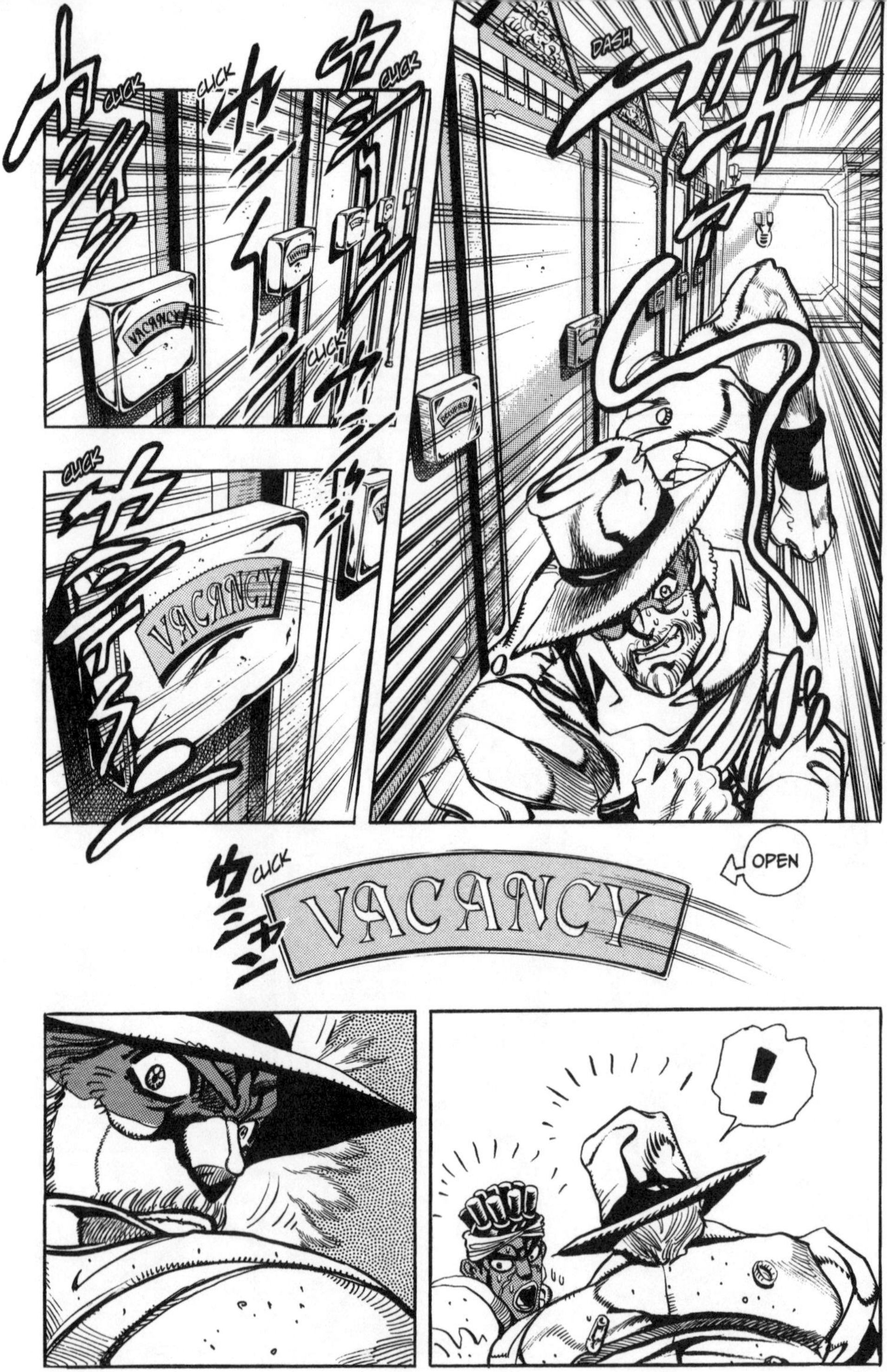

DASH
CLICK
CLICK
CLICK
CLICK
VACANCY
CLICK
VACANCY
CLICK
VACANCY
OPEN
!

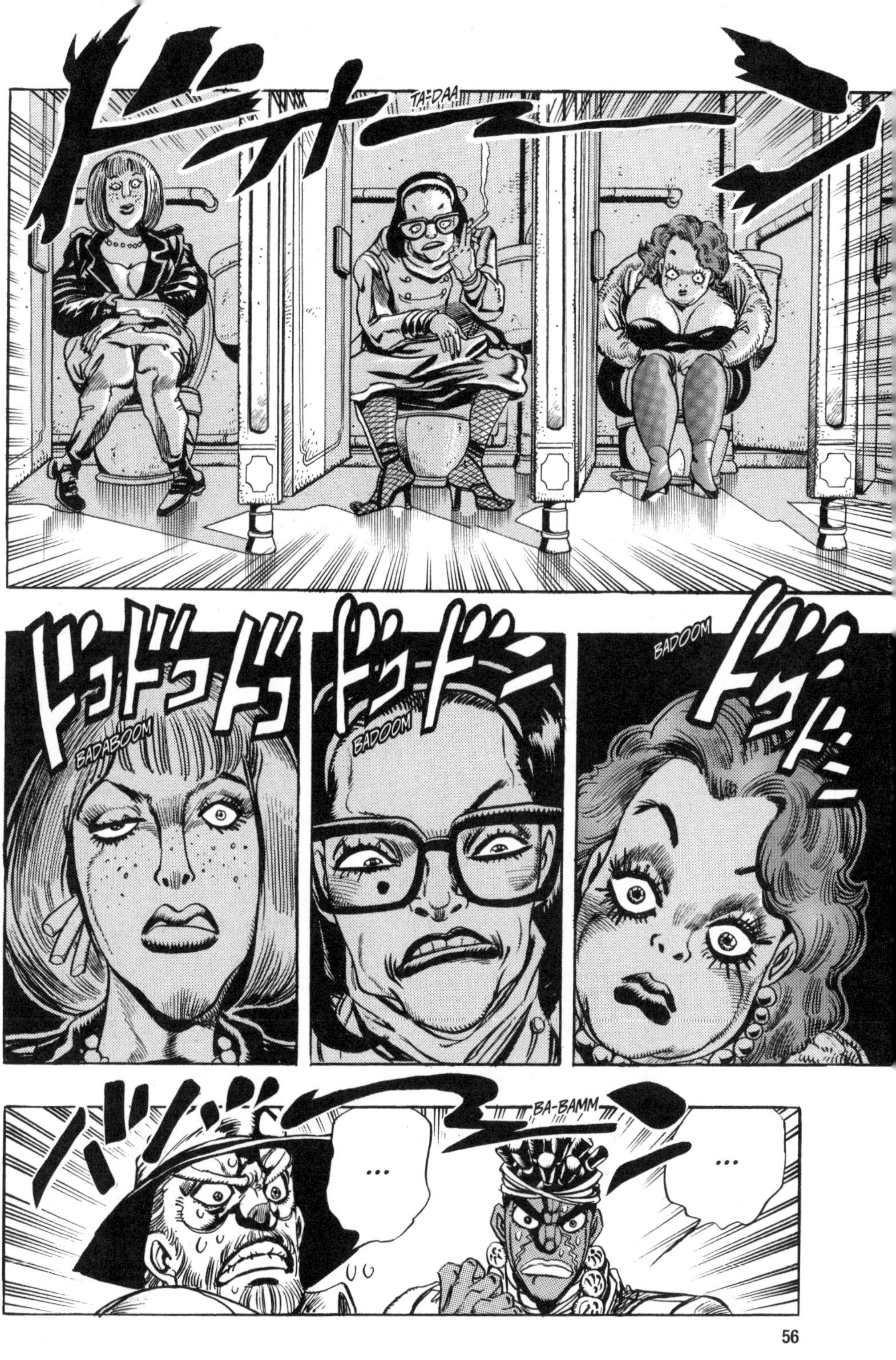
TA-DAA
BADOOM
BADOOM
BADABOOM
BA-BAMM
...
...

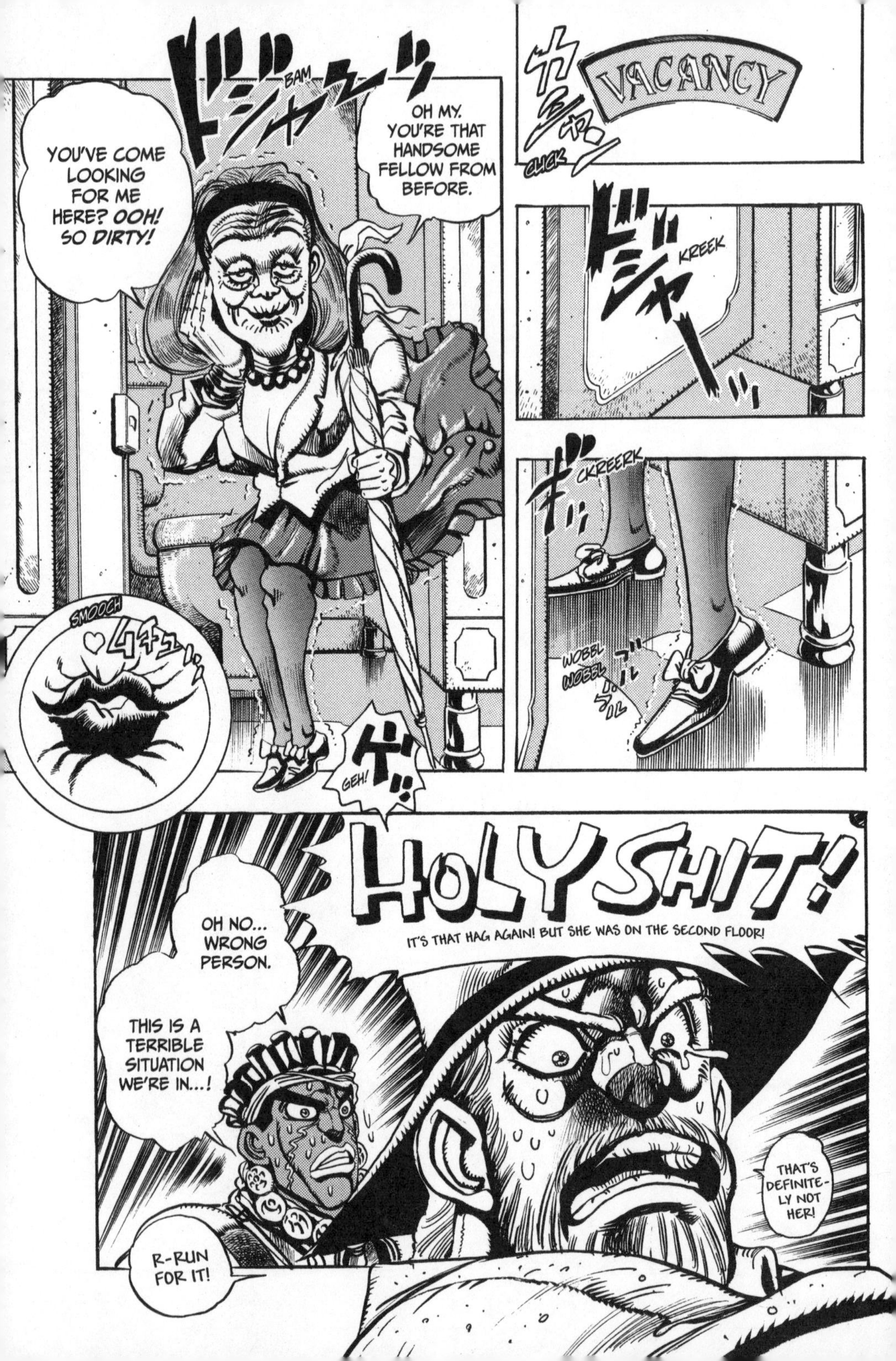

VACANCY
CLICK
KREEK
CKREERK
WOBBL WOBBL
BAM
OH MY. YOU'RE THAT HANDSOME FELLOW FROM BEFORE.
YOU'VE COME LOOKING FOR ME HERE? *OOH!* SO *DIRTY!*
SMOOCH
GEH!
HOLY SHIT!
IT'S THAT HAG AGAIN! BUT SHE WAS ON THE SECOND FLOOR!
THAT'S DEFINITE-LY NOT HER!
OH NO... WRONG PERSON.
THIS IS A TERRIBLE SITUATION WE'RE IN...!
R-RUN FOR IT!

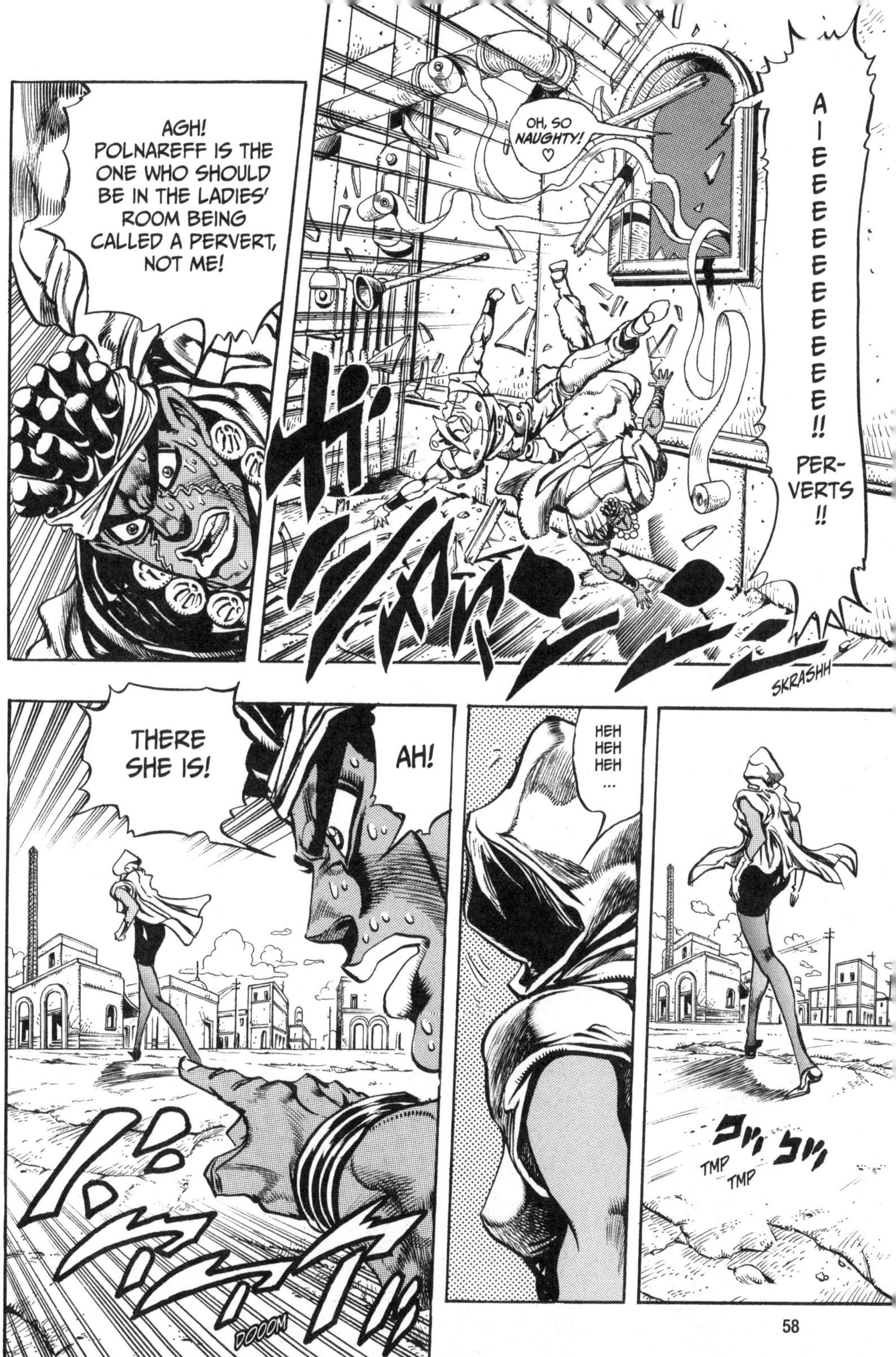
AIEEEEEEEEEEE!!
PERVERTS!!
OH, SO NAUGHTY! ♡
SKRASHH
AGH! POLNAREFF IS THE ONE WHO SHOULD BE IN THE LADIES' ROOM BEING CALLED A PERVERT, NOT ME!
TMP TMP
HEH HEH HEH ...
AH!
THERE SHE IS!
DOOOM

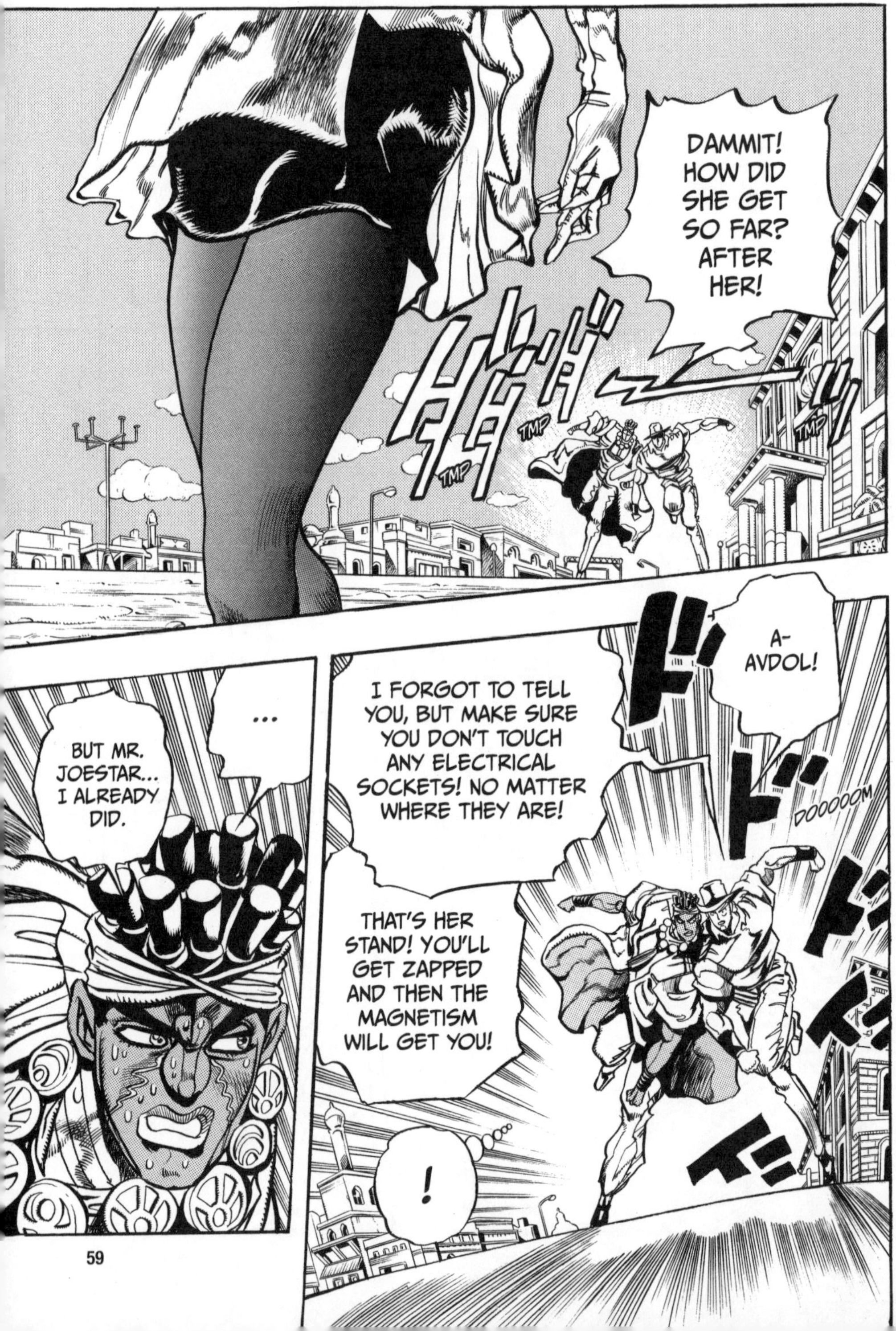
DAMMIT! HOW DID SHE GET SO FAR? AFTER HER!
TMP
TMP
TMP
A- AVDOL!
DOOOOOM
I FORGOT TO TELL YOU, BUT MAKE SURE YOU DON'T TOUCH ANY ELECTRICAL SOCKETS! NO MATTER WHERE THEY ARE!
THAT'S HER STAND! YOU'LL GET ZAPPED AND THEN THE MAGNETISM WILL GET YOU!
!
...
BUT MR. JOESTAR... I ALREADY DID.

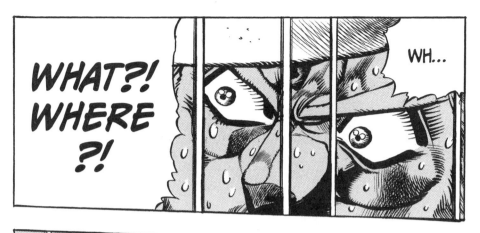

WH...

WHAT?! WHERE ?!

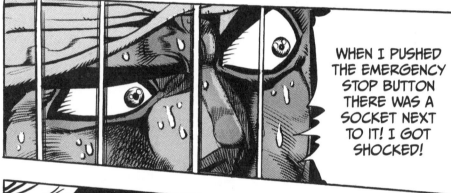

WHEN I PUSHED THE EMERGENCY STOP BUTTON THERE WAS A SOCKET NEXT TO IT! I GOT SHOCKED!

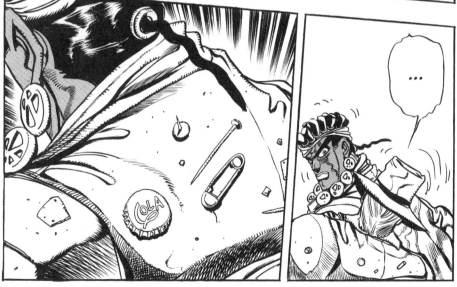

...

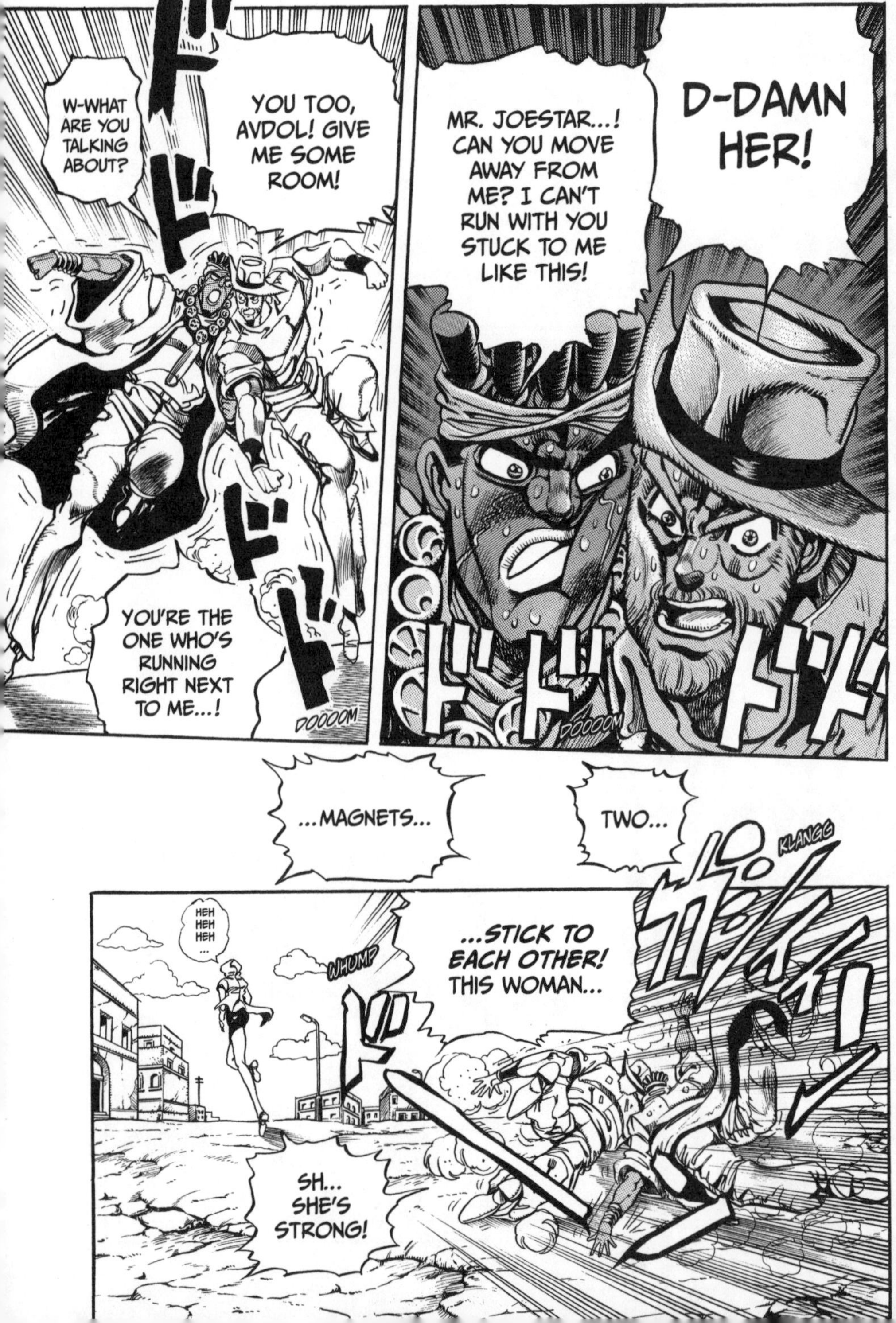
D-DAMN HER!
MR. JOESTAR...! CAN YOU MOVE AWAY FROM ME? I CAN'T RUN WITH YOU STUCK TO ME LIKE THIS!
DOOOOM
YOU TOO, AVDOL! GIVE ME SOME ROOM!
W-WHAT ARE YOU TALKING ABOUT?
YOU'RE THE ONE WHO'S RUNNING RIGHT NEXT TO ME...!
DOOOOM
TWO...
...MAGNETS...
KLANGG
...STICK TO EACH OTHER! THIS WOMAN...
WHUMP
HEH HEH HEH ...
SH... SHE'S STRONG!

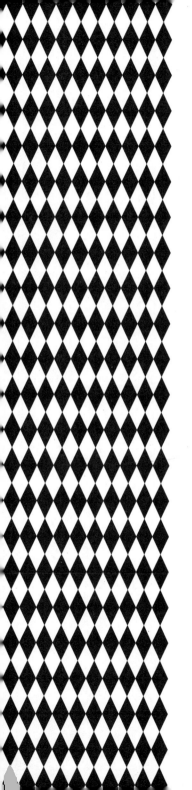
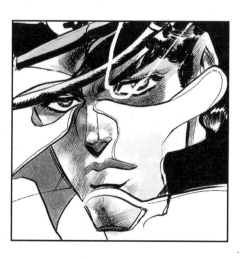

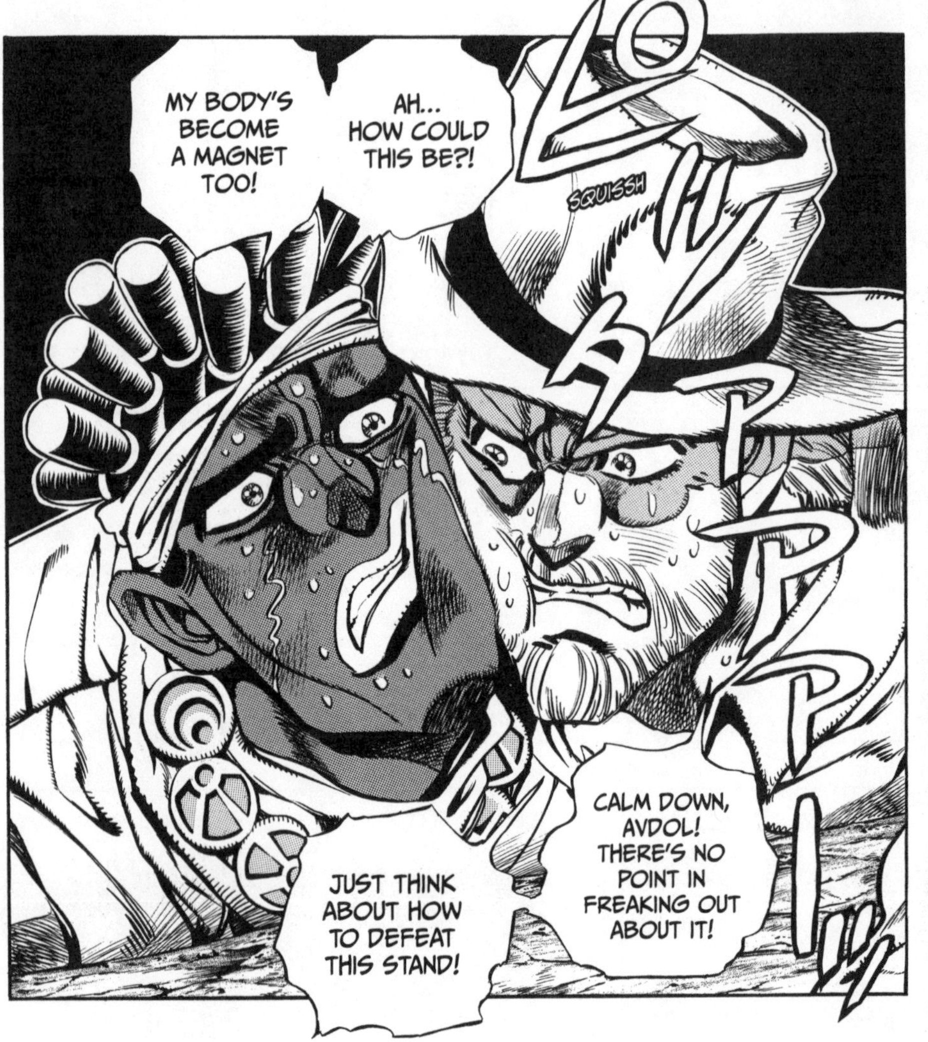
AH... HOW COULD THIS BE?!
MY BODY'S BECOME A MAGNET TOO!
SQUISSH
CALM DOWN, AVDOL! THERE'S NO POINT IN FREAKING OUT ABOUT IT!
JUST THINK ABOUT HOW TO DEFEAT THIS STAND!

CHAPTER 89: "Bast" Mariah PART 4

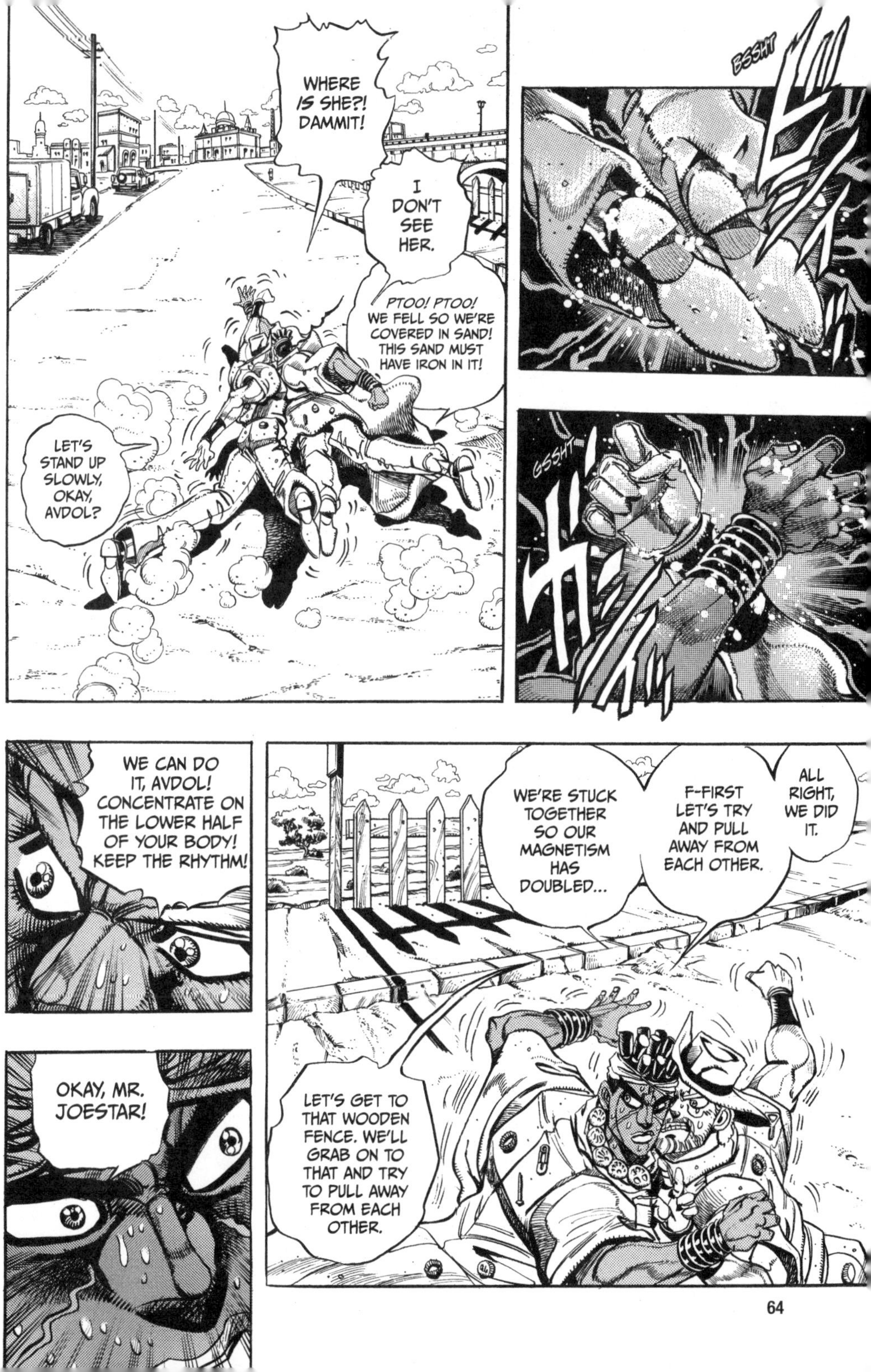
BSSHT
GSSHT
WHERE IS SHE?! DAMMIT!
I DON'T SEE HER.
PTOO! PTOO! WE FELL SO WE'RE COVERED IN SAND! THIS SAND MUST HAVE IRON IN IT!
LET'S STAND UP SLOWLY, OKAY, AVDOL?
ALL RIGHT, WE DID IT.
F-FIRST LET'S TRY AND PULL AWAY FROM EACH OTHER.
WE'RE STUCK TOGETHER SO OUR MAGNETISM HAS DOUBLED...
LET'S GET TO THAT WOODEN FENCE. WE'LL GRAB ON TO THAT AND TRY TO PULL AWAY FROM EACH OTHER.
WE CAN DO IT, AVDOL! CONCENTRATE ON THE LOWER HALF OF YOUR BODY! KEEP THE RHYTHM!
OKAY, MR. JOESTAR!

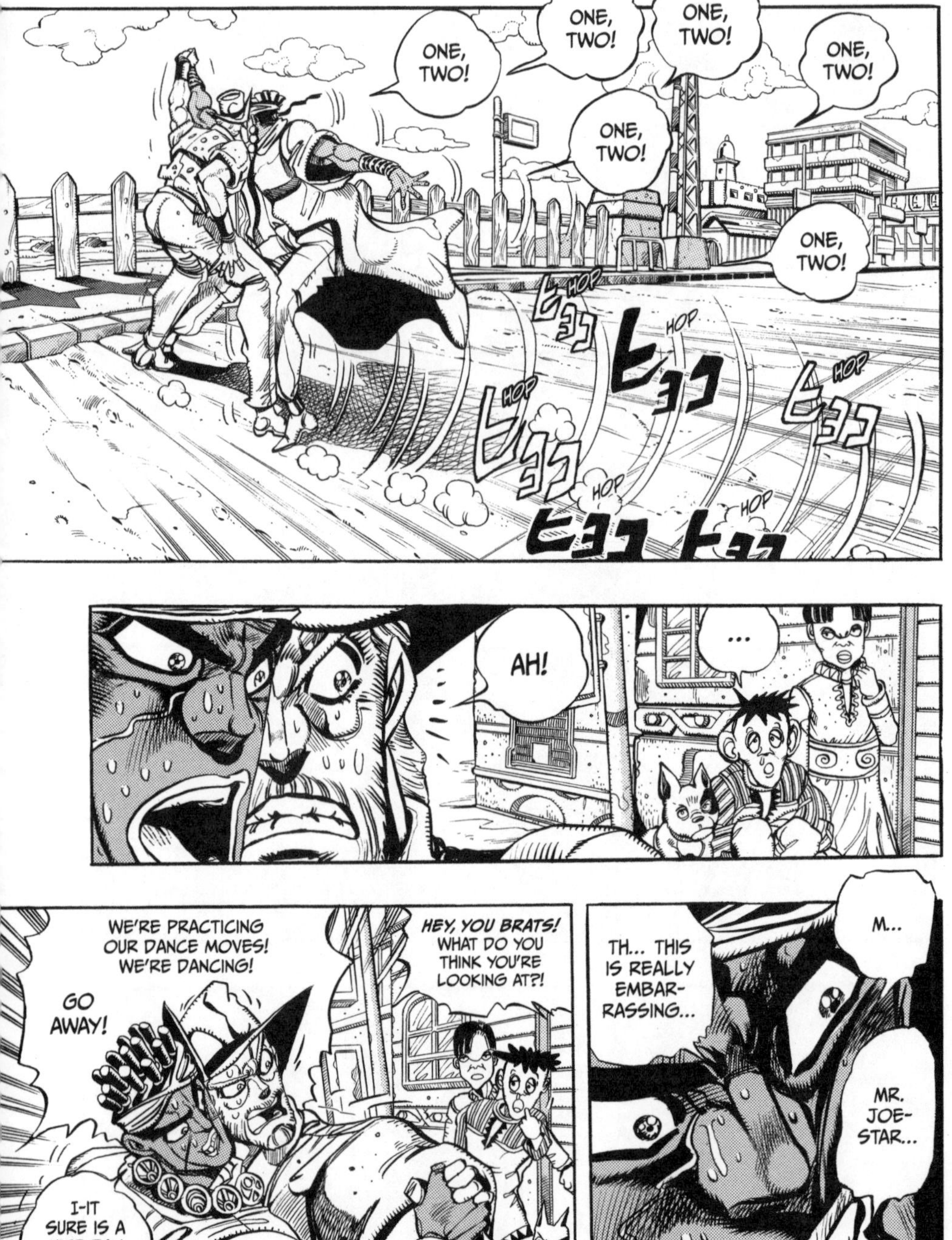
ONE, TWO!
ONE, TWO!
ONE, TWO!
ONE, TWO!
ONE, TWO!
ONE, TWO!
ヒョコ HOP
ヒョコ HOP
ヒョコ HOP
ヒョコ HOP
ヒョコ HOP
ヒョコ HOP
...
AH!
M...
TH... THIS IS REALLY EMBARRASSING...
MR. JOESTAR...
HEY, YOU BRATS! WHAT DO YOU THINK YOU'RE LOOKING AT?!
WE'RE PRACTICING OUR DANCE MOVES! WE'RE DANCING!
GO AWAY!
I-IT SURE IS A NICE DAY TO DANCE OUTSIDE!

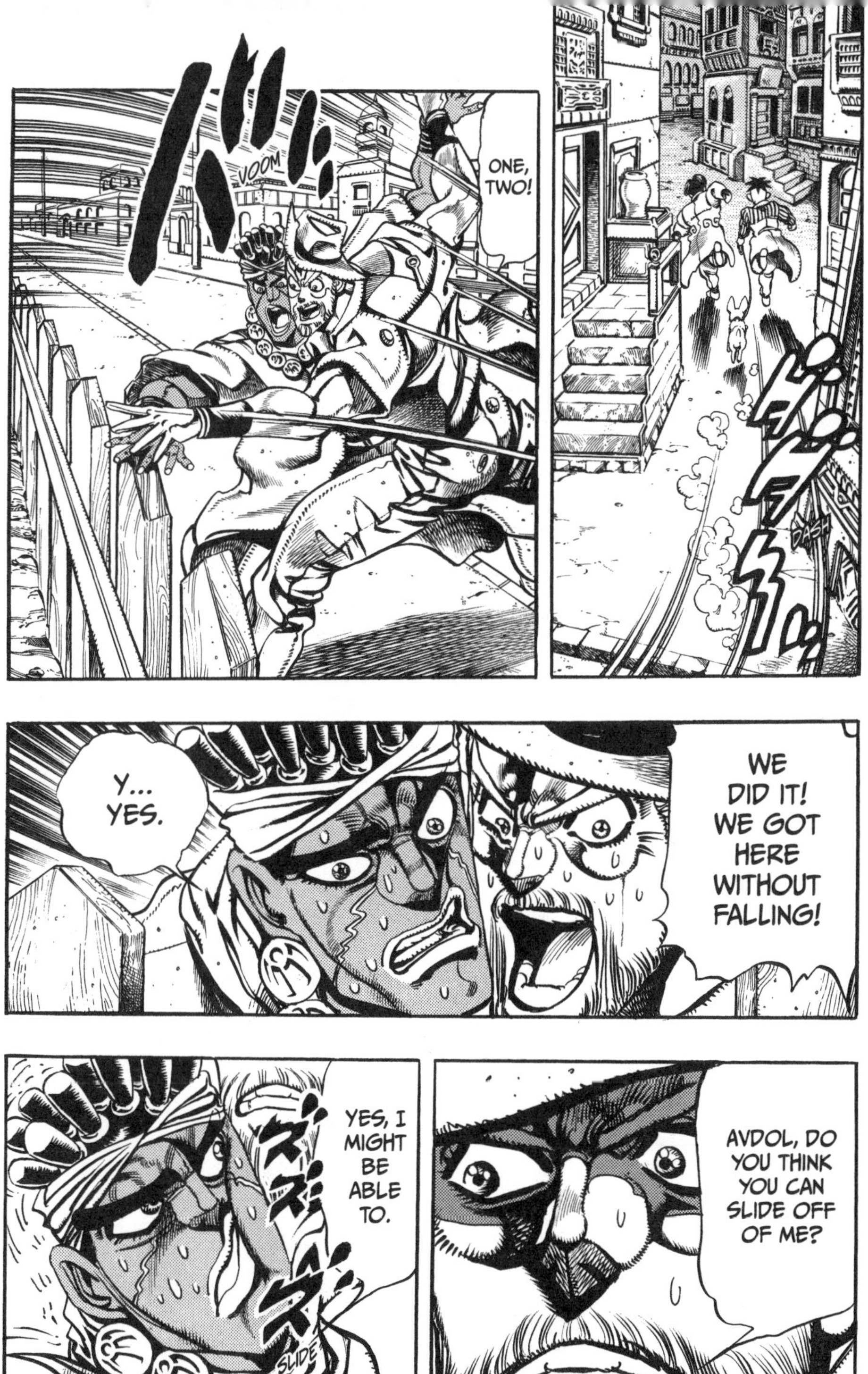
DASH
ONE, TWO!
VOOM
WE DID IT! WE GOT HERE WITHOUT FALLING!
Y... YES.
AVDOL, DO YOU THINK YOU CAN SLIDE OFF OF ME?
YES, I MIGHT BE ABLE TO.
SLIDE

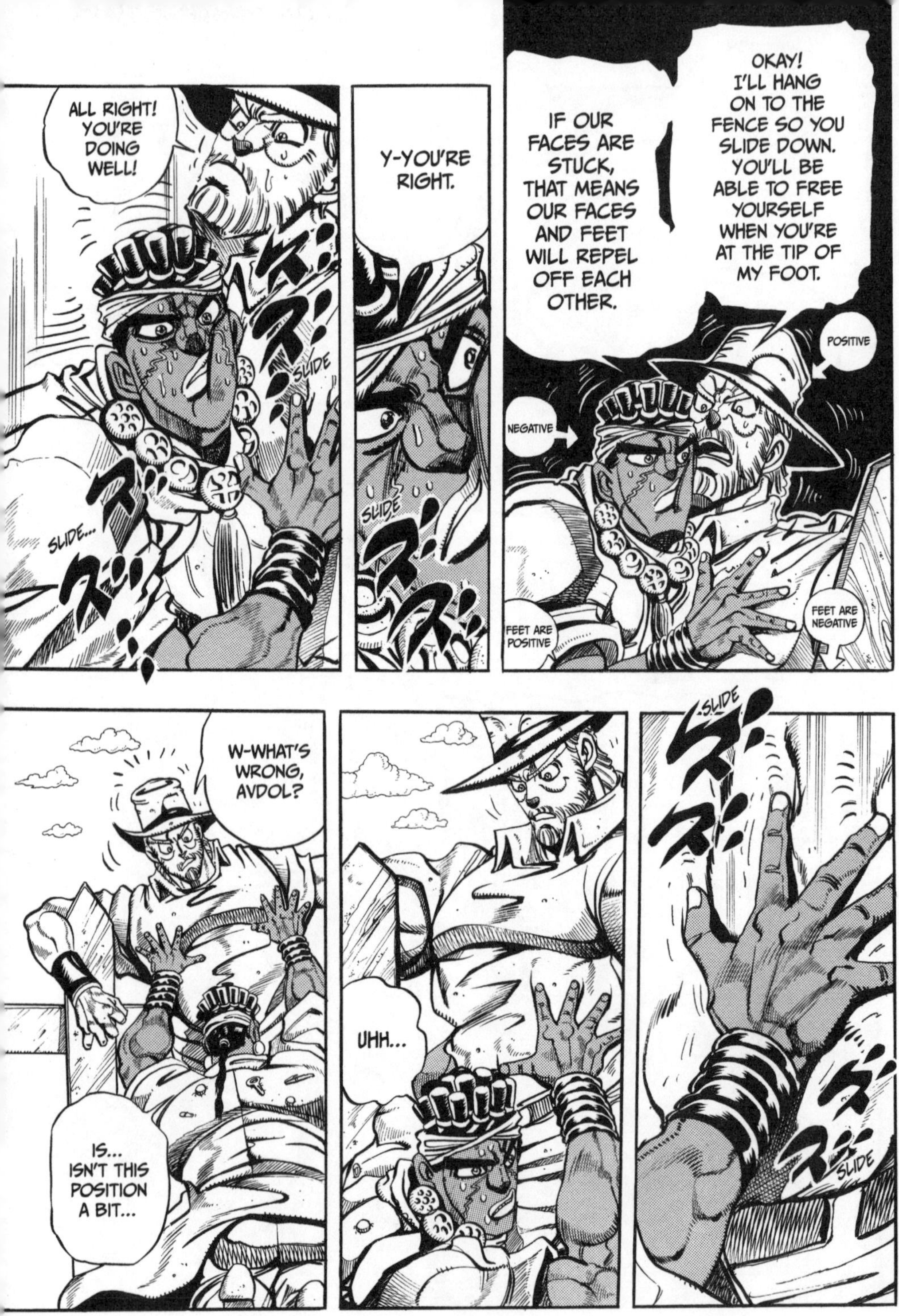
OKAY! I'LL HANG ON TO THE FENCE SO YOU SLIDE DOWN. YOU'LL BE ABLE TO FREE YOURSELF WHEN YOU'RE AT THE TIP OF MY FOOT.
IF OUR FACES ARE STUCK, THAT MEANS OUR FACES AND FEET WILL REPEL OFF EACH OTHER.
POSITIVE
NEGATIVE
FEET ARE NEGATIVE
FEET ARE POSITIVE
Y-YOU'RE RIGHT.
SLIDE
ALL RIGHT! YOU'RE DOING WELL!
SLIDE
SLIDE...
SLIDE
SLIDE
UHH...
W-WHAT'S WRONG, AVDOL?
IS... ISN'T THIS POSITION A BIT...

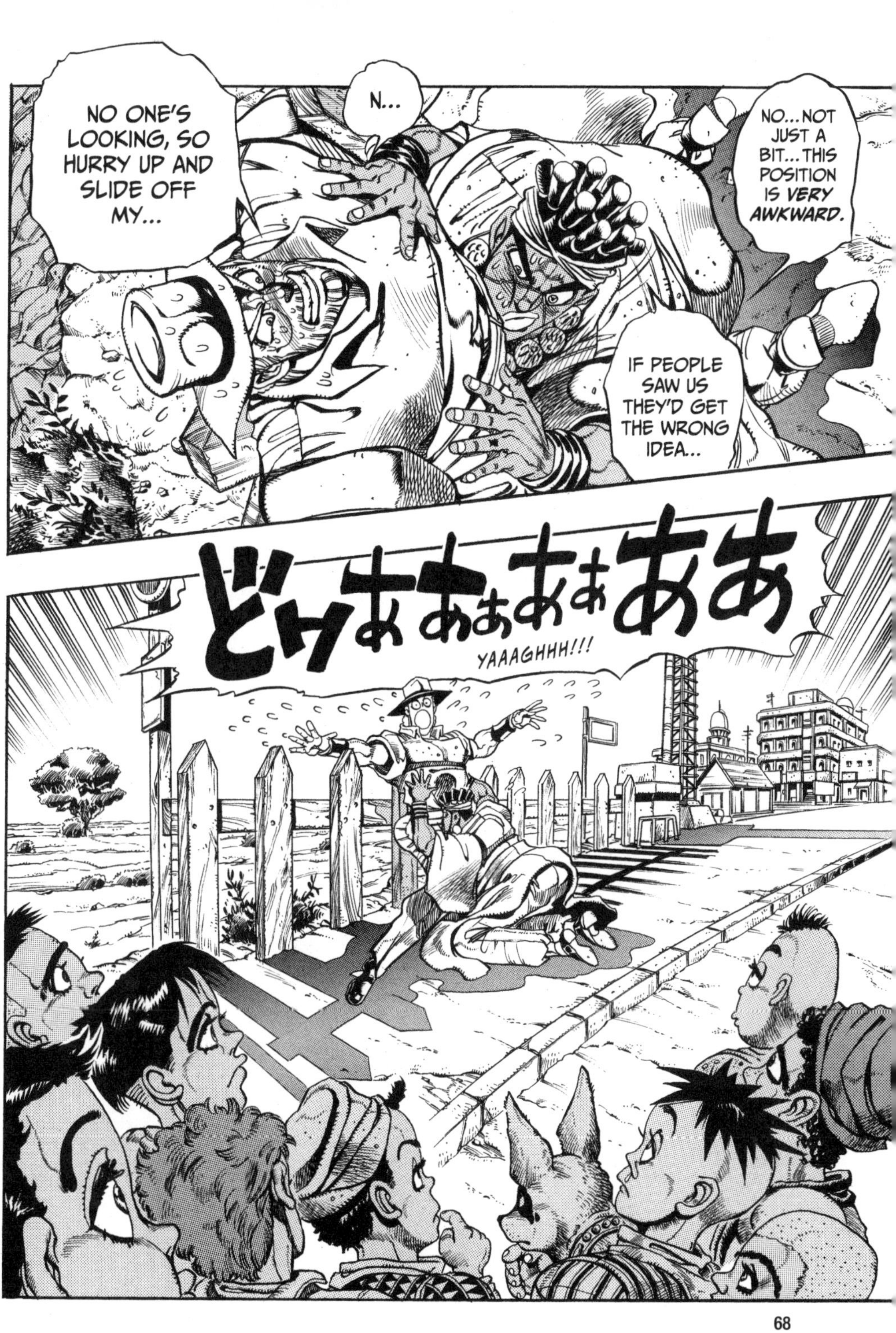
NO...NOT JUST A BIT...THIS POSITION IS *VERY AWKWARD.*
IF PEOPLE SAW US THEY'D GET THE WRONG IDEA...
N...
NO ONE'S LOOKING, SO HURRY UP AND SLIDE OFF MY...
どゥあああぁあぁああ
YAAAGHHH!!!

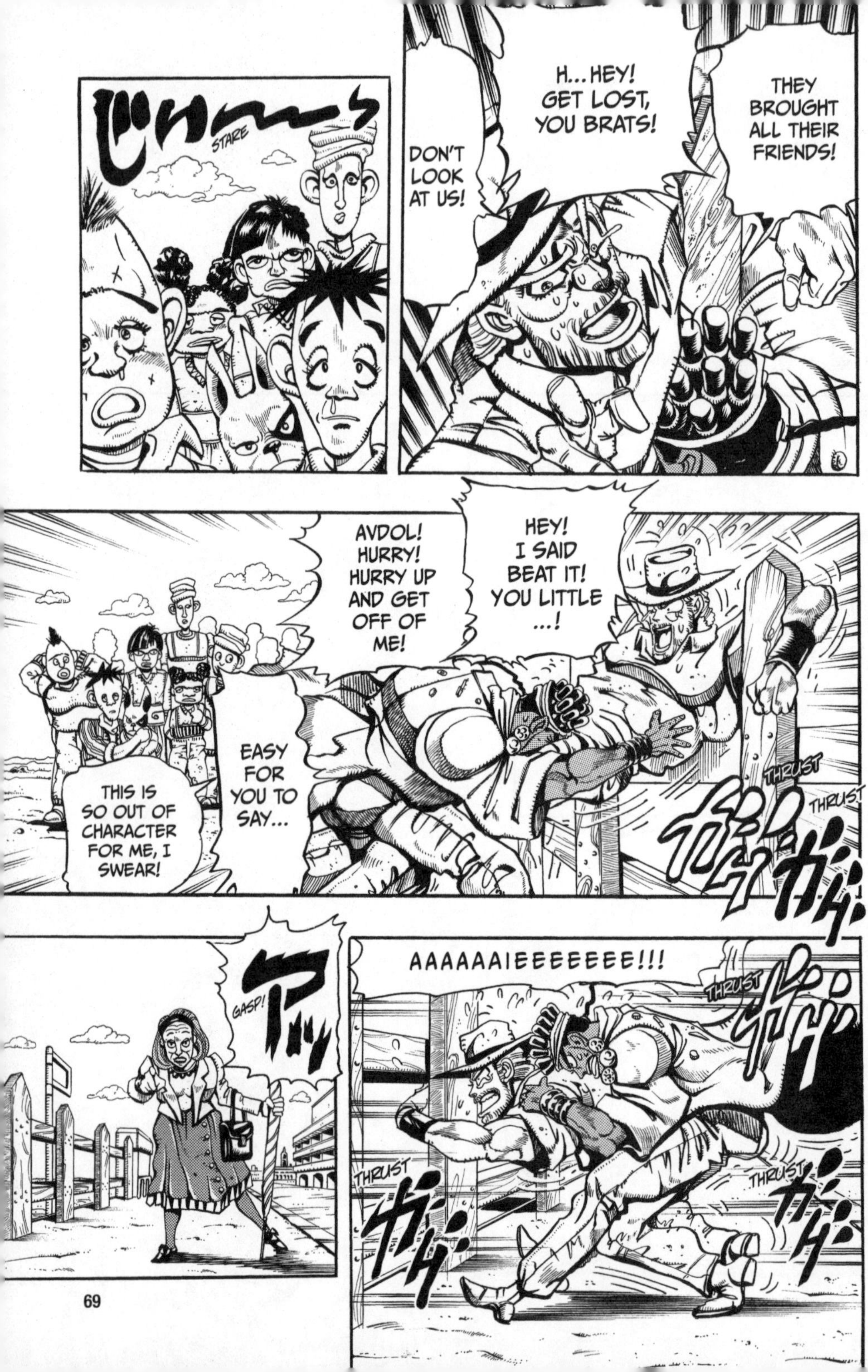
THEY BROUGHT ALL THEIR FRIENDS!
H... HEY! GET LOST, YOU BRATS!
DON'T LOOK AT US!
STARE
HEY! I SAID BEAT IT! YOU LITTLE ...!
AVDOL! HURRY! HURRY UP AND GET OFF OF ME!
THRUST
THRUST
EASY FOR YOU TO SAY...
THIS IS SO OUT OF CHARACTER FOR ME, I SWEAR!
AAAAAAIEEEEEEE!!!
THRUST
THRUST
THRUST
GASP!

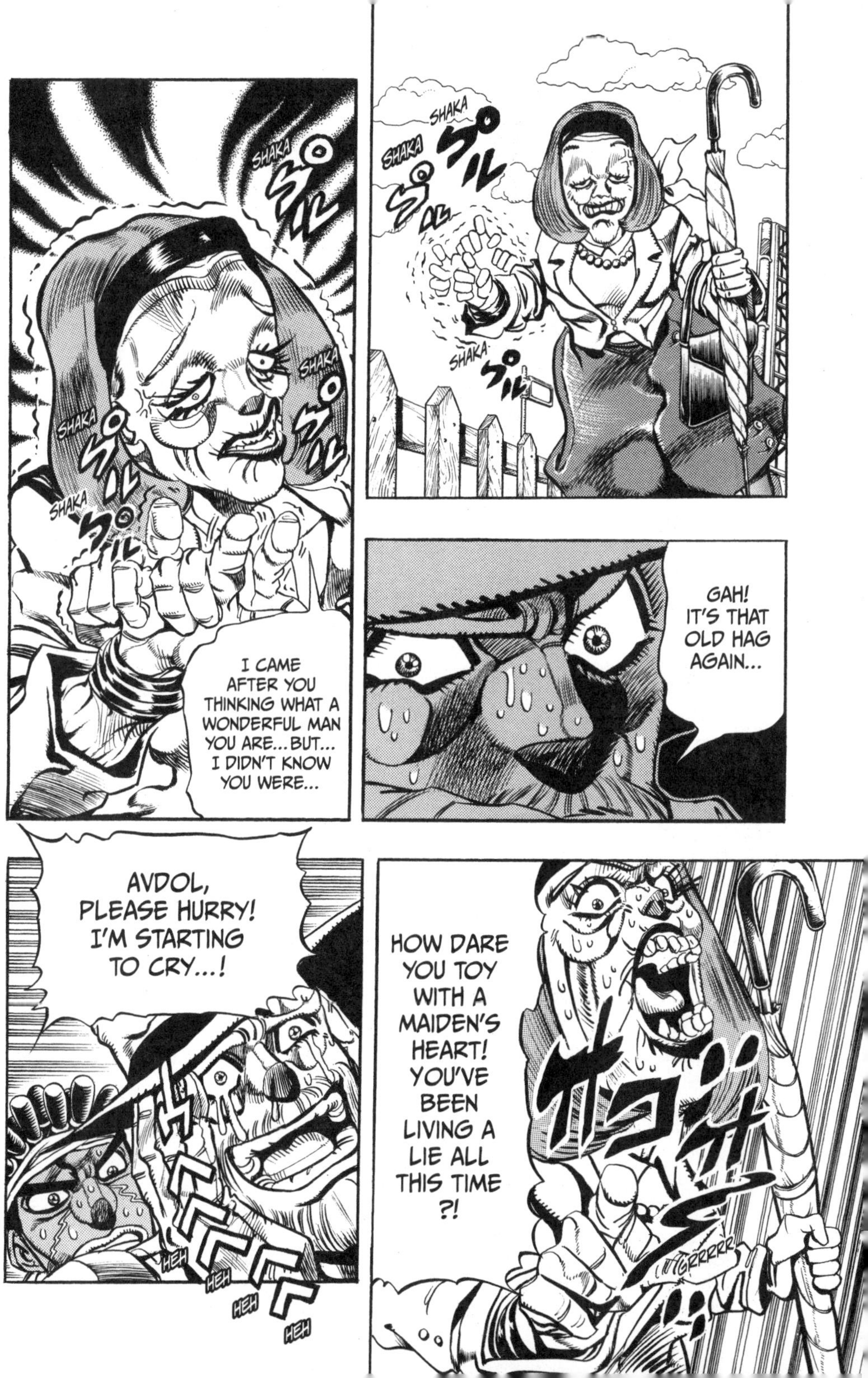
SHAKA
SHAKA
SHAKA
GAH! IT'S THAT OLD HAG AGAIN...
SHAKA
SHAKA
SHAKA
SHAKA
I CAME AFTER YOU THINKING WHAT A WONDERFUL MAN YOU ARE...BUT... I DIDN'T KNOW YOU WERE...
HOW DARE YOU TOY WITH A MAIDEN'S HEART! YOU'VE BEEN LIVING A LIE ALL THIS TIME ?!
GRRRRR
AVDOL, PLEASE HURRY! I'M STARTING TO CRY...!
HEH
HEH
HEH
HEH

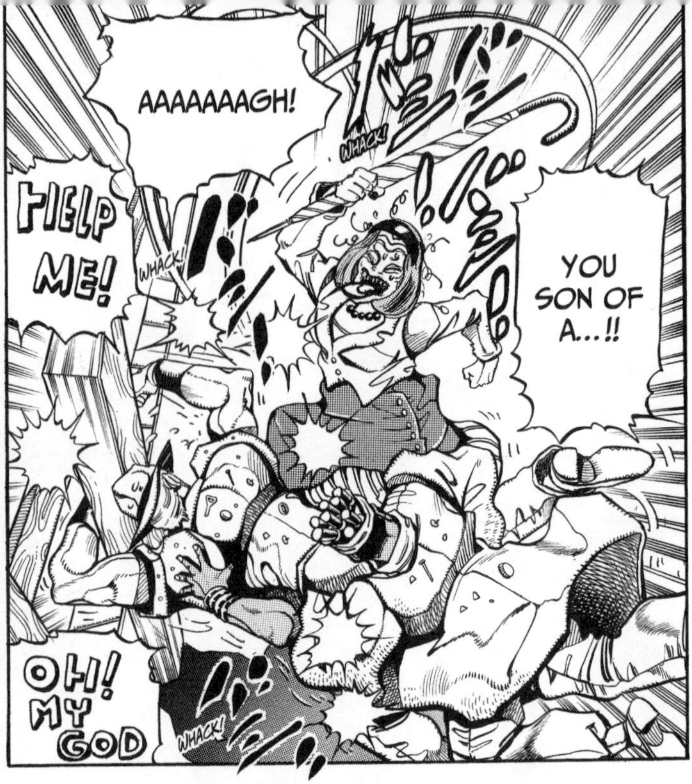
AAAAAAAGH!
WHACK!
YOU SON OF A...!!
HELP ME!
WHACK!
OH! MY GOD
WHACK!
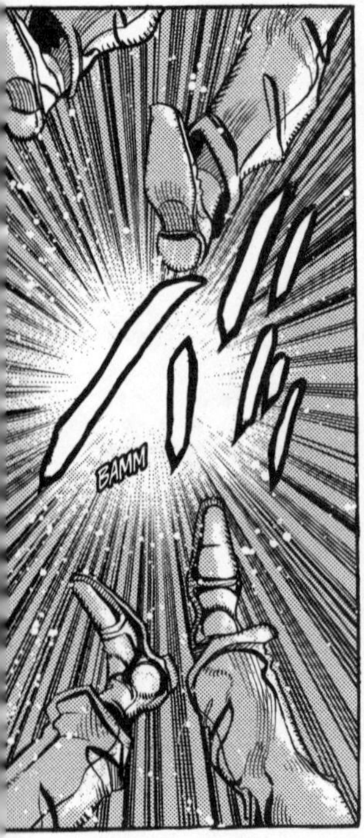
BAMM
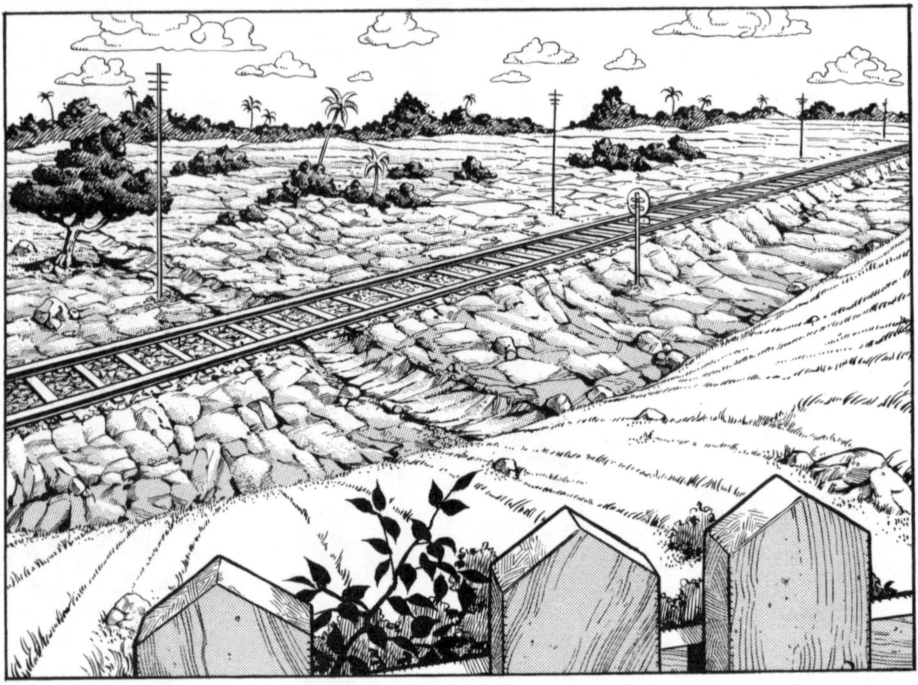

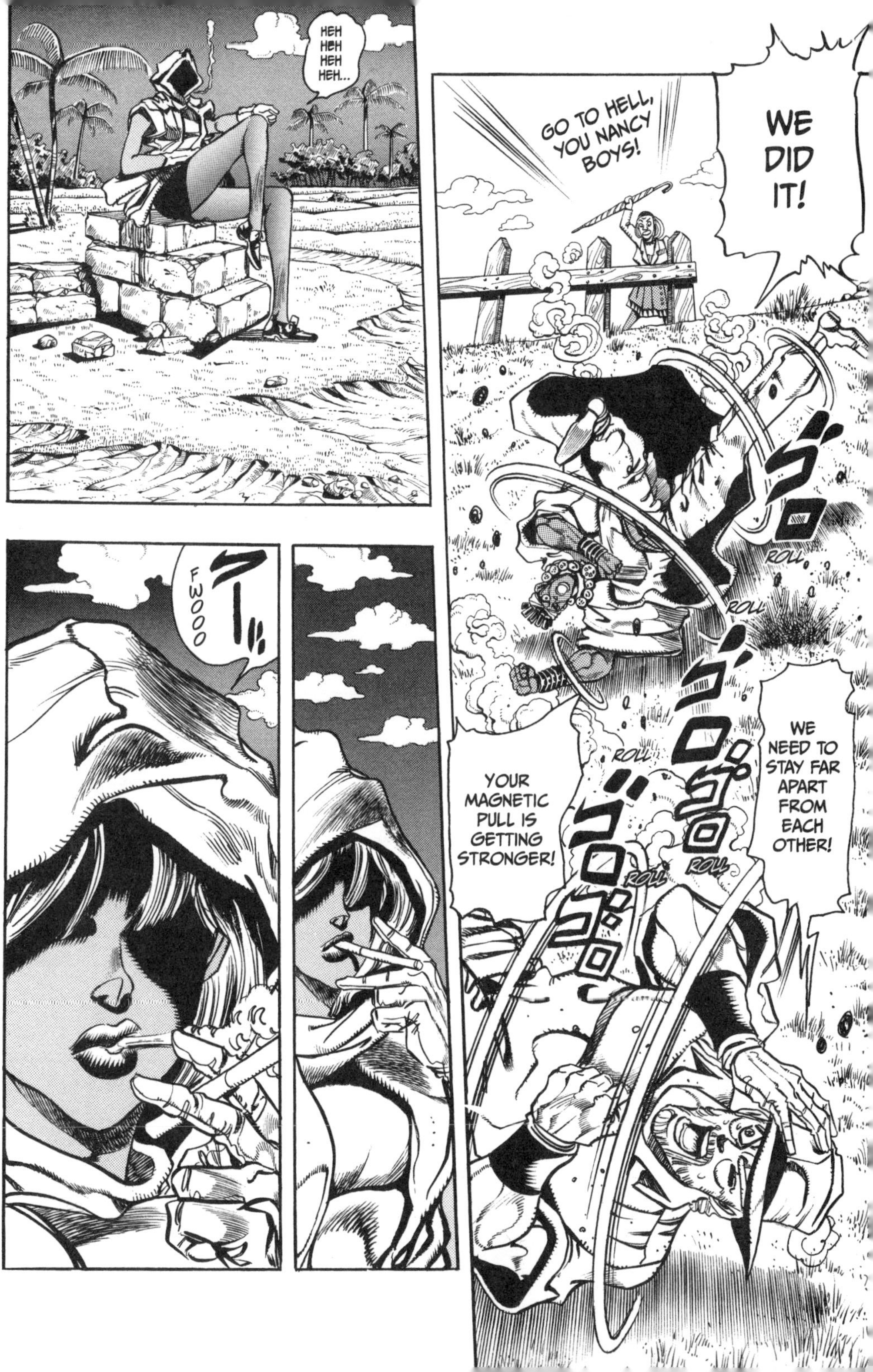
WE DID IT!
GO TO HELL, YOU NANCY BOYS!
ROLL
ROLL
WE NEED TO STAY FAR APART FROM EACH OTHER!
YOUR MAGNETIC PULL IS GETTING STRONGER!
ROLL
ROLL
ROLL
HEH HEH HEH HEH...
FWOOO

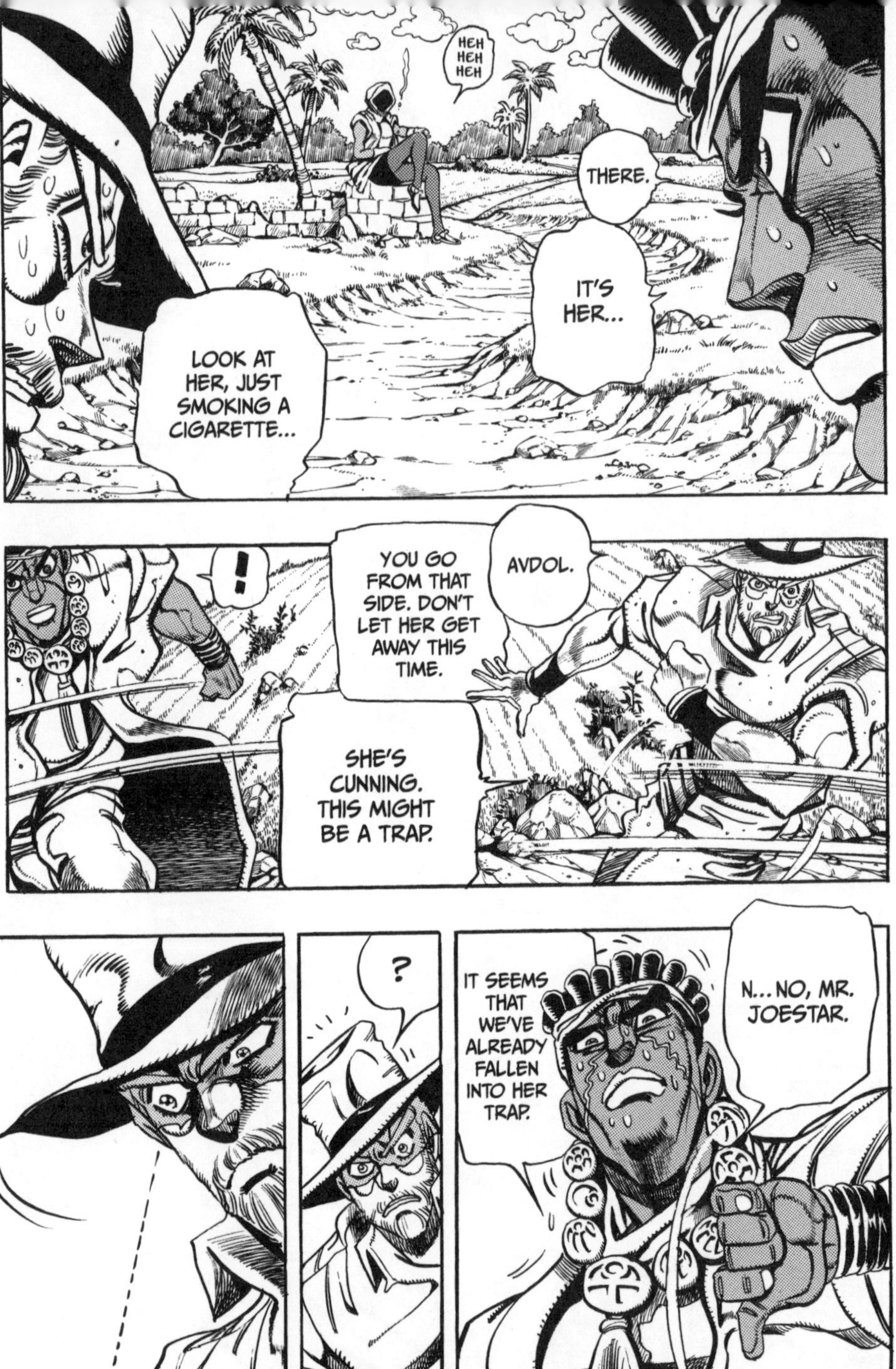
THERE.
IT'S HER...
HEH HEH HEH
LOOK AT HER, JUST SMOKING A CIGARETTE...
AVDOL.
YOU GO FROM THAT SIDE. DON'T LET HER GET AWAY THIS TIME.
SHE'S CUNNING. THIS MIGHT BE A TRAP.
!
N... NO, MR. JOESTAR.
IT SEEMS THAT WE'VE ALREADY FALLEN INTO HER TRAP.
?

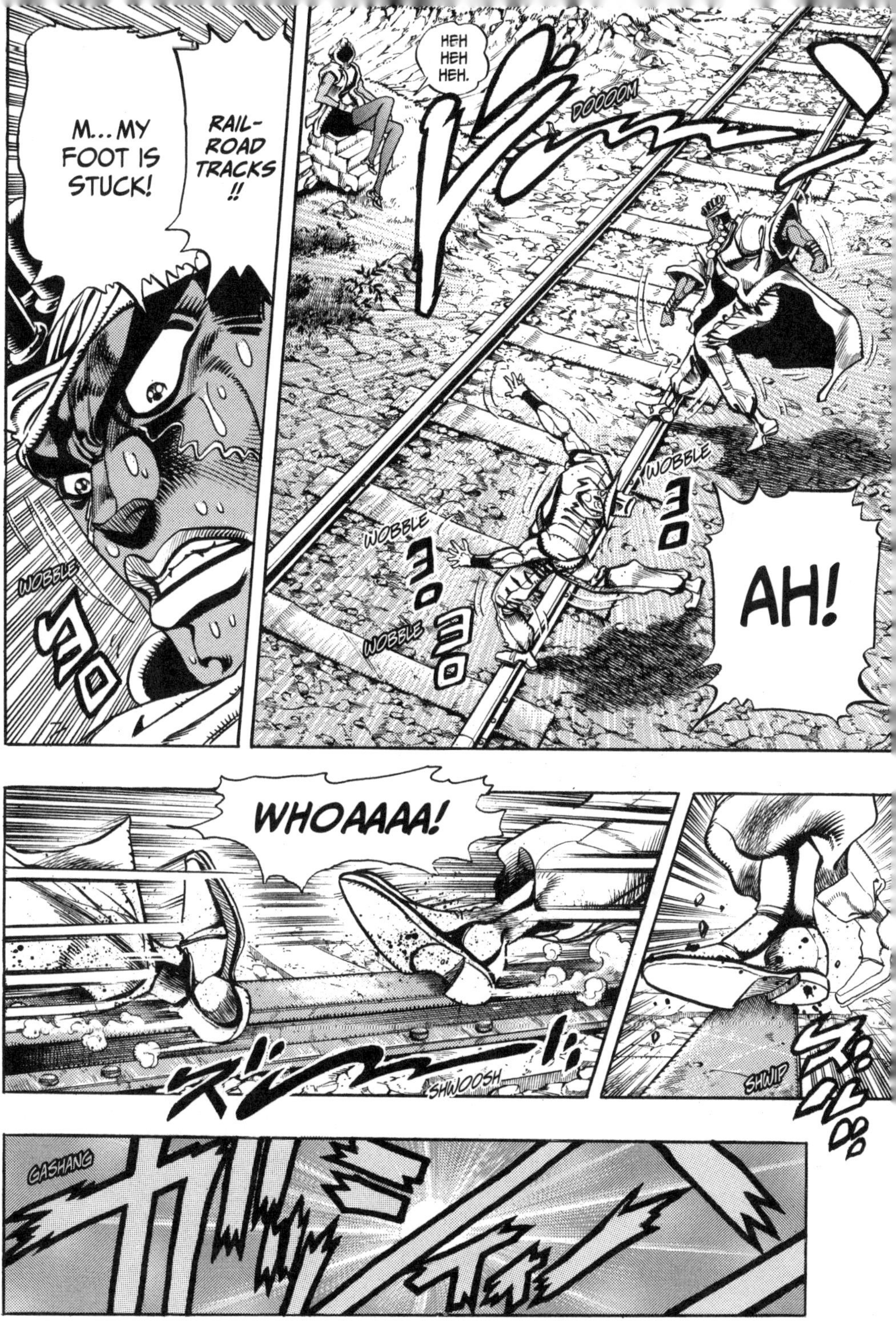
HEH HEH HEH.
DOOOOM
WOBBLE
AH!
WOBBLE
WOBBLE
RAIL-ROAD TRACKS !!
M...MY FOOT IS STUCK!
WOBBLE
SHWIP
WHOAAAA!
SHWOOSH
GASHANG

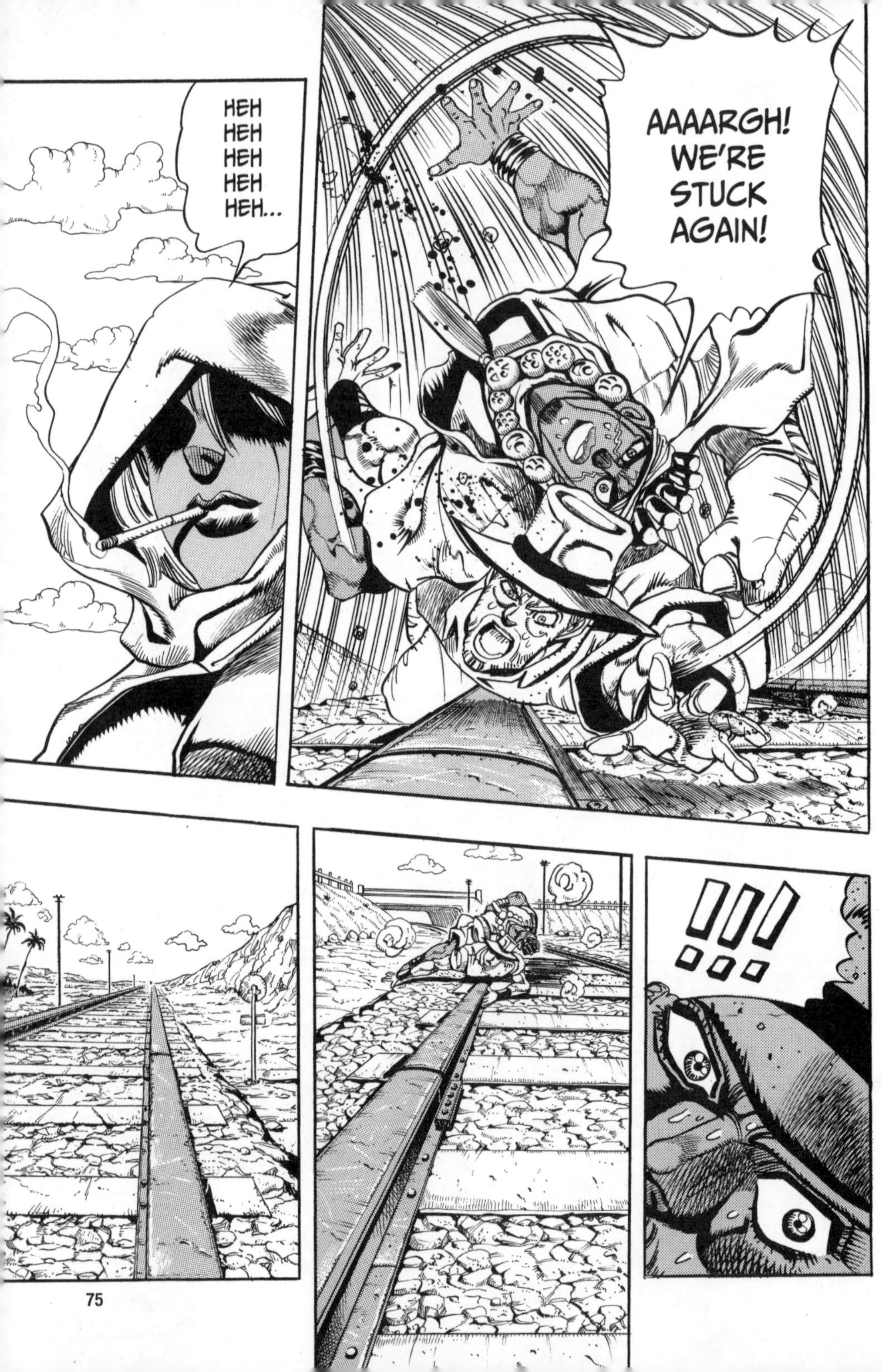
AAAARGH! WE'RE STUCK AGAIN!
HEH HEH HEH HEH HEH...
!!!

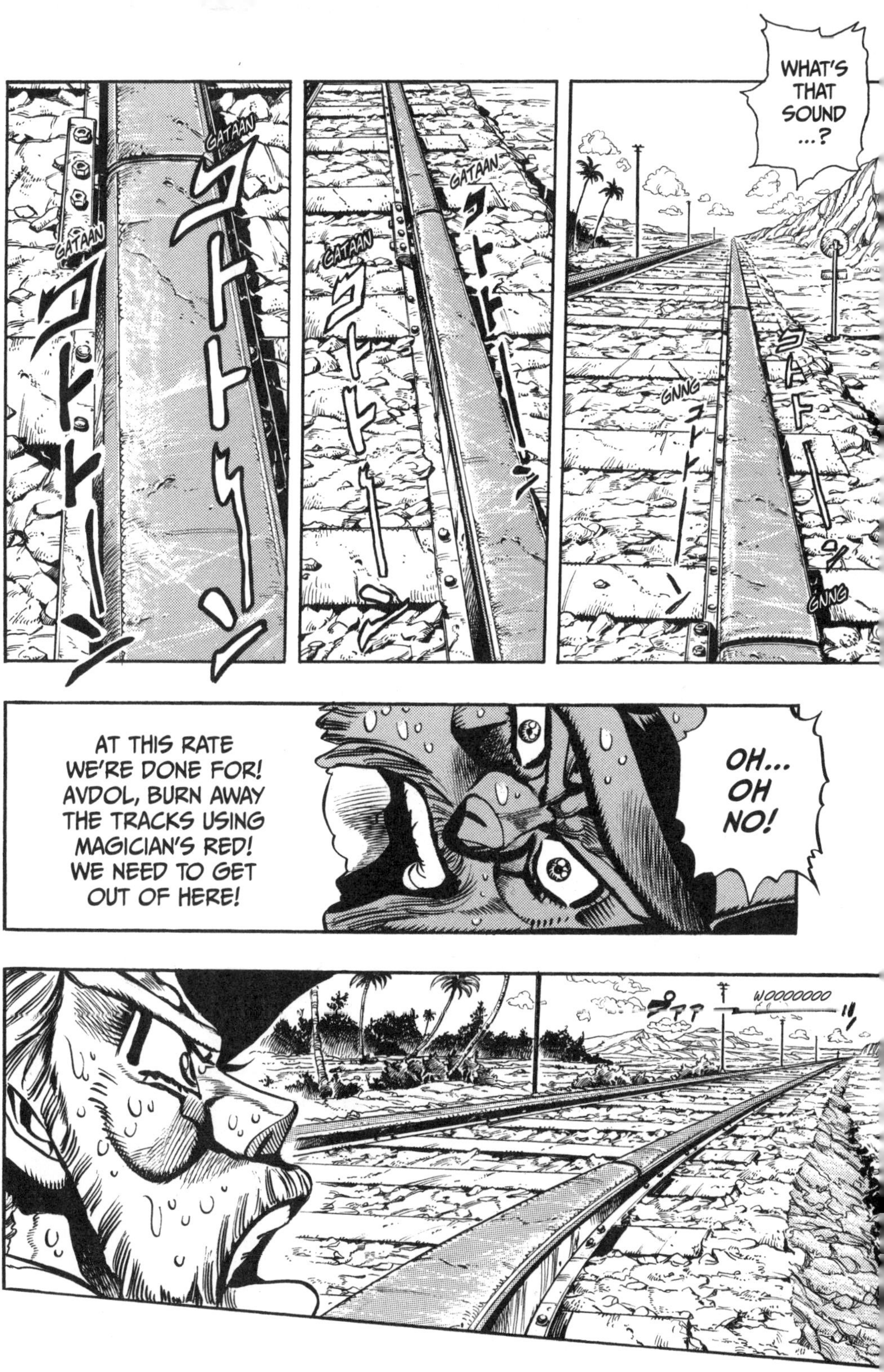
WHAT'S THAT SOUND ...?
GNNG
GNNG
GATAAN
GATAAN
GATAAN
GATAAN
OH... OH NO!
AT THIS RATE WE'RE DONE FOR! AVDOL, BURN AWAY THE TRACKS USING MAGICIAN'S RED! WE NEED TO GET OUT OF HERE!
WOOOOOOO

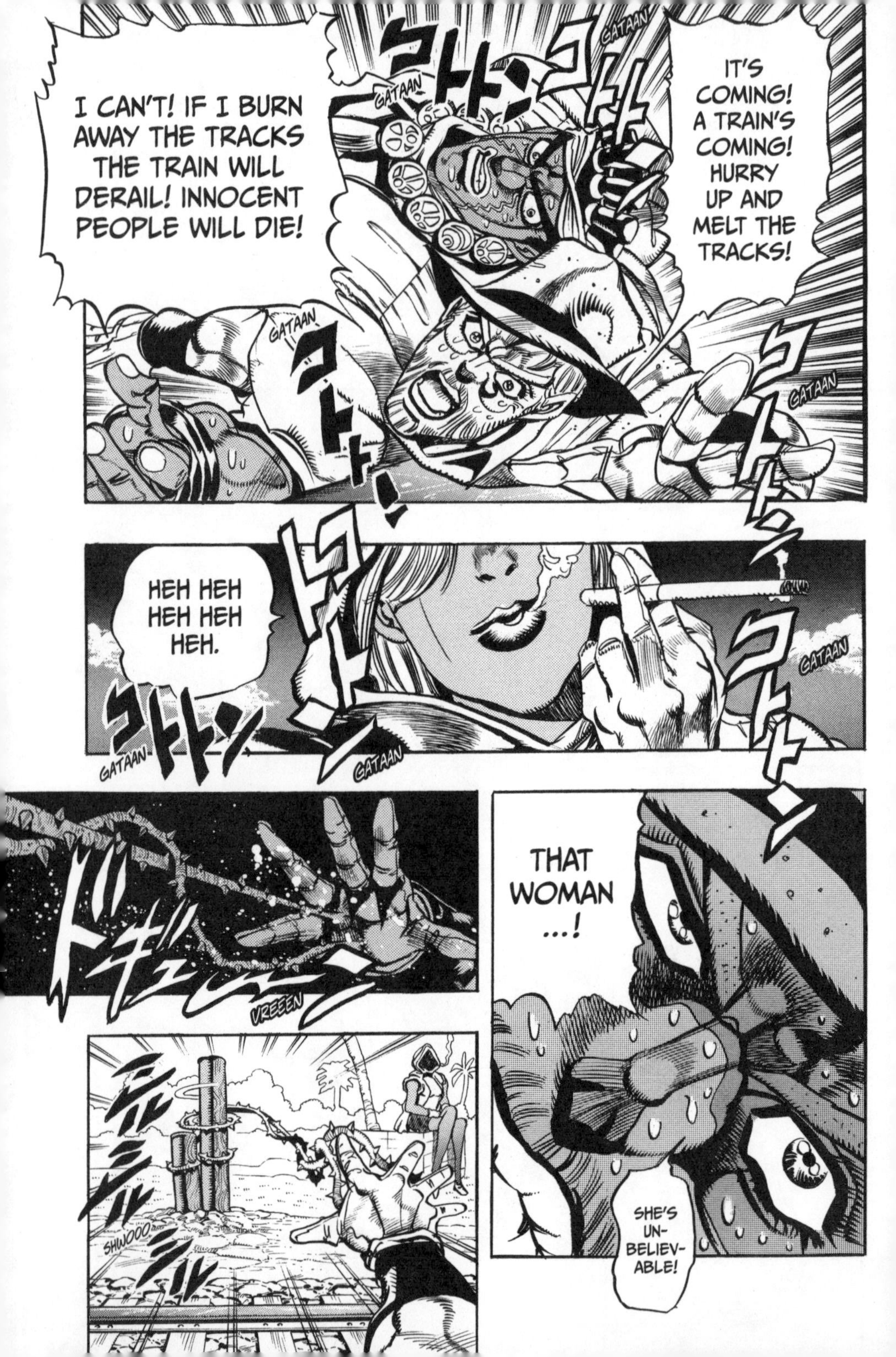
GATAAN
IT'S COMING! A TRAIN'S COMING! HURRY UP AND MELT THE TRACKS!
GATAAN
I CAN'T! IF I BURN AWAY THE TRACKS THE TRAIN WILL DERAIL! INNOCENT PEOPLE WILL DIE!
GATAAN
GATAAN
GATAAN
HEH HEH HEH HEH HEH.
GATAAN
GATAAN
THAT WOMAN ...!
SHE'S UN-BELIEV-ABLE!
VREEEN
SHWOOO

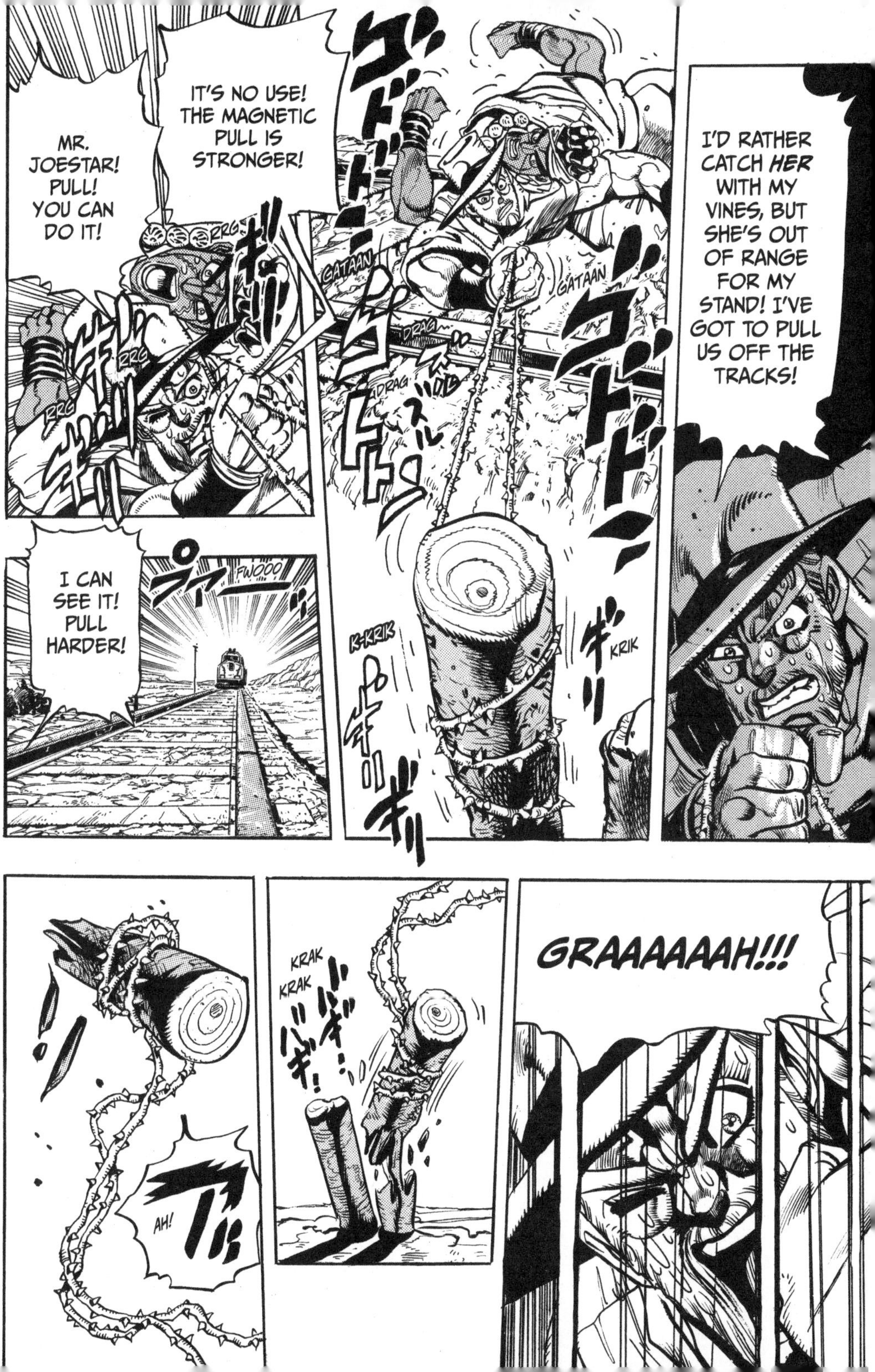
I'D RATHER CATCH HER WITH MY VINES, BUT SHE'S OUT OF RANGE FOR MY STAND! I'VE GOT TO PULL US OFF THE TRACKS!
GATAAN
GATAAN
DRAG
DRAG
K-KRIK
KRIK
IT'S NO USE! THE MAGNETIC PULL IS STRONGER!
MR. JOESTAR! PULL! YOU CAN DO IT!
RRG
RRG
RRG
FWOOO
I CAN SEE IT! PULL HARDER!
GRAAAAAAH!!!
KRAK
KRAK
AH!

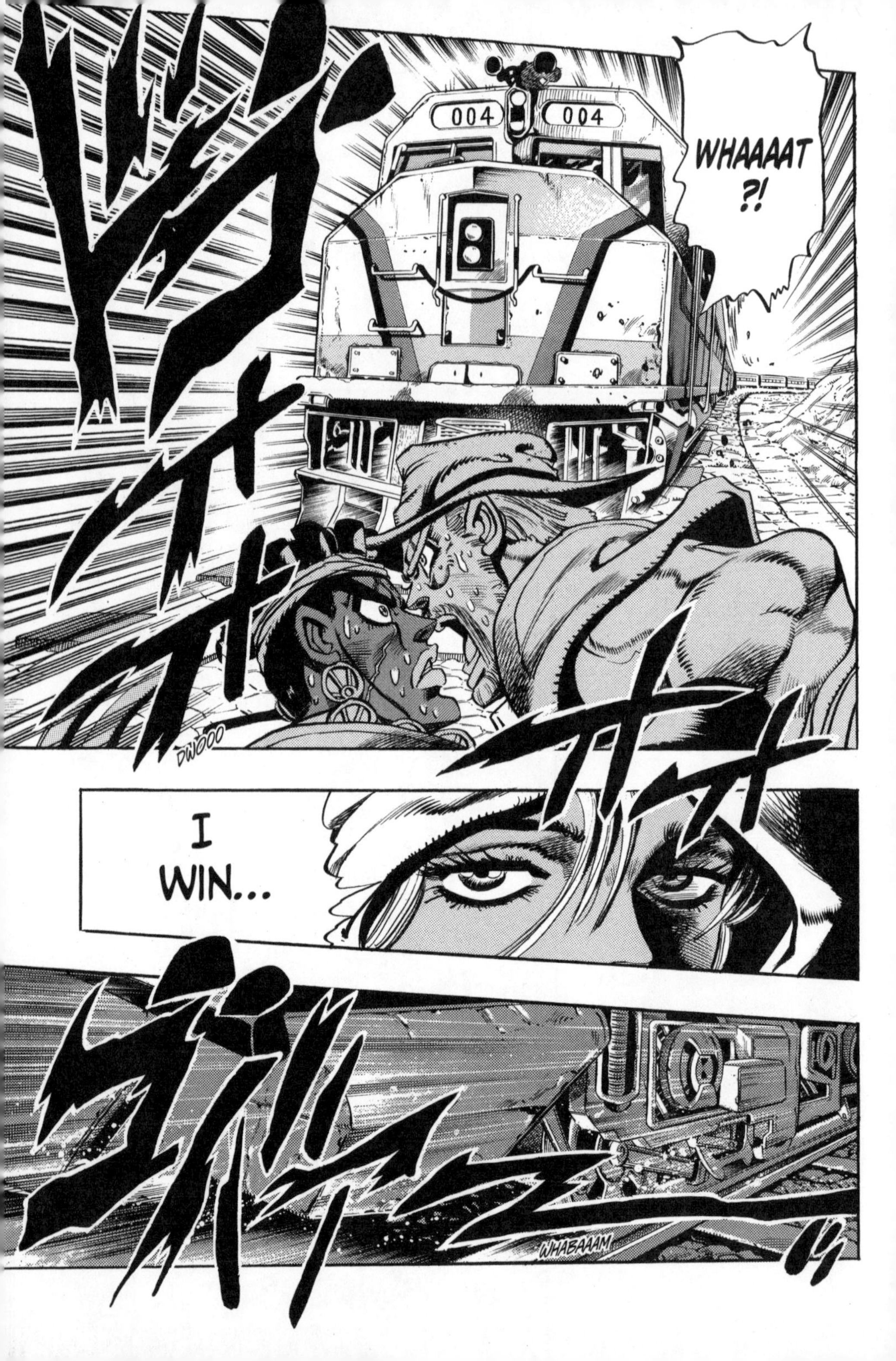
004
004
WHAAAAT ?!
DWOOO
I WIN...
WHABAAAM

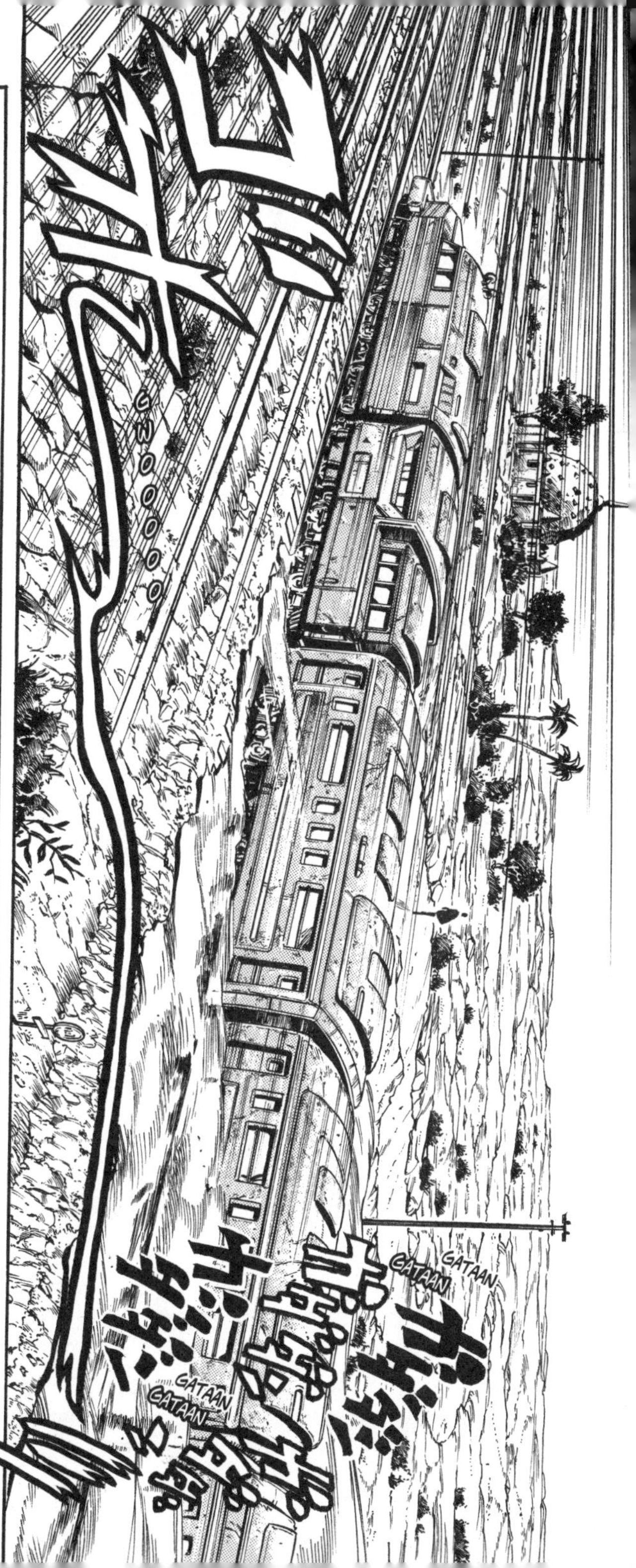
UWOOOOO
GATAAN
GATAAN
GATAAN
GATAAN
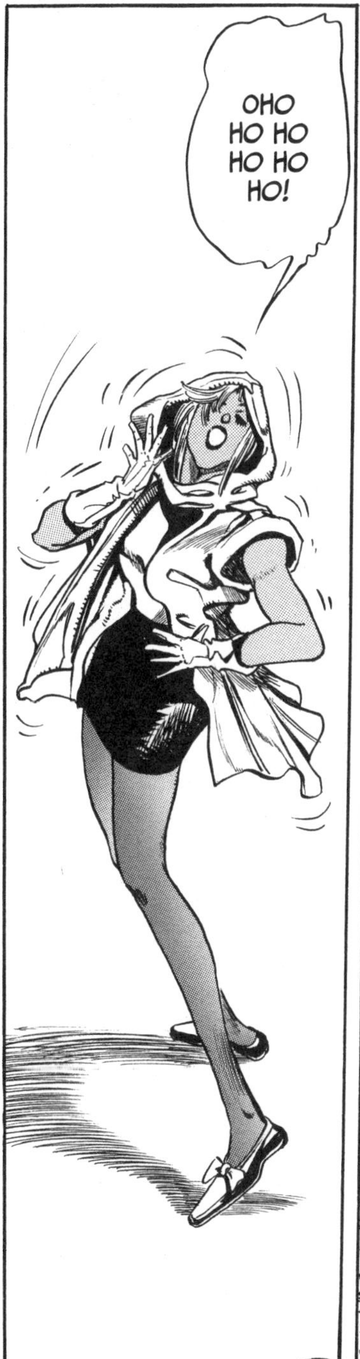
OHO HO HO HO HO HO!

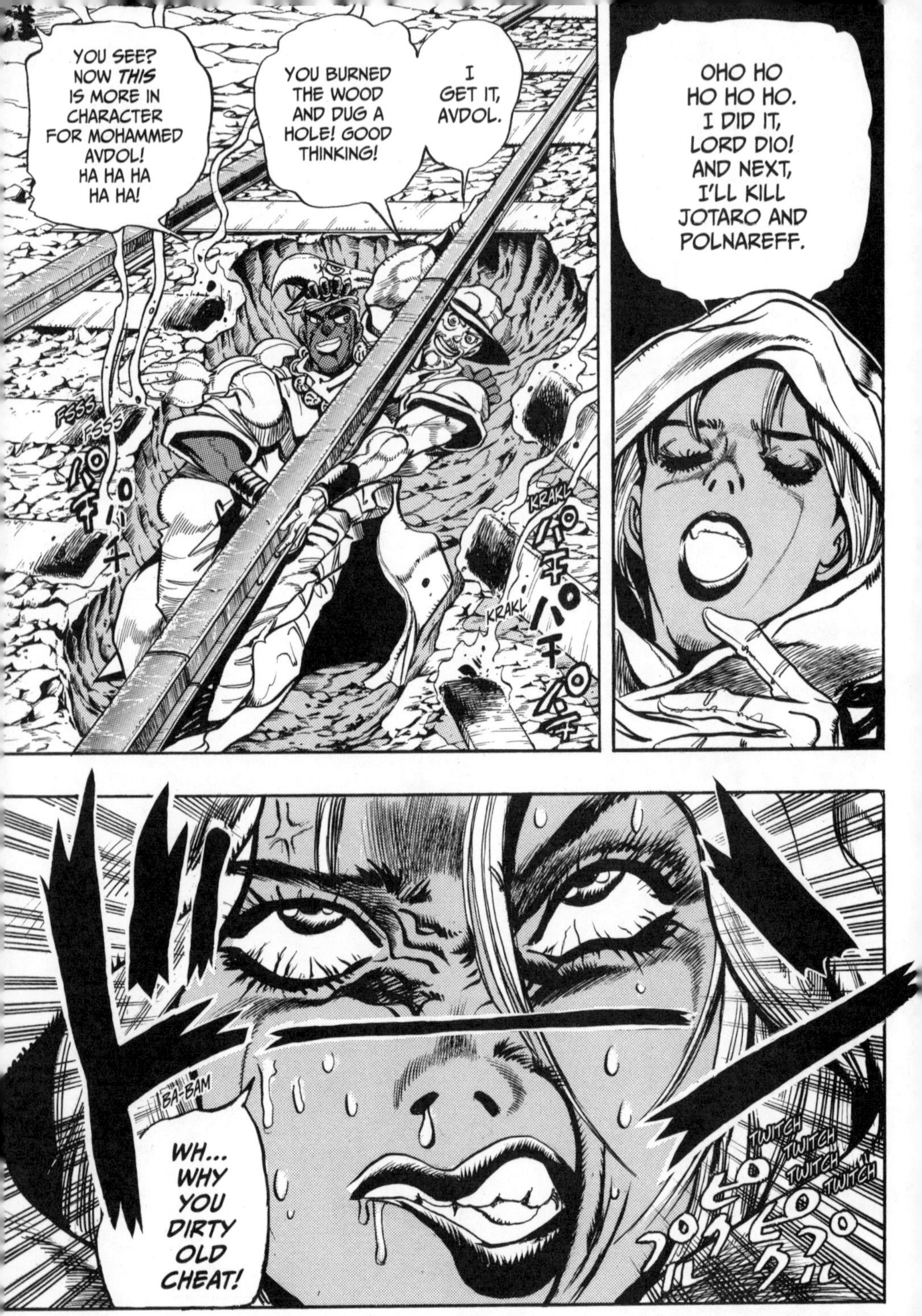
OHO HO HO HO HO. I DID IT, LORD DIO! AND NEXT, I'LL KILL JOTARO AND POLNAREFF.
I GET IT, AVDOL.
YOU BURNED THE WOOD AND DUG A HOLE! GOOD THINKING!
YOU SEE? NOW *THIS* IS MORE IN CHARACTER FOR MOHAMMED AVDOL! HA HA HA HA HA!
FSSS
FSSS
KRAKL
KRAKL
TWITCH TWITCH TWITCH TWITCH
BA-BAM
WH... WHY YOU DIRTY OLD CHEAT!

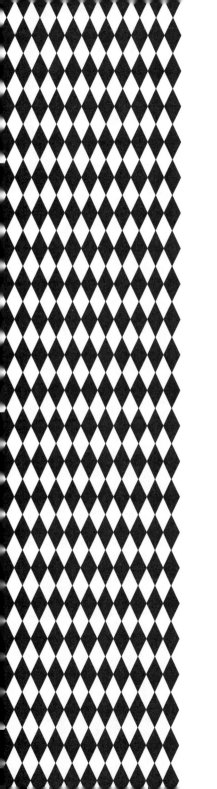
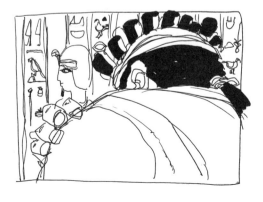

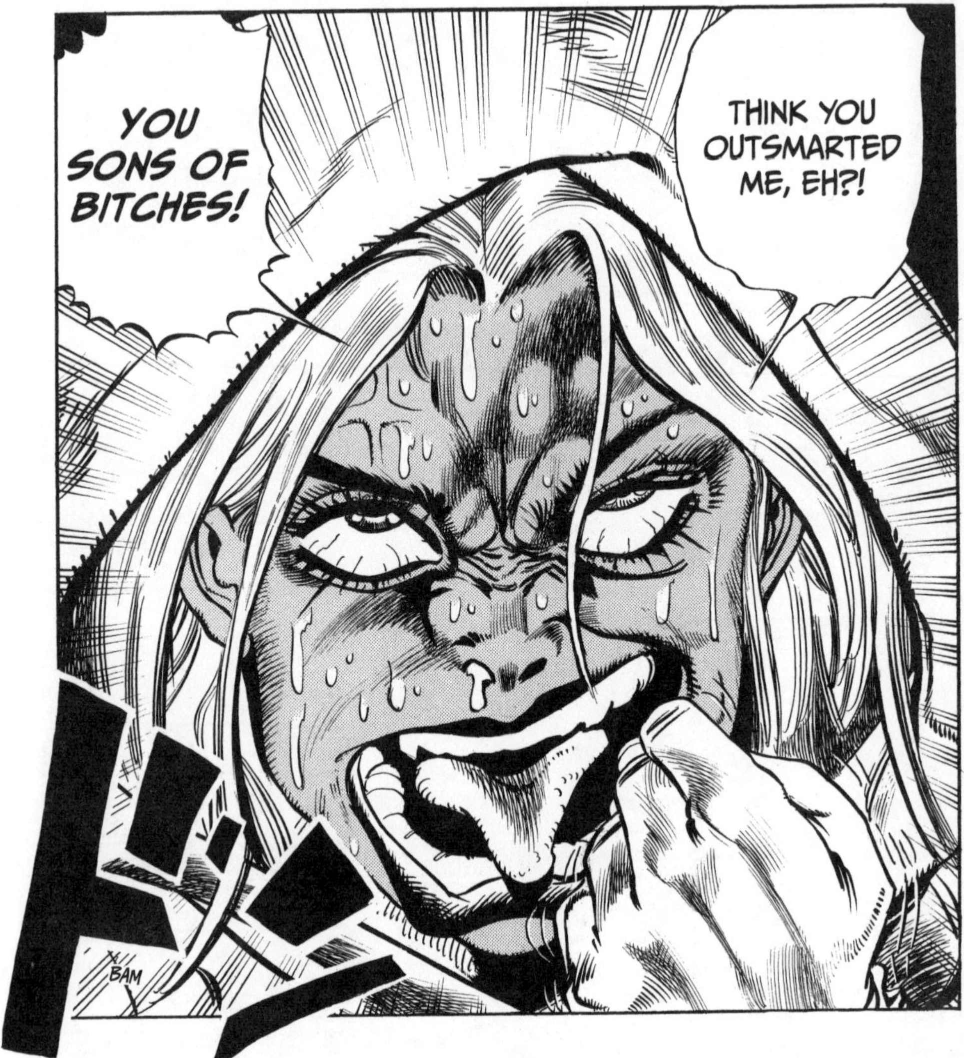
THINK YOU OUTSMARTED ME, EH?!
YOU SONS OF BITCHES!
BAM

CHAPTER 90: “Bast” Mariah PART 5

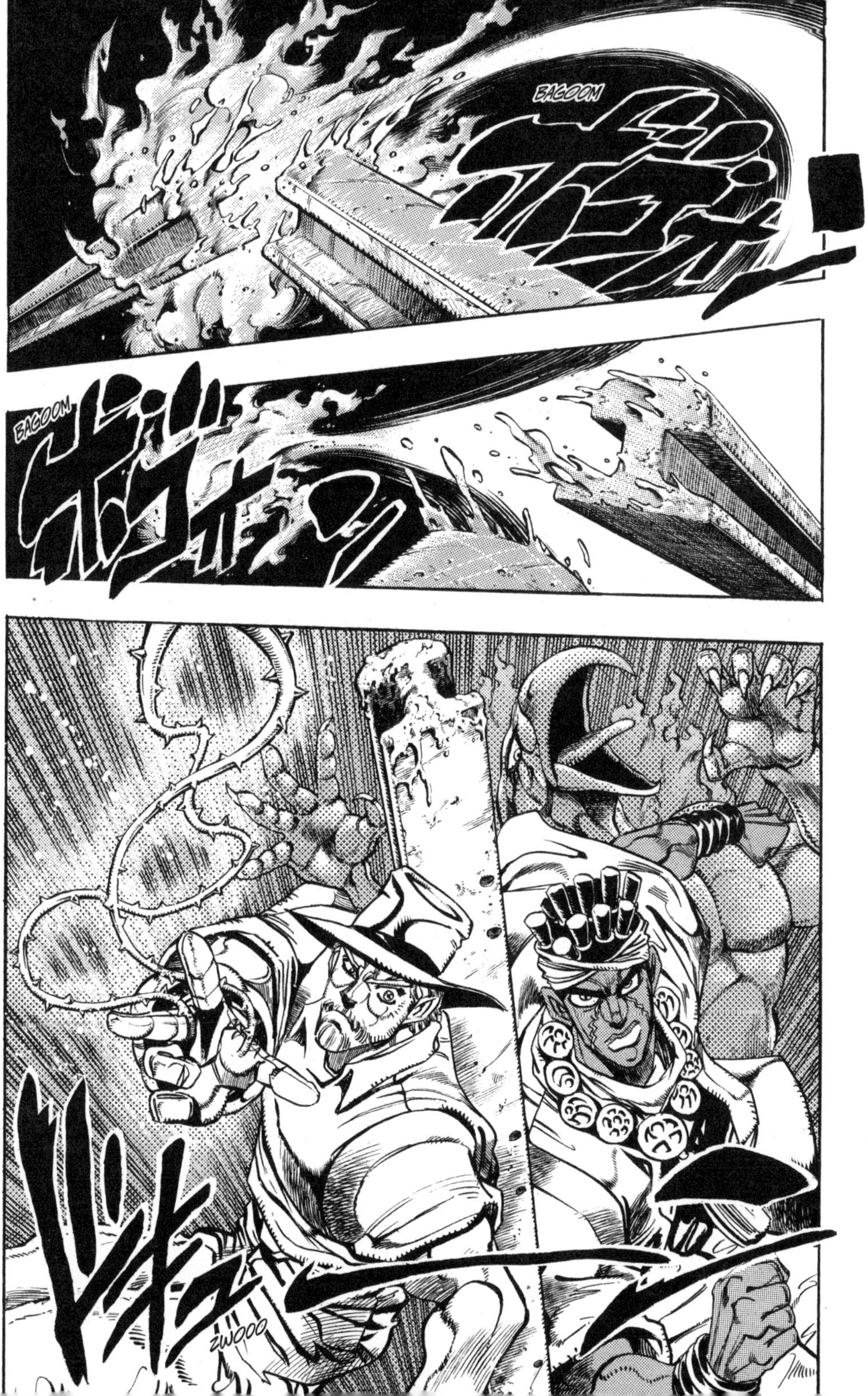
BAGOOM
BAGOOM
ZWOOO

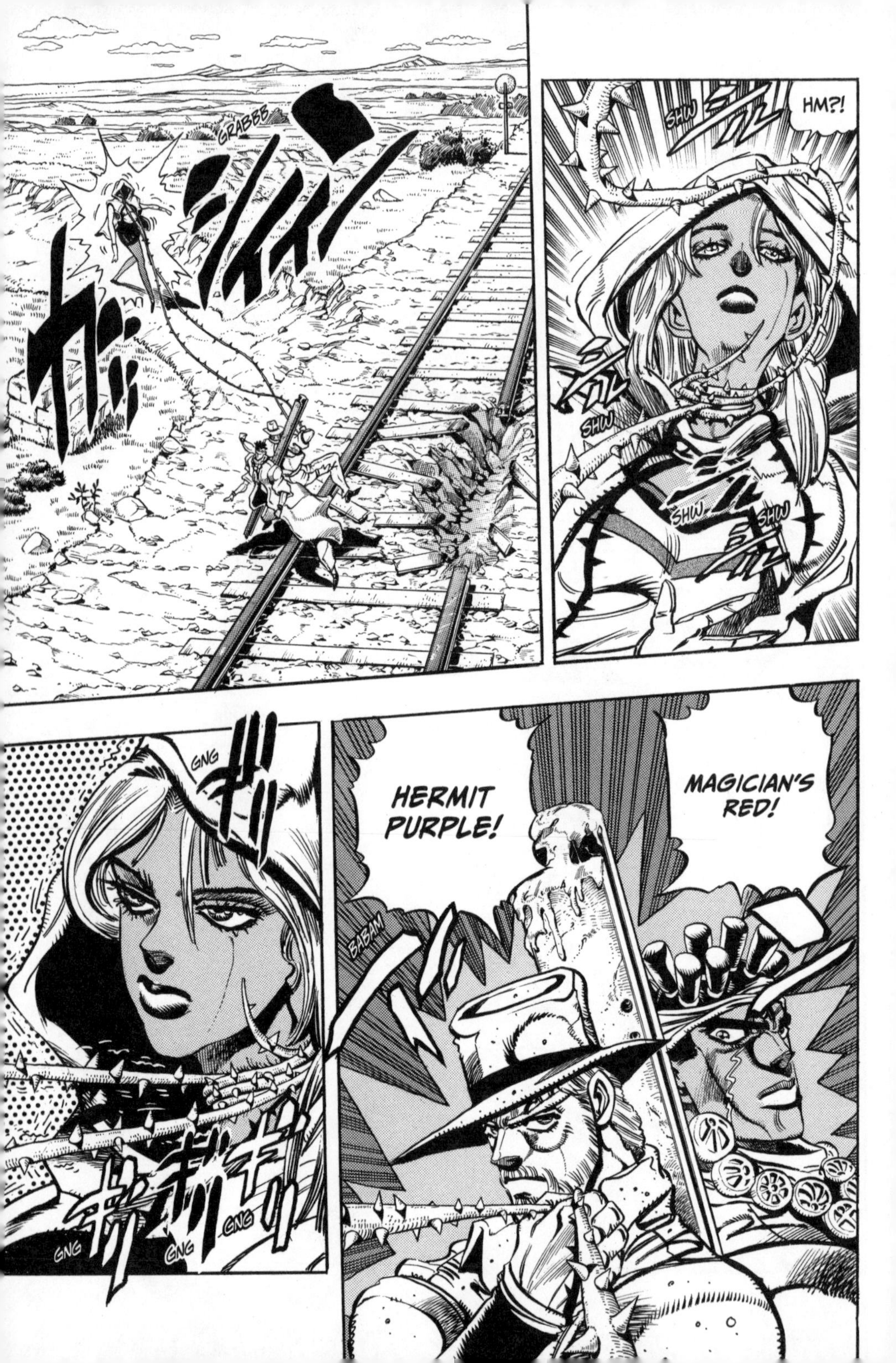
HM?!
SHW
SHW
SHW
SHW
GRABBBB
MAGICIAN'S RED!
HERMIT PURPLE!
BABAM
GNG
GNG
GNG
GNG

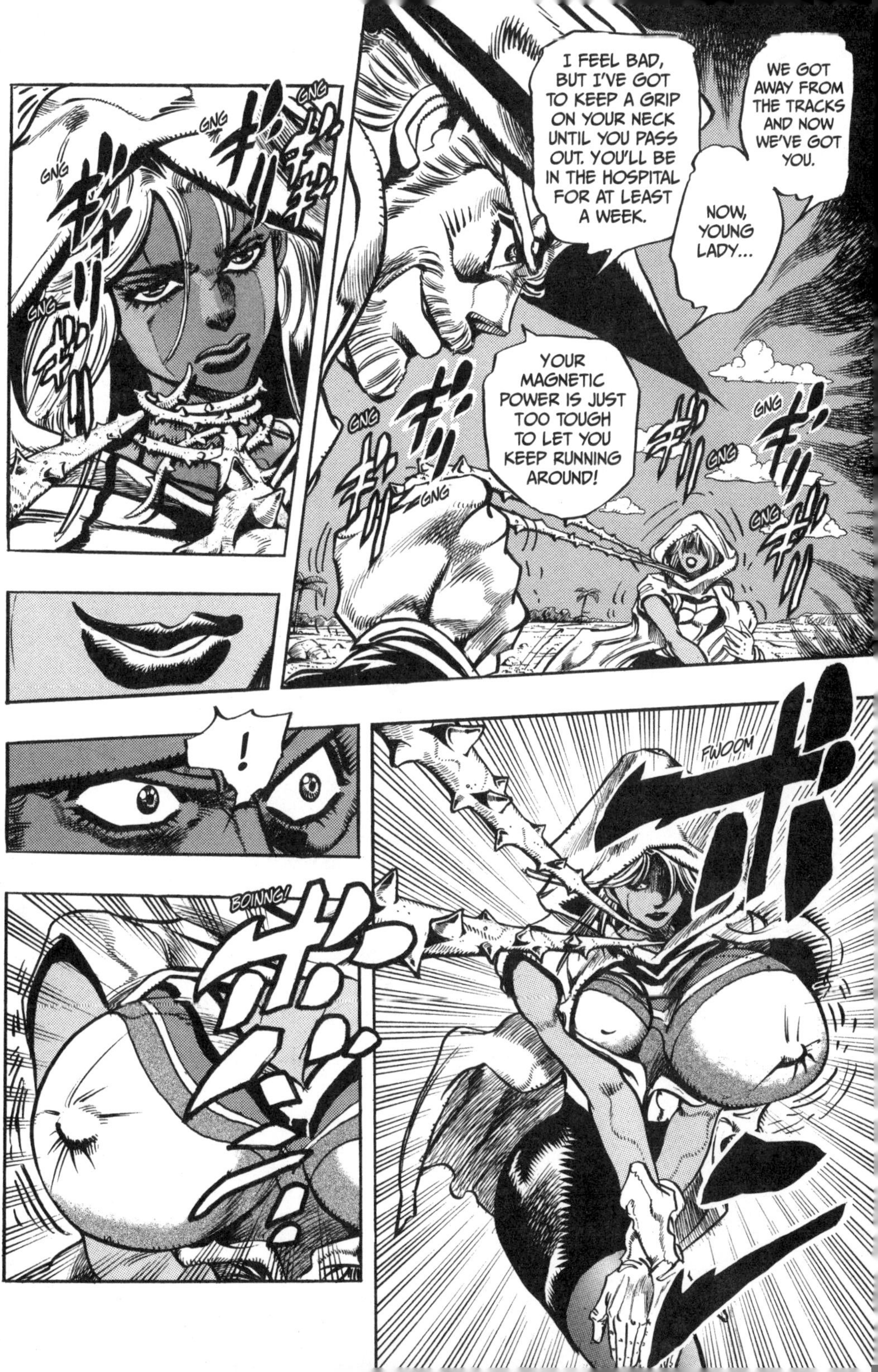
WE GOT AWAY FROM THE TRACKS AND NOW WE'VE GOT YOU.
NOW, YOUNG LADY...
I FEEL BAD, BUT I'VE GOT TO KEEP A GRIP ON YOUR NECK UNTIL YOU PASS OUT. YOU'LL BE IN THE HOSPITAL FOR AT LEAST A WEEK.
GNG
GNG
GNG
YOUR MAGNETIC POWER IS JUST TOO TOUGH TO LET YOU KEEP RUNNING AROUND!
GNG
GNG
GNG
GNG
GNG
GNG
GNG
FWOOM
!
BOINNG!

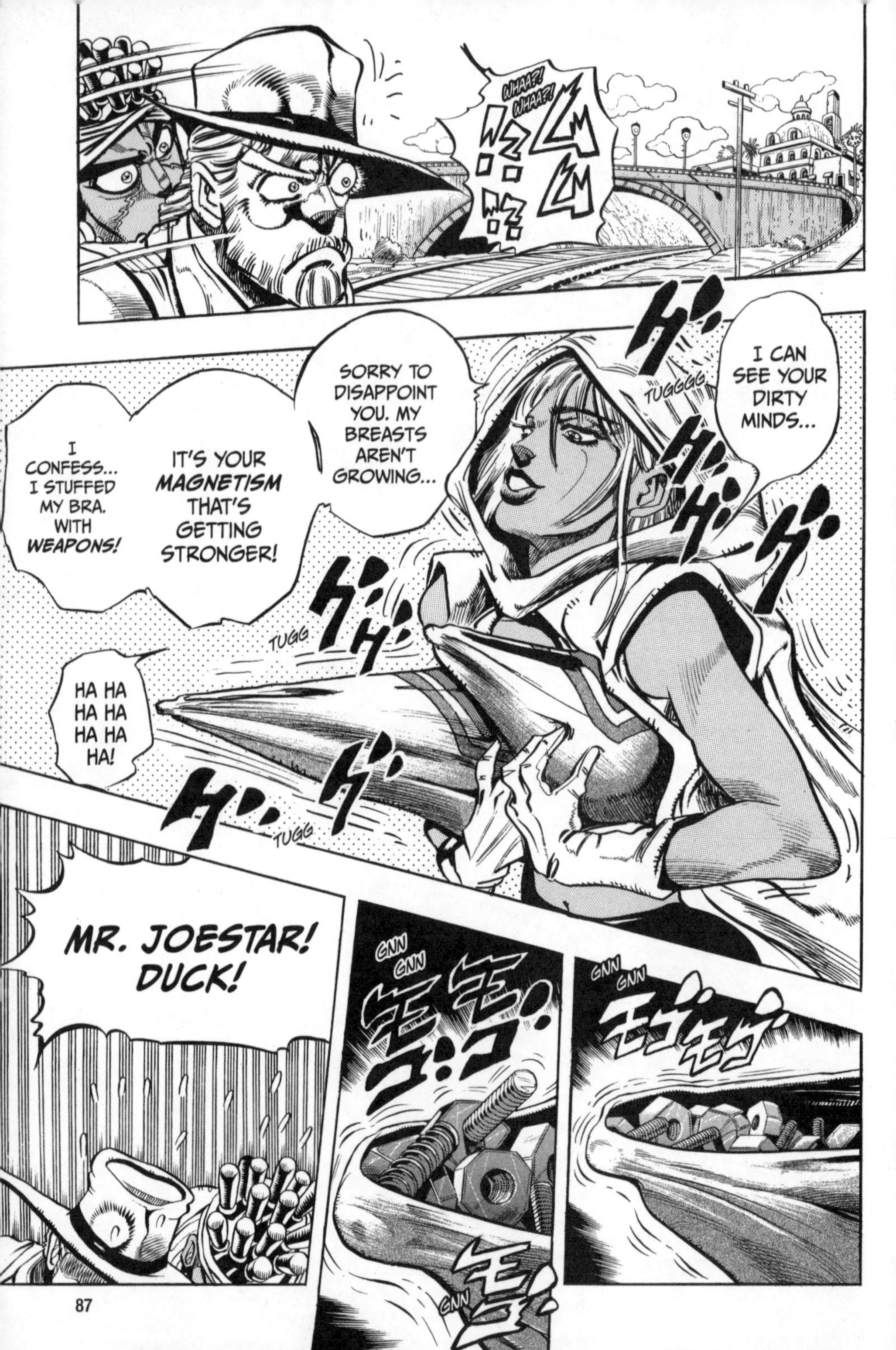
WHAA?! WHAA?!
I CAN SEE YOUR DIRTY MINDS...
TUGGGG
SORRY TO DISAPPOINT YOU. MY BREASTS AREN'T GROWING...
IT'S YOUR *MAGNETISM* THAT'S GETTING STRONGER!
I CONFESS... I STUFFED MY BRA. WITH *WEAPONS!*
TUGG
HA HA HA HA HA HA HA!
TUGG
GNN GNN
GNN GNN
GNN
MR. JOESTAR! DUCK!

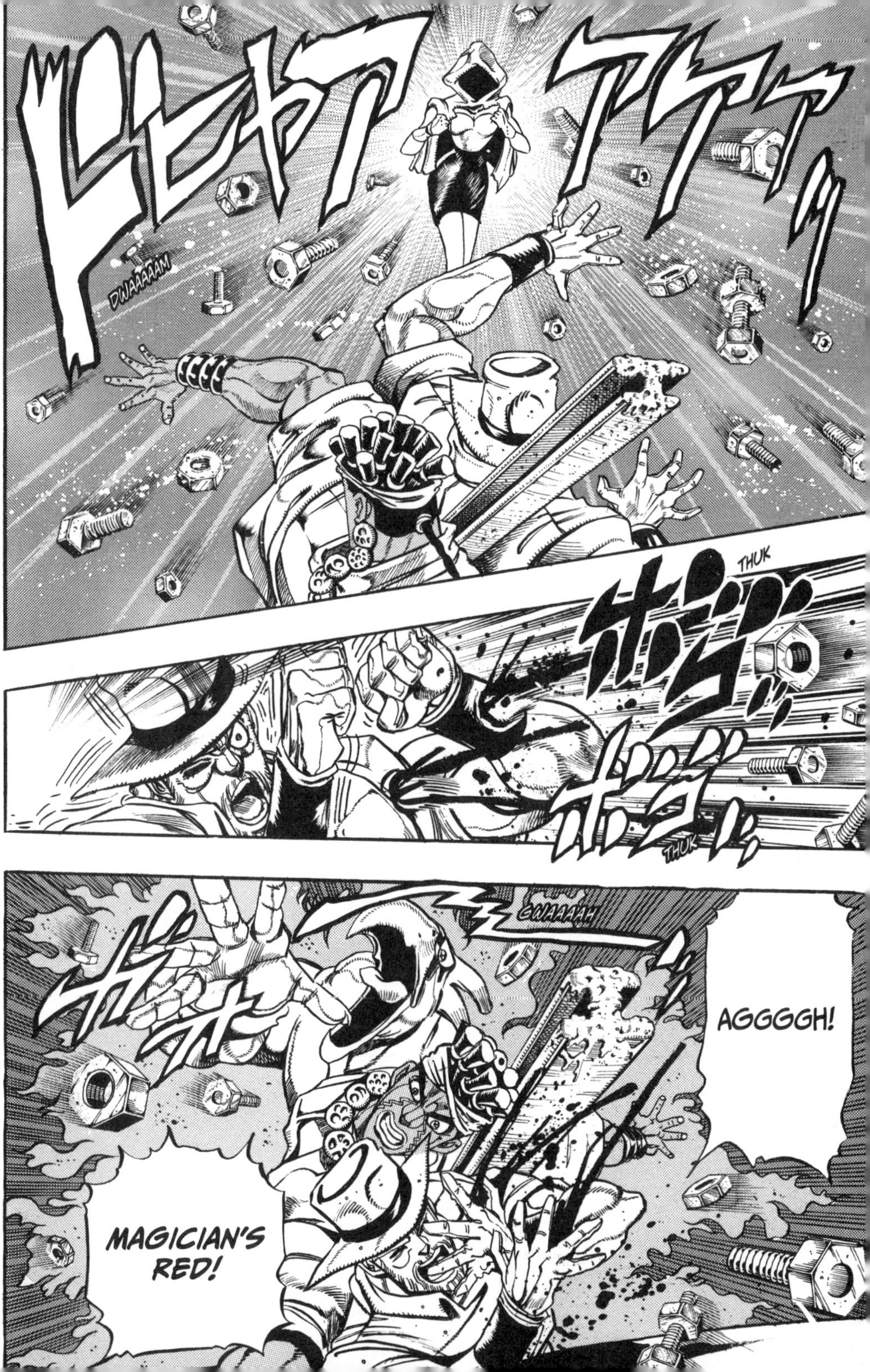
DWAAAAAM
THUK
THUK
AGGGGH!
GWAAAAH
MAGICIAN'S RED!

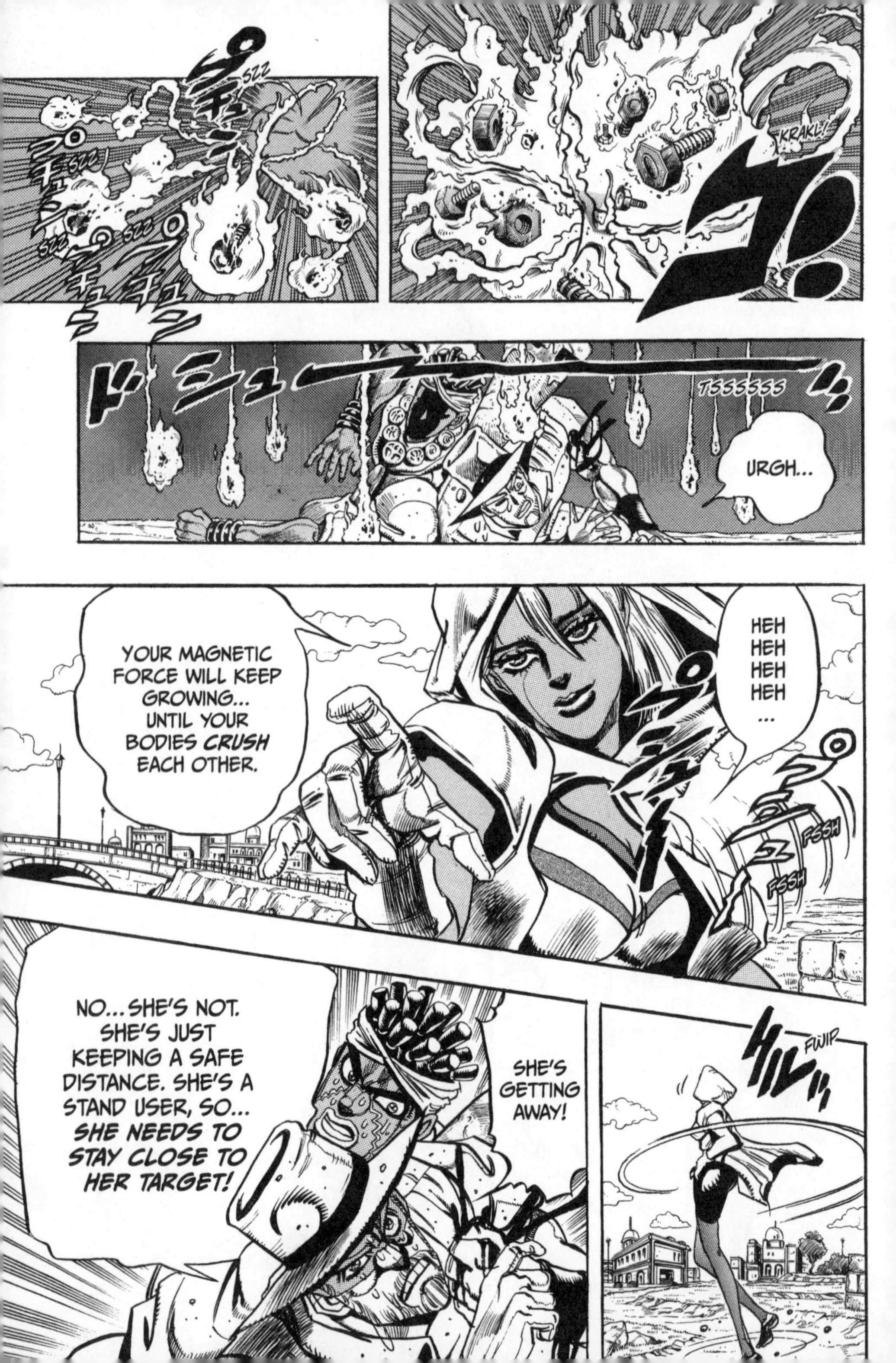

KRAKL!
SZZ
SZZ
SZZ
SZZ
TSSSSSS
URGH...
HEH HEH HEH HEH ...
FSSH
FSSH
YOUR MAGNETIC FORCE WILL KEEP GROWING... UNTIL YOUR BODIES CRUSH EACH OTHER.
FWIP
SHE'S GETTING AWAY!
NO...SHE'S NOT. SHE'S JUST KEEPING A SAFE DISTANCE. SHE'S A STAND USER, SO... SHE NEEDS TO STAY CLOSE TO HER TARGET!

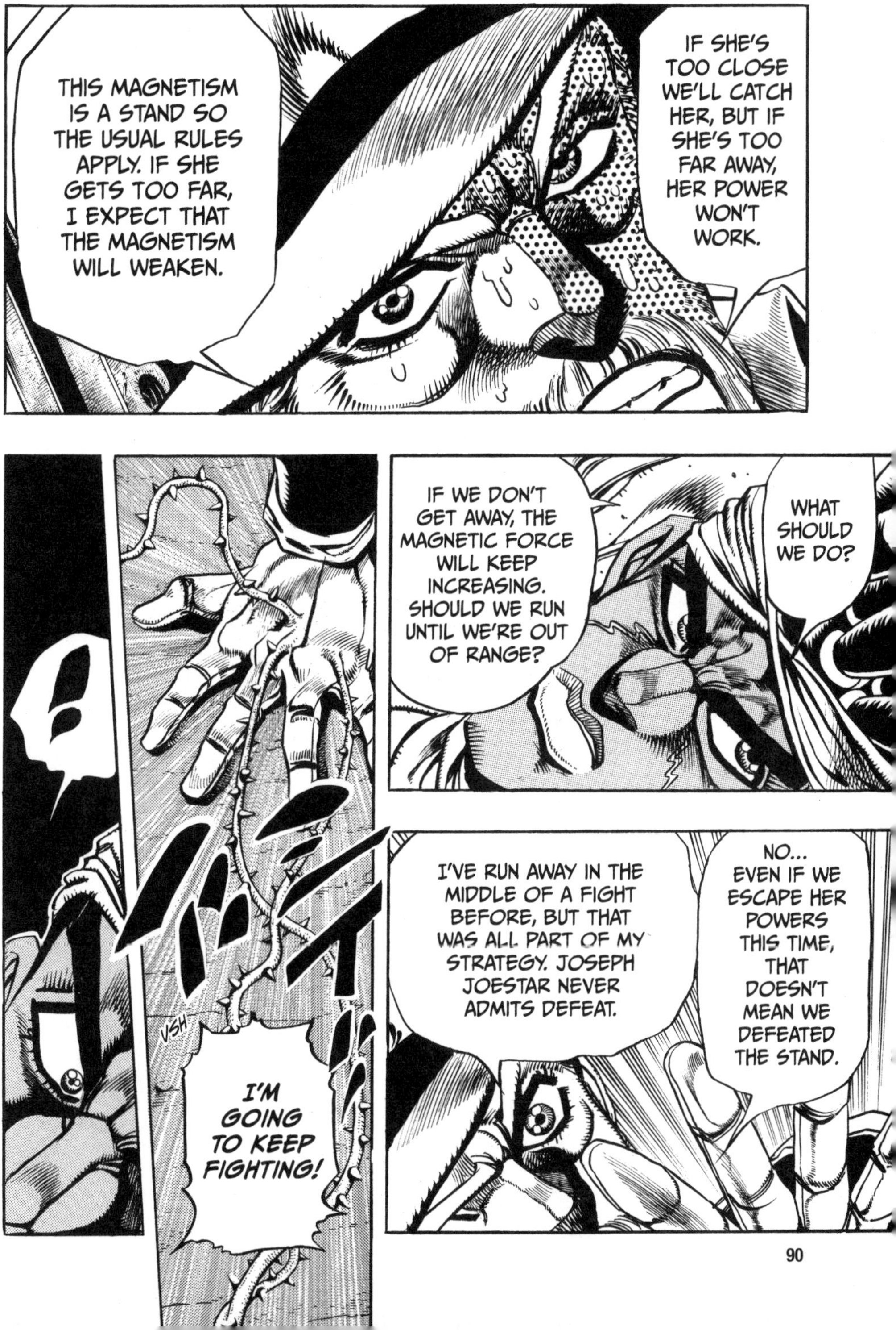
IF SHE'S TOO CLOSE WE'LL CATCH HER, BUT IF SHE'S TOO FAR AWAY, HER POWER WON'T WORK.
THIS MAGNETISM IS A STAND SO THE USUAL RULES APPLY. IF SHE GETS TOO FAR, I EXPECT THAT THE MAGNETISM WILL WEAKEN.
WHAT SHOULD WE DO?
IF WE DON'T GET AWAY, THE MAGNETIC FORCE WILL KEEP INCREASING. SHOULD WE RUN UNTIL WE'RE OUT OF RANGE?
NO... EVEN IF WE ESCAPE HER POWERS THIS TIME, THAT DOESN'T MEAN WE DEFEATED THE STAND.
I'VE RUN AWAY IN THE MIDDLE OF A FIGHT BEFORE, BUT THAT WAS ALL PART OF MY STRATEGY. JOSEPH JOESTAR NEVER ADMITS DEFEAT.
VSH
I'M GOING TO KEEP FIGHTING!

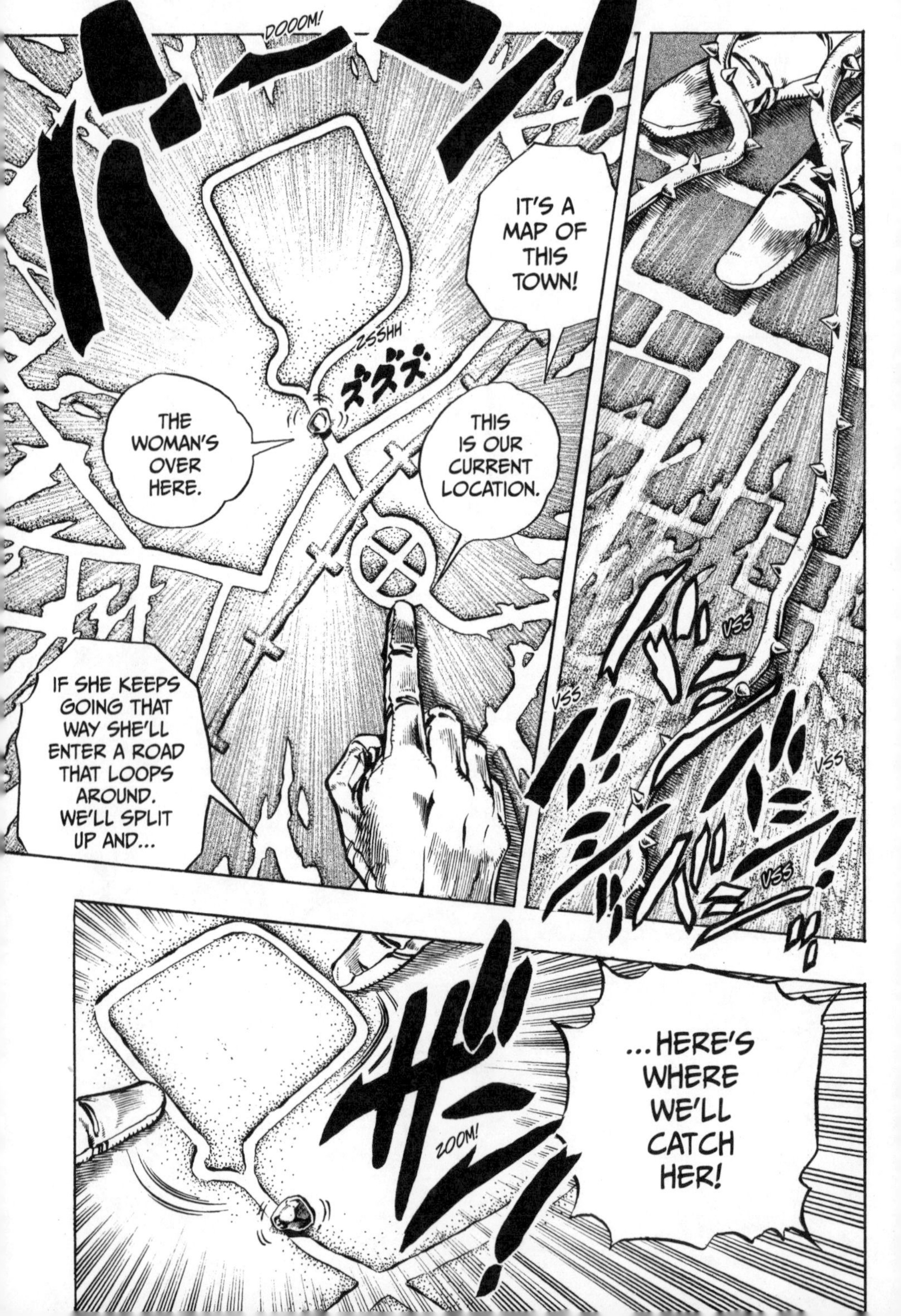
VSS
VSS
VSS
VSS
DOOOM!
IT'S A MAP OF THIS TOWN!
ZSSHH
ズズズ
THIS IS OUR CURRENT LOCATION.
THE WOMAN'S OVER HERE.
IF SHE KEEPS GOING THAT WAY SHE'LL ENTER A ROAD THAT LOOPS AROUND. WE'LL SPLIT UP AND...
...HERE'S WHERE WE'LL CATCH HER!
ZOOM!

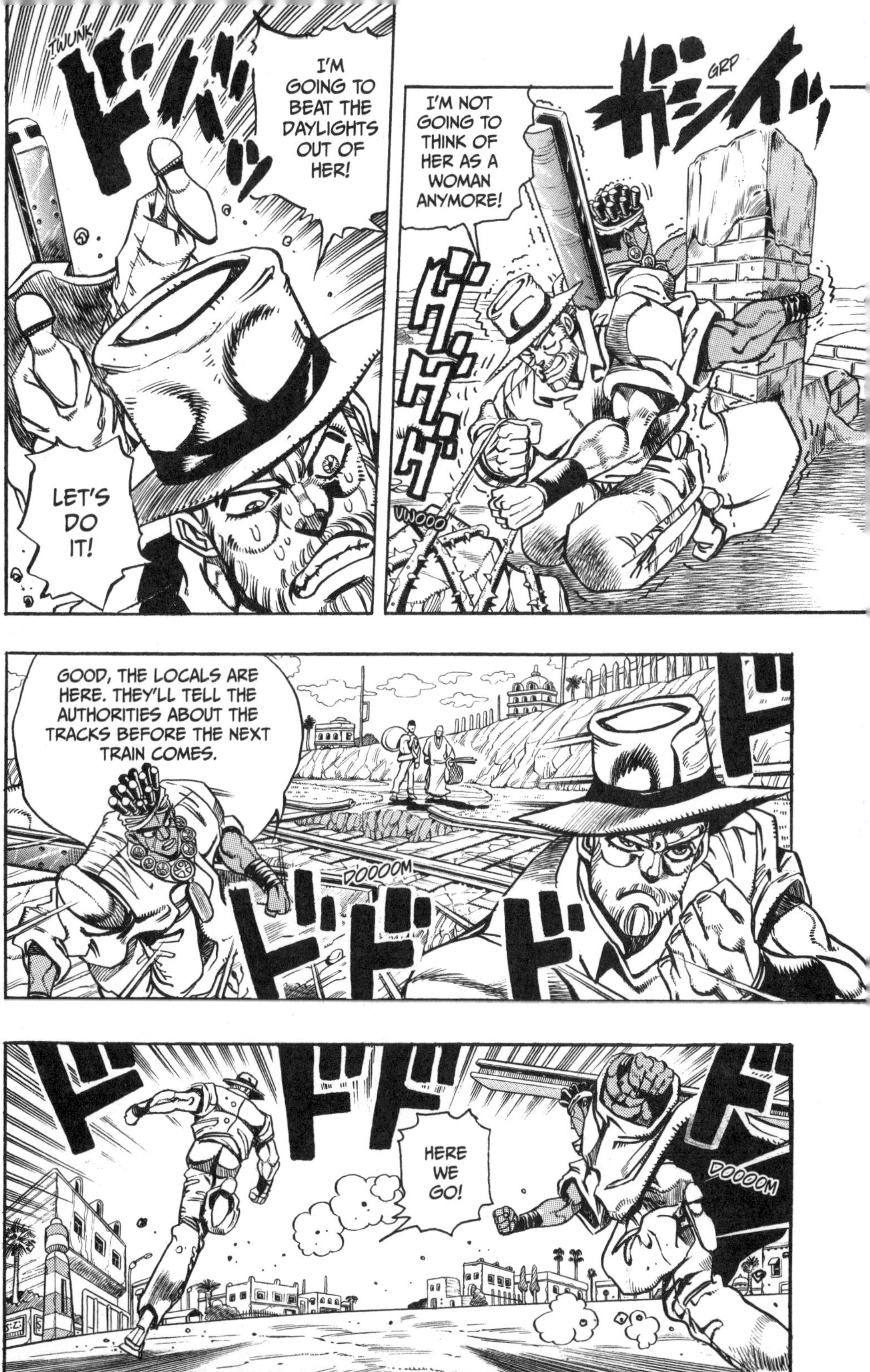
GRP
I'M NOT GOING TO THINK OF HER AS A WOMAN ANYMORE!
UWOOO
TWUNK
I'M GOING TO BEAT THE DAYLIGHTS OUT OF HER!
LET'S DO IT!
GOOD, THE LOCALS ARE HERE. THEY'LL TELL THE AUTHORITIES ABOUT THE TRACKS BEFORE THE NEXT TRAIN COMES.
DOOOOM
HERE WE GO!
DOOOOM

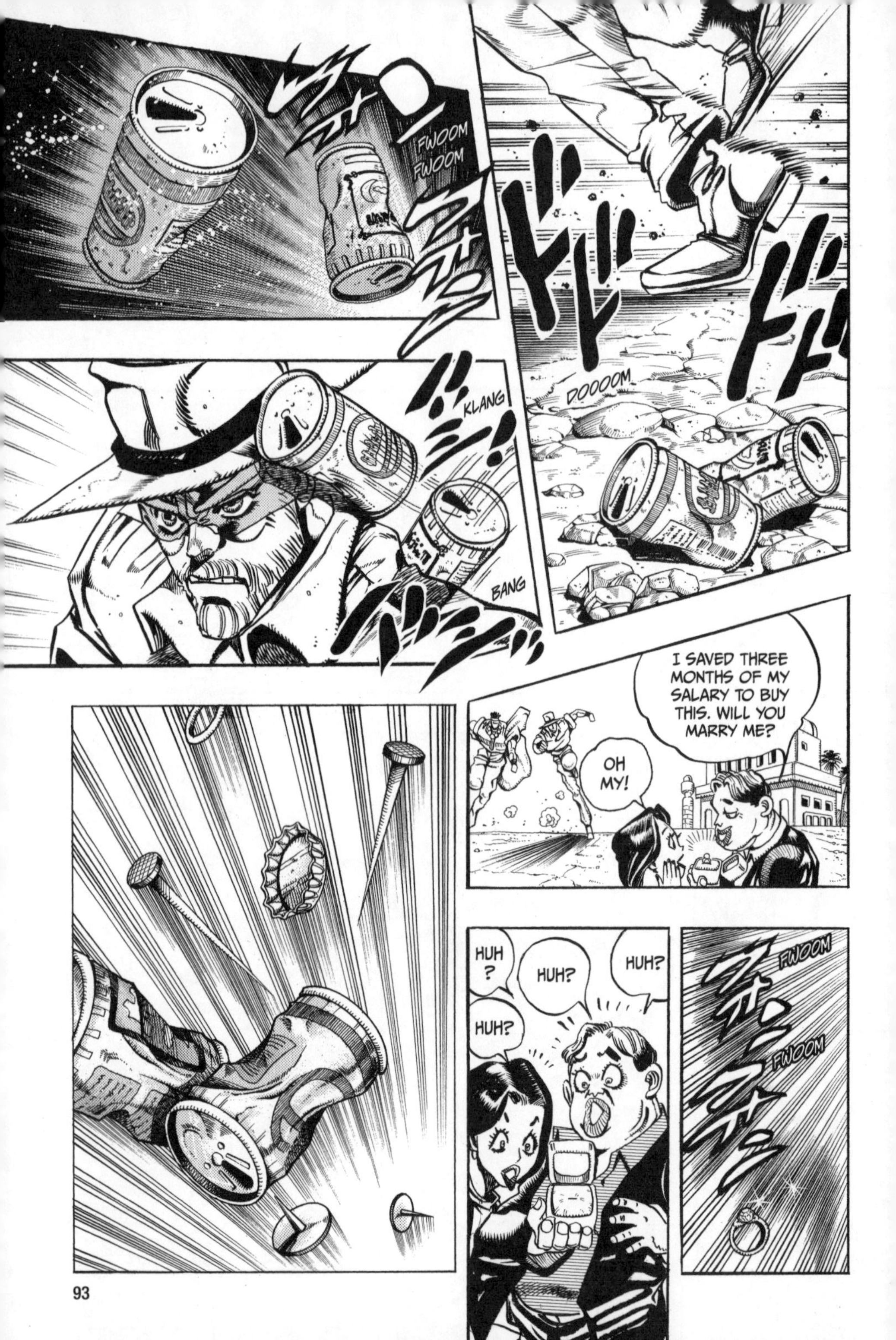
DOOOOM
FWOOM
FWOOM
KLANG
BANG
I SAVED THREE MONTHS OF MY SALARY TO BUY THIS. WILL YOU MARRY ME?
OH MY!
FWOOM
FWOOM
HUH?
HUH?
HUH ?
HUH?

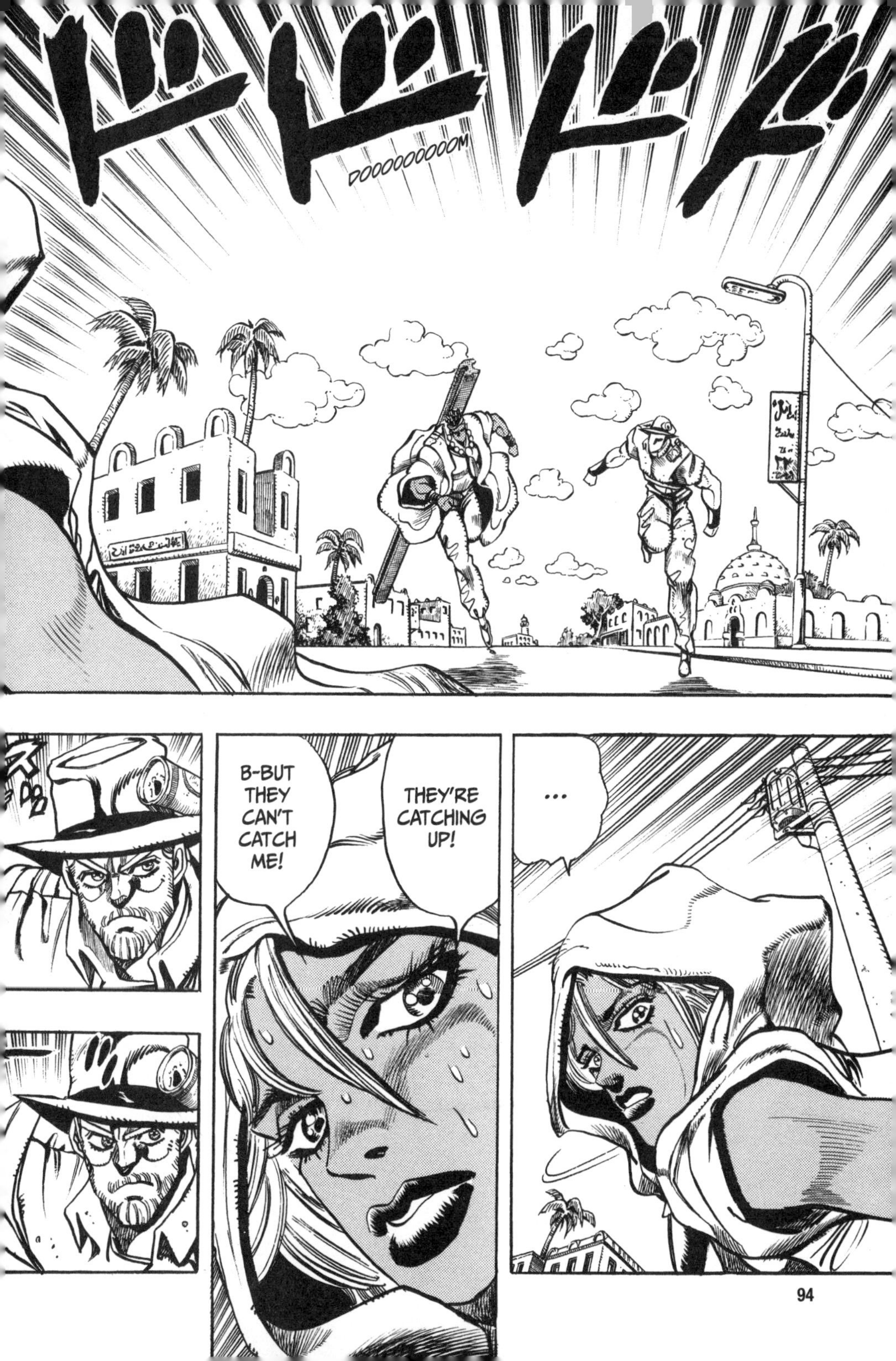
DOOOOOOOOOM
...
THEY'RE CATCHING UP!
B-BUT THEY CAN'T CATCH ME!

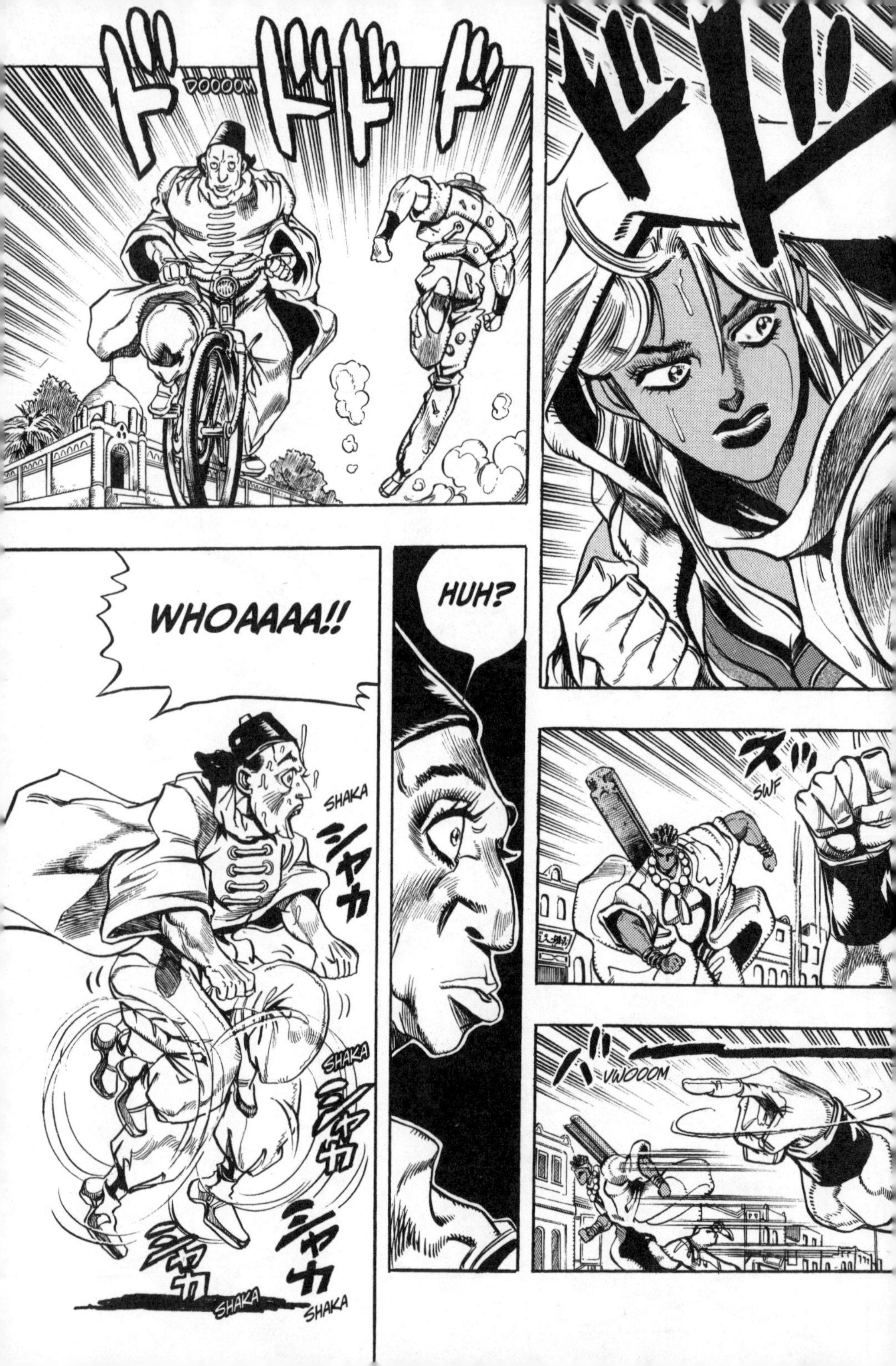

ドドド
ドドドド
DOOOOM
ズッ
SWF
バ
VWOOOM
HUH?
WHOAAAA!!
SHAKA
シャカ
SHAKA
シャカ
シャカ
SHAKA
シャカ
SHAKA

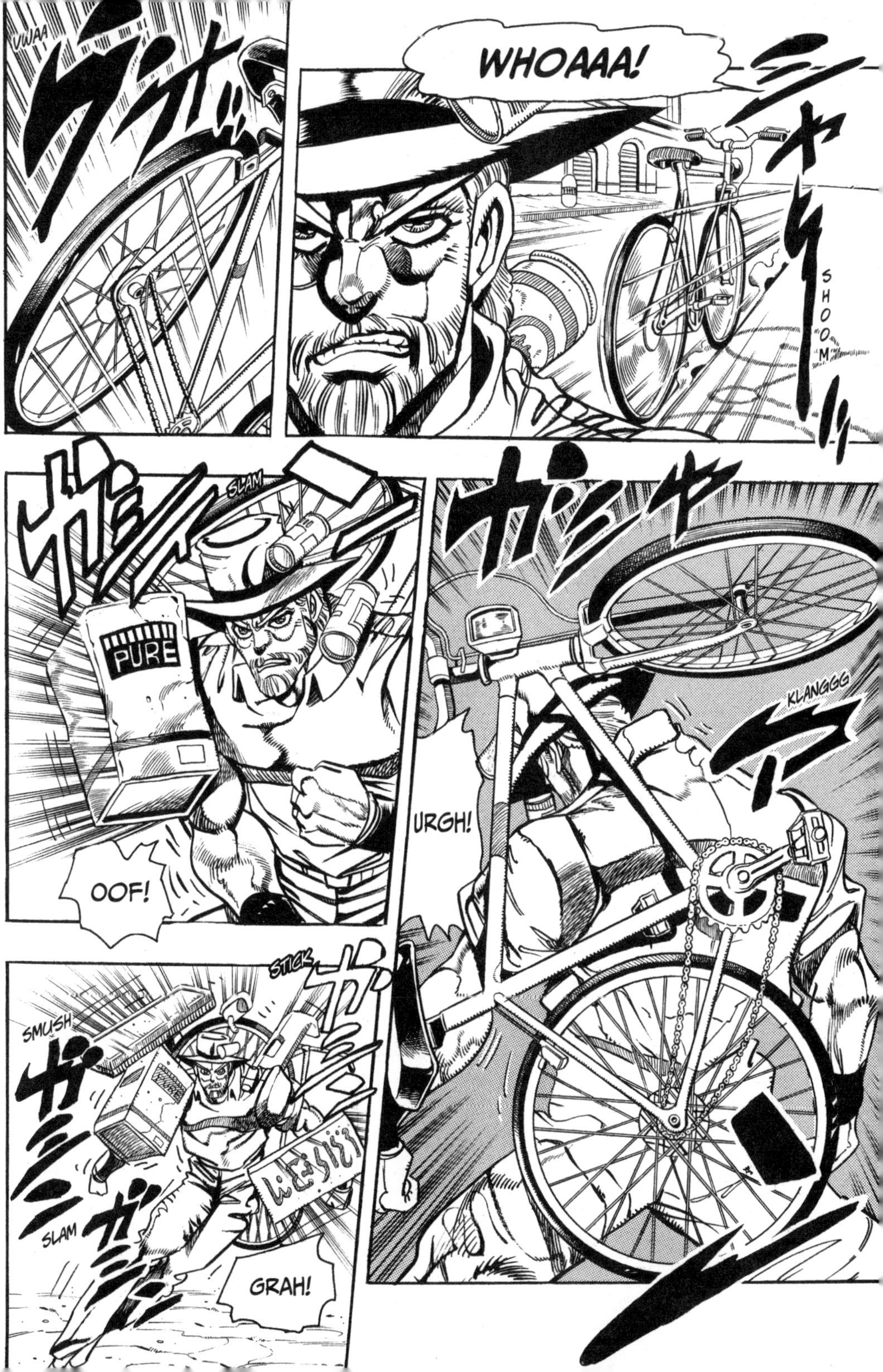
WHOAAA!
SHOOM
UWAA
KLANGGG
URGH!
SLAM
OOF!
STICK
SMUSH
SLAM
GRAH!

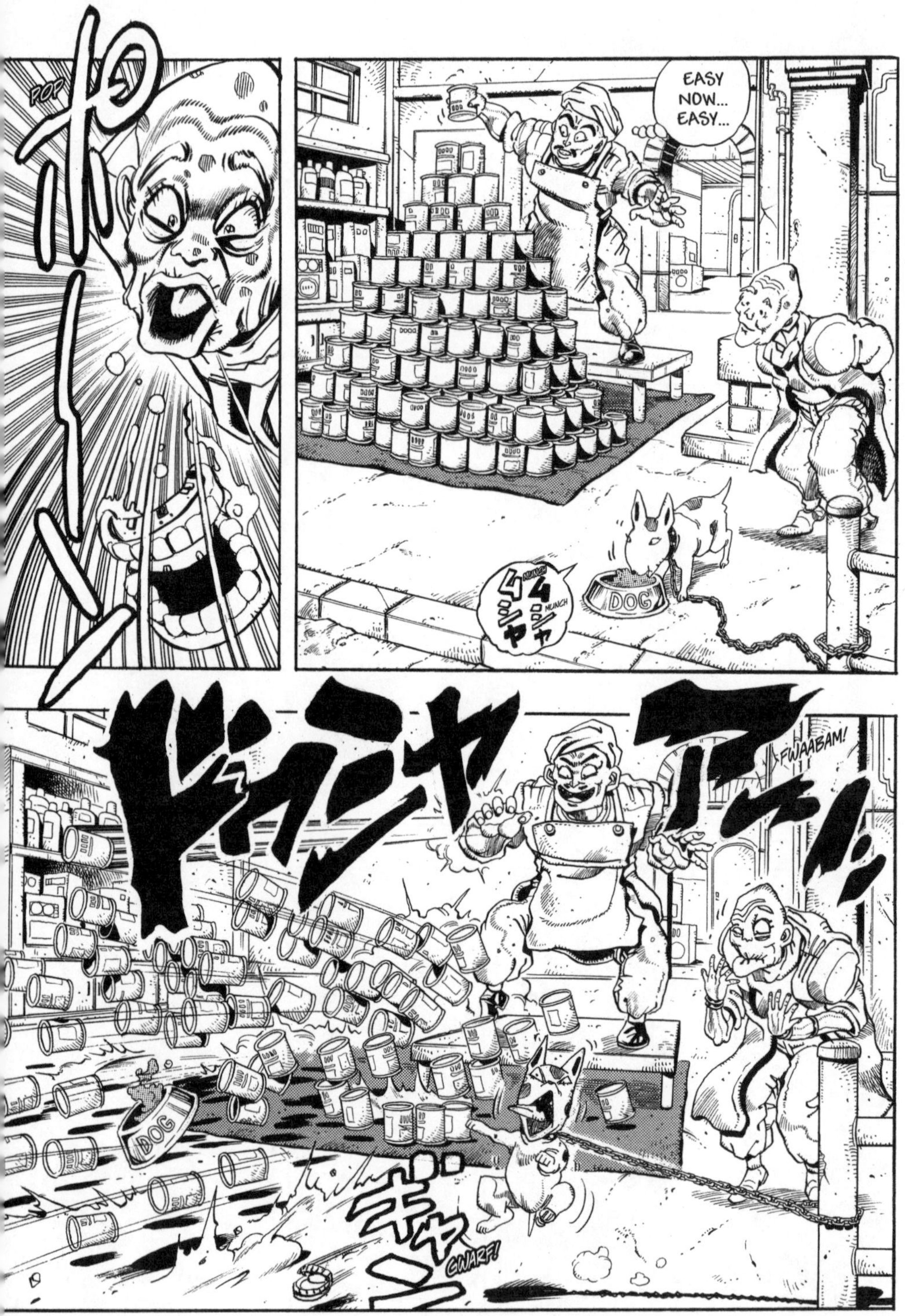
EASY NOW... EASY...
MUNCH MUNCH
ムシャ ムシャ
POP
FWAABAM!
GWARF!

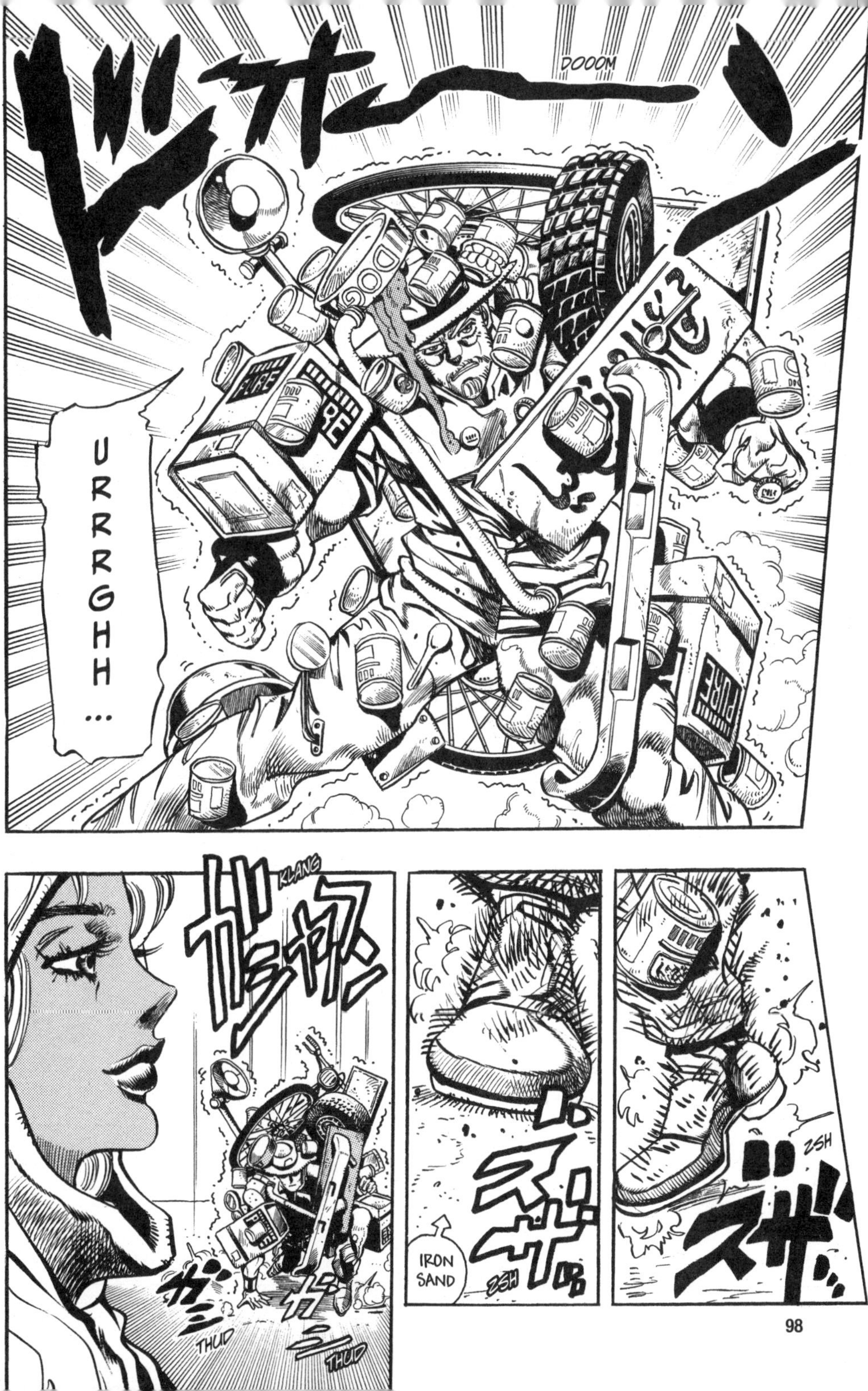
DOOOM
URRRGHH...
ZSH
IRON SAND
ZSH
KLANG
THUD
THUD

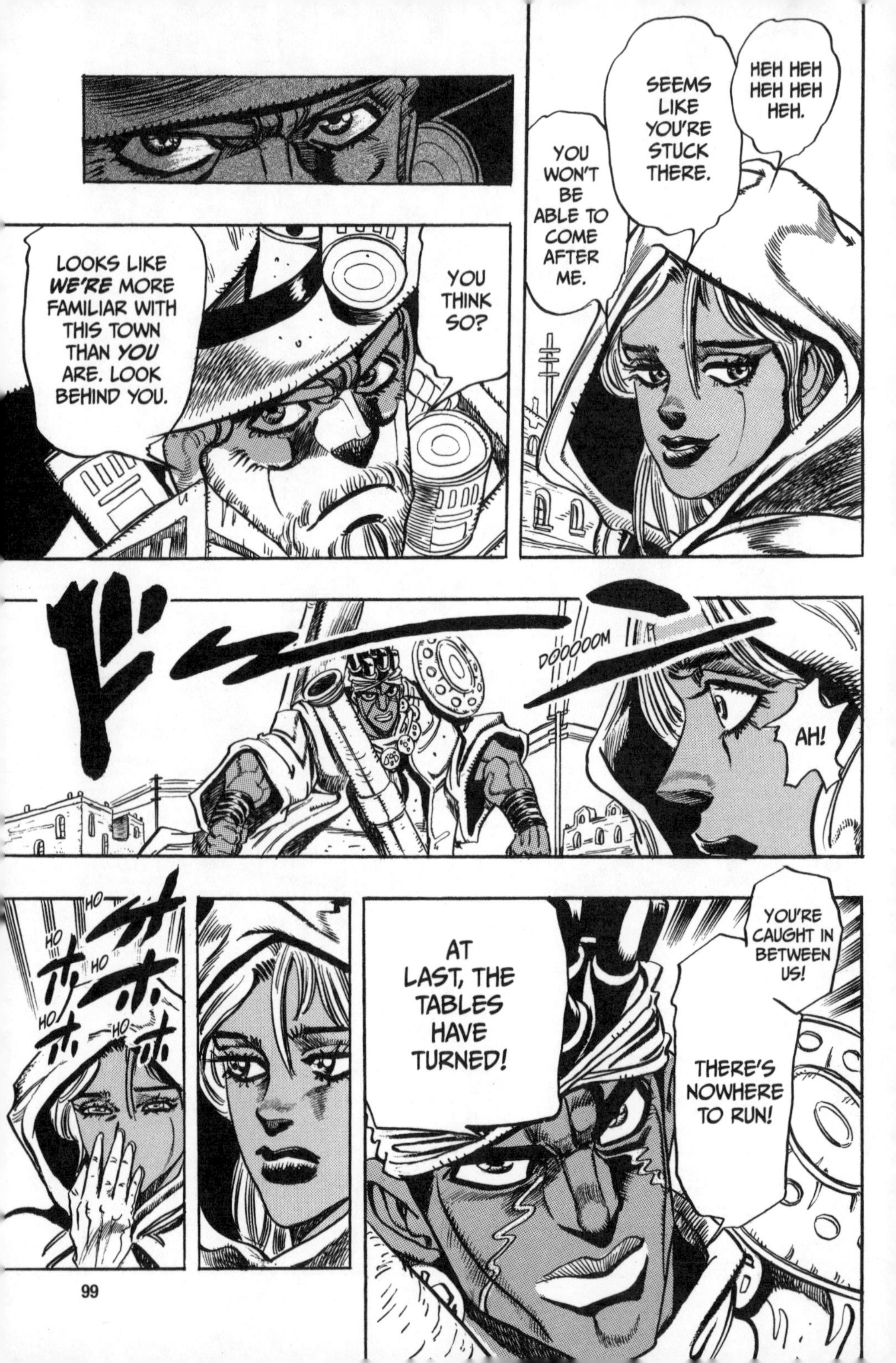
HEH HEH HEH HEH HEH.
SEEMS LIKE YOU'RE STUCK THERE.
YOU WON'T BE ABLE TO COME AFTER ME.
YOU THINK SO?
LOOKS LIKE *WE'RE* MORE FAMILIAR WITH THIS TOWN THAN *YOU* ARE. LOOK BEHIND YOU.
DOOOOOM
AH!
YOU'RE CAUGHT IN BETWEEN US!
AT LAST, THE TABLES HAVE TURNED!
THERE'S NOWHERE TO RUN!
HO HO HO HO HO

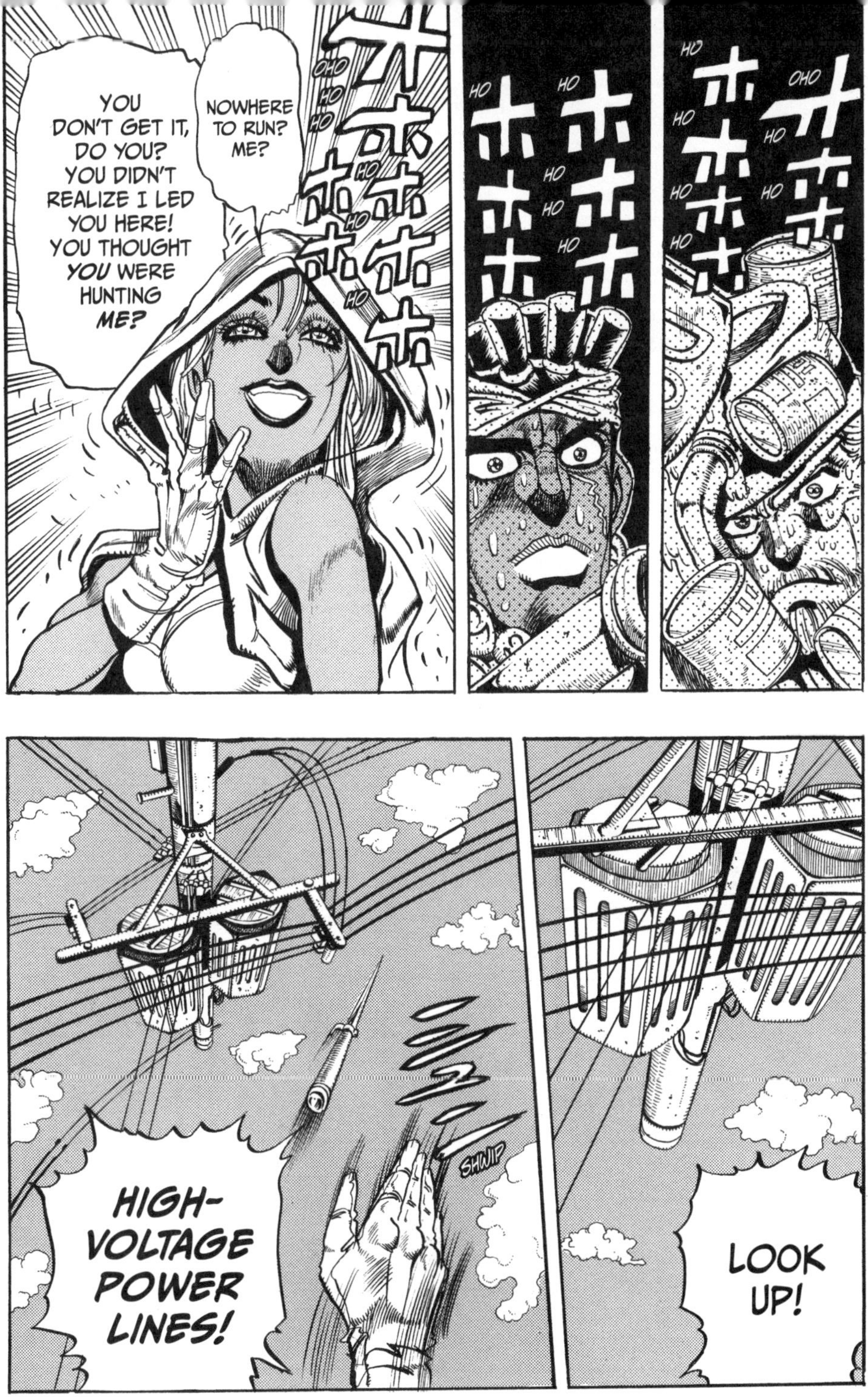
OHO HO HO HO HO HO HO HO HO
HO HO HO HO HO
NOWHERE TO RUN? ME?
YOU DON'T GET IT, DO YOU? YOU DIDN'T REALIZE I LED YOU HERE! YOU THOUGHT *YOU* WERE HUNTING *ME?*
OHO HO HO HO HO
LOOK UP!
SHWIP
HIGH-VOLTAGE POWER LINES!

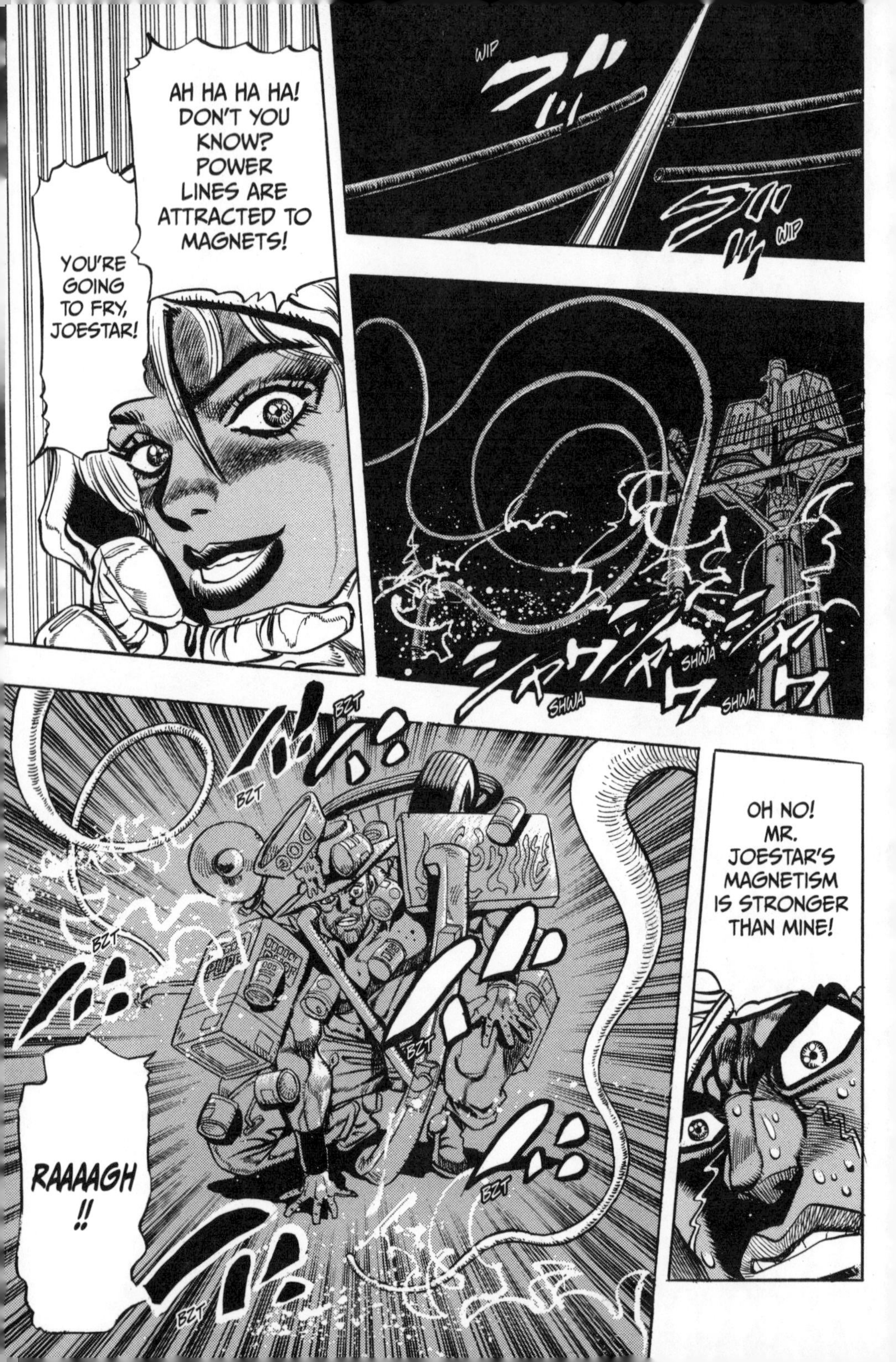
WIP
WIP
SHWA
SHWA
SHWA
AH HA HA HA! DON'T YOU KNOW? POWER LINES ARE ATTRACTED TO MAGNETS!
YOU'RE GOING TO FRY, JOESTAR!
OH NO! MR. JOESTAR'S MAGNETISM IS STRONGER THAN MINE!
BZT
BZT
BZT
BZT
BZT
BZT
RAAAAGH !!

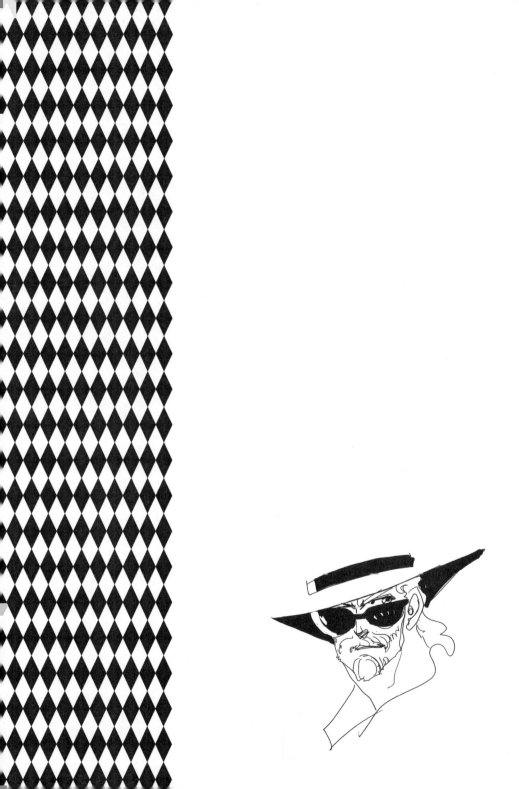

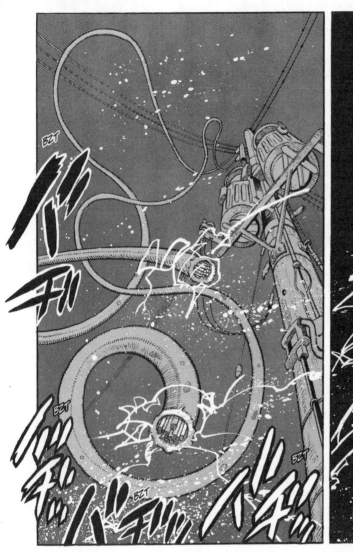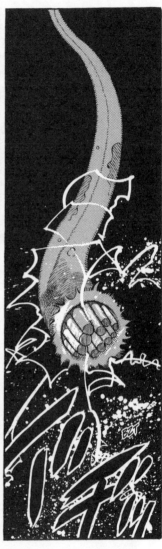

CHAPTER 91: "Bast" Mariah PART 6

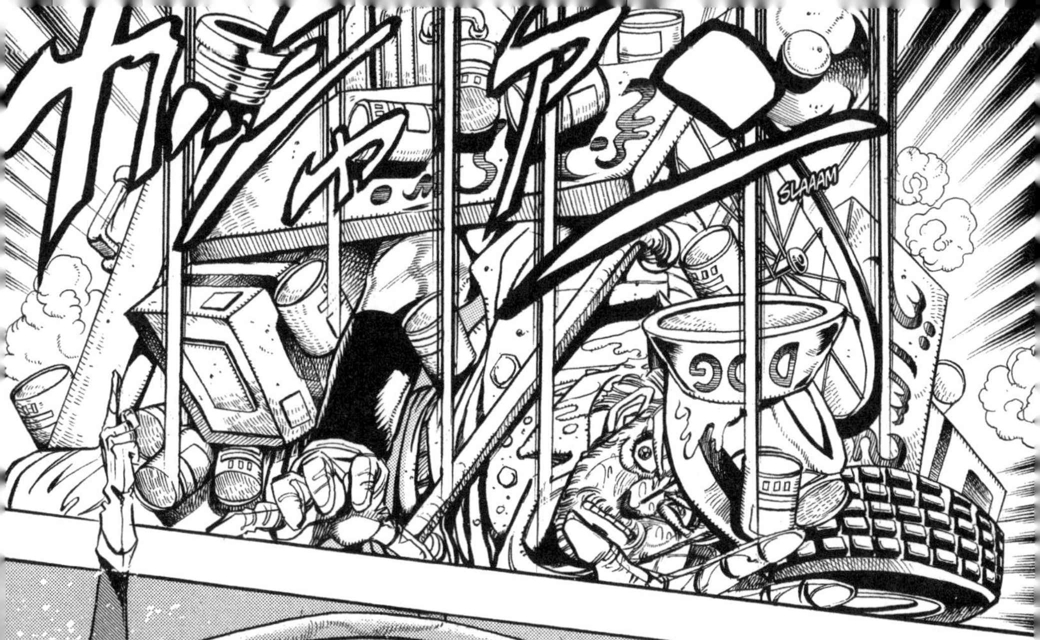
SLAAAM

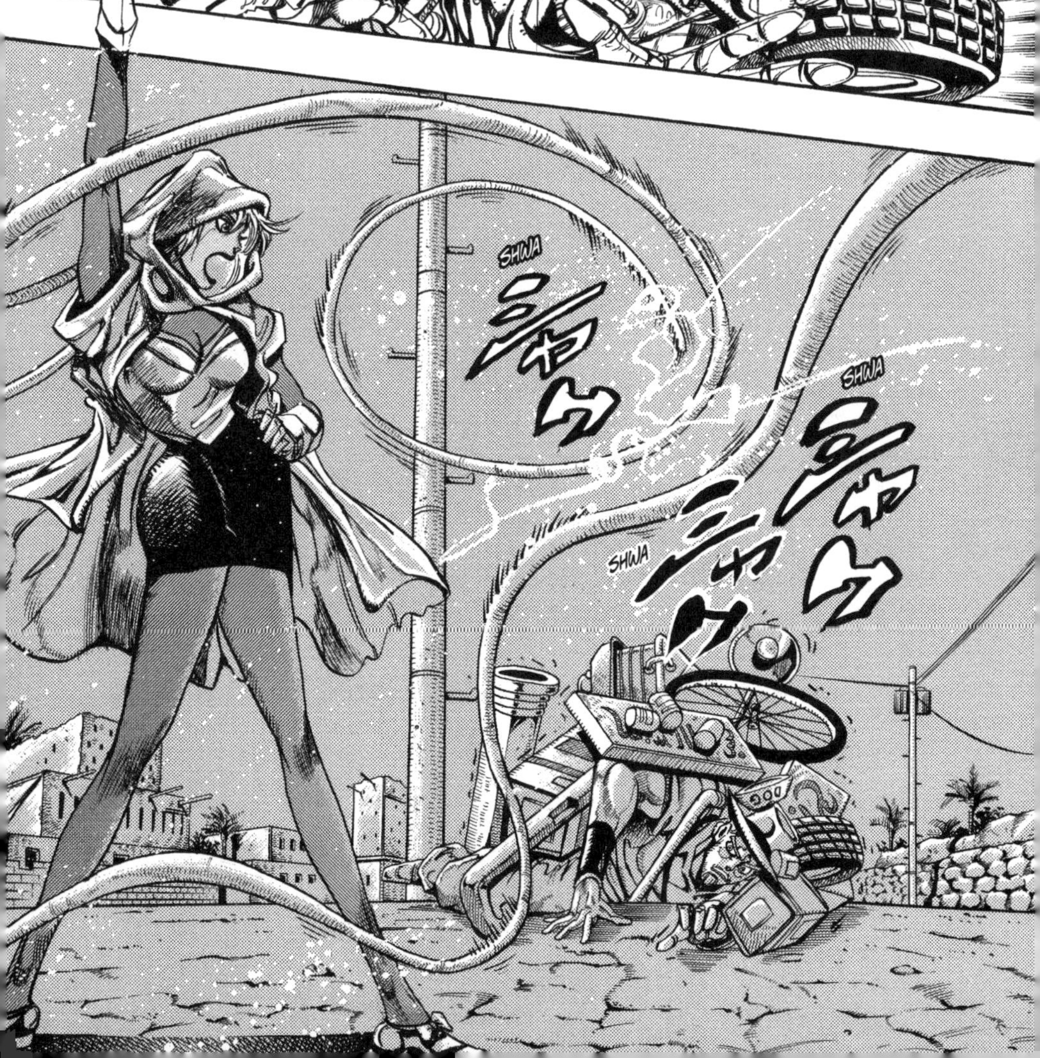
SHWA
SHWA
SHWA

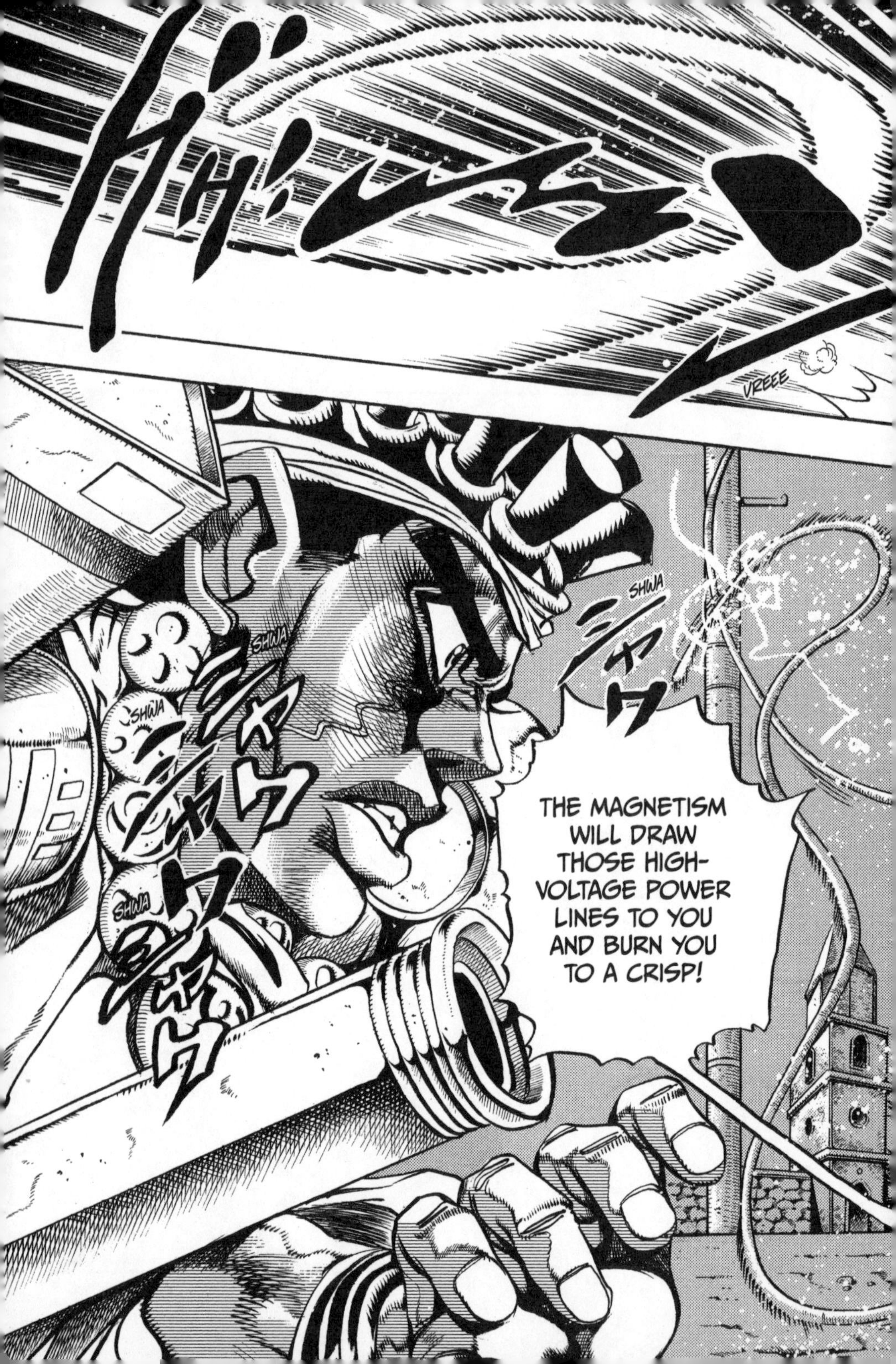
VREEE
SHWA
THE MAGNETISM WILL DRAW THOSE HIGH-VOLTAGE POWER LINES TO YOU AND BURN YOU TO A CRISP!
SHWA
SHWA
SHWA

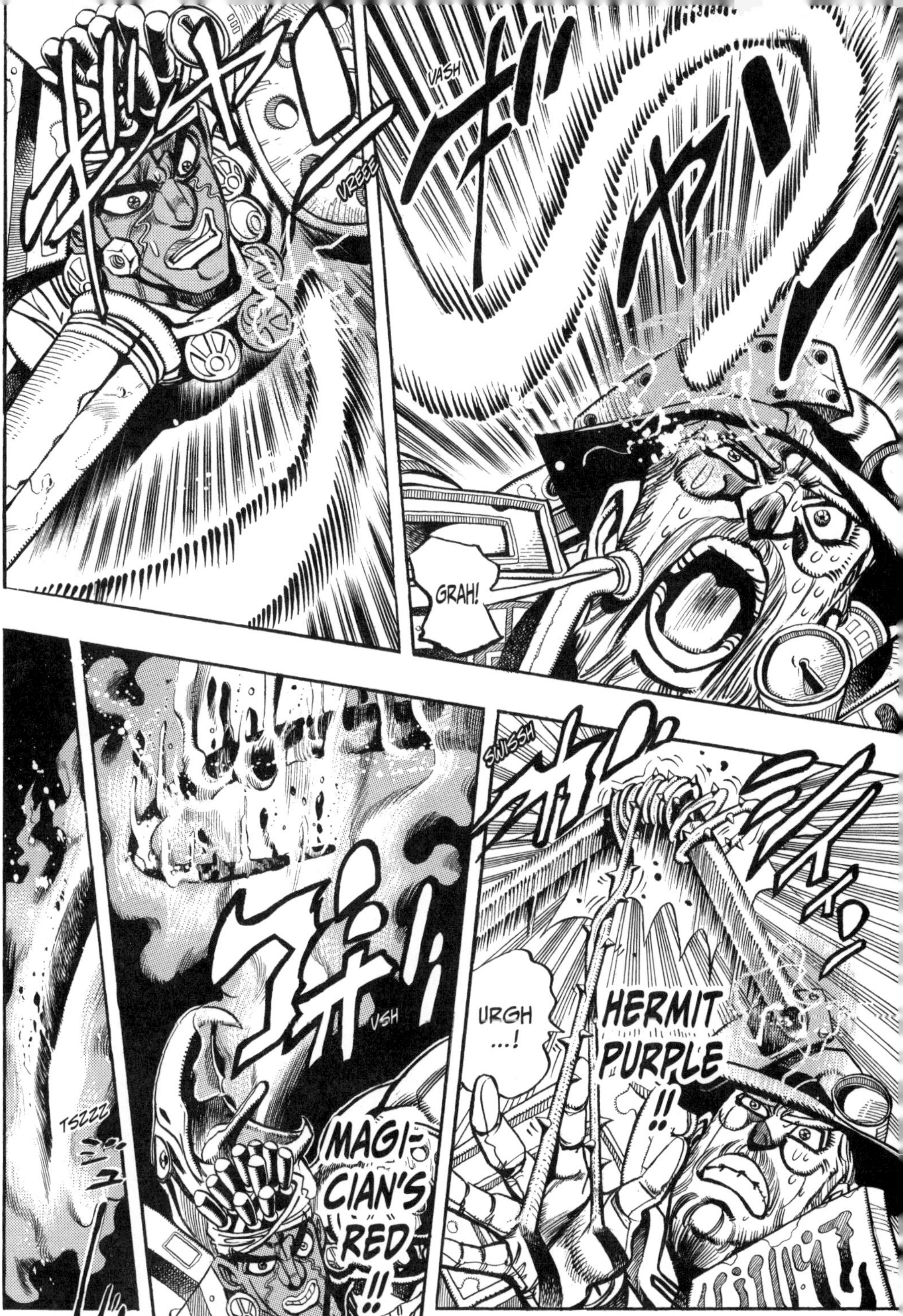
VASH
GRAH!
VREEE
SWISSH
URGH ...!
HERMIT PURPLE!!
VSH
MAGICIAN'S RED!!
TSZZZ

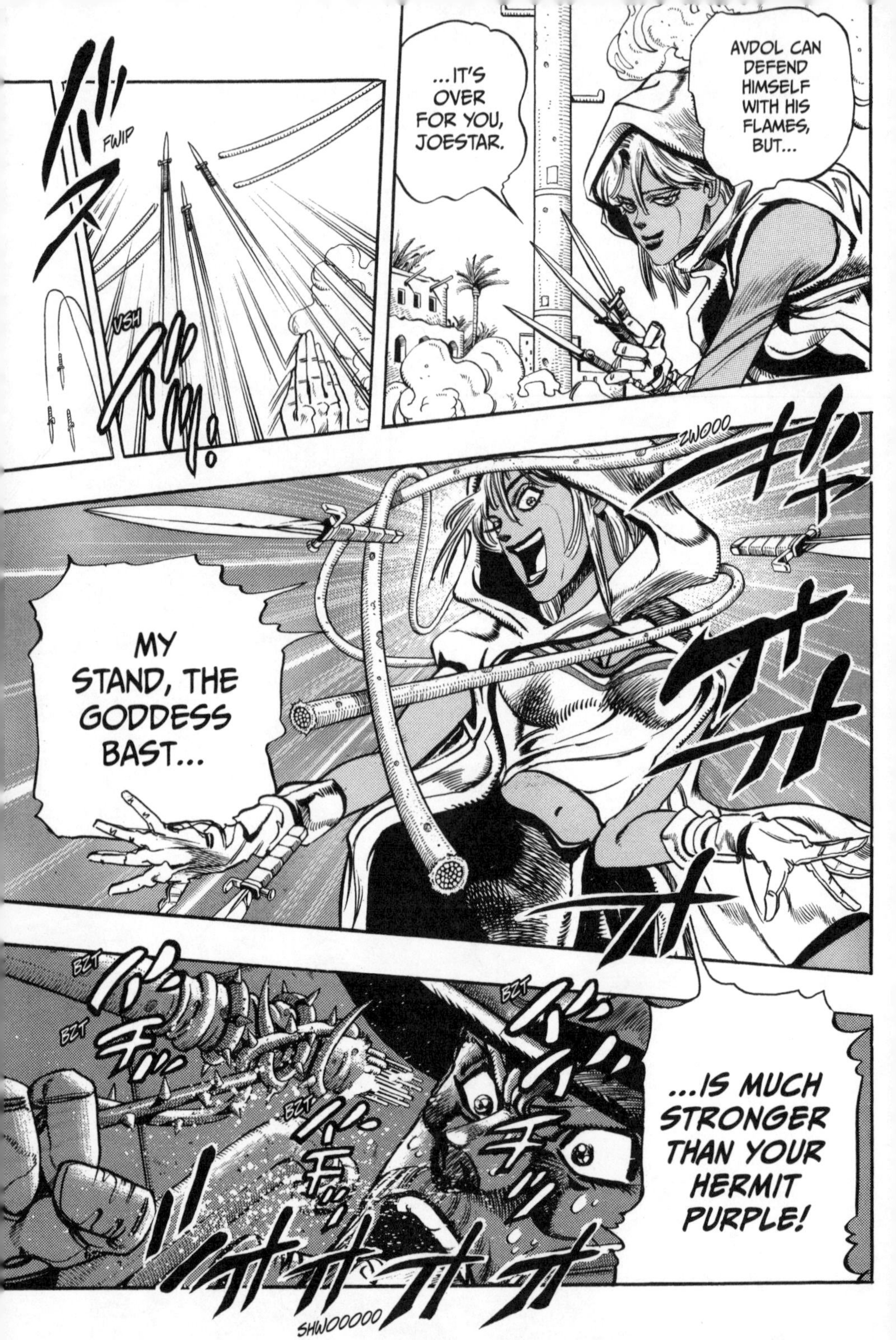
AVDOL CAN DEFEND HIMSELF WITH HIS FLAMES, BUT...
...IT'S OVER FOR YOU, JOESTAR.
FWIP
VSH
ZWOOO
MY STAND, THE GODDESS BAST...
...IS MUCH STRONGER THAN YOUR HERMIT PURPLE!
BZT
BZT
BZT
BZT
SHWOOOOO

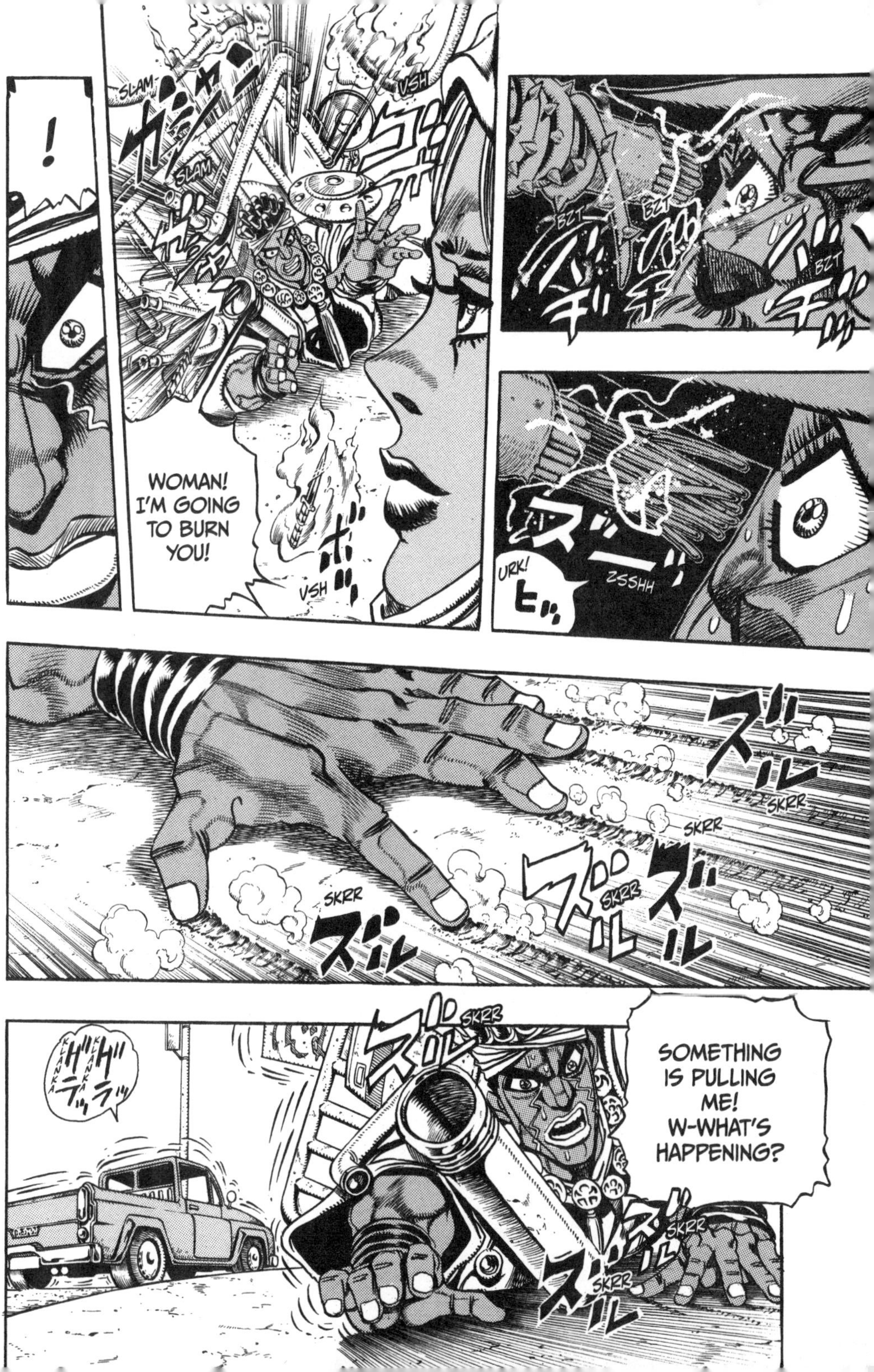
BZT
BZT
BZT
URK!
ZSSHH
SLAM
SLAM
VSH
WOMAN! I'M GOING TO BURN YOU!
VSH
!
SKRR
SKRR
SKRR
SKRR
SOMETHING IS PULLING ME! W-WHAT'S HAPPENING?
SKRR
KLANKA KLANKA
SKRR
SKRR

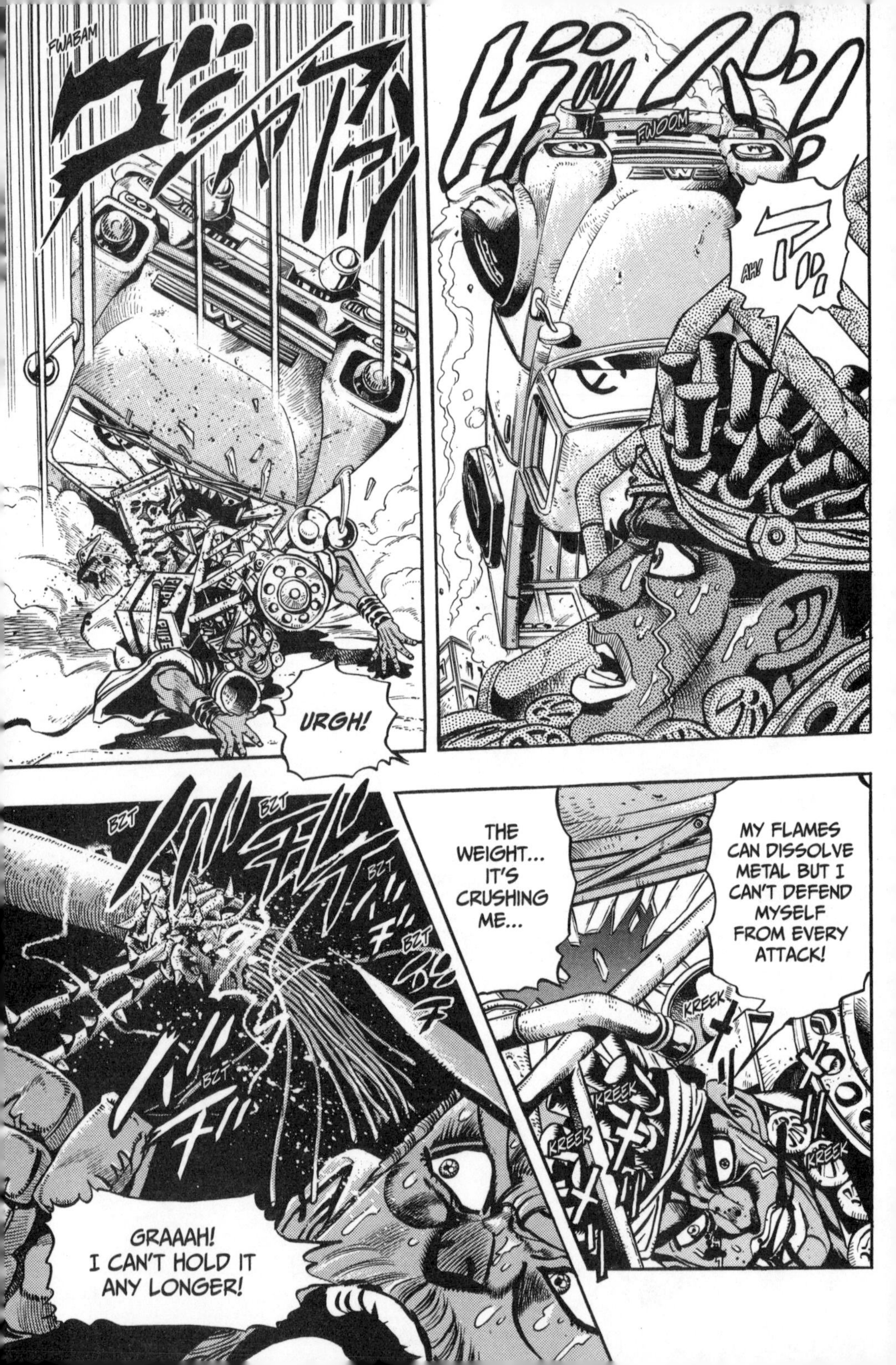

FWOOM
AH!
FWABAM
URGH!
MY FLAMES CAN DISSOLVE METAL BUT I CAN'T DEFEND MYSELF FROM EVERY ATTACK!
THE WEIGHT... IT'S CRUSHING ME...
KREEK
KREEK
KREEK
KREEK
BZT
BZT
BZT
BZT
BZT
GRAAAH! I CAN'T HOLD IT ANY LONGER!

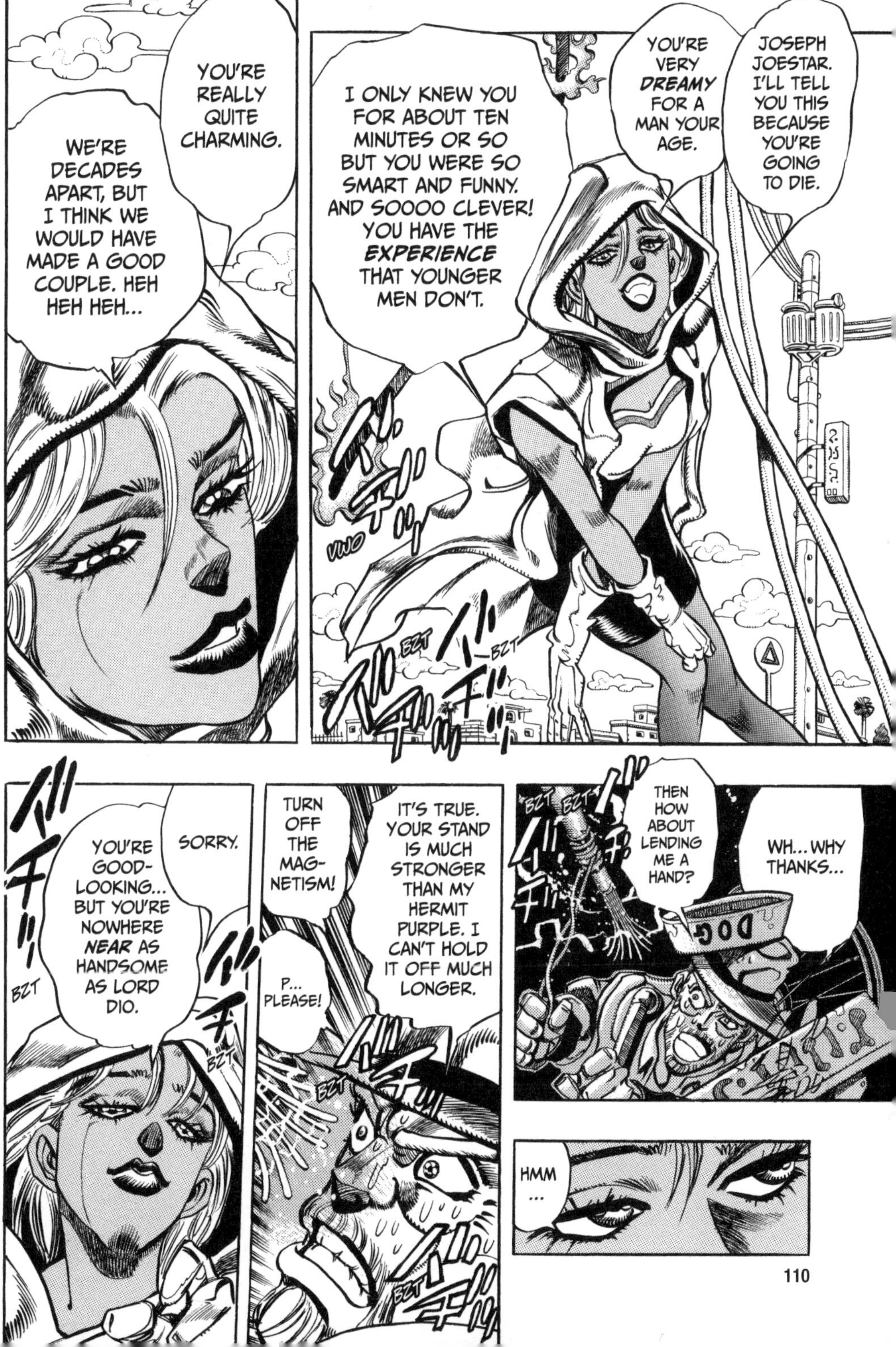
JOSEPH JOESTAR. I'LL TELL YOU THIS BECAUSE YOU'RE GOING TO DIE.
YOU'RE VERY *DREAMY* FOR A MAN YOUR AGE.
I ONLY KNEW YOU FOR ABOUT TEN MINUTES OR SO BUT YOU WERE SO SMART AND FUNNY. AND SOOOO CLEVER! YOU HAVE THE *EXPERIENCE* THAT YOUNGER MEN DON'T.
VWO
BZT
BZT
YOU'RE REALLY QUITE CHARMING.
WE'RE DECADES APART, BUT I THINK WE WOULD HAVE MADE A GOOD COUPLE. HEH HEH HEH...
WH...WHY THANKS...
THEN HOW ABOUT LENDING ME A HAND?
BZT BZT
HMM ...
IT'S TRUE. YOUR STAND IS MUCH STRONGER THAN MY HERMIT PURPLE. I CAN'T HOLD IT OFF MUCH LONGER.
TURN OFF THE MAG- NETISM!
P... PLEASE!
BZT
BZT
SORRY.
YOU'RE GOOD-LOOKING... BUT YOU'RE NOWHERE *NEAR* AS HANDSOME AS LORD DIO.
BZT
BZT

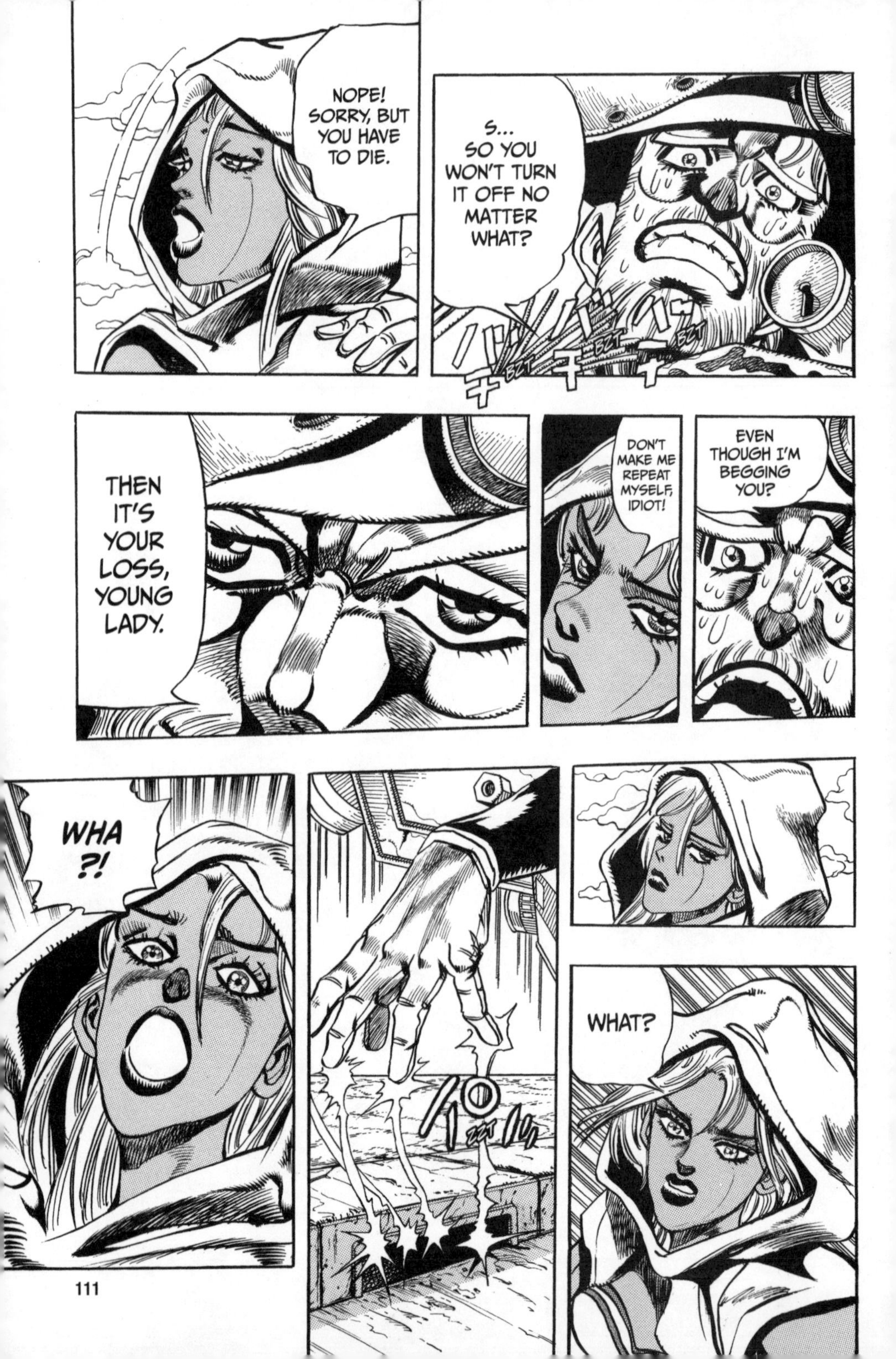
S...
SO YOU WON'T TURN IT OFF NO MATTER WHAT?
BZT BZT BZT BZT
NOPE! SORRY, BUT YOU HAVE TO DIE.
EVEN THOUGH I'M BEGGING YOU?
DON'T MAKE ME REPEAT MYSELF, IDIOT!
THEN IT'S YOUR LOSS, YOUNG LADY.
WHAT?
BZT
WHA ?!

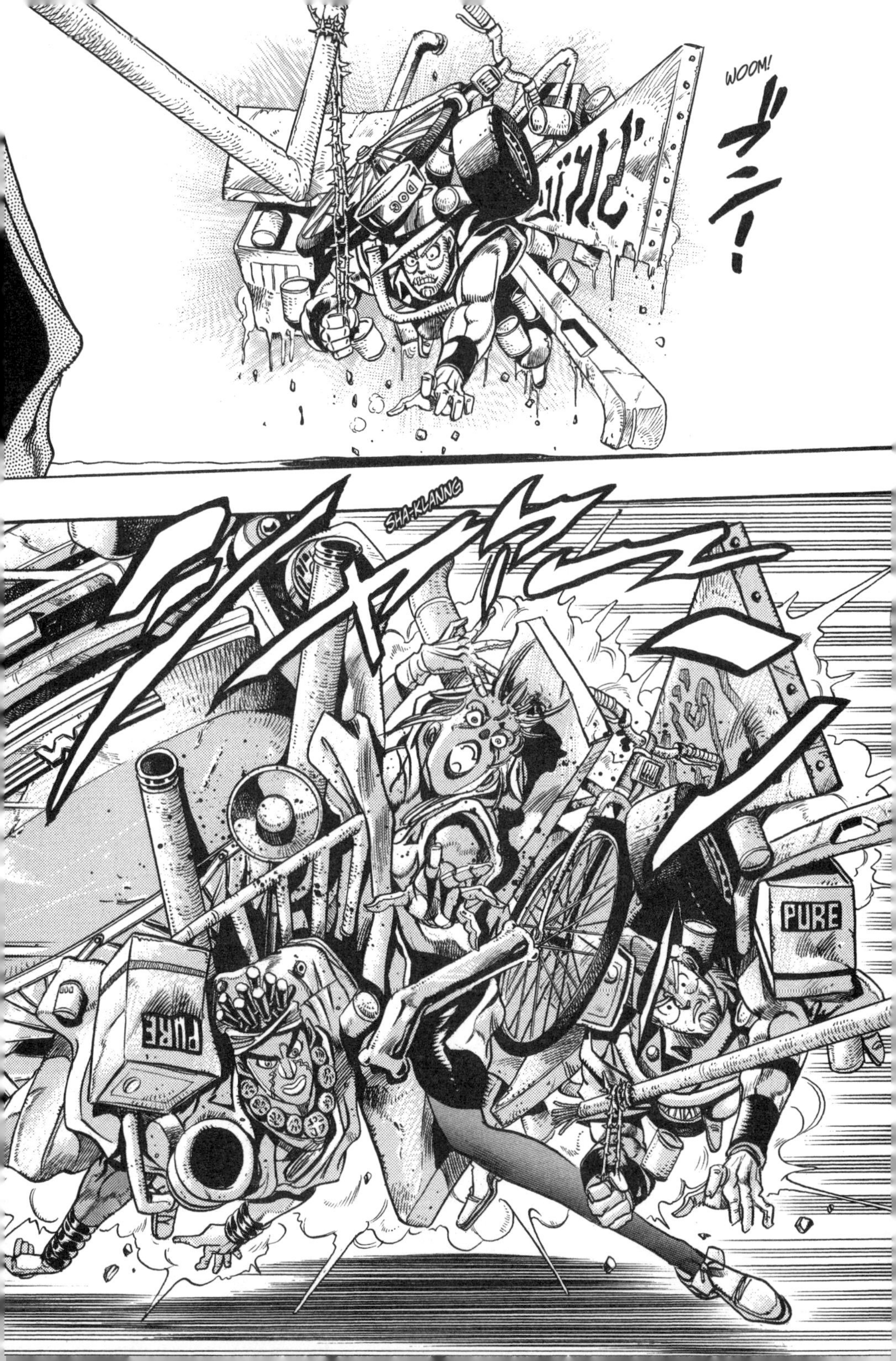
WOOM!
DOG
SHA-KLANNG
PURE
PURE

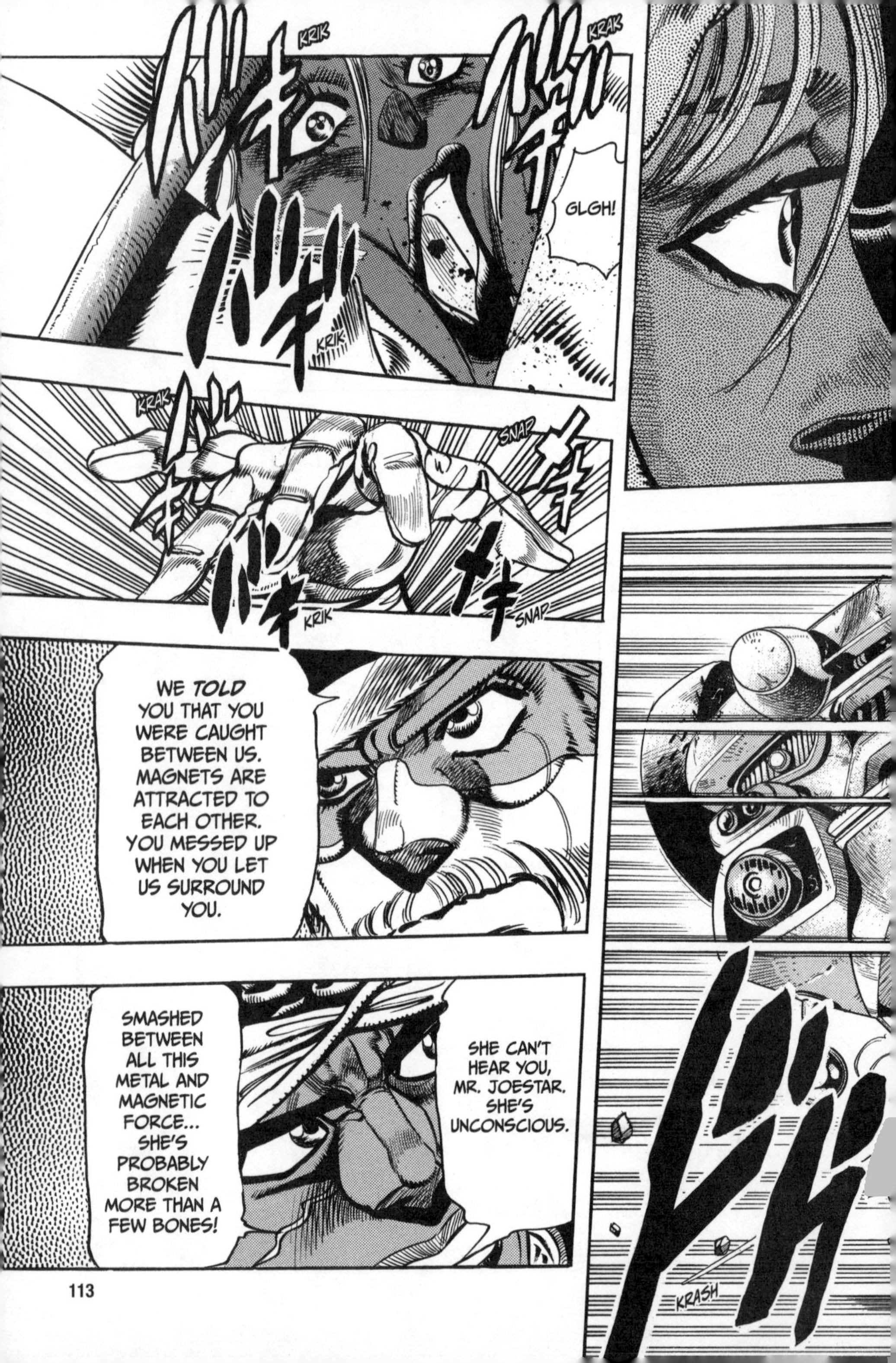

KRAK
KRIK
GLGH!
KRIK
SNAP
KRAK
SNAP
KRIK
KRASH
WE *TOLD* YOU THAT YOU WERE CAUGHT BETWEEN US. MAGNETS ARE ATTRACTED TO EACH OTHER. YOU MESSED UP WHEN YOU LET US SURROUND YOU.
SMASHED BETWEEN ALL THIS METAL AND MAGNETIC FORCE... SHE'S PROBABLY BROKEN MORE THAN A FEW BONES!
SHE CAN'T HEAR YOU, MR. JOESTAR. SHE'S UNCONSCIOUS.

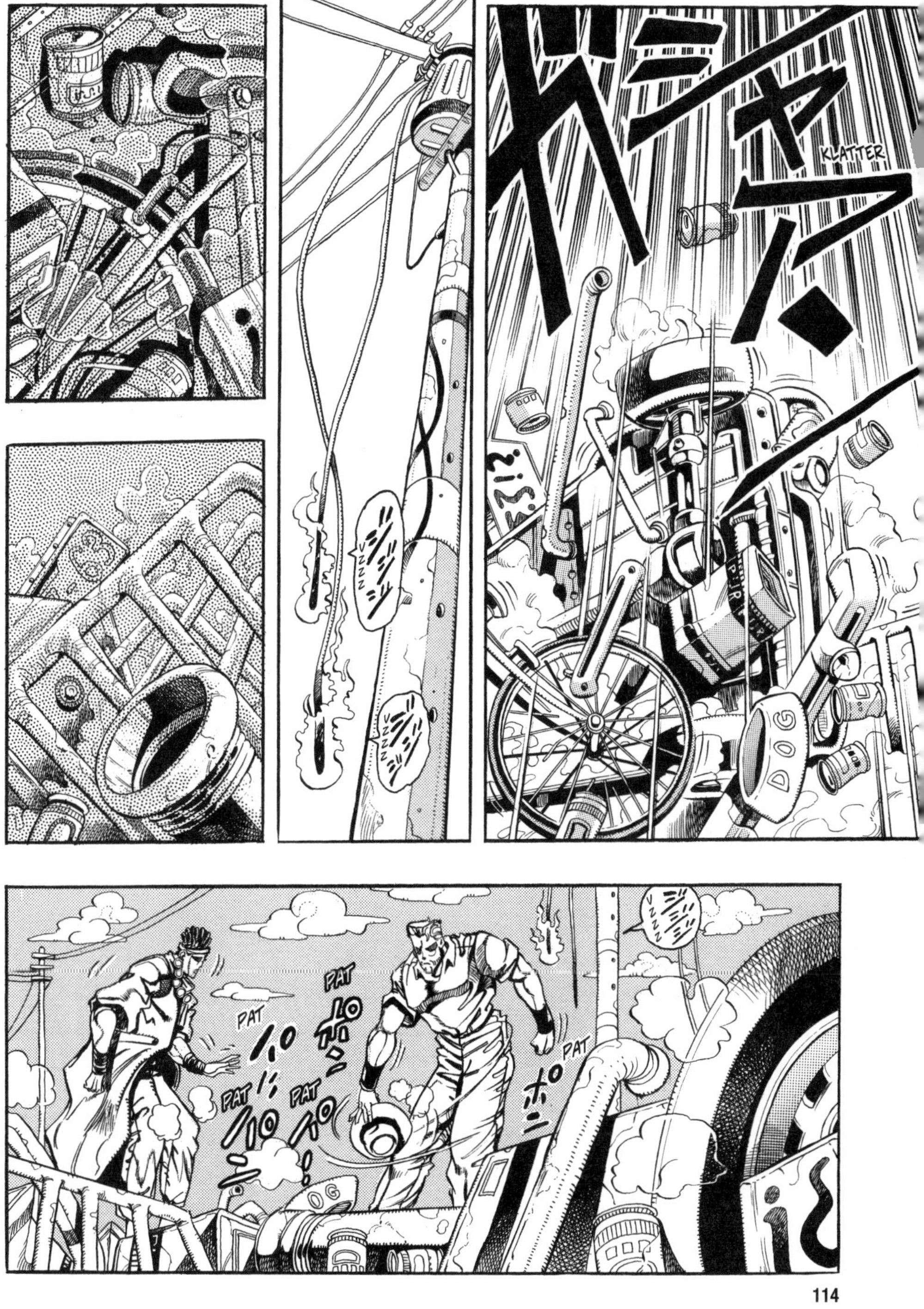
KLATTER
VZZZ
VZZZ
VZZZ
PAT
PAT
PAT
PAT
PAT

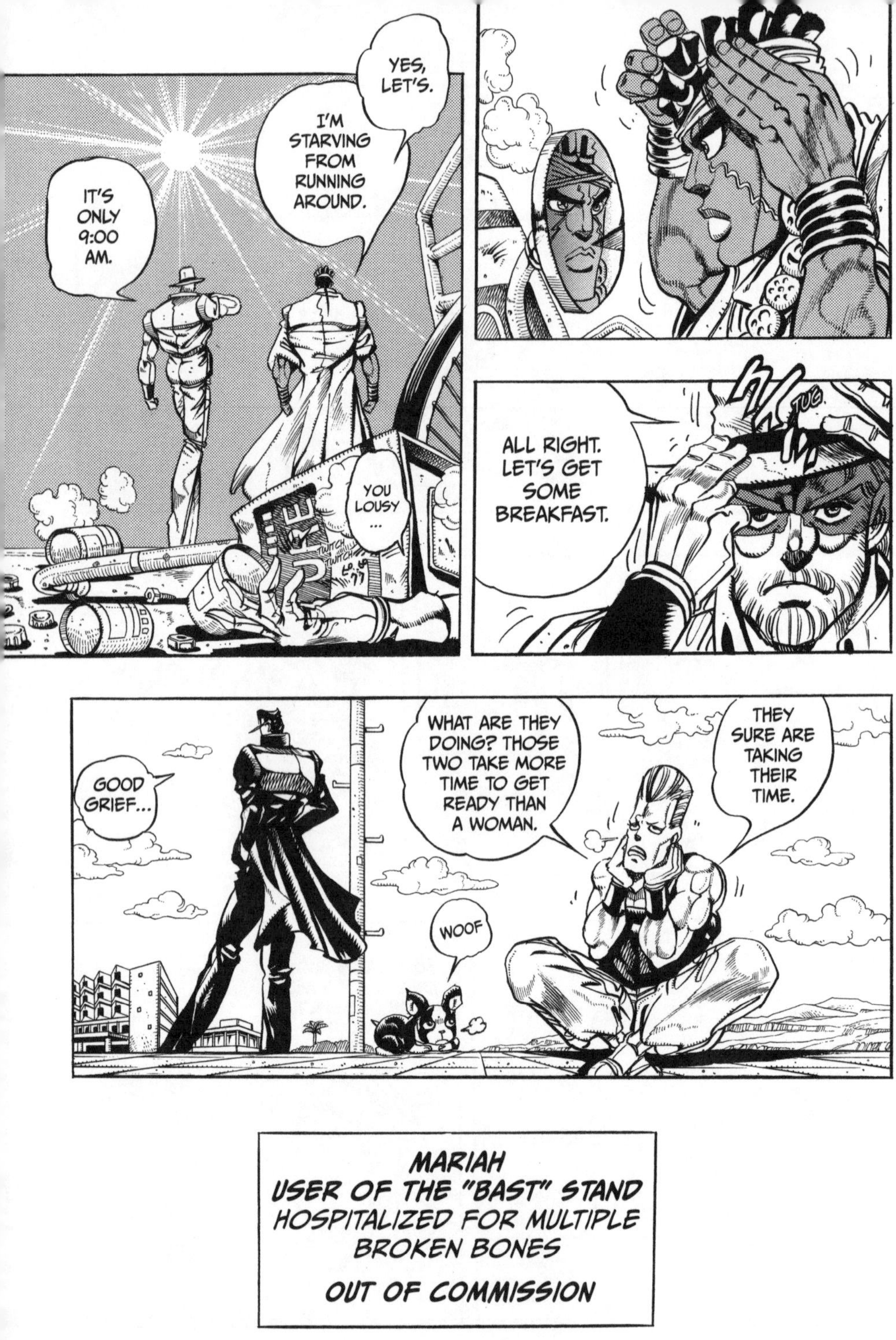
TUG
ALL RIGHT. LET'S GET SOME BREAKFAST.
YES, LET'S.
I'M STARVING FROM RUNNING AROUND.
IT'S ONLY 9:00 AM.
YOU LOUSY ...
TWITCH TWITCH
THEY SURE ARE TAKING THEIR TIME.
WHAT ARE THEY DOING? THOSE TWO TAKE MORE TIME TO GET READY THAN A WOMAN.
WOOF
GOOD GRIEF...

MARIAH
USER OF THE "BAST" STAND
HOSPITALIZED FOR MULTIPLE BROKEN BONES

OUT OF COMMISSION

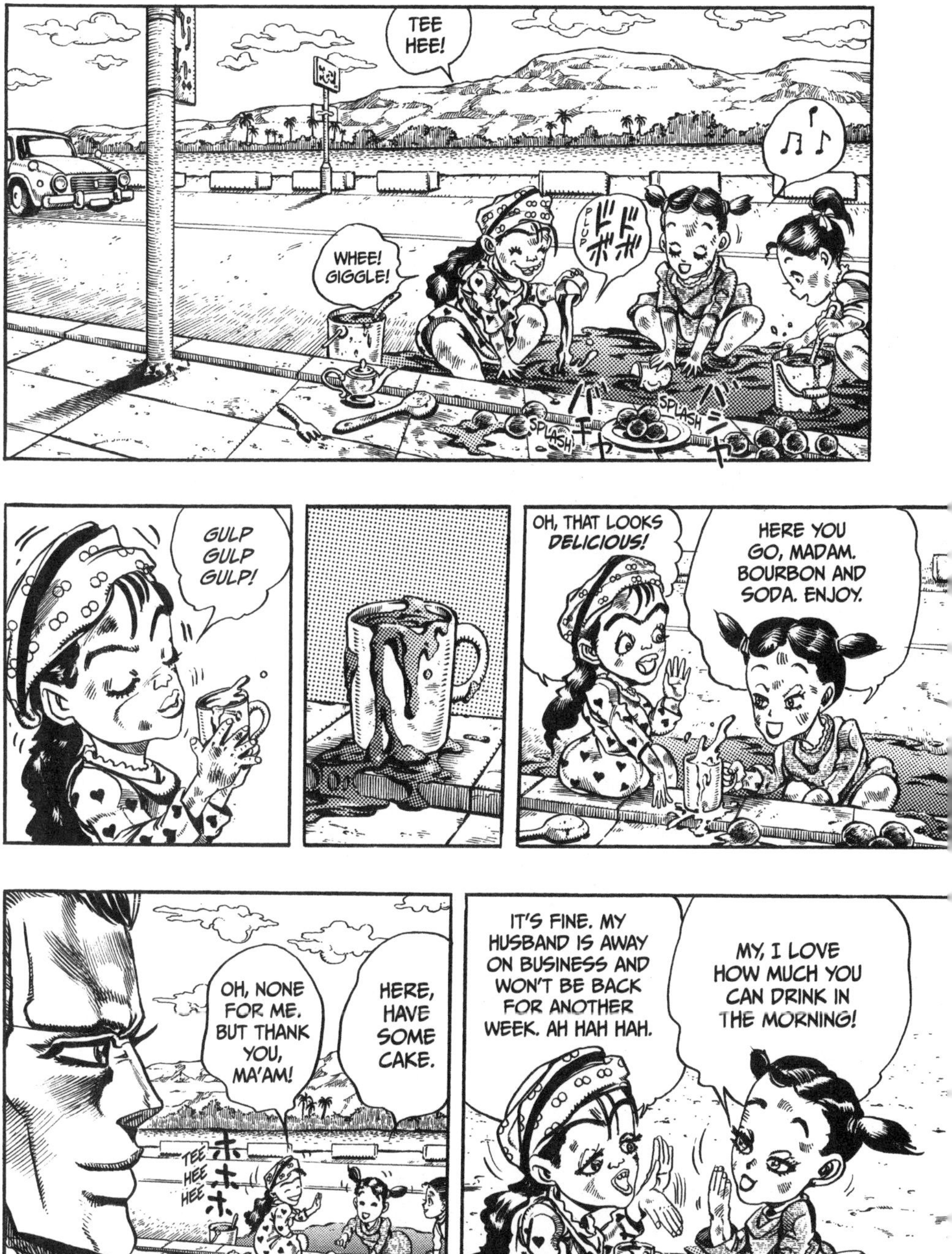
TEE HEE!
PLUP ドボドボ
WHEE! GIGGLE!
SPLASH
SPLASH
HERE YOU GO, MADAM. BOURBON AND SODA. ENJOY.
OH, THAT LOOKS DELICIOUS!
GULP GULP GULP!
MY, I LOVE HOW MUCH YOU CAN DRINK IN THE MORNING!
IT'S FINE. MY HUSBAND IS AWAY ON BUSINESS AND WON'T BE BACK FOR ANOTHER WEEK. AH HAH HAH.
HERE, HAVE SOME CAKE.
OH, NONE FOR ME. BUT THANK YOU, MA'AM!
TEE HEE HEE ホホホ

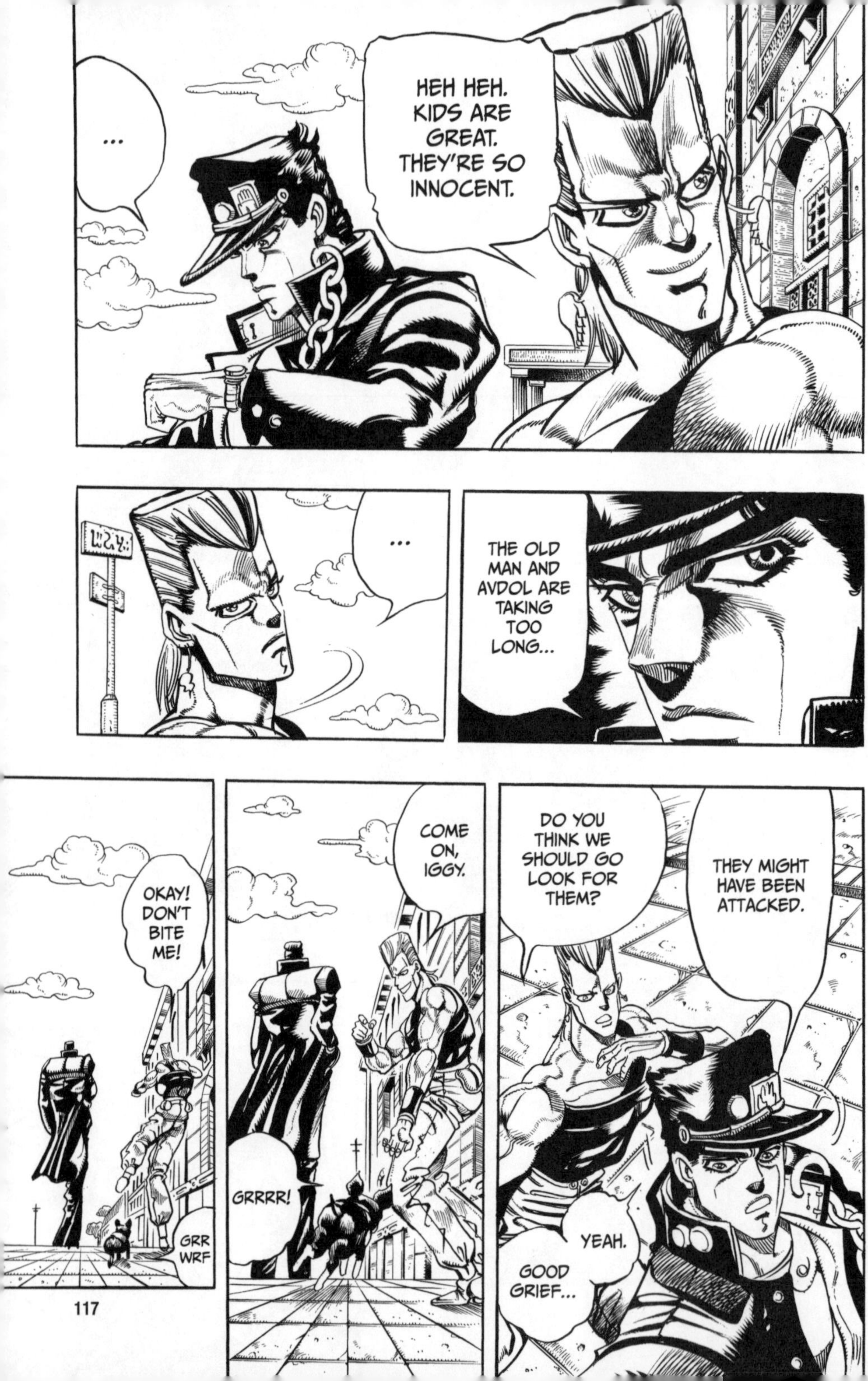
HEH HEH. KIDS ARE GREAT. THEY'RE SO INNOCENT.
...
THE OLD MAN AND AVDOL ARE TAKING TOO LONG...
...
THEY MIGHT HAVE BEEN ATTACKED.
DO YOU THINK WE SHOULD GO LOOK FOR THEM?
YEAH.
GOOD GRIEF...
COME ON, IGGY.
GRRRR!
OKAY! DON'T BITE ME!
GRR WRF

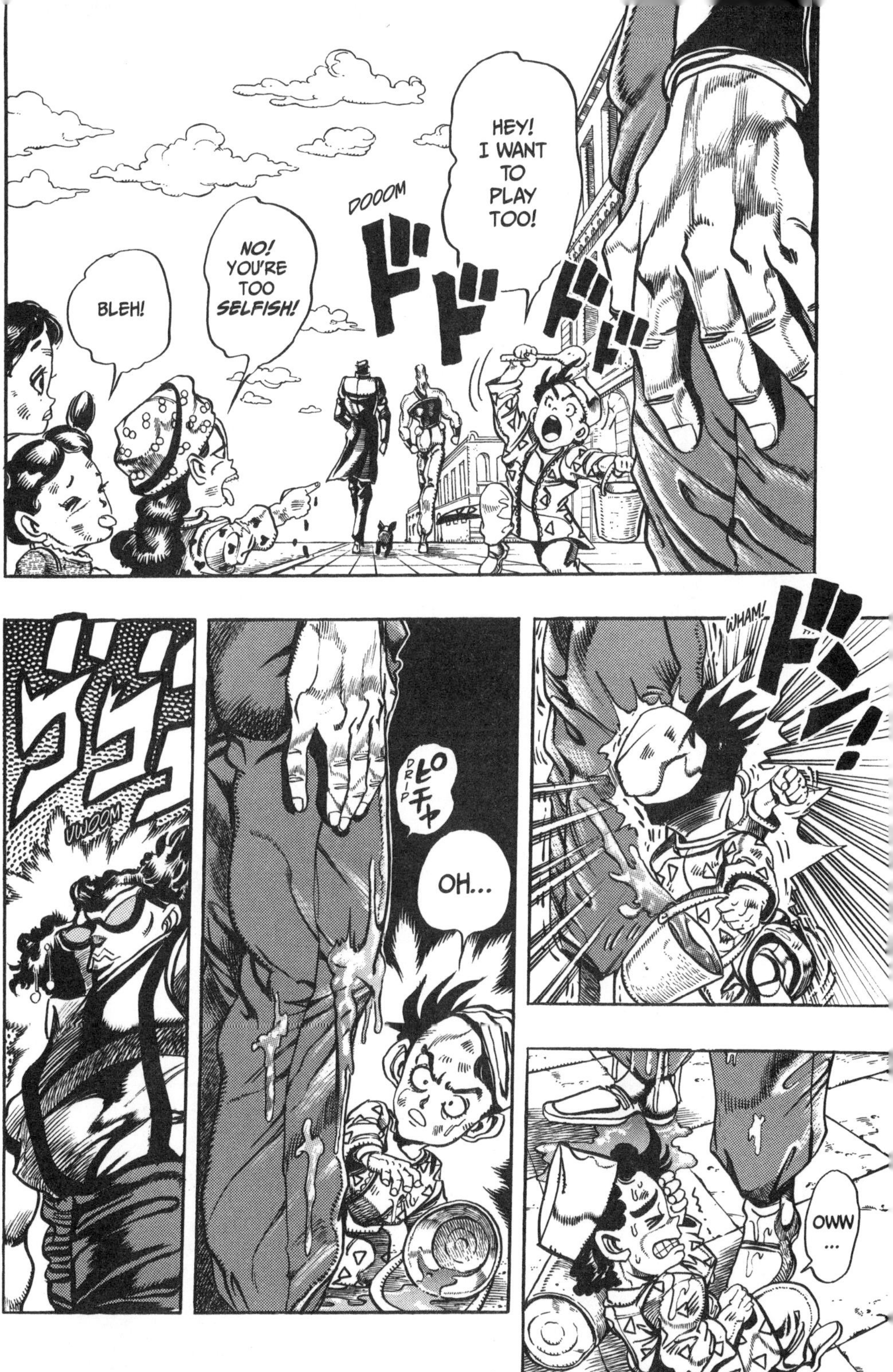
HEY! I WANT TO PLAY TOO!
DOOOM
NO! YOU'RE TOO SELFISH!
BLEH!
WHAM!
DRIP
OH...
UWOOM
OWW ...

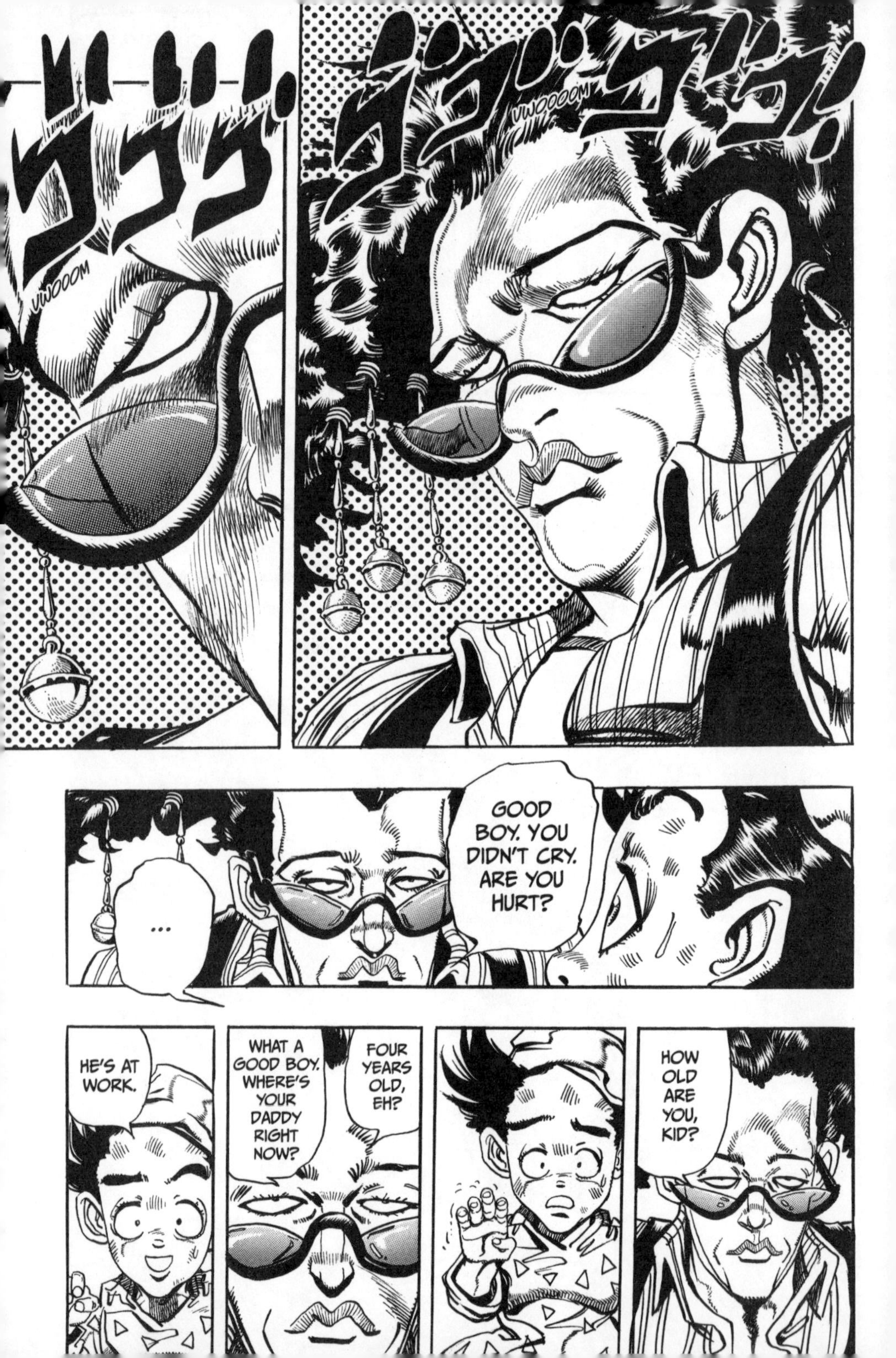
VWOOOM
VWOOOM
GOOD BOY. YOU DIDN'T CRY. ARE YOU HURT?
...
HOW OLD ARE YOU, KID?
FOUR YEARS OLD, EH?
WHAT A GOOD BOY. WHERE'S YOUR DADDY RIGHT NOW?
HE'S AT WORK.

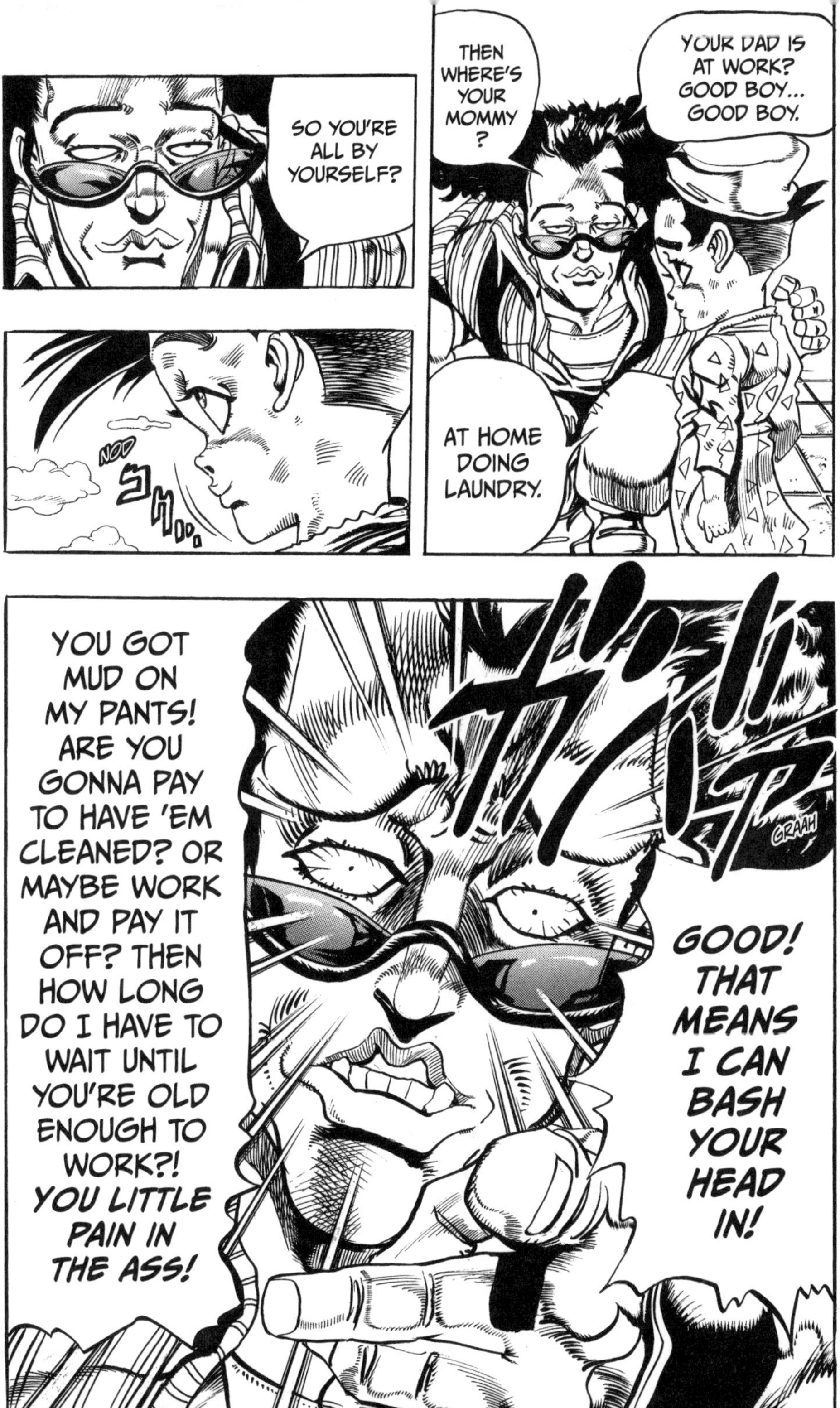
YOUR DAD IS AT WORK? GOOD BOY... GOOD BOY.
THEN WHERE'S YOUR MOMMY ?
AT HOME DOING LAUNDRY.
SO YOU'RE ALL BY YOURSELF?
NOD
GRAAH
YOU GOT MUD ON MY PANTS! ARE YOU GONNA PAY TO HAVE 'EM CLEANED? OR MAYBE WORK AND PAY IT OFF? THEN HOW LONG DO I HAVE TO WAIT UNTIL YOU'RE OLD ENOUGH TO WORK?! YOU LITTLE PAIN IN THE ASS!
GOOD! THAT MEANS I CAN BASH YOUR HEAD IN!

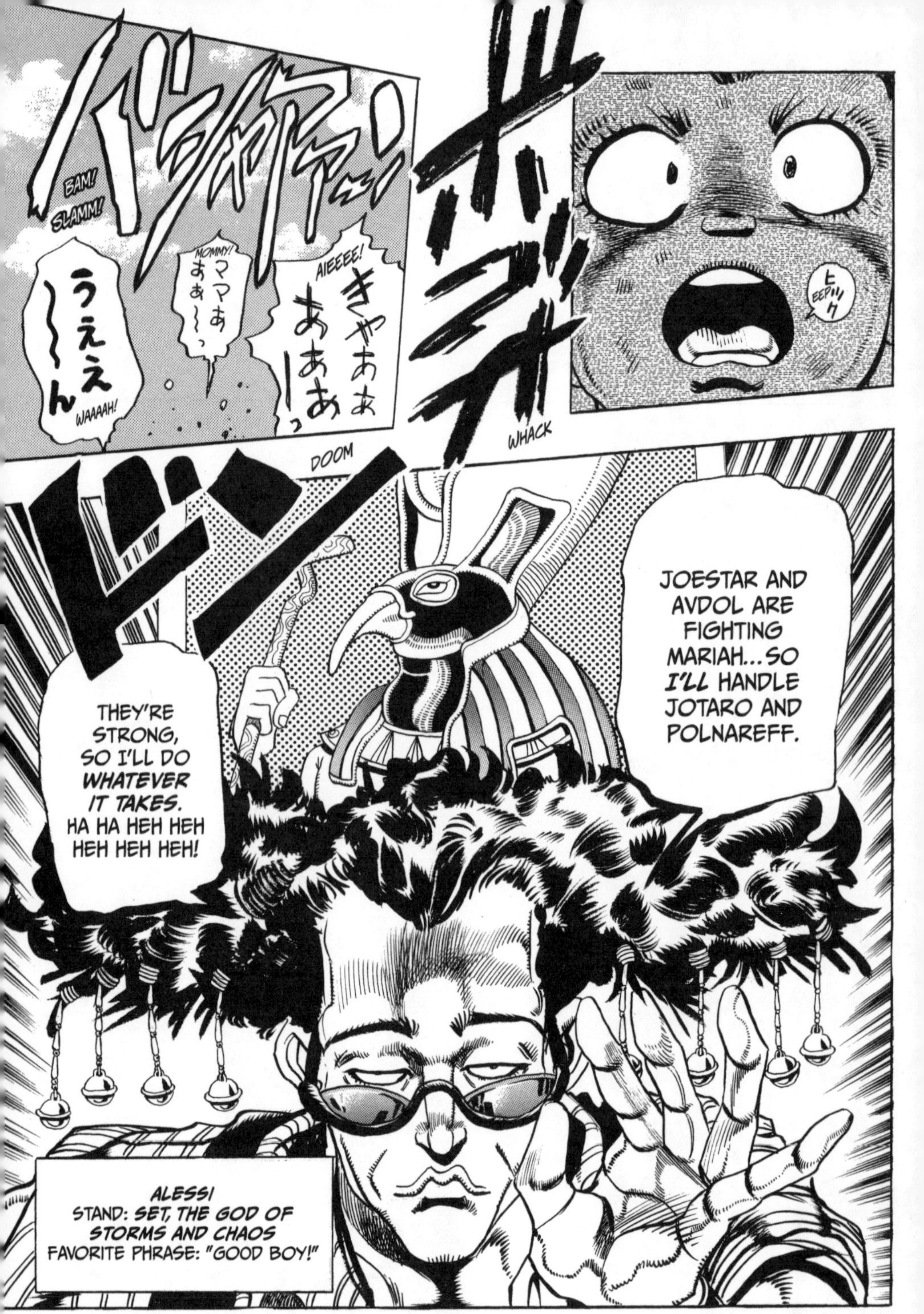
ヒック
EEP!
WHACK
AIEEEE!
きゃあああああっ
MOMMY!
ママあぁ〜っ
BAM!
SLAMM!
うえぇ〜〜ん
WAAAAH!
JOESTAR AND AVDOL ARE FIGHTING MARIAH...SO *I'LL* HANDLE JOTARO AND POLNAREFF.
DOOM
THEY'RE STRONG, SO I'LL DO ***WHATEVER IT TAKES***. HA HA HEH HEH HEH HEH HEH!
ALESSI
STAND: ***SET, THE GOD OF STORMS AND CHAOS***
FAVORITE PHRASE: "GOOD BOY!"

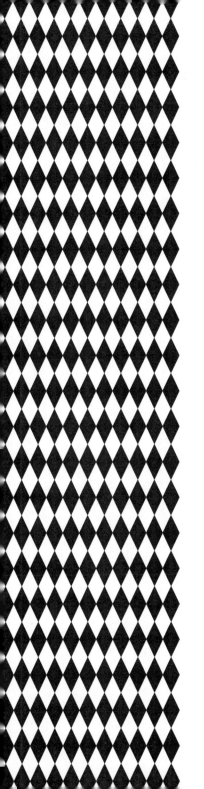

JoJo's

BIZARRE ADVENTURE

CHAPTER 92: "Set" Alessi PART 1

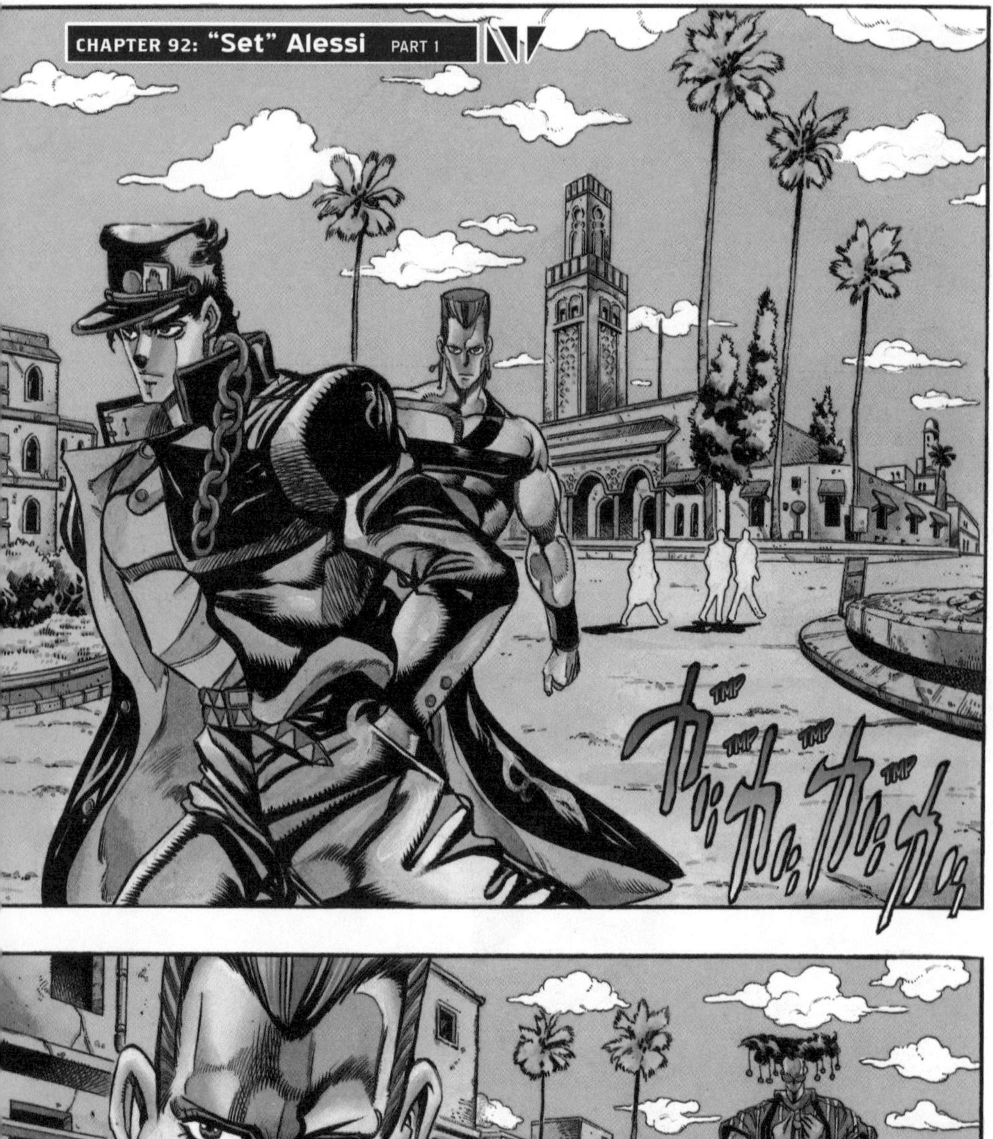
TMP
TMP
TMP
TMP

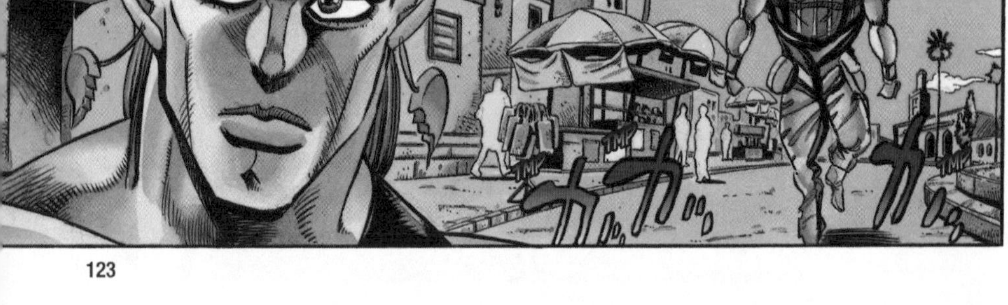
TMP
TMP
TMP

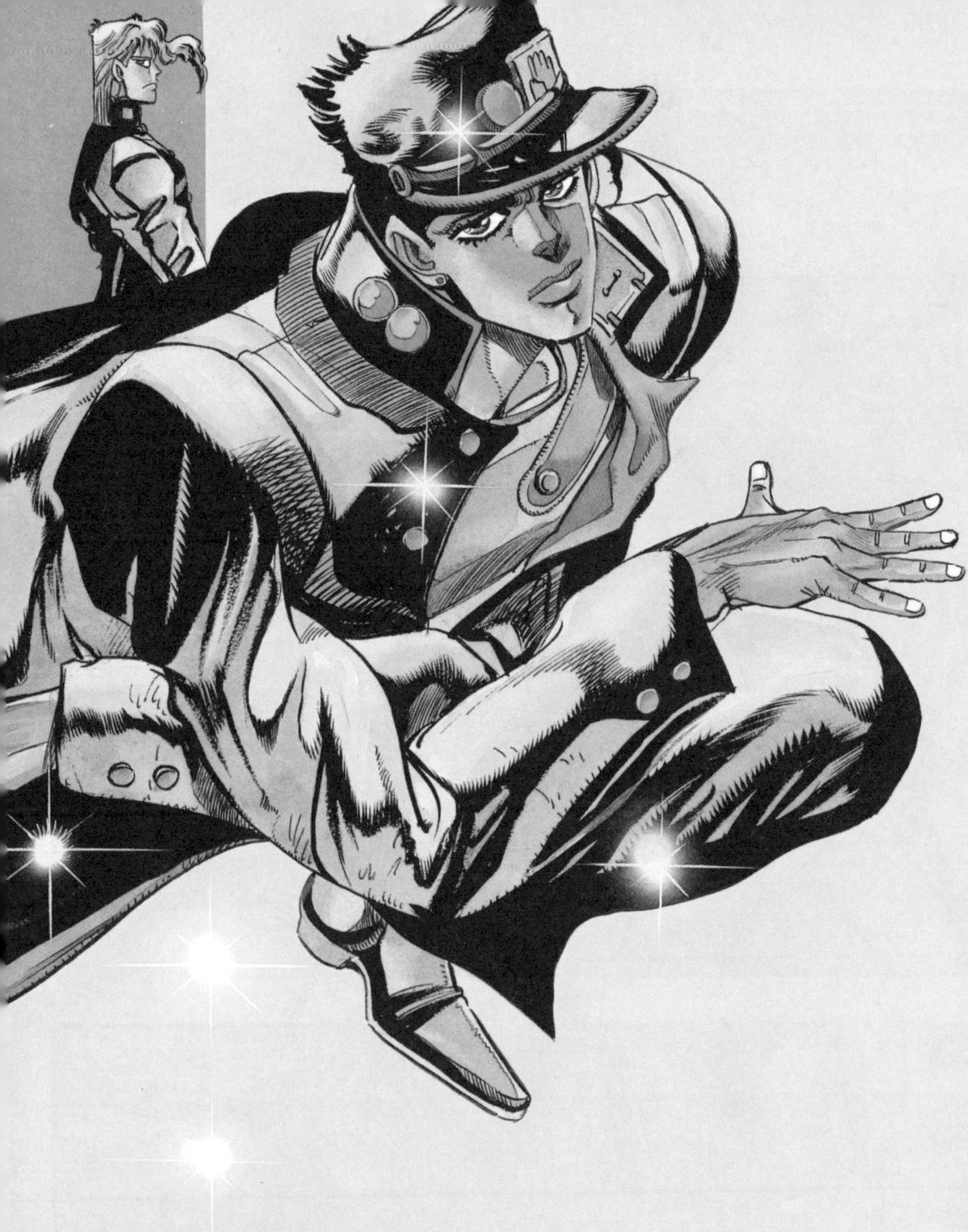

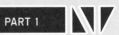

CHAPTER 92: “Set” Alessi PART 1

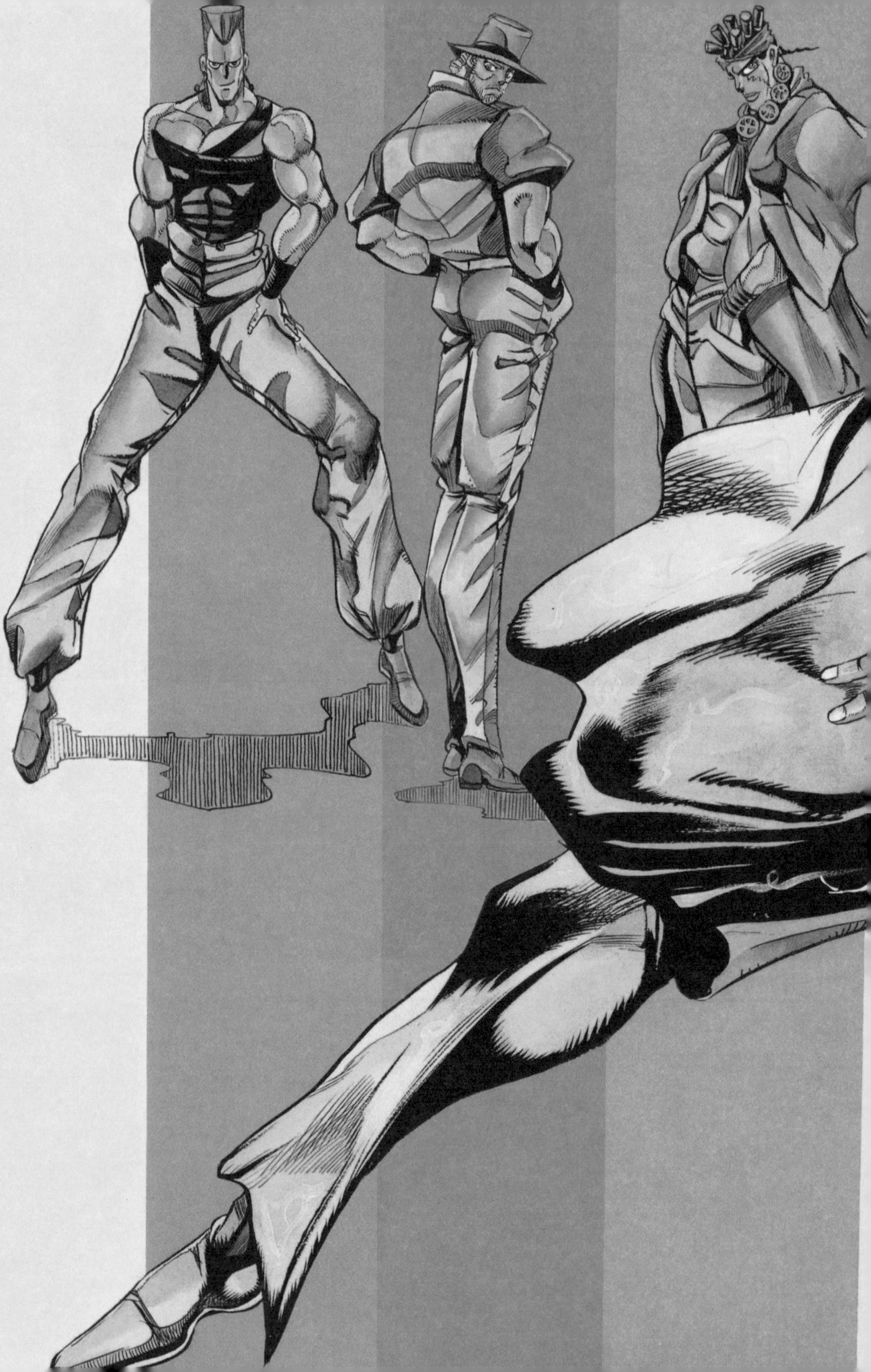

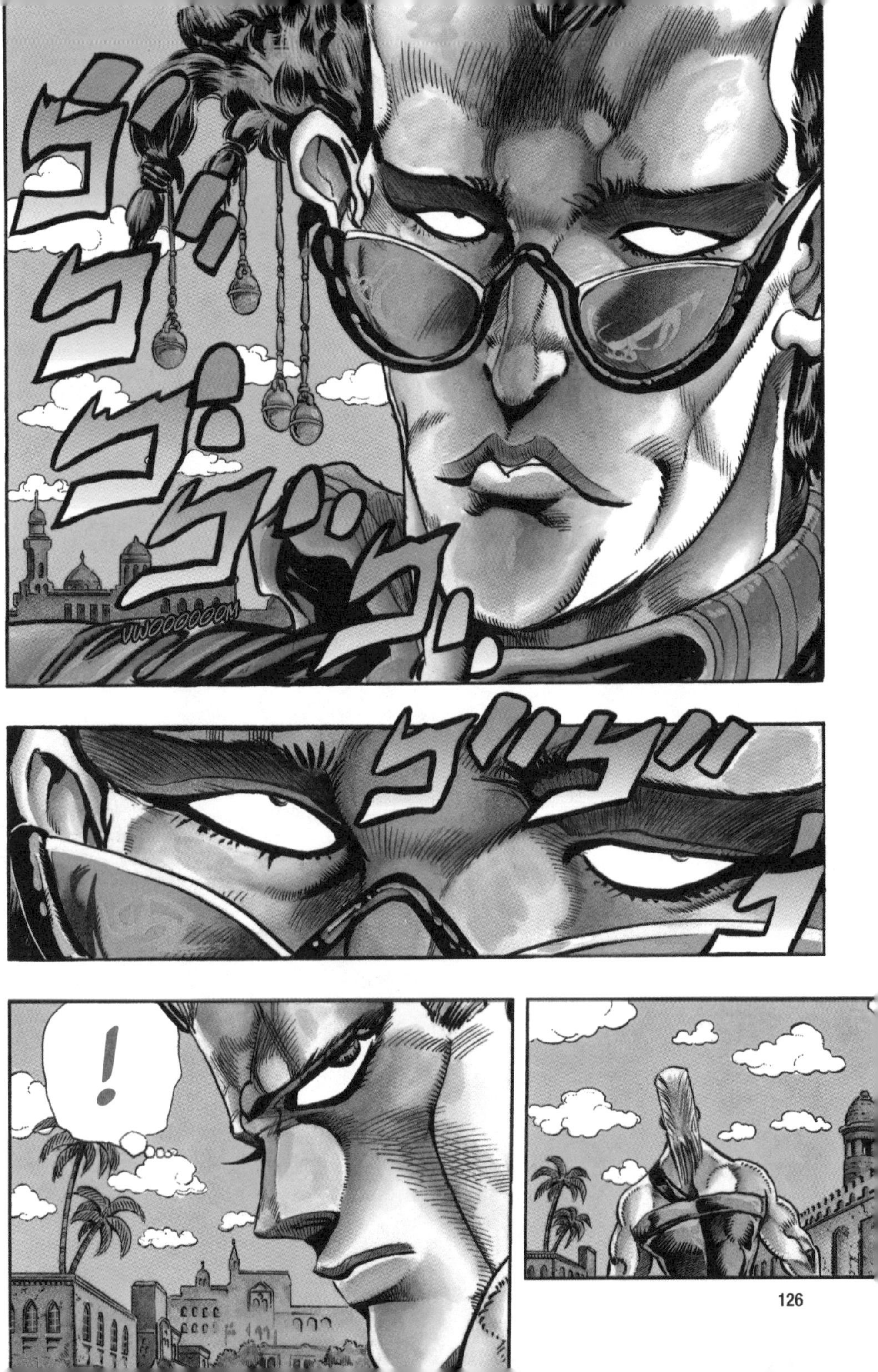
VWOOOOOOM
!

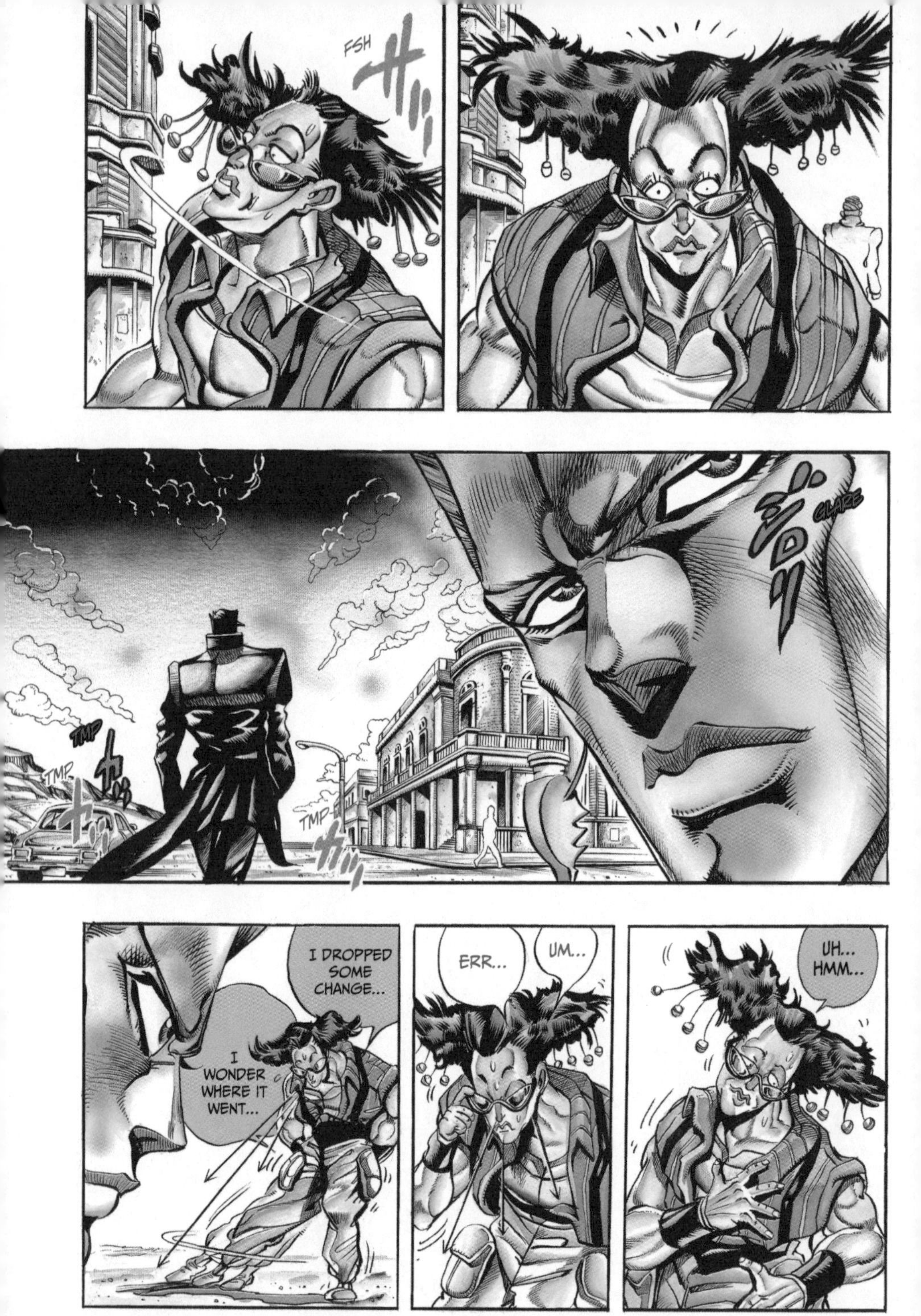
FSH
GLARE
TMP
TMP
TMP
UH... HMM...
UM...
ERR...
I DROPPED SOME CHANGE...
I WONDER WHERE IT WENT...

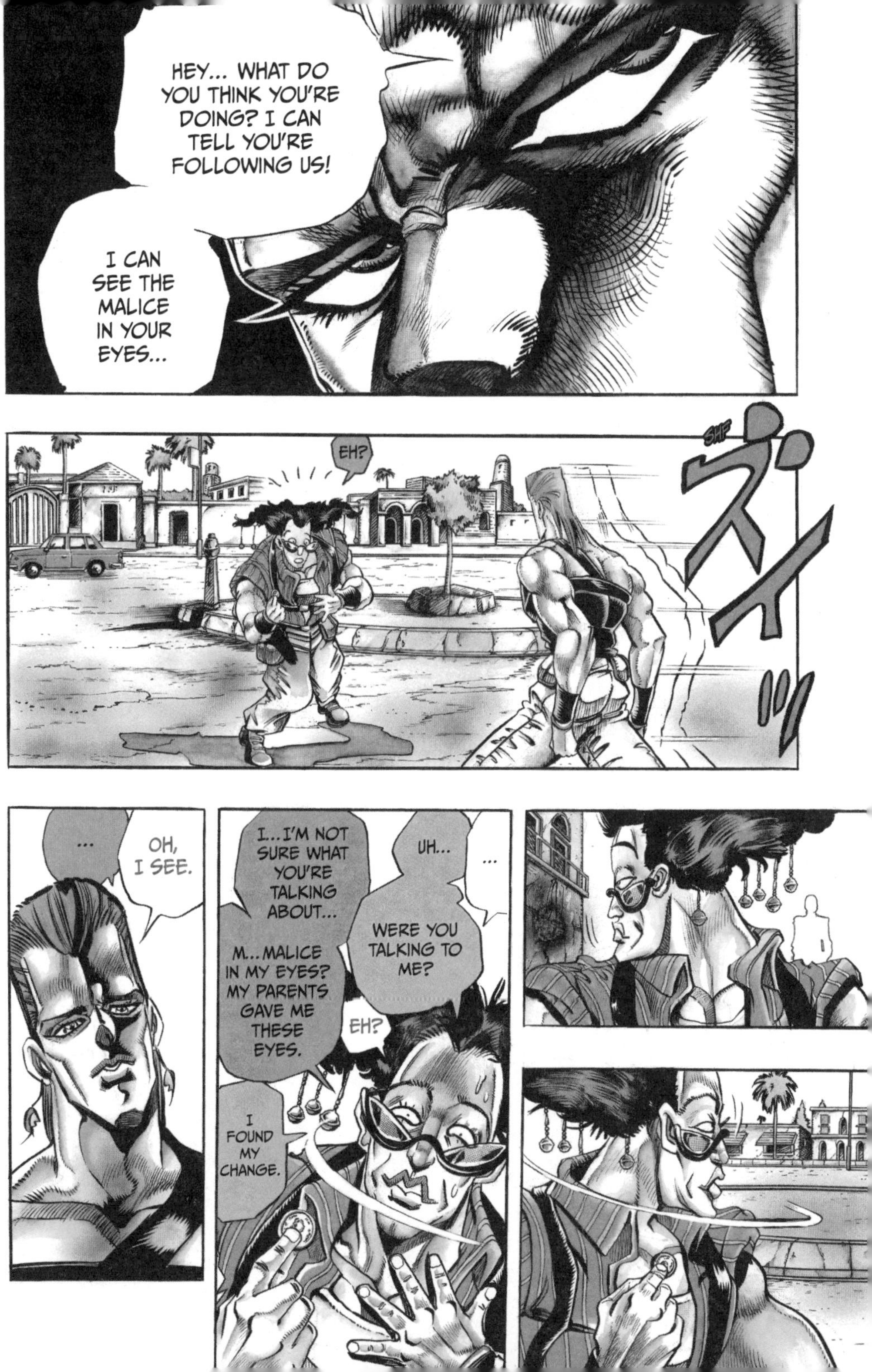
HEY... WHAT DO YOU THINK YOU'RE DOING? I CAN TELL YOU'RE FOLLOWING US!
I CAN SEE THE MALICE IN YOUR EYES...
SHF
EH?
...
UH...
WERE YOU TALKING TO ME?
I...I'M NOT SURE WHAT YOU'RE TALKING ABOUT...
M...MALICE IN MY EYES? MY PARENTS GAVE ME THESE EYES.
EH?
I FOUND MY CHANGE.
OH, I SEE.
...

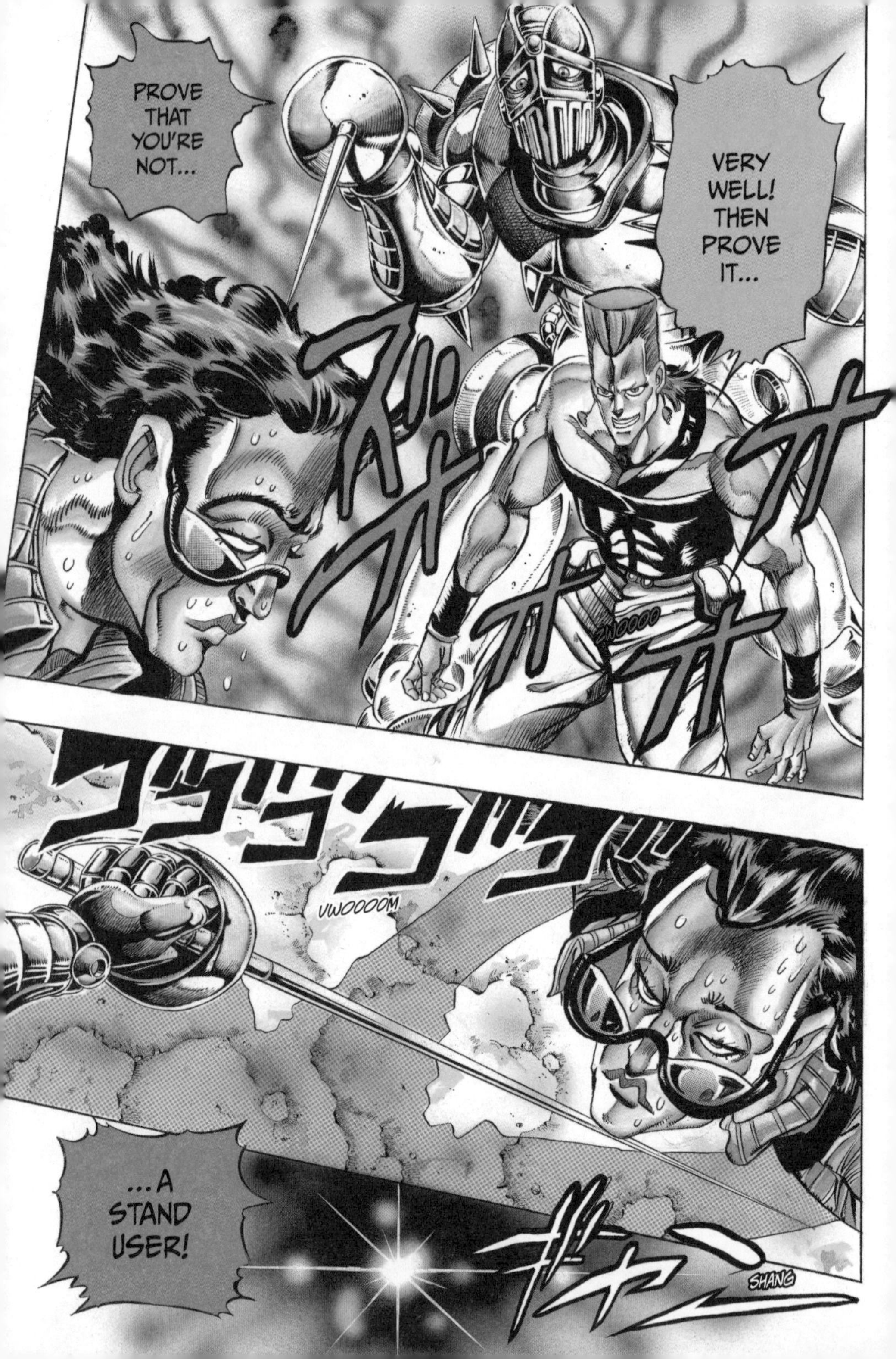
VERY WELL! THEN PROVE IT...
PROVE THAT YOU'RE NOT...
ZWOOOO
VWOOOOM
...A STAND USER!
SHANG

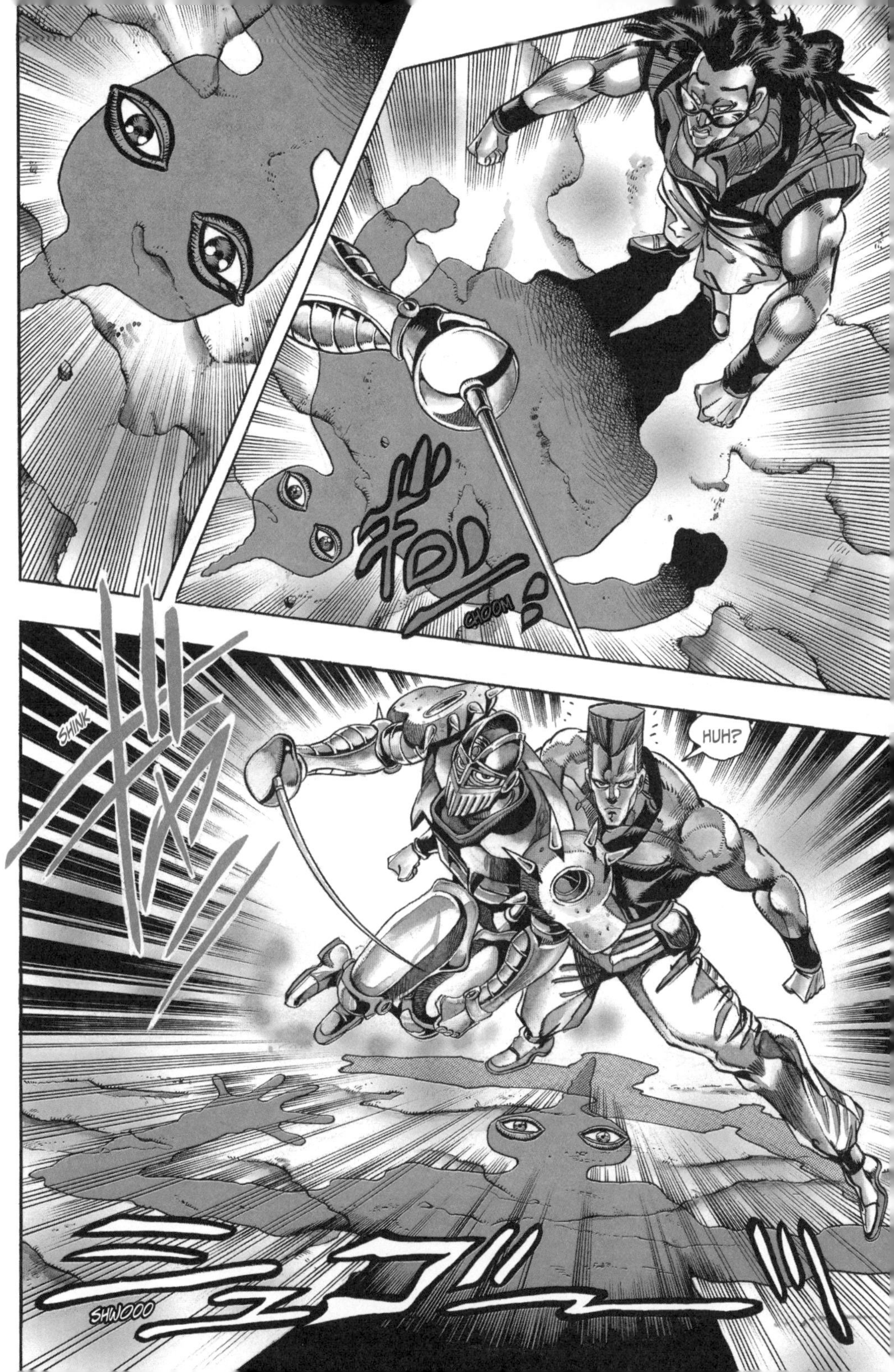
CHOOM
HUH?
SHINK
SHWOOO

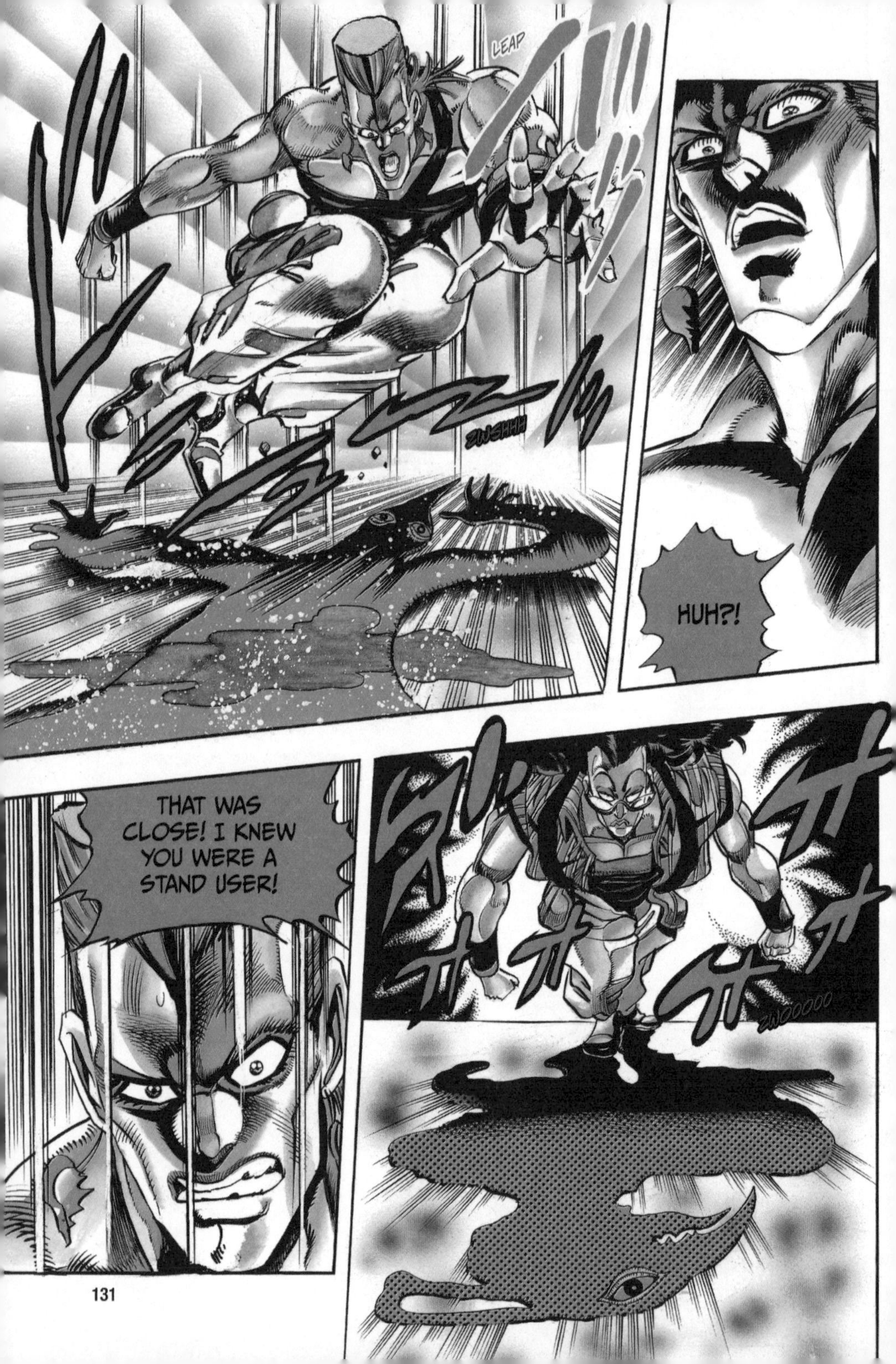
HUH?!
LEAP
ZWSHHH
ZWOOOOO
THAT WAS CLOSE! I KNEW YOU WERE A STAND USER!

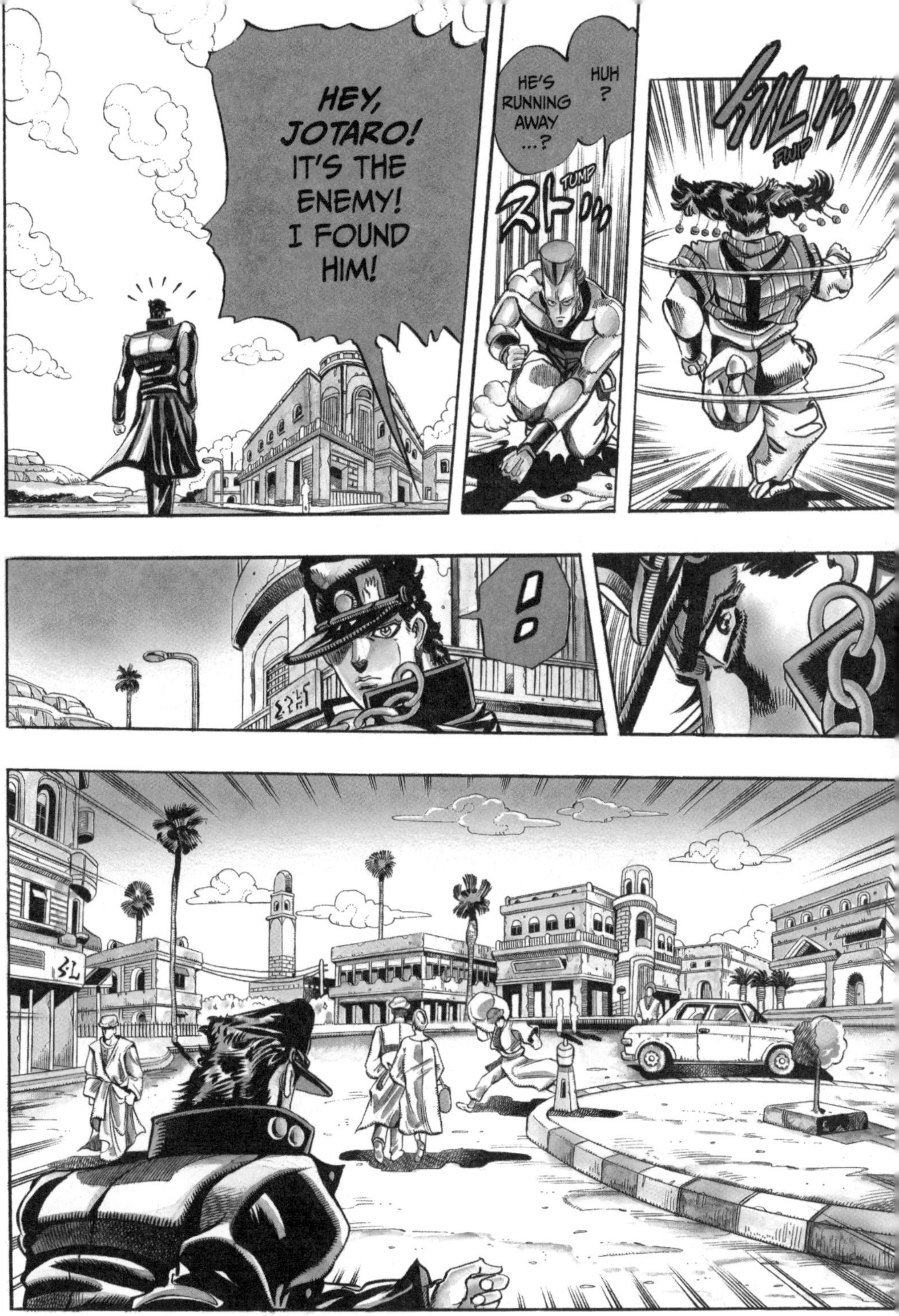

FWIP
HUH ?
HE'S RUNNING AWAY ...?
TUMP
HEY, JOTARO! IT'S THE ENEMY! I FOUND HIM!
!!

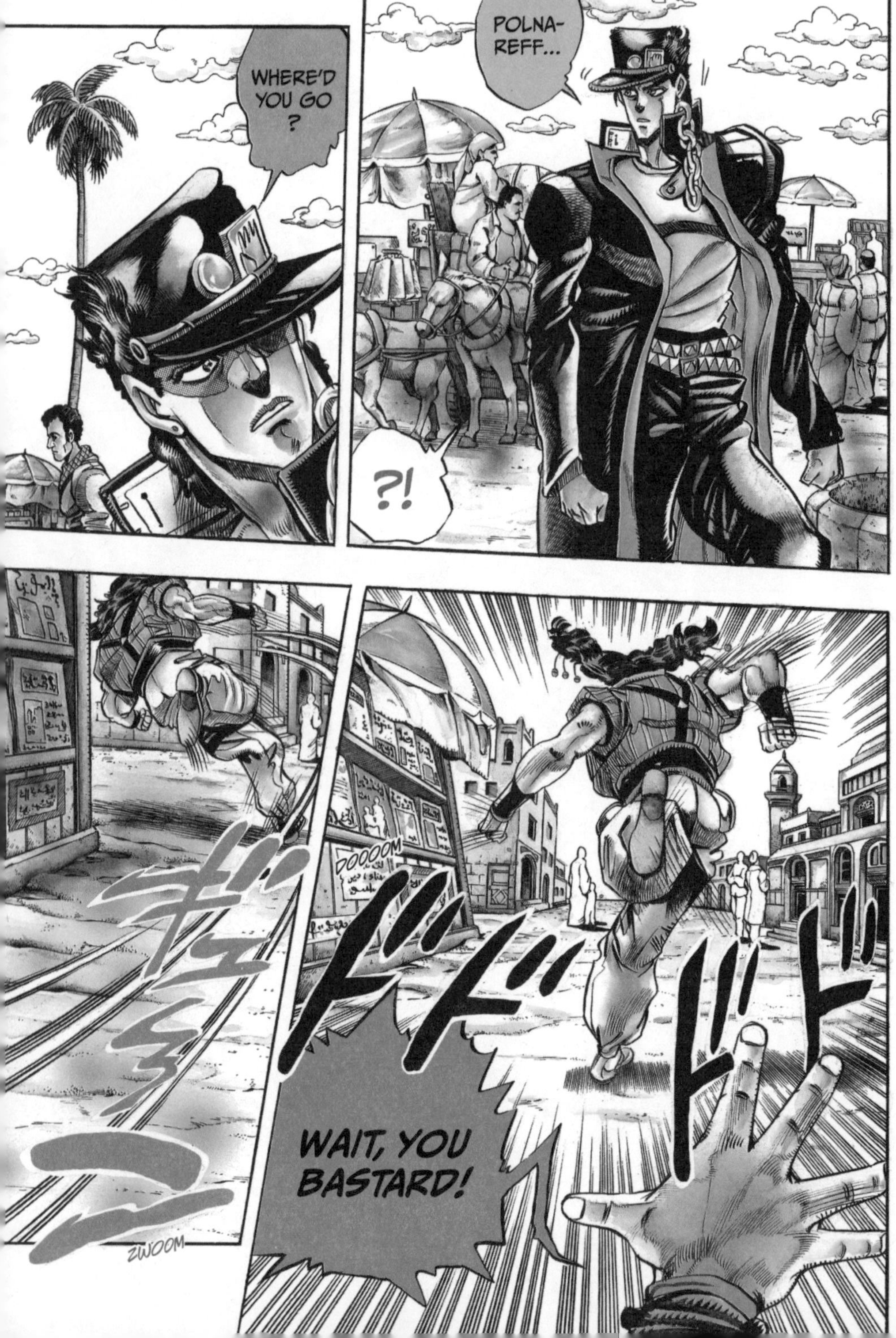
POLNA-REFF...
?!
WHERE'D YOU GO ?
DOOOOM
WAIT, YOU BASTARD!
ZWOOM

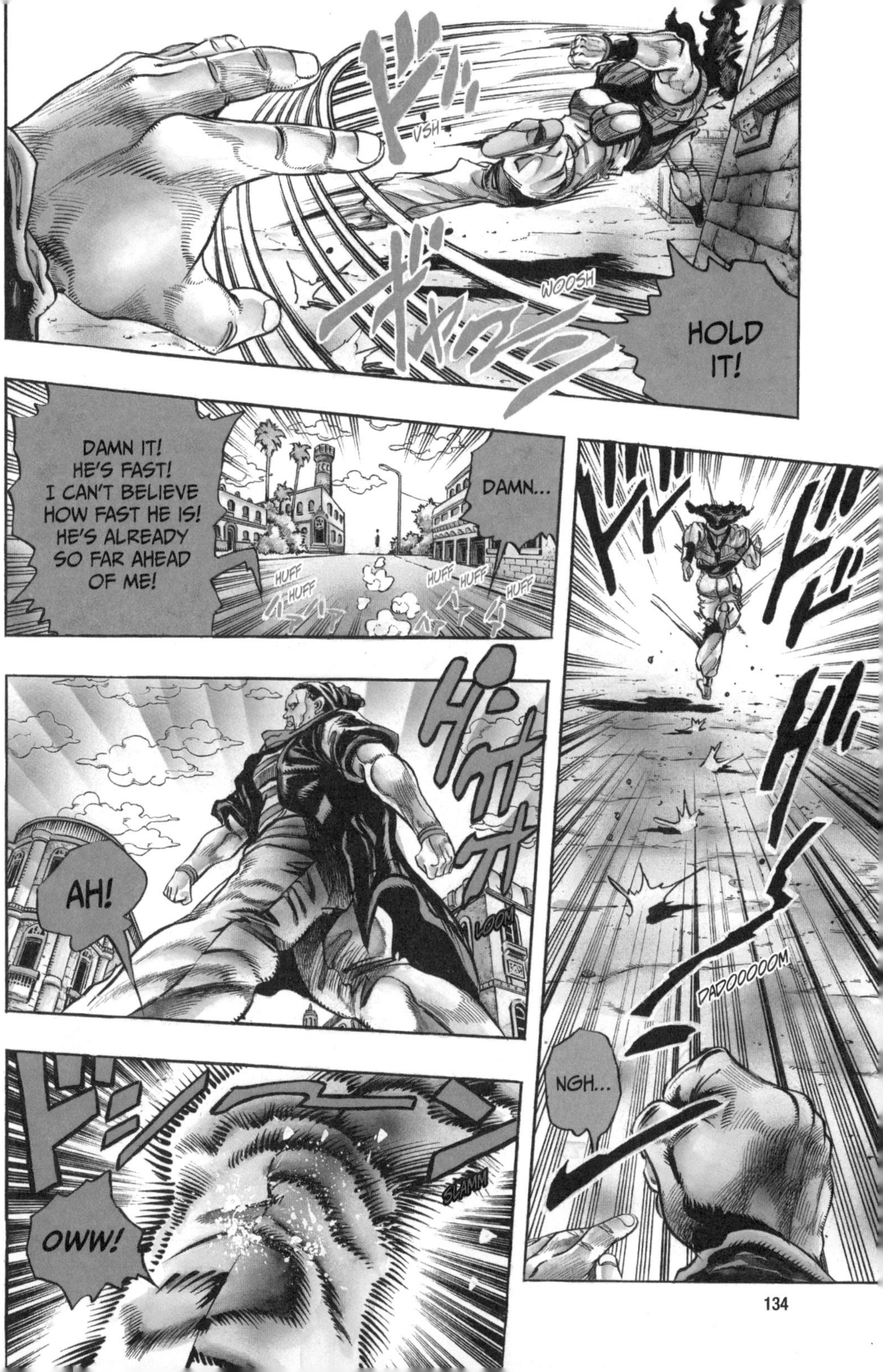
VSH
WOOSH
HOLD IT!
DADOOOOOM
NGH...
DAMN...
DAMN IT! HE'S FAST! I CAN'T BELIEVE HOW FAST HE IS! HE'S ALREADY SO FAR AHEAD OF ME!
HUFF
HUFF
HUFF
HUFF
HUFF
LOOM
AH!
SLAMM
OWW!

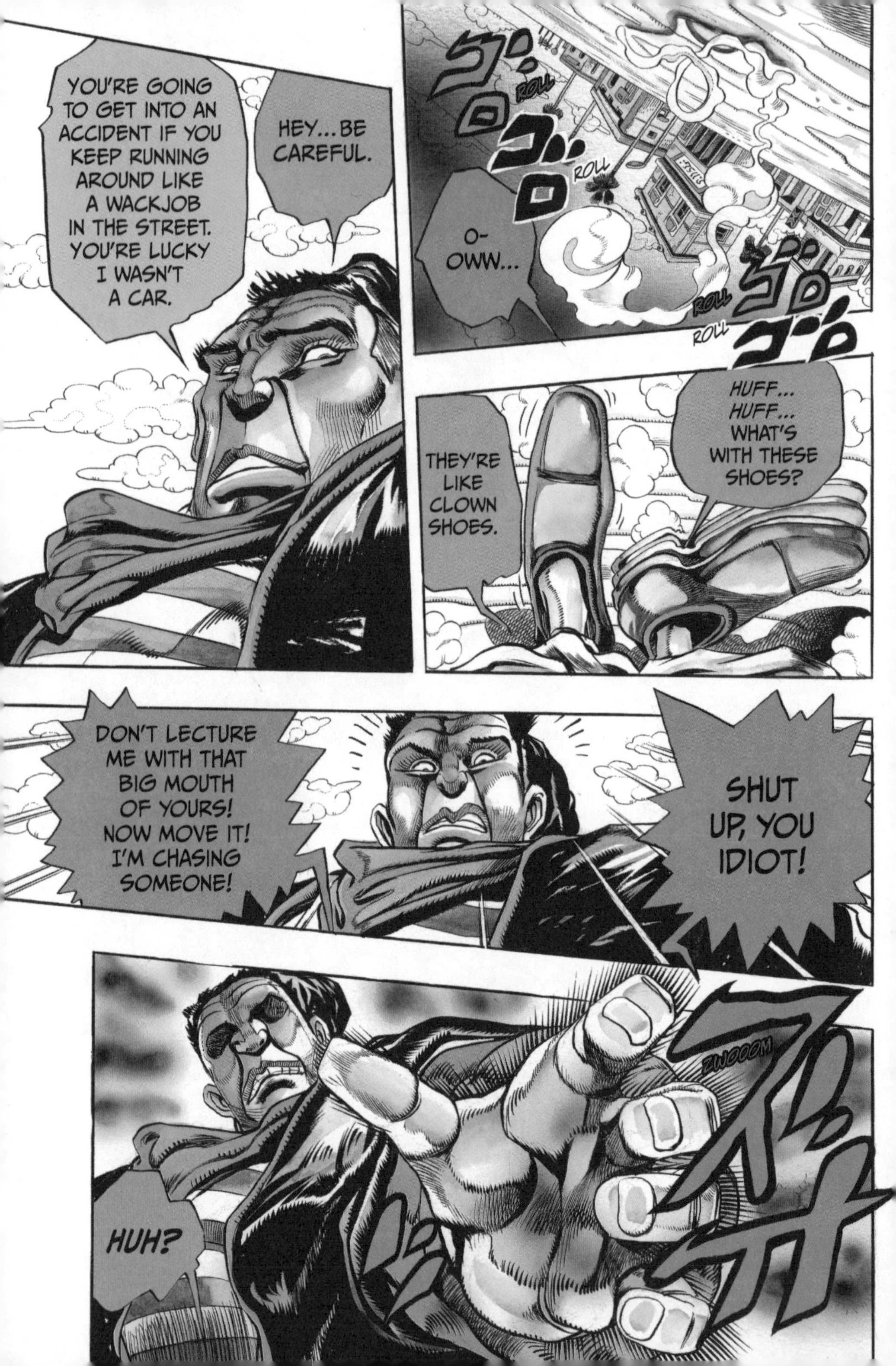
ROLL
ROLL
O-OWW...
ROLL
ROLL
HUFF... HUFF... WHAT'S WITH THESE SHOES?
THEY'RE LIKE CLOWN SHOES.
HEY... BE CAREFUL.
YOU'RE GOING TO GET INTO AN ACCIDENT IF YOU KEEP RUNNING AROUND LIKE A WACKJOB IN THE STREET. YOU'RE LUCKY I WASN'T A CAR.
SHUT UP, YOU IDIOT!
DON'T LECTURE ME WITH THAT BIG MOUTH OF YOURS! NOW MOVE IT! I'M CHASING SOMEONE!
ZWOOOM
HUH?

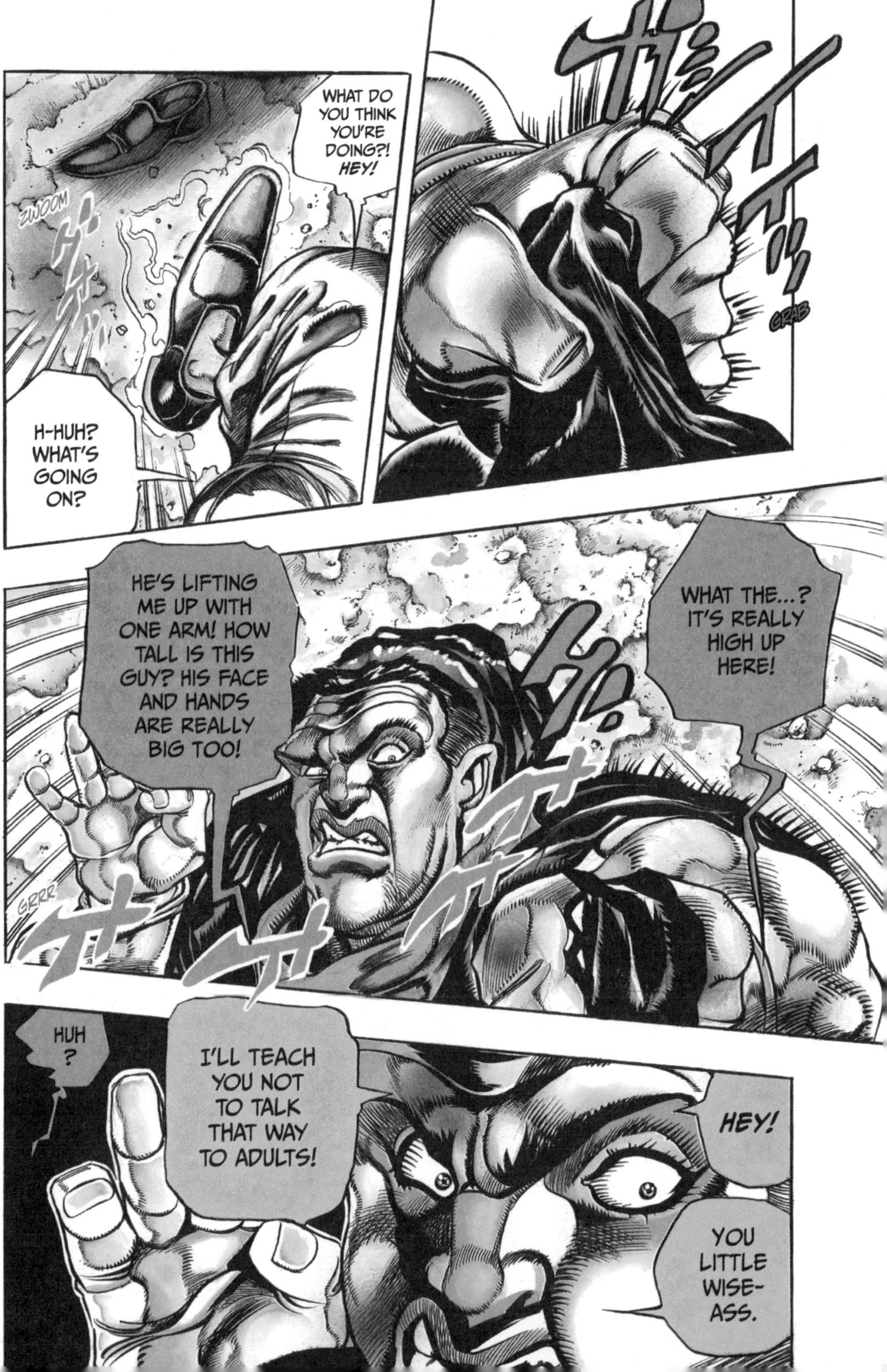
GRAB
WHAT DO YOU THINK YOU'RE DOING?! HEY!
ZWOOM
H-HUH? WHAT'S GOING ON?
WHAT THE...? IT'S REALLY HIGH UP HERE!
HE'S LIFTING ME UP WITH ONE ARM! HOW TALL IS THIS GUY? HIS FACE AND HANDS ARE REALLY BIG TOO!
GRRR
I'LL TEACH YOU NOT TO TALK THAT WAY TO ADULTS!
HEY!
YOU LITTLE WISE-ASS.
HUH?

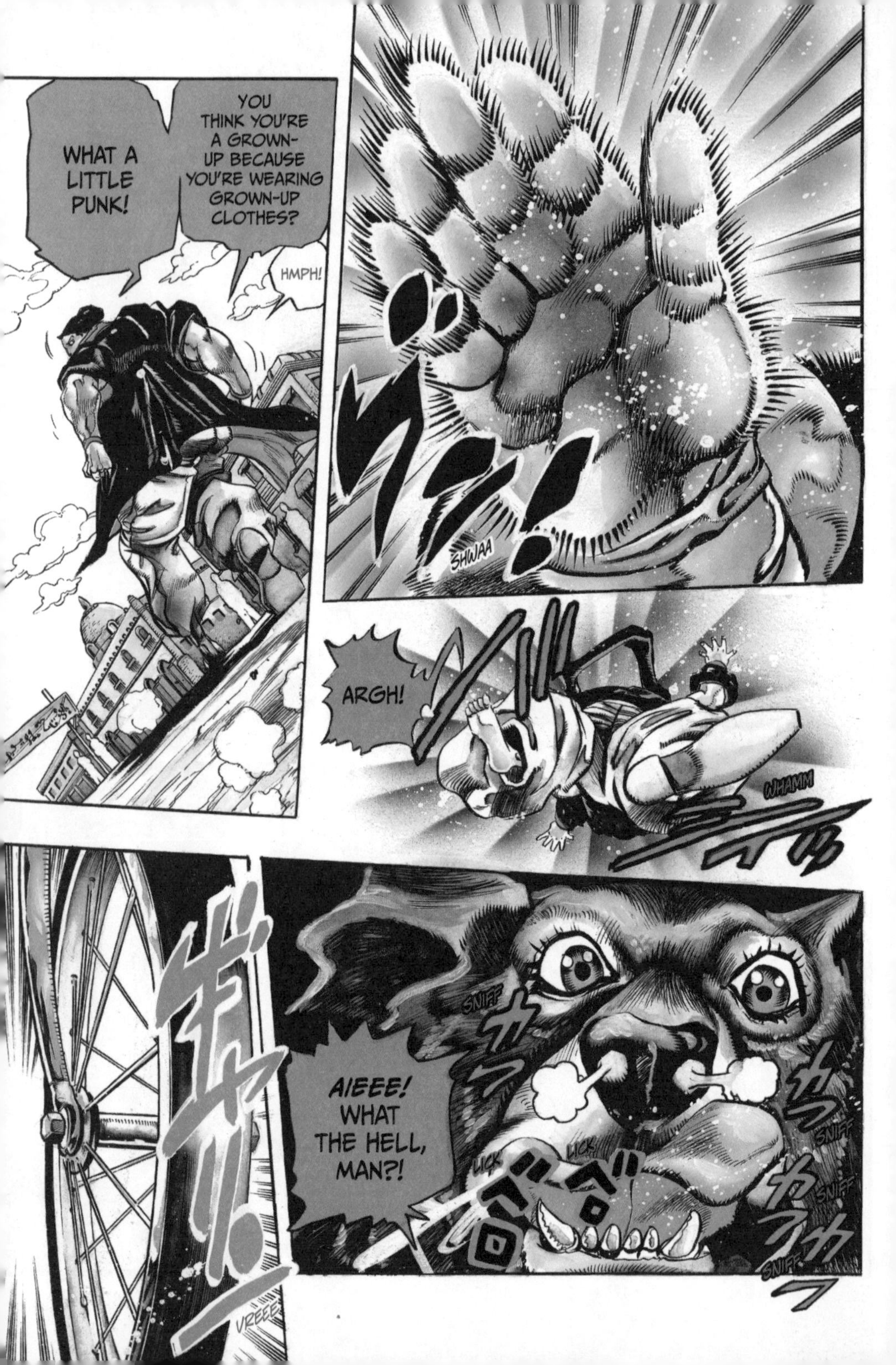
SHWAA
ARGH!
WHAMM
WHAT A LITTLE PUNK!
YOU THINK YOU'RE A GROWN-UP BECAUSE YOU'RE WEARING GROWN-UP CLOTHES?
HMPH!
SNIFF
SNIFF
SNIFF
SNIFF
LICK
LICK
AIEEE! WHAT THE HELL, MAN?!
VREEE

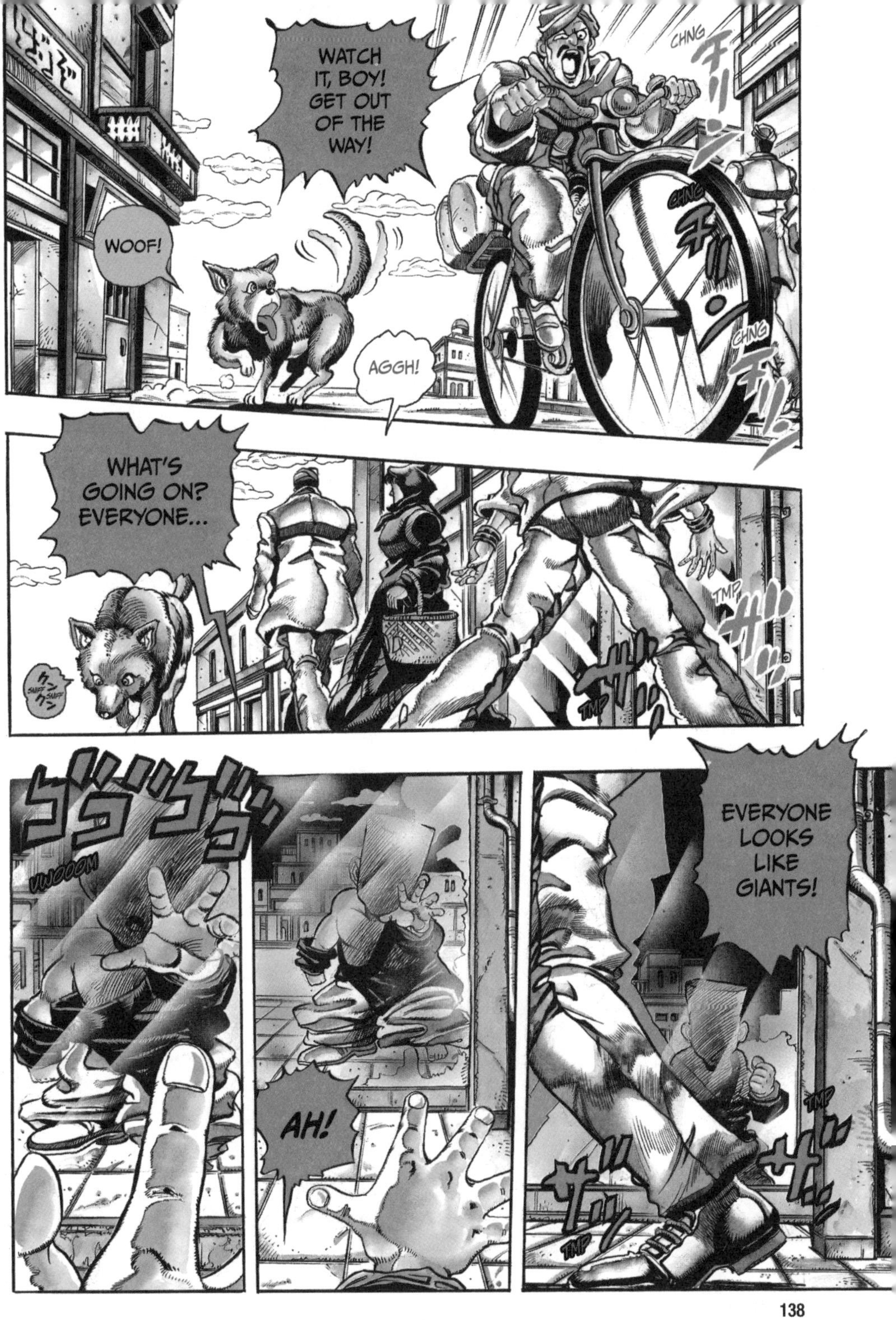
CHNG
WATCH IT, BOY! GET OUT OF THE WAY!
CHNG
CHNG
WOOF!
AGGH!
TMP
WHAT'S GOING ON? EVERYONE...
TMP
SNIFF SNIFF
EVERYONE LOOKS LIKE GIANTS!
TMP
TMP
AH!
VWOOOM

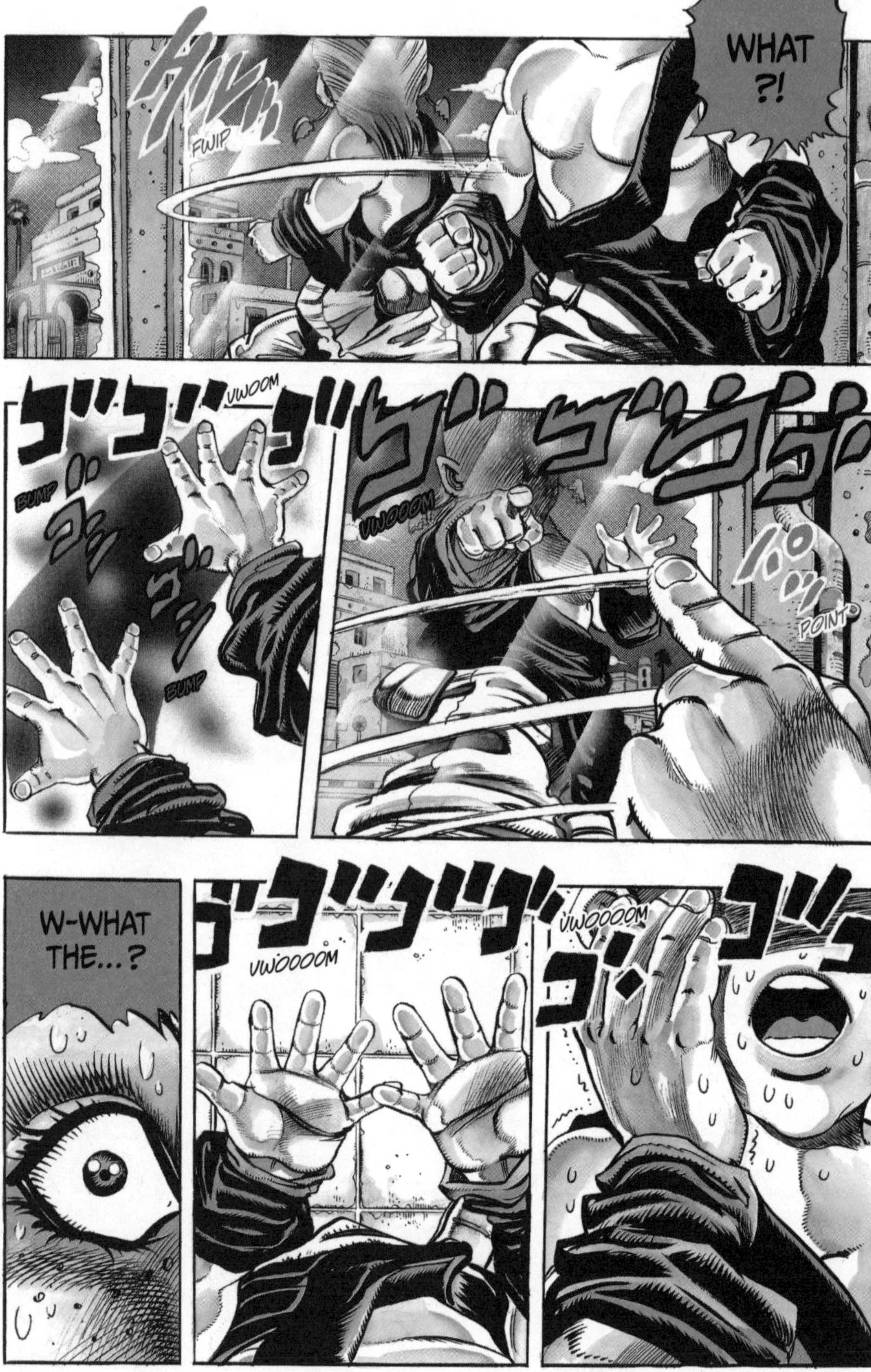
WHAT ?!
FWIP
POINT
VWOOOM
VWOOM
BUMP
BUMP
VWOOOOM
VWOOOOM
W-WHAT THE...?

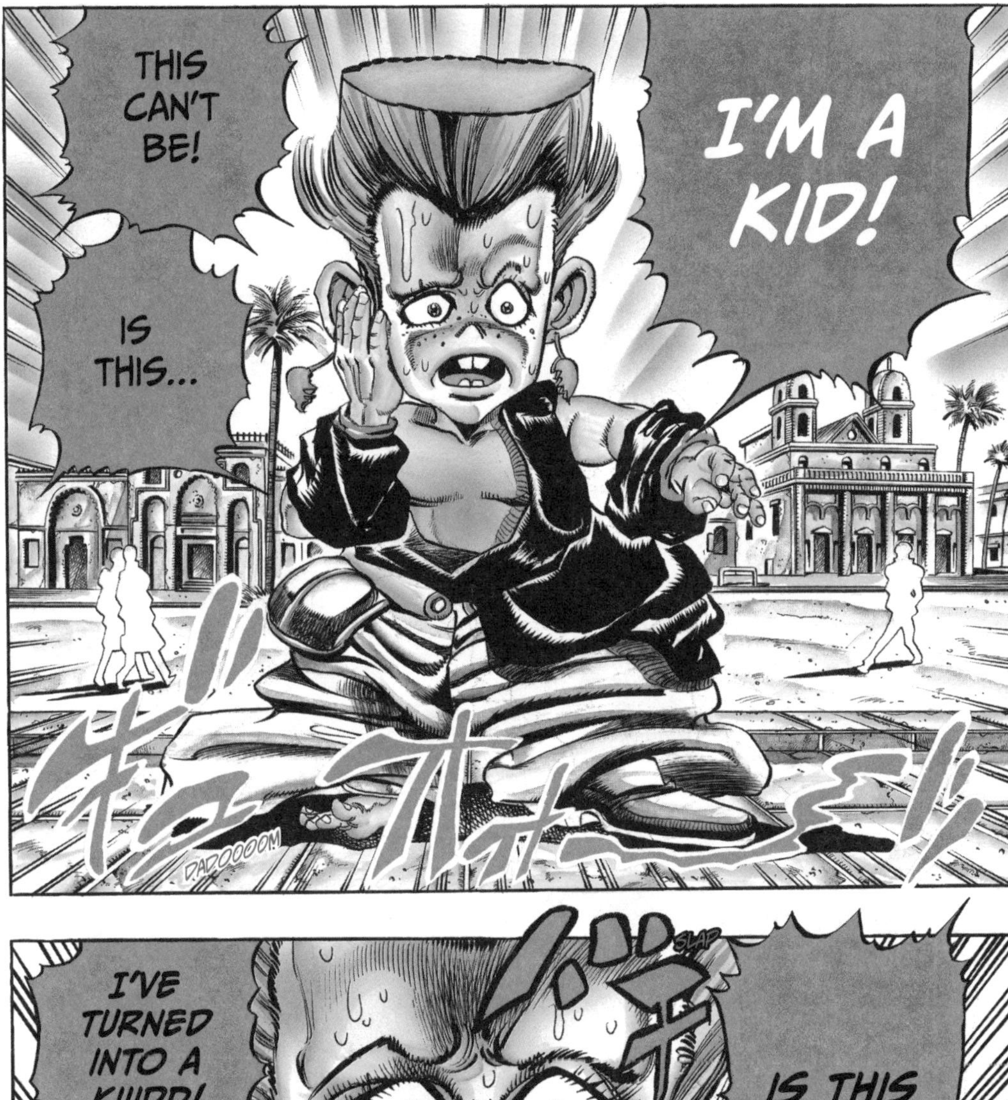
I'M A KID!
THIS CAN'T BE!
IS THIS...
DADOOOOM

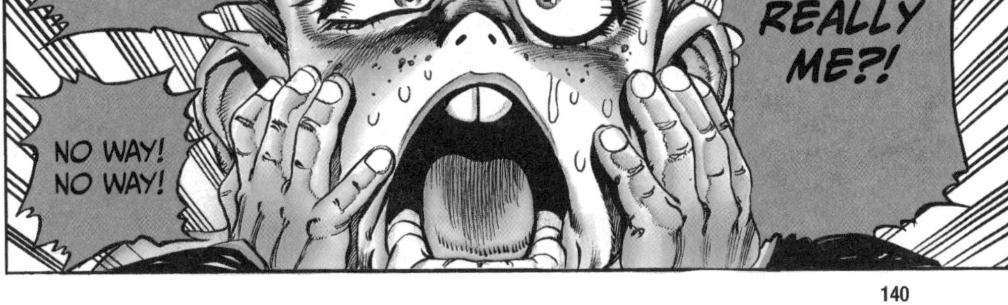
SLAP
IS THIS REALLY ME?!
I'VE TURNED INTO A KIIIDD!
NO WAY! NO WAY!

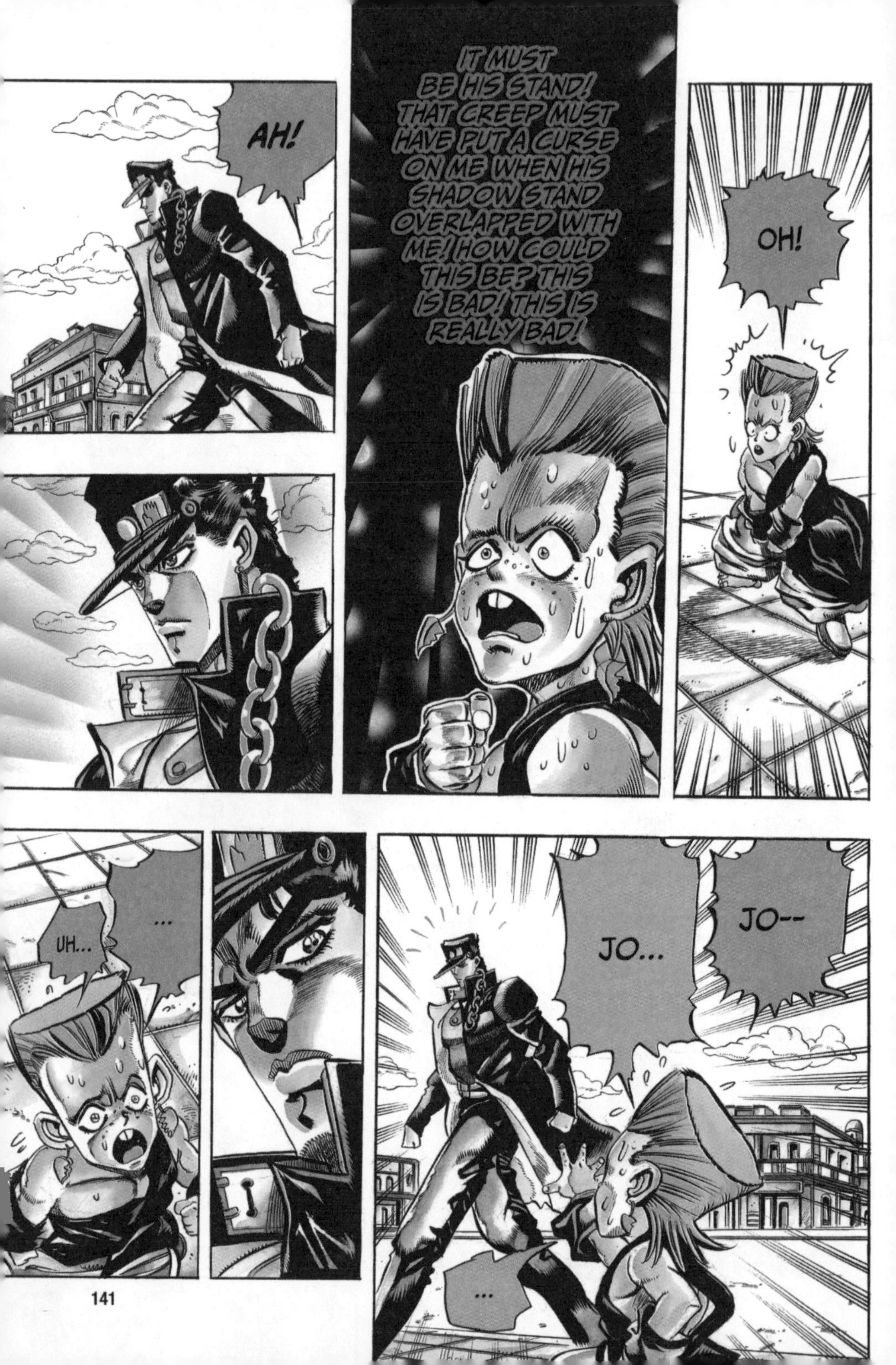

OH!
IT MUST BE HIS STAND! THAT CREEP MUST HAVE PUT A CURSE ON ME WHEN HIS SHADOW STAND OVERLAPPED WITH ME! HOW COULD THIS BE? THIS IS BAD! THIS IS REALLY BAD!
AH!
JO--
JO...
...
...
UH...

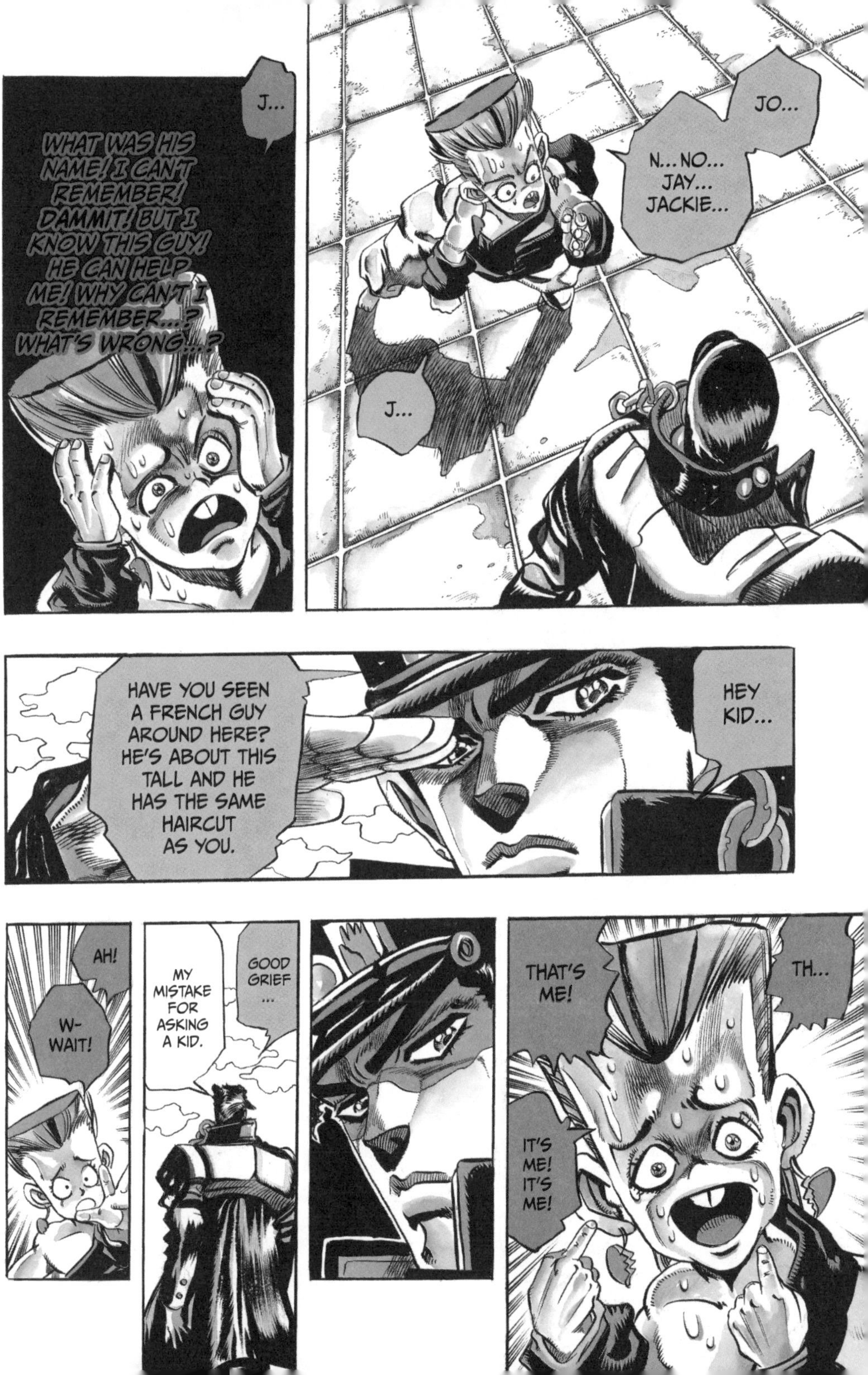
JO...
N...NO... JAY... JACKIE...
J...
J...
WHAT WAS HIS NAME! I CAN'T REMEMBER! DAMMIT! BUT I KNOW THIS GUY! HE CAN HELP ME! WHY CAN'T I REMEMBER...? WHAT'S WRONG...?
HEY KID...
HAVE YOU SEEN A FRENCH GUY AROUND HERE? HE'S ABOUT THIS TALL AND HE HAS THE SAME HAIRCUT AS YOU.
TH...
THAT'S ME!
IT'S ME! IT'S ME!
GOOD GRIEF ...
MY MISTAKE FOR ASKING A KID.
AH!
W-WAIT!

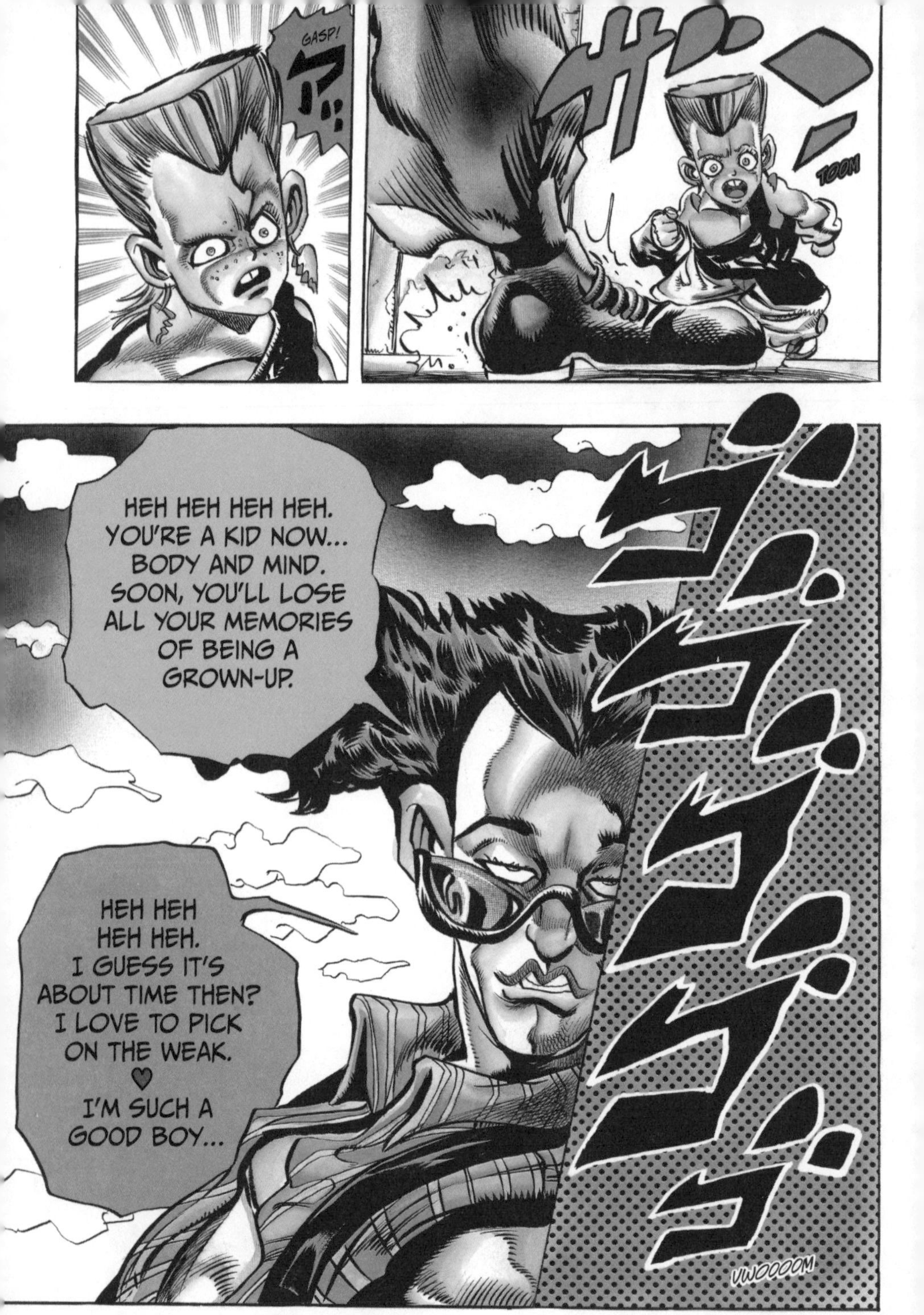
TOOM
GASP!
HEH HEH HEH HEH. YOU'RE A KID NOW... BODY AND MIND. SOON, YOU'LL LOSE ALL YOUR MEMORIES OF BEING A GROWN-UP.
HEH HEH HEH HEH. I GUESS IT'S ABOUT TIME THEN? I LOVE TO PICK ON THE WEAK. ♥ I'M SUCH A GOOD BOY...
VWOOOOM

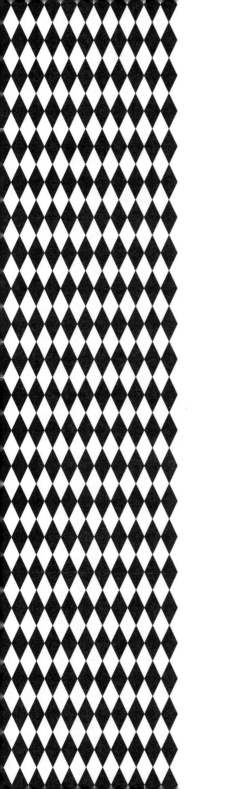

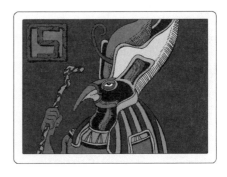

CHAPTER 93: "Set" Alessi PART 2

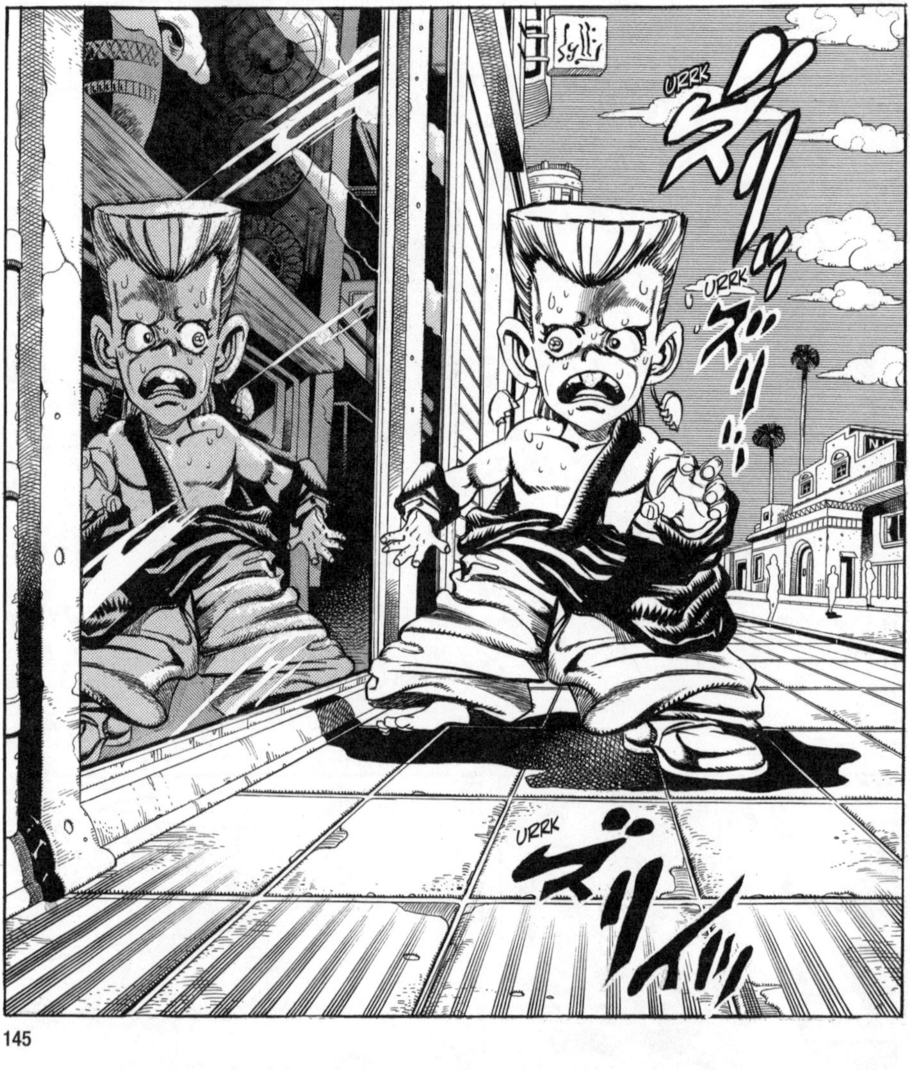
URRK
URRK
URRK

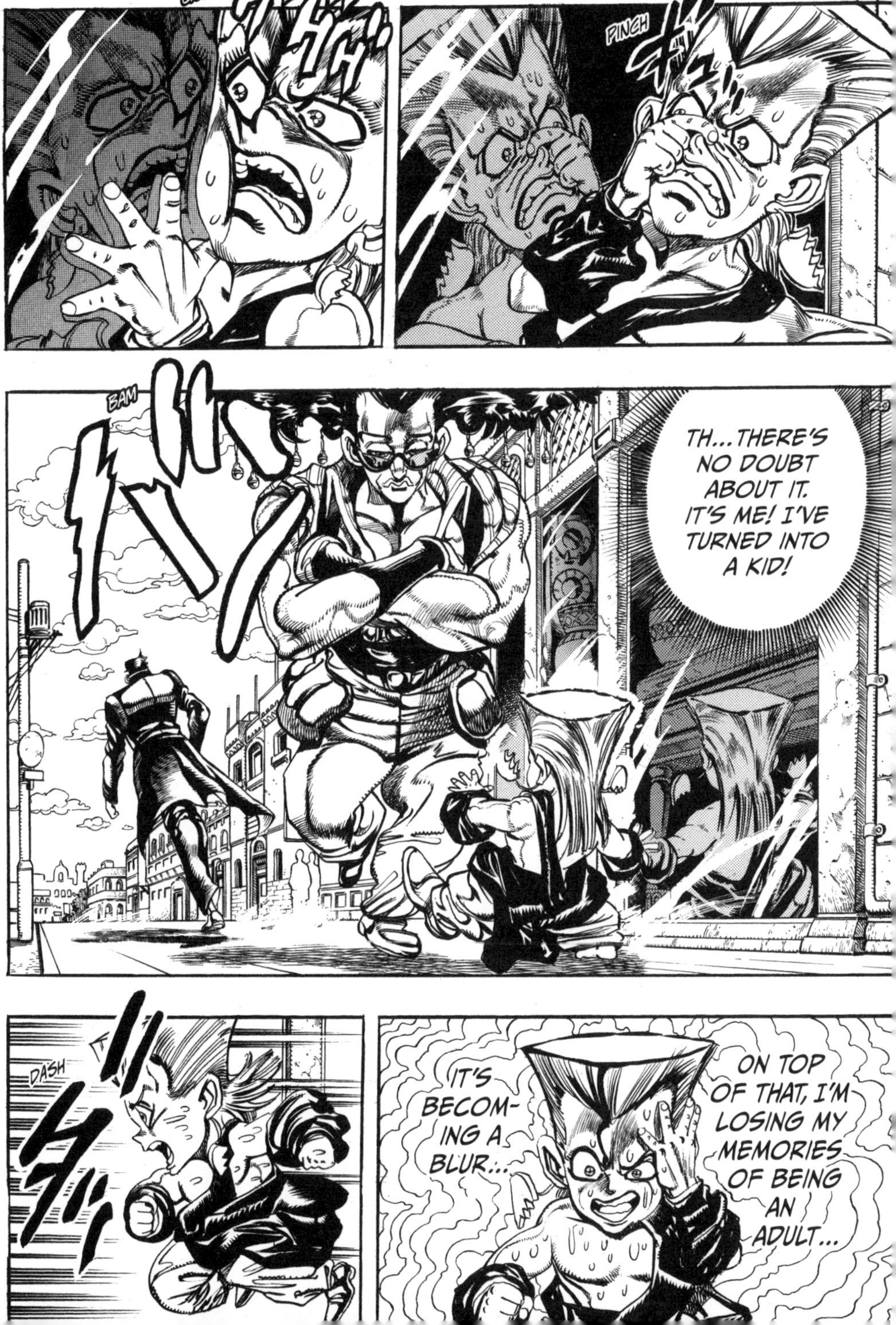
PINCH
GUHHH
BAM
TH...THERE'S NO DOUBT ABOUT IT. IT'S ME! I'VE TURNED INTO A KID!
ON TOP OF THAT, I'M LOSING MY MEMORIES OF BEING AN ADULT...
IT'S BECOMING A BLUR...
DASH

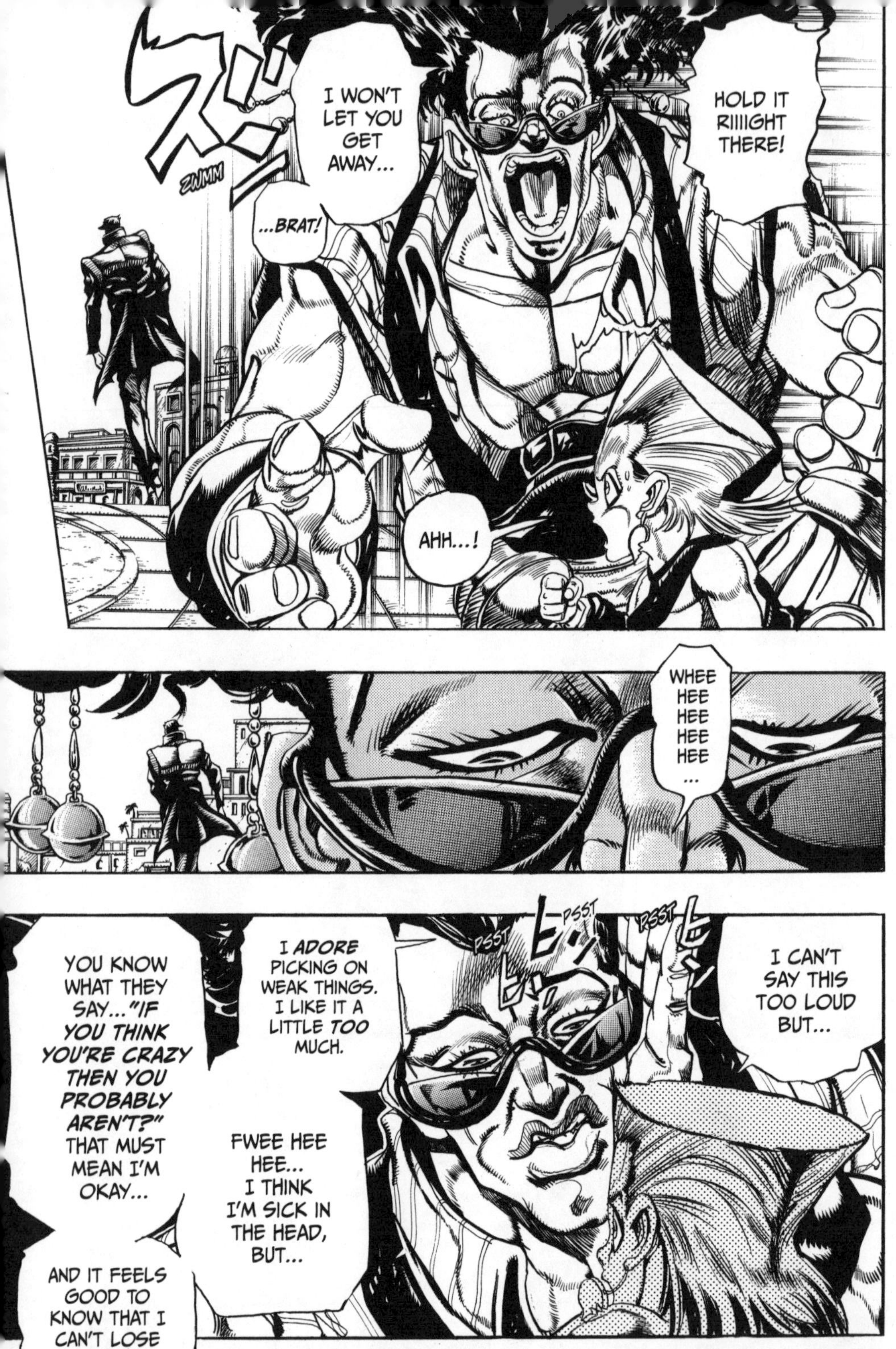
HOLD IT RIIIIGHT THERE!
ZWMM
I WON'T LET YOU GET AWAY...
...BRAT!
AHH...!
WHEE HEE HEE HEE HEE ...
PSST
PSST
PSST
I CAN'T SAY THIS TOO LOUD BUT...
I *ADORE* PICKING ON WEAK THINGS. I LIKE IT A LITTLE *TOO* MUCH.
FWEE HEE HEE... I THINK I'M SICK IN THE HEAD, BUT...
YOU KNOW WHAT THEY SAY... *"IF YOU THINK YOU'RE CRAZY THEN YOU PROBABLY AREN'T?"* THAT MUST MEAN I'M OKAY...
AND IT FEELS GOOD TO KNOW THAT I CAN'T LOSE TO A KID...

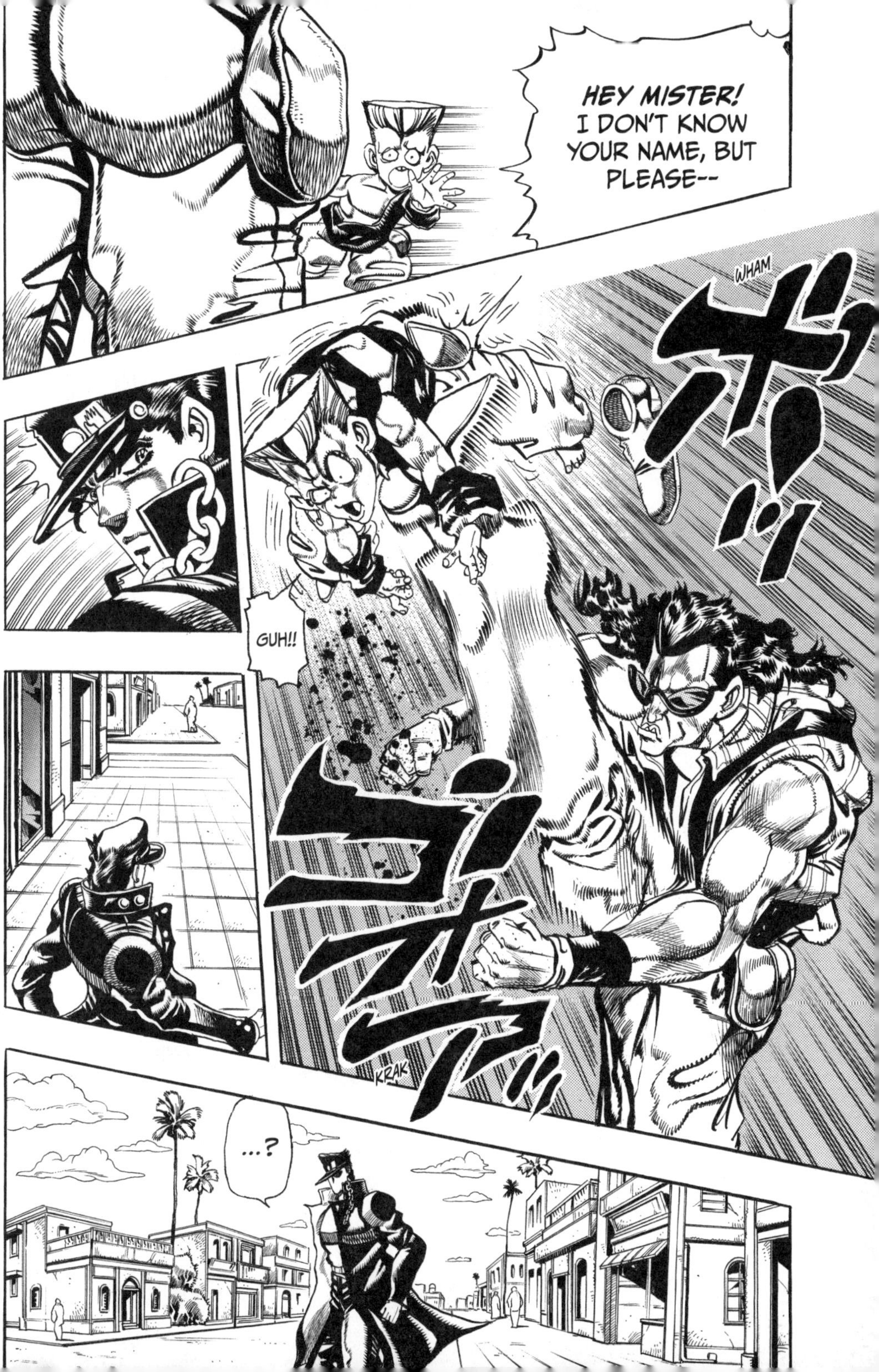

HEY MISTER! I DON'T KNOW YOUR NAME, BUT PLEASE--
WHAM
GUH!!
KRAK
...?

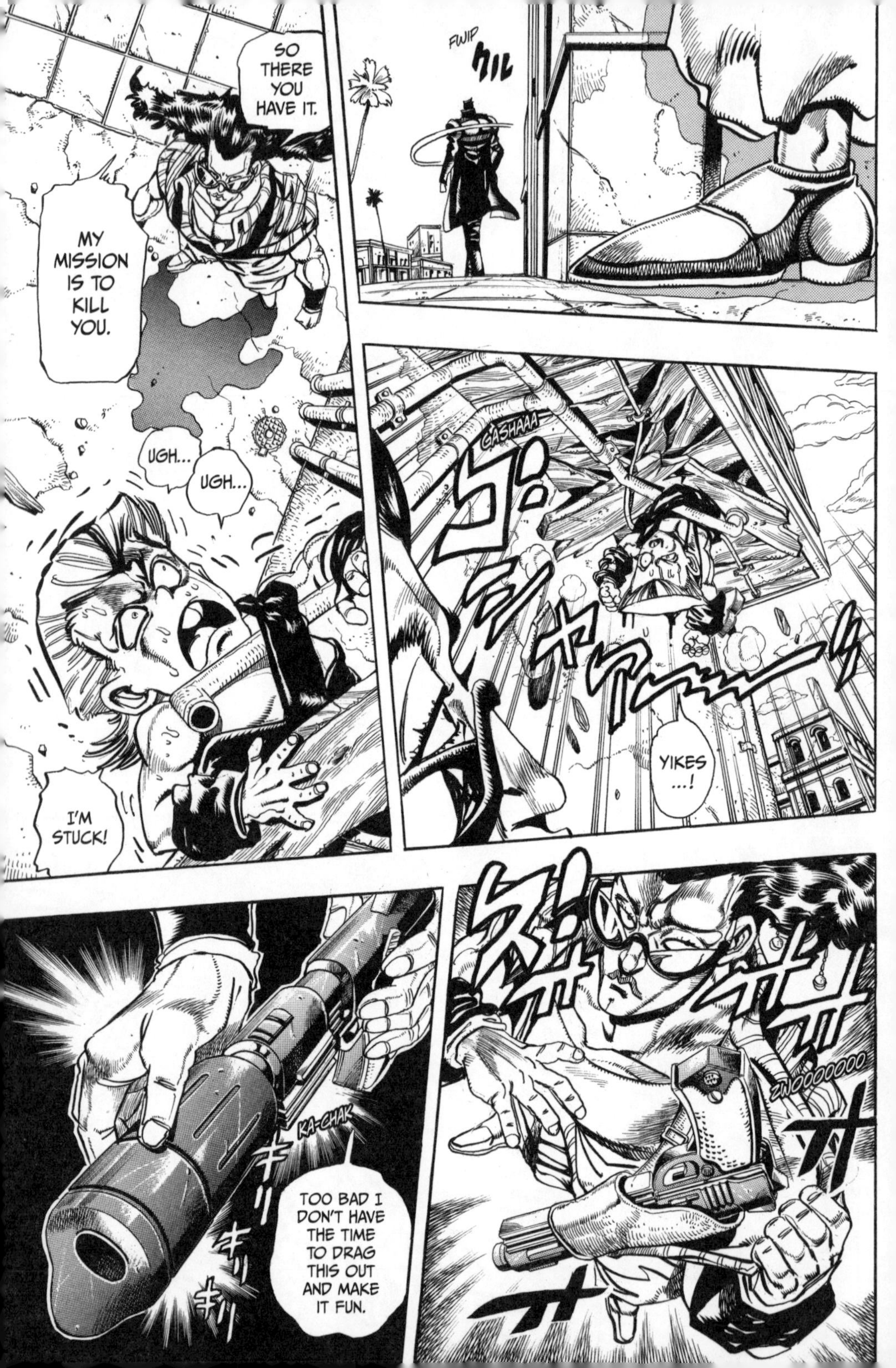
FWIP
クル
GASHAAA
YIKES ...!
SO THERE YOU HAVE IT.
MY MISSION IS TO KILL YOU.
UGH...
UGH...
I'M STUCK!
ZWOOOOOOO
KA-CHAK
TOO BAD I DON'T HAVE THE TIME TO DRAG THIS OUT AND MAKE IT FUN.

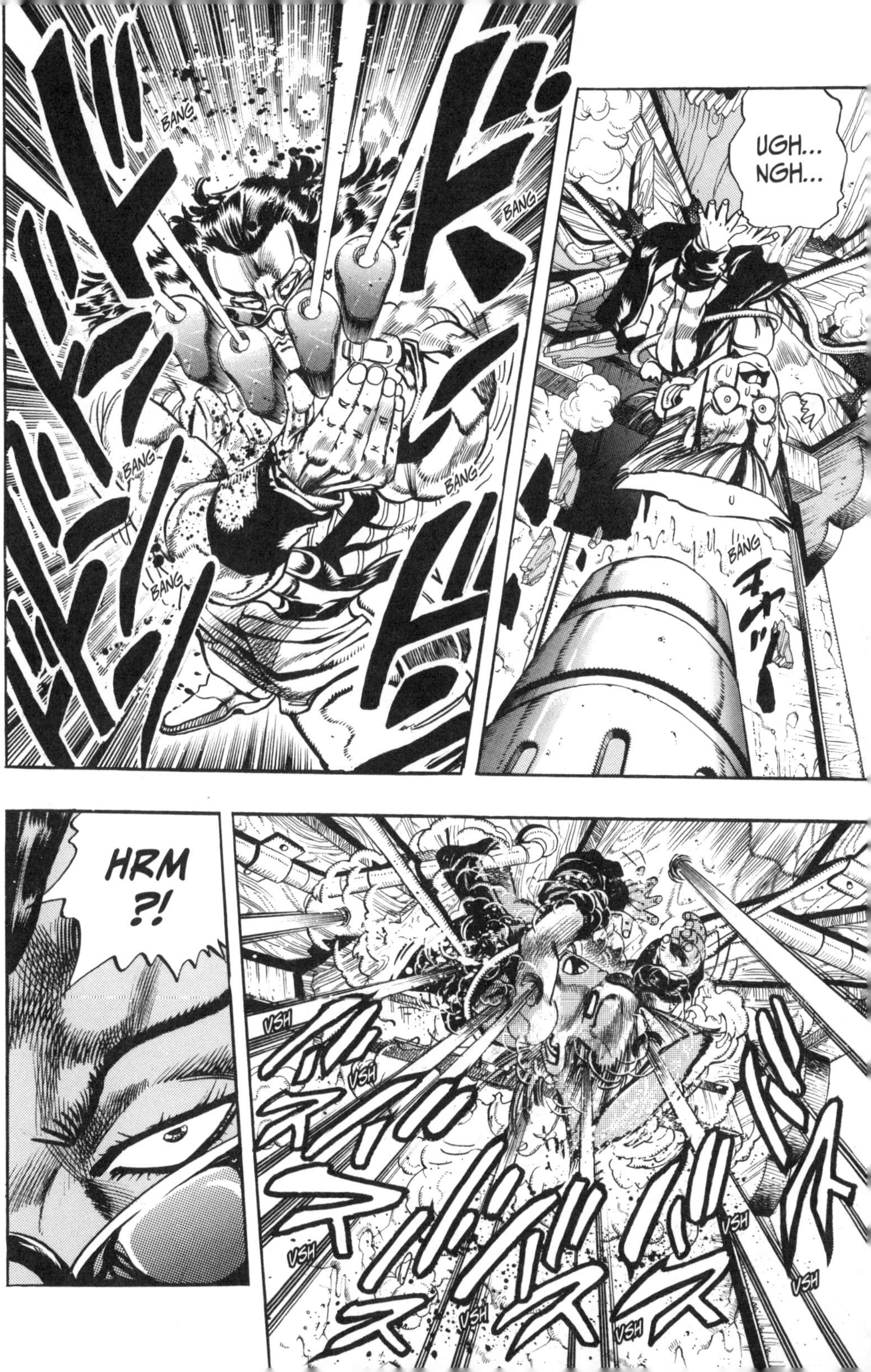
UGH... NGH...
BANG
BANG
BANG
BANG
BANG
BANG
VSH
VSH
VSH
VSH
VSH
VSH
VSH
HRM ?!

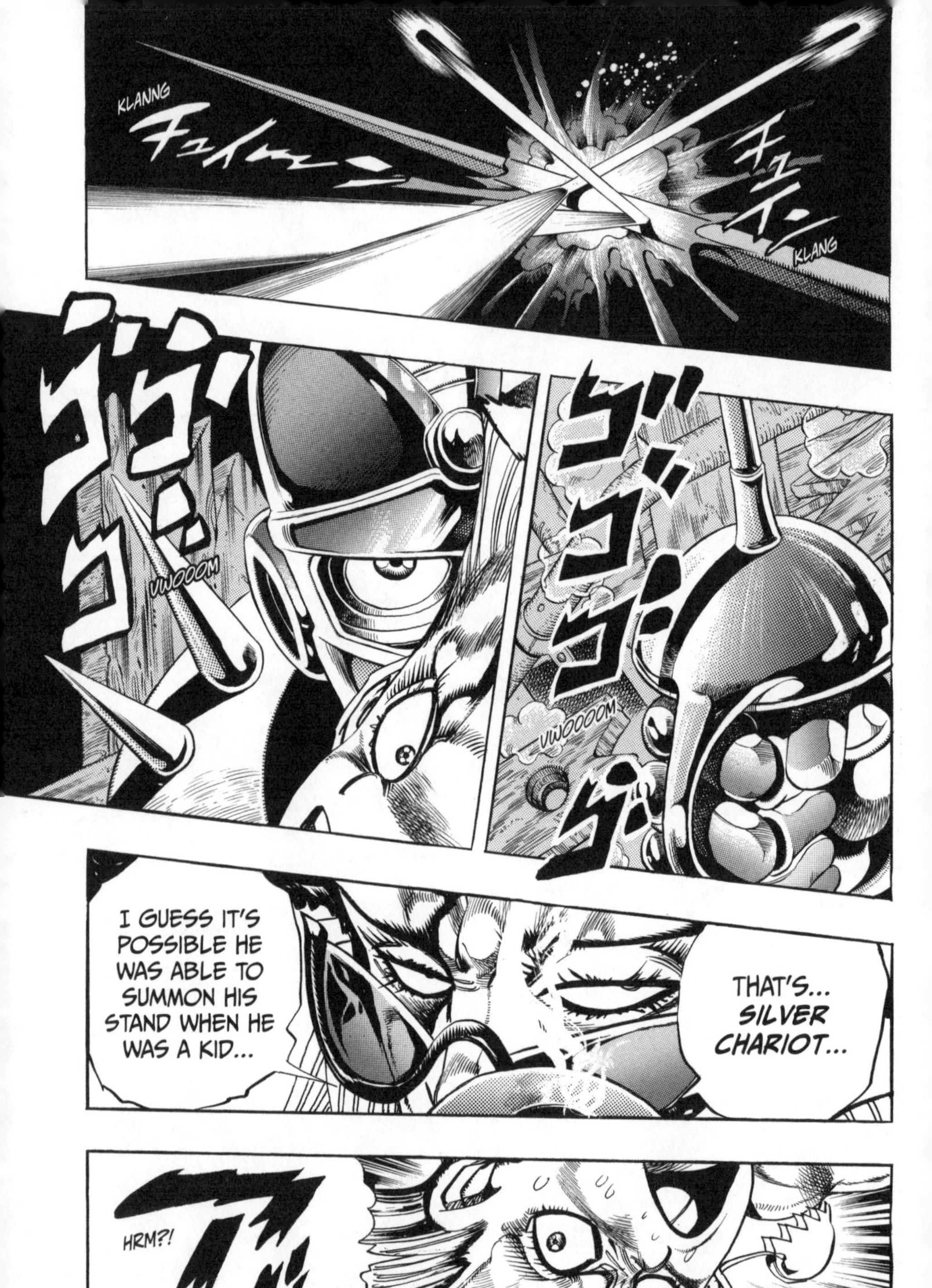
KLANNG
KLANG
VWOOOOM
VWOOOM
THAT'S... SILVER CHARIOT...
I GUESS IT'S POSSIBLE HE WAS ABLE TO SUMMON HIS STAND WHEN HE WAS A KID...
HRM?!

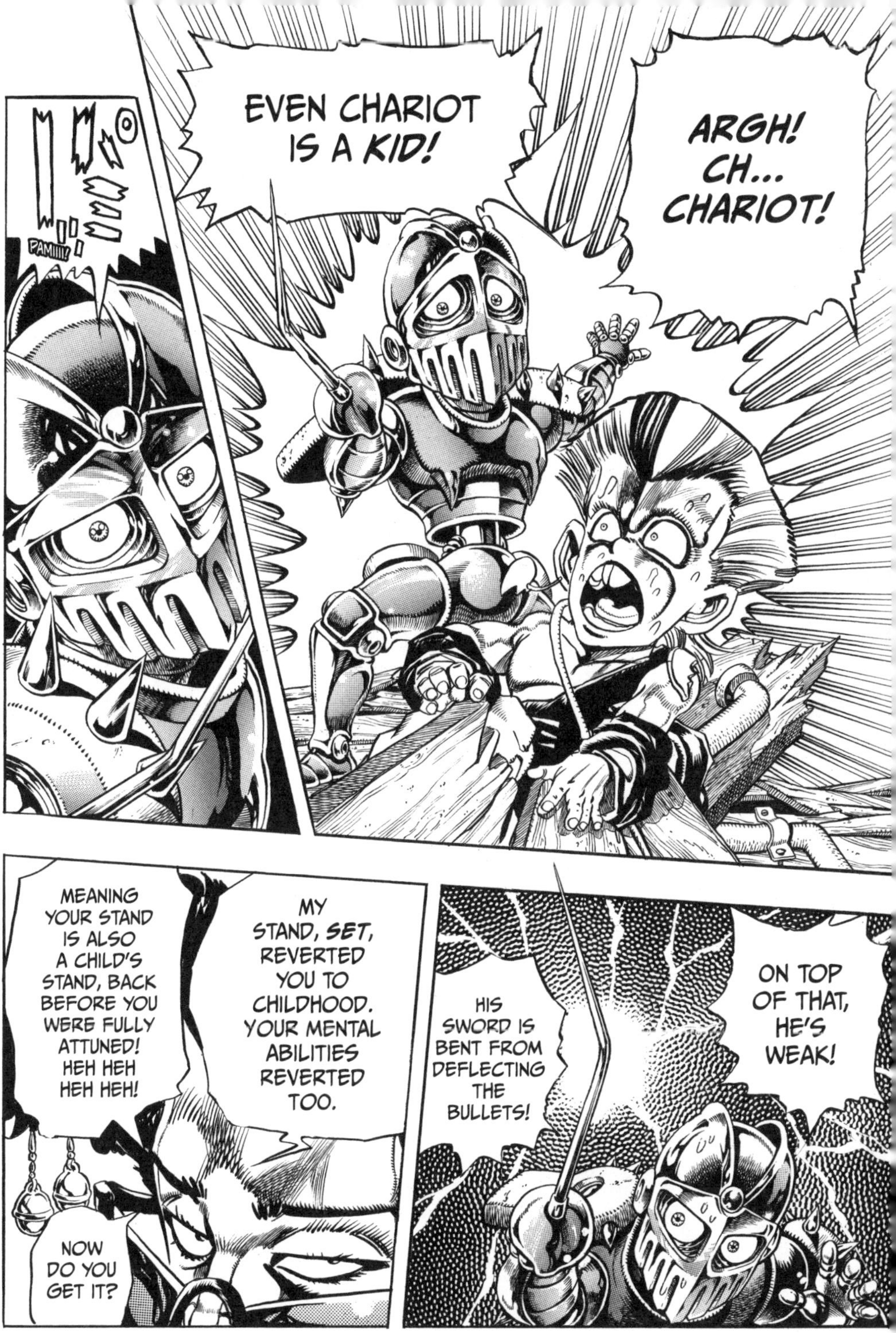
ARGH! CH... CHARIOT!
EVEN CHARIOT IS A KID!
PAMIIII!
ON TOP OF THAT, HE'S WEAK!
HIS SWORD IS BENT FROM DEFLECTING THE BULLETS!
MY STAND, SET, REVERTED YOU TO CHILDHOOD. YOUR MENTAL ABILITIES REVERTED TOO.
MEANING YOUR STAND IS ALSO A CHILD'S STAND, BACK BEFORE YOU WERE FULLY ATTUNED! HEH HEH HEH HEH!
NOW DO YOU GET IT?

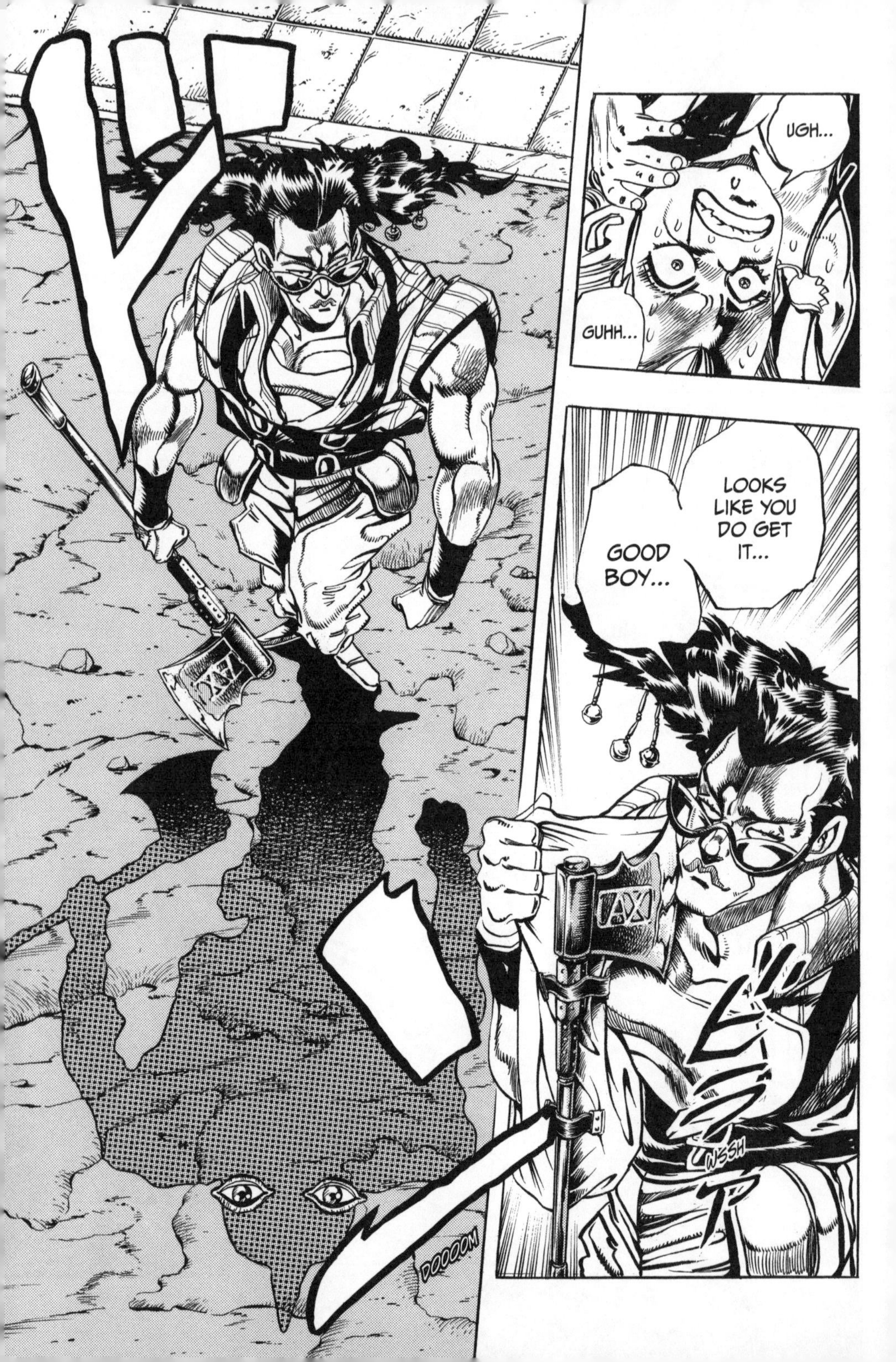
UGH...
GUHH...
LOOKS LIKE YOU DO GET IT...
GOOD BOY...
WSSH
DOOOOM

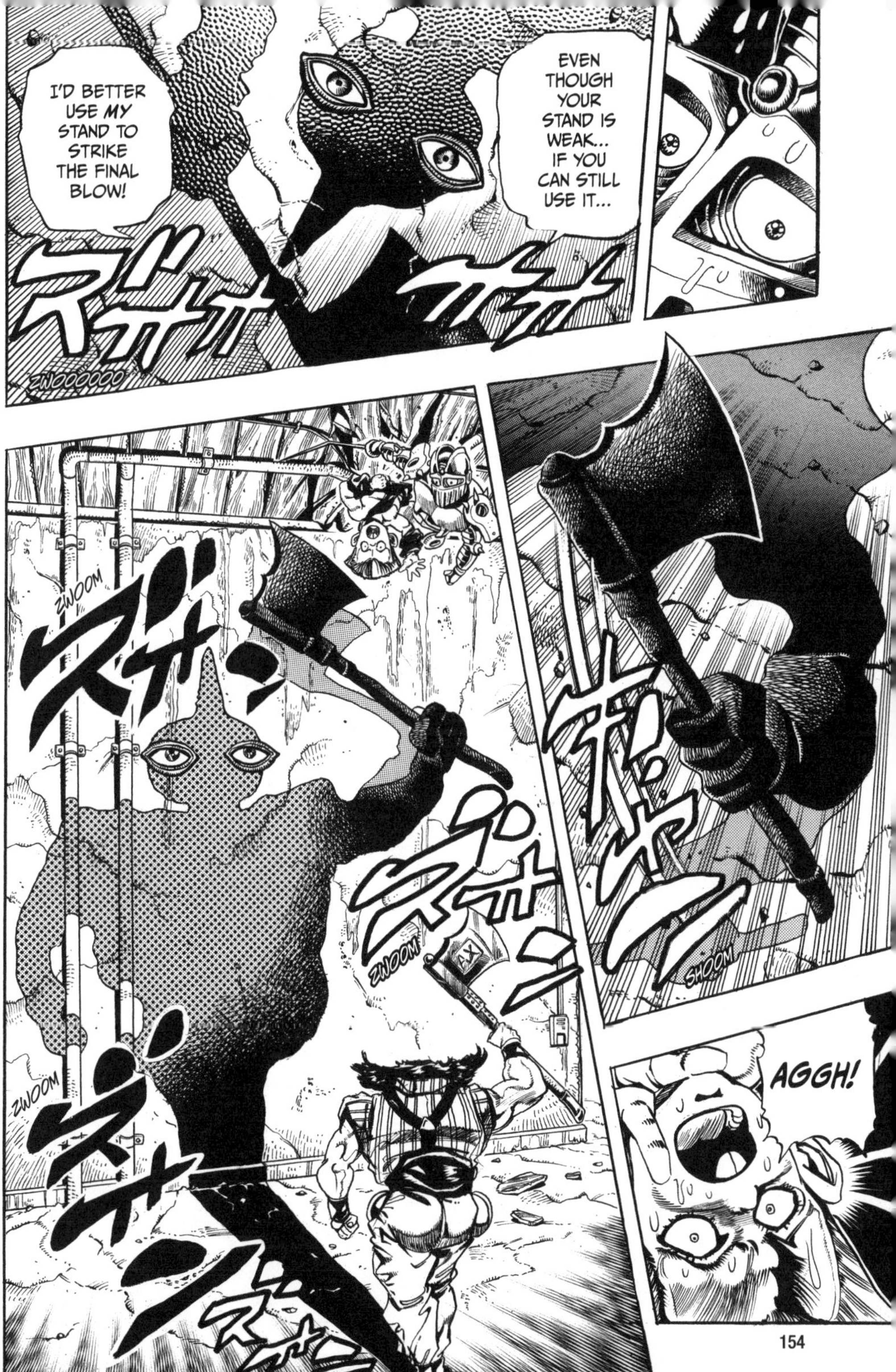
EVEN THOUGH YOUR STAND IS WEAK... IF YOU CAN STILL USE IT...
I'D BETTER USE MY STAND TO STRIKE THE FINAL BLOW!
ZWOOOOOO
SHOOM
AGGH!
ZWOOM
ZWOOM
ZWOOM

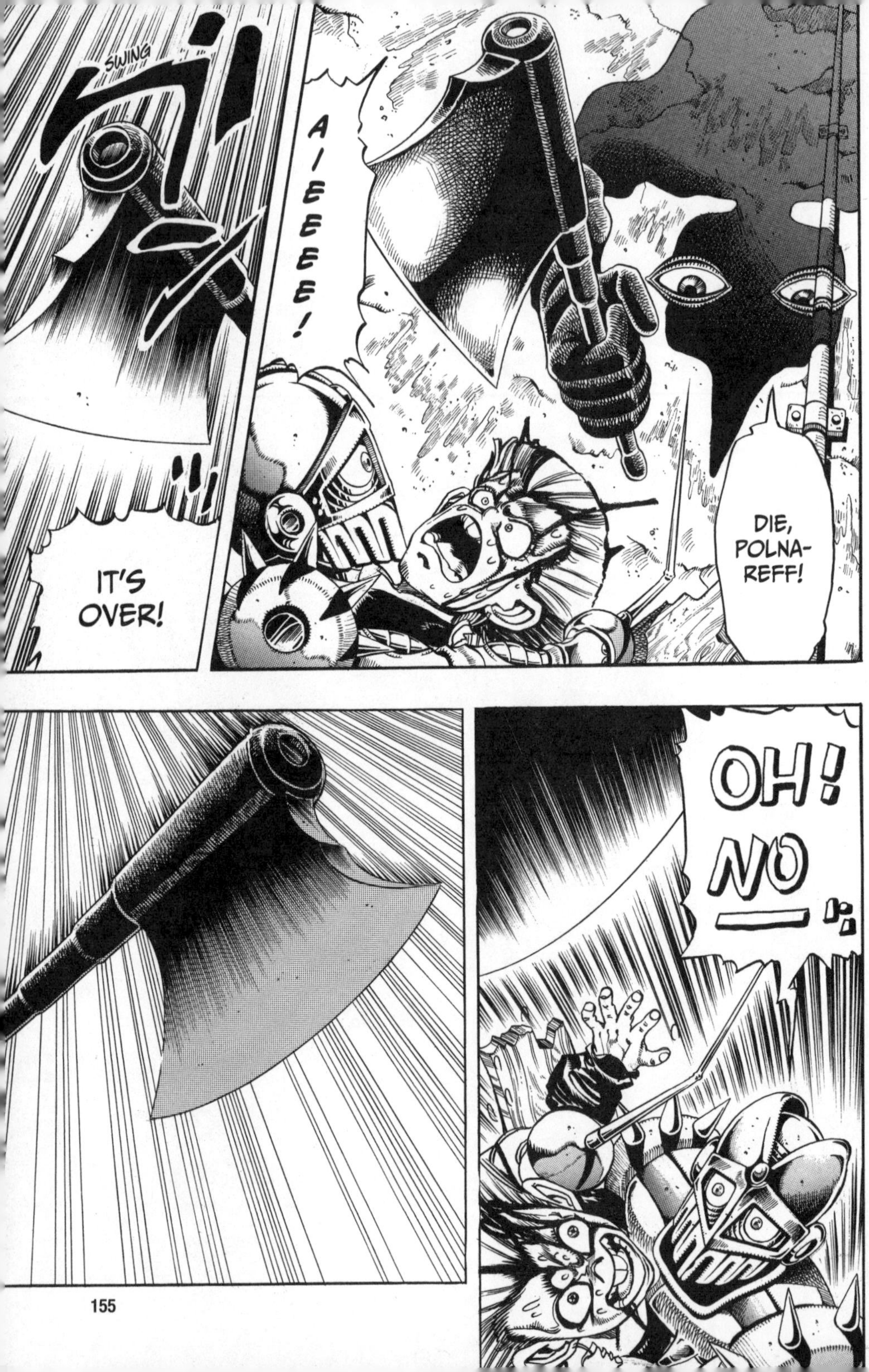
DIE, POLNAREFF!
AIEEEEE!
SWING
IT'S OVER!
OH! NO—!

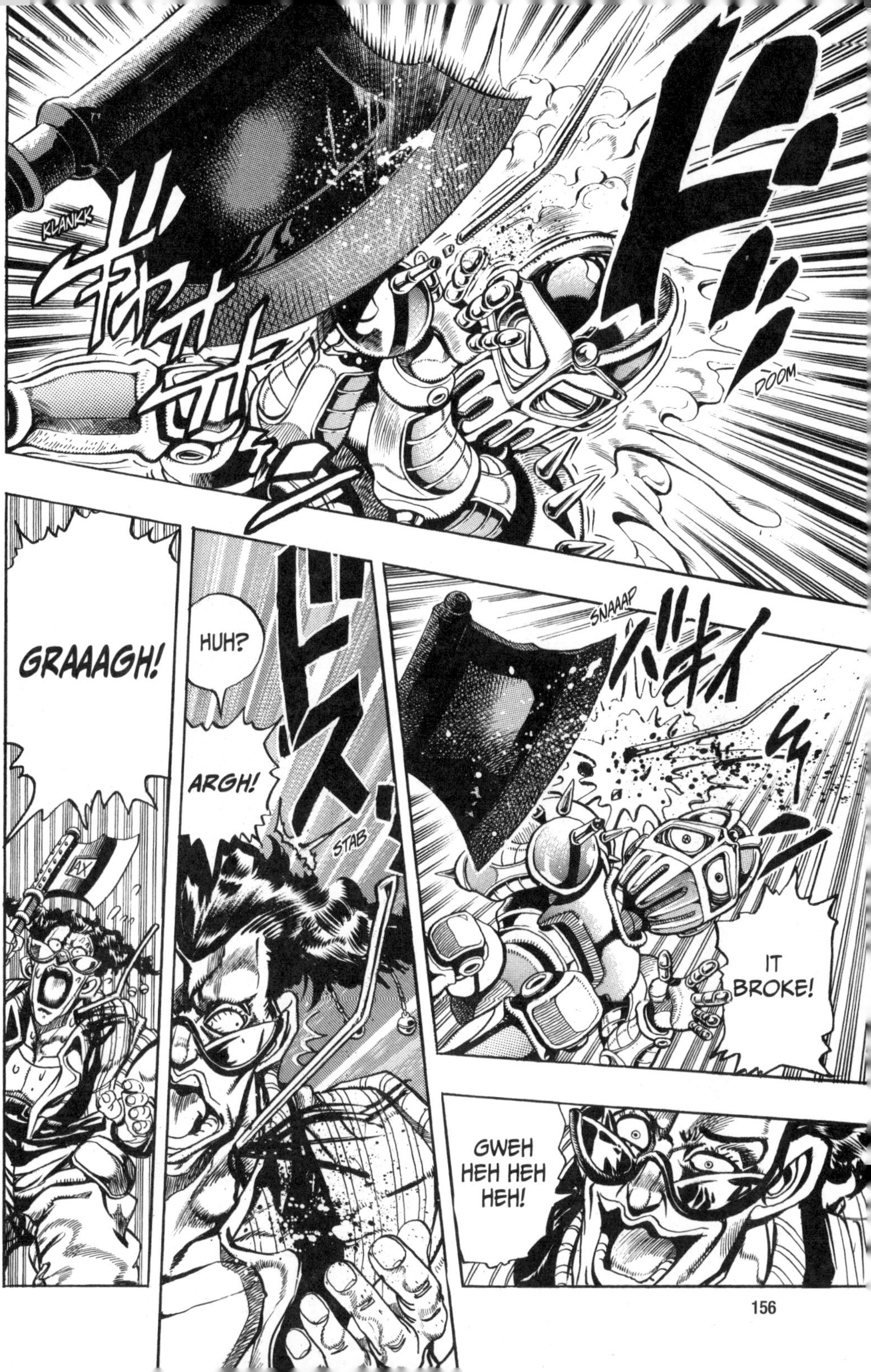

KLANKK
DOOM
SNAAAP
IT BROKE!
GWEH HEH HEH HEH!
HUH?
ARGH!
STAB
GRAAAGH!

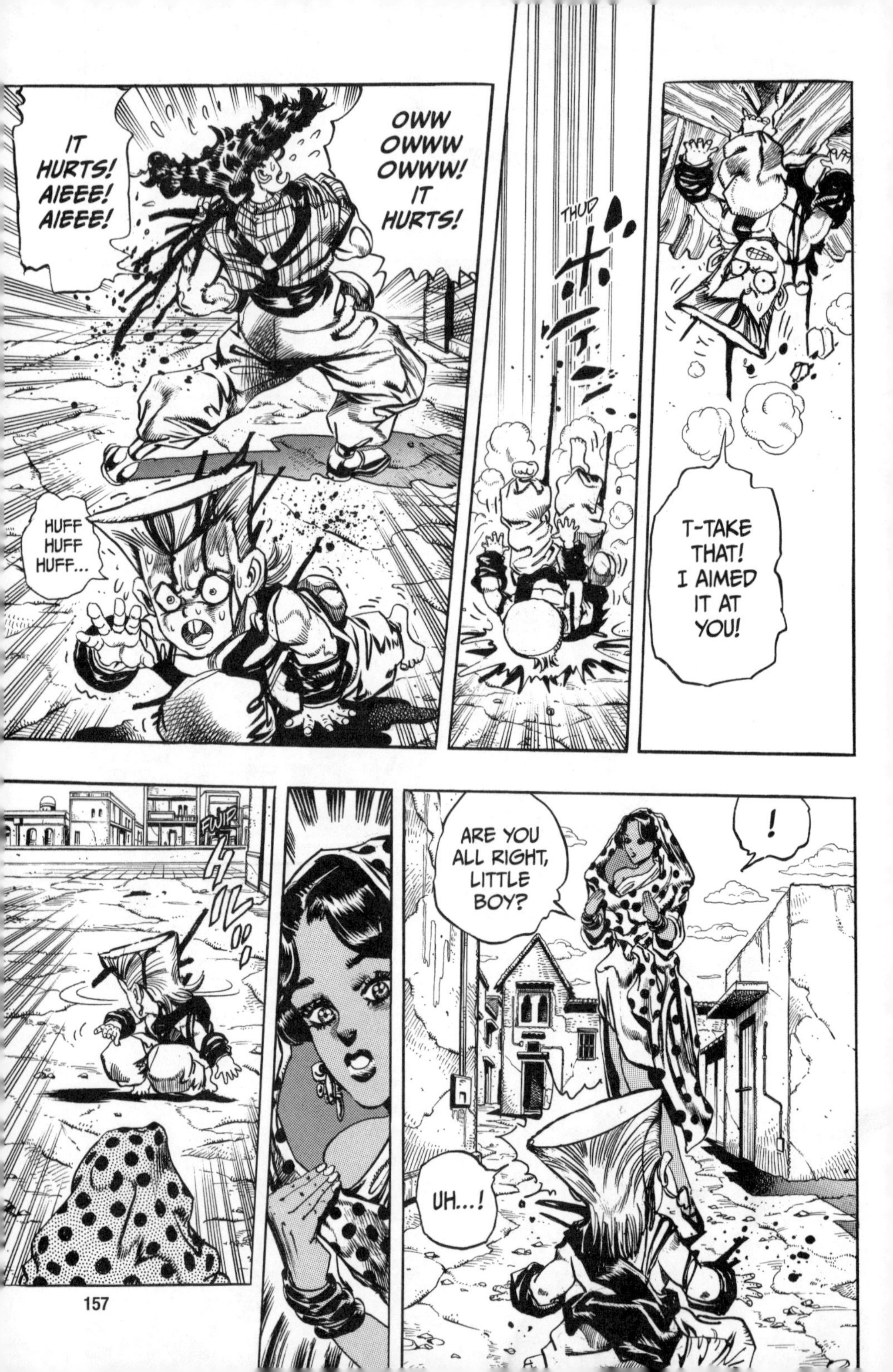
T-TAKE THAT! I AIMED IT AT YOU!
THUD
OWW OWWW OWWW! IT HURTS!
IT HURTS! AIEEE! AIEEE!
HUFF HUFF HUFF...
!
ARE YOU ALL RIGHT, LITTLE BOY?
UH...!
FWIP

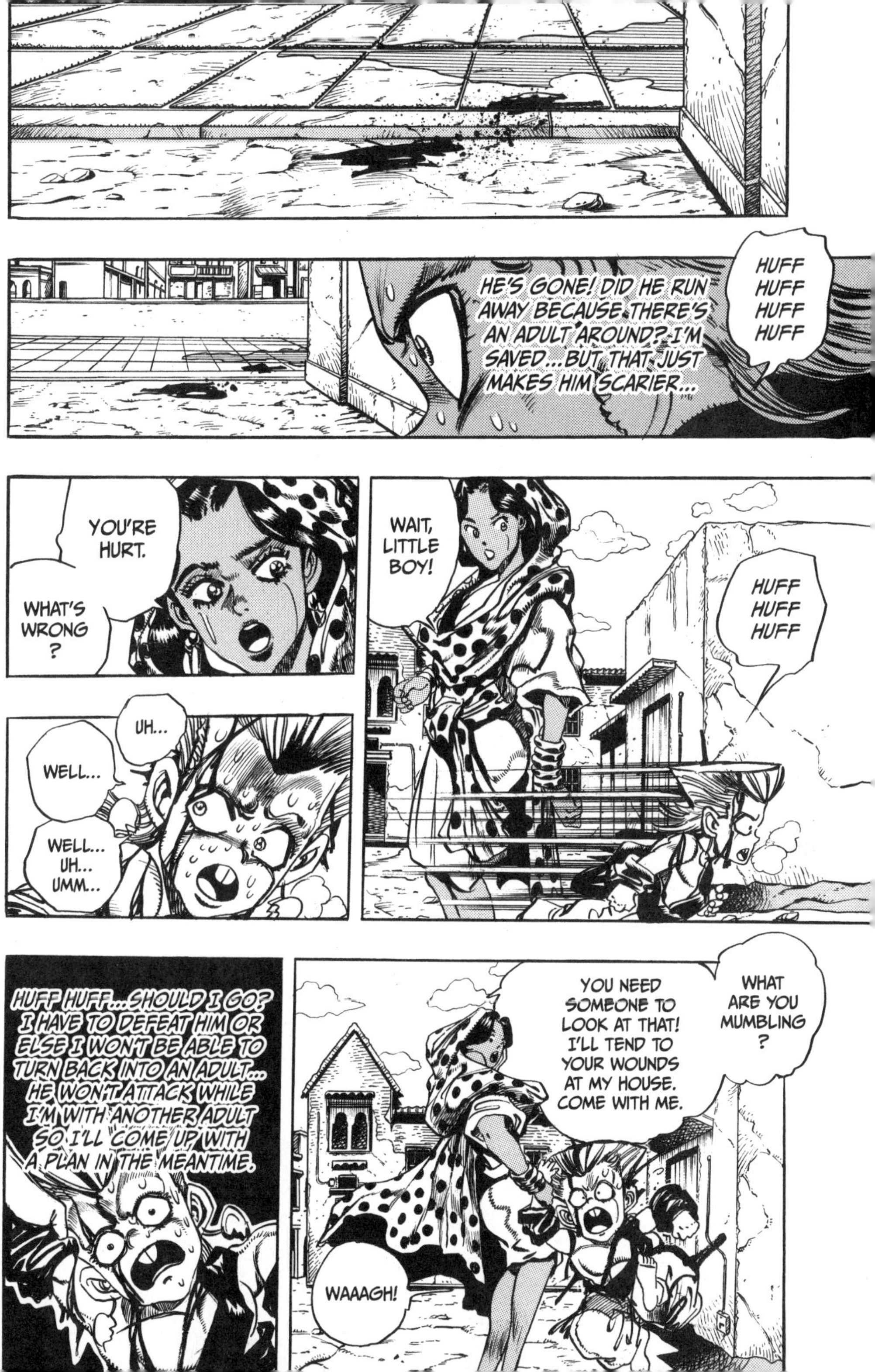
HUFF HUFF HUFF HUFF
HE'S GONE! DID HE RUN AWAY BECAUSE THERE'S AN ADULT AROUND? I'M SAVED...BUT THAT JUST MAKES HIM SCARIER...
WAIT, LITTLE BOY!
HUFF HUFF HUFF
YOU'RE HURT.
WHAT'S WRONG?
UH...
WELL...
WELL... UH... UMM...
WHAT ARE YOU MUMBLING?
YOU NEED SOMEONE TO LOOK AT THAT! I'LL TEND TO YOUR WOUNDS AT MY HOUSE. COME WITH ME.
WAAAGH!
HUFF HUFF...SHOULD I GO? I HAVE TO DEFEAT HIM OR ELSE I WON'T BE ABLE TO TURN BACK INTO AN ADULT... HE WON'T ATTACK WHILE I'M WITH ANOTHER ADULT SO I'LL COME UP WITH A PLAN IN THE MEANTIME.

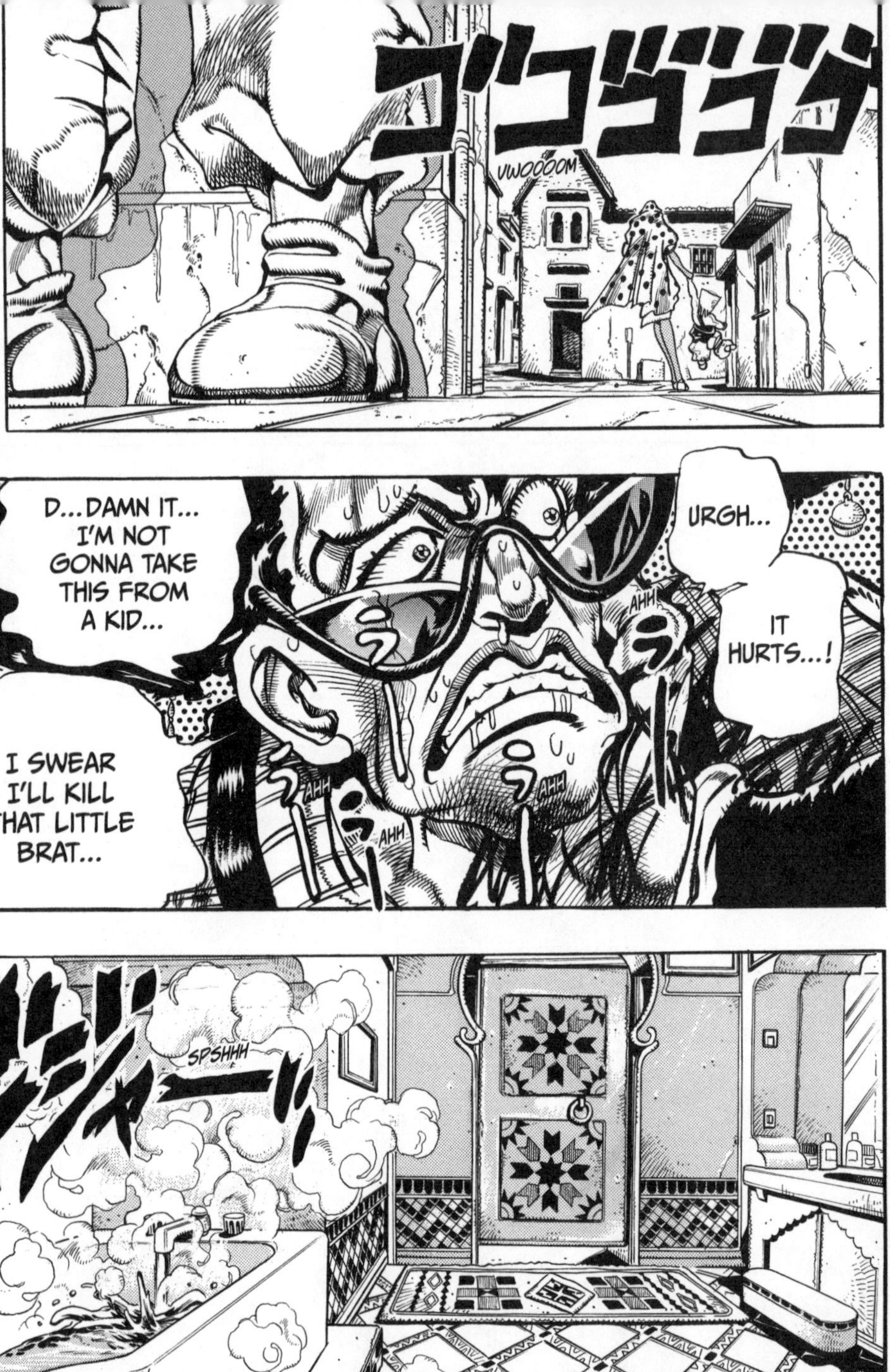
VWOOOOM
URGH...
IT HURTS...!
AHH
D...DAMN IT... I'M NOT GONNA TAKE THIS FROM A KID...
I SWEAR I'LL KILL THAT LITTLE BRAT...
AHH
AHH
AHH
SPSHHH

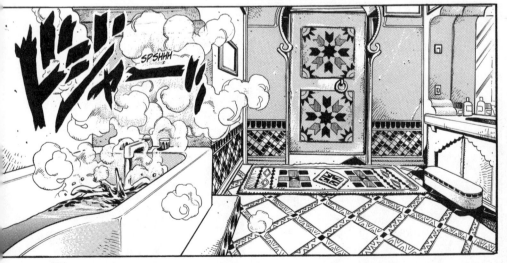

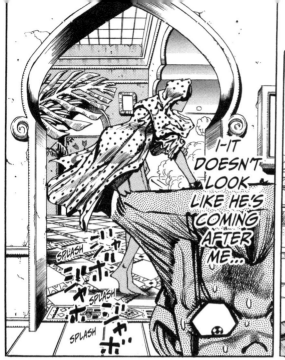

I-IT DOESN'T LOOK LIKE HE'S COMING AFTER ME...

SPLASH

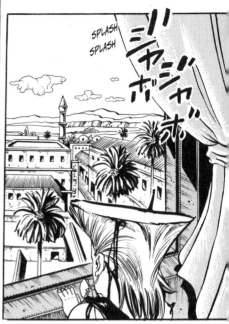

SPLASH SPLASH

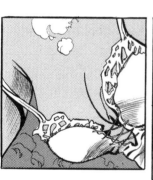

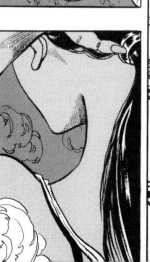

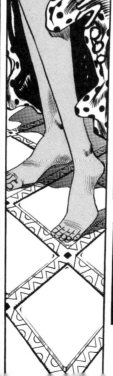

FWD

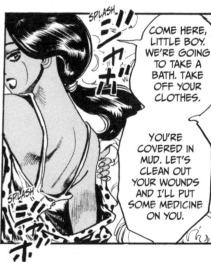

SPLASH

COME HERE, LITTLE BOY. WE'RE GOING TO TAKE A BATH. TAKE OFF YOUR CLOTHES.

YOU'RE COVERED IN MUD. LET'S CLEAN OUT YOUR WOUNDS AND I'LL PUT SOME MEDICINE ON YOU.

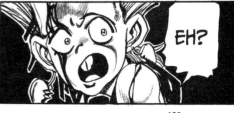

EH?

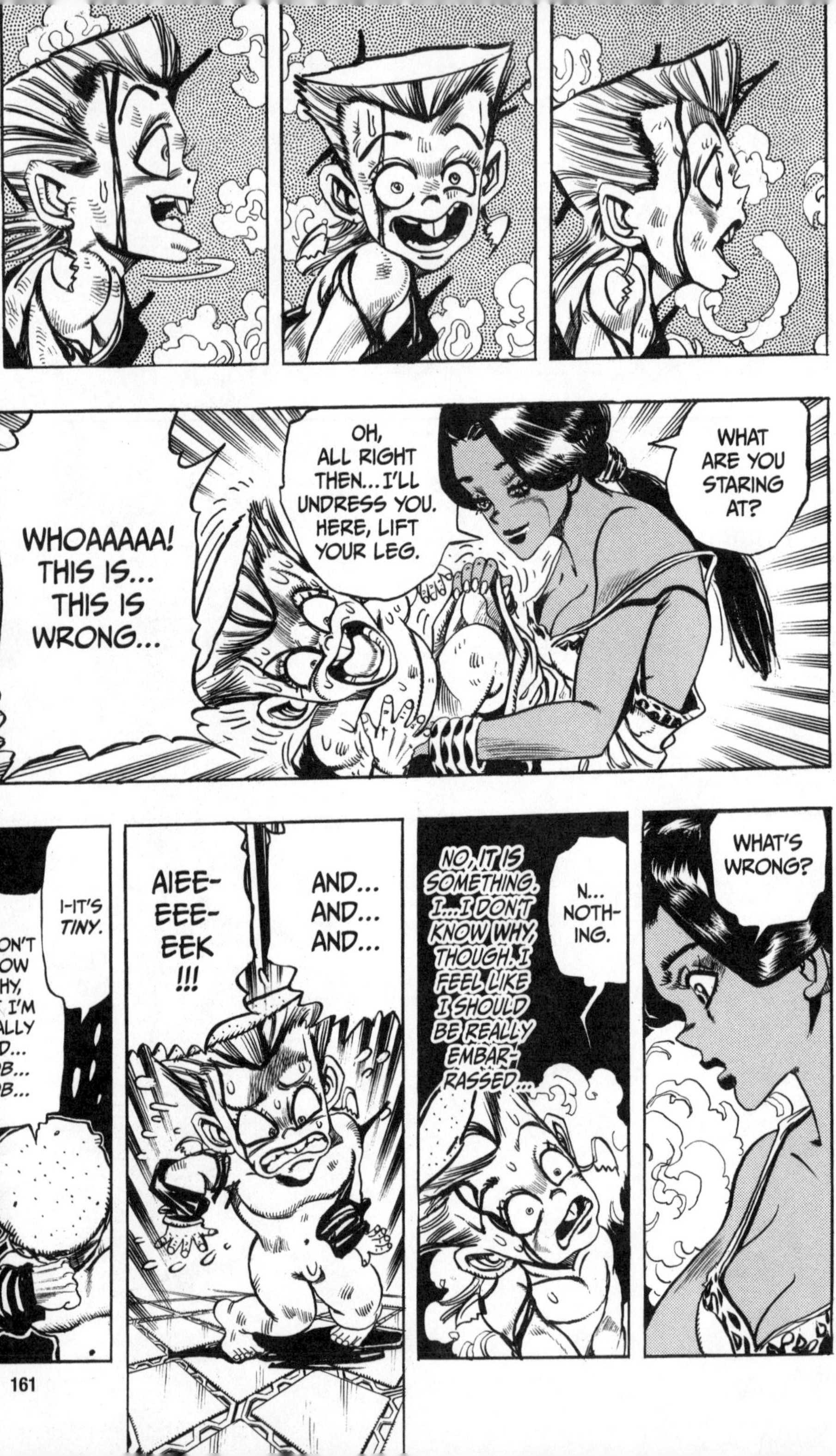
WHAT ARE YOU STARING AT?
OH, ALL RIGHT THEN... I'LL UNDRESS YOU. HERE, LIFT YOUR LEG.
WHOAAAAA! THIS IS... THIS IS WRONG...
WHAT'S WRONG?
N... NOTH-ING.
NO, IT IS SOMETHING. I...I DON'T KNOW WHY, THOUGH. I FEEL LIKE I SHOULD BE REALLY EMBARRASSED...
AND... AND... AND...
AIEE-EEE-EEK!!!
I-IT'S TINY.
I DON'T KNOW WHY, BUT I'M REALLY SAD... SOB... SOB...

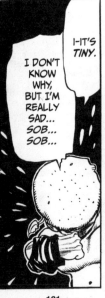

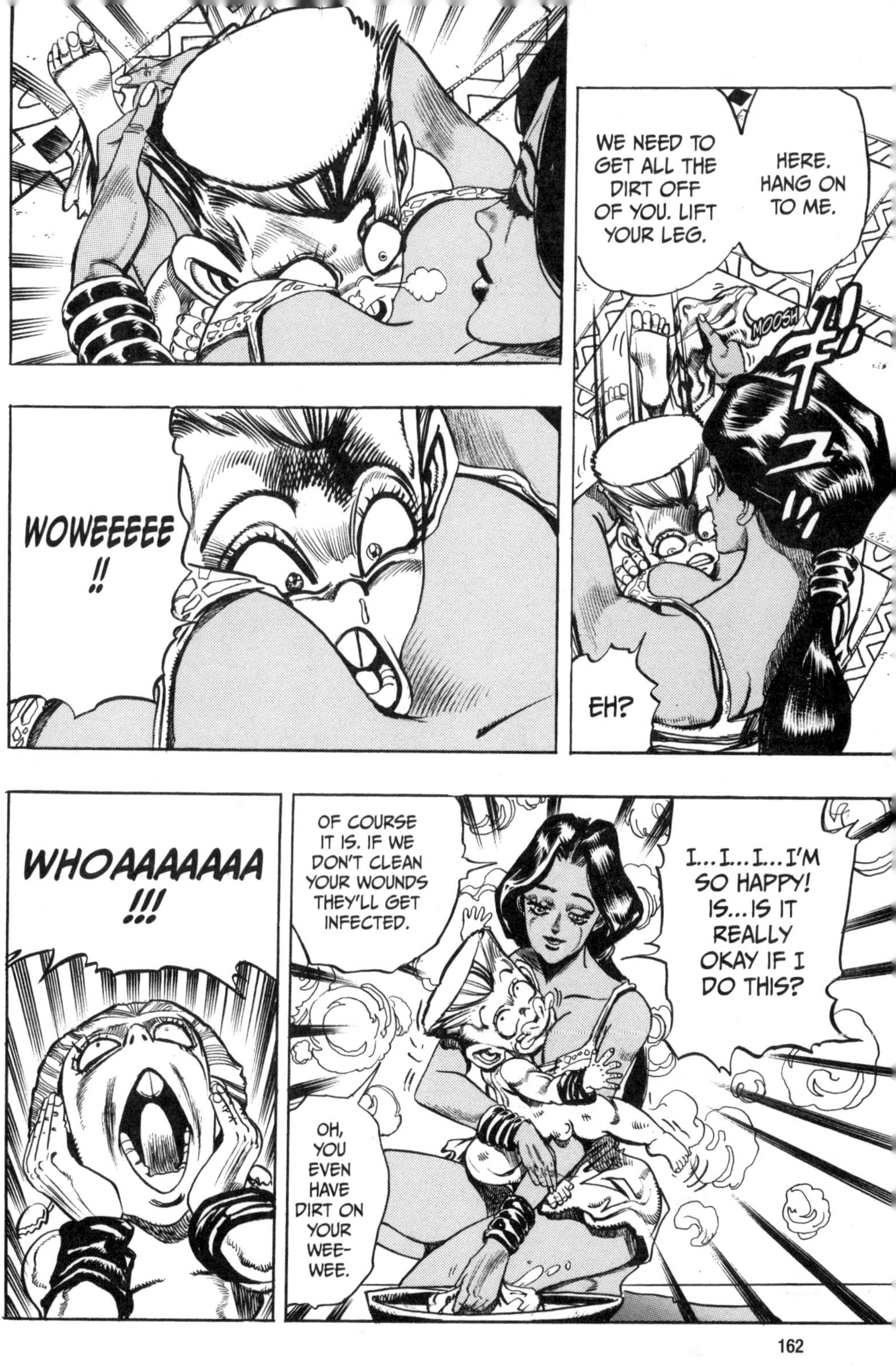
HERE. HANG ON TO ME.
WE NEED TO GET ALL THE DIRT OFF OF YOU. LIFT YOUR LEG.
MOOSH
EH?
WOWEEEEE!!
I...I...I...I'M SO HAPPY! IS...IS IT REALLY OKAY IF I DO THIS?
OF COURSE IT IS. IF WE DON'T CLEAN YOUR WOUNDS THEY'LL GET INFECTED.
OH, YOU EVEN HAVE DIRT ON YOUR WEE-WEE.
WHOAAAAAAA!!!

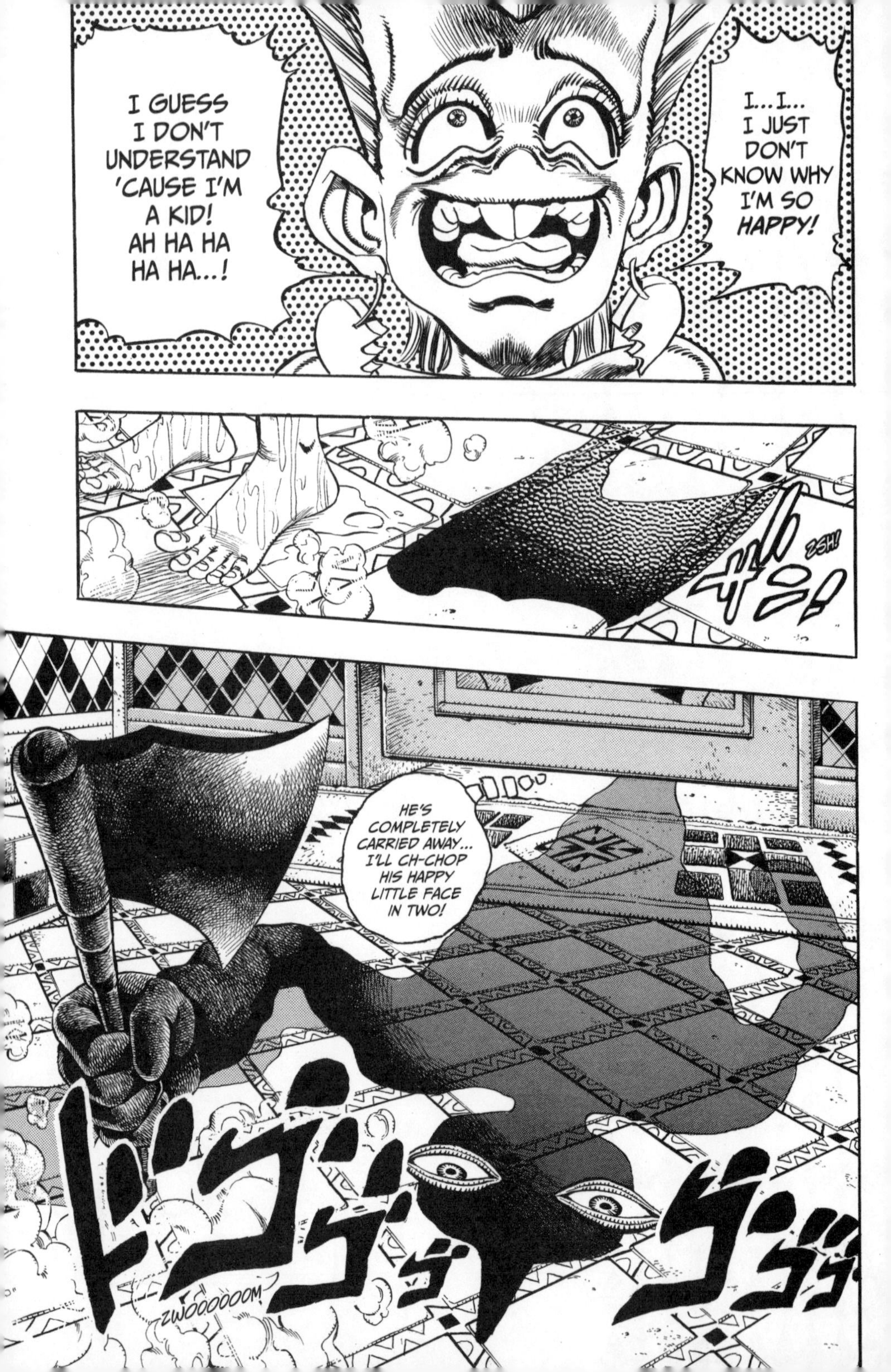
I... I...
I JUST DON'T KNOW WHY I'M SO *HAPPY!*
I GUESS I DON'T UNDERSTAND 'CAUSE I'M A KID! AH HA HA HA HA...!
ZSH!
HE'S COMPLETELY CARRIED AWAY... I'LL CH-CHOP HIS HAPPY LITTLE FACE IN TWO!
ZWOOOOOOM

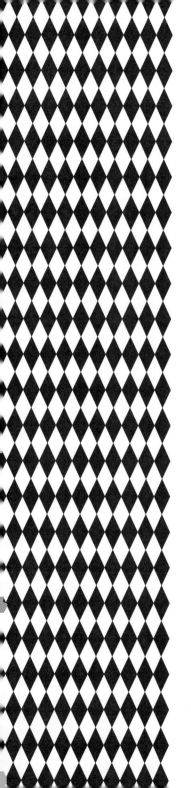
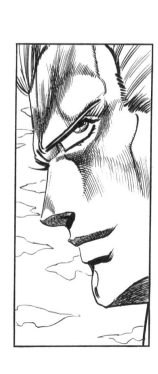

CHAPTER 94: "Set" Alessi PART 3

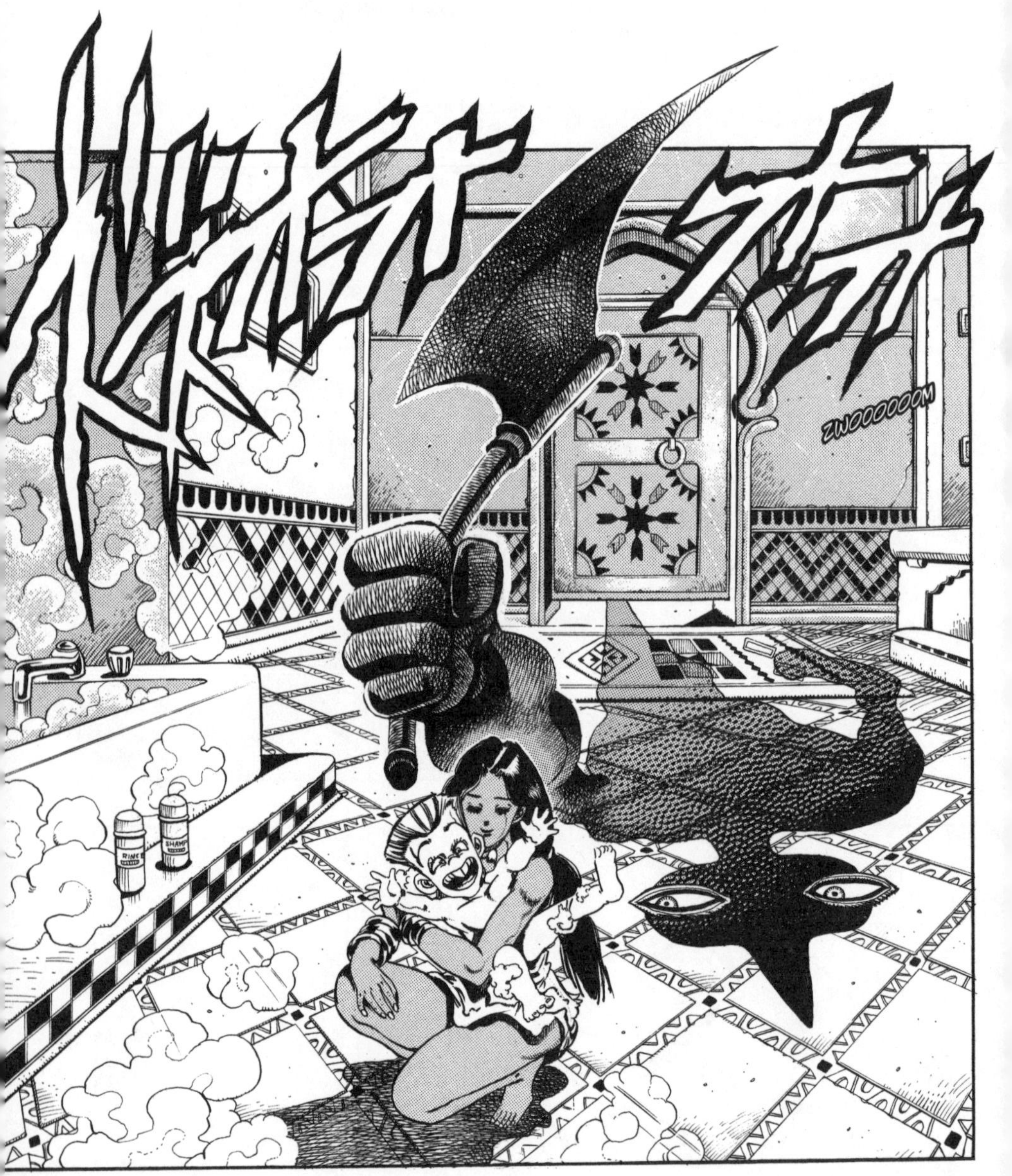
ZWOOOOOOM

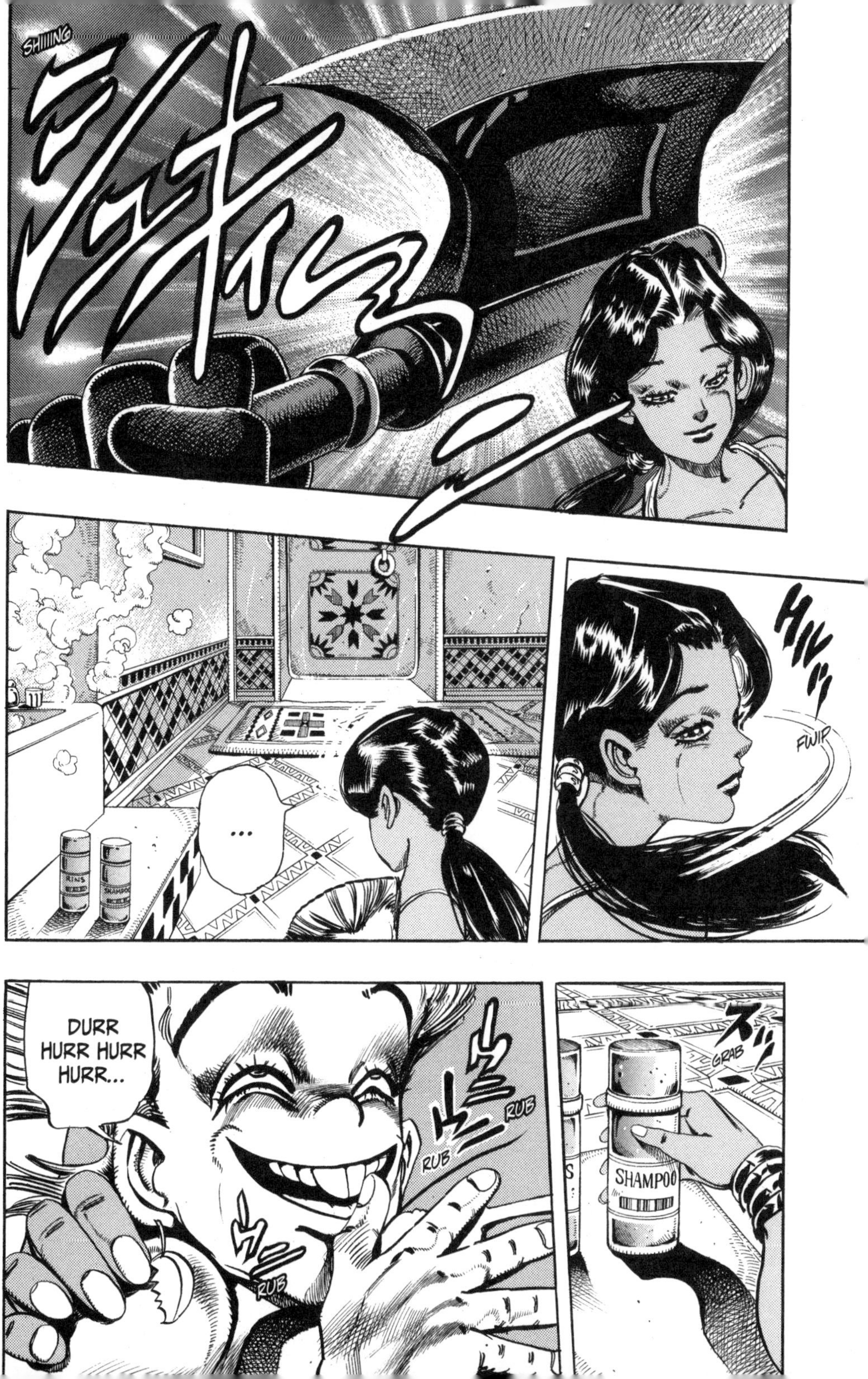
SHIIING
FWIP
...
RINS
SHAMPOO
GRAB
SHAMPOO
DURR HURR HURR HURR...
RUB
RUB
RUB

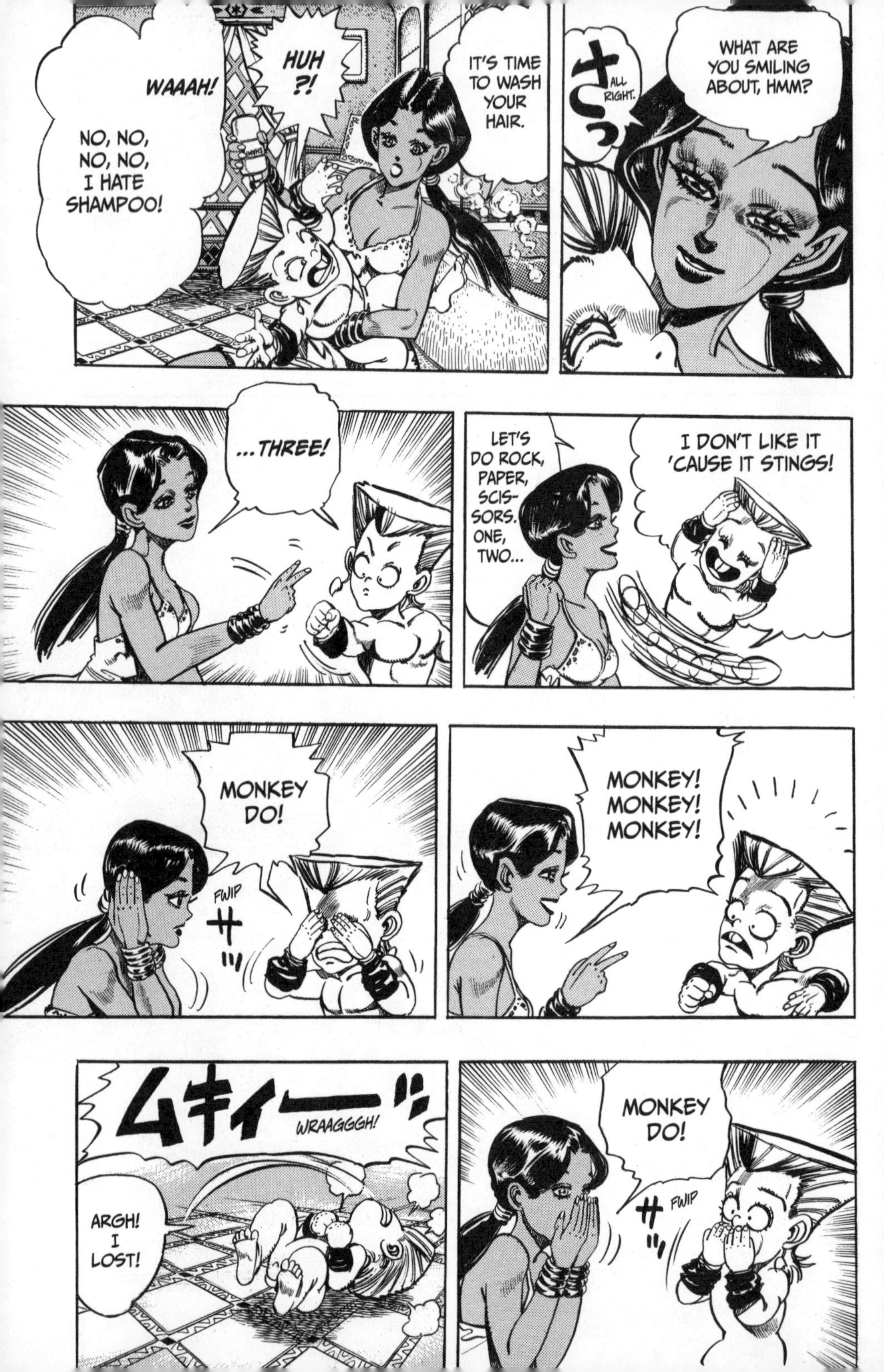
さっ
ALL RIGHT.
WHAT ARE YOU SMILING ABOUT, HMM?
IT'S TIME TO WASH YOUR HAIR.
HUH ?!
WAAAH!
NO, NO, NO, NO, I HATE SHAMPOO!
I DON'T LIKE IT 'CAUSE IT STINGS!
LET'S DO ROCK, PAPER, SCIS-SORS. ONE, TWO...
...THREE!
MONKEY! MONKEY! MONKEY!
MONKEY DO!
FWIP
MONKEY DO!
FWIP
ムキィーッ
WRAAGGGH!
ARGH! I LOST!

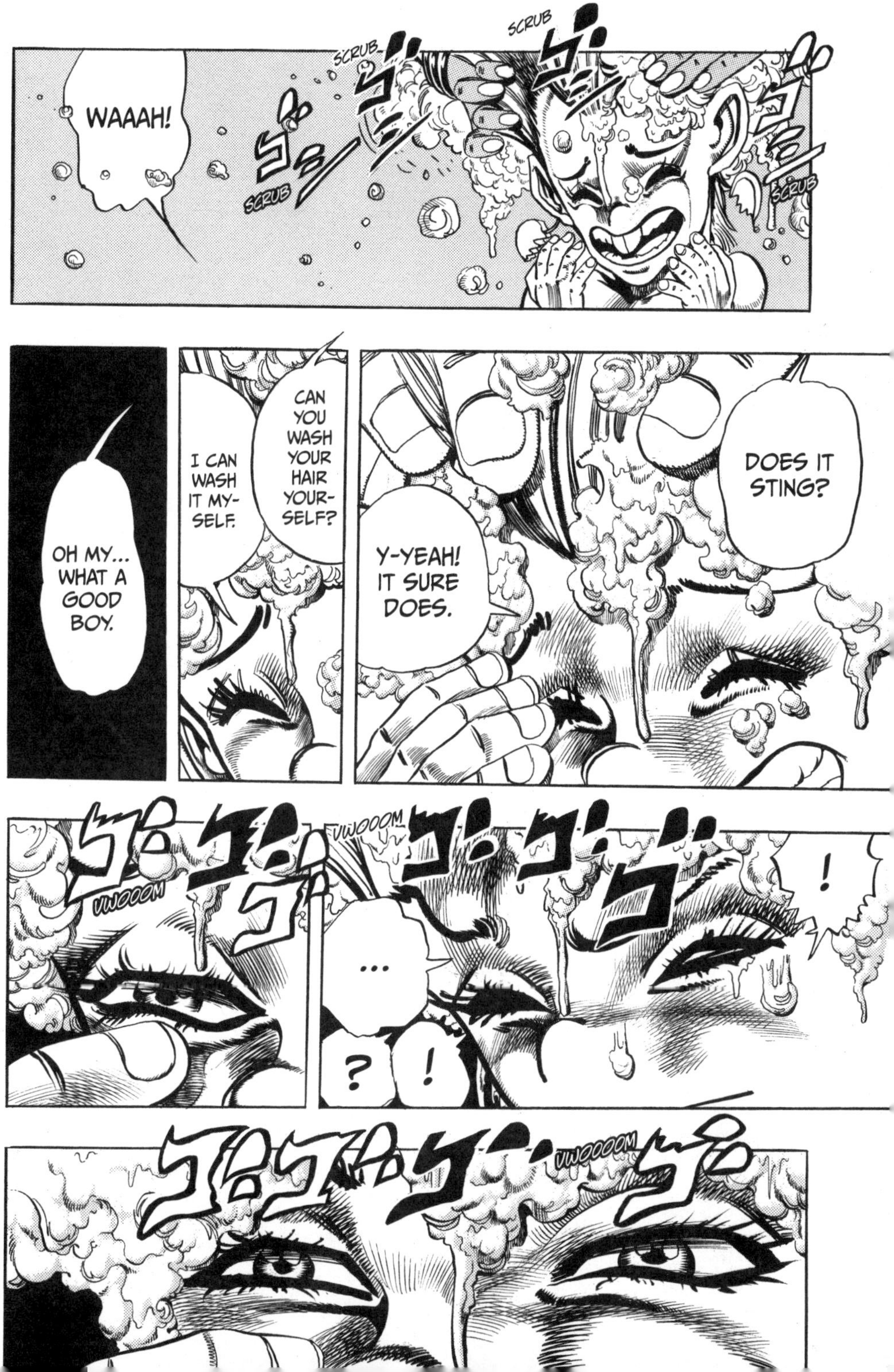
SCRUB
SCRUB
SCRUB
SCRUB
WAAAH!
DOES IT STING?
Y-YEAH! IT SURE DOES.
CAN YOU WASH YOUR HAIR YOURSELF?
I CAN WASH IT MYSELF.
OH MY... WHAT A GOOD BOY.
VWOOOM
!
...
?!
VWOOOM
VWOOOOM

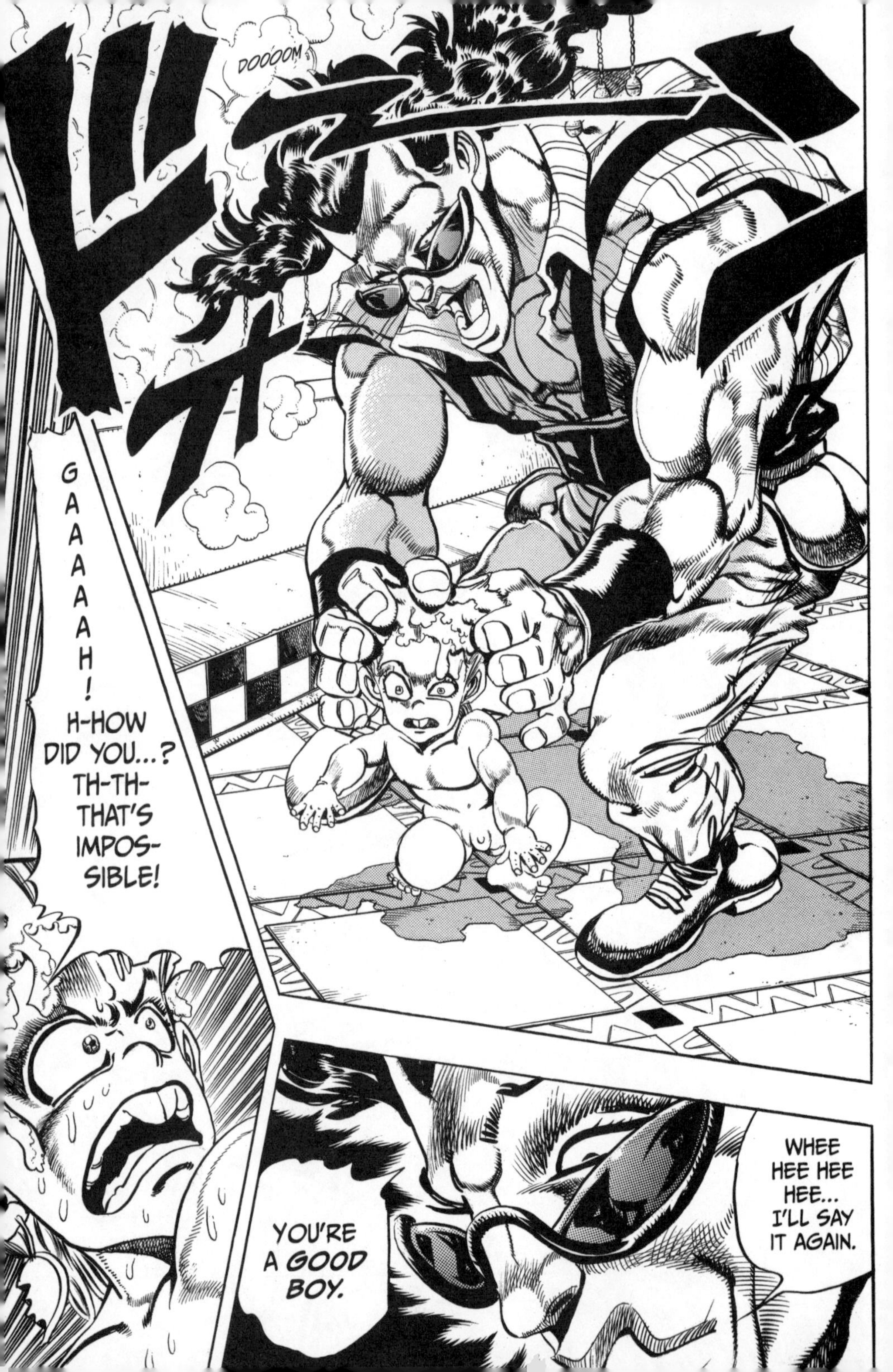
DOOOOM
GAAAAAAH! H-HOW DID YOU...? TH-TH-THAT'S IMPOS-SIBLE!
WHEE HEE HEE HEE... I'LL SAY IT AGAIN.
YOU'RE A GOOD BOY.

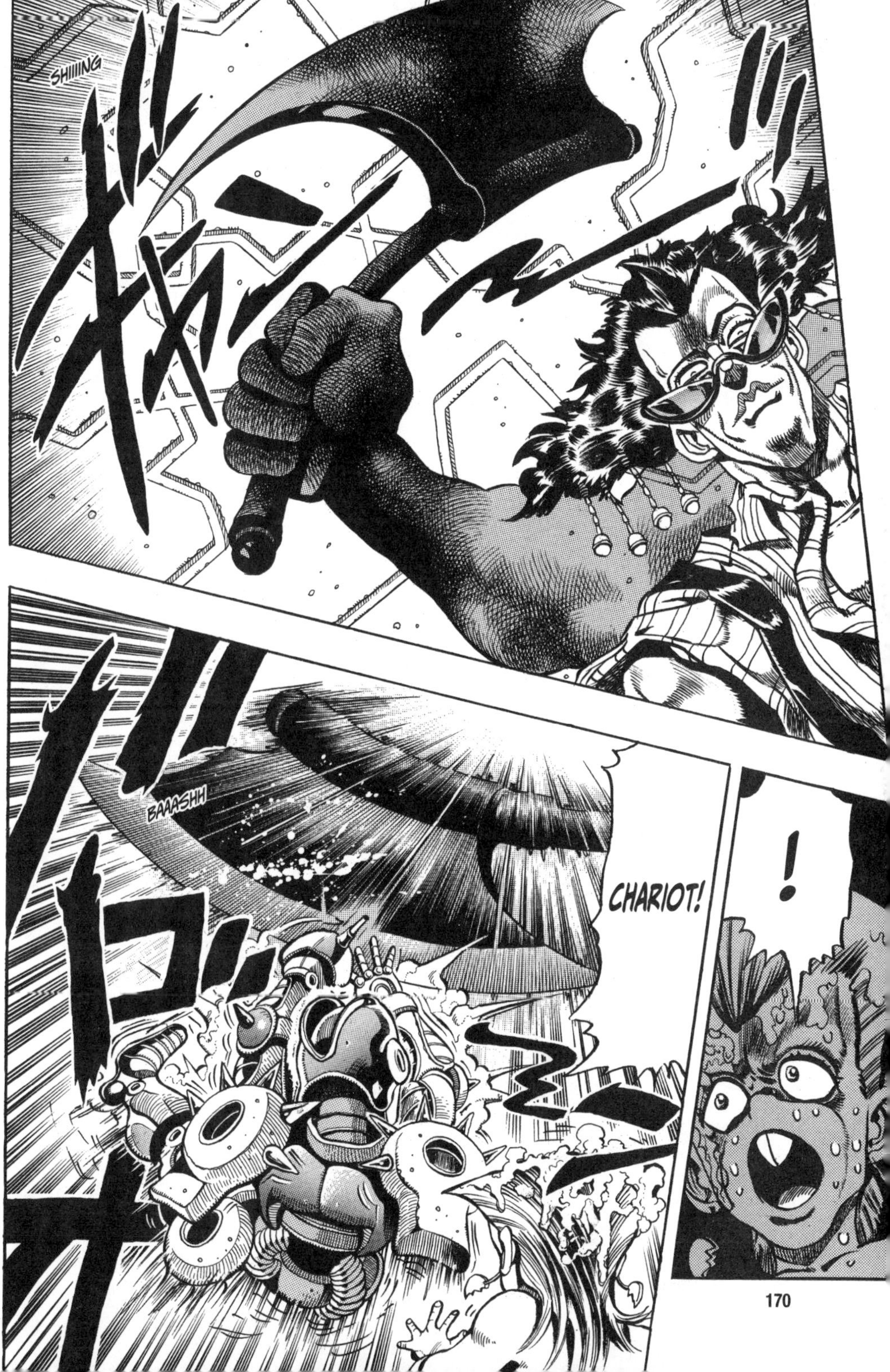
SHIIING
!
BAAASHH
CHARIOT!

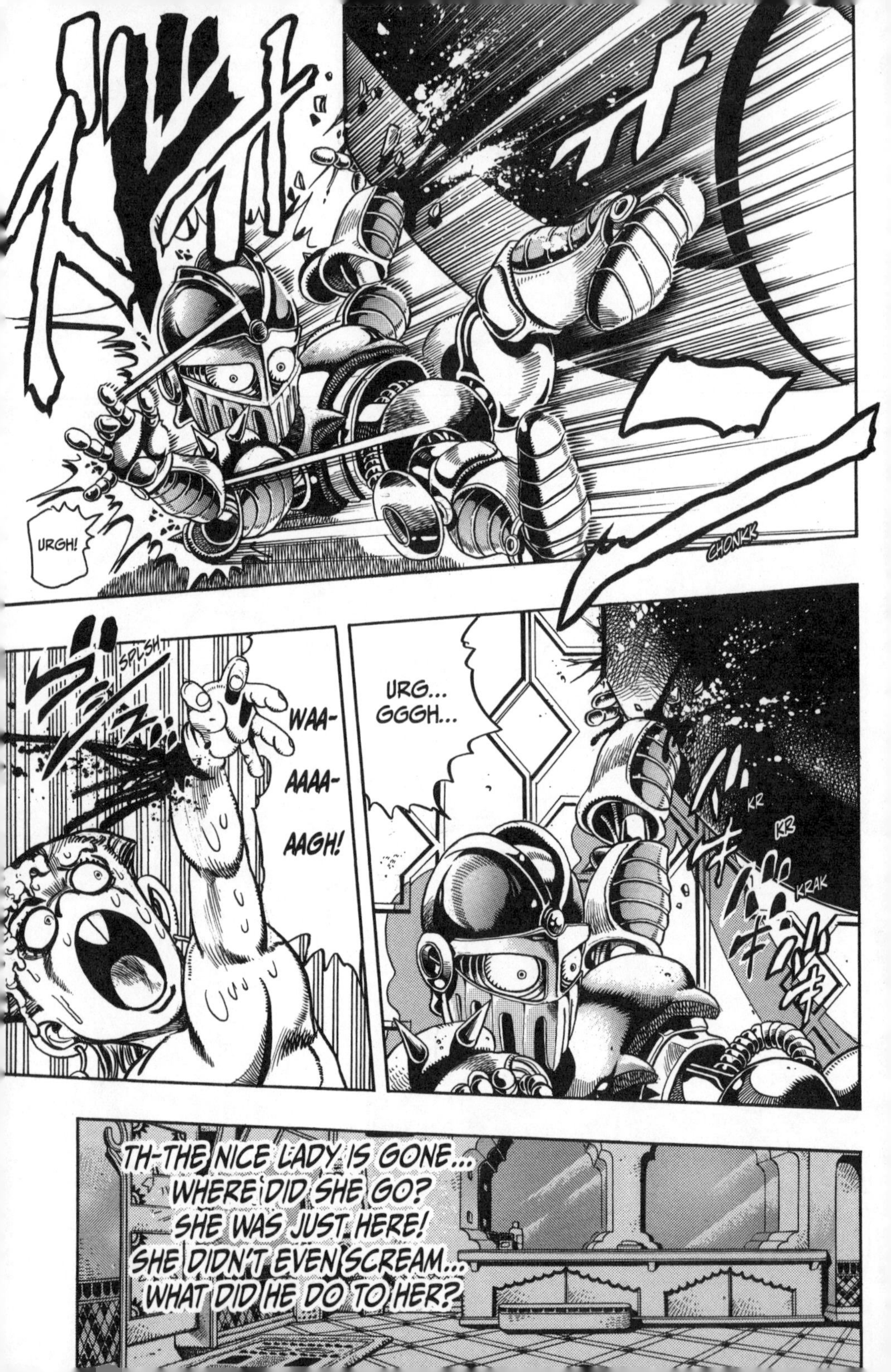
CHONKK
URGH!
URG... GGGH...
KR
KR
KRAK
SPLSH
WAA- AAAA- AAGH!
TH-THE NICE LADY IS GONE... WHERE DID SHE GO? SHE WAS JUST HERE! SHE DIDN'T EVEN SCREAM... WHAT DID HE DO TO HER?

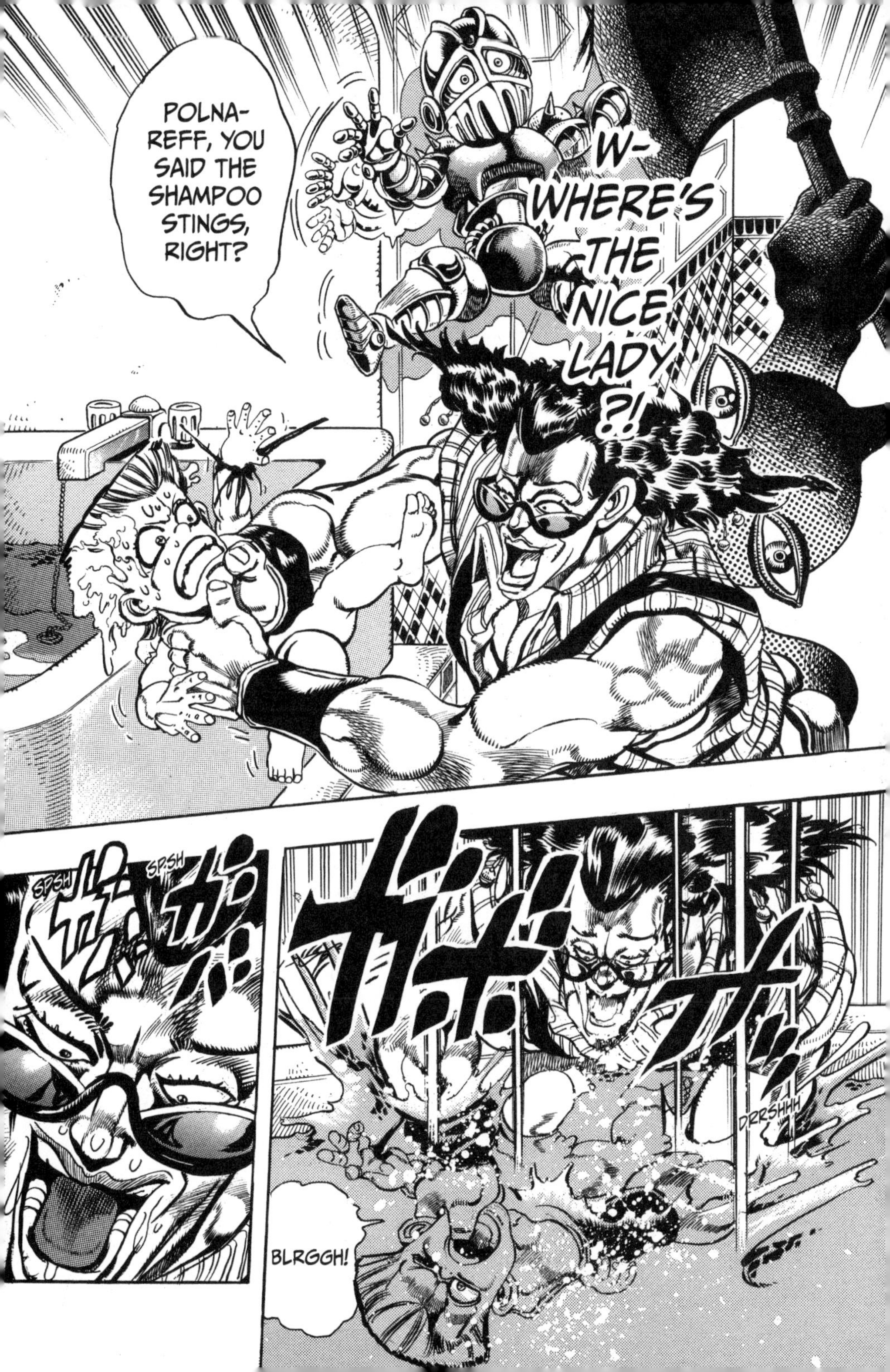
W-WHERE'S THE NICE LADY?!
POLNA-REFF, YOU SAID THE SHAMPOO STINGS, RIGHT?
DRRSHHH
BLRGGH!
SPSH
SPSH

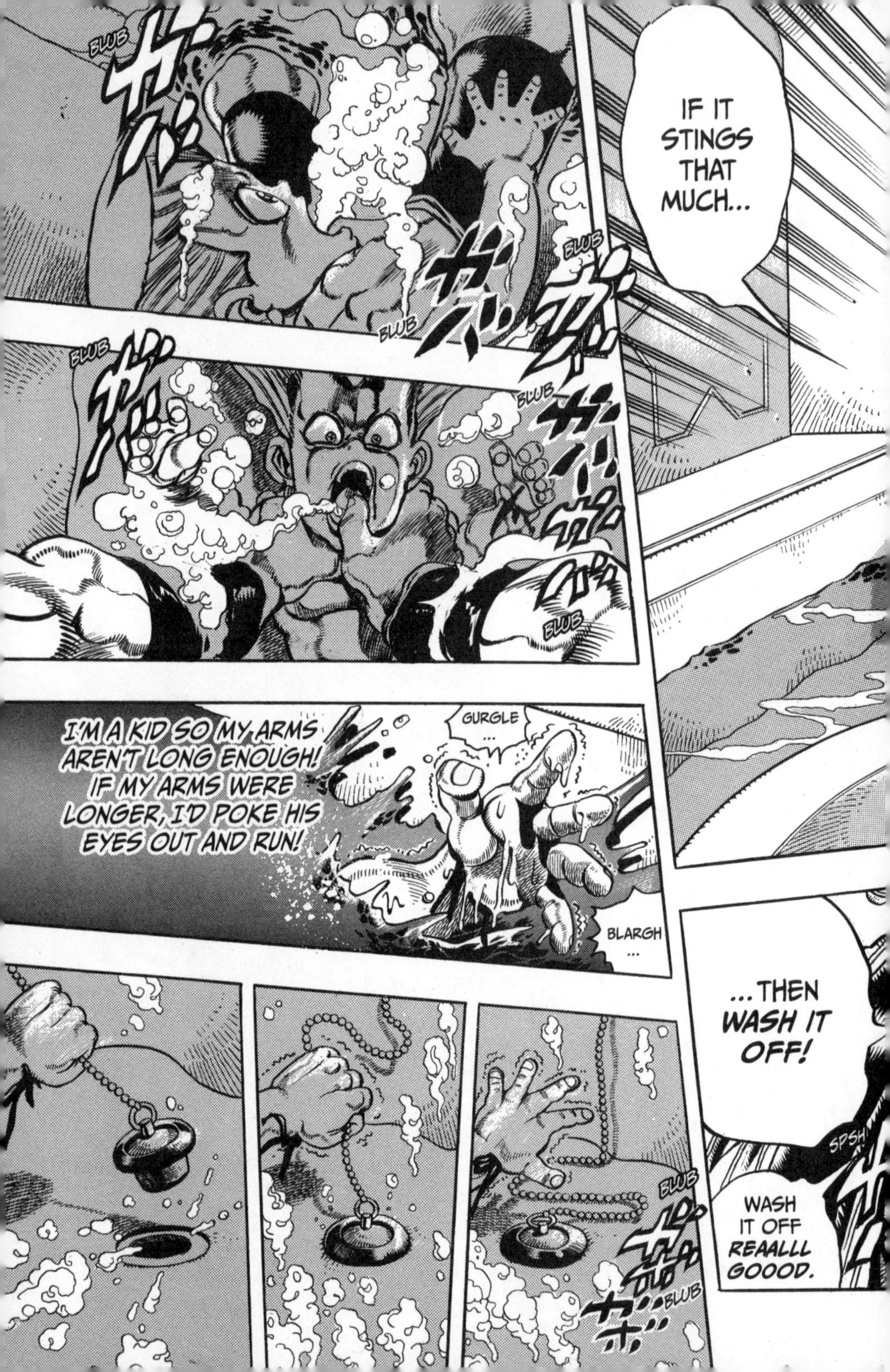
IF IT STINGS THAT MUCH...
BLUB
BLUB
BLUB
BLUB
BLUB
BLUB
I'M A KID SO MY ARMS AREN'T LONG ENOUGH! IF MY ARMS WERE LONGER, I'D POKE HIS EYES OUT AND RUN!
GURGLE ...
BLARGH ...
...THEN WASH IT OFF!
SPSH
WASH IT OFF REAALLL GOOOD.
BLUB
BLUB

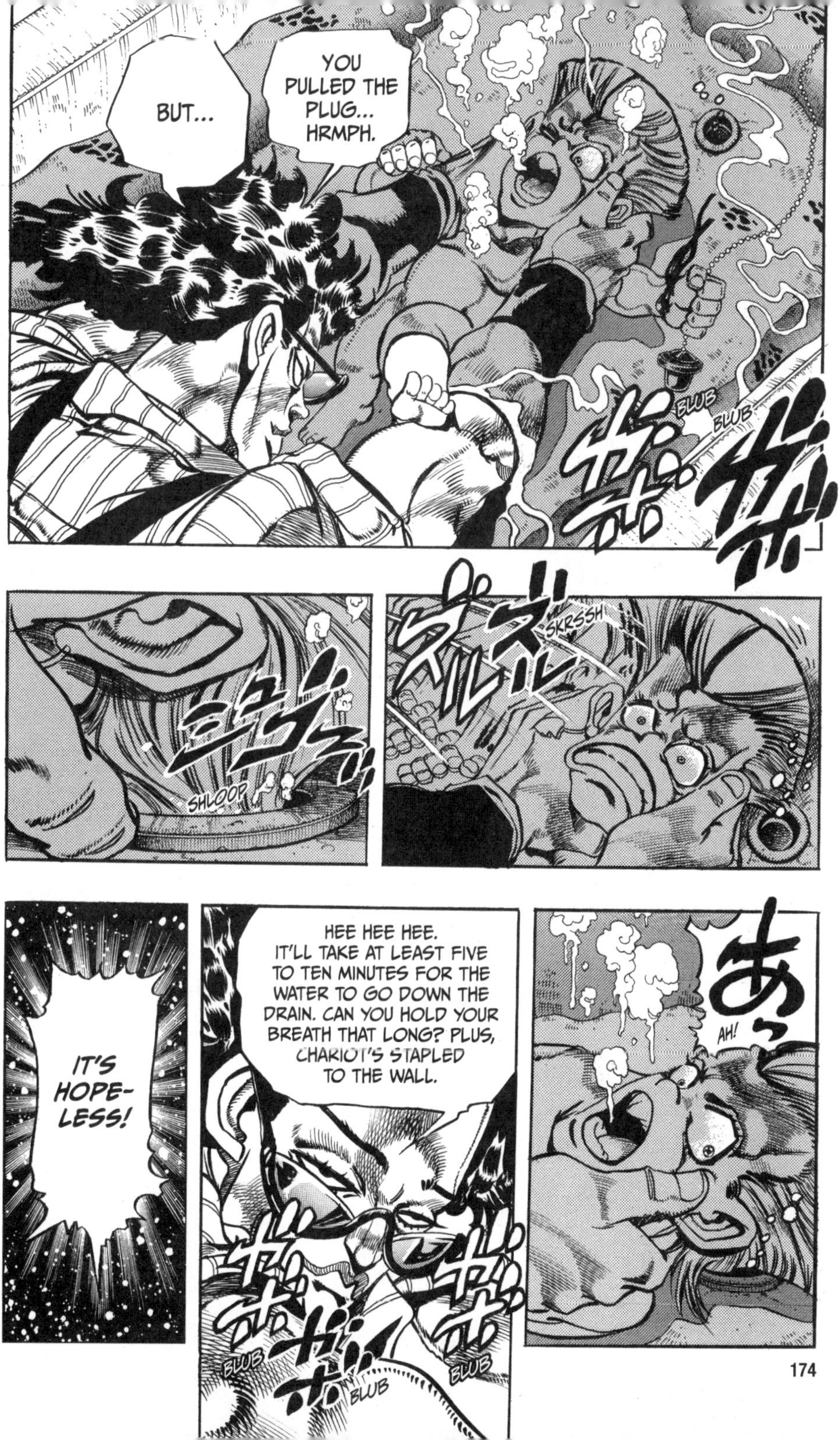
YOU PULLED THE PLUG... HRMPH.
BUT...
BLUB
BLUB
SKRSSH
SHLOOP
AH!
HEE HEE HEE. IT'LL TAKE AT LEAST FIVE TO TEN MINUTES FOR THE WATER TO GO DOWN THE DRAIN. CAN YOU HOLD YOUR BREATH THAT LONG? PLUS, CHARIOT'S STAPLED TO THE WALL.
BLUB
BLUB
BLUB
IT'S HOPE-LESS!

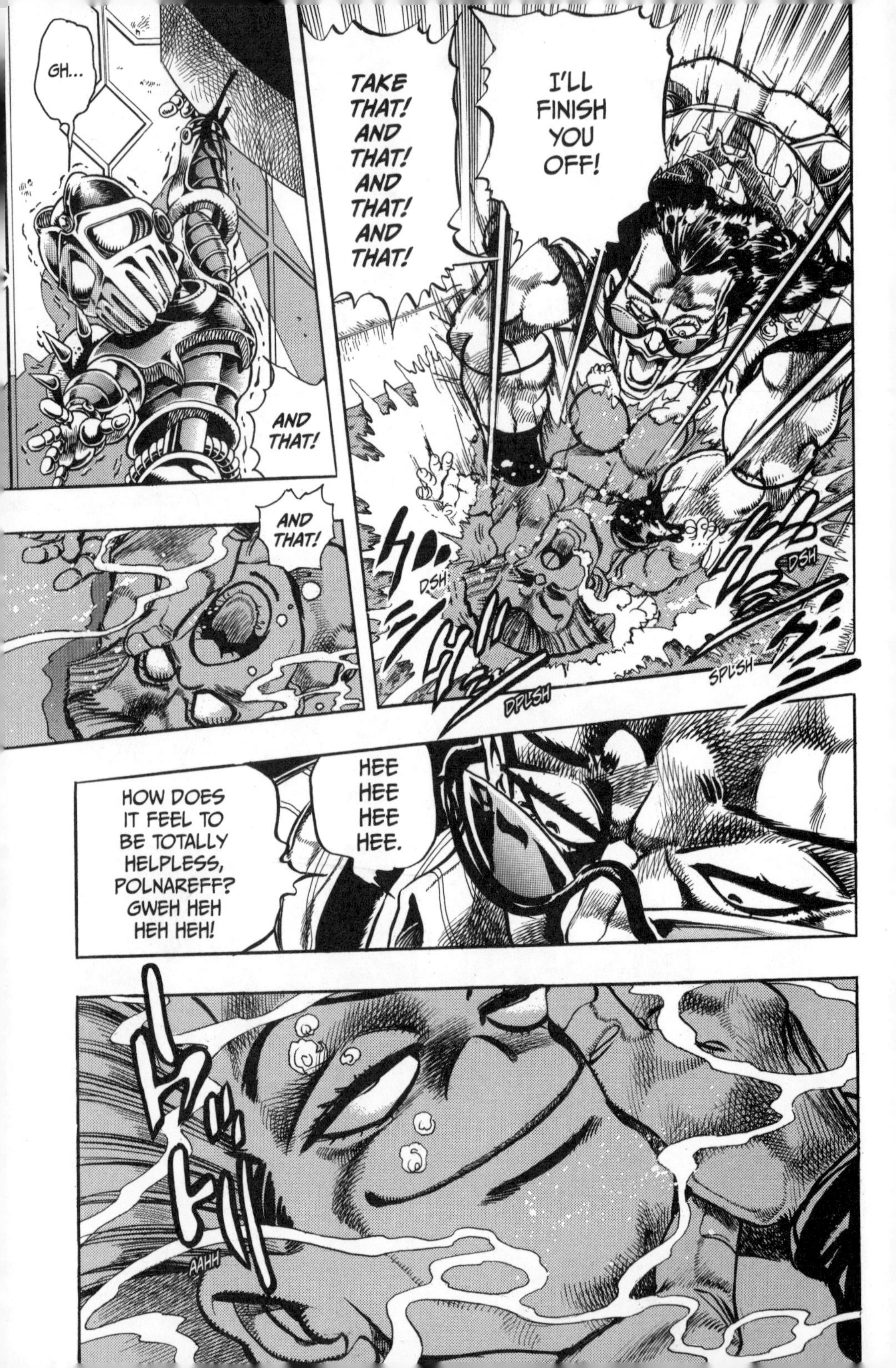
I'LL FINISH YOU OFF!
TAKE THAT! AND THAT! AND THAT! AND THAT!
DSH
DSH
SPLSH
DPLSH
GH...
AND THAT!
AND THAT!
HEE HEE HEE HEE.
HOW DOES IT FEEL TO BE TOTALLY HELPLESS, POLNAREFF? GWEH HEH HEH HEH!
AAHH

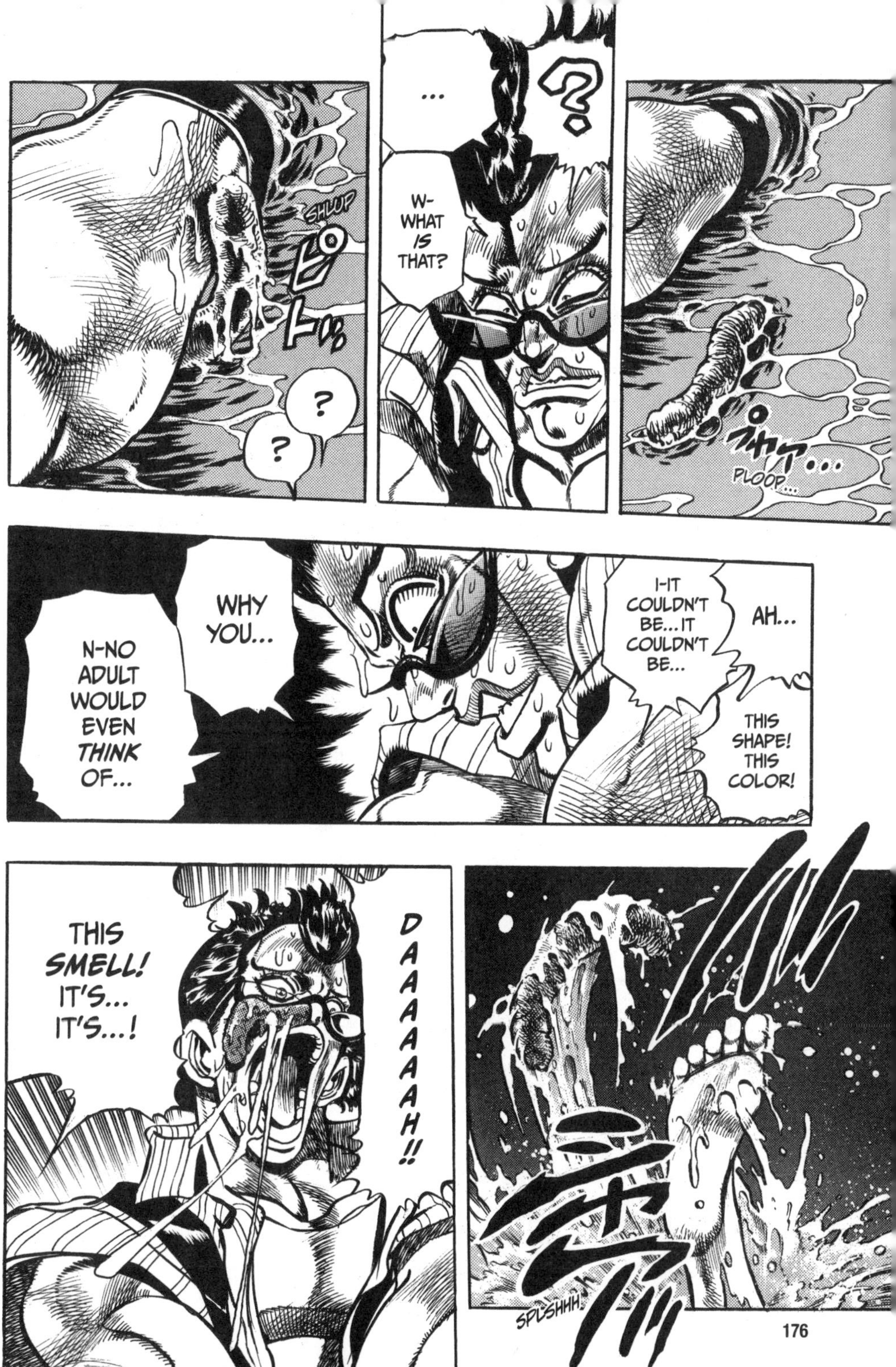
PLOOP...
...
?
W-WHAT IS THAT?
SHLUP
?
?
AH...
THIS SHAPE! THIS COLOR!
I-IT COULDN'T BE...IT COULDN'T BE...
WHY YOU...
N-NO ADULT WOULD EVEN THINK OF...
SPLSHHH
DAAAAAAAAH!!
THIS SMELL! IT'S... IT'S...!

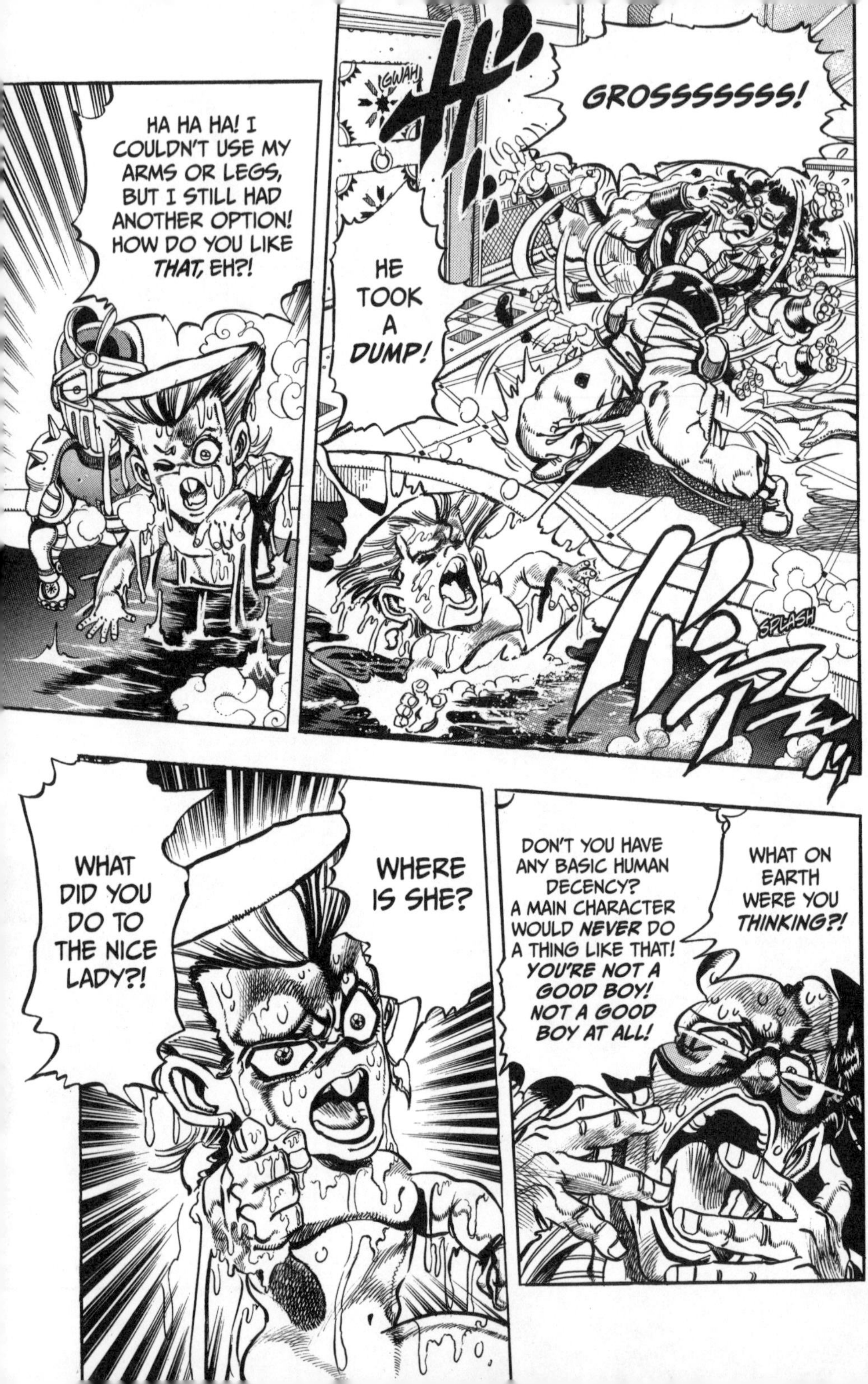
GWAH
GROSSSSSSS!
HE TOOK A DUMP!
SPLASH
HA HA HA! I COULDN'T USE MY ARMS OR LEGS, BUT I STILL HAD ANOTHER OPTION! HOW DO YOU LIKE THAT, EH?!
WHAT ON EARTH WERE YOU THINKING?!
DON'T YOU HAVE ANY BASIC HUMAN DECENCY? A MAIN CHARACTER WOULD NEVER DO A THING LIKE THAT! YOU'RE NOT A GOOD BOY! NOT A GOOD BOY AT ALL!
WHERE IS SHE?
WHAT DID YOU DO TO THE NICE LADY?!

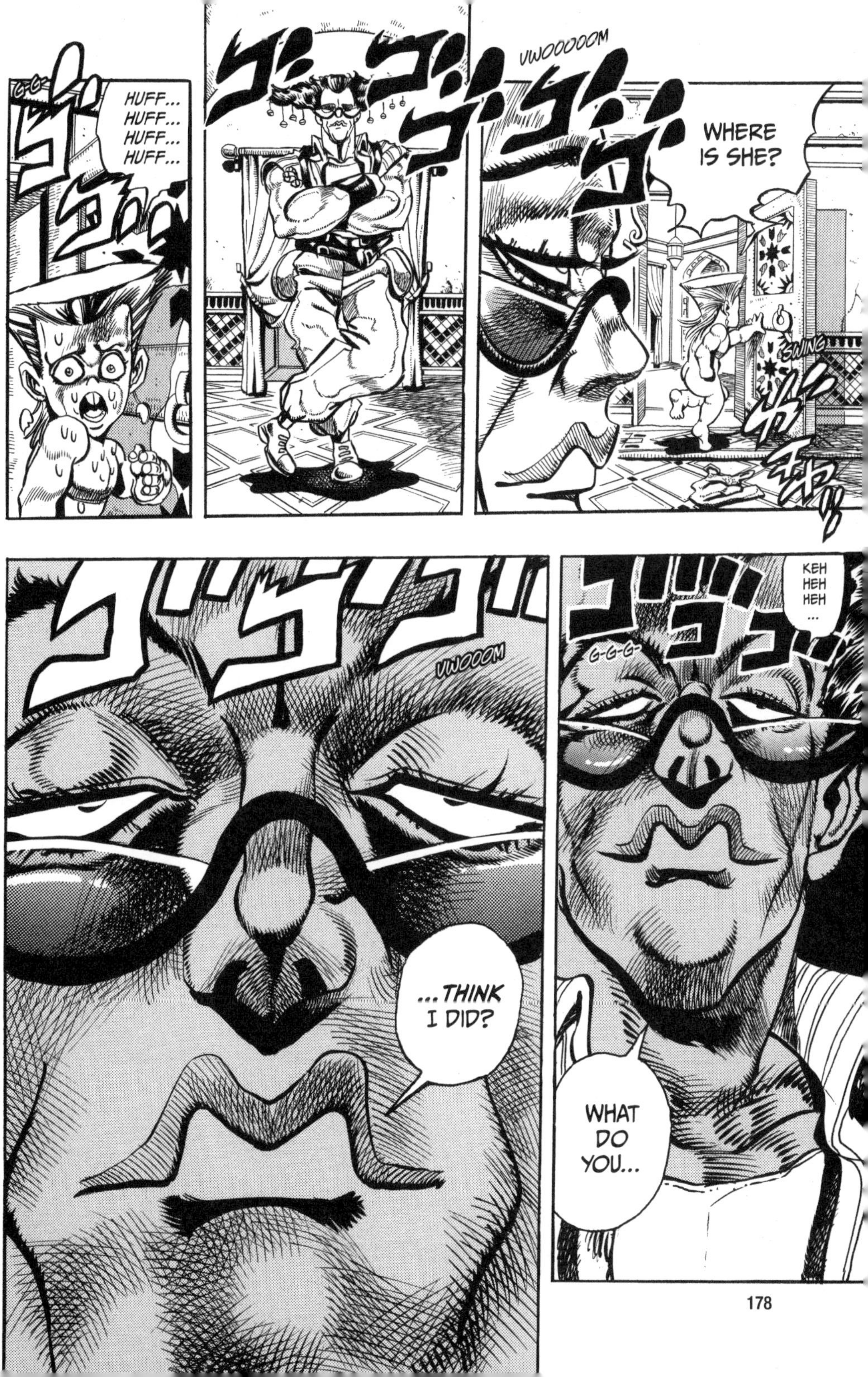
VWOOOOOM
WHERE IS SHE?
SWING
HUFF... HUFF... HUFF... HUFF...
KEH HEH HEH ...
G-G-G-
WHAT DO YOU...
VWOOOM
...THINK I DID?

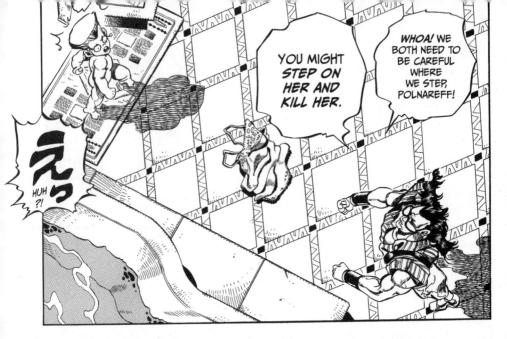

WHOA! WE BOTH NEED TO BE CAREFUL WHERE WE STEP, POLNAREFF!

YOU MIGHT **STEP ON HER** AND **KILL HER.**

えっ
HUH ?!

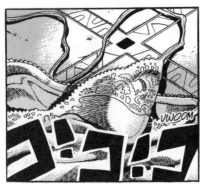

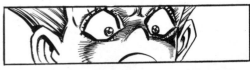

...

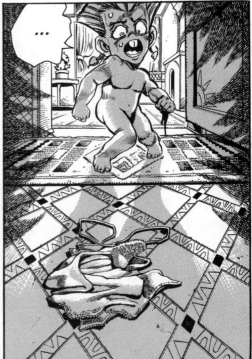

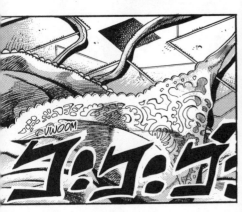

179

VWOOOOM
UGH...
UGH... UGH...
UGH.
WIGGLE
WIGGLE
WIGGLE
WIGGLE
UGH... UGH...
UGH...
UGH... UGH...
WIGGLE
WIGGLE
N...NO WAY...
TH...THIS CAN'T BE HAPPENING...

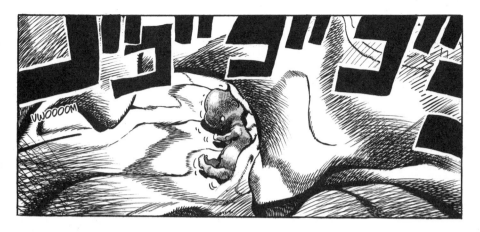

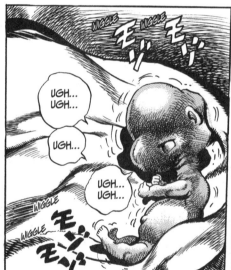

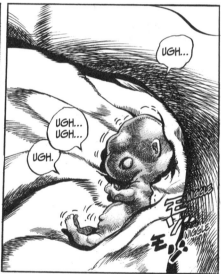

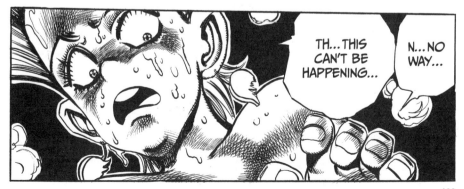

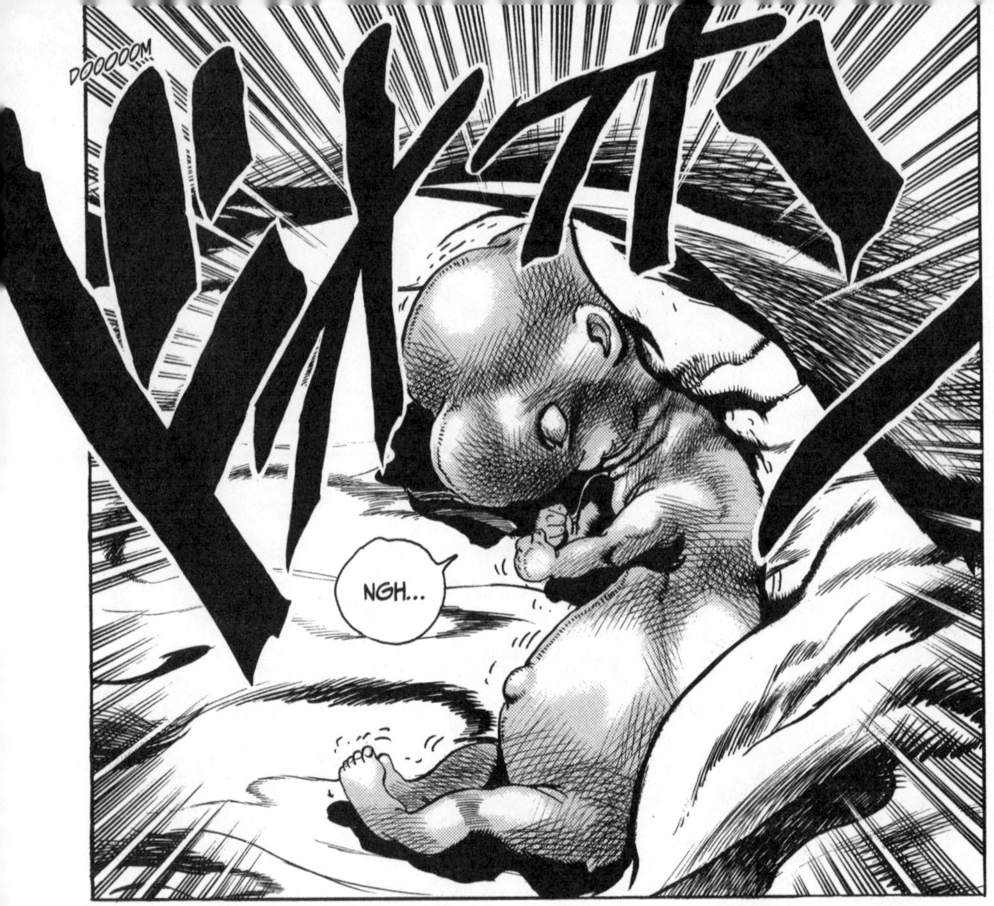
DOOOOOM
NGH...

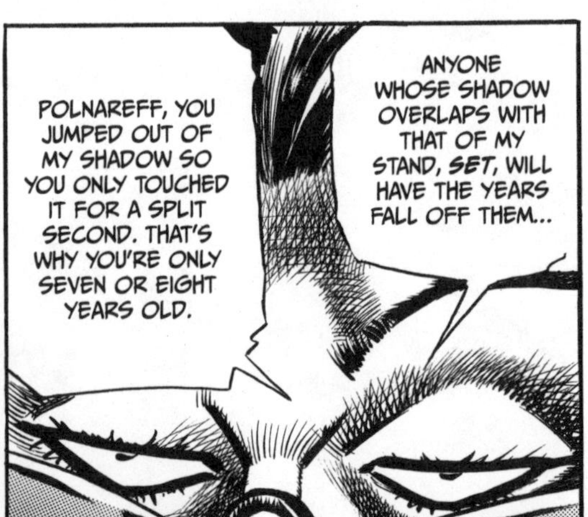
ANYONE WHOSE SHADOW OVERLAPS WITH THAT OF MY STAND, *SET*, WILL HAVE THE YEARS FALL OFF THEM...
POLNAREFF, YOU JUMPED OUT OF MY SHADOW SO YOU ONLY TOUCHED IT FOR A SPLIT SECOND. THAT'S WHY YOU'RE ONLY SEVEN OR EIGHT YEARS OLD.

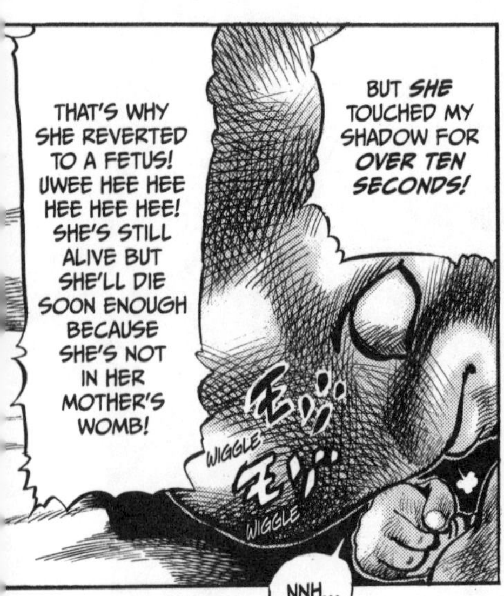
BUT ***SHE*** TOUCHED MY SHADOW FOR ***OVER TEN SECONDS!***
THAT'S WHY SHE REVERTED TO A FETUS! UWEE HEE HEE HEE HEE HEE! SHE'S STILL ALIVE BUT SHE'LL DIE SOON ENOUGH BECAUSE SHE'S NOT IN HER MOTHER'S WOMB!
WIGGLE
WIGGLE
NNH...

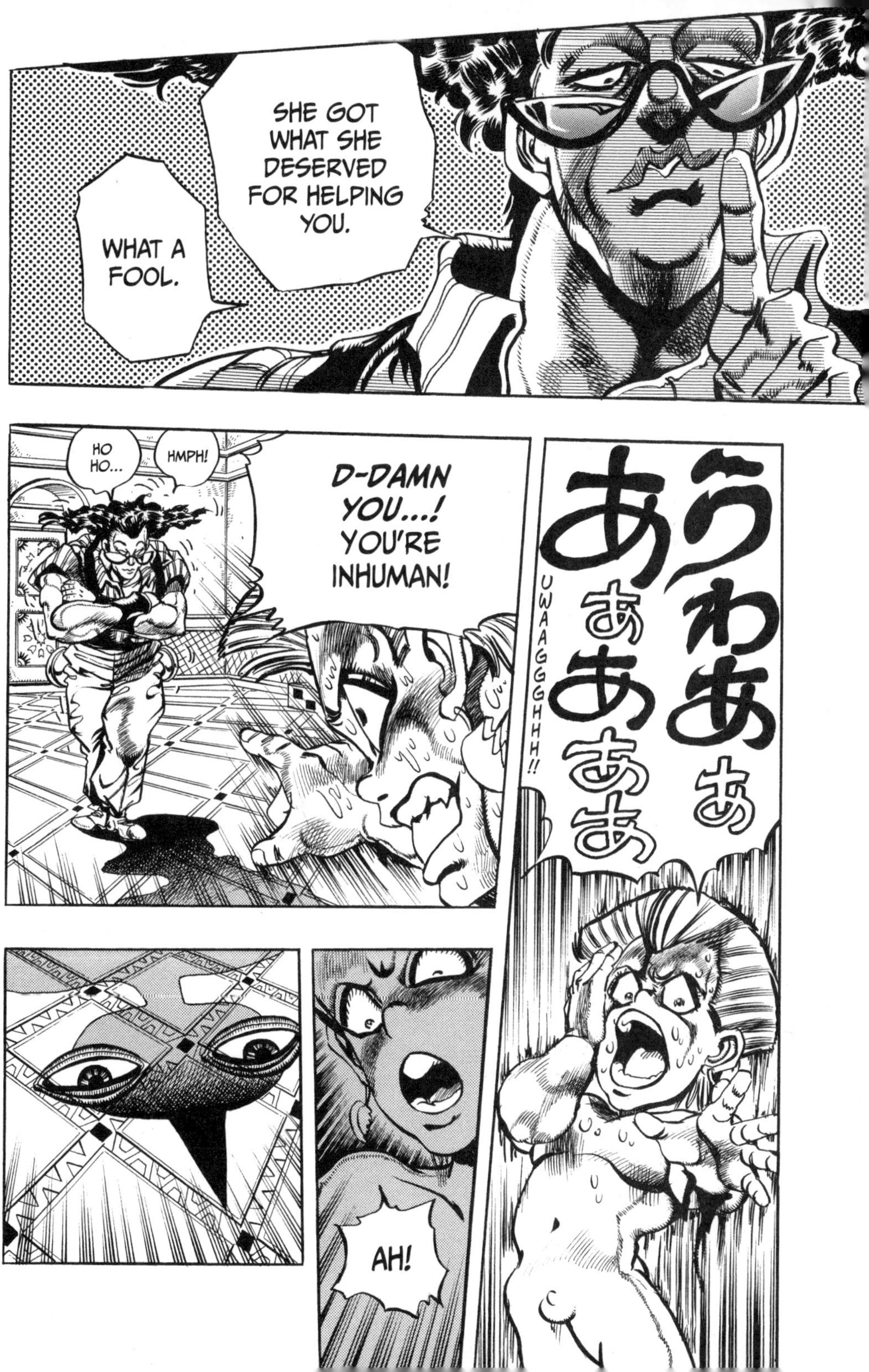
SHE GOT WHAT SHE DESERVED FOR HELPING YOU.
WHAT A FOOL.
うわああああああ
UWAAAGGGHHH!!
D-DAMN YOU...! YOU'RE INHUMAN!
HO HO...
HMPH!
AH!

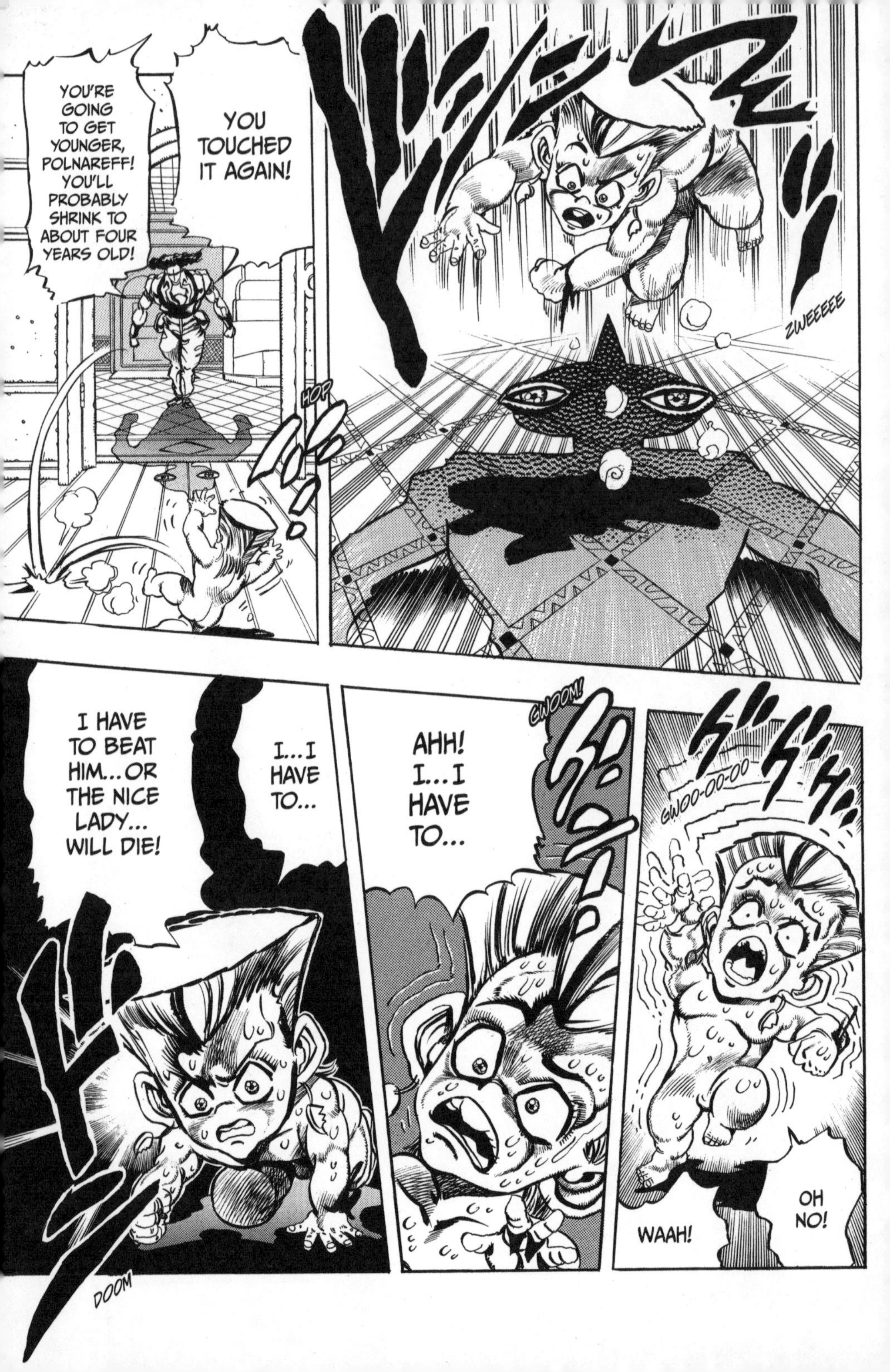
ZWEEEEE
YOU TOUCHED IT AGAIN!
YOU'RE GOING TO GET YOUNGER, POLNAREFF! YOU'LL PROBABLY SHRINK TO ABOUT FOUR YEARS OLD!
HOP
GWOO-OO-OO
OH NO!
WAAH!
CWOOM!
AHH! I...I HAVE TO...
I...I HAVE TO...
I HAVE TO BEAT HIM...OR THE NICE LADY... WILL DIE!
DOOM

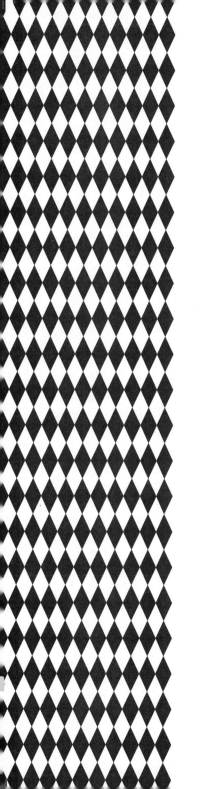

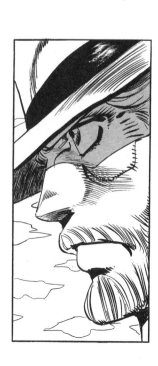

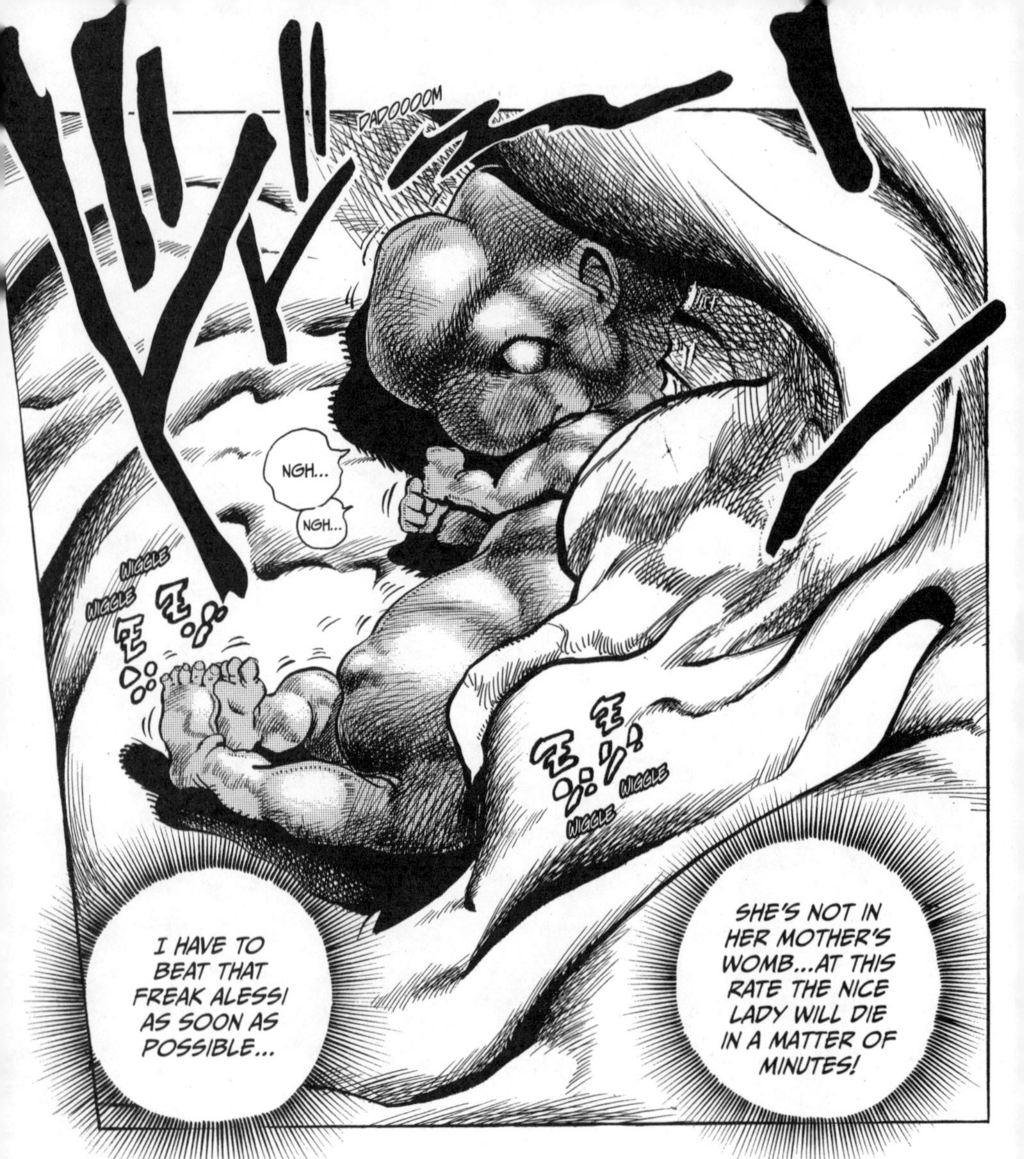
DADOOOOM
NGH...
NGH...
WIGGLE WIGGLE
WIGGLE WIGGLE
SHE'S NOT IN HER MOTHER'S WOMB...AT THIS RATE THE NICE LADY WILL DIE IN A MATTER OF MINUTES!
I HAVE TO BEAT THAT FREAK ALESSI AS SOON AS POSSIBLE...

CHAPTER 95: "Set" Alessi PART 4

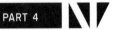

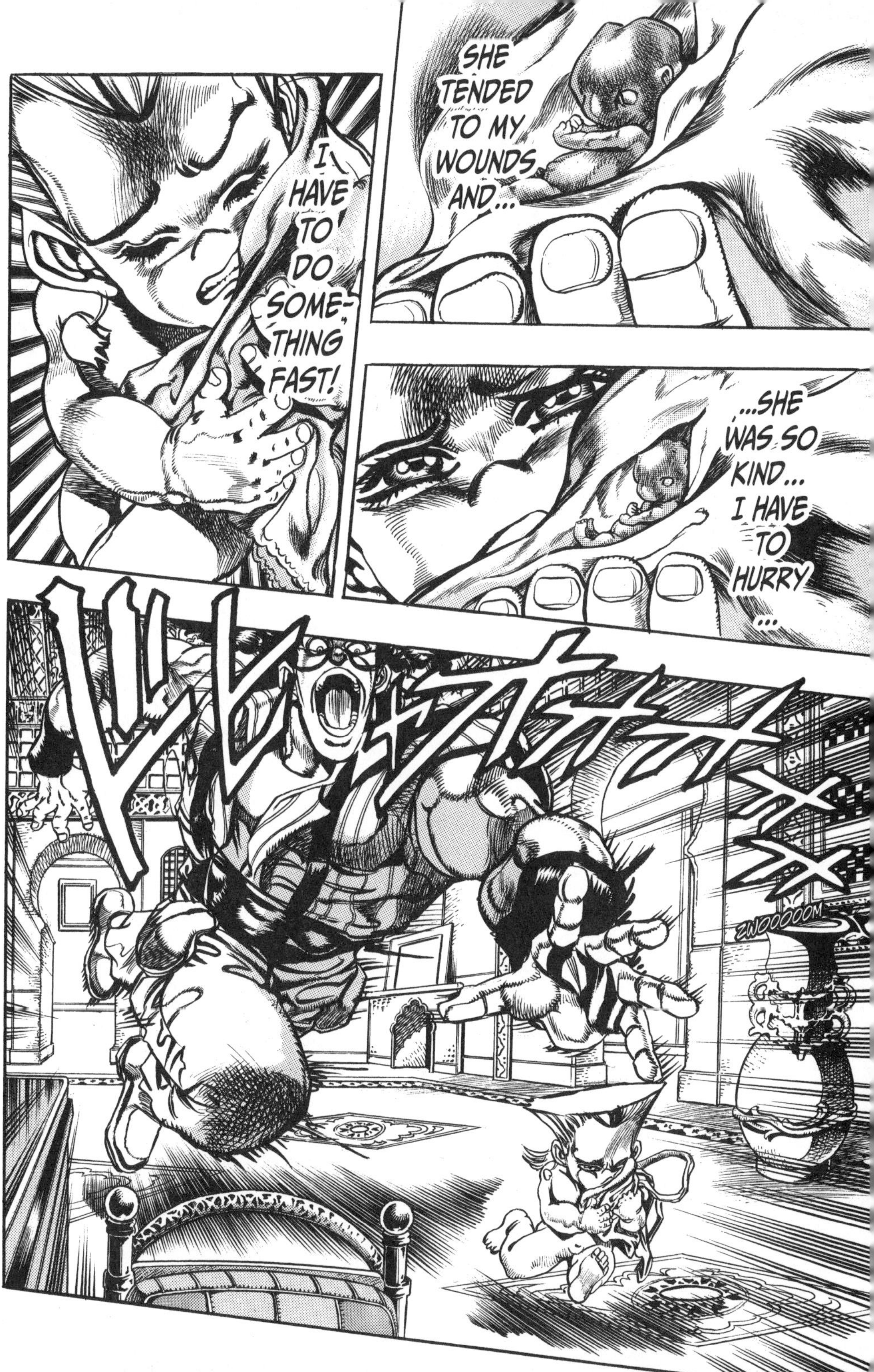
SHE TENDED TO MY WOUNDS AND...
...SHE WAS SO KIND... I HAVE TO HURRY...
I HAVE TO DO SOME-THING FAST!
ZWOOOOOM

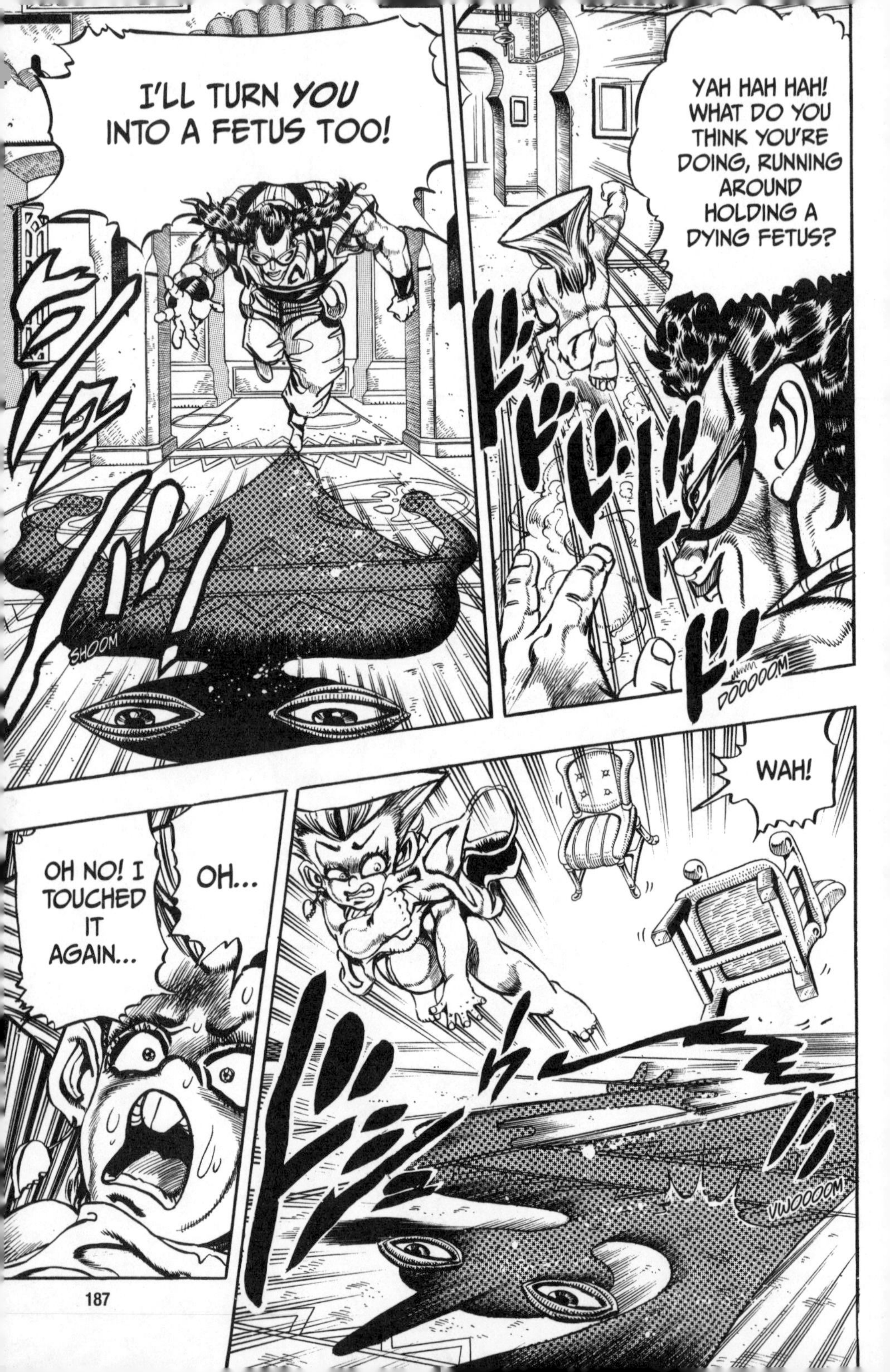
YAH HAH HAH! WHAT DO YOU THINK YOU'RE DOING, RUNNING AROUND HOLDING A DYING FETUS?
DOOOOOM
I'LL TURN *YOU* INTO A FETUS TOO!
SHOOM
WAH!
VWOOOOM
OH...
OH NO! I TOUCHED IT AGAIN...

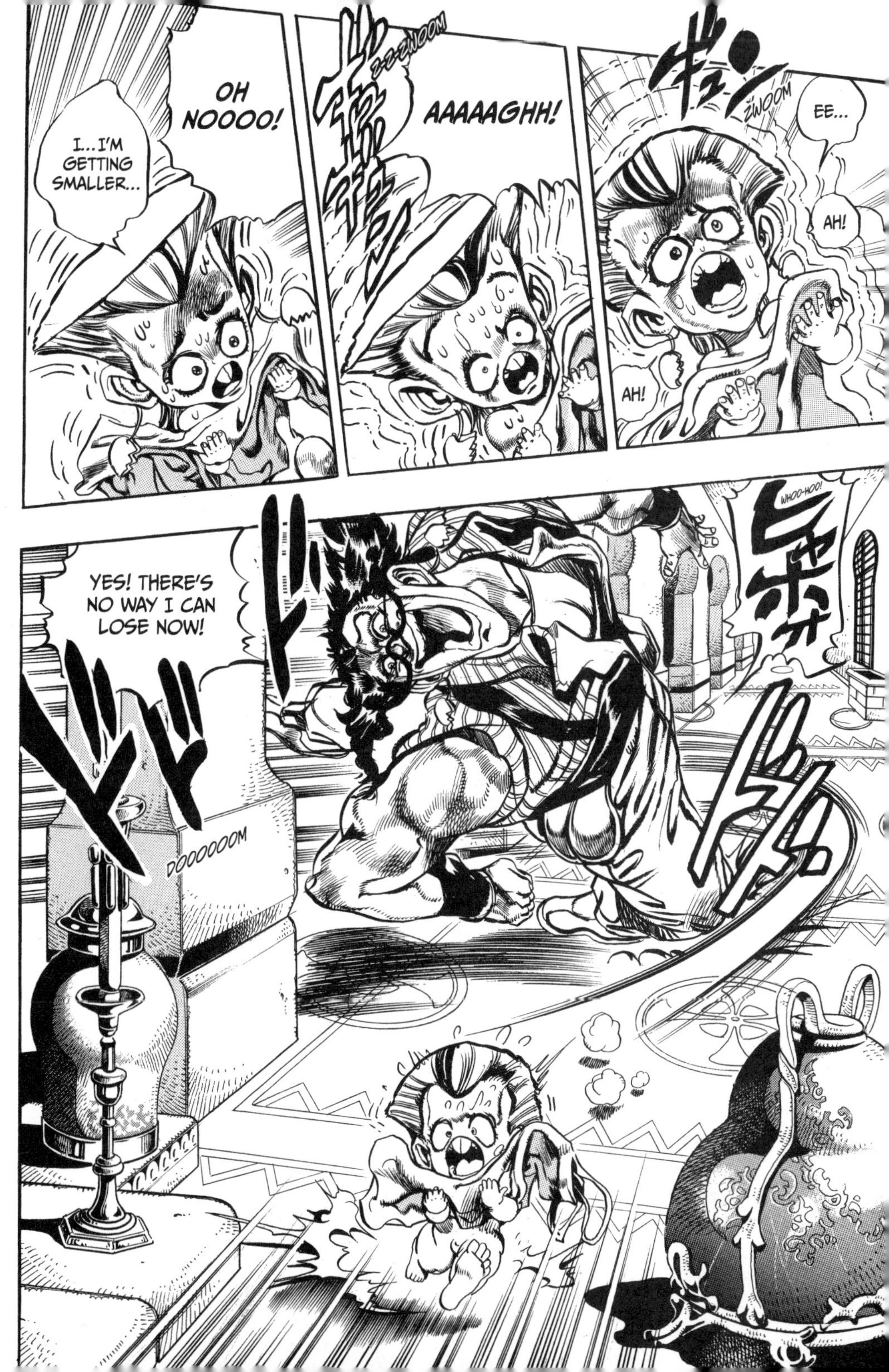
ZWOOM
EE...
AH!
AH!
Z-Z-ZWOOM
AAAAAGHH!
OH NOOOO!
I...I'M GETTING SMALLER...
WHOO-HOO!
YES! THERE'S NO WAY I CAN LOSE NOW!
DOOOOOOM

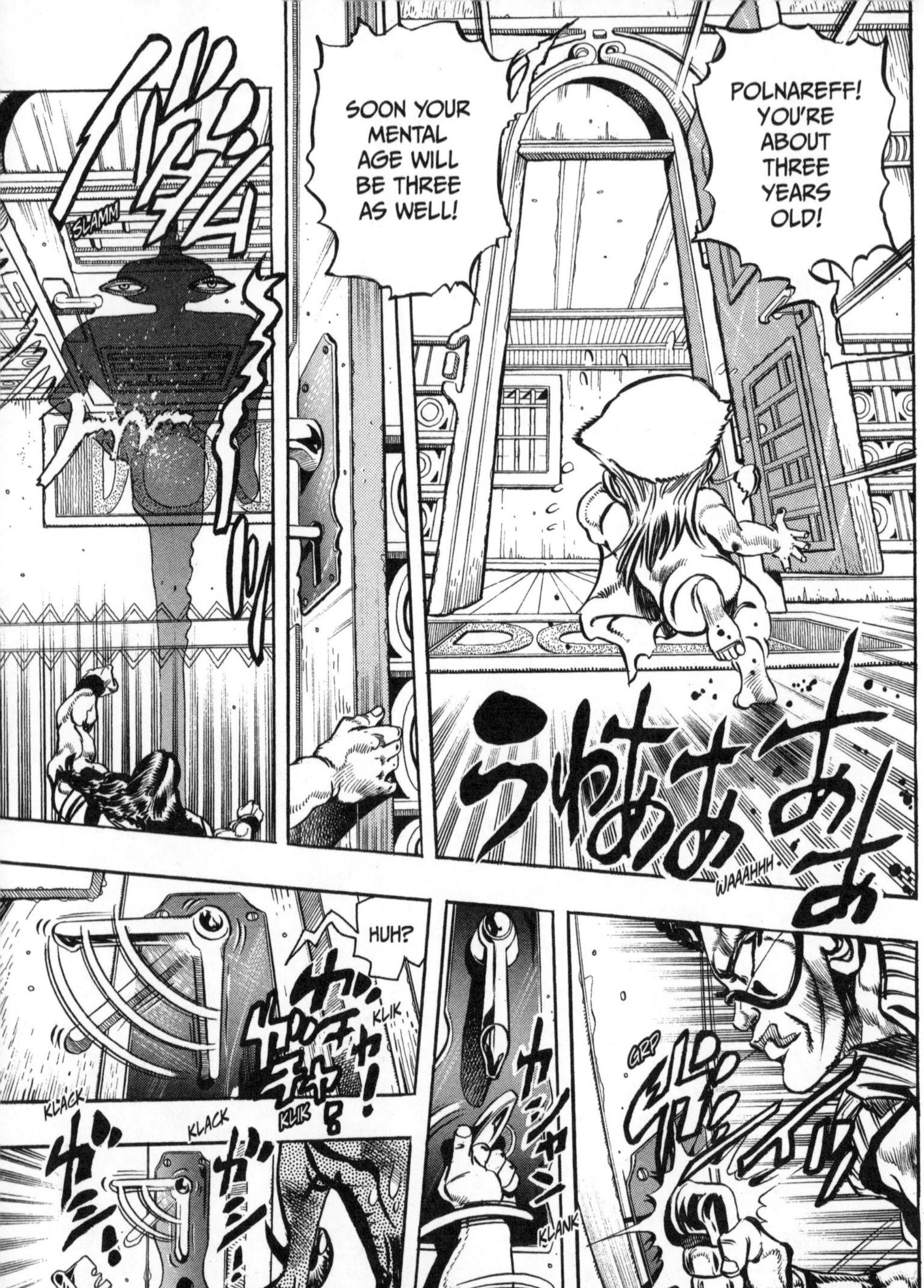
POLNAREFF! YOU'RE ABOUT THREE YEARS OLD!
SOON YOUR MENTAL AGE WILL BE THREE AS WELL!
WAAAHHH
SLAMM
GRP
KLANK
HUH?
KLIK
KLIK
KLACK
KLACK
HUFF HUFF
HUFF HUFF

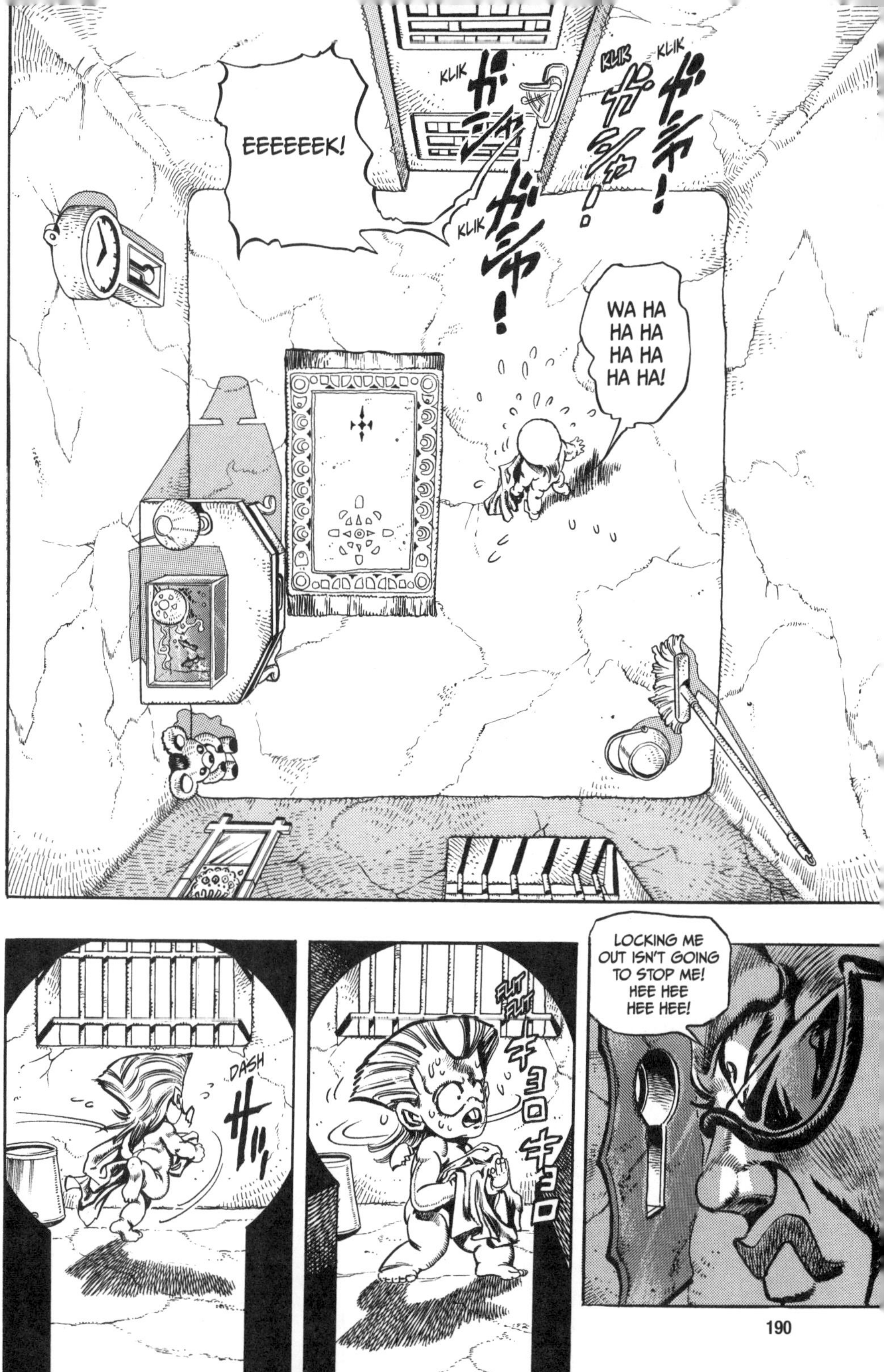
KLIK
KLIK
KLIK
KLIK
EEEEEEK!
WA HA HA HA HA HA HA HA!
LOCKING ME OUT ISN'T GOING TO STOP ME! HEE HEE HEE HEE!
FLIT FLIT
キョロキョロ
DASH
ザッ

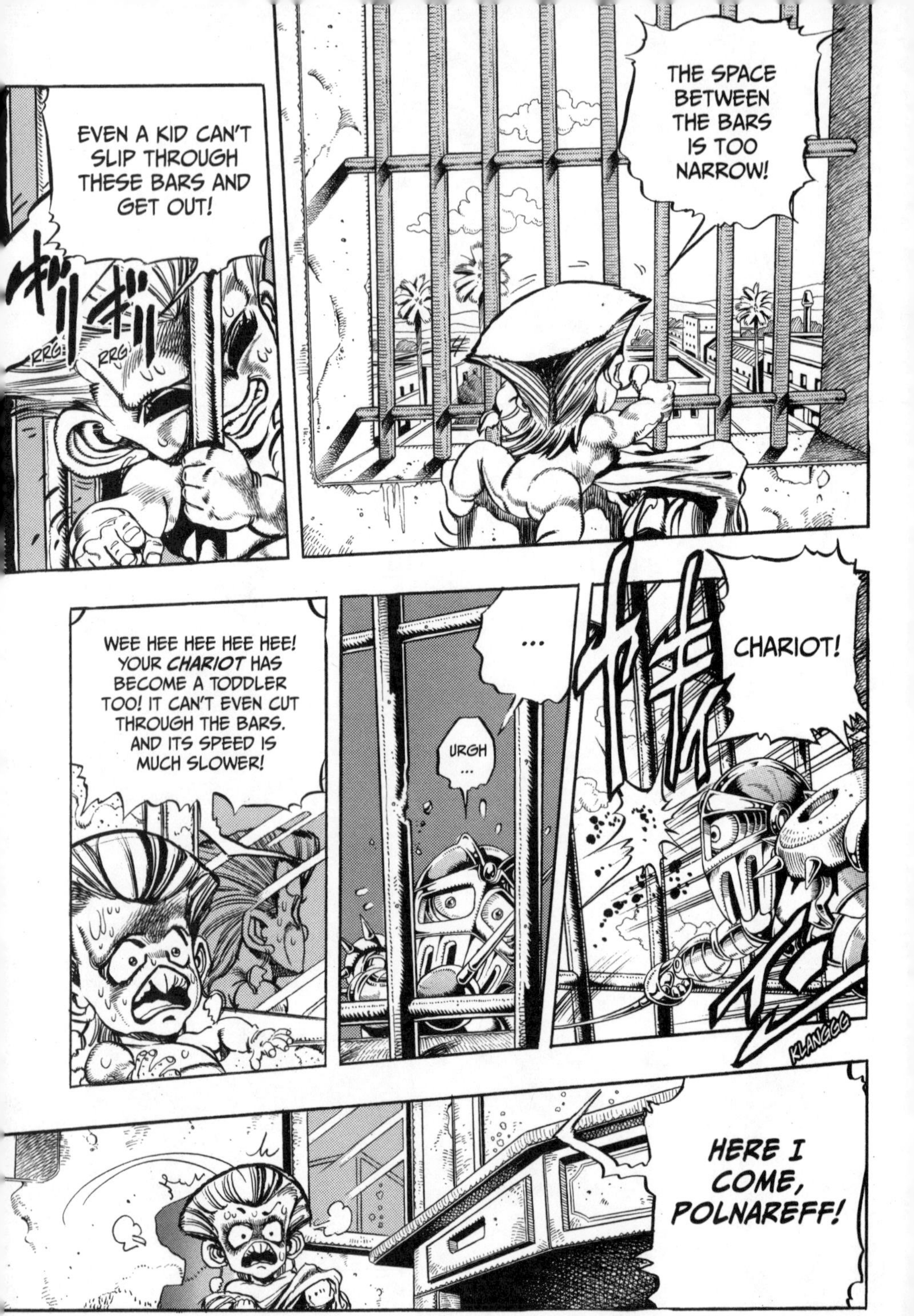
THE SPACE BETWEEN THE BARS IS TOO NARROW!
EVEN A KID CAN'T SLIP THROUGH THESE BARS AND GET OUT!
RRG
RRG
CHARIOT!
KLANGGG
...
URGH ...
WEE HEE HEE HEE HEE! YOUR *CHARIOT* HAS BECOME A TODDLER TOO! IT CAN'T EVEN CUT THROUGH THE BARS. AND ITS SPEED IS MUCH SLOWER!
HERE I COME, POLNAREFF!

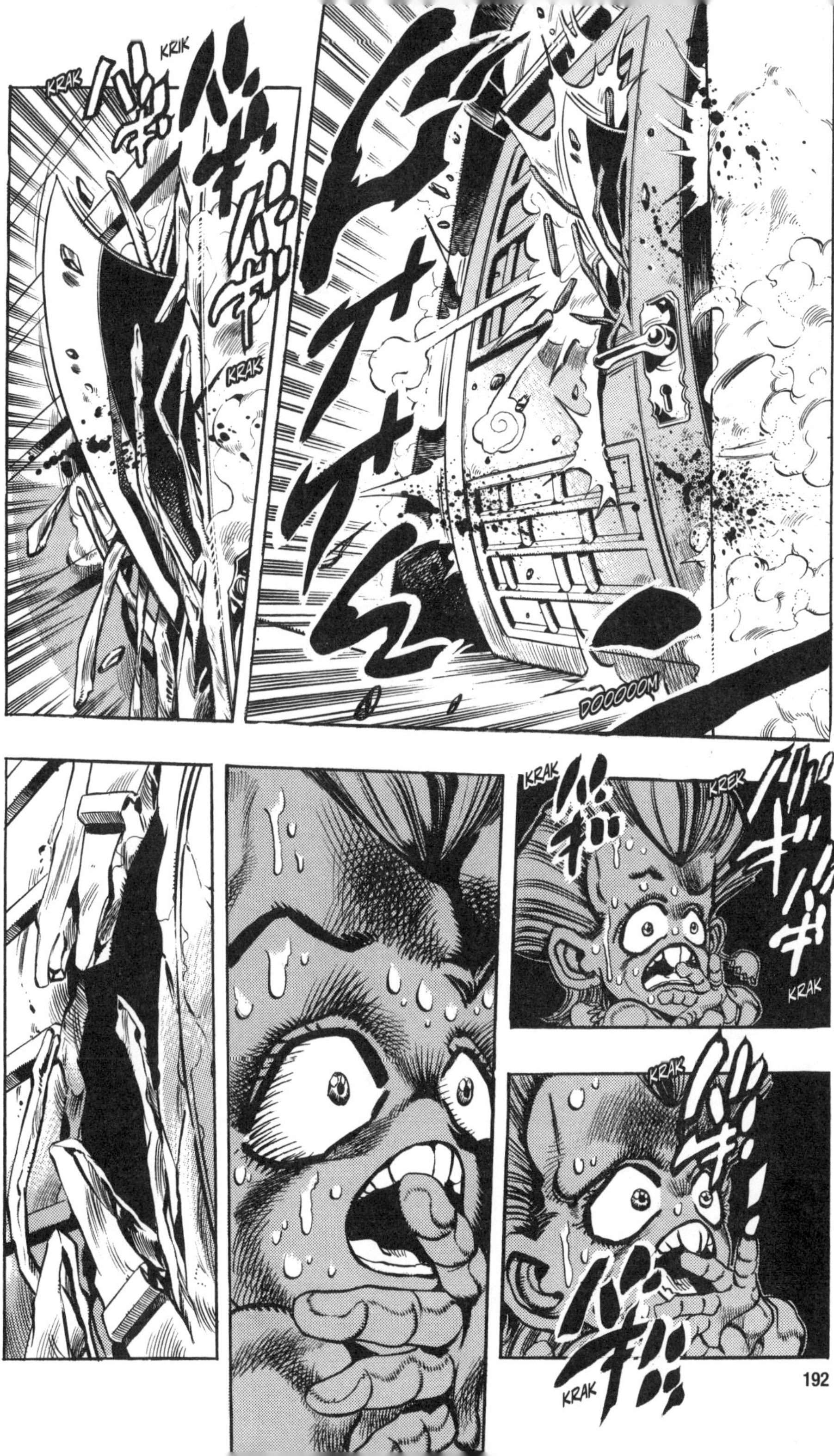
DOOOOOM
KRIK
KRAK
KRAK
KRAK
KREK
KRAK
KRAK
KRAK

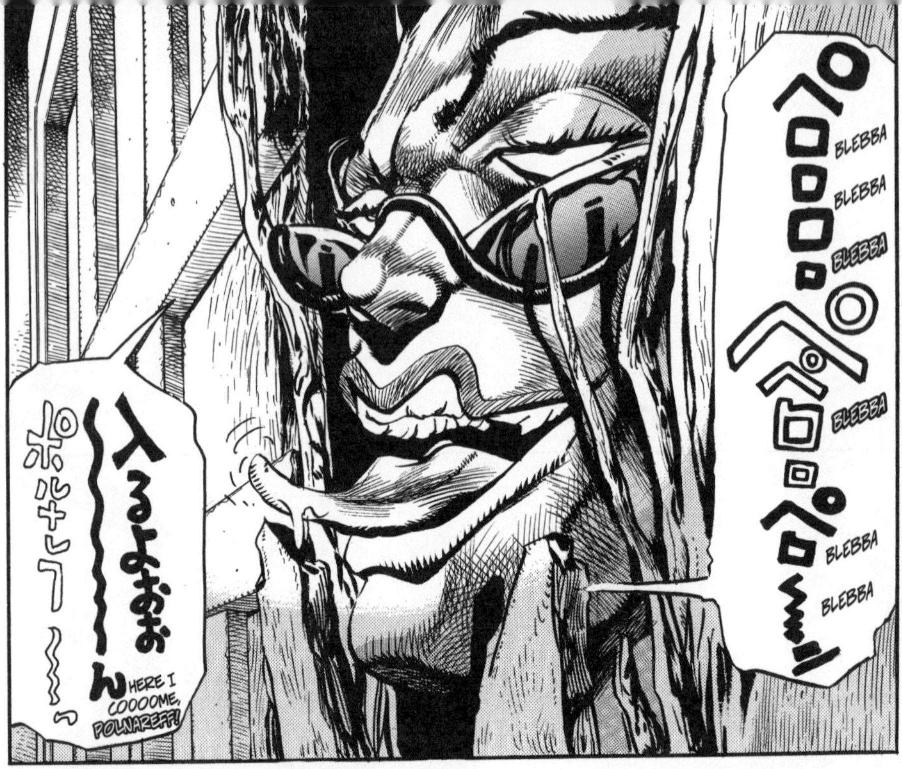
ペロロロロロ〜ペロペロペロ〜ッ
BLEBBA BLEBBA BLEBBA BLEBBA BLEBBA BLEBBA
入るよおお〜〜〜ん ポルナレフ〜〜〜
HERE I COOOOME, POLNAREFF!

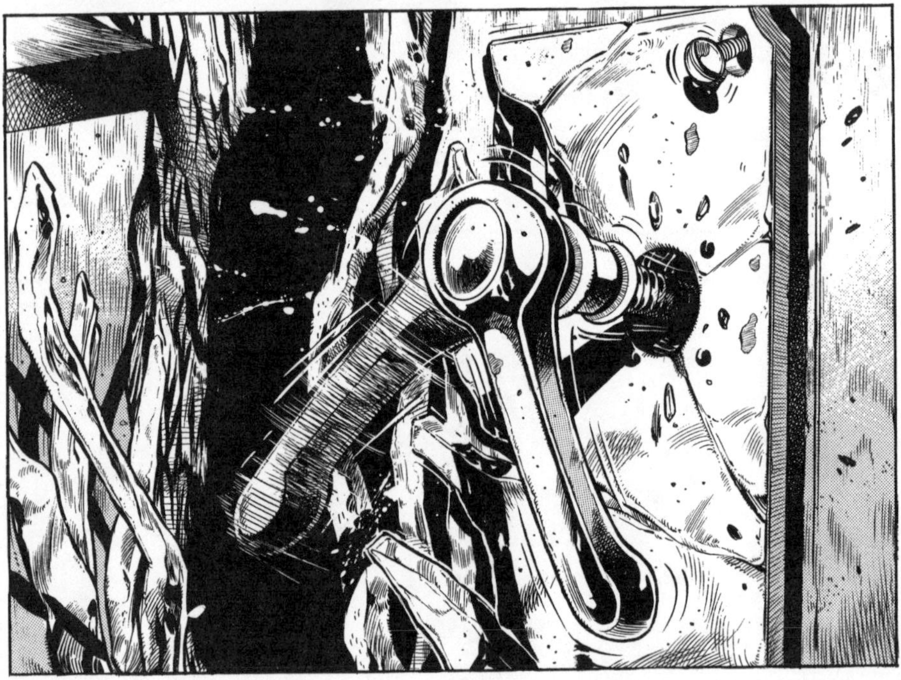

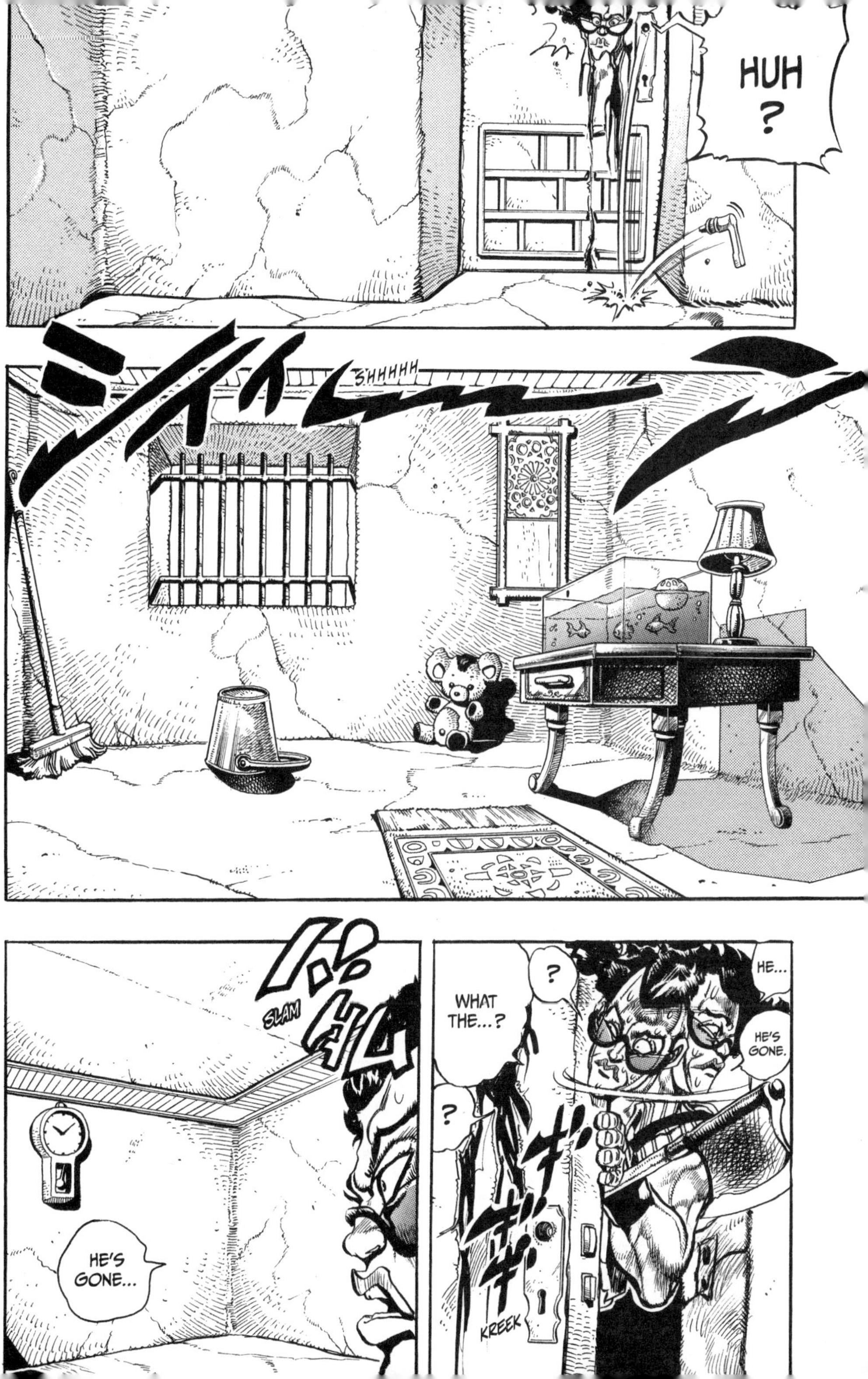
HUH ?
SHHHHH
HE...
HE'S GONE.
?
WHAT THE...?
?
KREEK
SLAM
HE'S GONE...

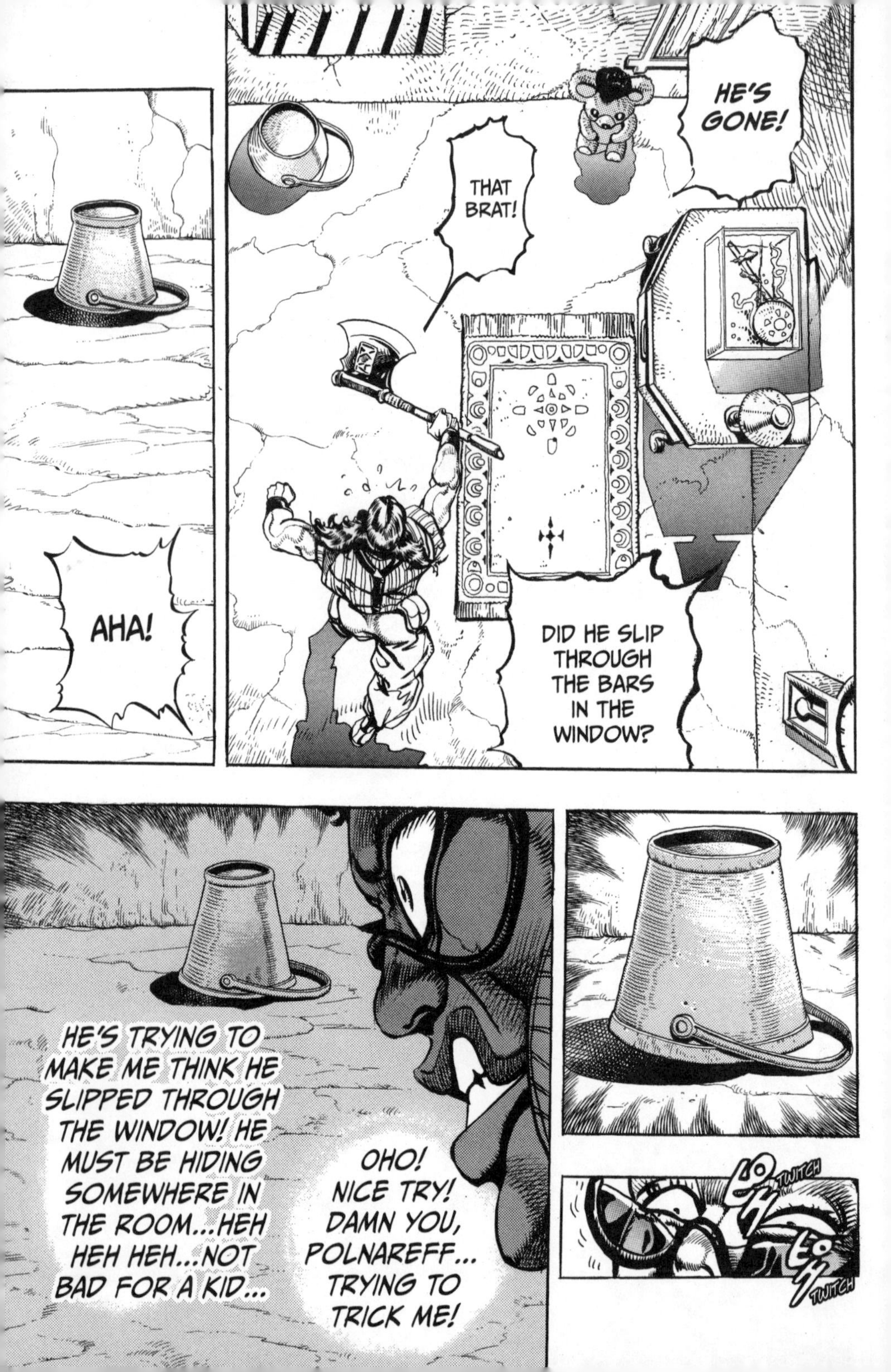
HE'S GONE!
THAT BRAT!
DID HE SLIP THROUGH THE BARS IN THE WINDOW?
AHA!
TWITCH TWITCH
OHO! NICE TRY! DAMN YOU, POLNAREFF... TRYING TO TRICK ME!
HE'S TRYING TO MAKE ME THINK HE SLIPPED THROUGH THE WINDOW! HE MUST BE HIDING SOMEWHERE IN THE ROOM...HEH HEH HEH...NOT BAD FOR A KID...

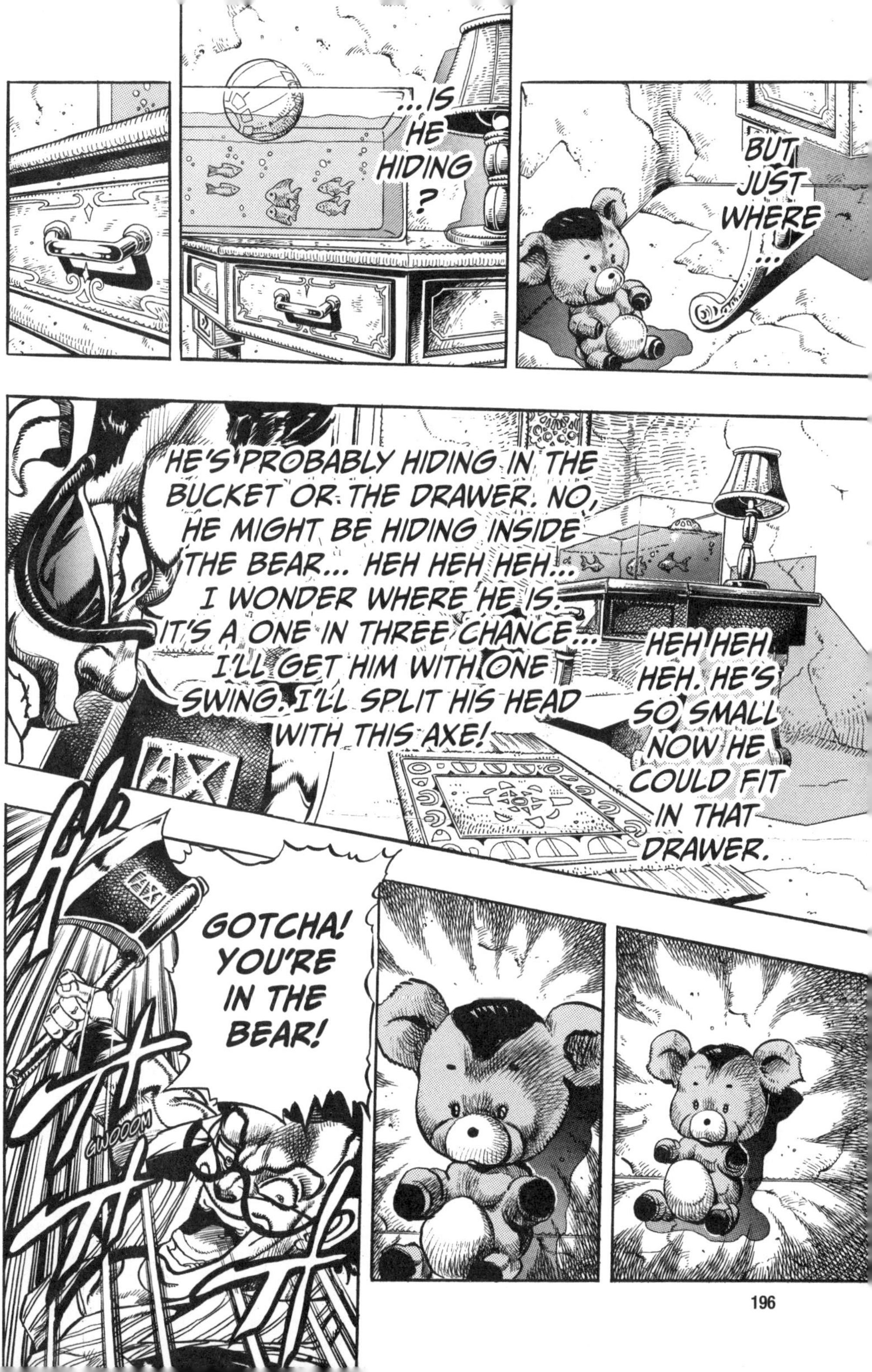
BUT JUST WHERE...
...IS HE HIDING?
HEH HEH HEH. HE'S SO SMALL NOW HE COULD FIT IN THAT DRAWER.
HE'S PROBABLY HIDING IN THE BUCKET OR THE DRAWER. NO, HE MIGHT BE HIDING INSIDE THE BEAR... HEH HEH HEH... I WONDER WHERE HE IS. IT'S A ONE IN THREE CHANCE... I'LL GET HIM WITH ONE SWING. I'LL SPLIT HIS HEAD WITH THIS AXE!
GOTCHA! YOU'RE IN THE BEAR!
GWOOOM

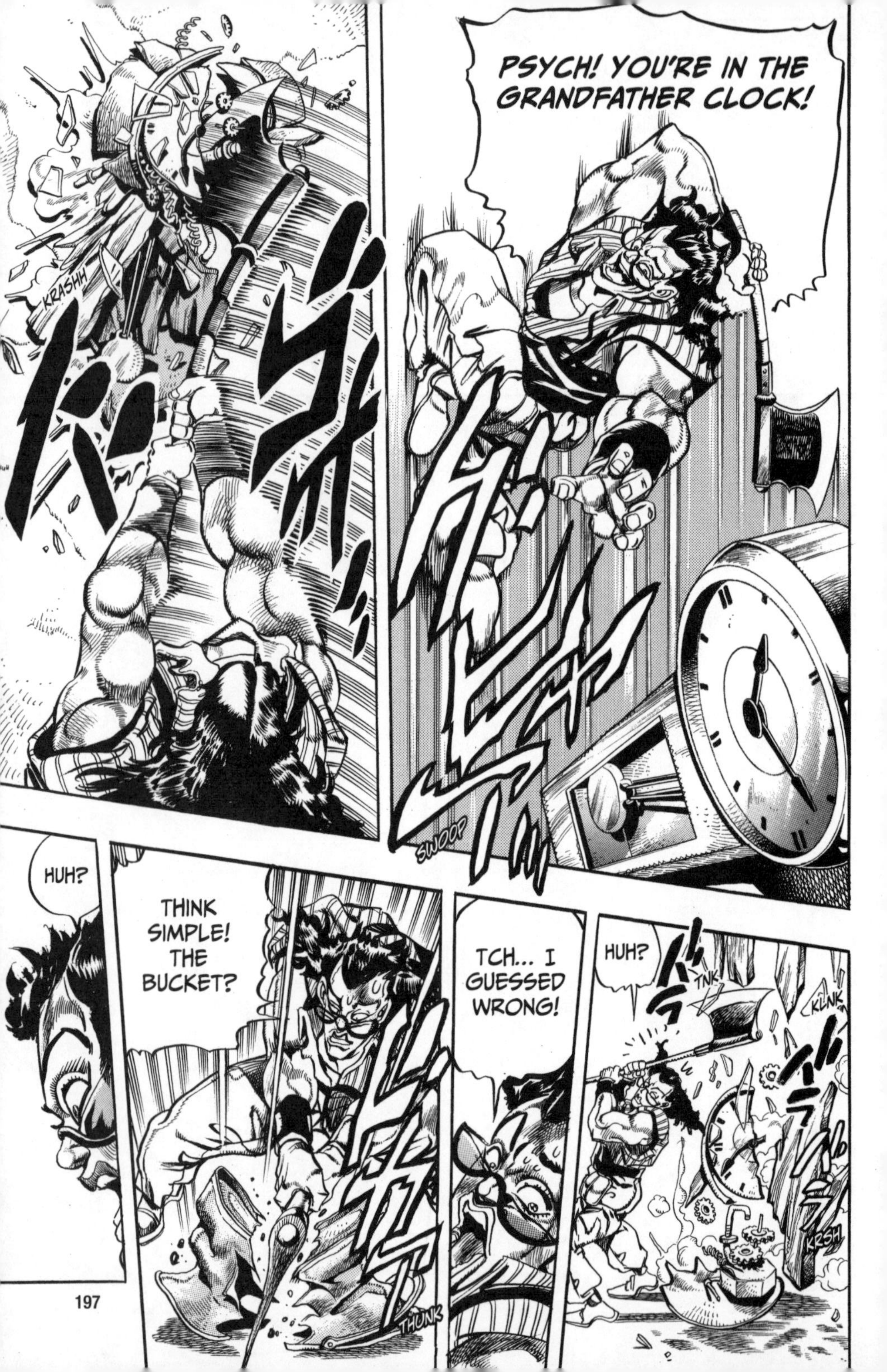
PSYCH! YOU'RE IN THE GRANDFATHER CLOCK!
SWOOP
KRASHH
HUH?
TNK
KLNK
KRSH
TCH... I GUESSED WRONG!
THINK SIMPLE! THE BUCKET?
THUNK
HUH?

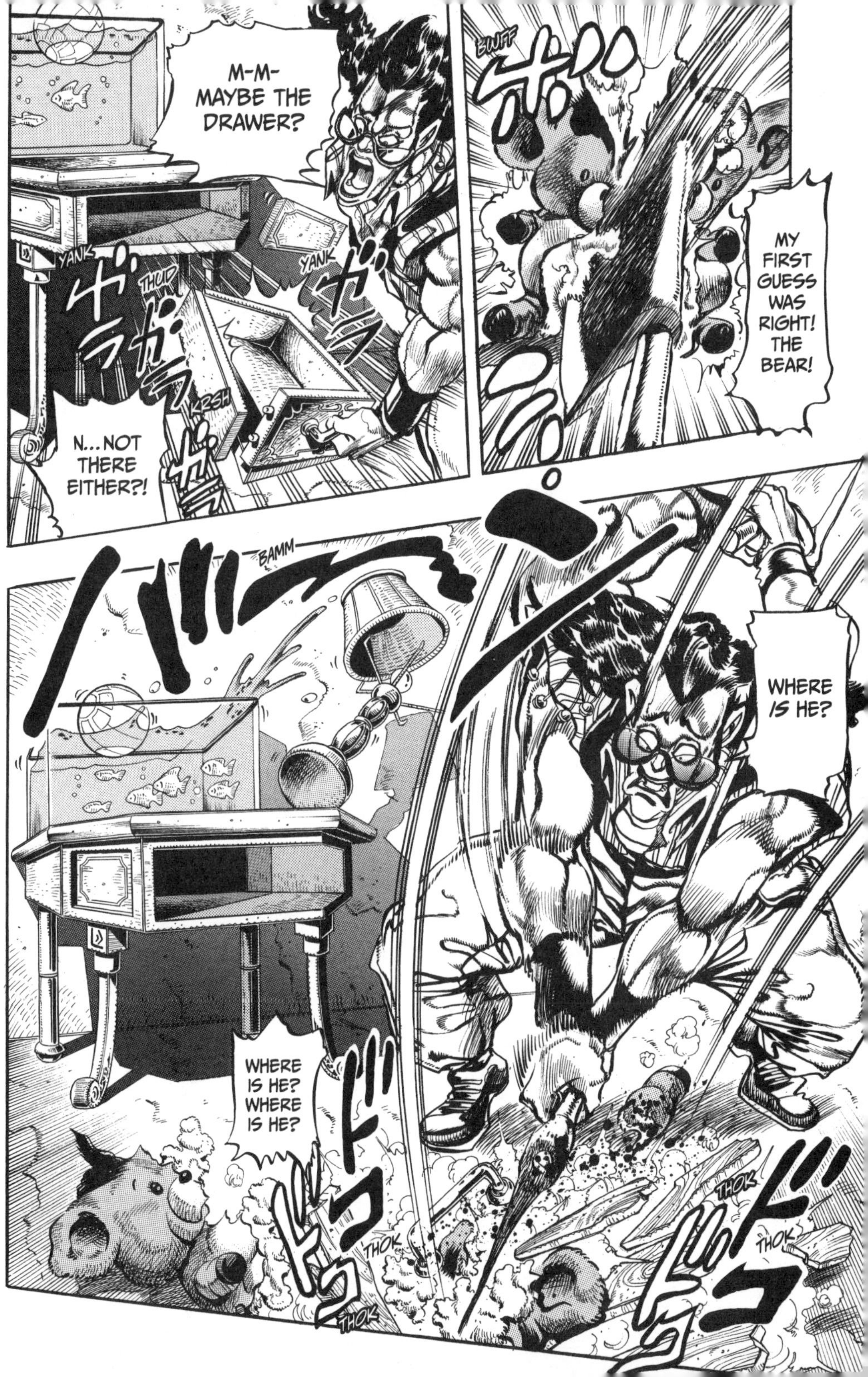

BWFF
MY FIRST GUESS WAS RIGHT! THE BEAR!
M-M-MAYBE THE DRAWER?
YANK
YANK
THUD
KRSH
N...NOT THERE EITHER?!
BAMM
WHERE IS HE?
THOK
THOK
WHERE IS HE? WHERE IS HE?
THOK
THOK

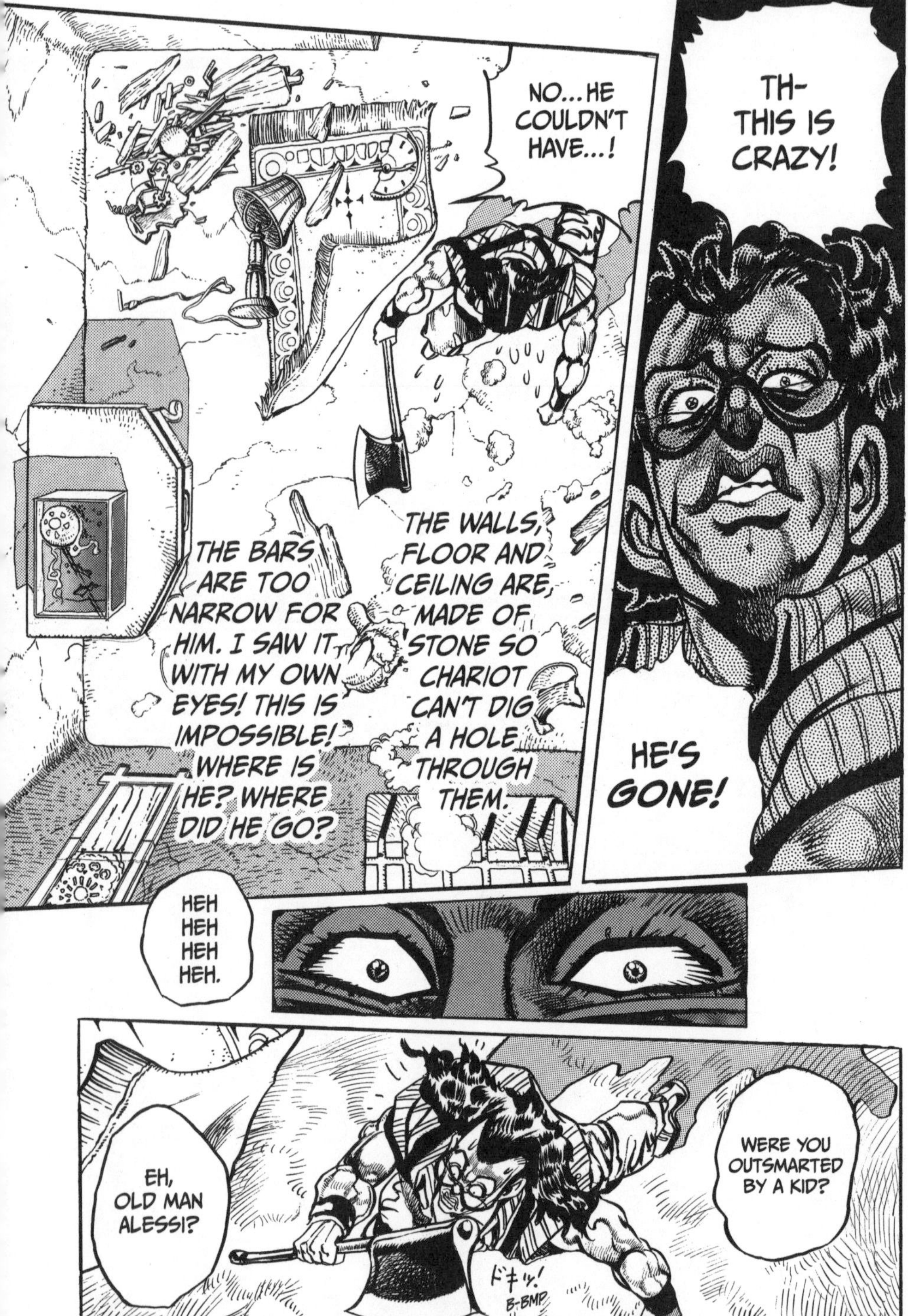
TH-THIS IS CRAZY!
HE'S GONE!
NO...HE COULDN'T HAVE...!
THE WALLS, FLOOR AND CEILING ARE MADE OF STONE SO CHARIOT CAN'T DIG A HOLE THROUGH THEM.
THE BARS ARE TOO NARROW FOR HIM. I SAW IT WITH MY OWN EYES! THIS IS IMPOSSIBLE! WHERE IS HE? WHERE DID HE GO?
HEH HEH HEH HEH.
WERE YOU OUTSMARTED BY A KID?
EH, OLD MAN ALESSI?
ドキッ!
B-BMP

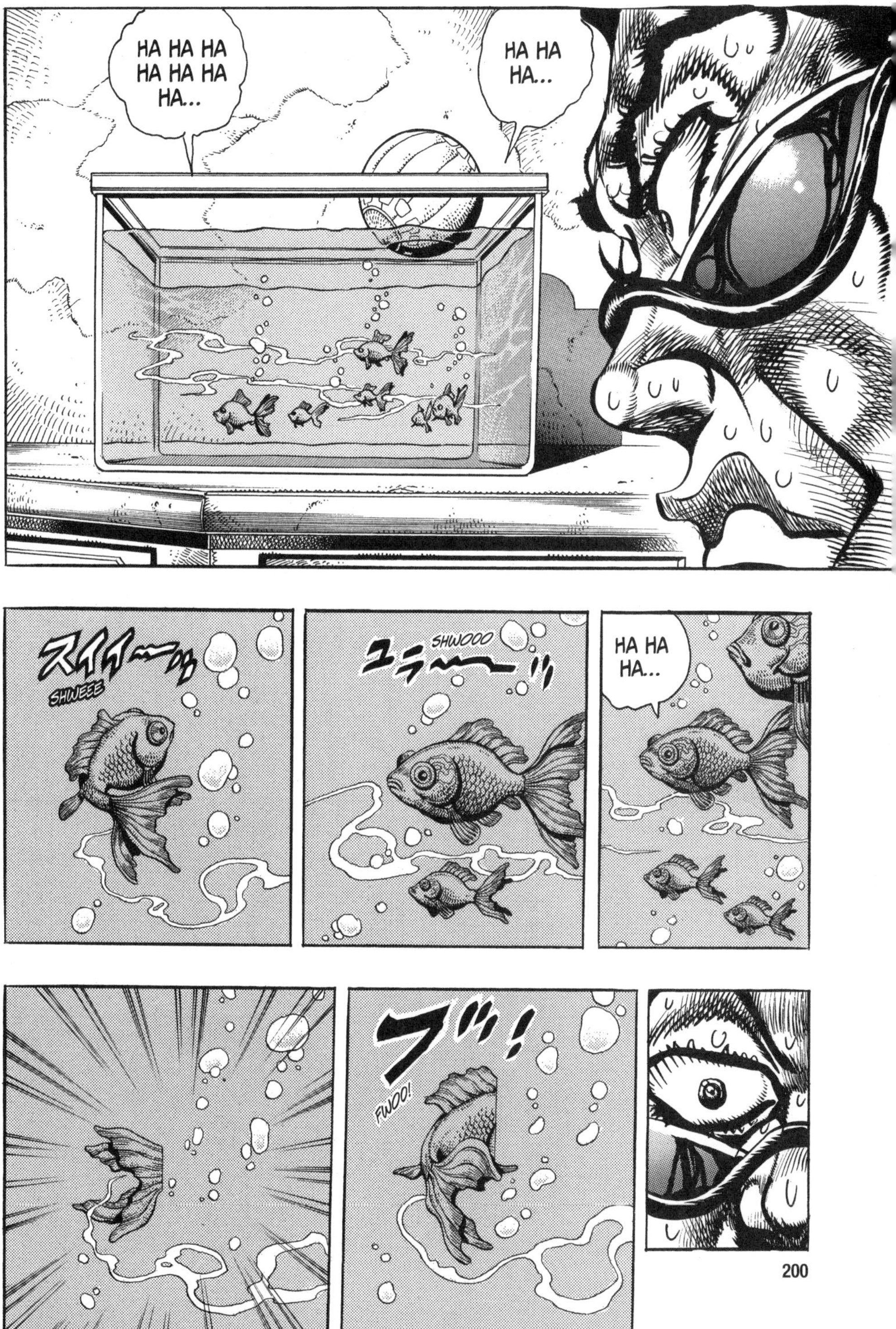
HA HA HA...
HA HA HA HA HA HA HA...
HA HA HA...
SHWOOO
SHWEEE
フッ!
FWOO!

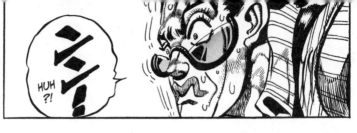

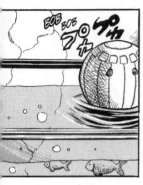

BOB BOB プゥ プゥゥ

ンシ！

HUH?!

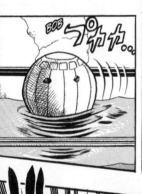

BOB プゥゥゥ...

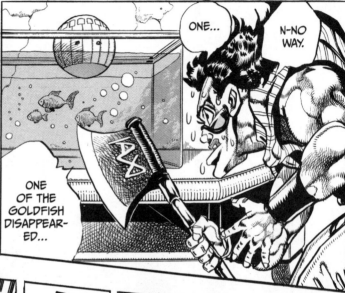

ONE...

N-NO WAY.

ONE OF THE GOLDFISH DISAPPEAR-ED...

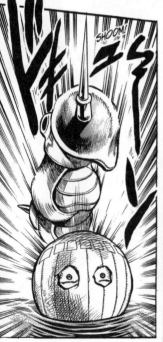

SHOOM!

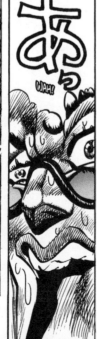

あっ

WAH!

コ

NGH?

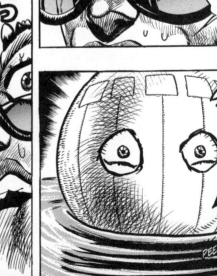

PEEK-A-BOO!

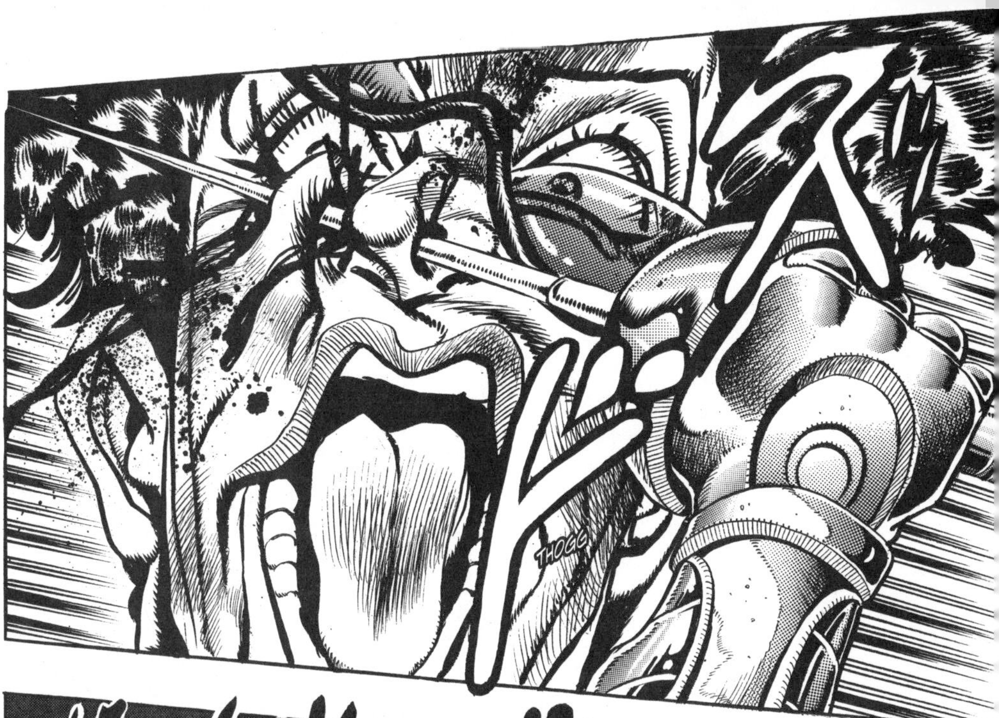
THOGG

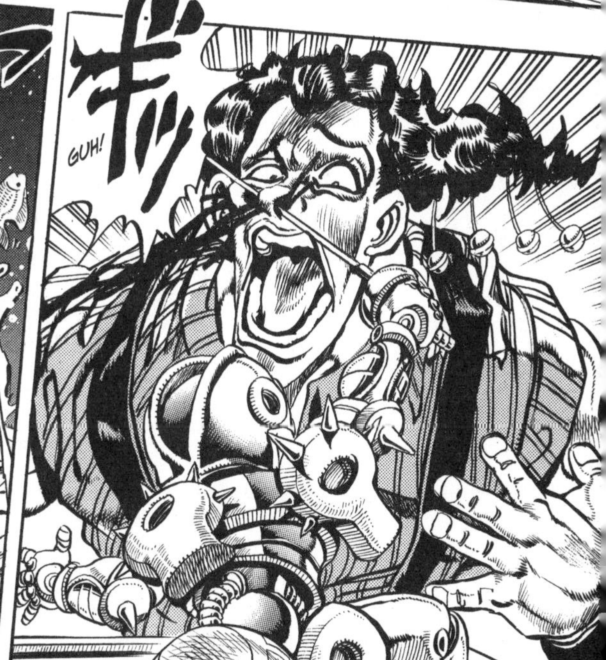
GUH!

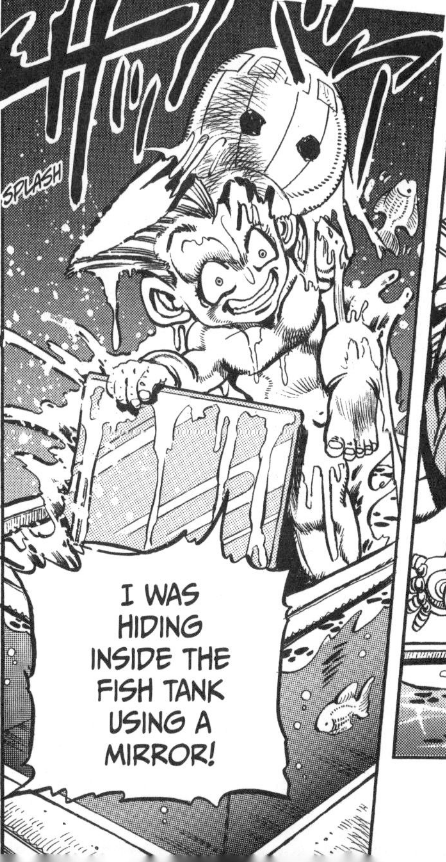
SPLASH
I WAS HIDING INSIDE THE FISH TANK USING A MIRROR!

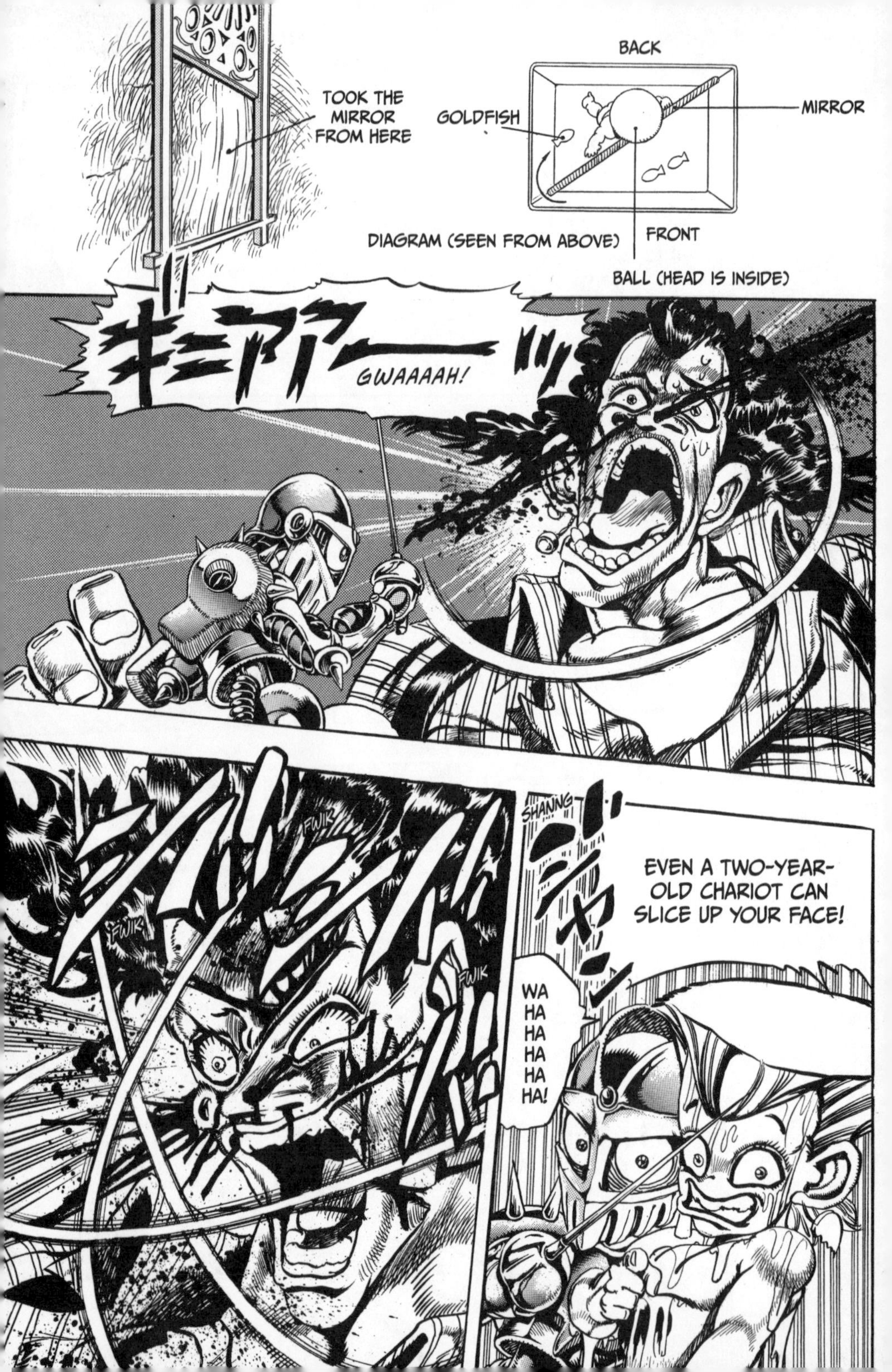
BACK
MIRROR
GOLDFISH
FRONT
DIAGRAM (SEEN FROM ABOVE)
BALL (HEAD IS INSIDE)
TOOK THE MIRROR FROM HERE
GWAAAAH!
SHANG
EVEN A TWO-YEAR-OLD CHARIOT CAN SLICE UP YOUR FACE!
WA HA HA HA HA HA!
FWIK
FWIK
FWIK

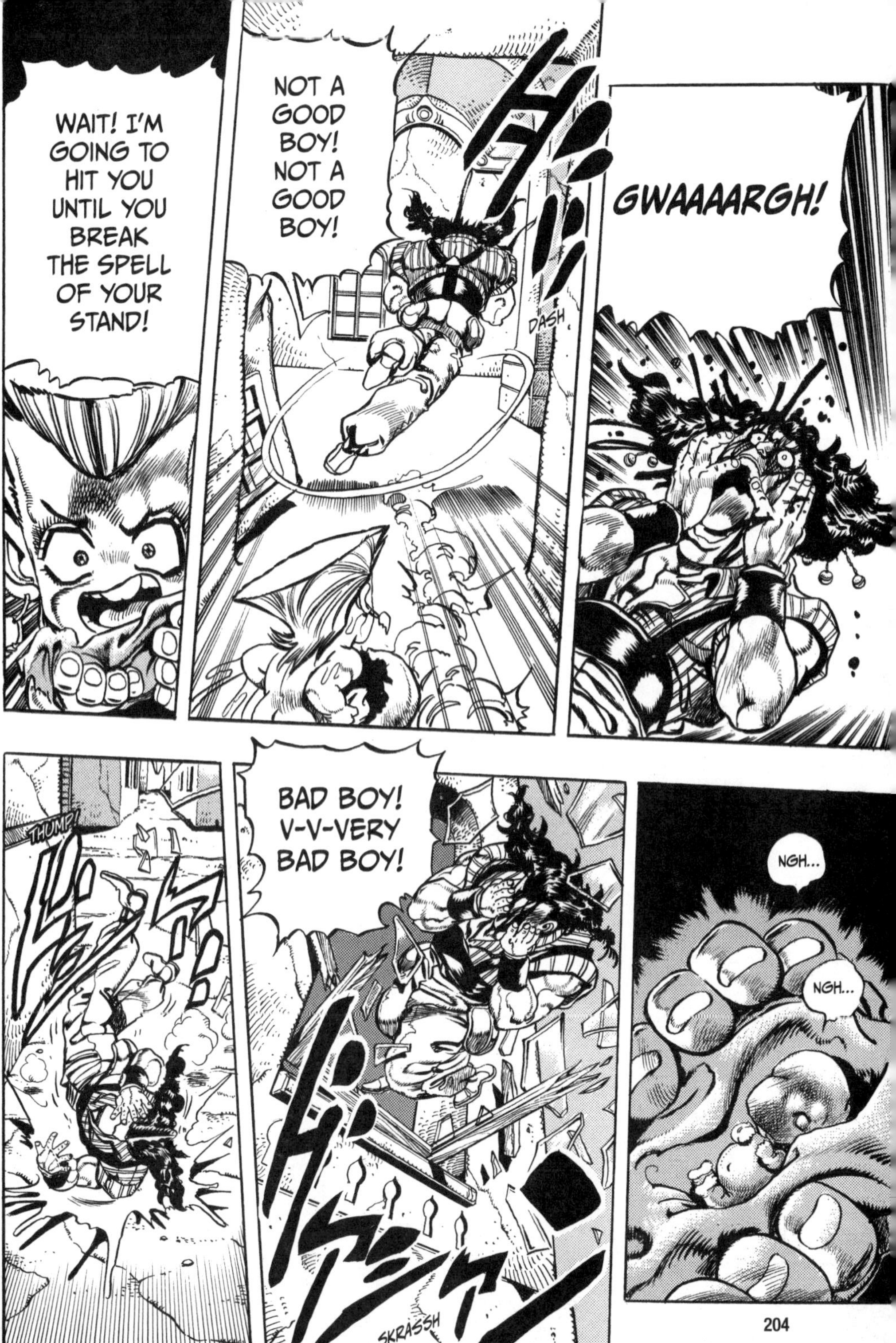
GWAAAARGH!
NOT A GOOD BOY! NOT A GOOD BOY!
DASH
WAIT! I'M GOING TO HIT YOU UNTIL YOU BREAK THE SPELL OF YOUR STAND!
NGH...
NGH...
BAD BOY! V-V-VERY BAD BOY!
SKRASSH
THUMP!

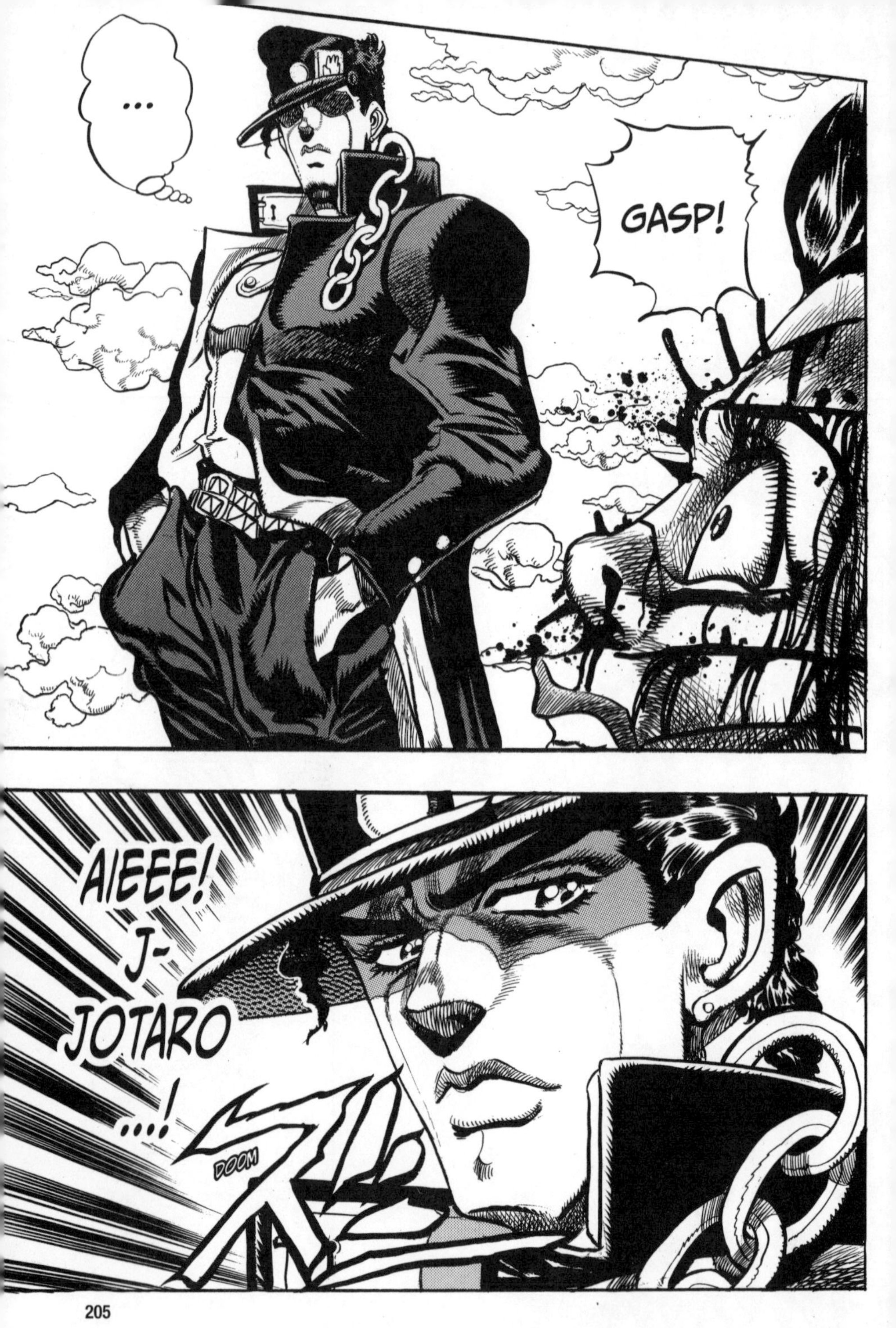
GASP!
...
AIEEE! J-JOTARO ...!
DOOM

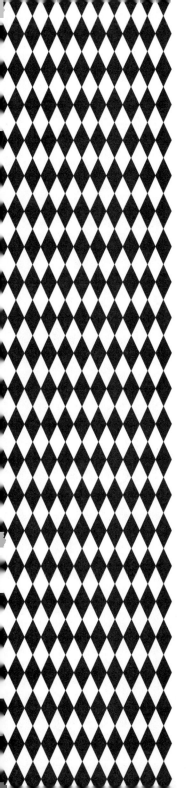
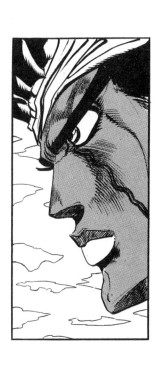

CHAPTER 96: "Set" Alessi PART 5

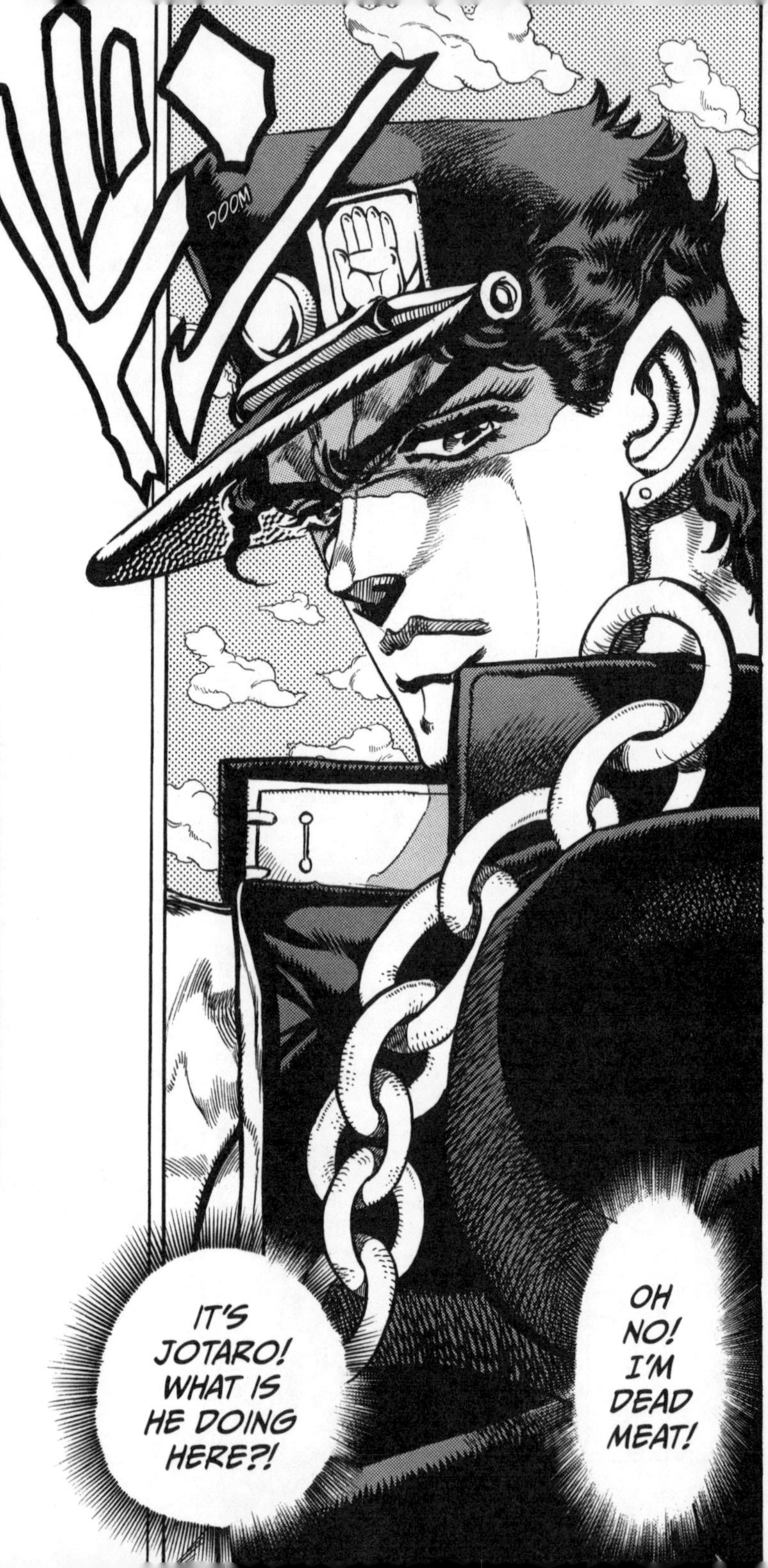

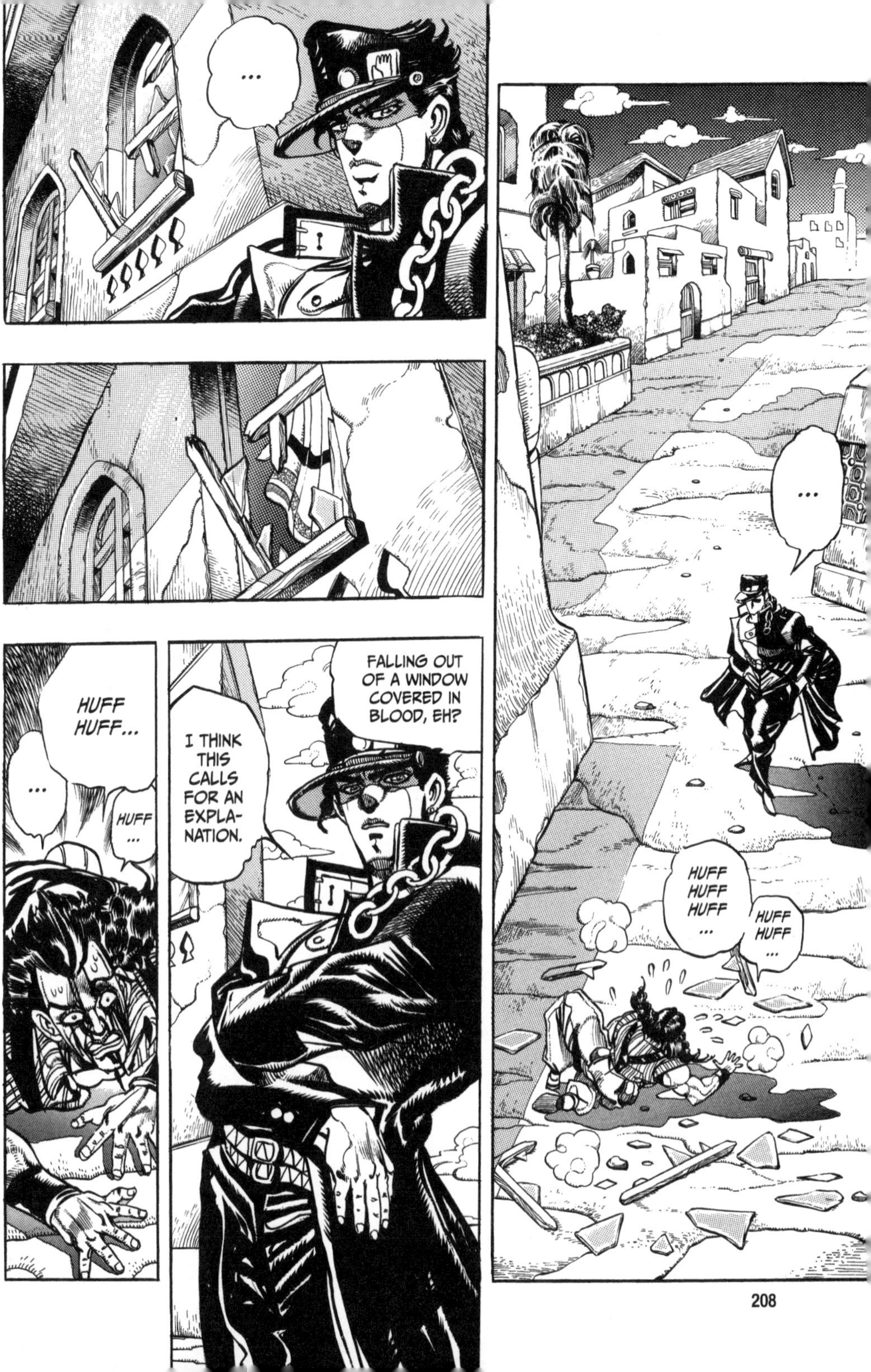
...
HUFF HUFF ...
HUFF HUFF HUFF ...
...
FALLING OUT OF A WINDOW COVERED IN BLOOD, EH?
I THINK THIS CALLS FOR AN EXPLANATION.
HUFF HUFF...
HUFF ...
...

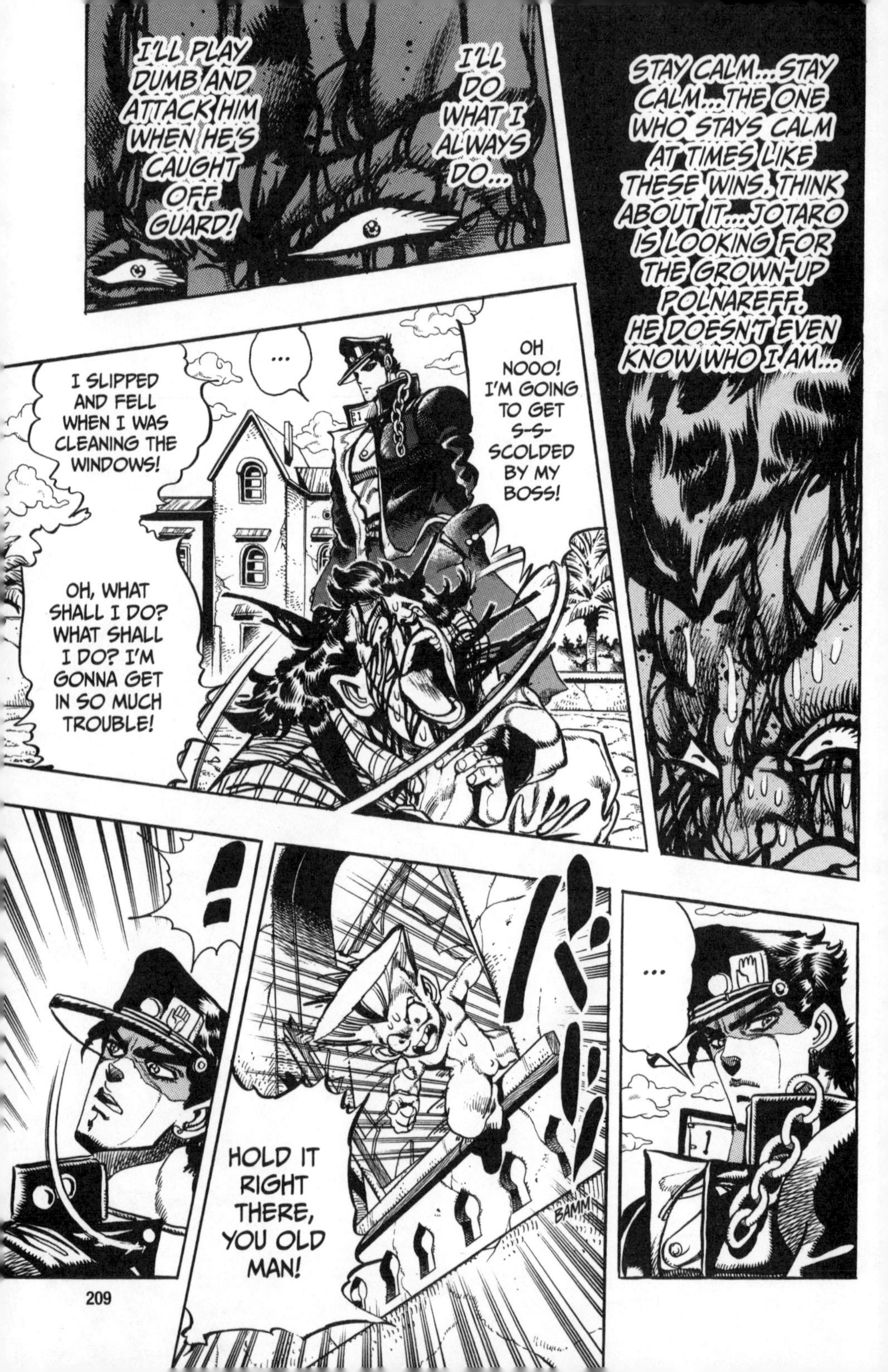
STAY CALM...STAY CALM...THE ONE WHO STAYS CALM AT TIMES LIKE THESE WINS. THINK ABOUT IT...JOTARO IS LOOKING FOR THE GROWN-UP POLNAREFF. HE DOESN'T EVEN KNOW WHO I AM...
I'LL DO WHAT I ALWAYS DO...
I'LL PLAY DUMB AND ATTACK HIM WHEN HE'S CAUGHT OFF GUARD!
OH NOOO! I'M GOING TO GET S-S-SCOLDED BY MY BOSS!
...
I SLIPPED AND FELL WHEN I WAS CLEANING THE WINDOWS!
OH, WHAT SHALL I DO? WHAT SHALL I DO? I'M GONNA GET IN SO MUCH TROUBLE!
...
BAMM
HOLD IT RIGHT THERE, YOU OLD MAN!
!

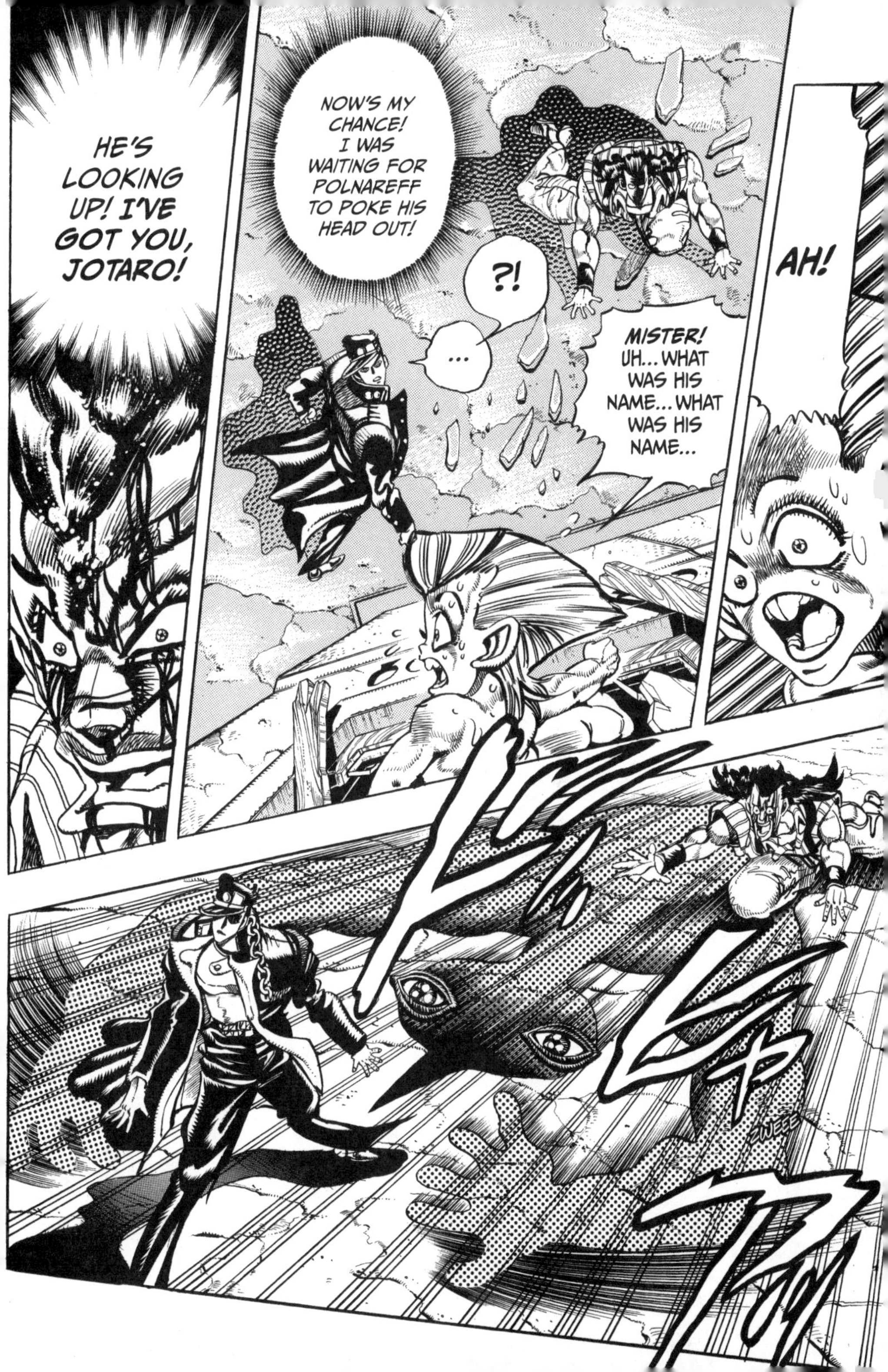
AH!
NOW'S MY CHANCE! I WAS WAITING FOR POLNAREFF TO POKE HIS HEAD OUT!
MISTER! UH... WHAT WAS HIS NAME... WHAT WAS HIS NAME...
?!
...
HE'S LOOKING UP! I'VE GOT YOU, JOTARO!
ZWEEE

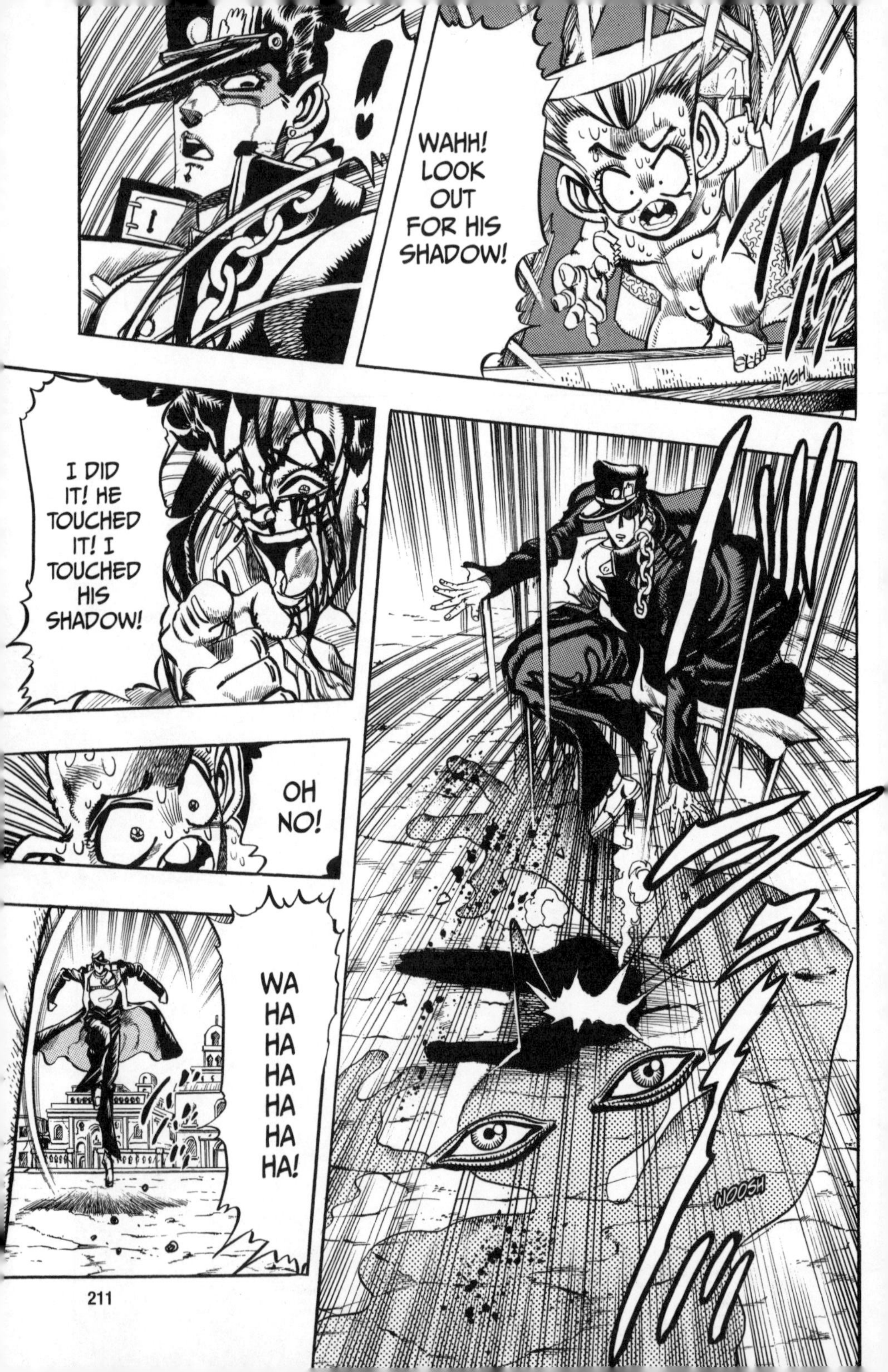
WAHH! LOOK OUT FOR HIS SHADOW!
AGH
!
WOOSH
I DID IT! HE TOUCHED IT! I TOUCHED HIS SHADOW!
OH NO!
WA HA HA HA HA HA HA!

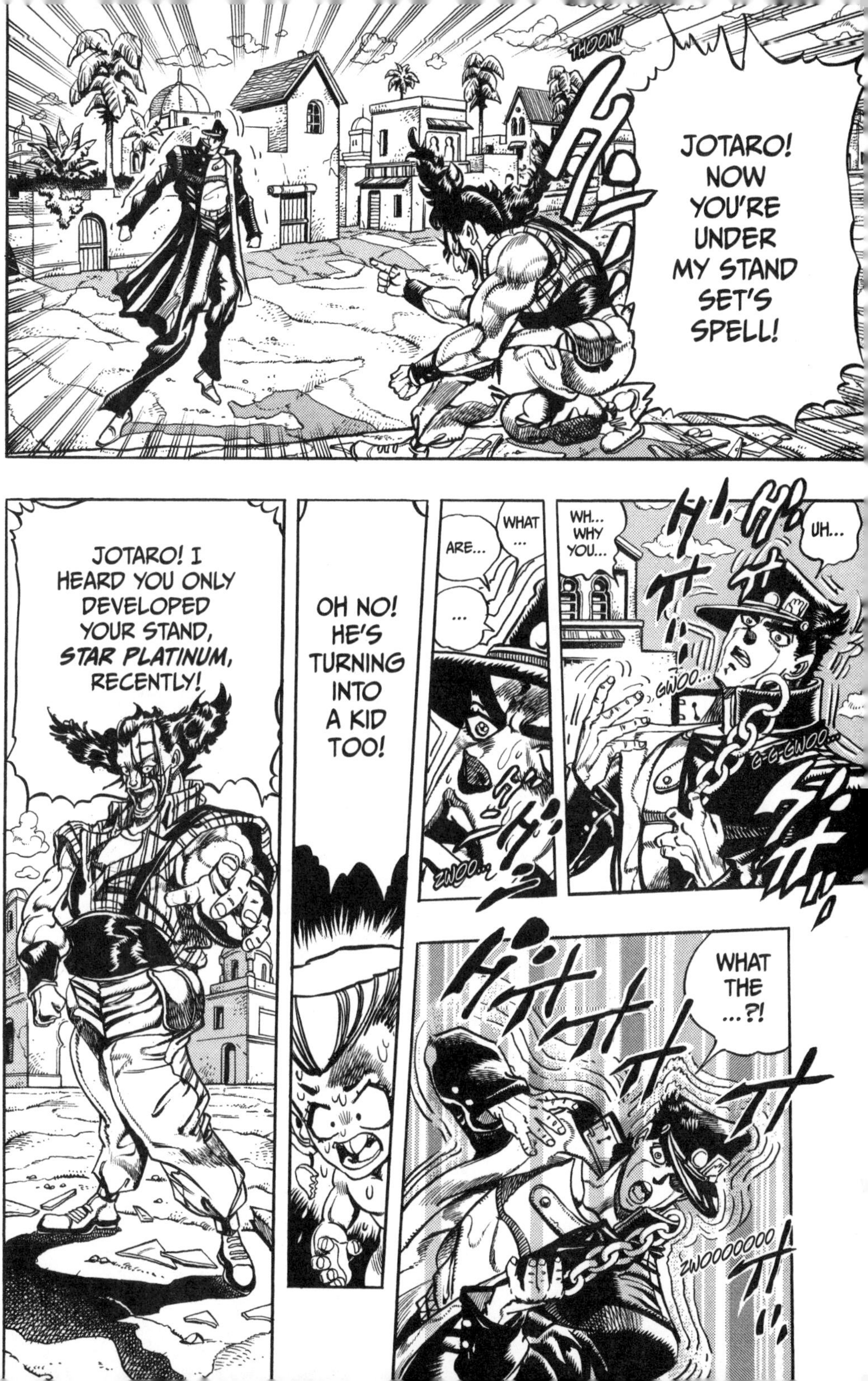
THOOM!
JOTARO! NOW YOU'RE UNDER MY STAND SET'S SPELL!
UH...
WH... WHY YOU...
GWOO...
G-G-GWOO...
WHAT ...
ARE...
...
ZWOO...
WHAT THE ...?!
ZWOOOOOOO
OH NO! HE'S TURNING INTO A KID TOO!
JOTARO! I HEARD YOU ONLY DEVELOPED YOUR STAND, STAR PLATINUM, RECENTLY!

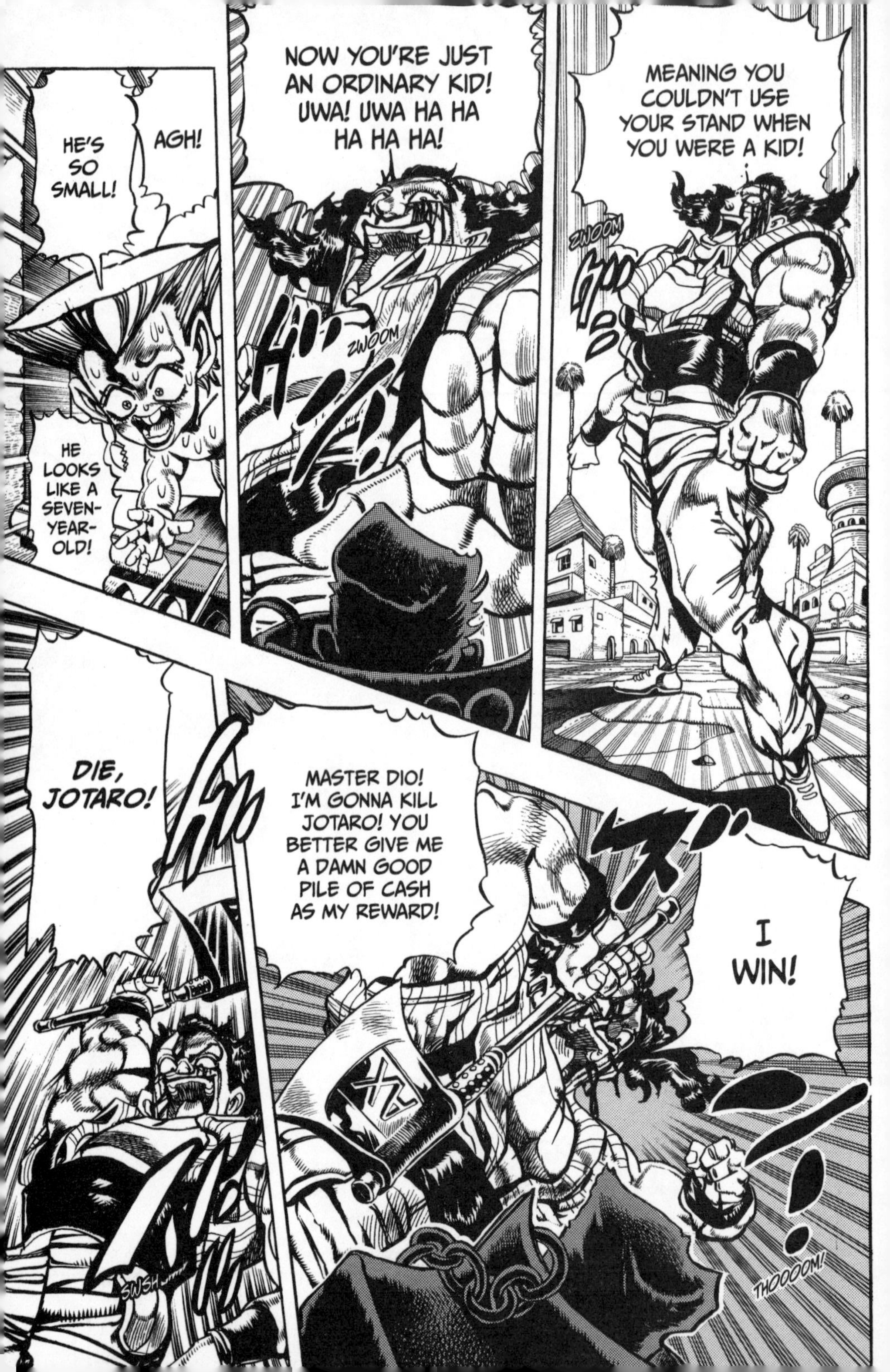
MEANING YOU COULDN'T USE YOUR STAND WHEN YOU WERE A KID!
ZWOOM
NOW YOU'RE JUST AN ORDINARY KID! UWA! UWA HA HA HA HA HA!
ZWOOM
AGH!
HE'S SO SMALL!
HE LOOKS LIKE A SEVEN-YEAR-OLD!
I WIN!
THOOOM!
MASTER DIO! I'M GONNA KILL JOTARO! YOU BETTER GIVE ME A DAMN GOOD PILE OF CASH AS MY REWARD!
DIE, JOTARO!
SWSH

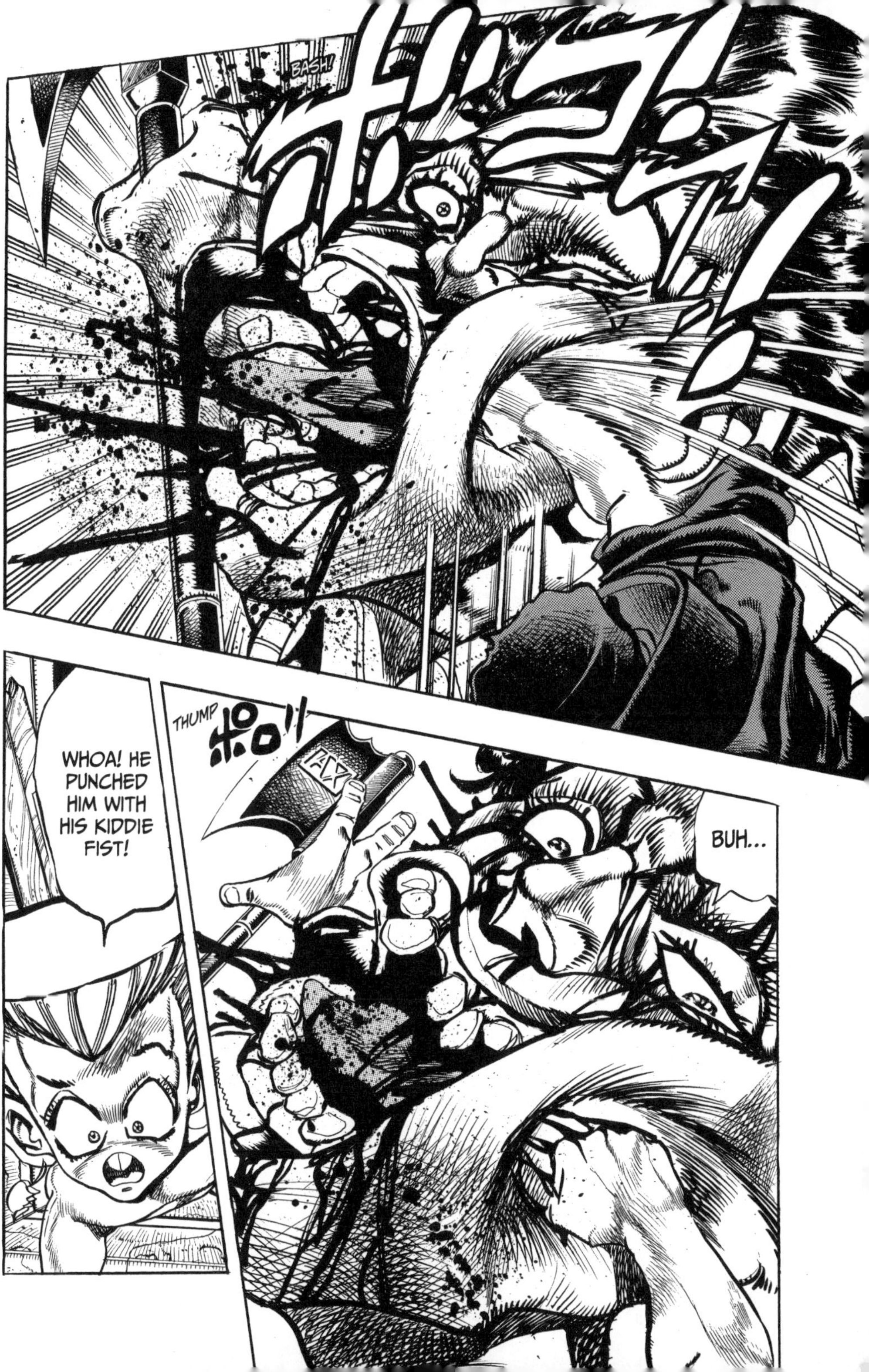
BASH!
THUMP
BUH...
WHOA! HE PUNCHED HIM WITH HIS KIDDIE FIST!

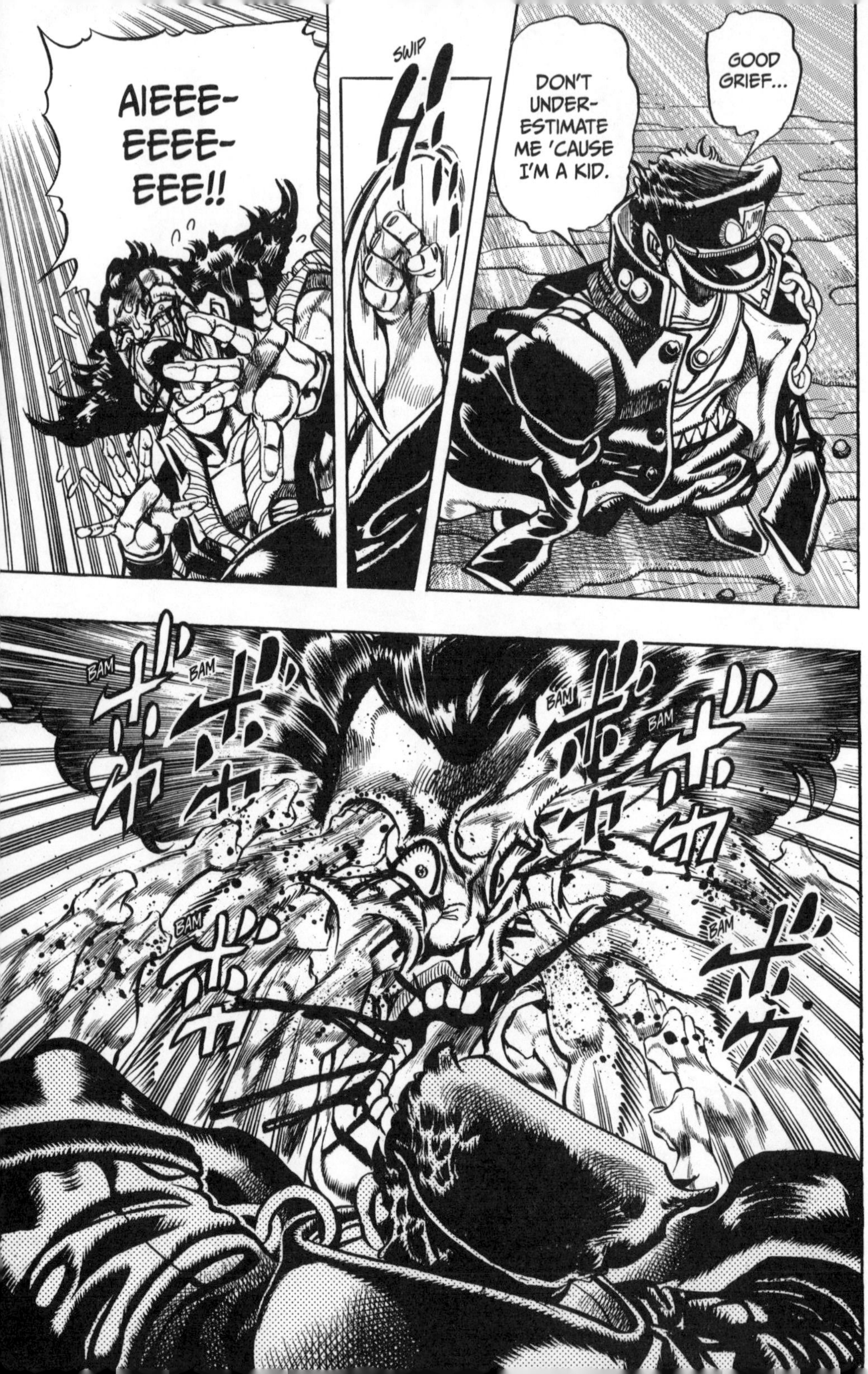
GOOD GRIEF...
DON'T UNDER-ESTIMATE ME 'CAUSE I'M A KID.
SWIP
AIEEE-EEEE-EEE!!
BAM
BAM
BAM
BAM
BAM
BAM

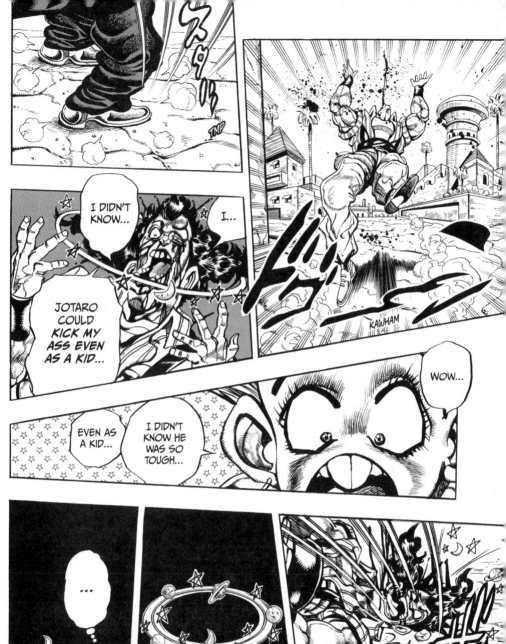

I DIDN'T KNOW...

I...

JOTARO COULD KICK MY ASS EVEN AS A KID...

EVEN AS A KID...

I DIDN'T KNOW HE WAS SO TOUGH...

WOW...

KAWHAM

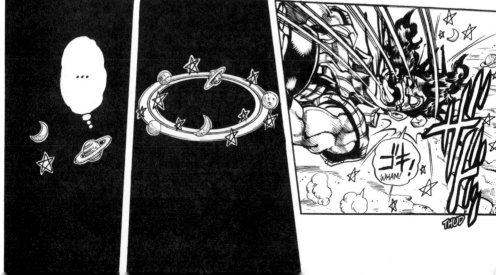

...

WHAM!

THUD

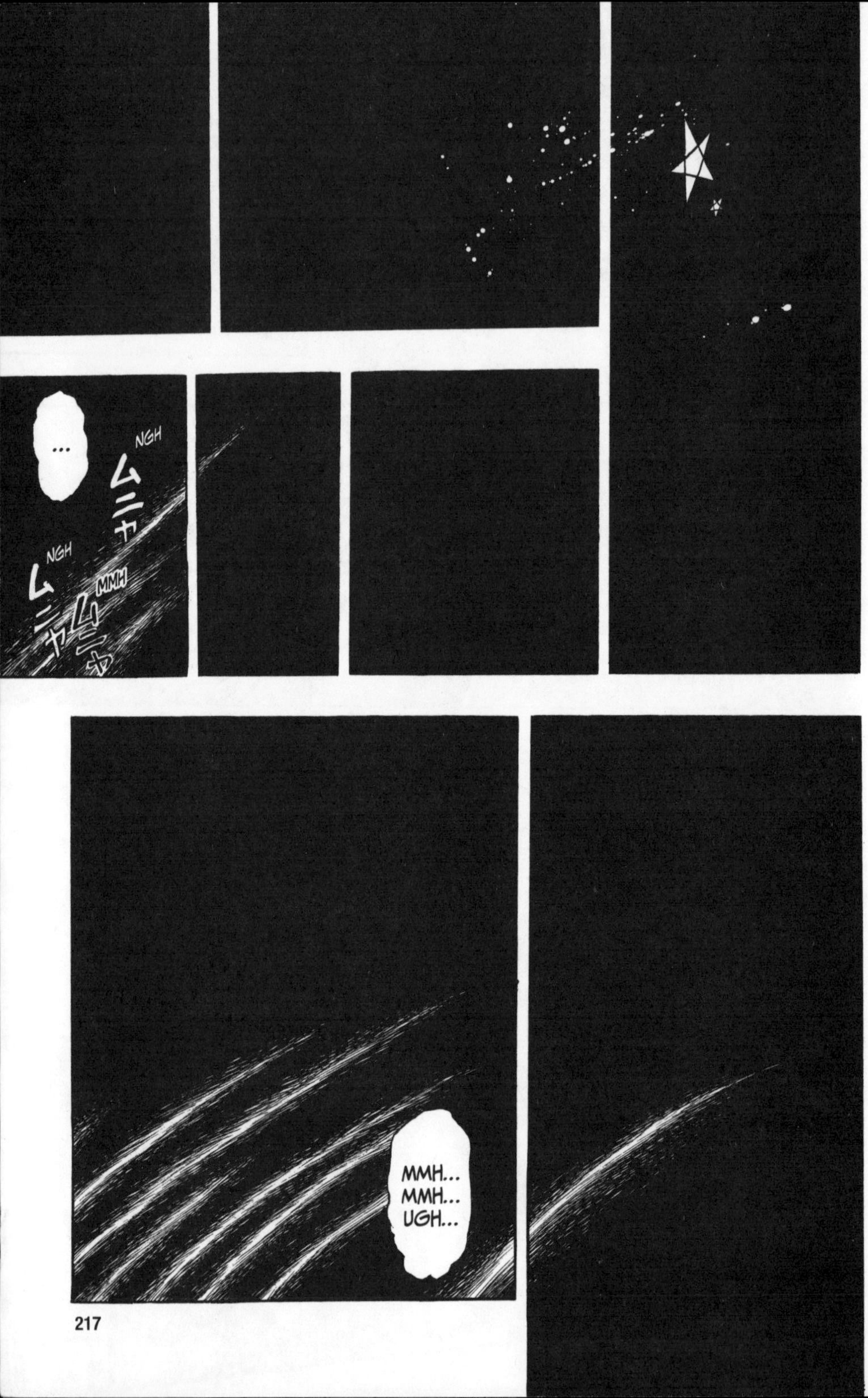
...
NGH
ムニャ
NGH
ムニャ
MMH
ムニャ
MMH... MMH... UGH...

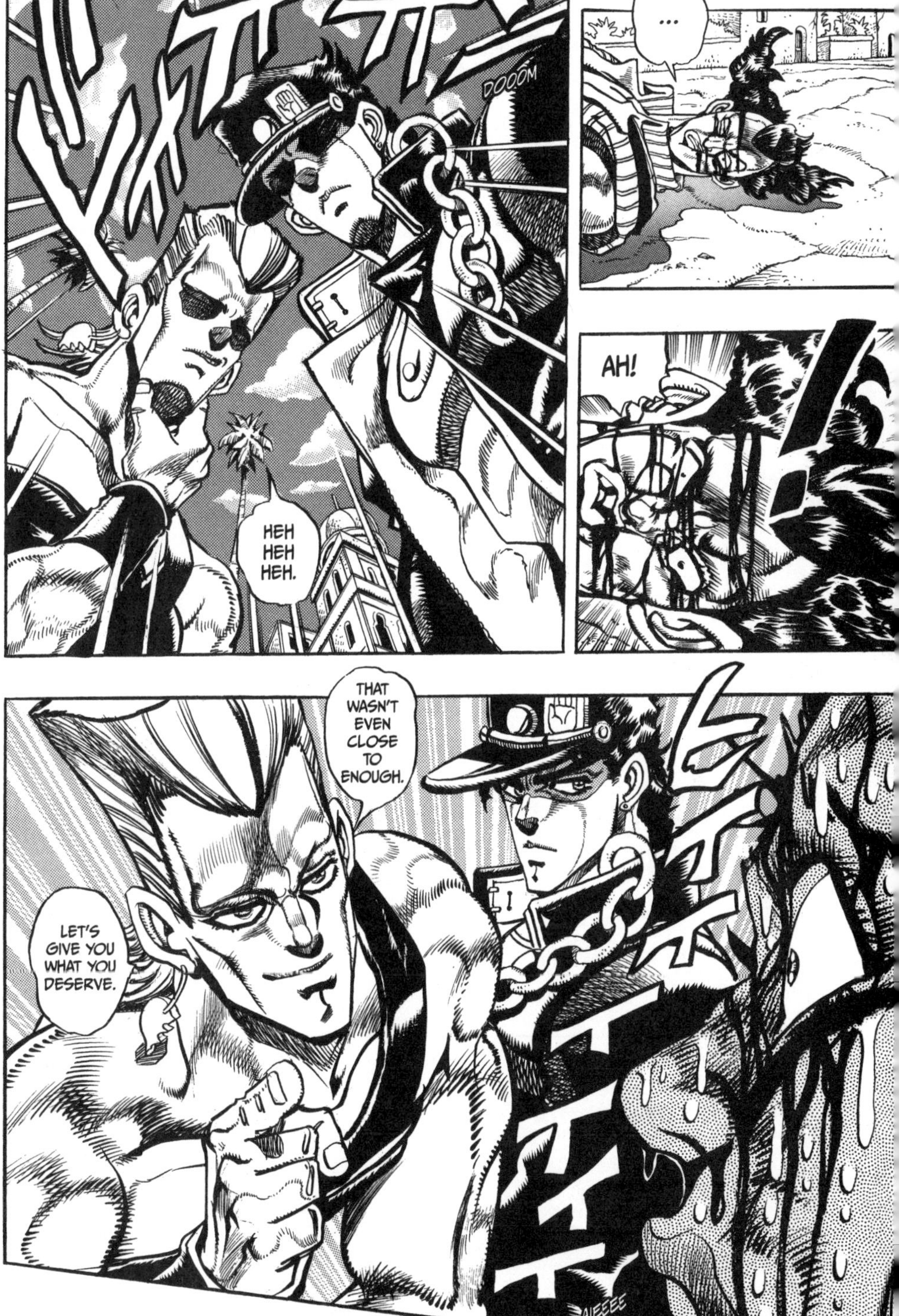
...
AH!
DOOOM
HEH HEH HEH.
THAT WASN'T EVEN CLOSE TO ENOUGH.
LET'S GIVE YOU WHAT YOU DESERVE.
AIEEEE

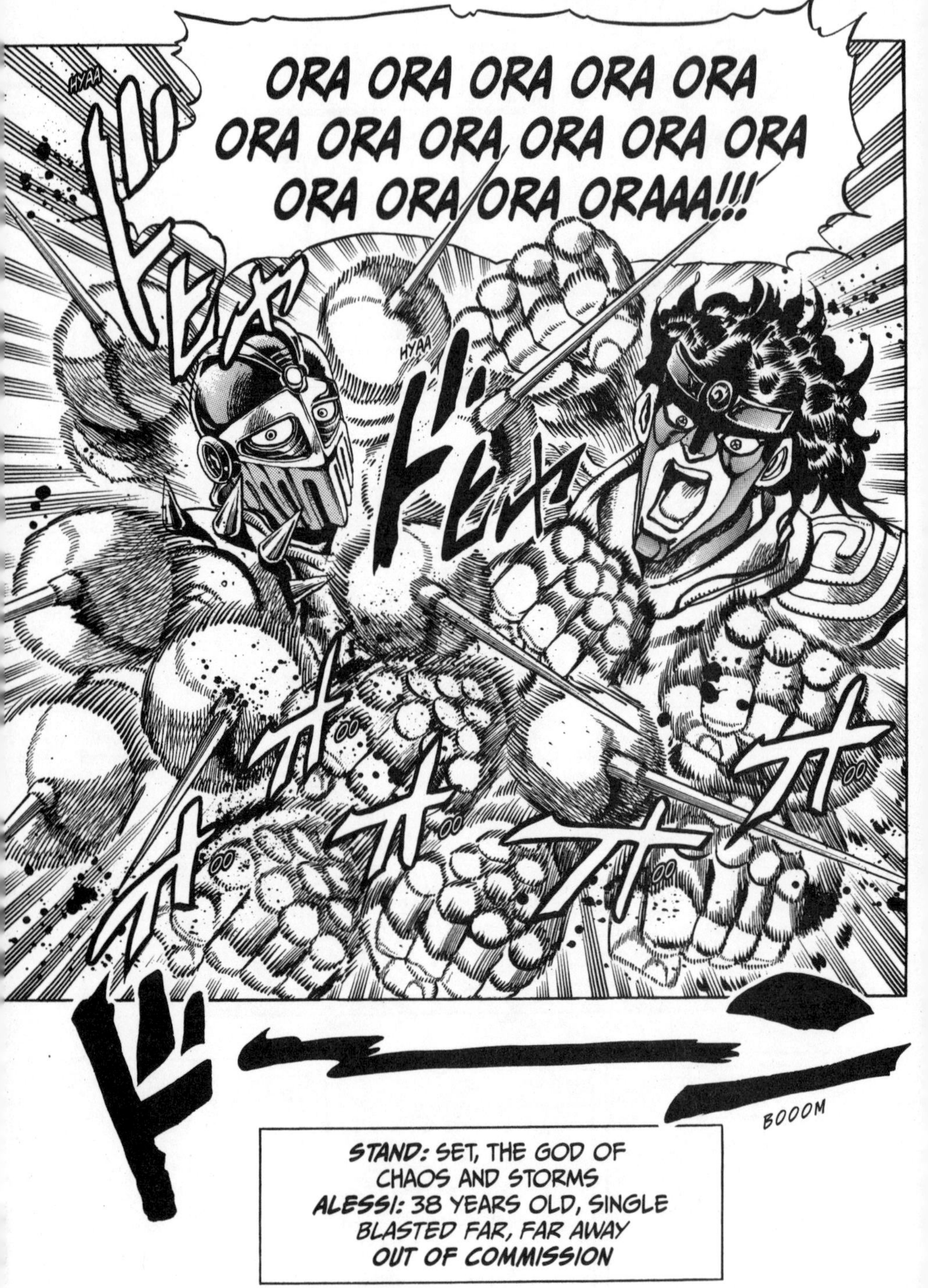
ORA ORA ORA ORA ORA ORA ORA ORA ORA ORA ORA ORA ORA ORA ORAAA!!!
HYAA
HYAA
BOOOM
STAND: SET, THE GOD OF CHAOS AND STORMS
ALESSI: 38 YEARS OLD, SINGLE
BLASTED FAR, FAR AWAY
OUT OF COMMISSION

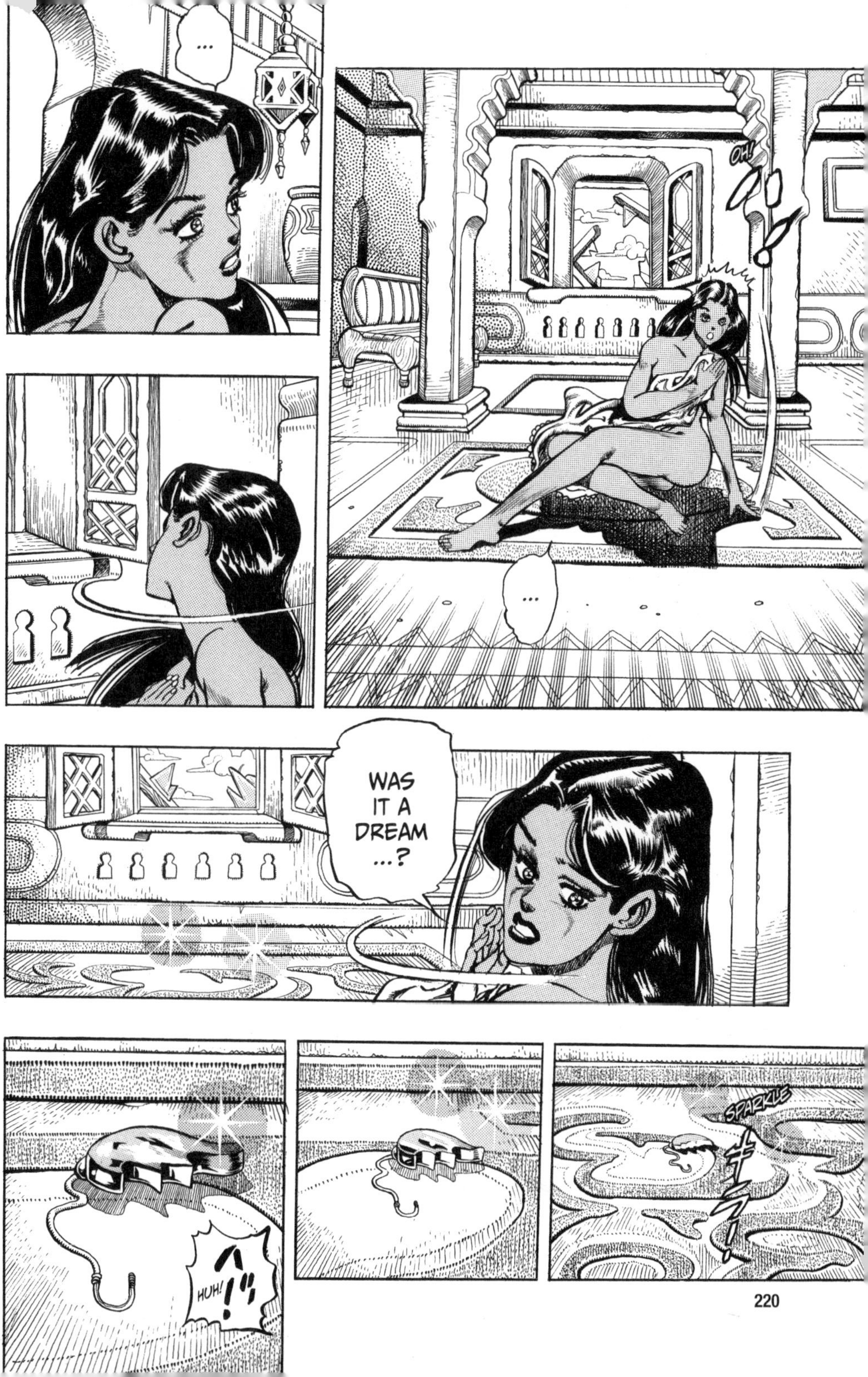

OH!
...
...
WAS IT A DREAM ...?
SPARKLE
HUH!

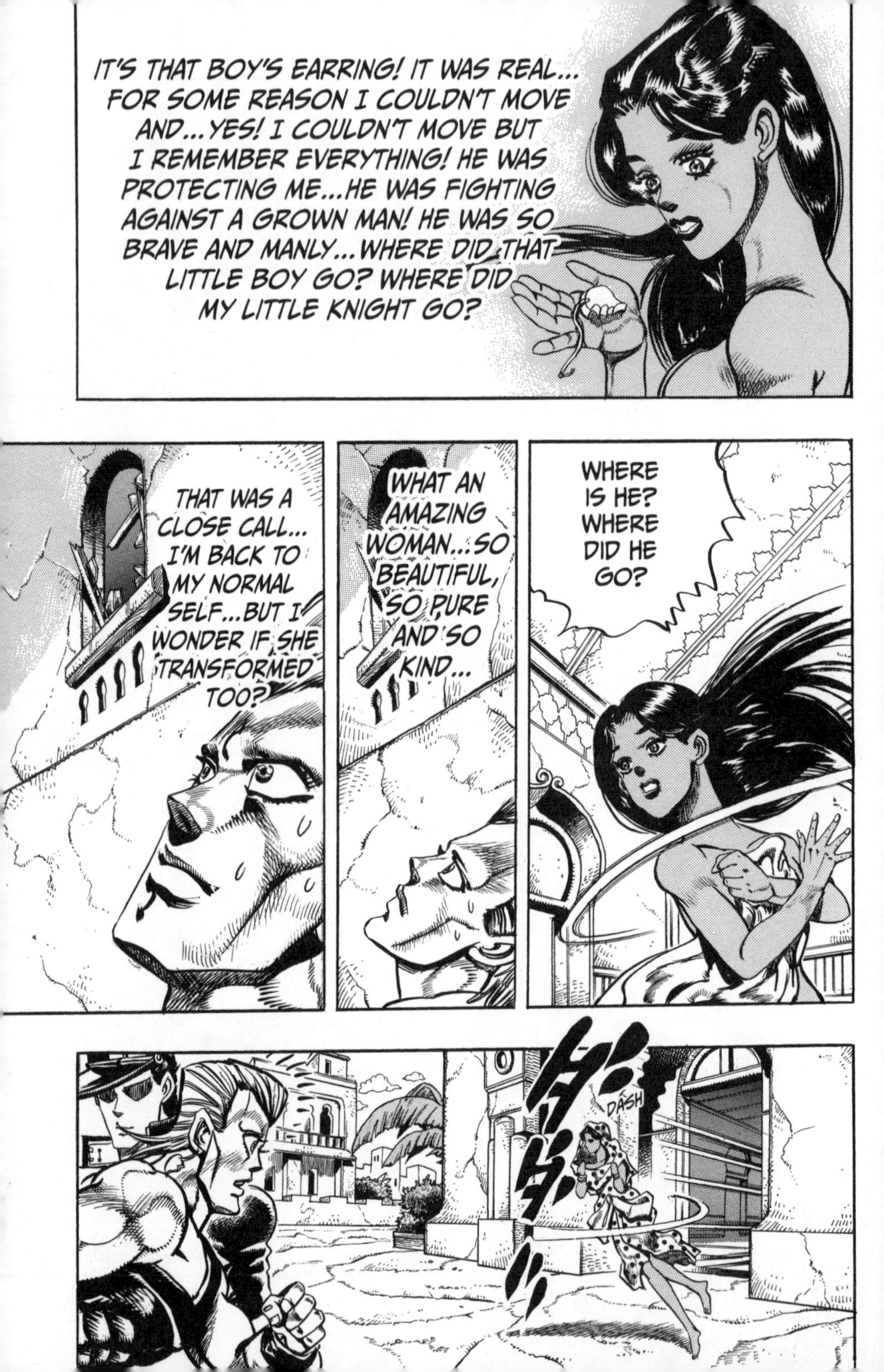
IT'S THAT BOY'S EARRING! IT WAS REAL... FOR SOME REASON I COULDN'T MOVE AND...YES! I COULDN'T MOVE BUT I REMEMBER EVERYTHING! HE WAS PROTECTING ME...HE WAS FIGHTING AGAINST A GROWN MAN! HE WAS SO BRAVE AND MANLY...WHERE DID THAT LITTLE BOY GO? WHERE DID MY LITTLE KNIGHT GO?
WHERE IS HE? WHERE DID HE GO?
WHAT AN AMAZING WOMAN...SO BEAUTIFUL, SO PURE AND SO KIND...
THAT WAS A CLOSE CALL... I'M BACK TO MY NORMAL SELF...BUT I WONDER IF SHE TRANSFORMED TOO?
DASH

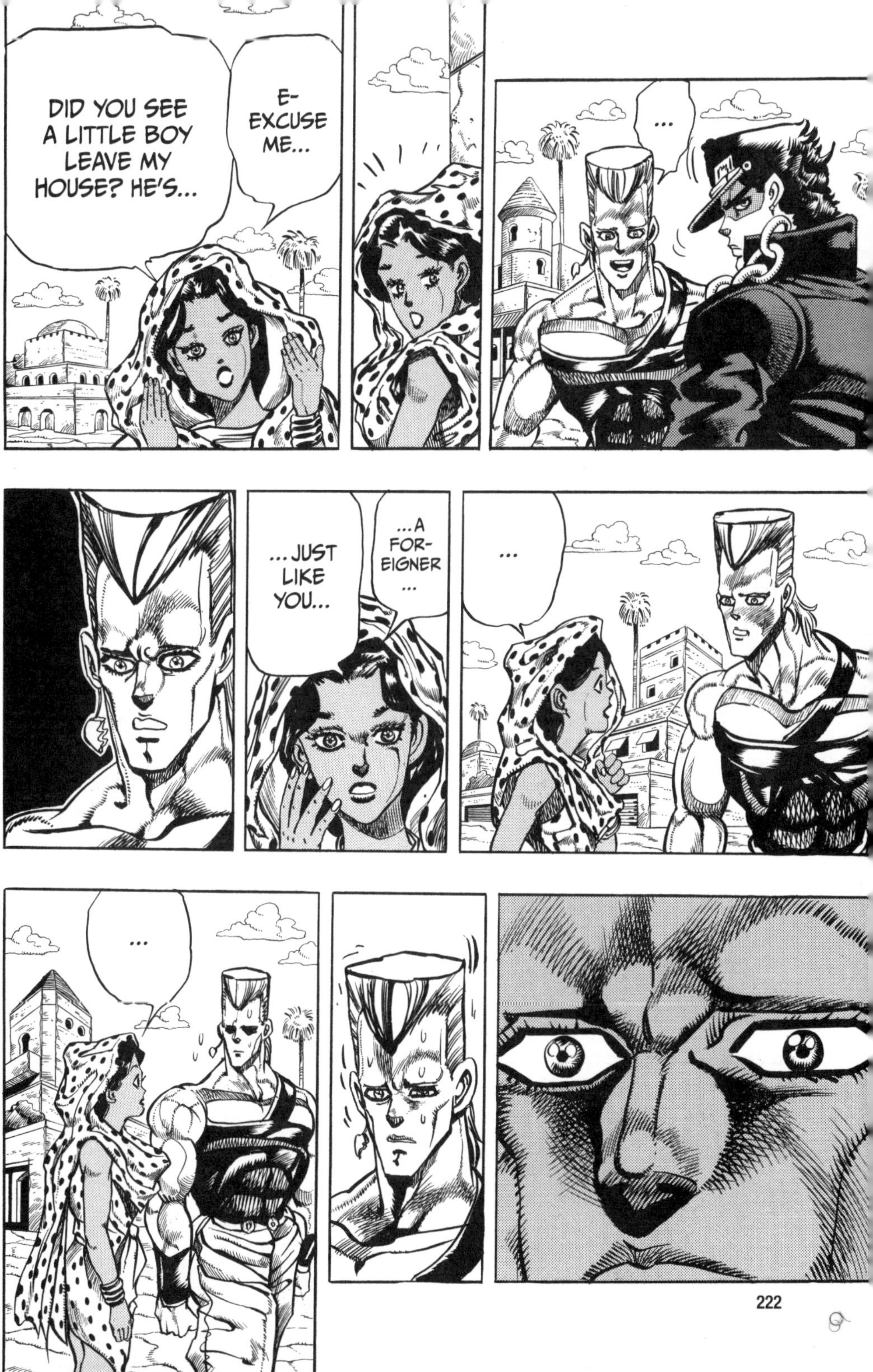
...
E- EXCUSE ME...
DID YOU SEE A LITTLE BOY LEAVE MY HOUSE? HE'S...
...
...A FOR- EIGNER ...
...JUST LIKE YOU...
...

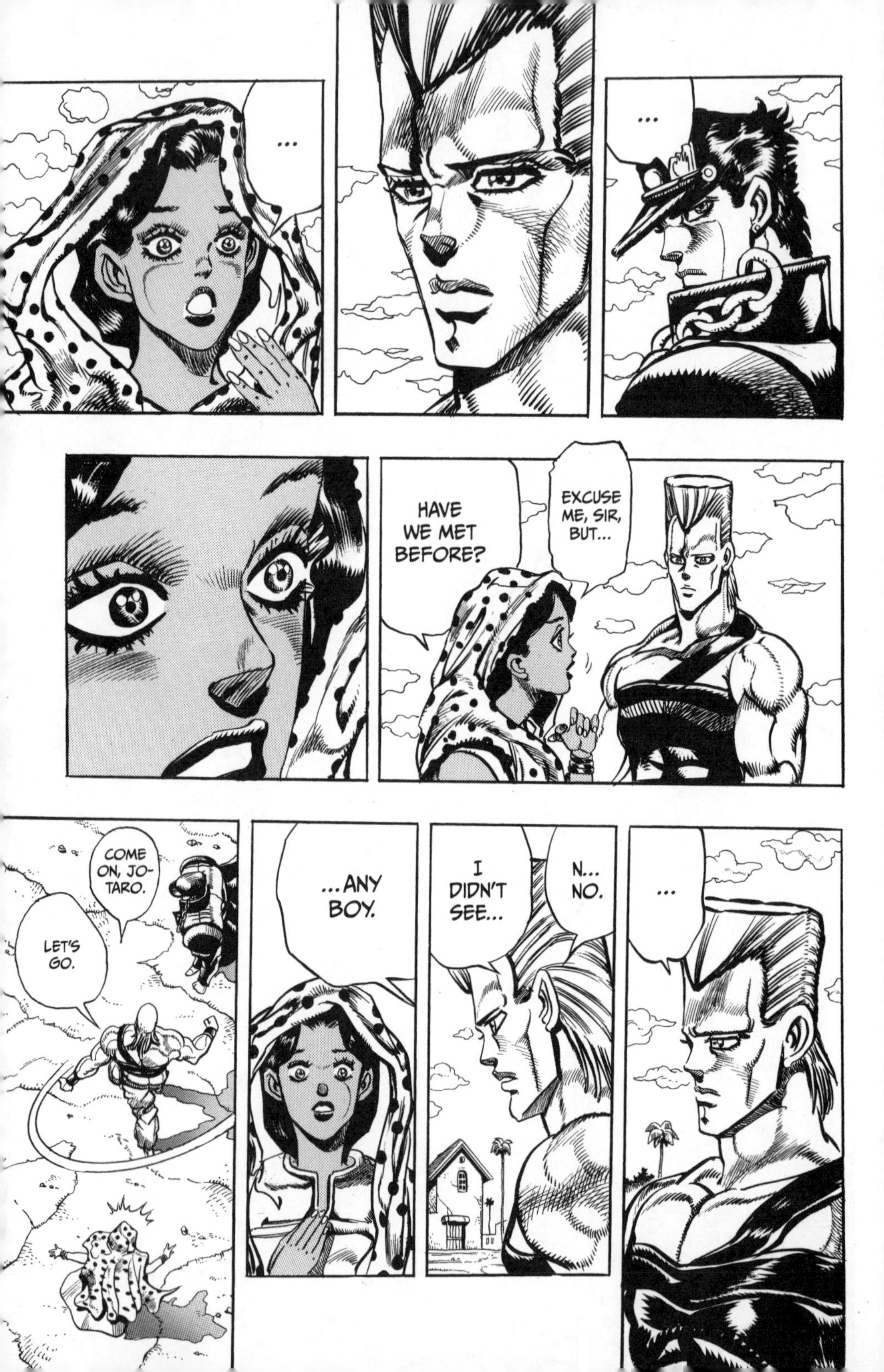
...
...
EXCUSE ME, SIR, BUT...
HAVE WE MET BEFORE?
...
N... NO.
I DIDN'T SEE...
...ANY BOY.
COME ON, JO-TARO.
LET'S GO.

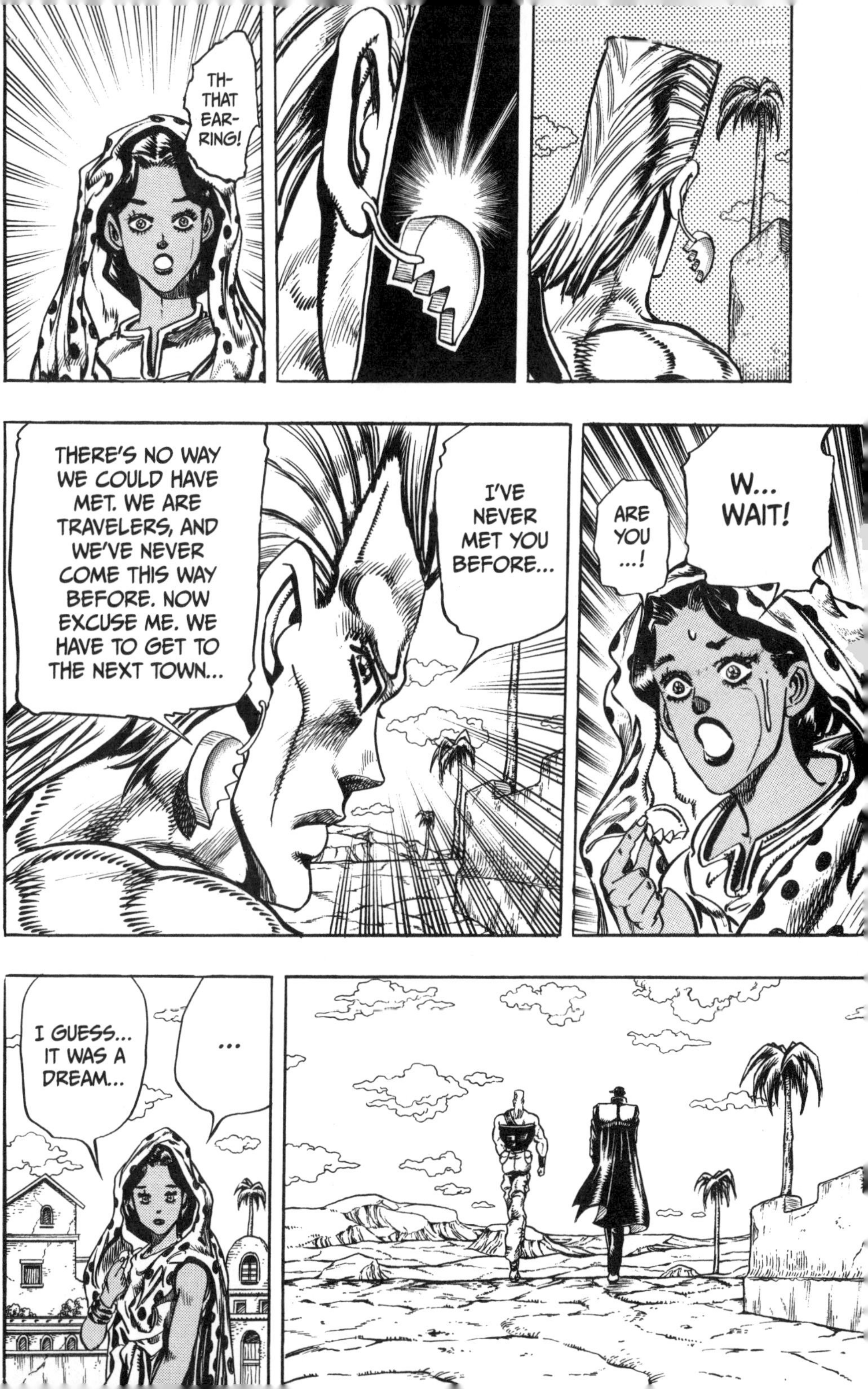
TH-THAT EAR-RING!
W... WAIT!
ARE YOU ...!
I'VE NEVER MET YOU BEFORE...
THERE'S NO WAY WE COULD HAVE MET. WE ARE TRAVELERS, AND WE'VE NEVER COME THIS WAY BEFORE. NOW EXCUSE ME. WE HAVE TO GET TO THE NEXT TOWN...
...
I GUESS... IT WAS A DREAM...

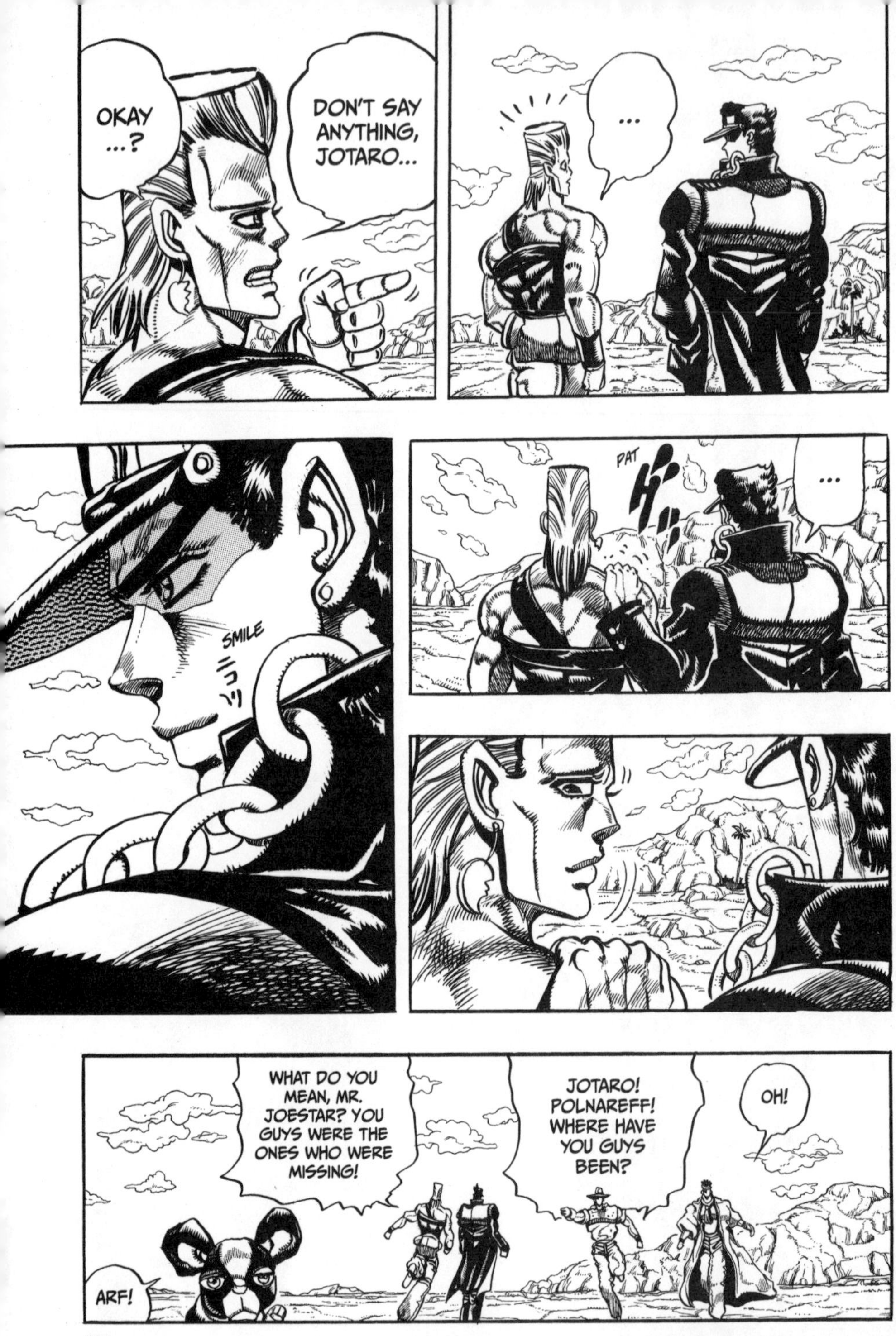
...
DON'T SAY ANYTHING, JOTARO...
OKAY ...?
PAT
...
SMILE
ニコッ
OH!
JOTARO! POLNAREFF! WHERE HAVE YOU GUYS BEEN?
WHAT DO YOU MEAN, MR. JOESTAR? YOU GUYS WERE THE ONES WHO WERE MISSING!
ARF!

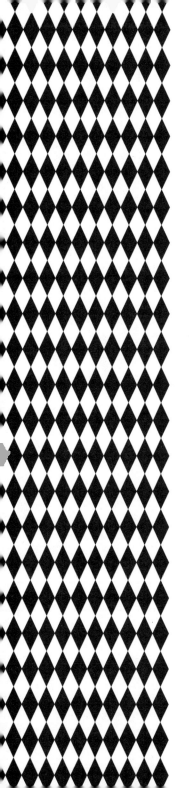

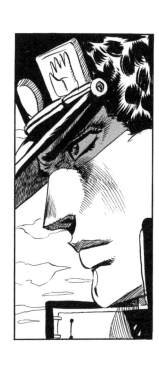

CHAPTER 97: The Man Who Shot DIO

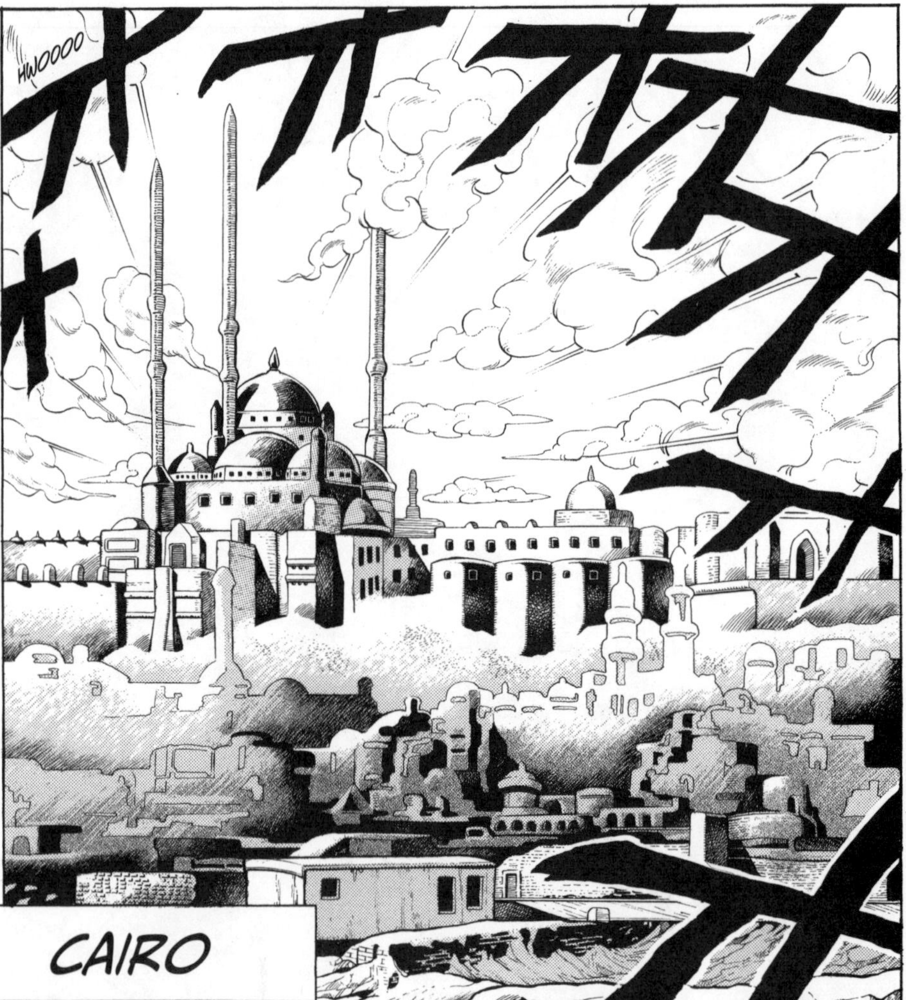
HWOOOO
CAIRO

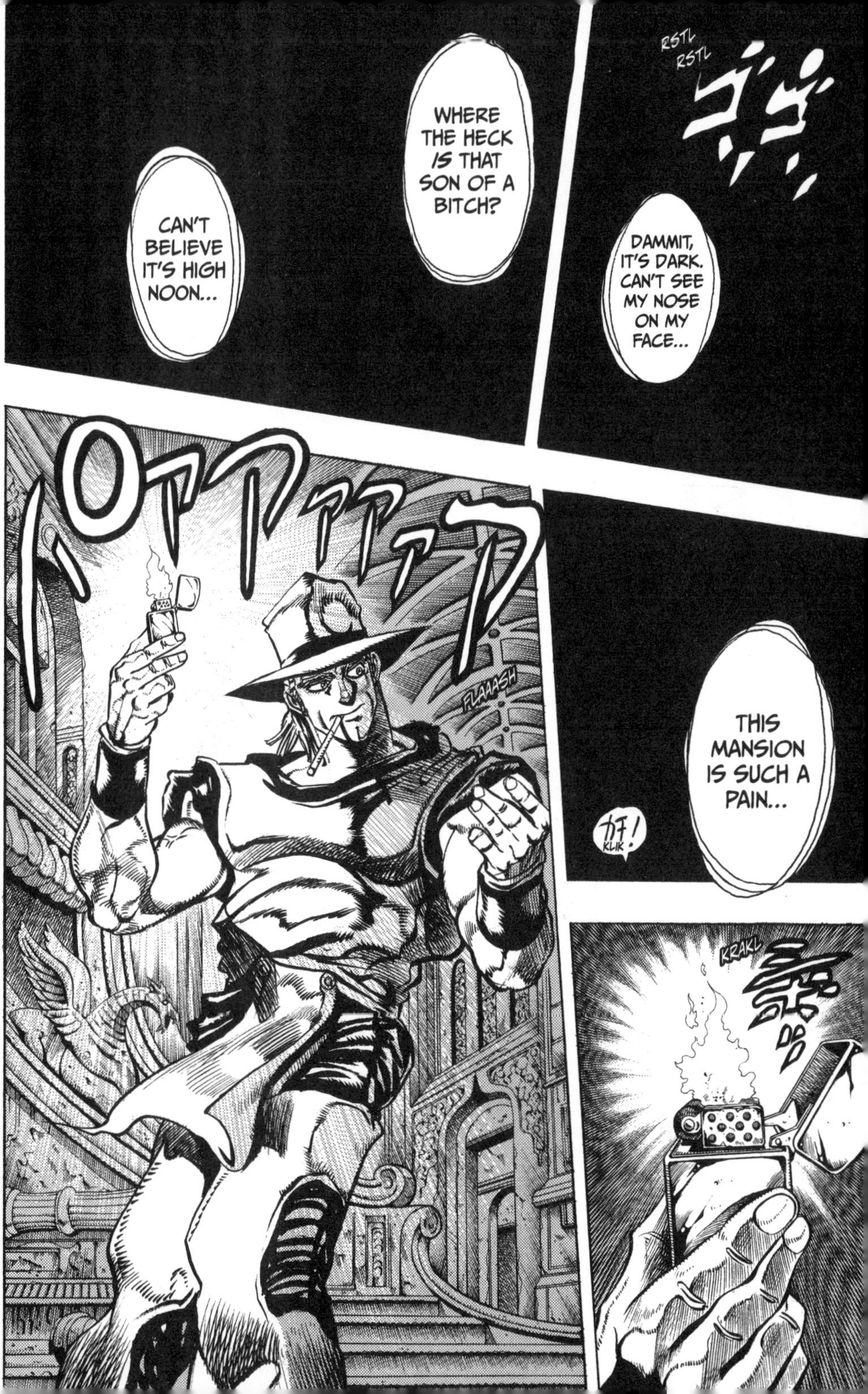

RSTL RSTL
DAMMIT, IT'S DARK. CAN'T SEE MY NOSE ON MY FACE...
WHERE THE HECK IS THAT SON OF A BITCH?
CAN'T BELIEVE IT'S HIGH NOON...
THIS MANSION IS SUCH A PAIN...
KLIK
KRAKL
FLAAASH

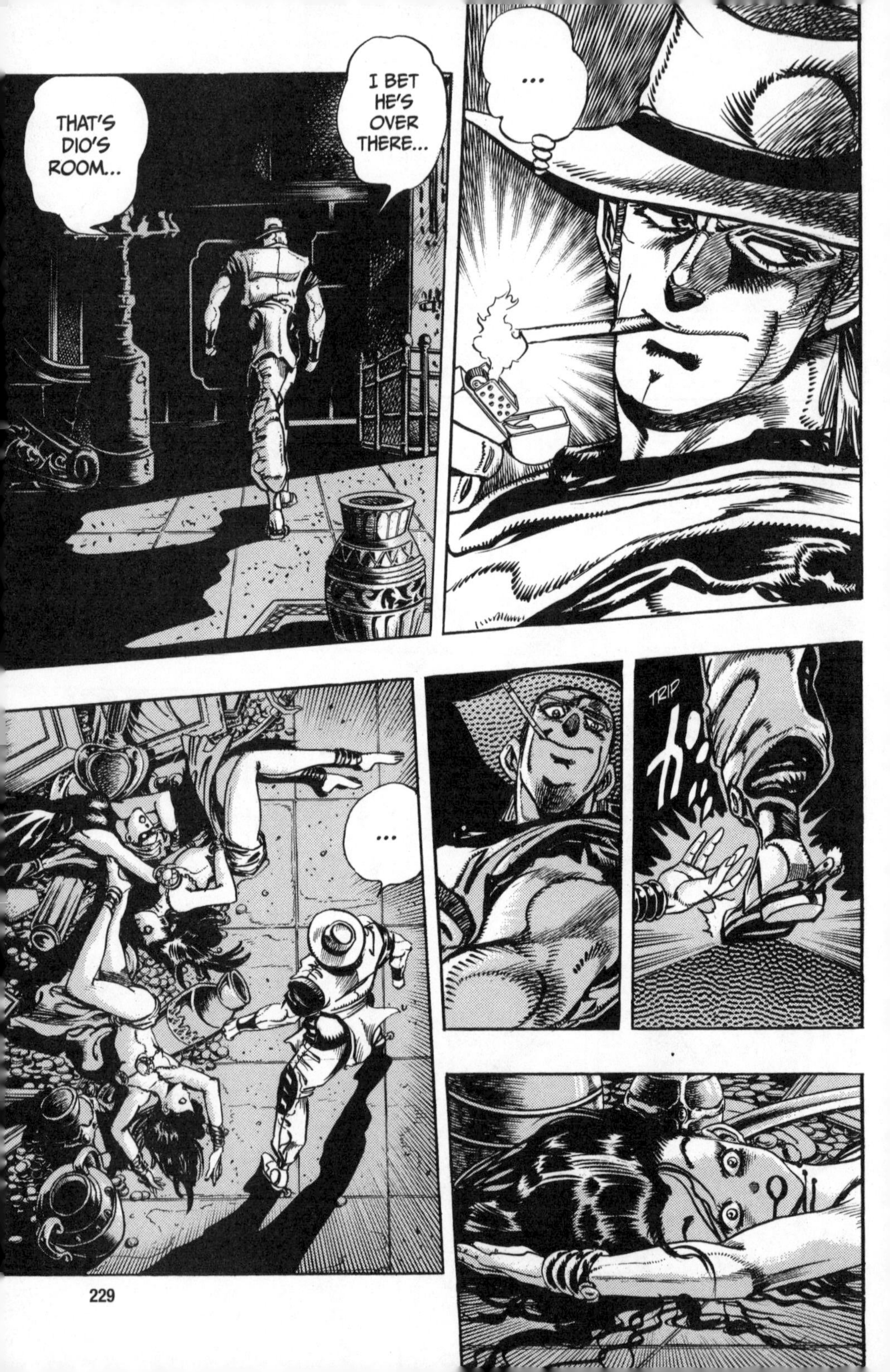
...
I BET HE'S OVER THERE...
THAT'S DIO'S ROOM...
TRIP
...

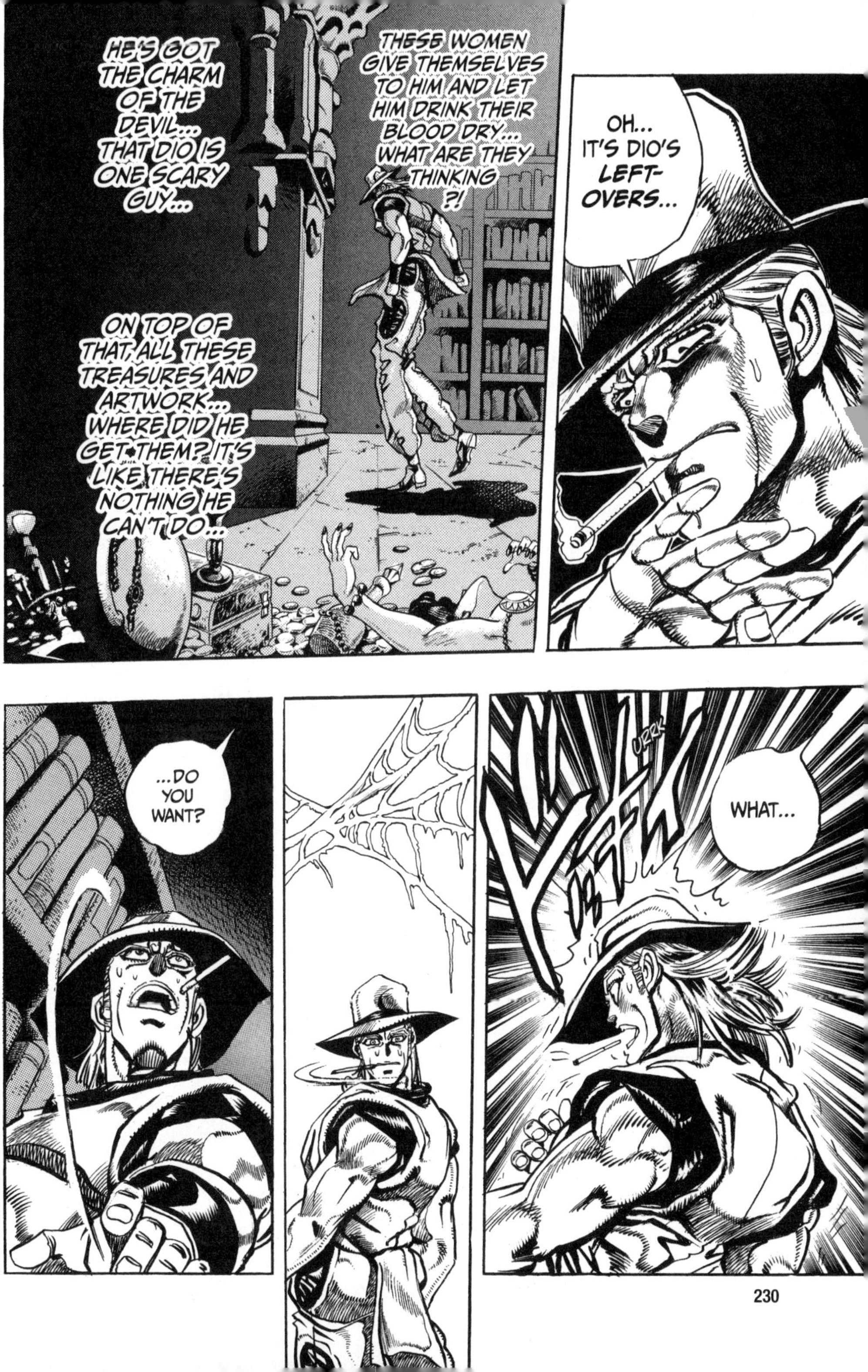
OH... IT'S DIO'S LEFT-OVERS...
THESE WOMEN GIVE THEMSELVES TO HIM AND LET HIM DRINK THEIR BLOOD DRY... WHAT ARE THEY THINKING?!
HE'S GOT THE CHARM OF THE DEVIL... THAT DIO IS ONE SCARY GUY...
ON TOP OF THAT, ALL THESE TREASURES AND ARTWORK... WHERE DID HE GET THEM? IT'S LIKE THERE'S NOTHING HE CAN'T DO...
URRK
WHAT...
...DO YOU WANT?

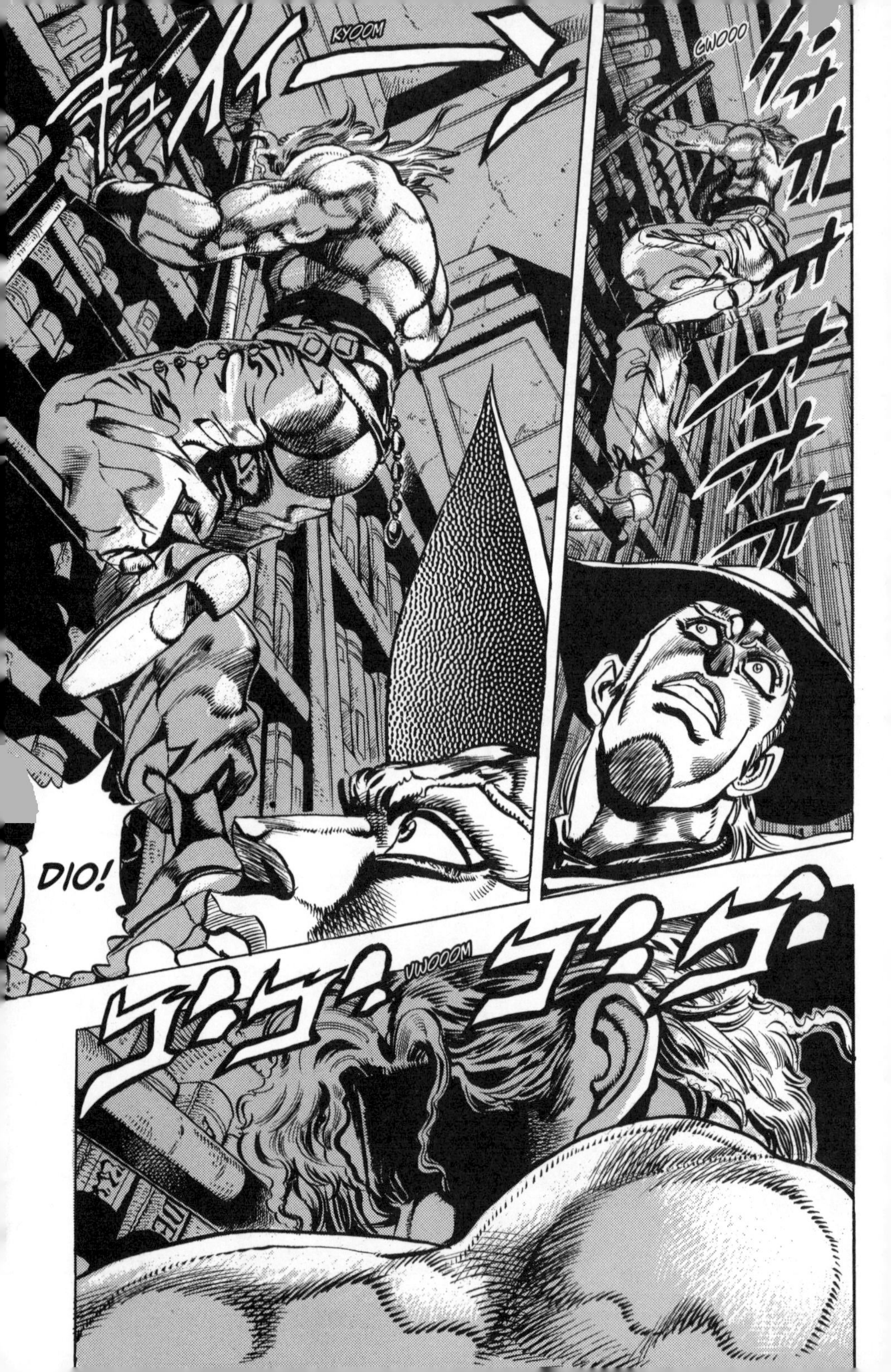
GWOOO
KYOOM
DIO!
VWOOOM

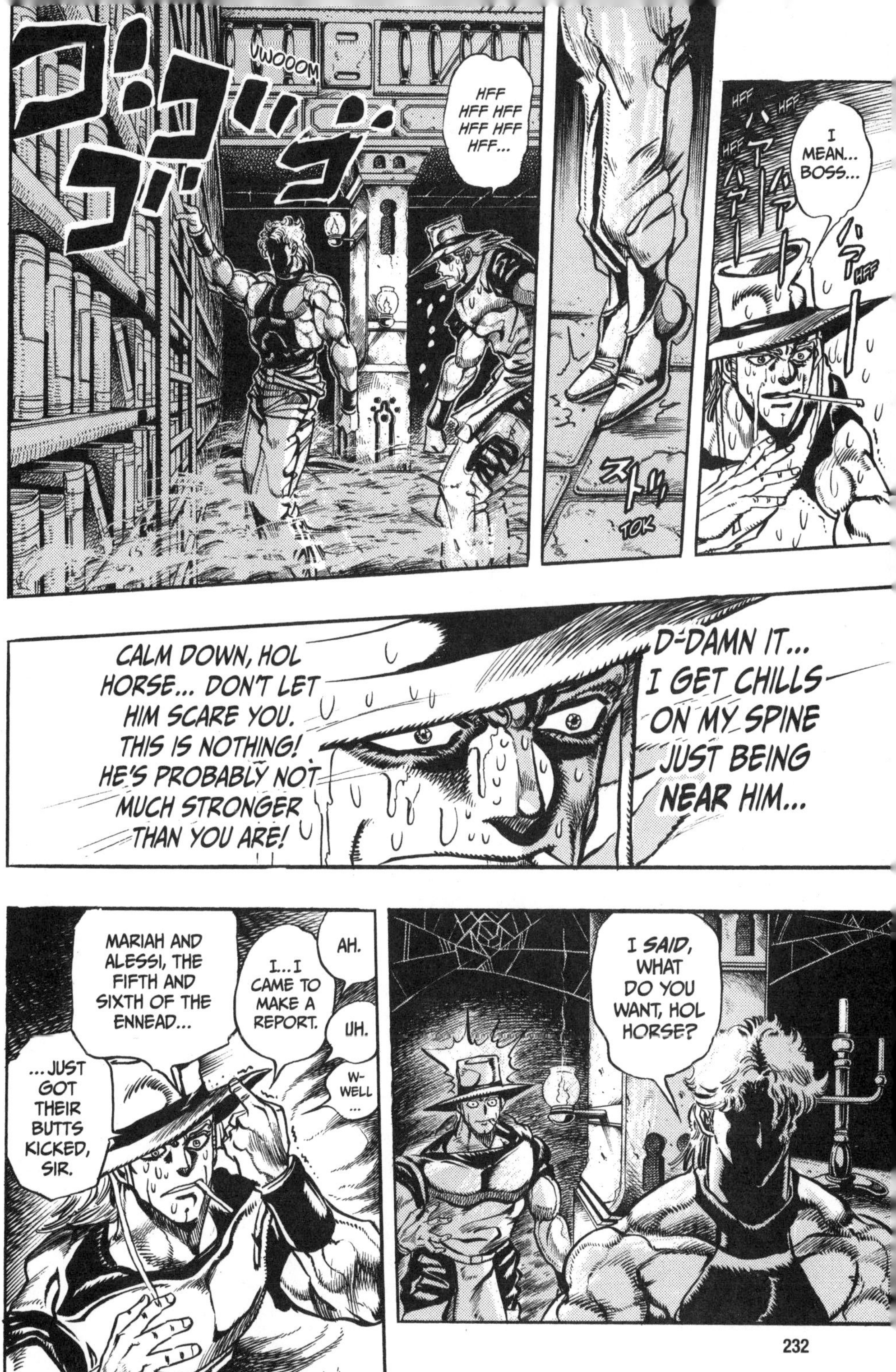
HFF
HFF
I MEAN... BOSS...
HFF
TOK
VWOOOM
HFF HFF HFF HFF HFF HFF...
D-DAMN IT... I GET CHILLS ON MY SPINE JUST BEING NEAR HIM...
CALM DOWN, HOL HORSE... DON'T LET HIM SCARE YOU. THIS IS NOTHING! HE'S PROBABLY NOT MUCH STRONGER THAN YOU ARE!
I SAID, WHAT DO YOU WANT, HOL HORSE?
AH.
UH.
W-WELL...
I...I CAME TO MAKE A REPORT.
MARIAH AND ALESSI, THE FIFTH AND SIXTH OF THE ENNEAD...
...JUST GOT THEIR BUTTS KICKED, SIR.

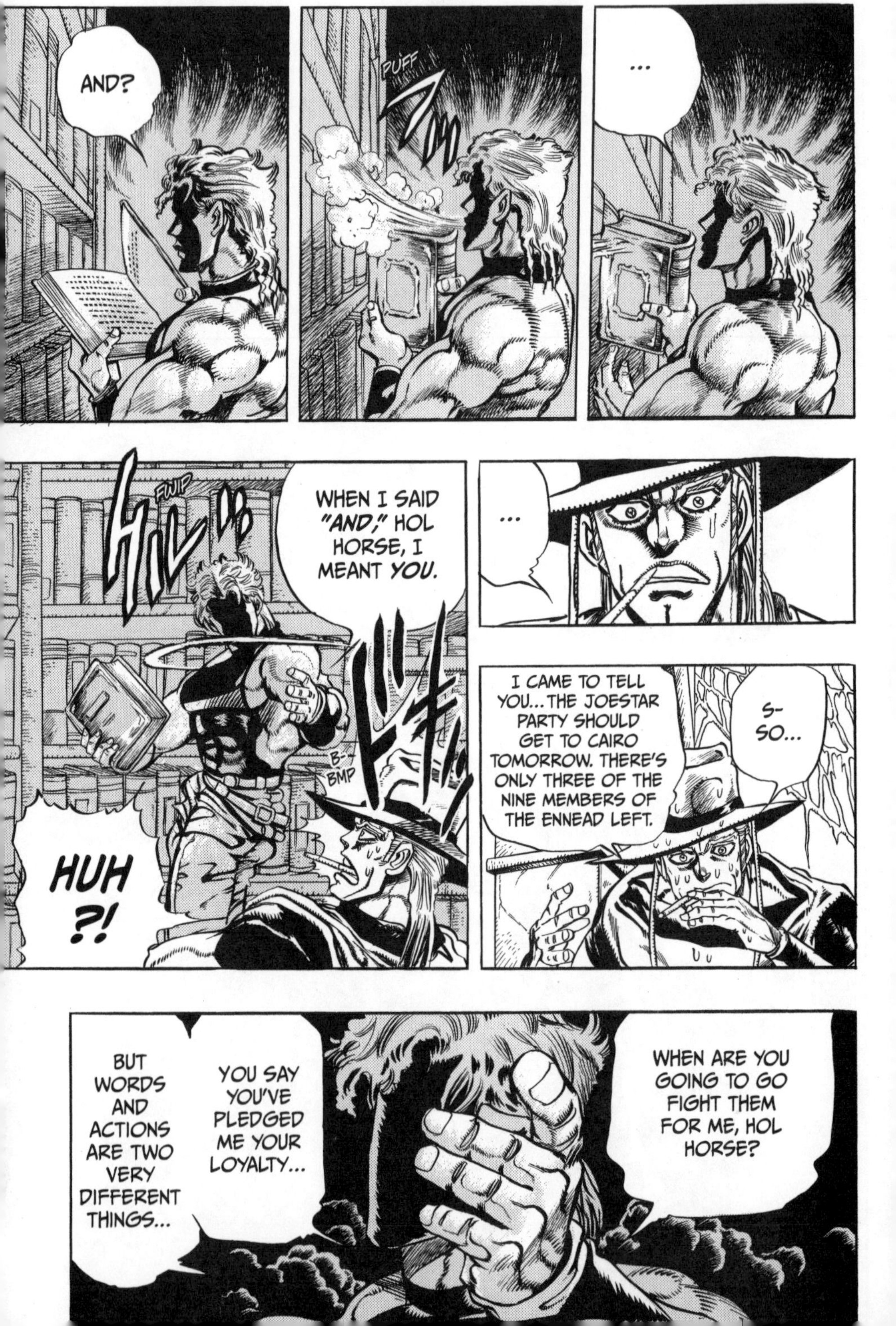
AND?
PUFF
...
FWIP
WHEN I SAID "AND," HOL HORSE, I MEANT YOU.
B-BMP
HUH?!
...
I CAME TO TELL YOU... THE JOESTAR PARTY SHOULD GET TO CAIRO TOMORROW. THERE'S ONLY THREE OF THE NINE MEMBERS OF THE ENNEAD LEFT.
S-SO...
YOU SAY YOU'VE PLEDGED ME YOUR LOYALTY...
BUT WORDS AND ACTIONS ARE TWO VERY DIFFERENT THINGS...
WHEN ARE YOU GOING TO GO FIGHT THEM FOR ME, HOL HORSE?

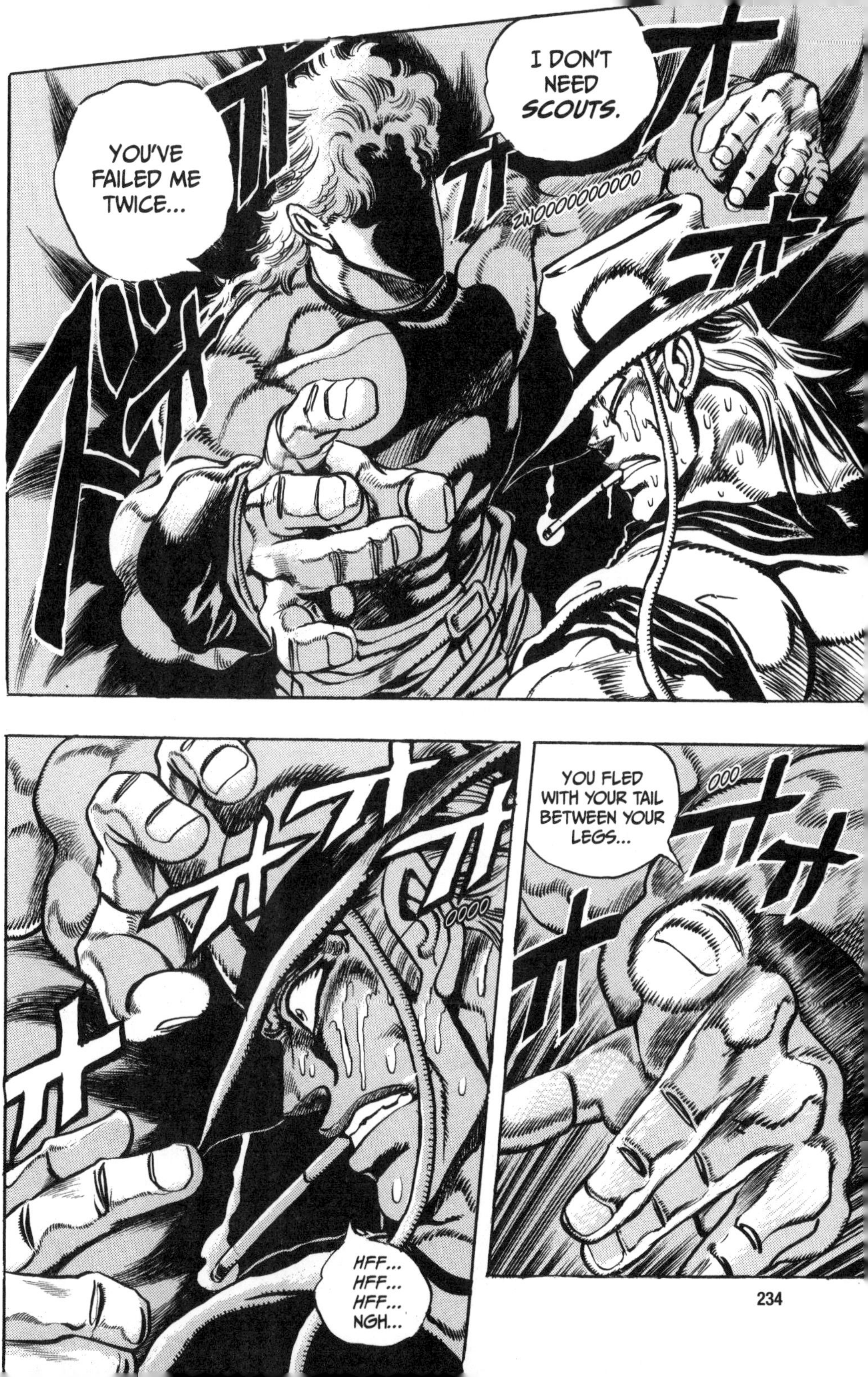
I DON'T NEED SCOUTS.
YOU'VE FAILED ME TWICE...
ZWOOOOOOOOOO
YOU FLED WITH YOUR TAIL BETWEEN YOUR LEGS...
OOO
OOOO
HFF... HFF... HFF... NGH...

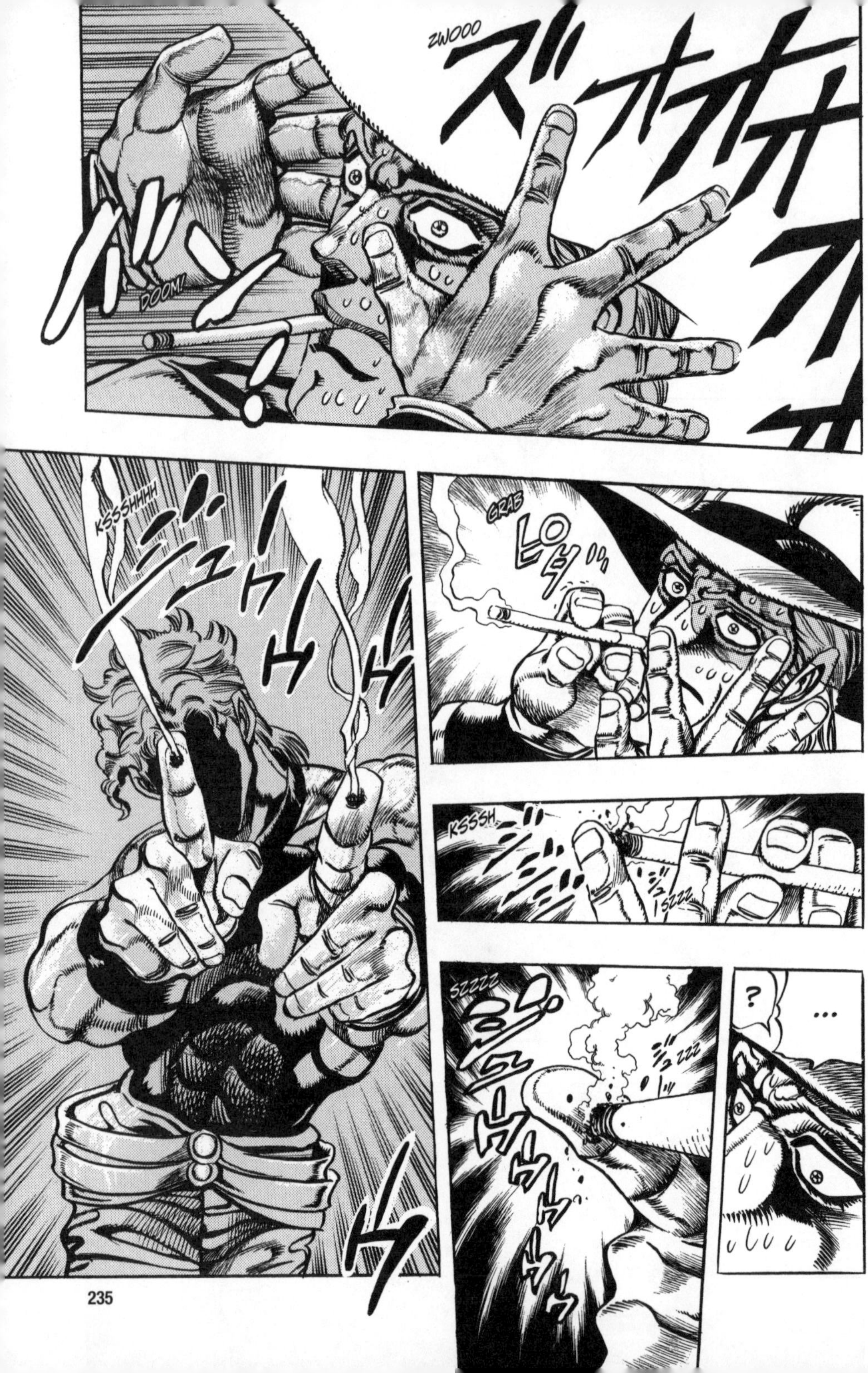
ZWOOO
DOOM!
GRAB
KSSSH
SZZZ
?
...
SZZZZ
ZZZ
KSSSHHHH

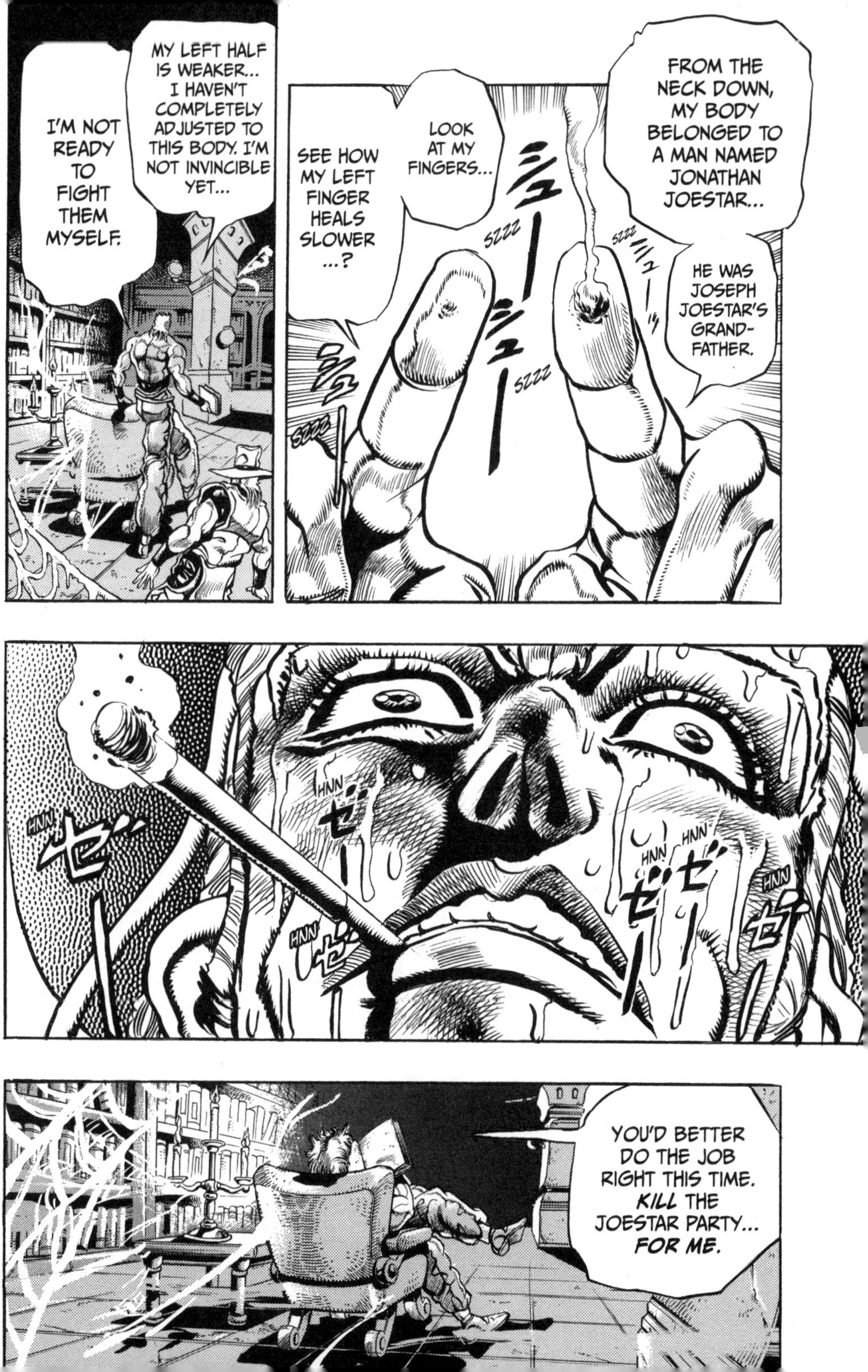
FROM THE NECK DOWN, MY BODY BELONGED TO A MAN NAMED JONATHAN JOESTAR...
SZZZ
HE WAS JOSEPH JOESTAR'S GRANDFATHER.
SZZZ
LOOK AT MY FINGERS...
SZZZ
SEE HOW MY LEFT FINGER HEALS SLOWER ...?
SZZZ
MY LEFT HALF IS WEAKER... I HAVEN'T COMPLETELY ADJUSTED TO THIS BODY. I'M NOT INVINCIBLE YET...
I'M NOT READY TO FIGHT THEM MYSELF.
HNN
HNN
HNN
HNN
HNN
HNN
YOU'D BETTER DO THE JOB RIGHT THIS TIME. *KILL* THE JOESTAR PARTY... ***FOR ME.***

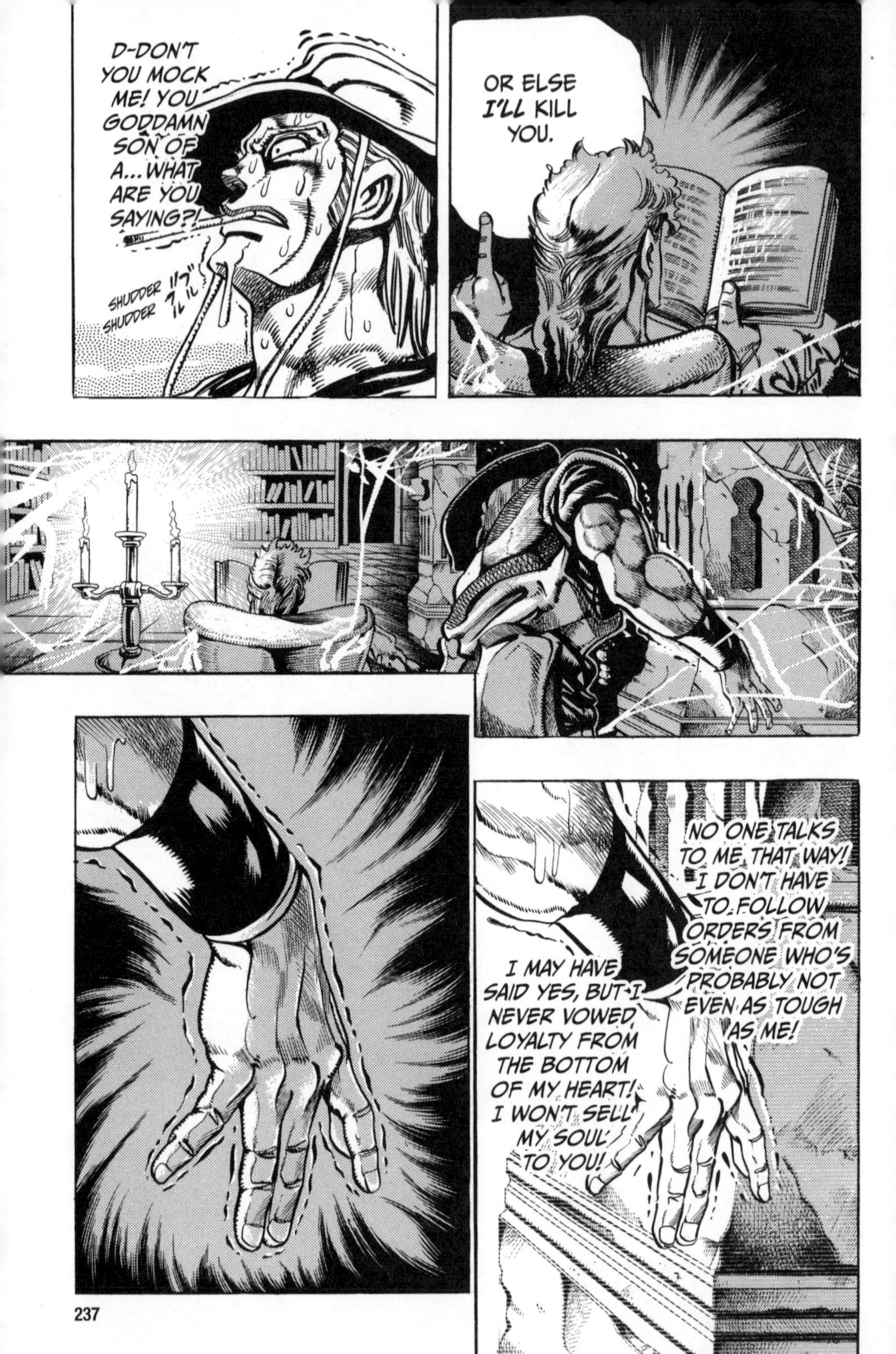
OR ELSE I'LL KILL YOU.
D-DON'T YOU MOCK ME! YOU GODDAMN SON OF A...WHAT ARE YOU SAYING?!
SHUDDER SHUDDER
NO ONE TALKS TO ME THAT WAY! I DON'T HAVE TO FOLLOW ORDERS FROM SOMEONE WHO'S PROBABLY NOT EVEN AS TOUGH AS ME!
I MAY HAVE SAID YES, BUT I NEVER VOWED LOYALTY FROM THE BOTTOM OF MY HEART! I WON'T SELL MY SOUL TO YOU!

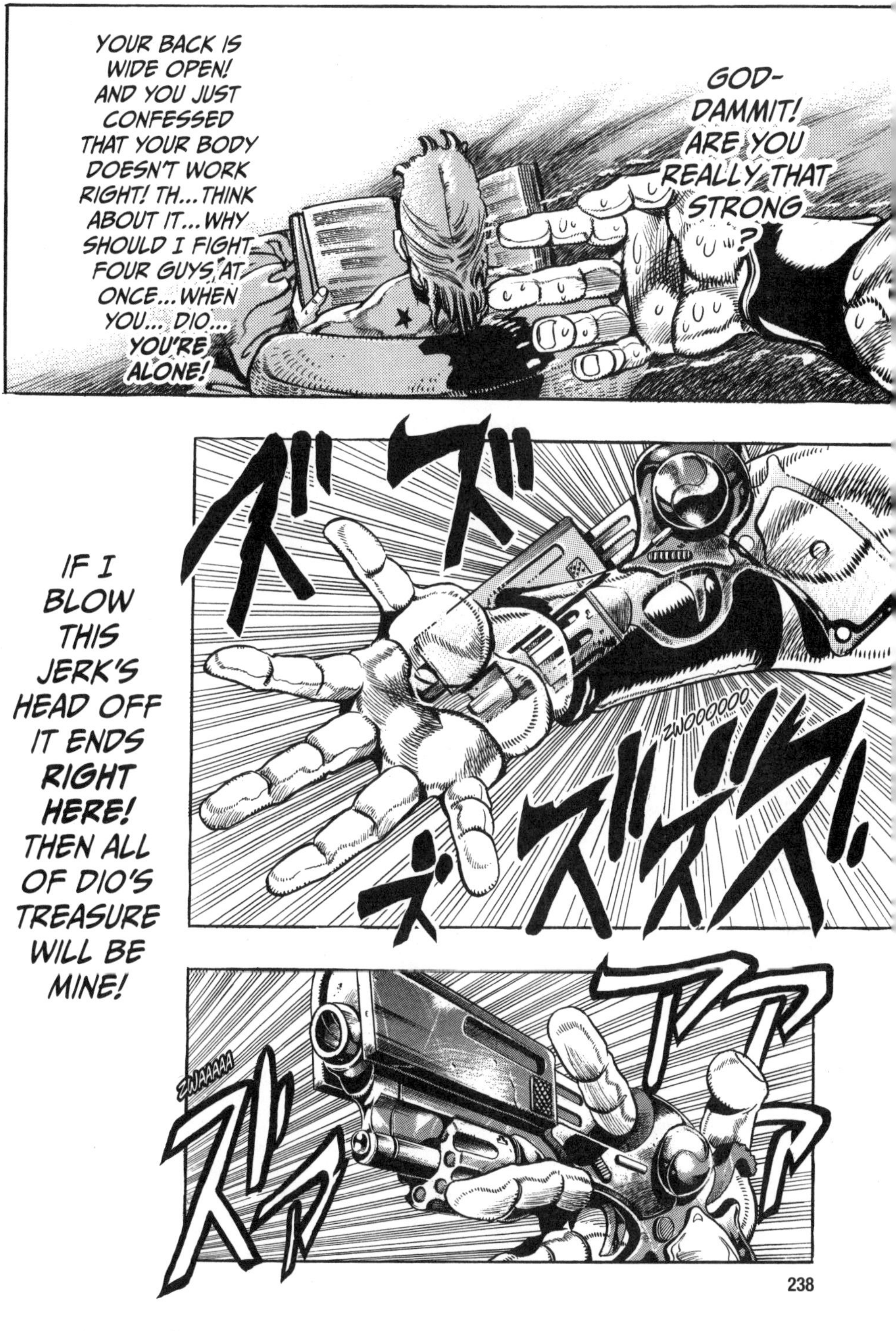

GOD-DAMMIT! ARE YOU REALLY THAT STRONG?
YOUR BACK IS WIDE OPEN! AND YOU JUST CONFESSED THAT YOUR BODY DOESN'T WORK RIGHT! TH...THINK ABOUT IT...WHY SHOULD I FIGHT FOUR GUYS AT ONCE...WHEN YOU... DIO... YOU'RE ALONE!
ZWOOOOOO
IF I BLOW THIS JERK'S HEAD OFF IT ENDS RIGHT HERE! THEN ALL OF DIO'S TREASURE WILL BE MINE!
ZWAAAAA

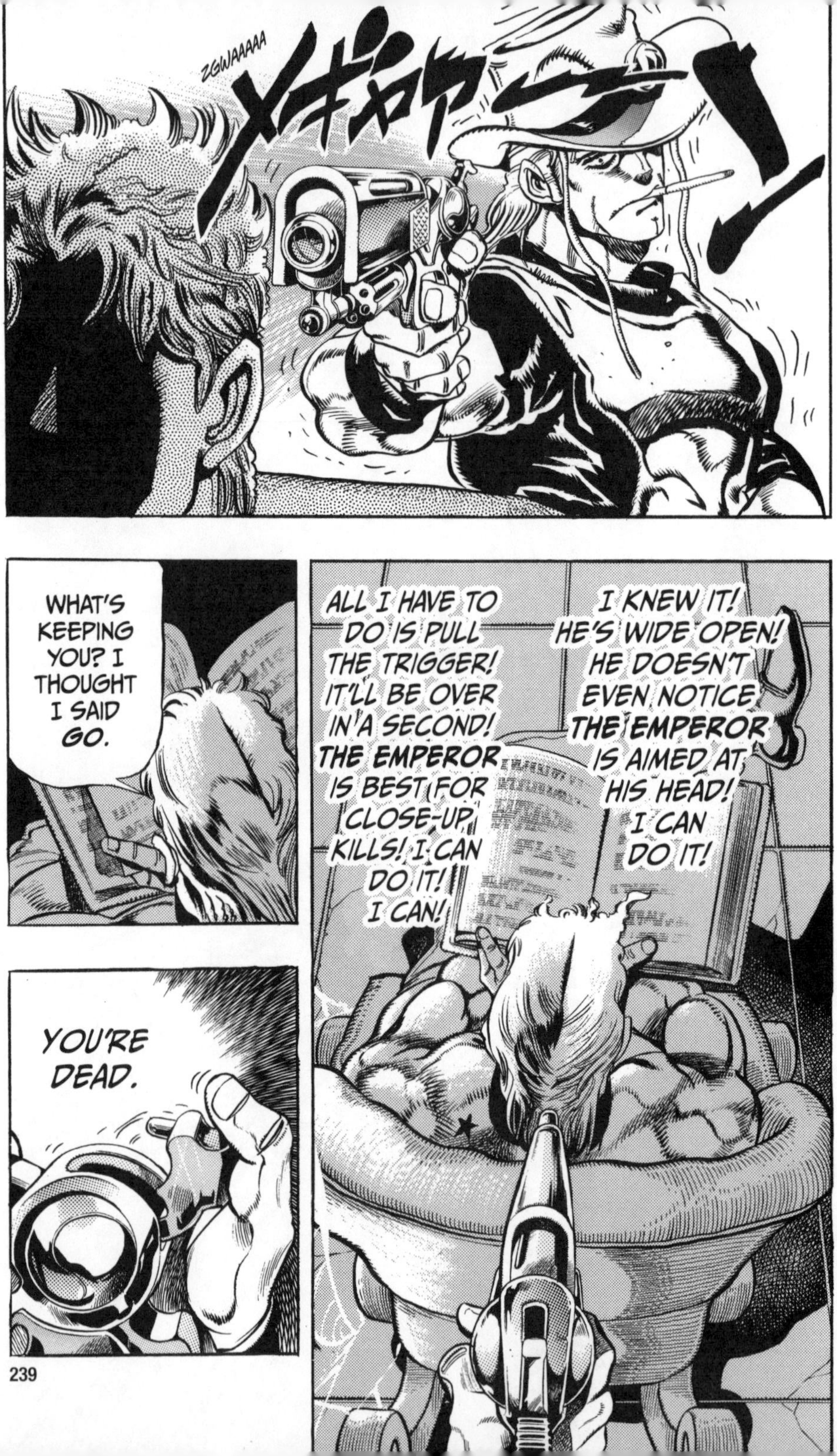
ZGWAAAAA
メギャアーン
I KNEW IT! HE'S WIDE OPEN! HE DOESN'T EVEN NOTICE THE EMPEROR IS AIMED AT HIS HEAD! I CAN DO IT!
ALL I HAVE TO DO IS PULL THE TRIGGER! IT'LL BE OVER IN A SECOND! THE EMPEROR IS BEST FOR CLOSE-UP KILLS! I CAN DO IT! I CAN!
WHAT'S KEEPING YOU? I THOUGHT I SAID GO.
YOU'RE DEAD.

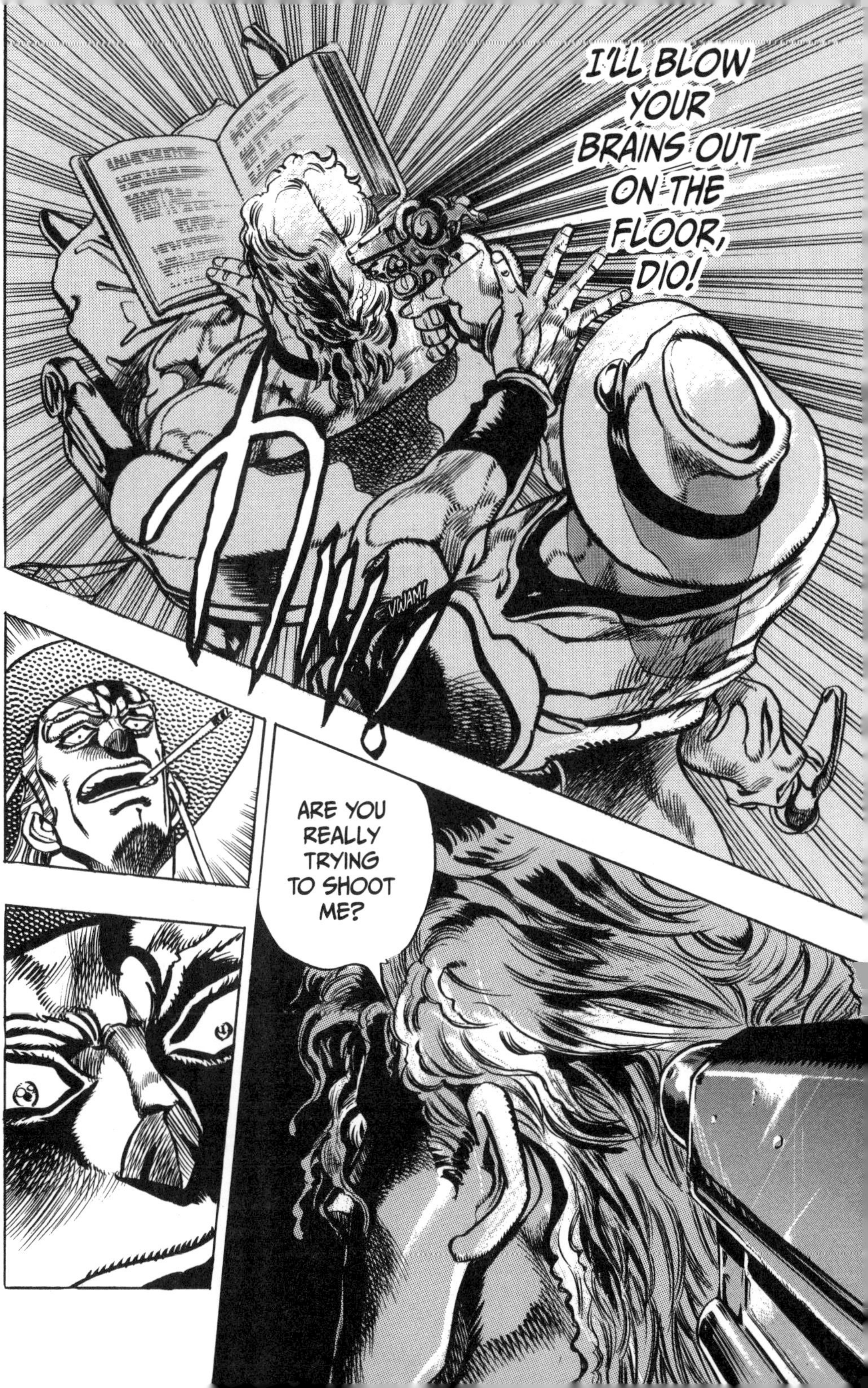
I'LL BLOW YOUR BRAINS OUT ON THE FLOOR, DIO!
VWAM!
ARE YOU REALLY TRYING TO SHOOT ME?

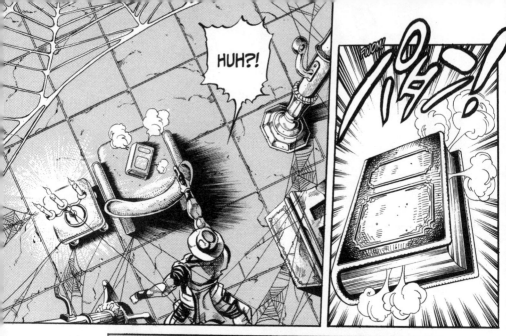

HUH?!

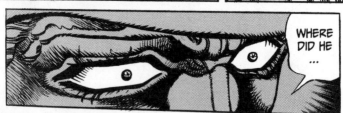

WHERE DID HE ...

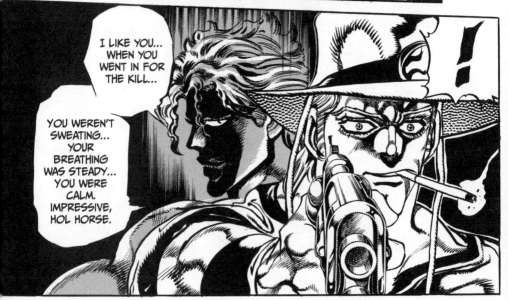

I LIKE YOU... WHEN YOU WENT IN FOR THE KILL...

YOU WEREN'T SWEATING... YOUR BREATHING WAS STEADY... YOU WERE CALM. IMPRESSIVE, HOL HORSE.

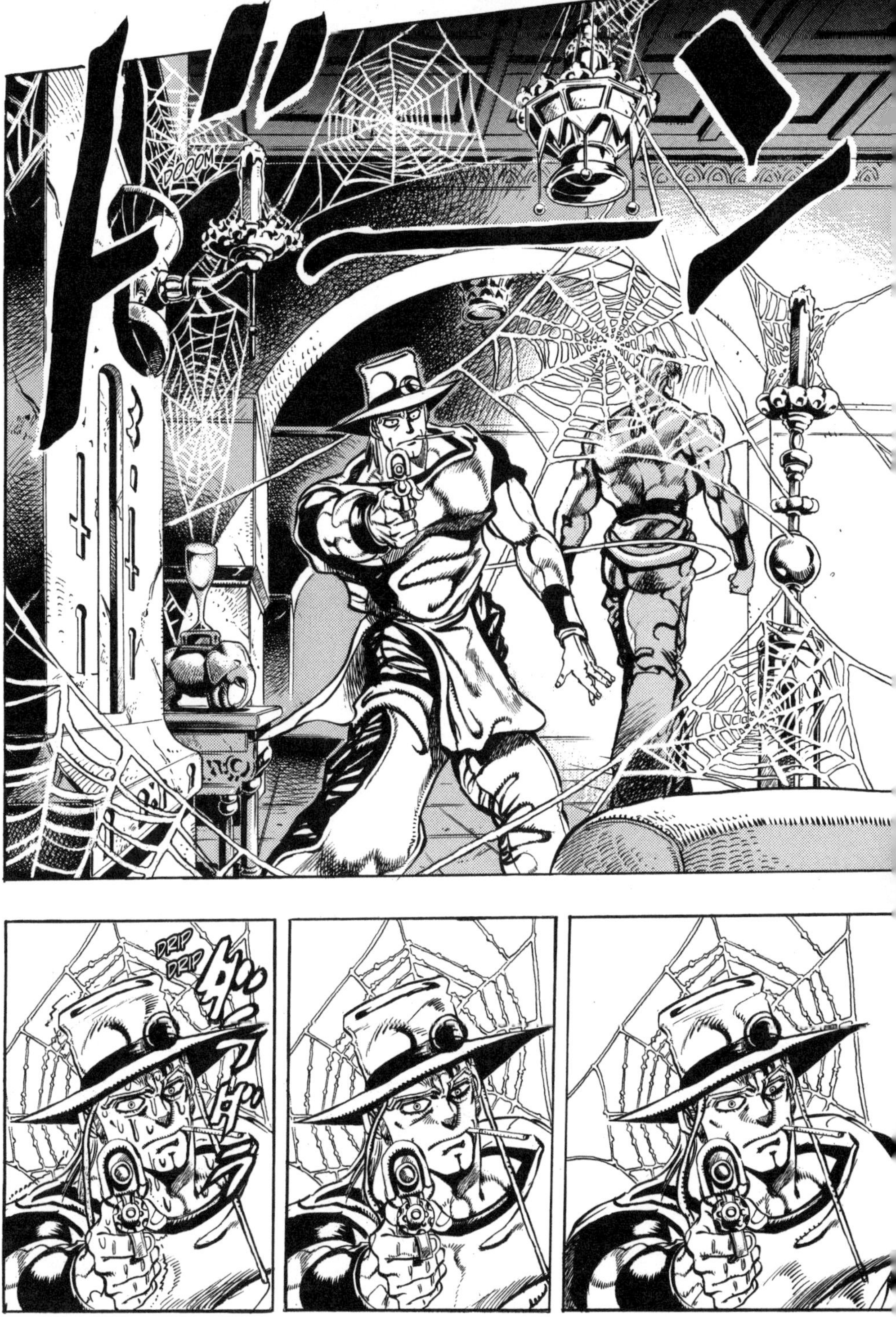
DOOOM
DRIP DRIP

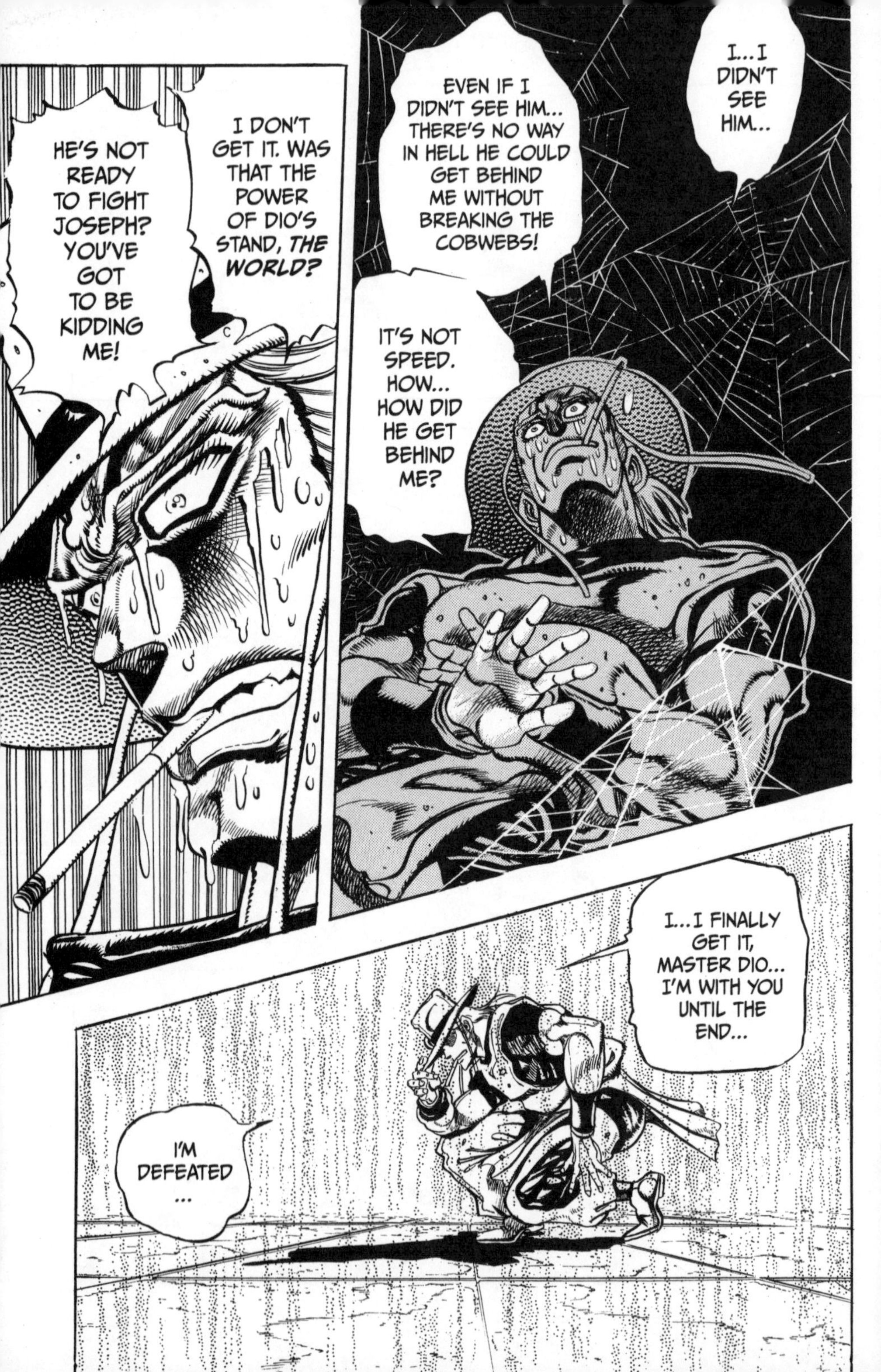
I...I DIDN'T SEE HIM...
EVEN IF I DIDN'T SEE HIM... THERE'S NO WAY IN HELL HE COULD GET BEHIND ME WITHOUT BREAKING THE COBWEBS!
IT'S NOT SPEED. HOW... HOW DID HE GET BEHIND ME?
I DON'T GET IT. WAS THAT THE POWER OF DIO'S STAND, *THE WORLD?*
HE'S NOT READY TO FIGHT JOSEPH? YOU'VE GOT TO BE KIDDING ME!
I...I FINALLY GET IT, MASTER DIO... I'M WITH YOU UNTIL THE END...
I'M DEFEATED ...

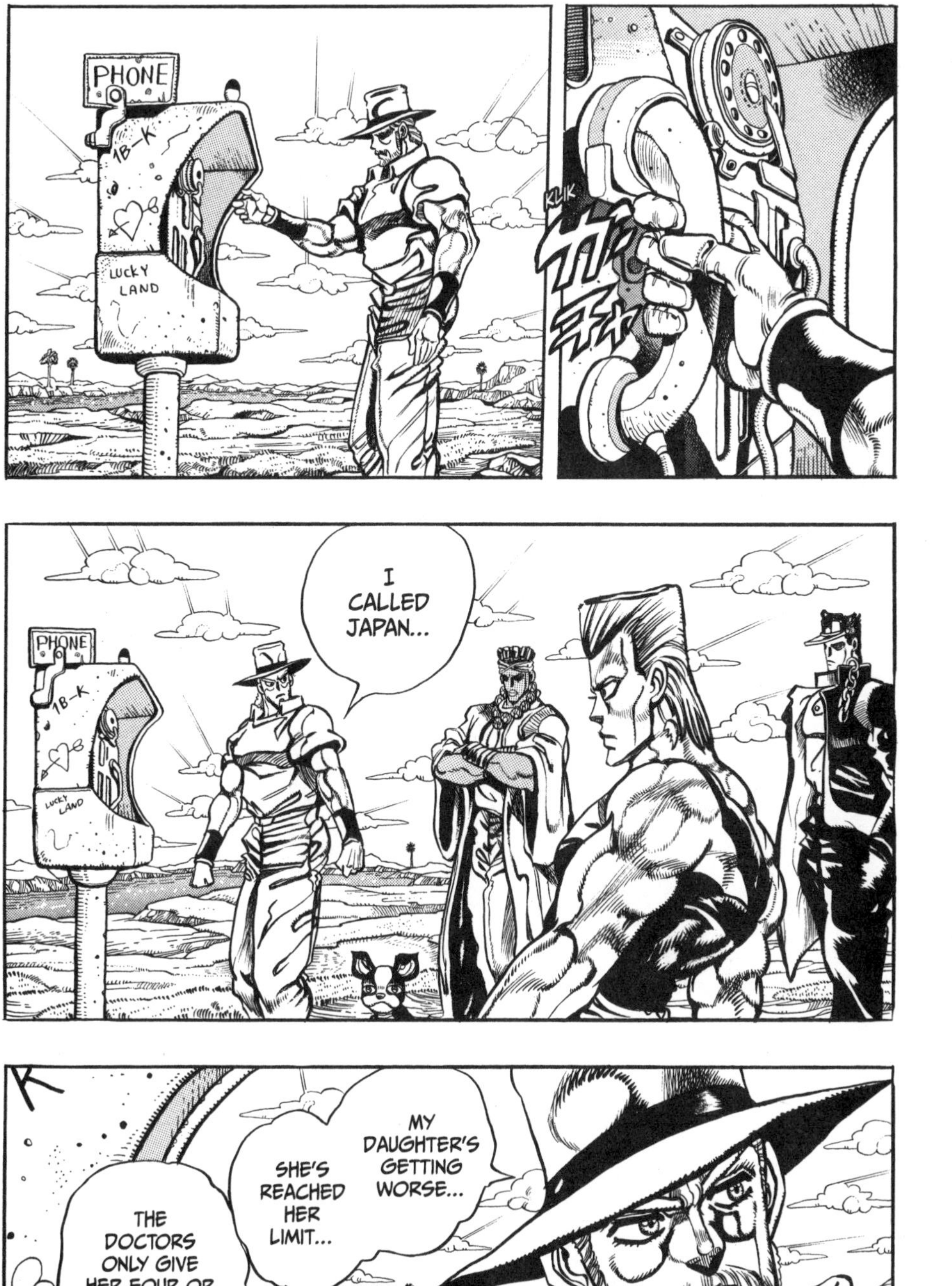
KLIK
カチャ
PHONE
1B-K
LUCKY LAND
PHONE
1B-K
LUCKY LAND
I CALLED JAPAN...
MY DAUGHTER'S GETTING WORSE...
SHE'S REACHED HER LIMIT...
THE DOCTORS ONLY GIVE HER FOUR OR FIVE DAYS...

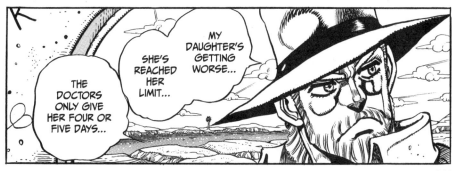

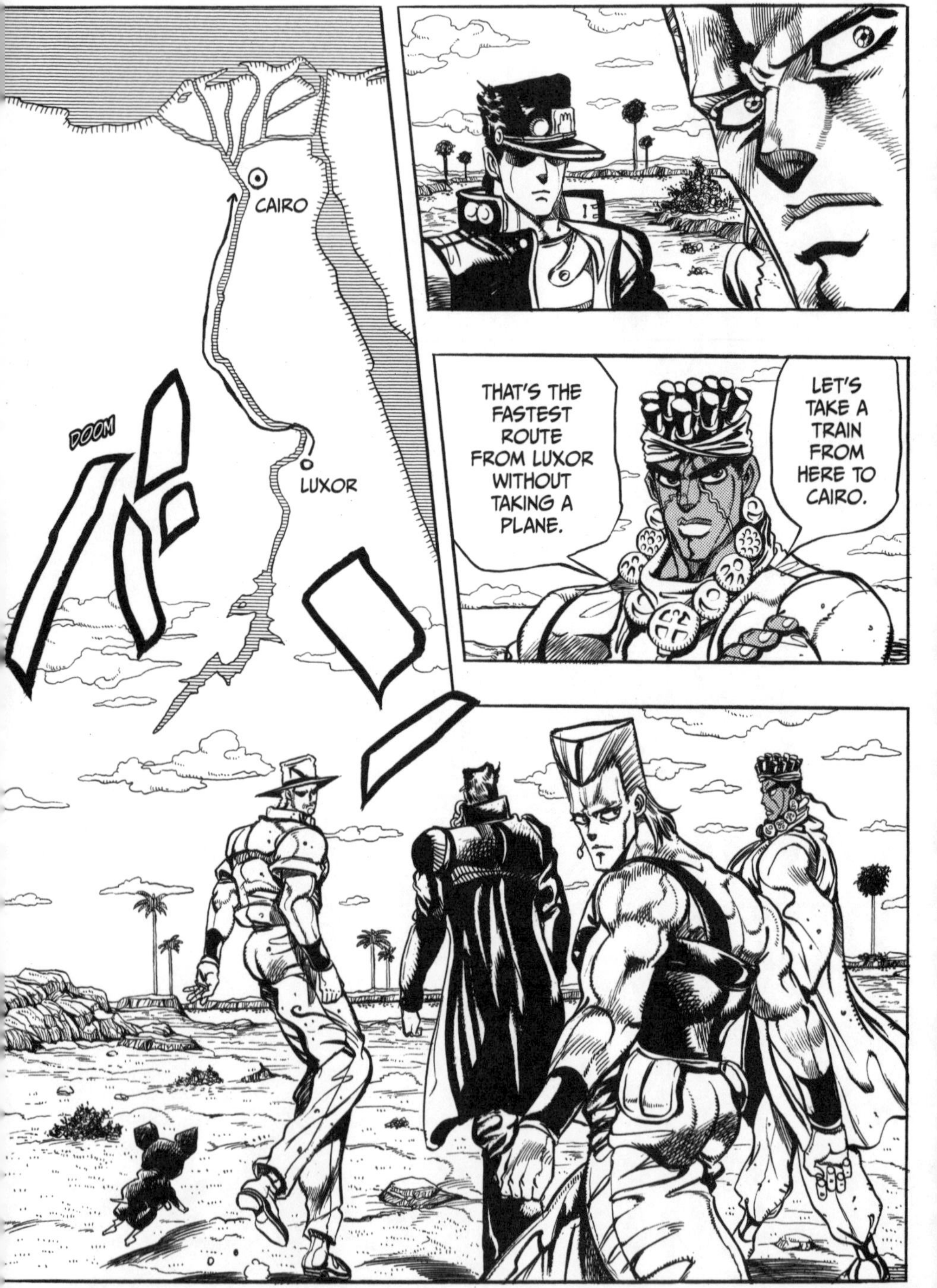
LET'S TAKE A TRAIN FROM HERE TO CAIRO.
THAT'S THE FASTEST ROUTE FROM LUXOR WITHOUT TAKING A PLANE.
CAIRO
LUXOR
DOOM

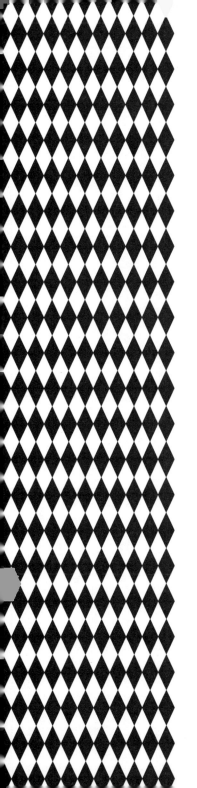

JoJo's
BIZARRE ADVENTURE

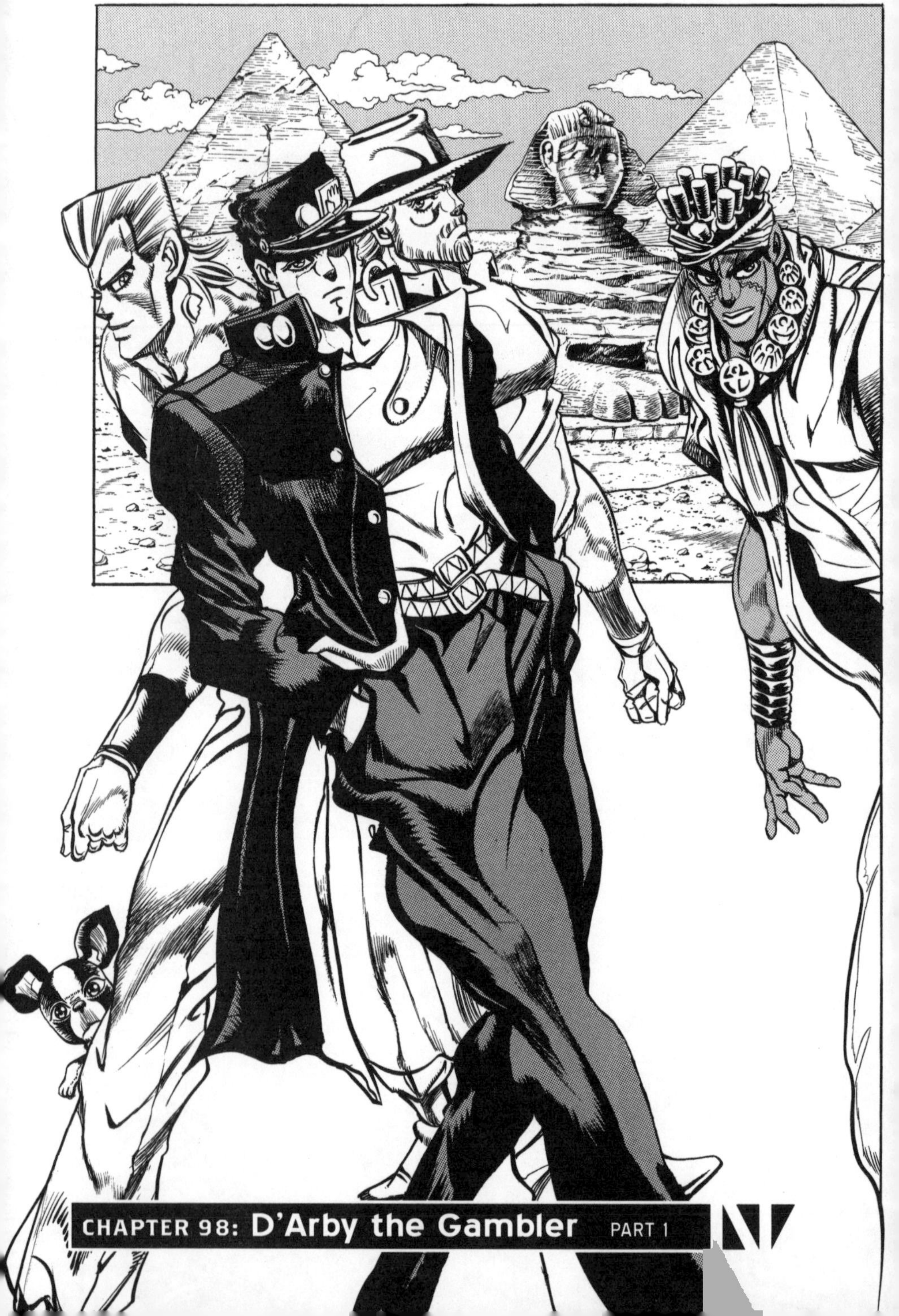
CHAPTER 98: D'Arby the Gambler PART 1

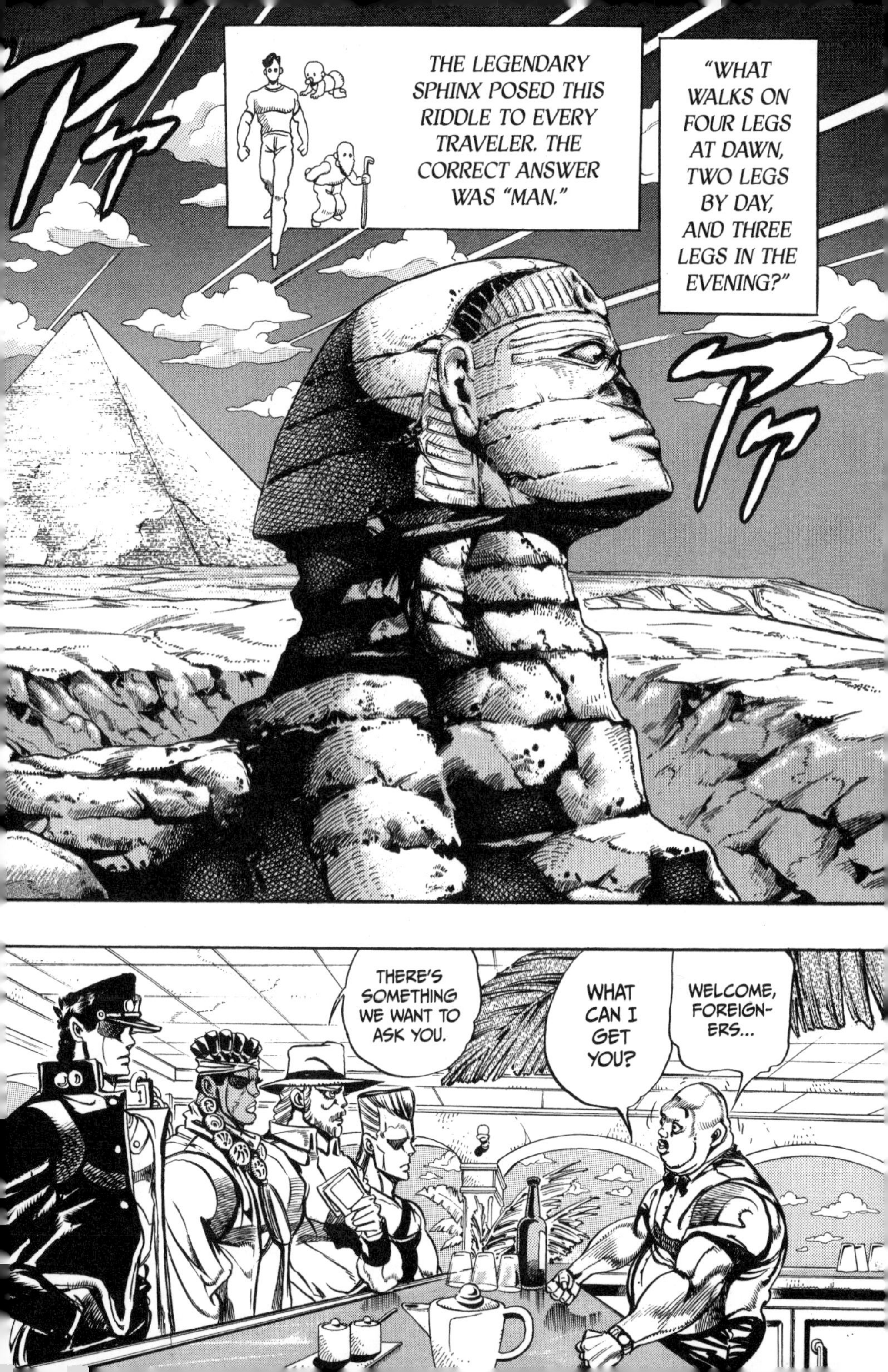
"WHAT WALKS ON FOUR LEGS AT DAWN, TWO LEGS BY DAY, AND THREE LEGS IN THE EVENING?"
THE LEGENDARY SPHINX POSED THIS RIDDLE TO EVERY TRAVELER. THE CORRECT ANSWER WAS "MAN."
アァ
アァ
WELCOME, FOREIGN-ERS...
WHAT CAN I GET YOU?
THERE'S SOMETHING WE WANT TO ASK YOU.

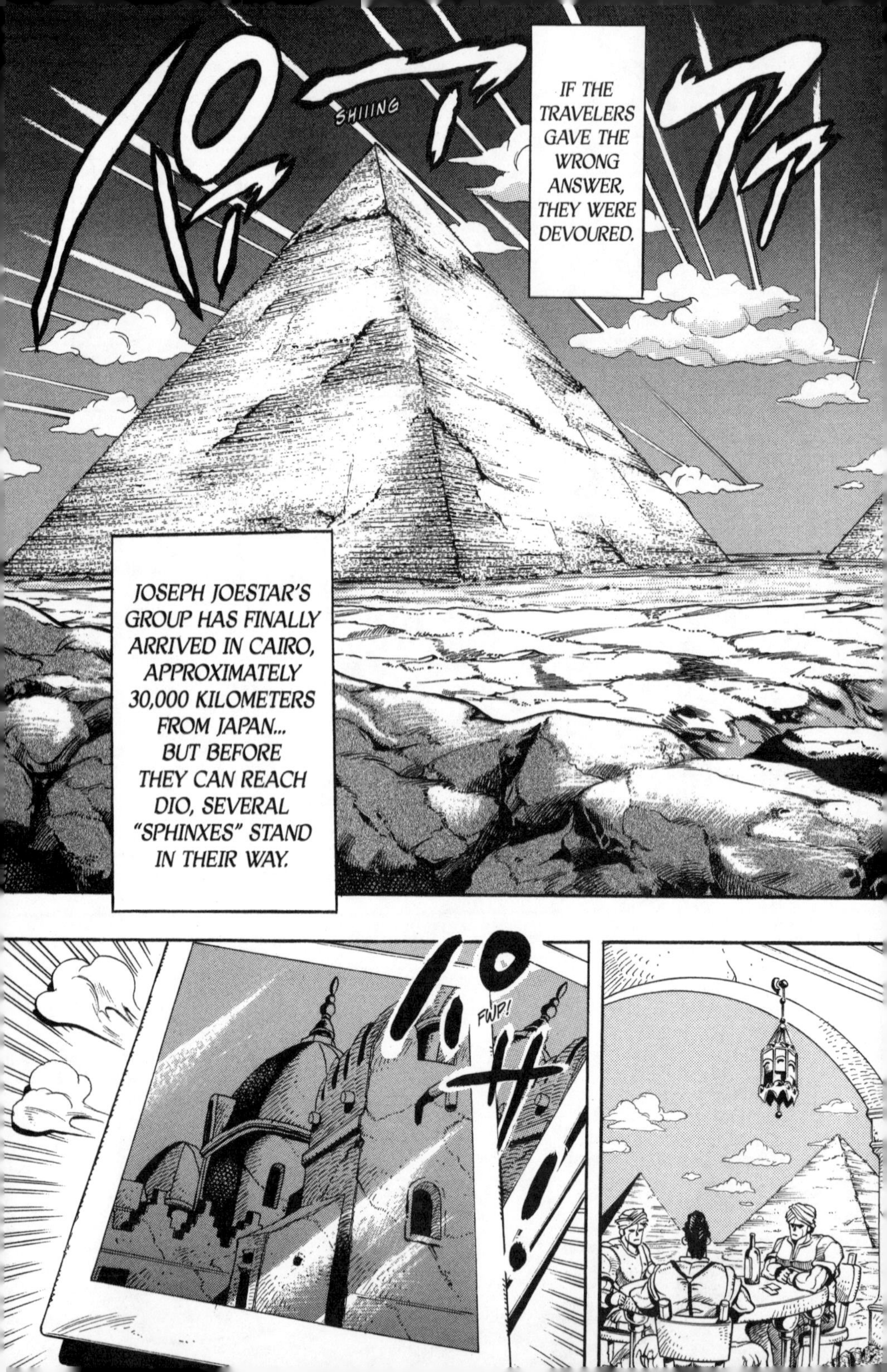
IF THE TRAVELERS GAVE THE WRONG ANSWER, THEY WERE DEVOURED.
SHIIING
JOSEPH JOESTAR'S GROUP HAS FINALLY ARRIVED IN CAIRO, APPROXIMATELY 30,000 KILOMETERS FROM JAPAN... BUT BEFORE THEY CAN REACH DIO, SEVERAL "SPHINXES" STAND IN THEIR WAY.
FWP!

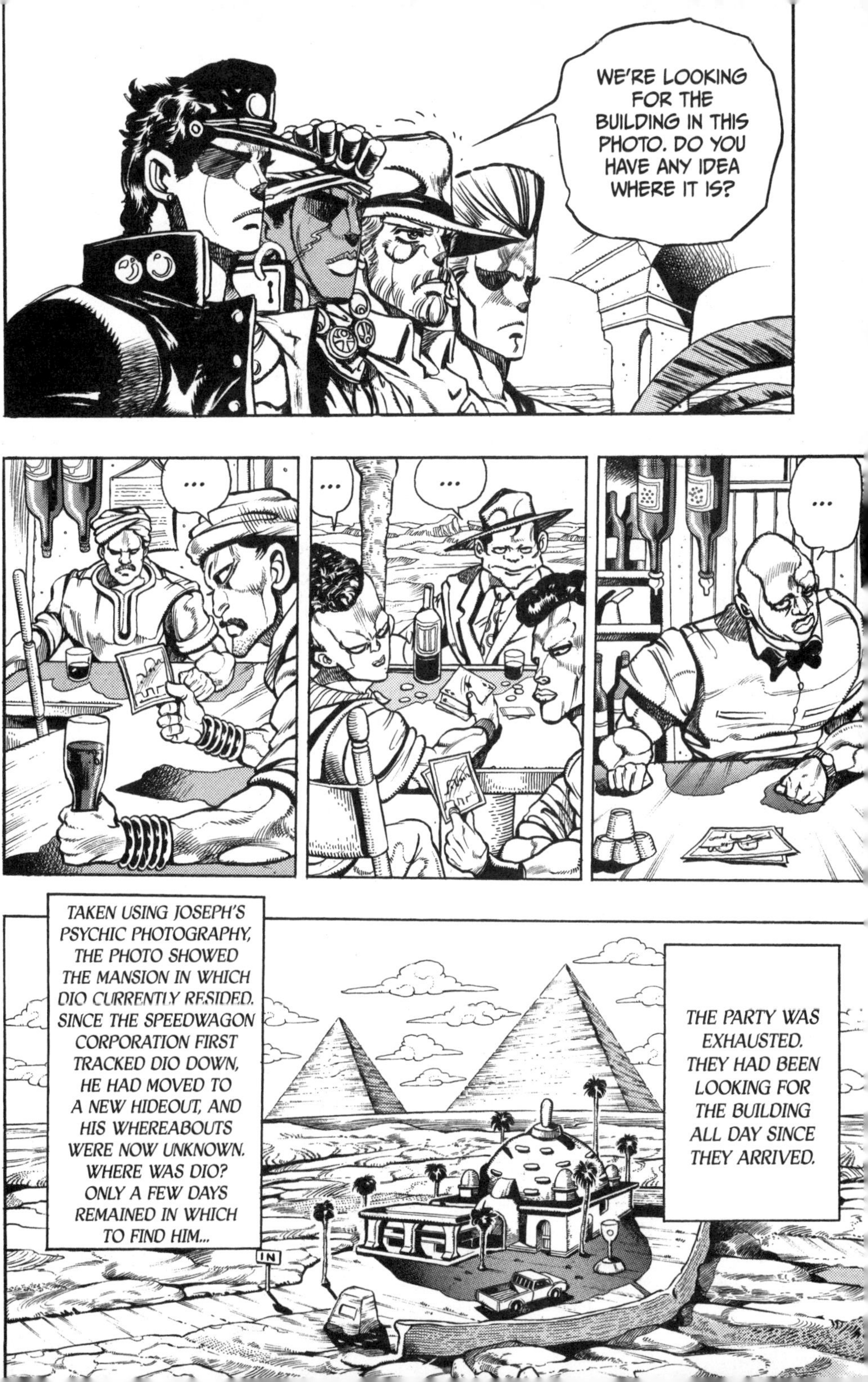
WE'RE LOOKING FOR THE BUILDING IN THIS PHOTO. DO YOU HAVE ANY IDEA WHERE IT IS?
...
...
...
...
THE PARTY WAS EXHAUSTED. THEY HAD BEEN LOOKING FOR THE BUILDING ALL DAY SINCE THEY ARRIVED.
TAKEN USING JOSEPH'S PSYCHIC PHOTOGRAPHY, THE PHOTO SHOWED THE MANSION IN WHICH DIO CURRENTLY RESIDED. SINCE THE SPEEDWAGON CORPORATION FIRST TRACKED DIO DOWN, HE HAD MOVED TO A NEW HIDEOUT, AND HIS WHEREABOUTS WERE NOW UNKNOWN. WHERE WAS DIO? ONLY A FEW DAYS REMAINED IN WHICH TO FIND HIM...
IN

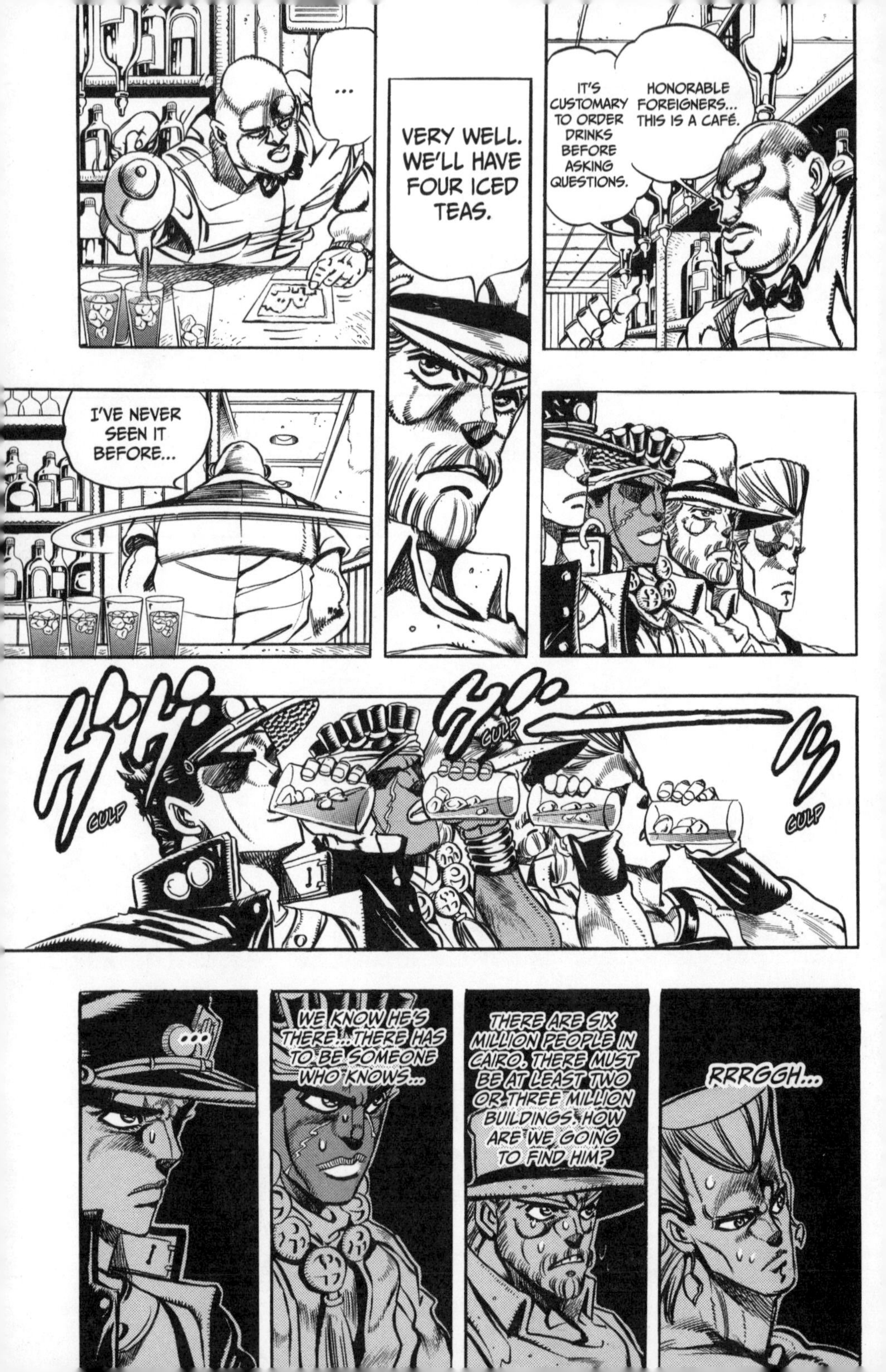
HONORABLE FOREIGNERS... THIS IS A CAFÉ.
IT'S CUSTOMARY TO ORDER DRINKS BEFORE ASKING QUESTIONS.
VERY WELL. WE'LL HAVE FOUR ICED TEAS.
...
I'VE NEVER SEEN IT BEFORE...
GULP
GULP
GULP
RRRGGH...
THERE ARE SIX MILLION PEOPLE IN CAIRO. THERE MUST BE AT LEAST TWO OR THREE MILLION BUILDINGS. HOW ARE WE GOING TO FIND HIM?
WE KNOW HE'S THERE... THERE HAS TO BE SOMEONE WHO KNOWS...
...

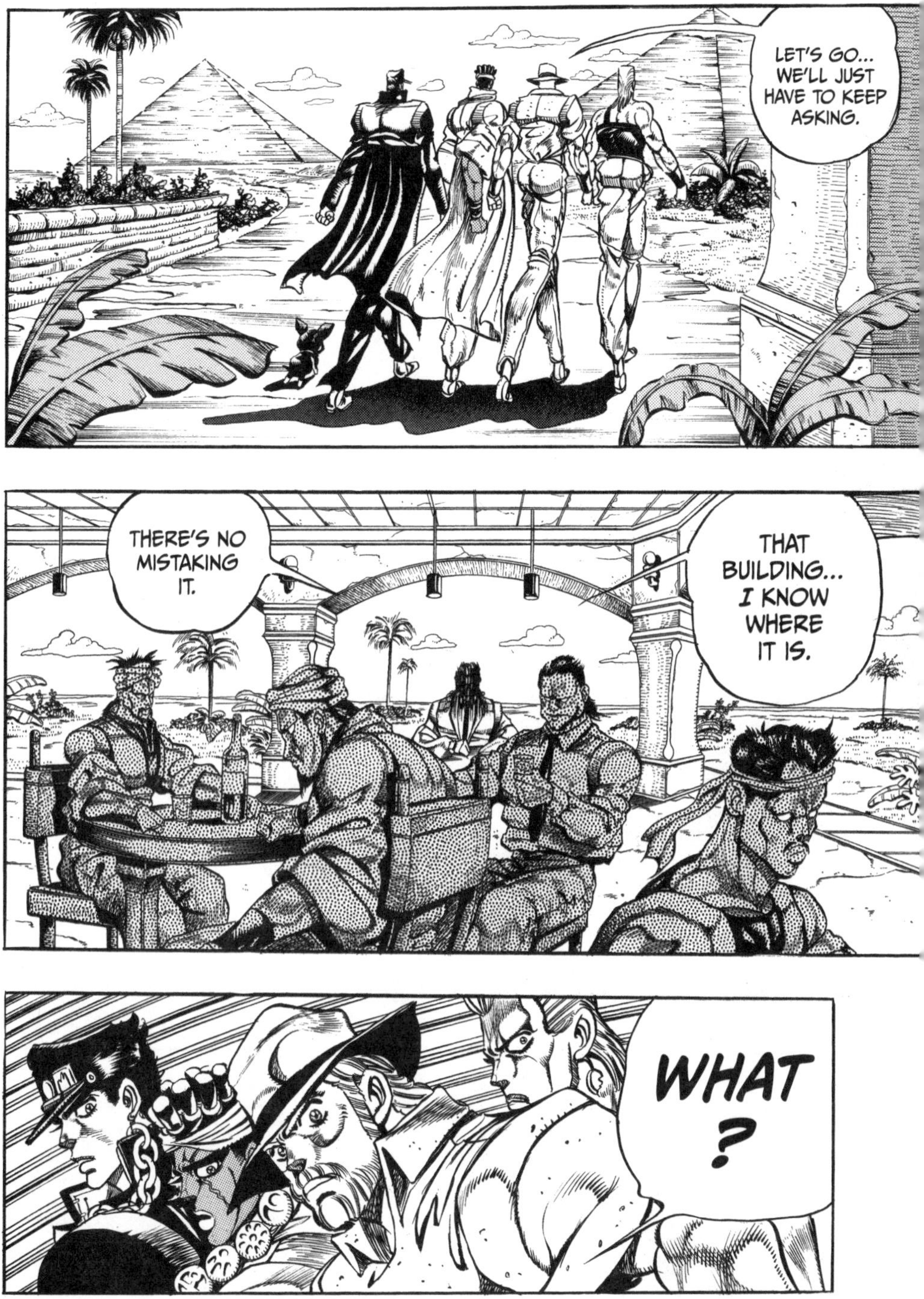
LET'S GO... WE'LL JUST HAVE TO KEEP ASKING.
THAT BUILDING... I KNOW WHERE IT IS.
THERE'S NO MISTAKING IT.
WHAT ?

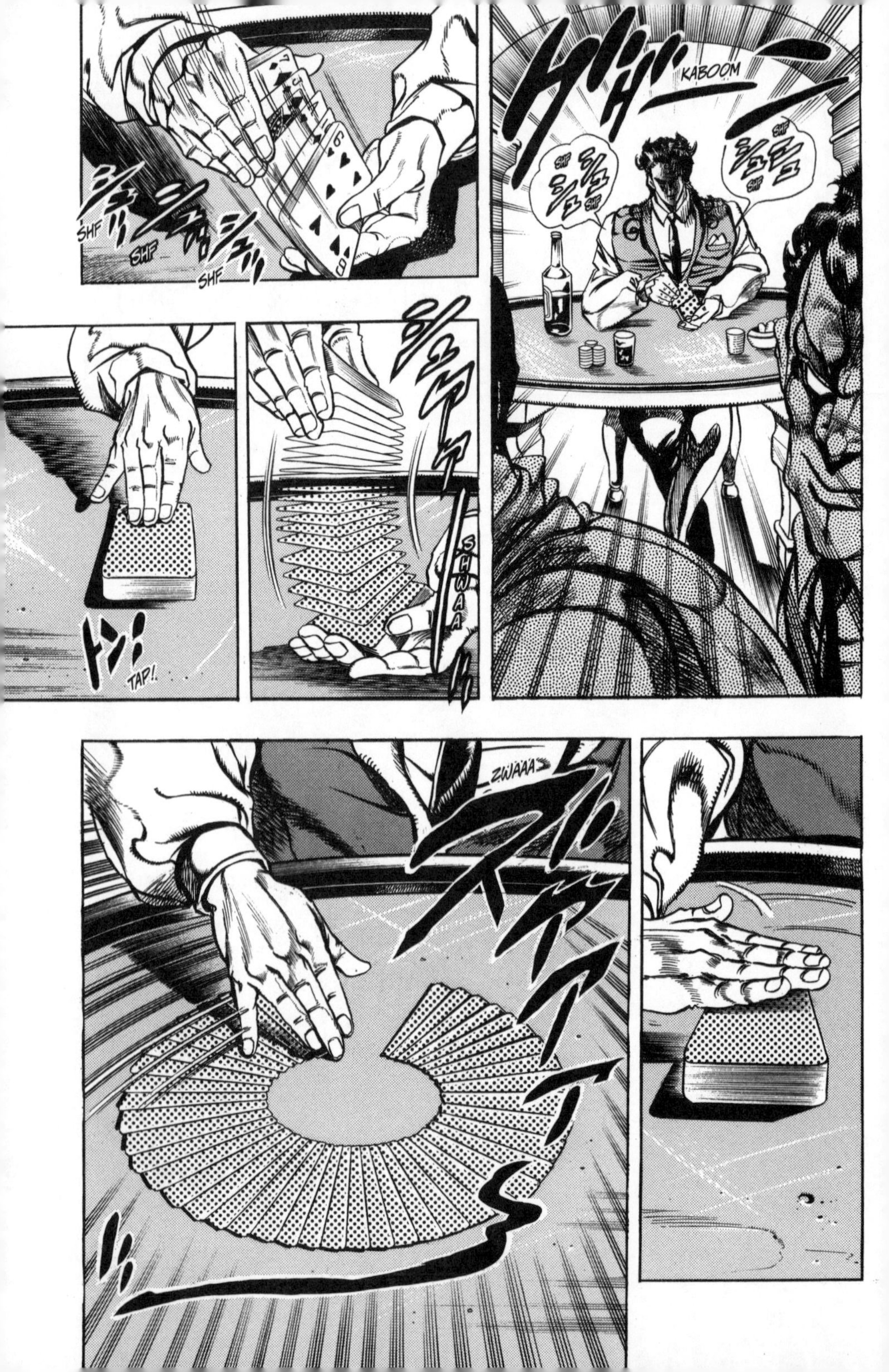
KABOOM
SHF SHF SHF
SHF SHF
SHF SHF SHF
SHWAAA
TAP!
ZWAAA

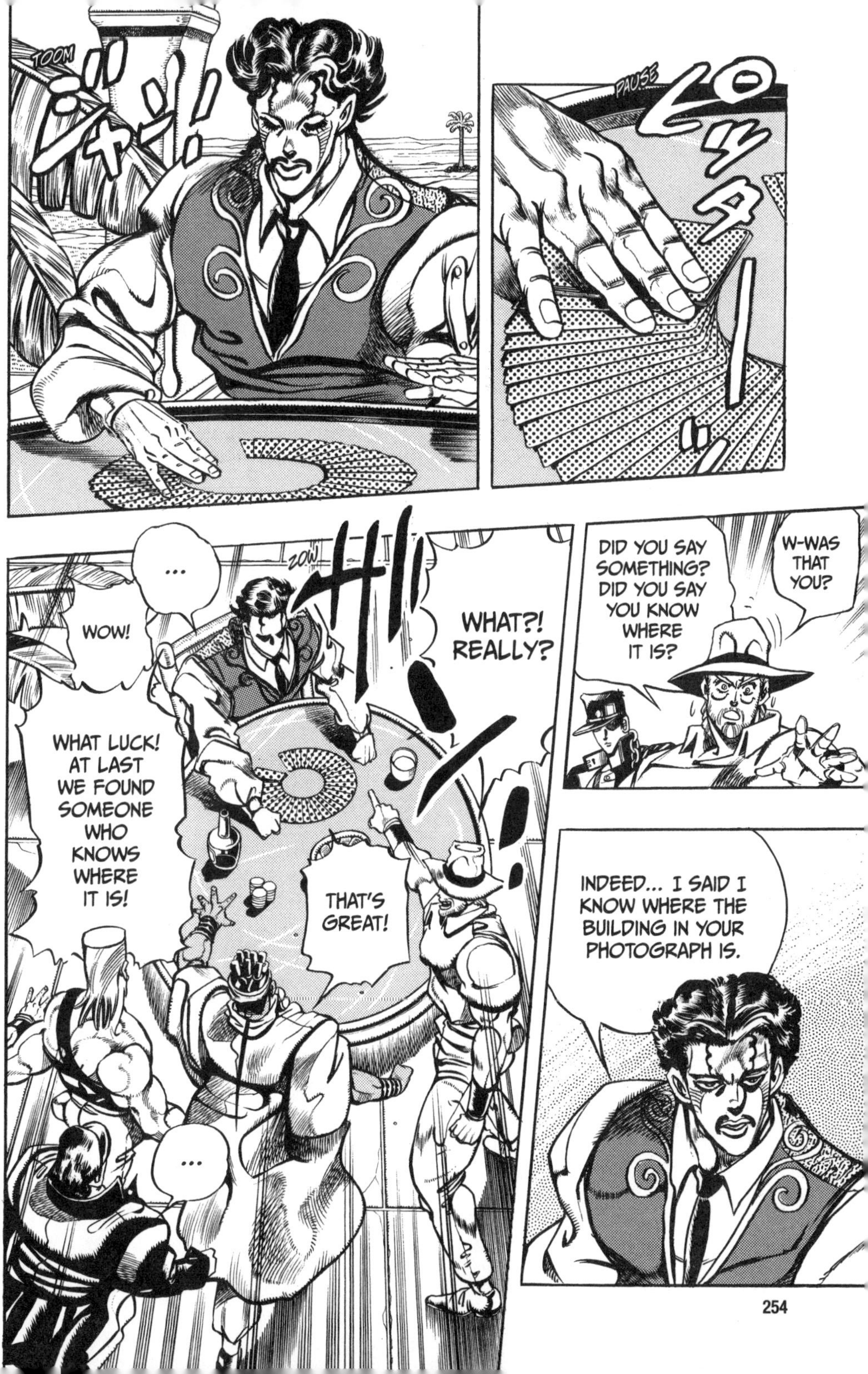
PAUSE
TOOM
W-WAS THAT YOU?
DID YOU SAY SOMETHING? DID YOU SAY YOU KNOW WHERE IT IS?
INDEED... I SAID I KNOW WHERE THE BUILDING IN YOUR PHOTOGRAPH IS.
ZOW
WHAT?! REALLY?
...
WOW!
WHAT LUCK! AT LAST WE FOUND SOMEONE WHO KNOWS WHERE IT IS!
THAT'S GREAT!
...

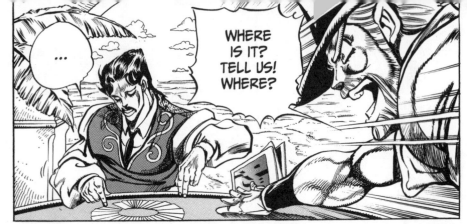

WHERE IS IT? TELL US! WHERE?

···

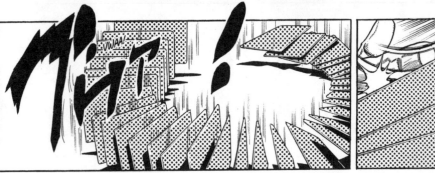

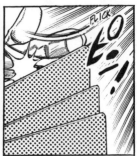

FLICK

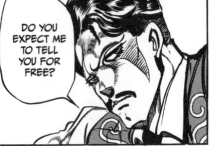

DO YOU EXPECT ME TO TELL YOU FOR FREE?

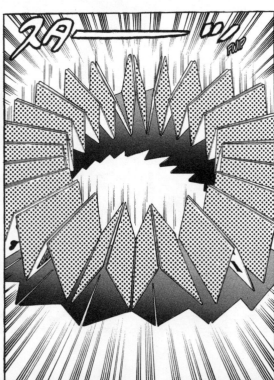

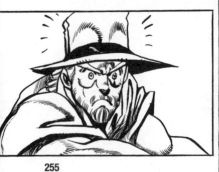

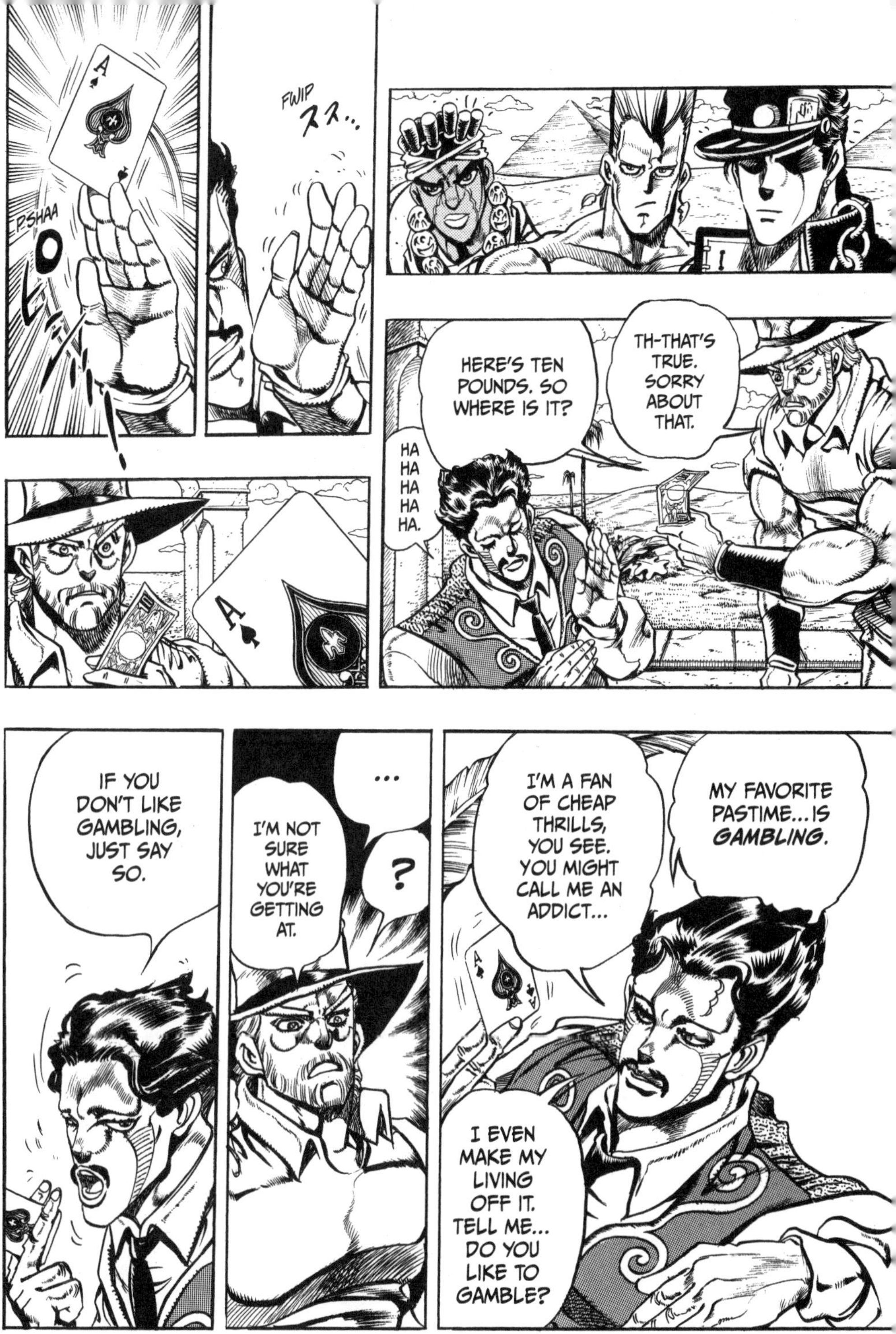
TH-THAT'S TRUE. SORRY ABOUT THAT.
HERE'S TEN POUNDS. SO WHERE IS IT?
HA HA HA HA HA.
FWIP
P.SHAA
MY FAVORITE PASTIME...IS ***GAMBLING***.
I'M A FAN OF CHEAP THRILLS, YOU SEE. YOU MIGHT CALL ME AN ADDICT...
I EVEN MAKE MY LIVING OFF IT. TELL ME... DO YOU LIKE TO GAMBLE?
...
?
I'M NOT SURE WHAT YOU'RE GETTING AT.
IF YOU DON'T LIKE GAMBLING, JUST SAY SO.

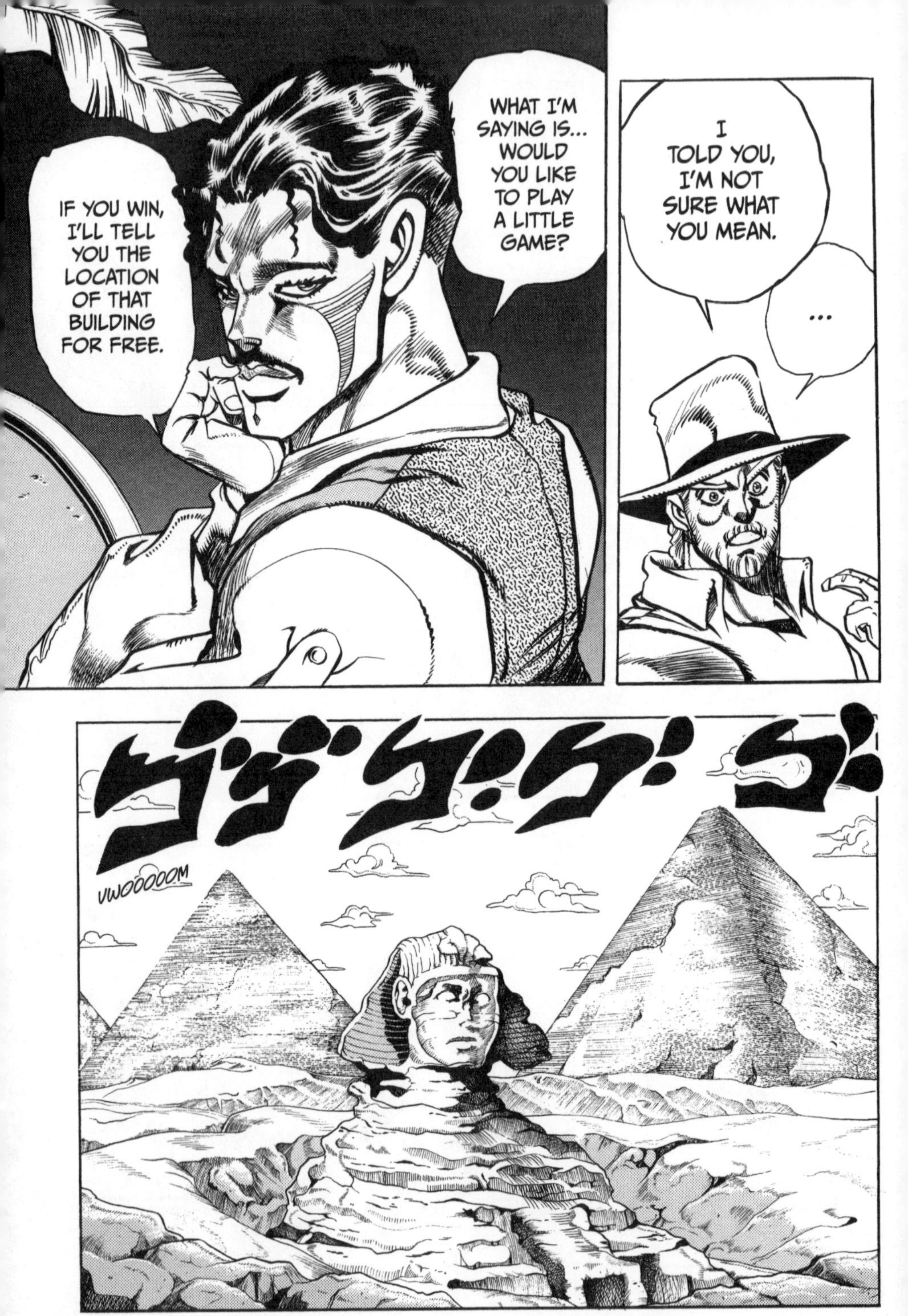
I TOLD YOU, I'M NOT SURE WHAT YOU MEAN.
...
WHAT I'M SAYING IS... WOULD YOU LIKE TO PLAY A LITTLE GAME?
IF YOU WIN, I'LL TELL YOU THE LOCATION OF THAT BUILDING FOR FREE.
VWOOOOOM

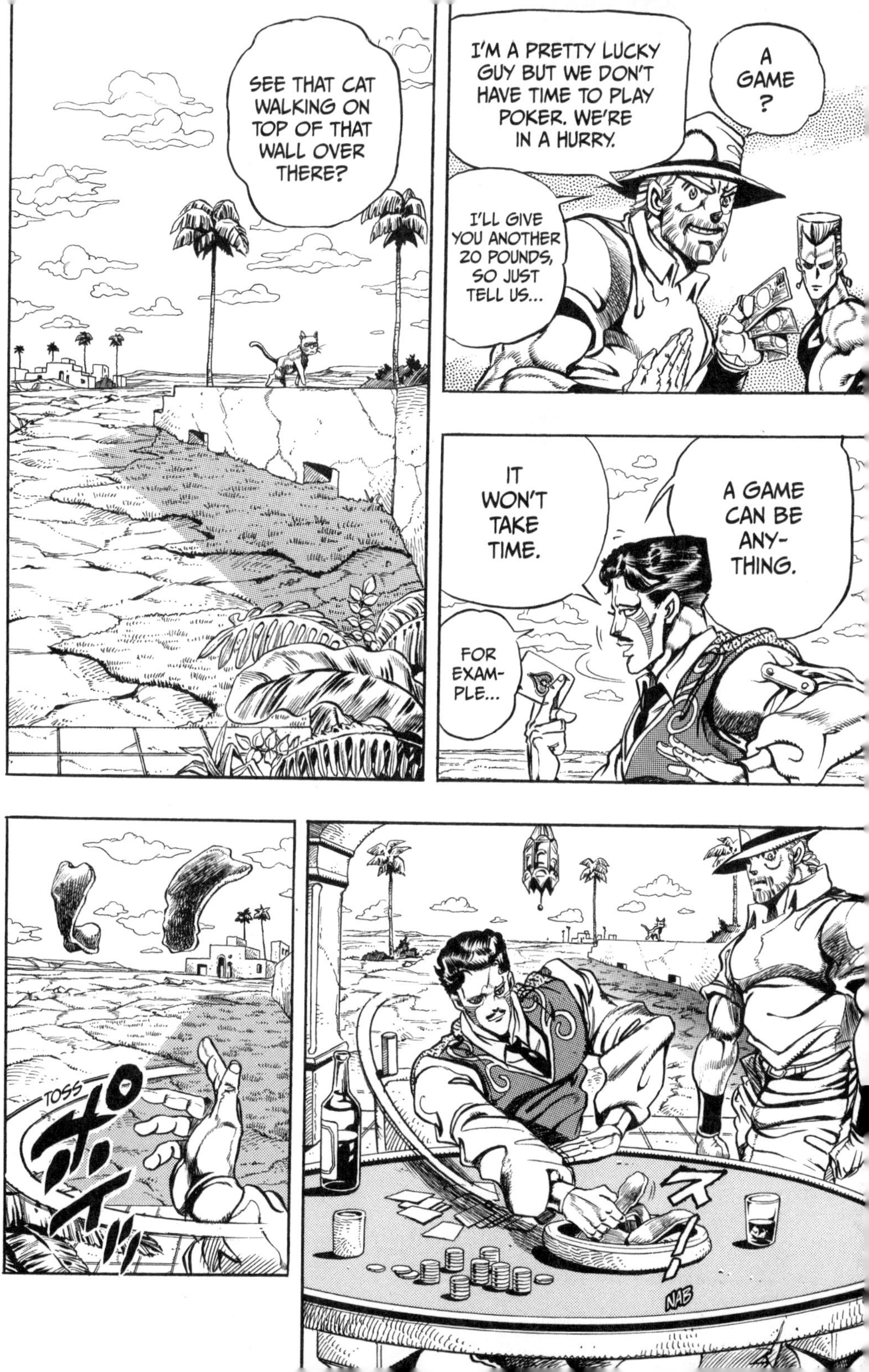
A GAME?
I'M A PRETTY LUCKY GUY BUT WE DON'T HAVE TIME TO PLAY POKER. WE'RE IN A HURRY.
I'LL GIVE YOU ANOTHER 20 POUNDS, SO JUST TELL US...
A GAME CAN BE ANY-THING.
IT WON'T TAKE TIME.
FOR EXAM-PLE...
SEE THAT CAT WALKING ON TOP OF THAT WALL OVER THERE?
NAB
TOSS

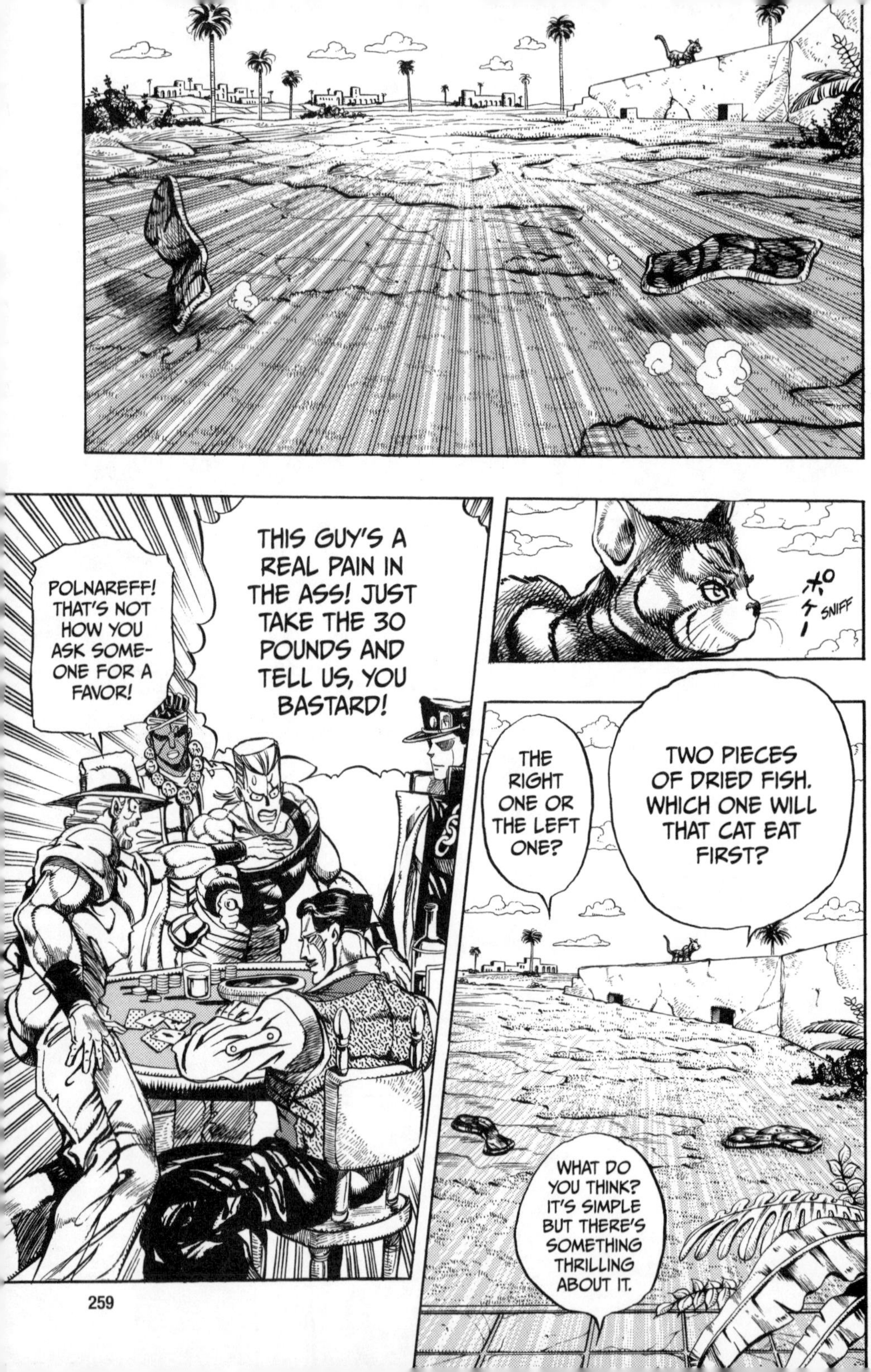
SNIFF
TWO PIECES OF DRIED FISH. WHICH ONE WILL THAT CAT EAT FIRST?
THE RIGHT ONE OR THE LEFT ONE?
WHAT DO YOU THINK? IT'S SIMPLE BUT THERE'S SOMETHING THRILLING ABOUT IT.
THIS GUY'S A REAL PAIN IN THE ASS! JUST TAKE THE 30 POUNDS AND TELL US, YOU BASTARD!
POLNAREFF! THAT'S NOT HOW YOU ASK SOME-ONE FOR A FAVOR!

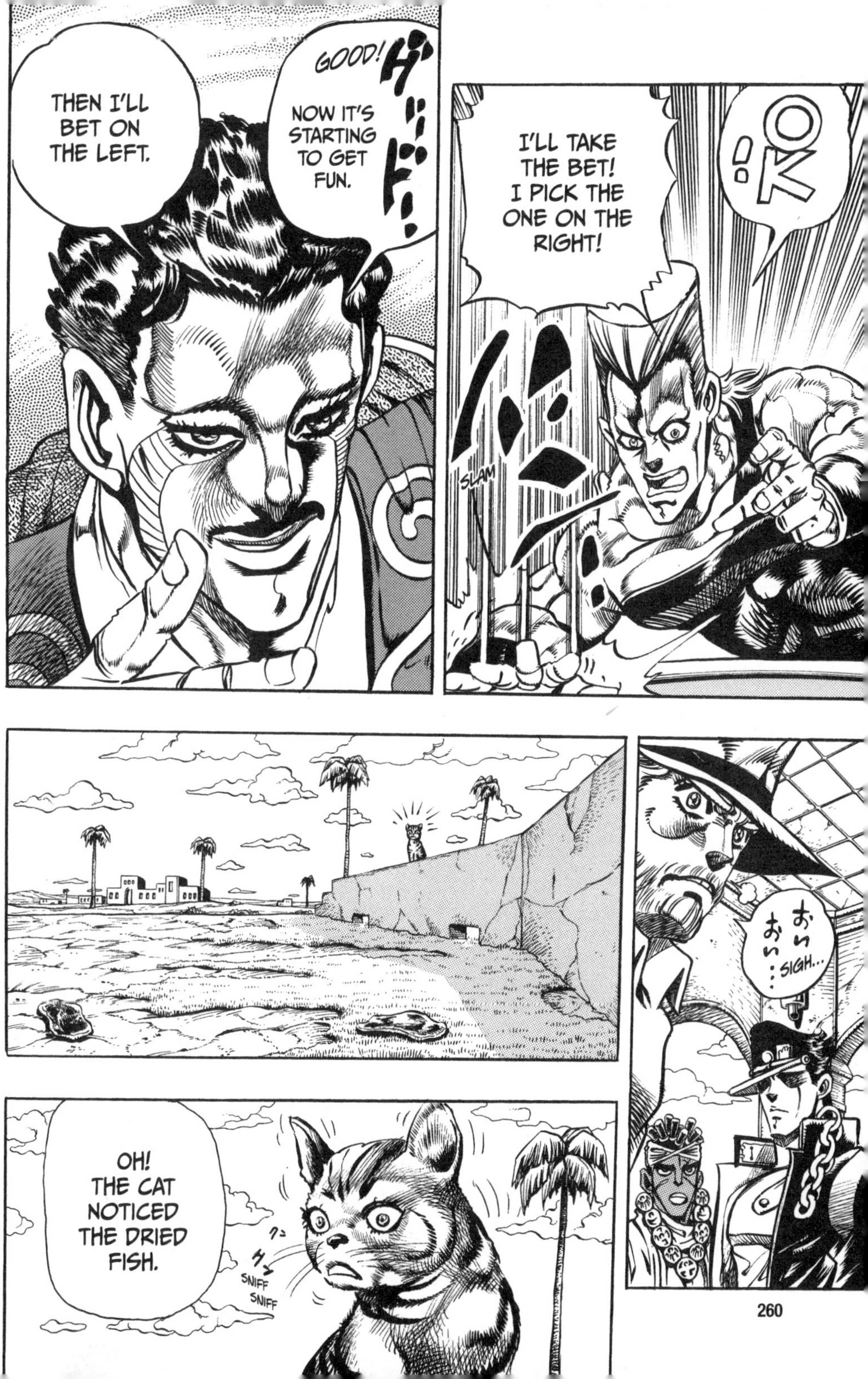

O.K!
I'LL TAKE THE BET! I PICK THE ONE ON THE RIGHT!
SLAM
GOOD!
NOW IT'S STARTING TO GET FUN.
THEN I'LL BET ON THE LEFT.
おい おい…
SIGH...
OH! THE CAT NOTICED THE DRIED FISH.
SNIFF SNIFF

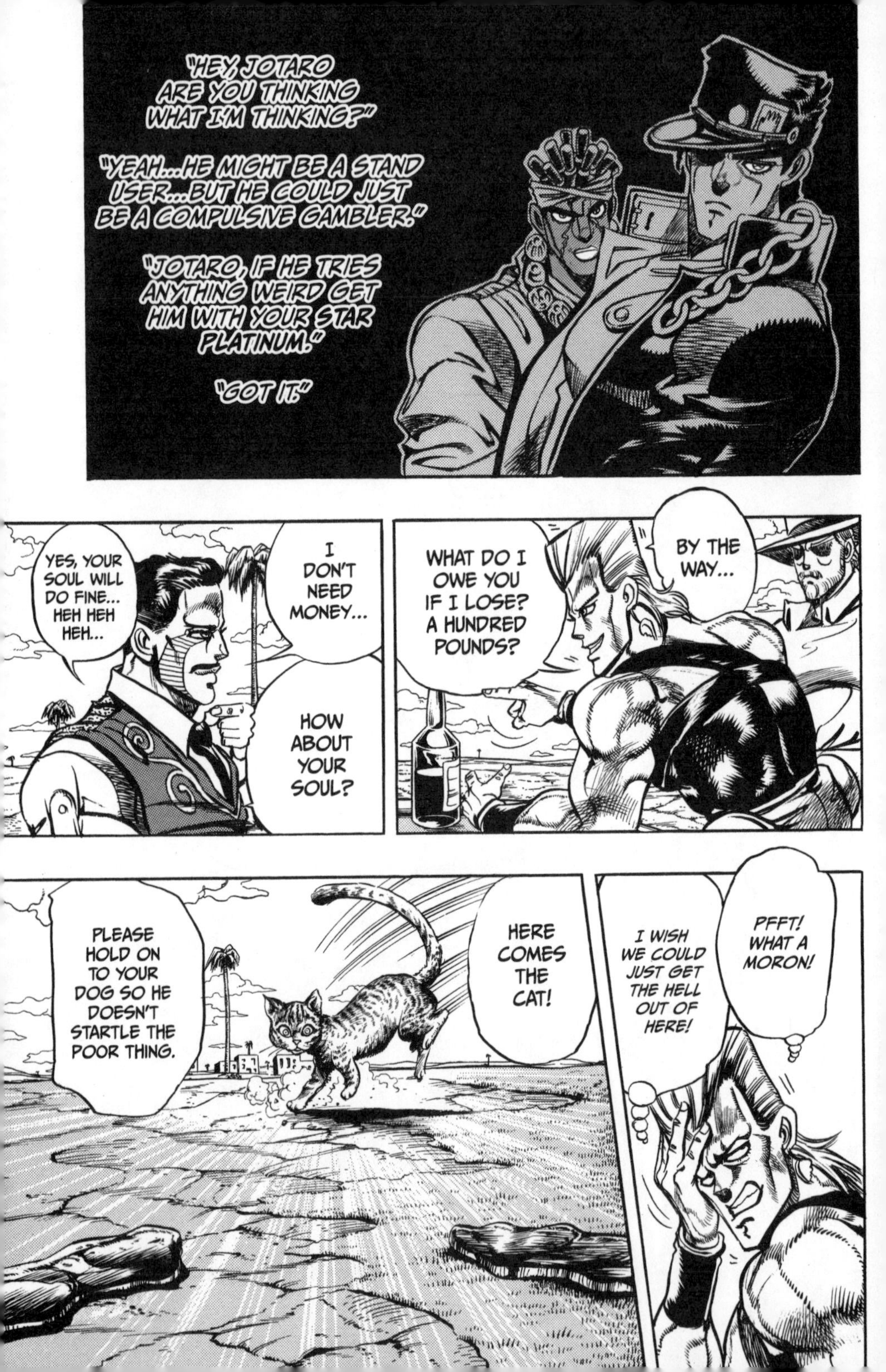
"HEY, JOTARO ARE YOU THINKING WHAT I'M THINKING?"
"YEAH...HE MIGHT BE A STAND USER...BUT HE COULD JUST BE A COMPULSIVE GAMBLER."
"JOTARO, IF HE TRIES ANYTHING WEIRD GET HIM WITH YOUR STAR PLATINUM."
"GOT IT."
BY THE WAY...
WHAT DO I OWE YOU IF I LOSE? A HUNDRED POUNDS?
I DON'T NEED MONEY...
HOW ABOUT YOUR SOUL?
YES, YOUR SOUL WILL DO FINE... HEH HEH HEH...
PFFT! WHAT A MORON!
I WISH WE COULD JUST GET THE HELL OUT OF HERE!
HERE COMES THE CAT!
PLEASE HOLD ON TO YOUR DOG SO HE DOESN'T STARTLE THE POOR THING.

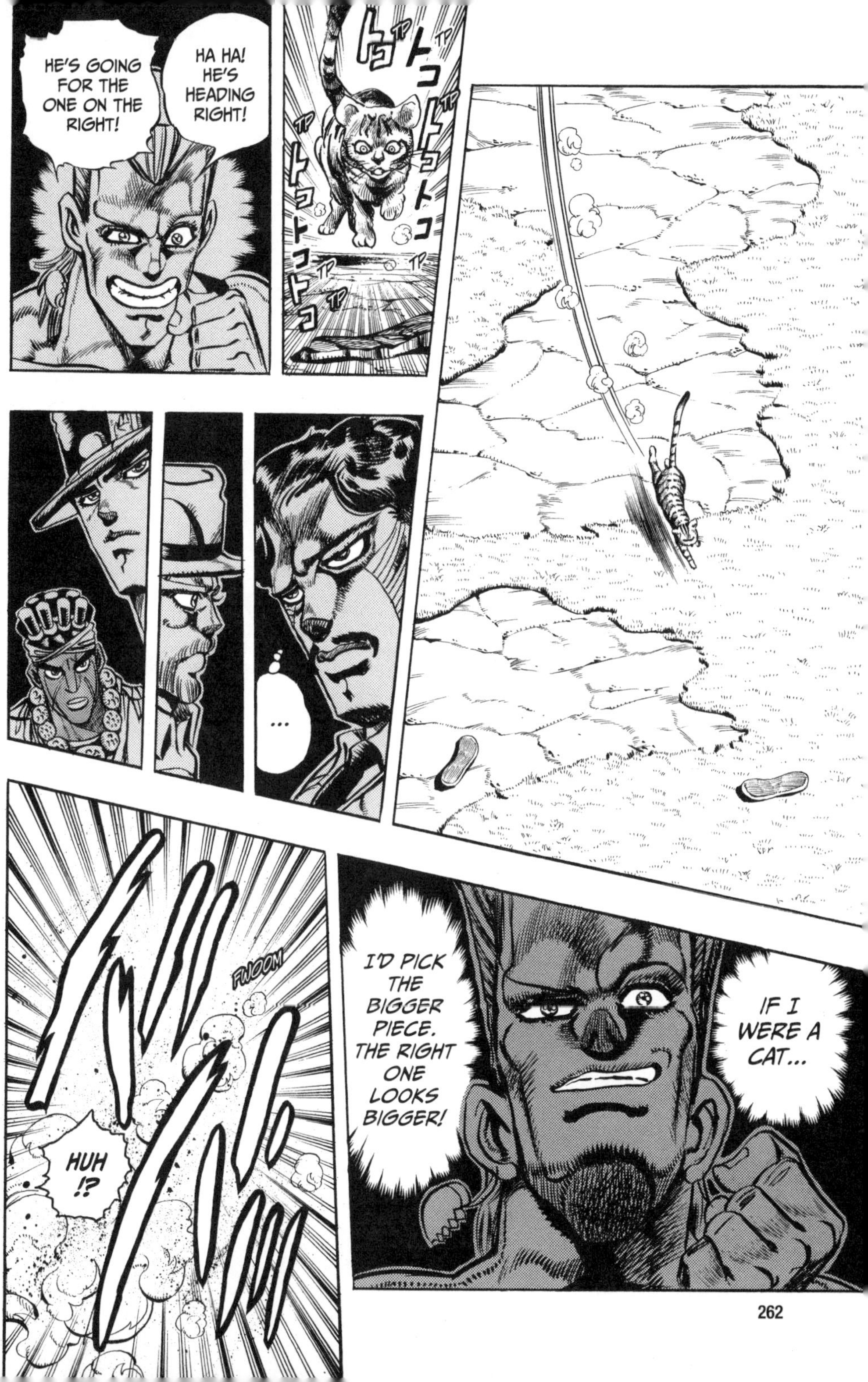
TP
HA HA! HE'S HEADING RIGHT!
HE'S GOING FOR THE ONE ON THE RIGHT!
...
IF I WERE A CAT...
I'D PICK THE BIGGER PIECE. THE RIGHT ONE LOOKS BIGGER!
FWOOM
HUH !?

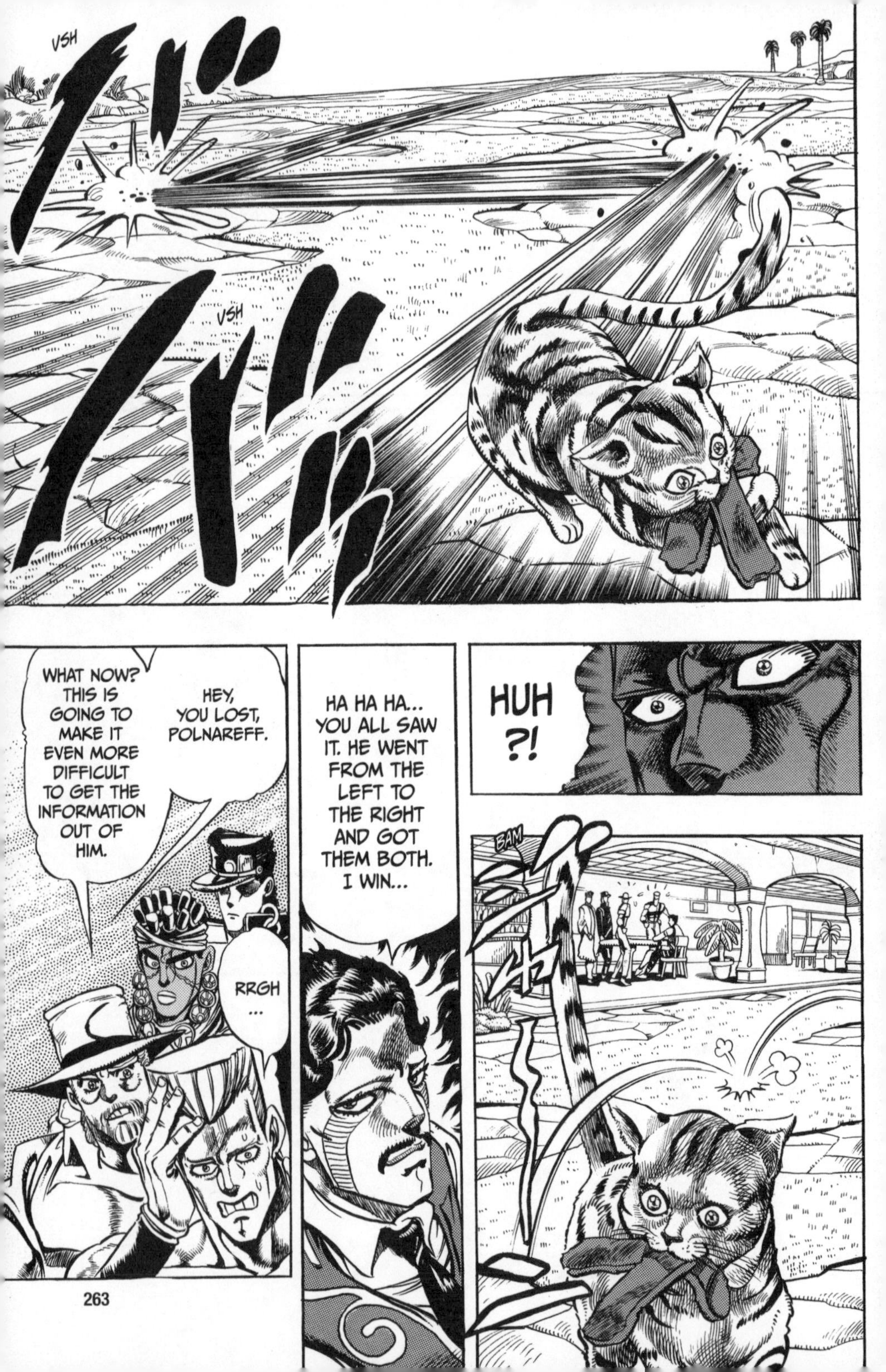
VSH
VSH
HUH ?!
BAM
HA HA HA... YOU ALL SAW IT. HE WENT FROM THE LEFT TO THE RIGHT AND GOT THEM BOTH. I WIN...
HEY, YOU LOST, POLNAREFF.
WHAT NOW? THIS IS GOING TO MAKE IT EVEN MORE DIFFICULT TO GET THE INFORMATION OUT OF HIM.
RRGH ...

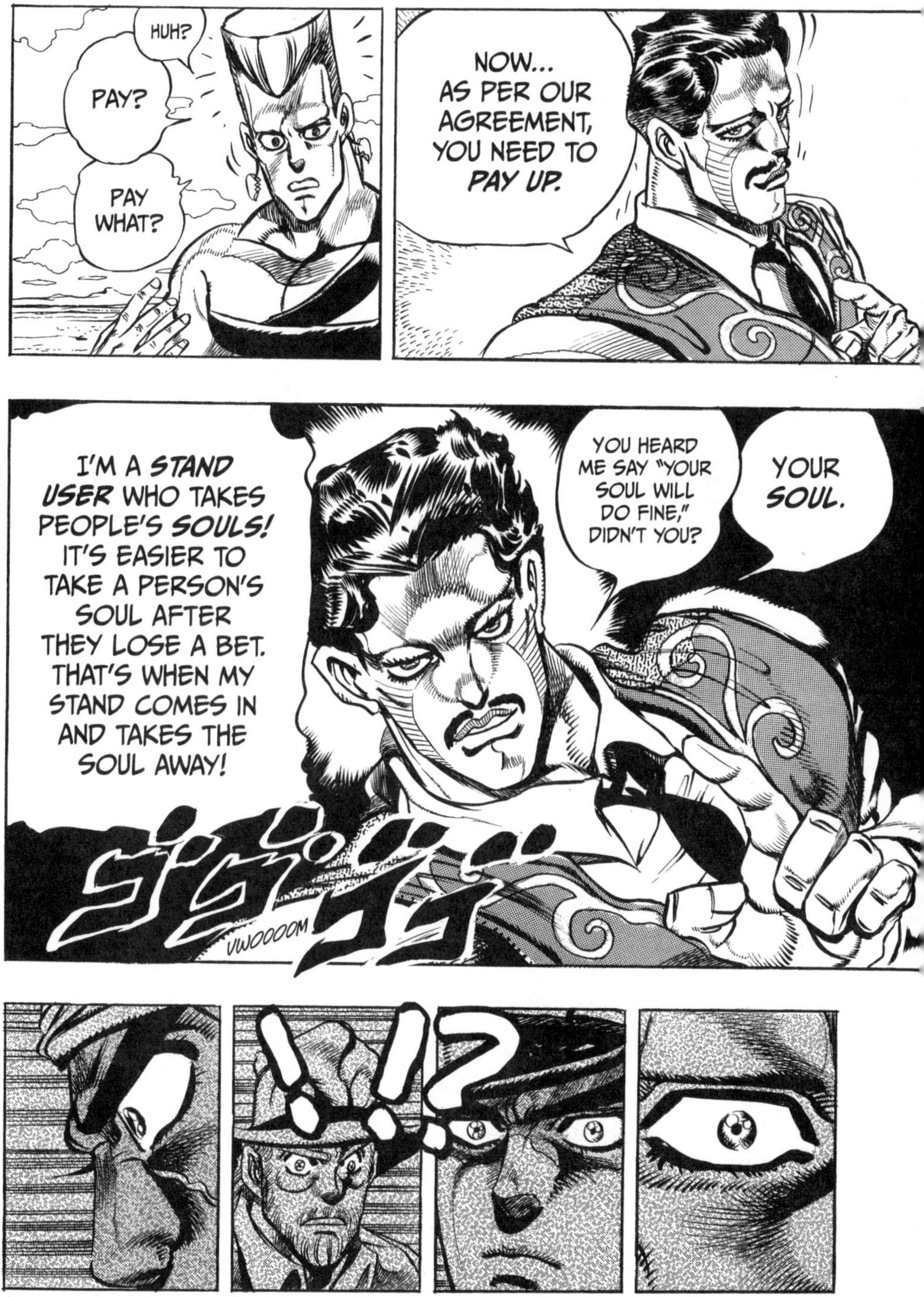
NOW... AS PER OUR AGREEMENT, YOU NEED TO PAY UP.
HUH?
PAY?
PAY WHAT?
YOUR SOUL.
YOU HEARD ME SAY "YOUR SOUL WILL DO FINE," DIDN'T YOU?
I'M A STAND USER WHO TAKES PEOPLE'S SOULS! IT'S EASIER TO TAKE A PERSON'S SOUL AFTER THEY LOSE A BET. THAT'S WHEN MY STAND COMES IN AND TAKES THE SOUL AWAY!
VWOOOOM
!!?

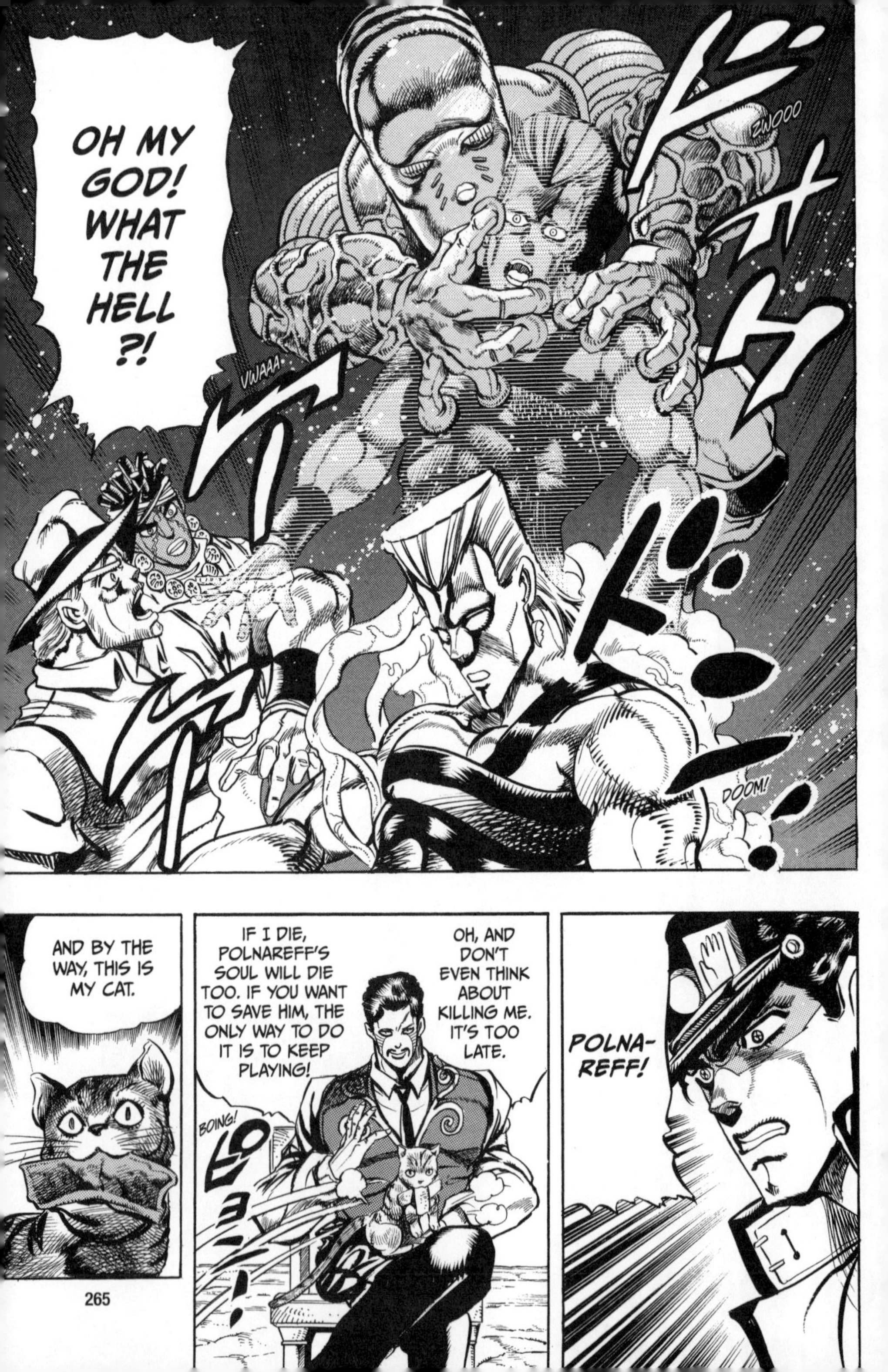

ZWOOO
OH MY GOD! WHAT THE HELL ?!
VWAAA
DOOM!
POLNA-REFF!
IF I DIE, POLNAREFF'S SOUL WILL DIE TOO. IF YOU WANT TO SAVE HIM, THE ONLY WAY TO DO IT IS TO KEEP PLAYING!
OH, AND DON'T EVEN THINK ABOUT KILLING ME. IT'S TOO LATE.
BOING!
AND BY THE WAY, THIS IS MY CAT.

OSIRIS
1

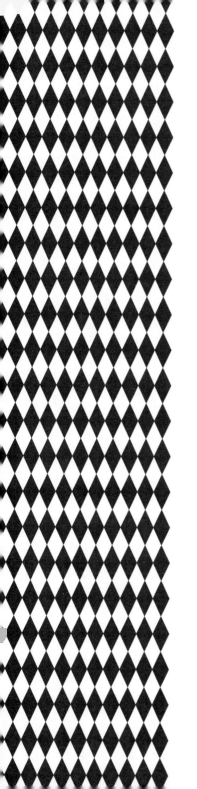

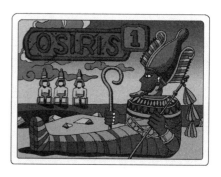

CHAPTER 99: D'Arby the Gambler PART 2

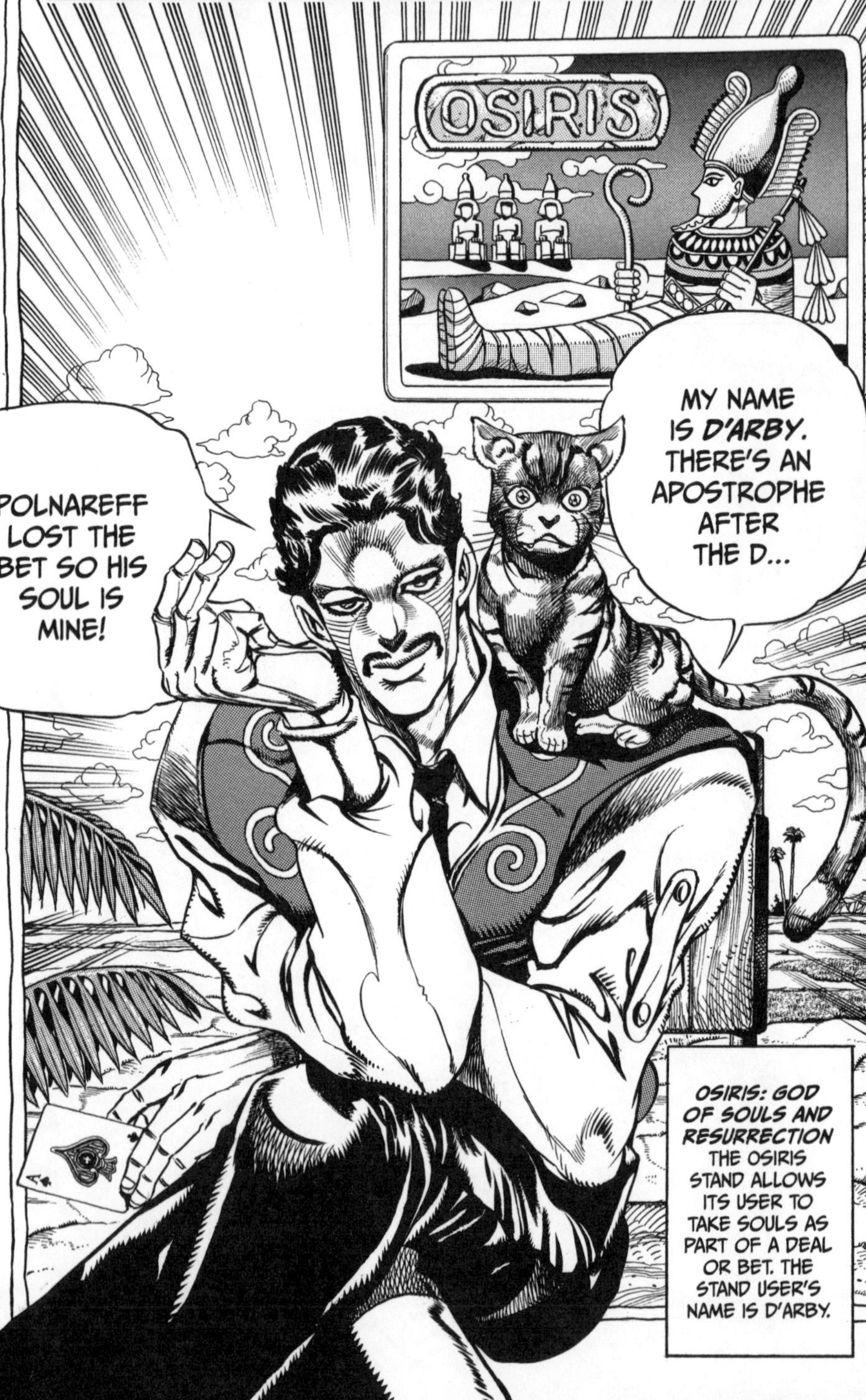
OSIRIS
MY NAME IS *D'ARBY*. THERE'S AN APOSTROPHE AFTER THE D...
POLNAREFF LOST THE BET SO HIS SOUL IS MINE!
OSIRIS: GOD OF SOULS AND RESURRECTION THE OSIRIS STAND ALLOWS ITS USER TO TAKE SOULS AS PART OF A DEAL OR BET. THE STAND USER'S NAME IS D'ARBY.

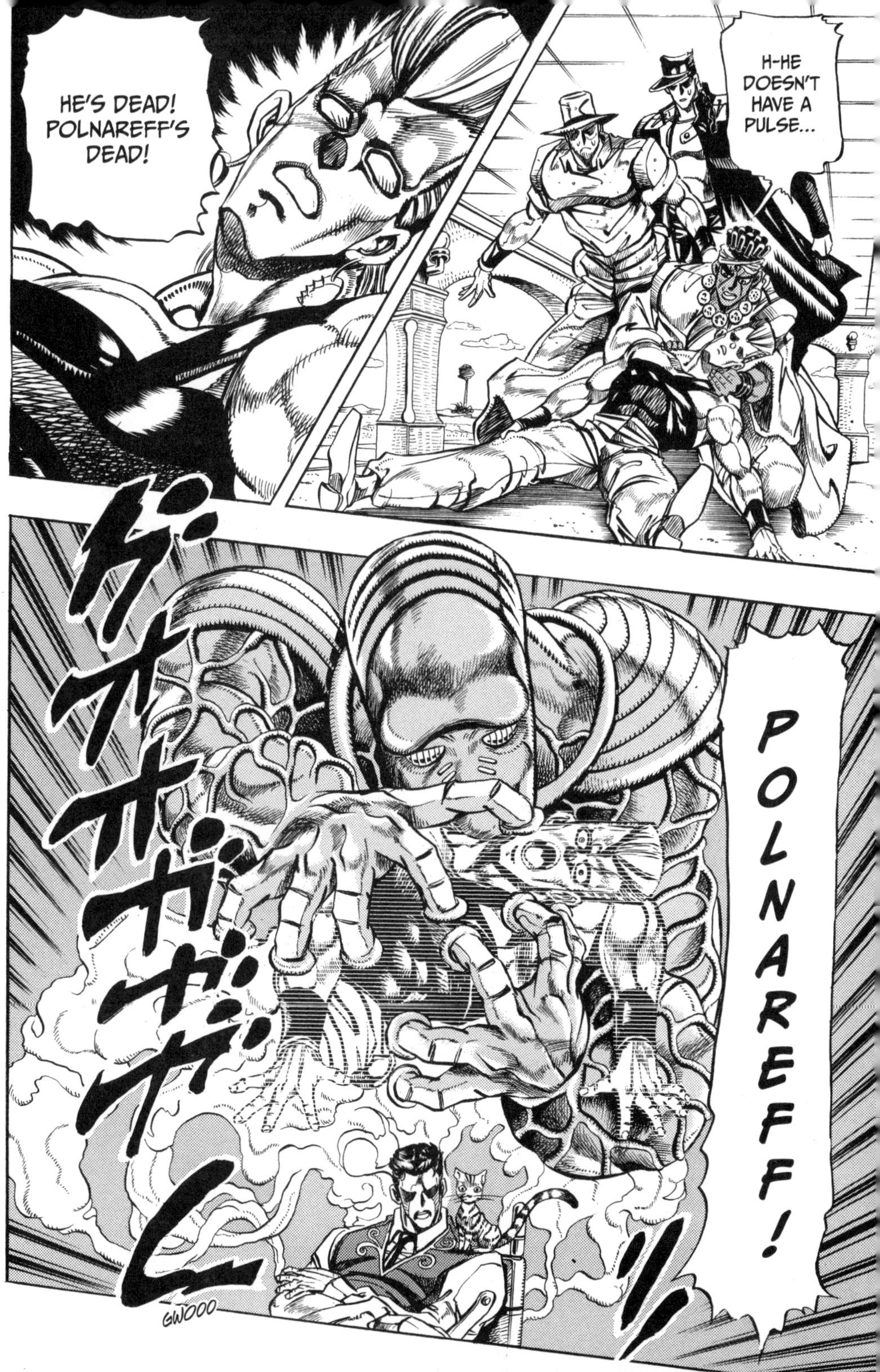
H-HE DOESN'T HAVE A PULSE...
HE'S DEAD! POLNAREFF'S DEAD!
POLNAREFF!
GWOOO

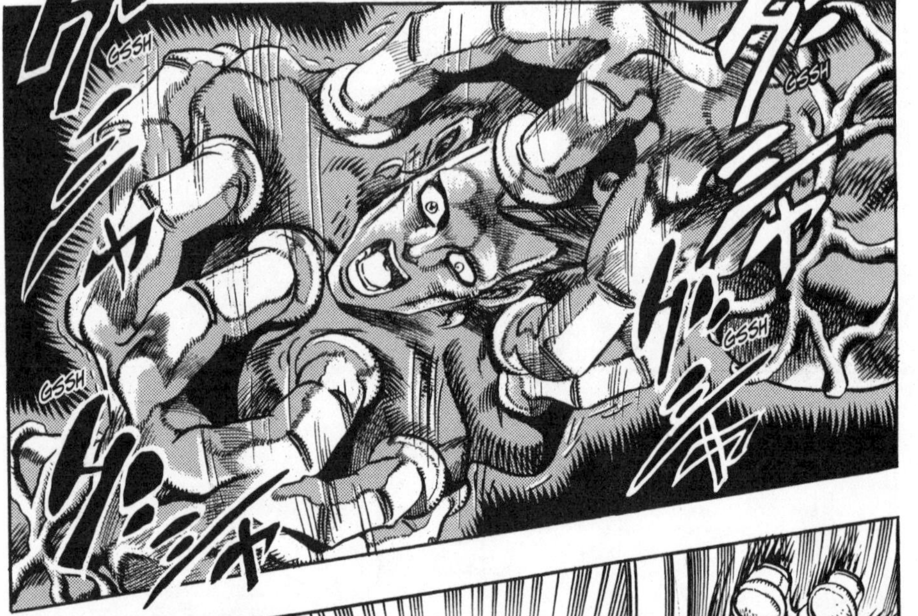
GSSH
GSSH
GSSH
GSSH
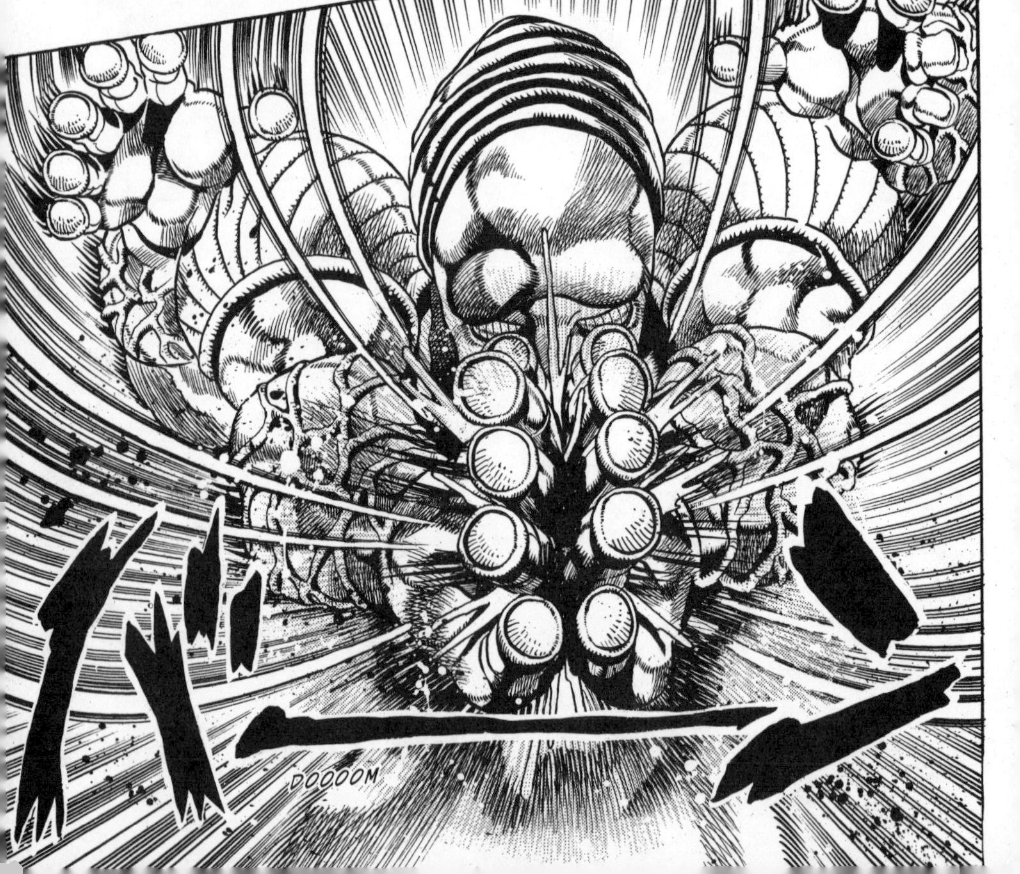
DOOOOM

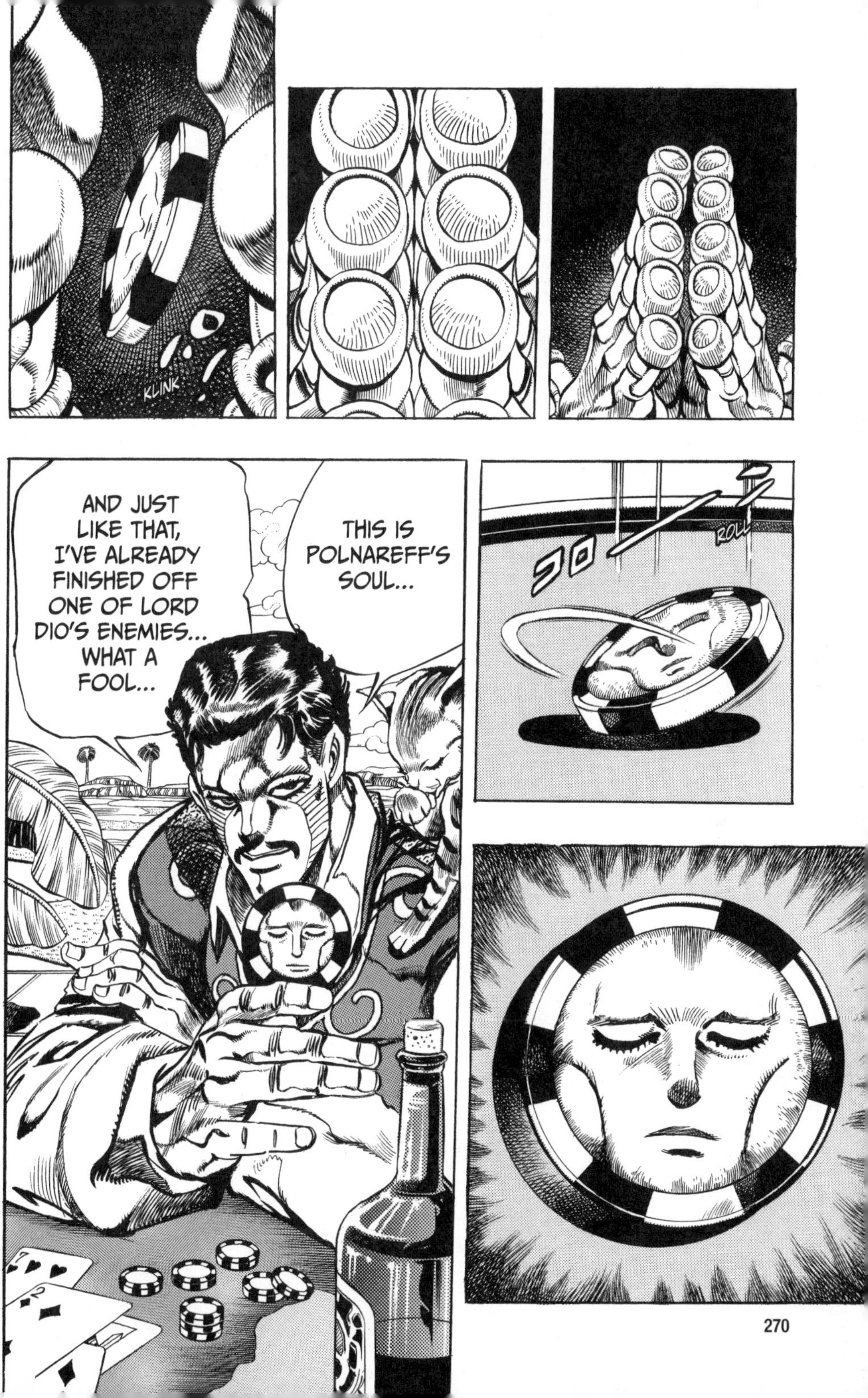
KLINK
コロ
ROLL
THIS IS POLNAREFF'S SOUL...
AND JUST LIKE THAT, I'VE ALREADY FINISHED OFF ONE OF LORD DIO'S ENEMIES... WHAT A FOOL...

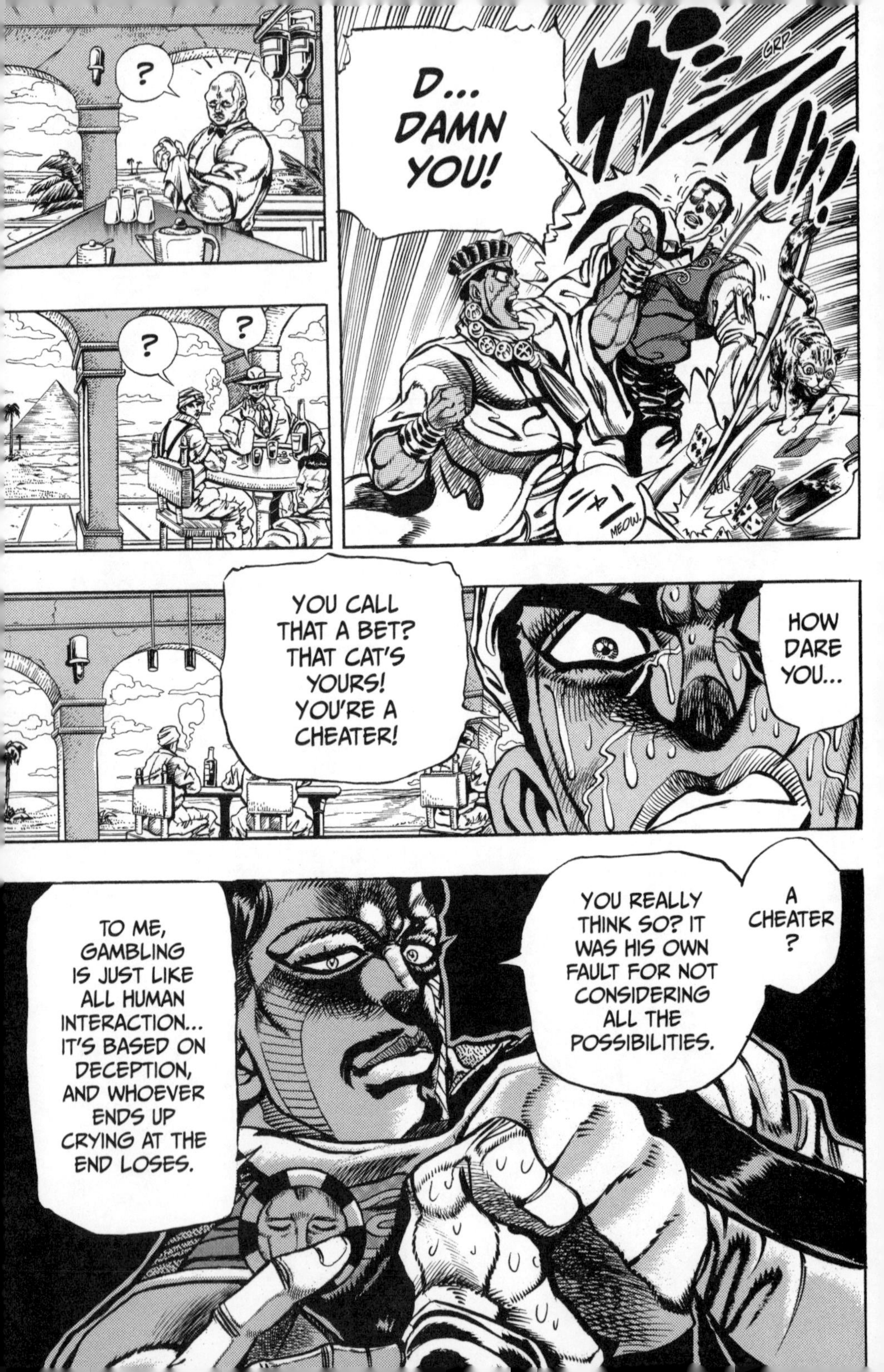
D... DAMN YOU!
GRP
MEOW.
?
?
?
HOW DARE YOU...
YOU CALL THAT A BET? THAT CAT'S YOURS! YOU'RE A CHEATER!
A CHEATER?
YOU REALLY THINK SO? IT WAS HIS OWN FAULT FOR NOT CONSIDERING ALL THE POSSIBILITIES.
TO ME, GAMBLING IS JUST LIKE ALL HUMAN INTERACTION... IT'S BASED ON DECEPTION, AND WHOEVER ENDS UP CRYING AT THE END LOSES.

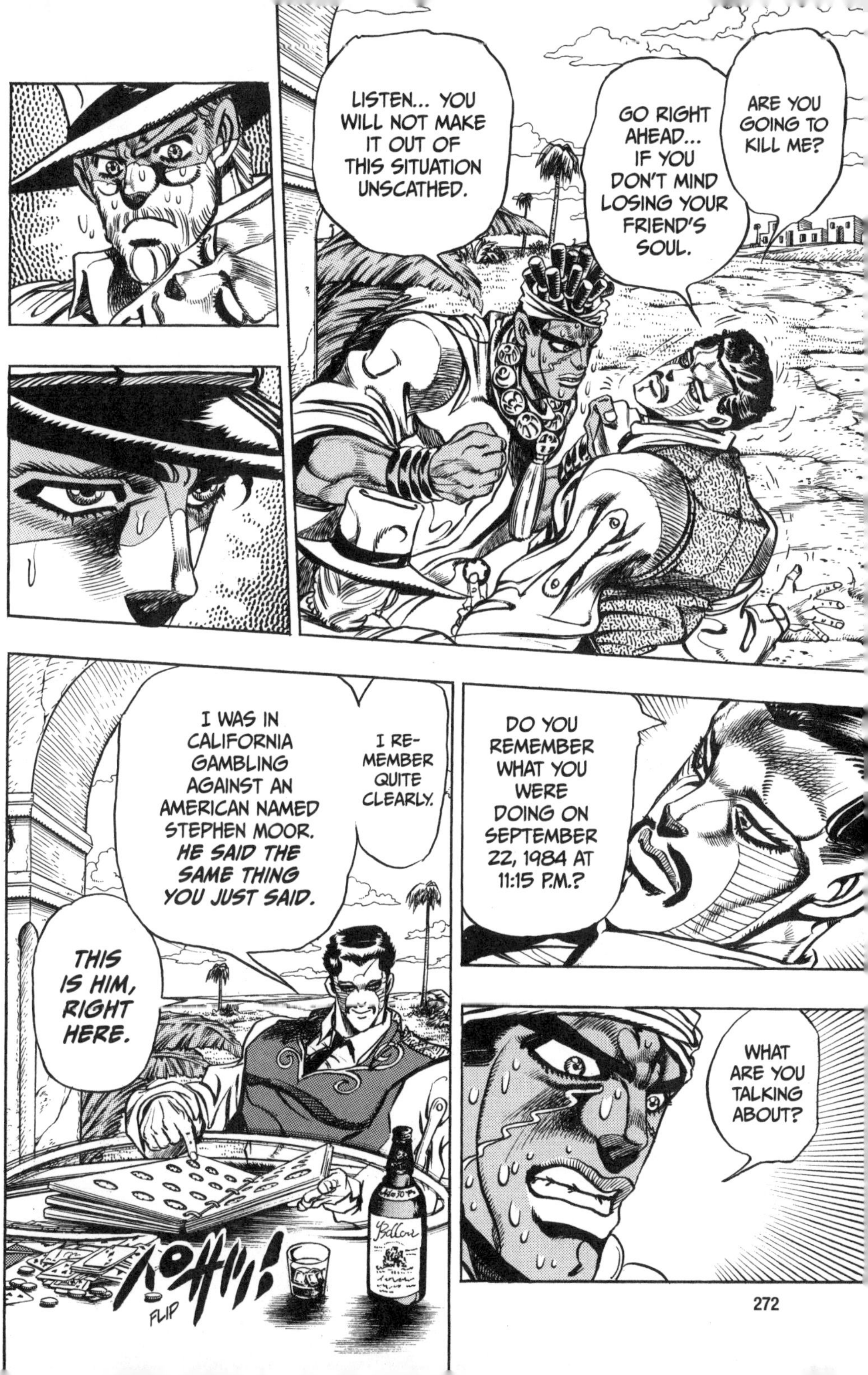
ARE YOU GOING TO KILL ME?
GO RIGHT AHEAD... IF YOU DON'T MIND LOSING YOUR FRIEND'S SOUL.
LISTEN... YOU WILL NOT MAKE IT OUT OF THIS SITUATION UNSCATHED.
DO YOU REMEMBER WHAT YOU WERE DOING ON SEPTEMBER 22, 1984 AT 11:15 P.M.?
WHAT ARE YOU TALKING ABOUT?
I RE-MEMBER QUITE CLEARLY.
I WAS IN CALIFORNIA GAMBLING AGAINST AN AMERICAN NAMED STEPHEN MOOR. *HE SAID THE SAME THING YOU JUST SAID.*
THIS IS HIM, RIGHT HERE.
FLIP

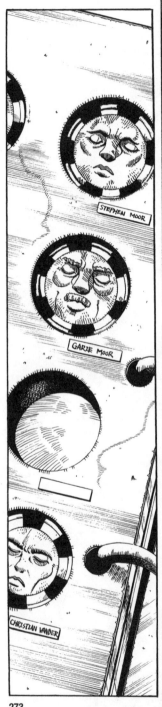

STEPHEN MOOR

GARIE MOOR

CHRISTIAN VANDER

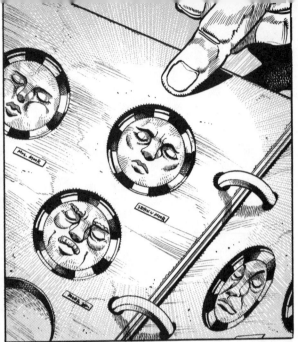

Mrs. Moor

Stephen Moor

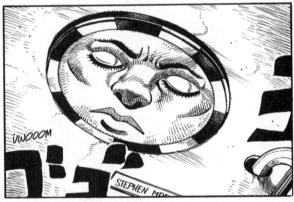

VWOOOM

STEPHEN MOOR

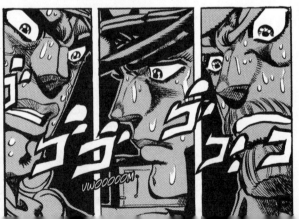

VWOOOOOM

273

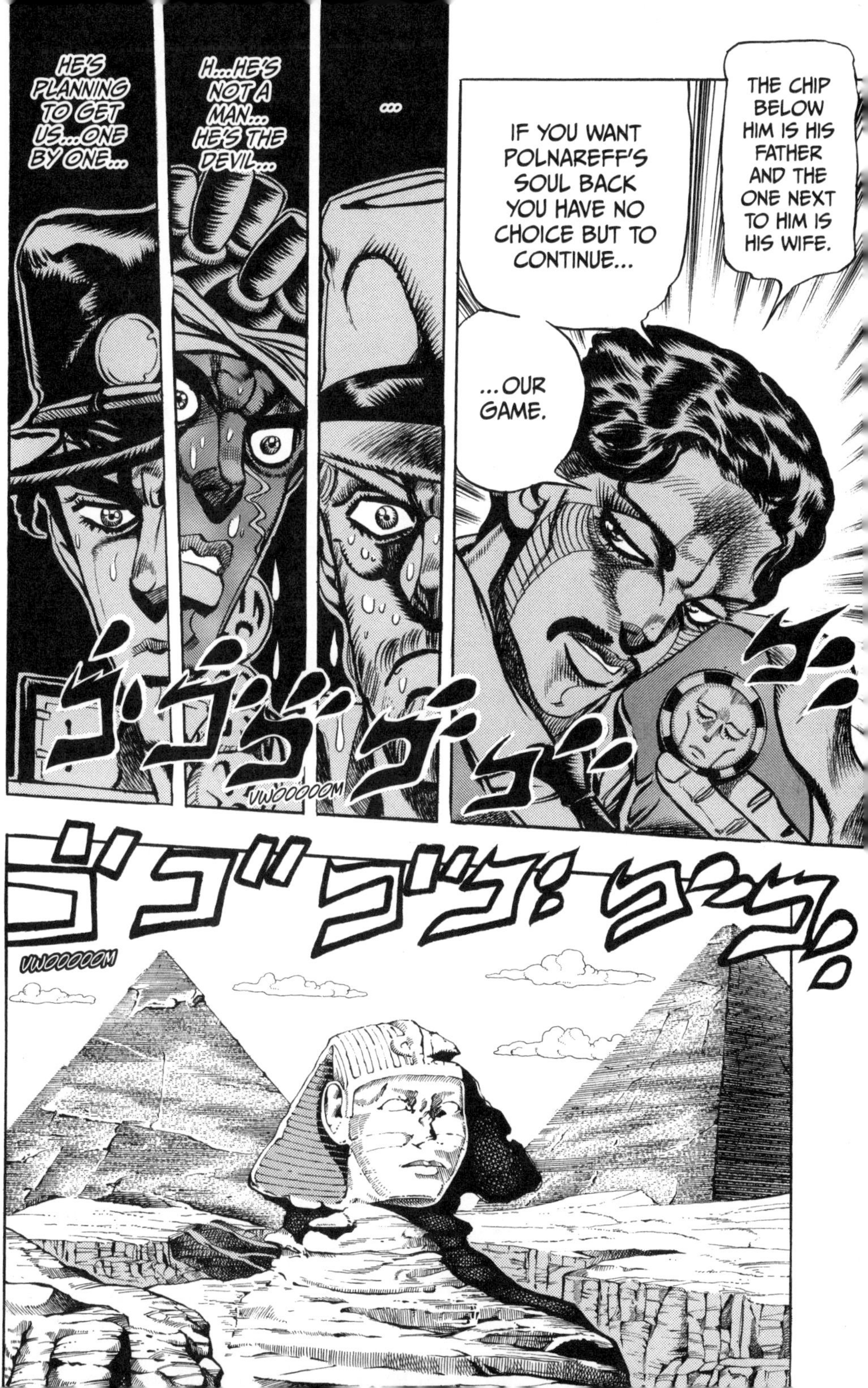
THE CHIP BELOW HIM IS HIS FATHER AND THE ONE NEXT TO HIM IS HIS WIFE.
IF YOU WANT POLNAREFF'S SOUL BACK YOU HAVE NO CHOICE BUT TO CONTINUE...
...OUR GAME.
...
H...HE'S NOT A MAN... HE'S THE DEVIL...
HE'S PLANNING TO GET US...ONE BY ONE...
VWOOOOOM
VWOOOOOM

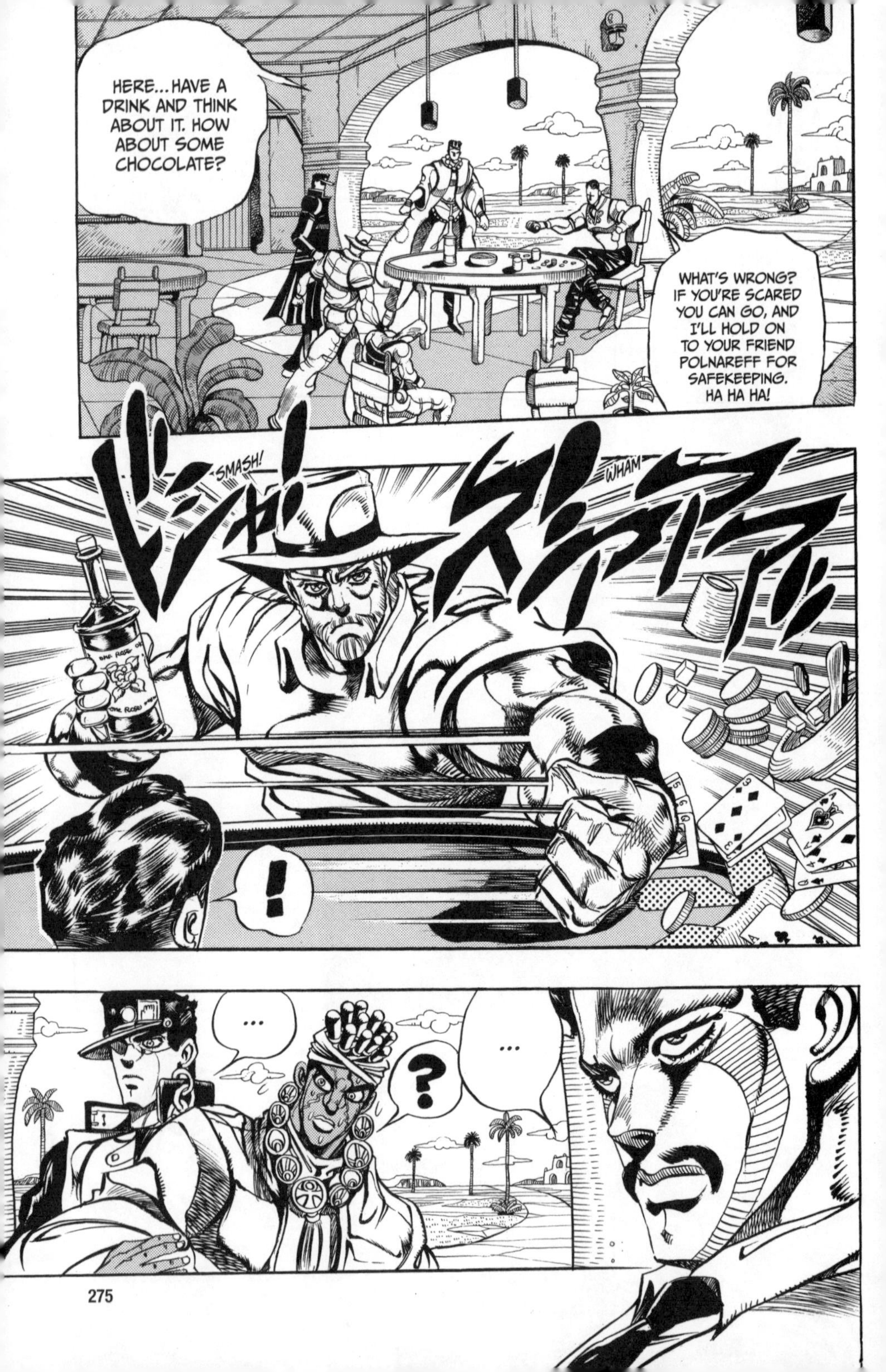
HERE... HAVE A DRINK AND THINK ABOUT IT. HOW ABOUT SOME CHOCOLATE?
WHAT'S WRONG? IF YOU'RE SCARED YOU CAN GO, AND I'LL HOLD ON TO YOUR FRIEND POLNAREFF FOR SAFEKEEPING. HA HA HA!
WHAM
SMASH!
!
...
?
...

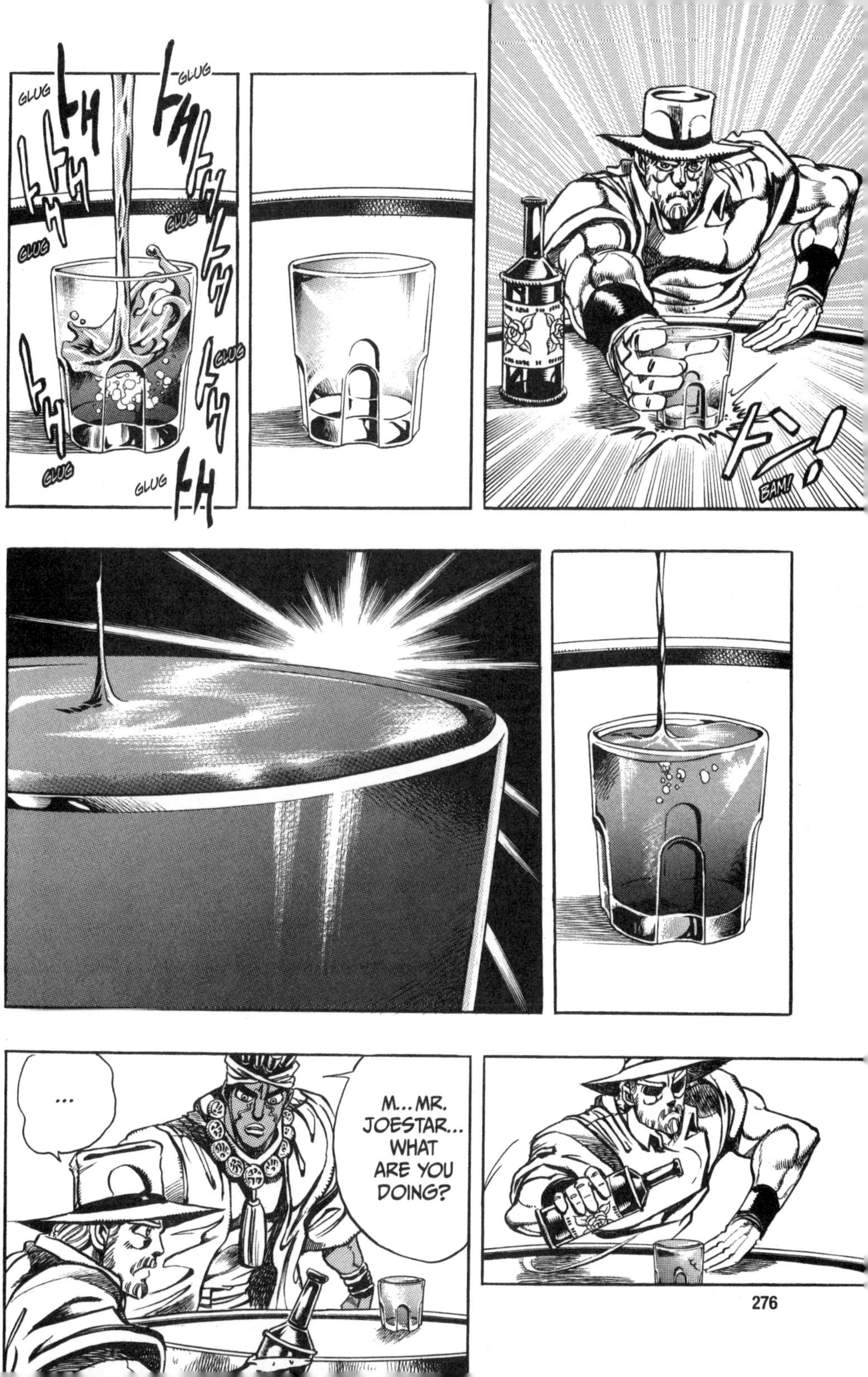
ドン!
BAM!
GLUG
GLUG
GLUG
GLUG
GLUG
GLUG
GLUG
M...MR. JOESTAR... WHAT ARE YOU DOING?
...

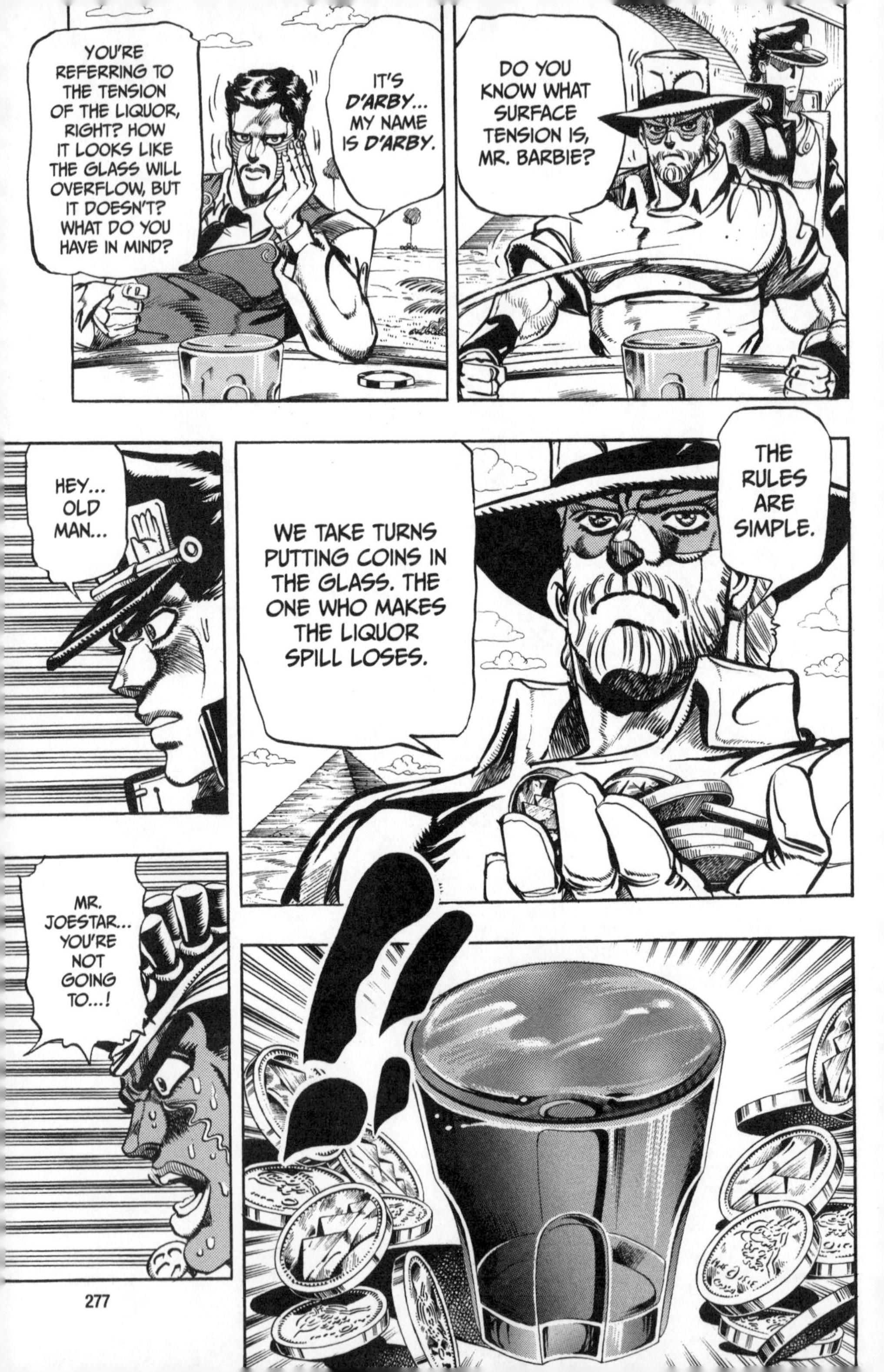

DO YOU KNOW WHAT SURFACE TENSION IS, MR. BARBIE?
IT'S D'ARBY... MY NAME IS D'ARBY.
YOU'RE REFERRING TO THE TENSION OF THE LIQUOR, RIGHT? HOW IT LOOKS LIKE THE GLASS WILL OVERFLOW, BUT IT DOESN'T? WHAT DO YOU HAVE IN MIND?
THE RULES ARE SIMPLE.
WE TAKE TURNS PUTTING COINS IN THE GLASS. THE ONE WHO MAKES THE LIQUOR SPILL LOSES.
HEY... OLD MAN...
MR. JOESTAR... YOU'RE NOT GOING TO...!

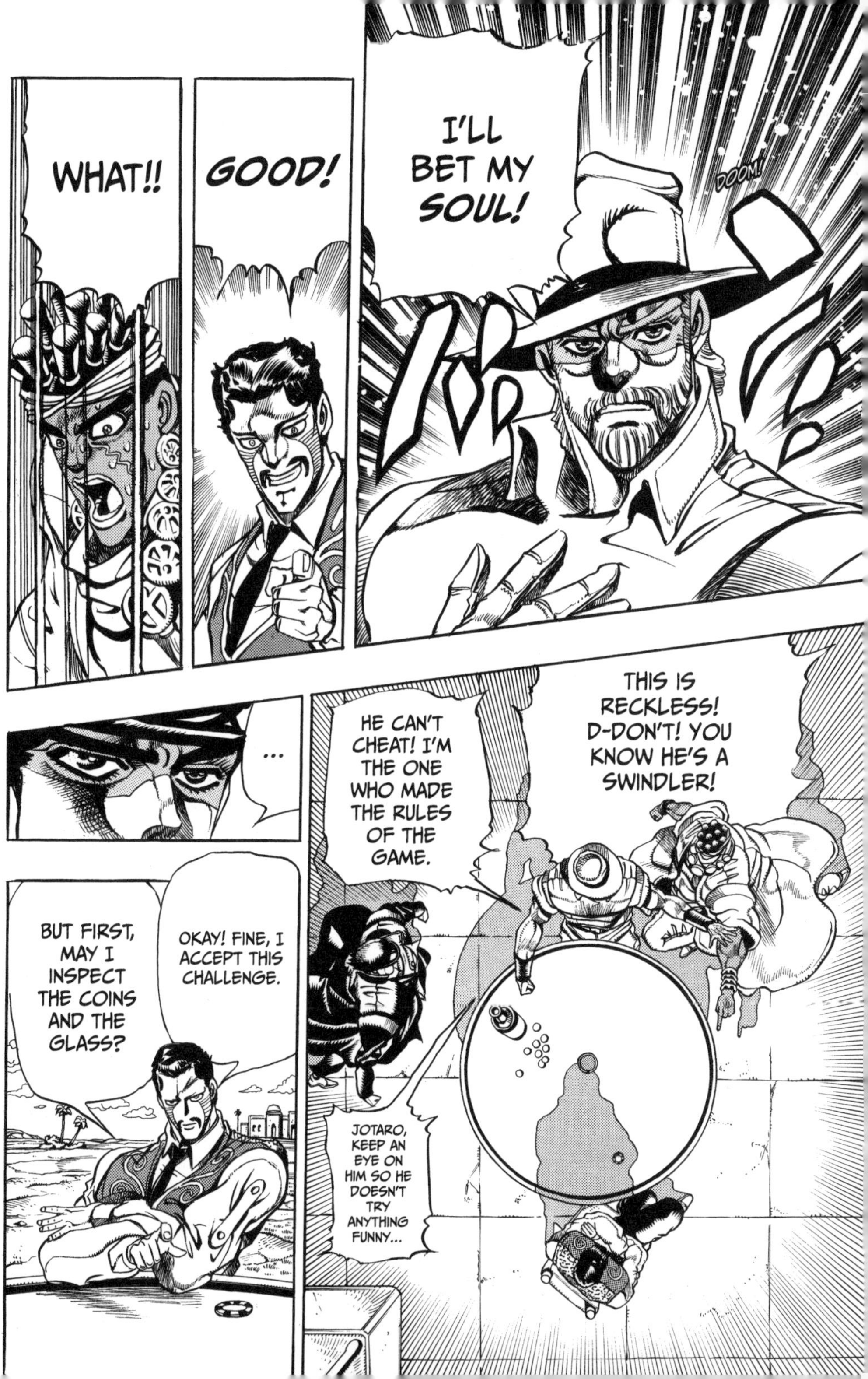
I'LL BET MY SOUL!
DOOM!
GOOD!
WHAT!!
THIS IS RECKLESS! D-DON'T! YOU KNOW HE'S A SWINDLER!
HE CAN'T CHEAT! I'M THE ONE WHO MADE THE RULES OF THE GAME.
JOTARO, KEEP AN EYE ON HIM SO HE DOESN'T TRY ANYTHING FUNNY...
...
OKAY! FINE, I ACCEPT THIS CHALLENGE.
BUT FIRST, MAY I INSPECT THE COINS AND THE GLASS?

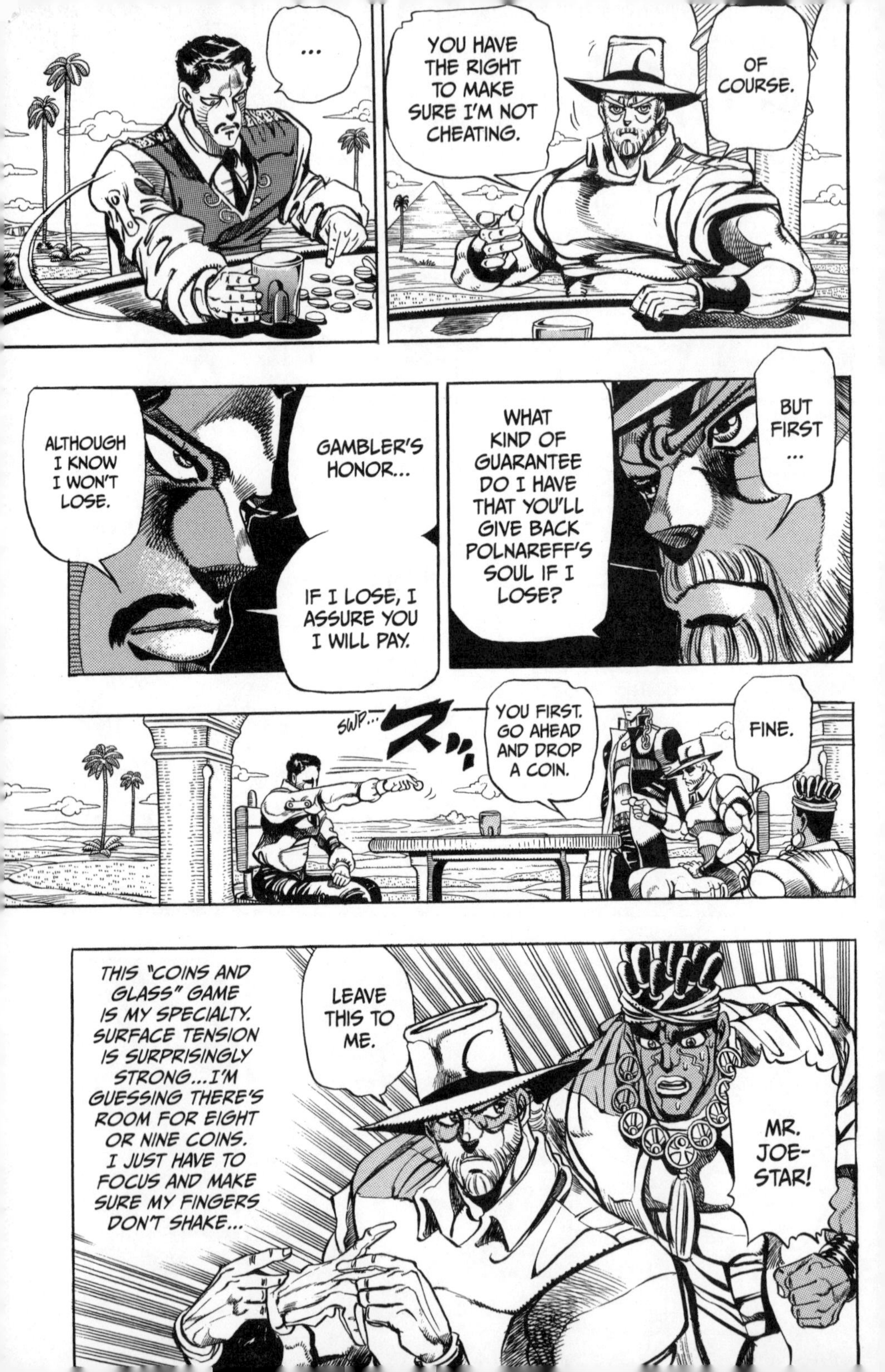
OF COURSE.
YOU HAVE THE RIGHT TO MAKE SURE I'M NOT CHEATING.
...
BUT FIRST ...
WHAT KIND OF GUARANTEE DO I HAVE THAT YOU'LL GIVE BACK POLNAREFF'S SOUL IF I LOSE?
GAMBLER'S HONOR...
IF I LOSE, I ASSURE YOU I WILL PAY.
ALTHOUGH I KNOW I WON'T LOSE.
FINE.
YOU FIRST. GO AHEAD AND DROP A COIN.
SWP...
MR. JOE-STAR!
LEAVE THIS TO ME.
THIS "COINS AND GLASS" GAME IS MY SPECIALTY. SURFACE TENSION IS SURPRISINGLY STRONG...I'M GUESSING THERE'S ROOM FOR EIGHT OR NINE COINS. I JUST HAVE TO FOCUS AND MAKE SURE MY FINGERS DON'T SHAKE...

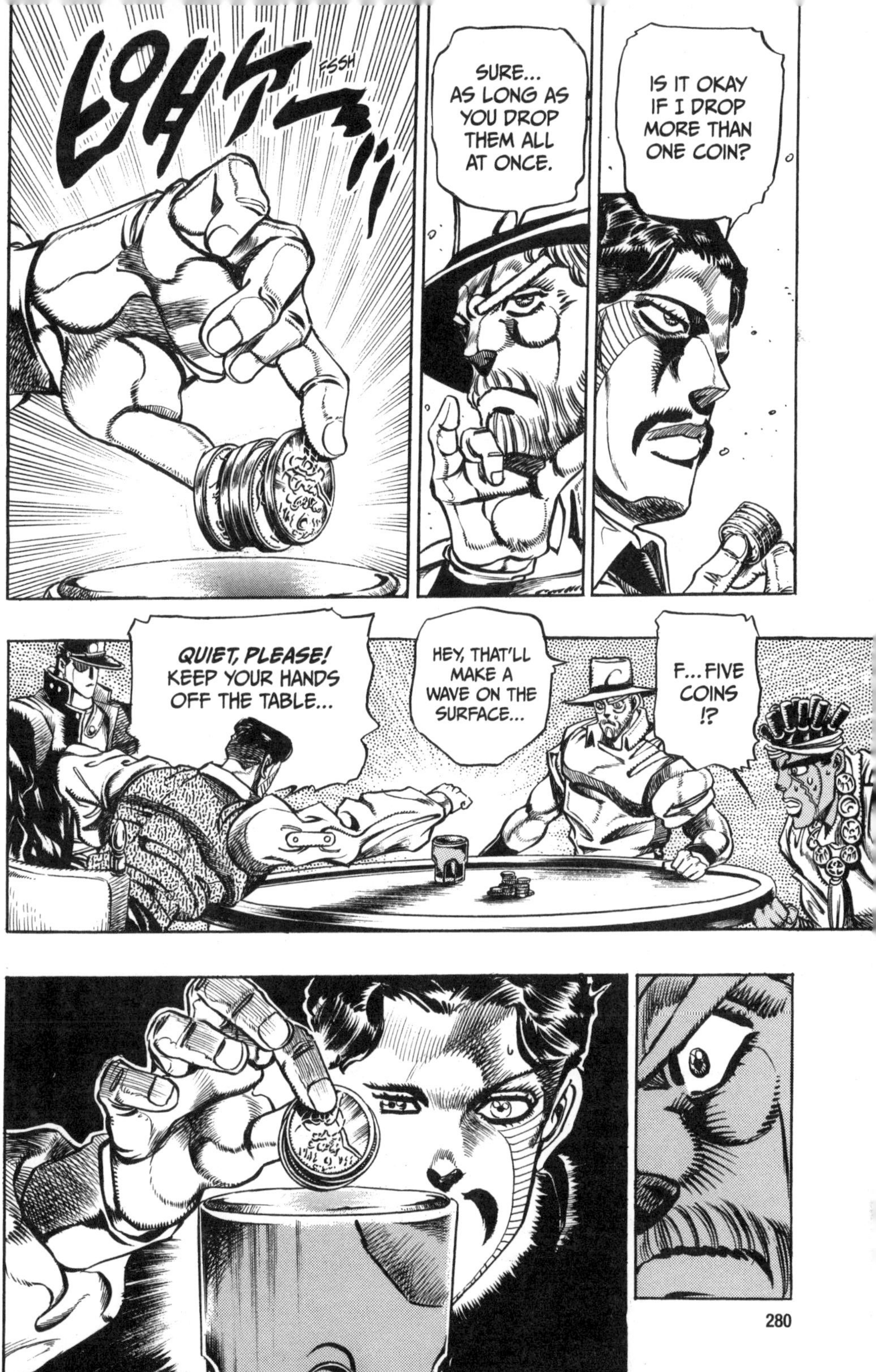
IS IT OKAY IF I DROP MORE THAN ONE COIN?
SURE... AS LONG AS YOU DROP THEM ALL AT ONCE.
FSSH
F...FIVE COINS !?
HEY, THAT'LL MAKE A WAVE ON THE SURFACE...
QUIET, PLEASE! KEEP YOUR HANDS OFF THE TABLE...

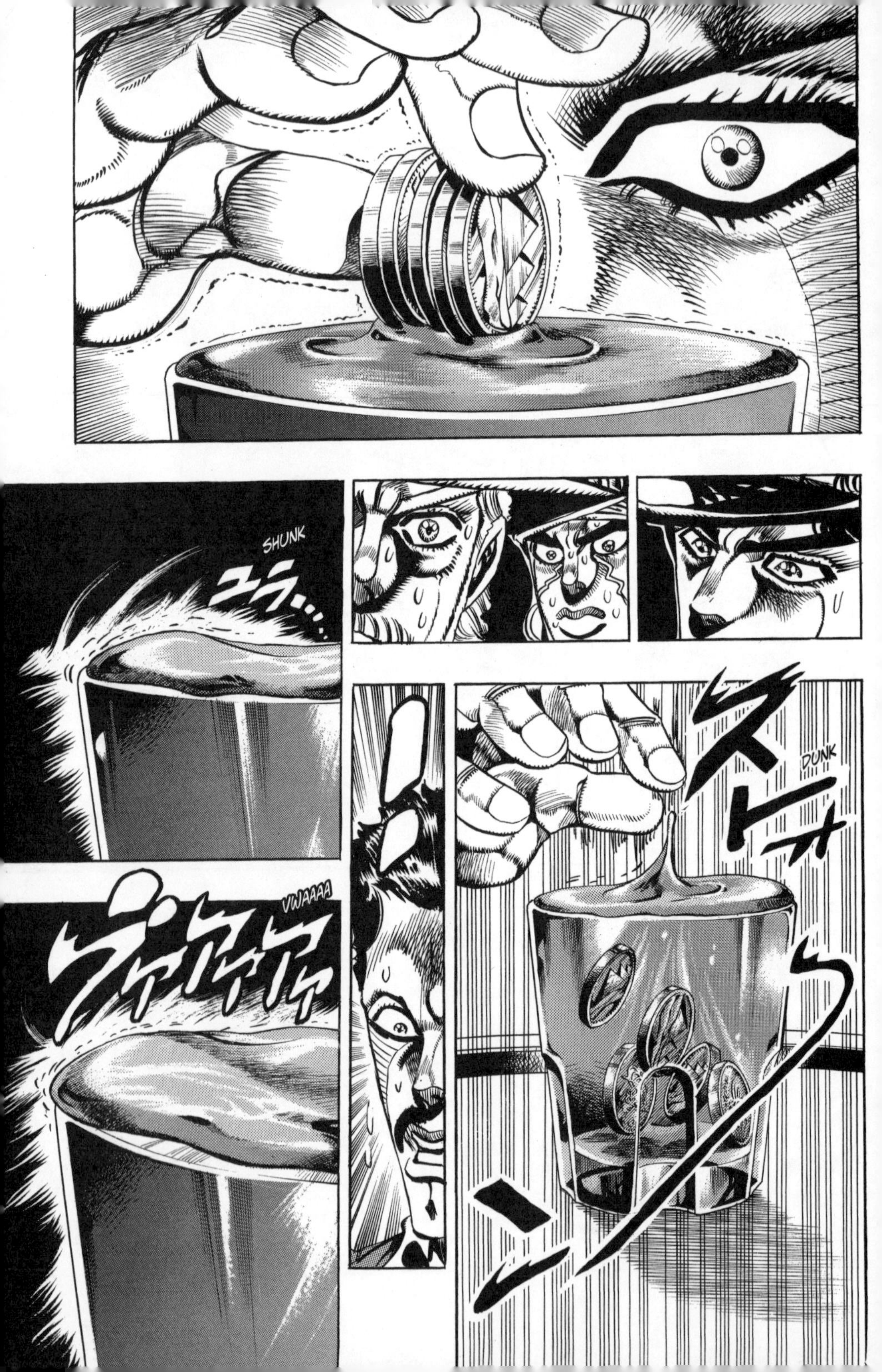
DUNK
SHUNK
VWAAAA

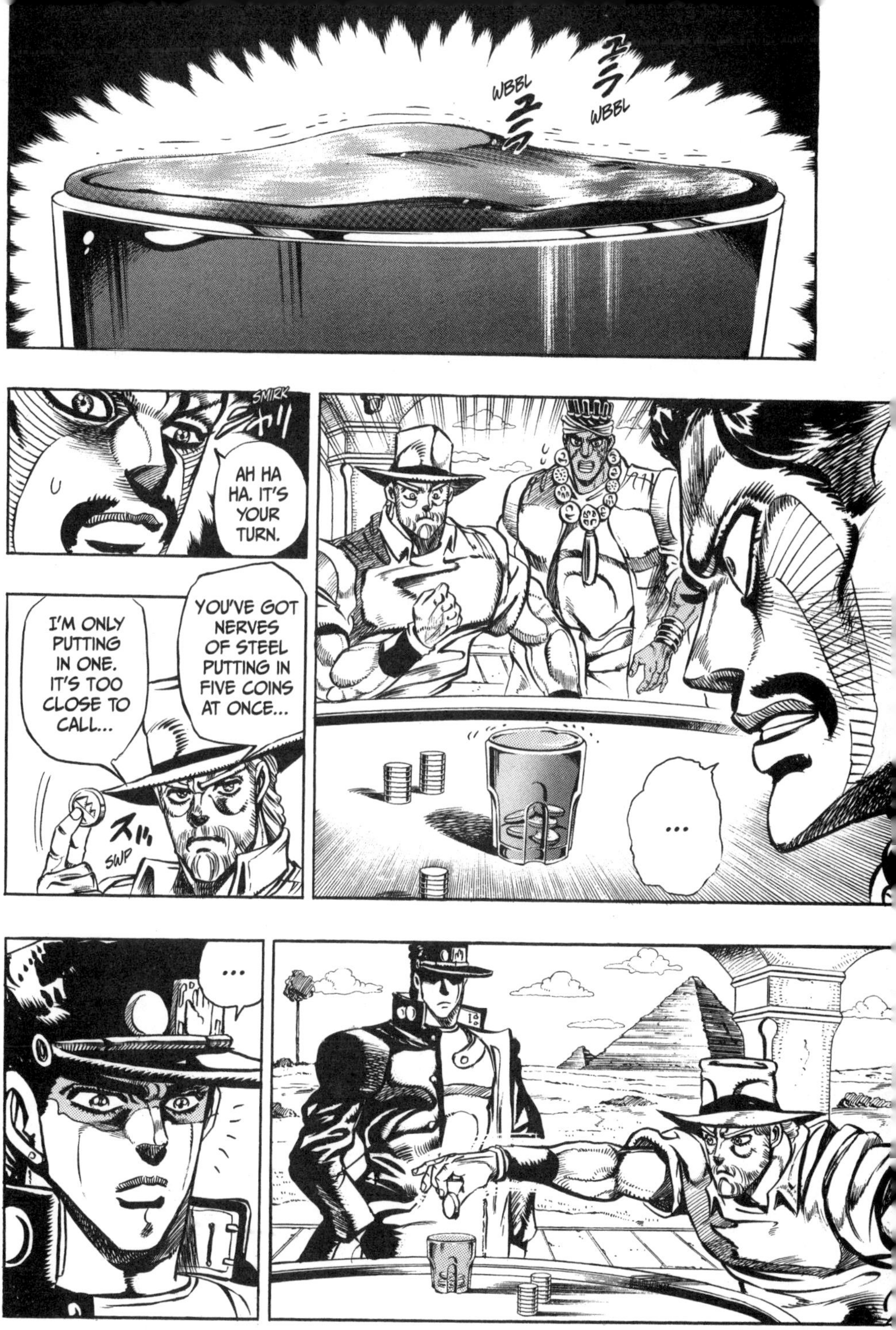
ユラ
WBBL
WBBL
ユラ
...
SMIRK
ニヤリ
AH HA HA. IT'S YOUR TURN.
YOU'VE GOT NERVES OF STEEL PUTTING IN FIVE COINS AT ONCE...
I'M ONLY PUTTING IN ONE. IT'S TOO CLOSE TO CALL...
ズッ
SWP
...

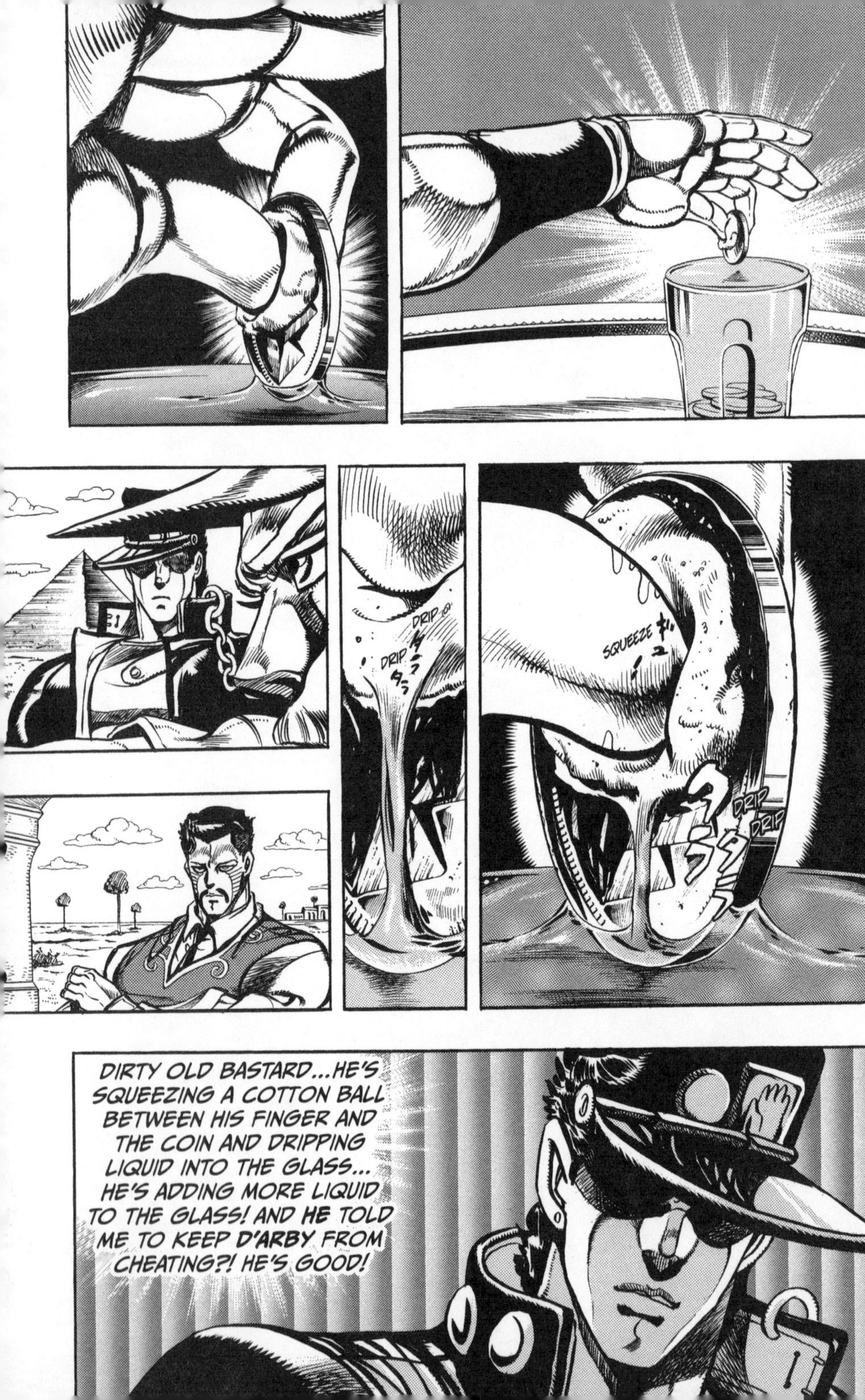
SQUEEZE
DRIP
DRIP
DRIP
DRIP
DIRTY OLD BASTARD...HE'S SQUEEZING A COTTON BALL BETWEEN HIS FINGER AND THE COIN AND DRIPPING LIQUID INTO THE GLASS... HE'S ADDING MORE LIQUID TO THE GLASS! AND **HE** TOLD ME TO KEEP **D'ARBY** FROM CHEATING?! HE'S GOOD!

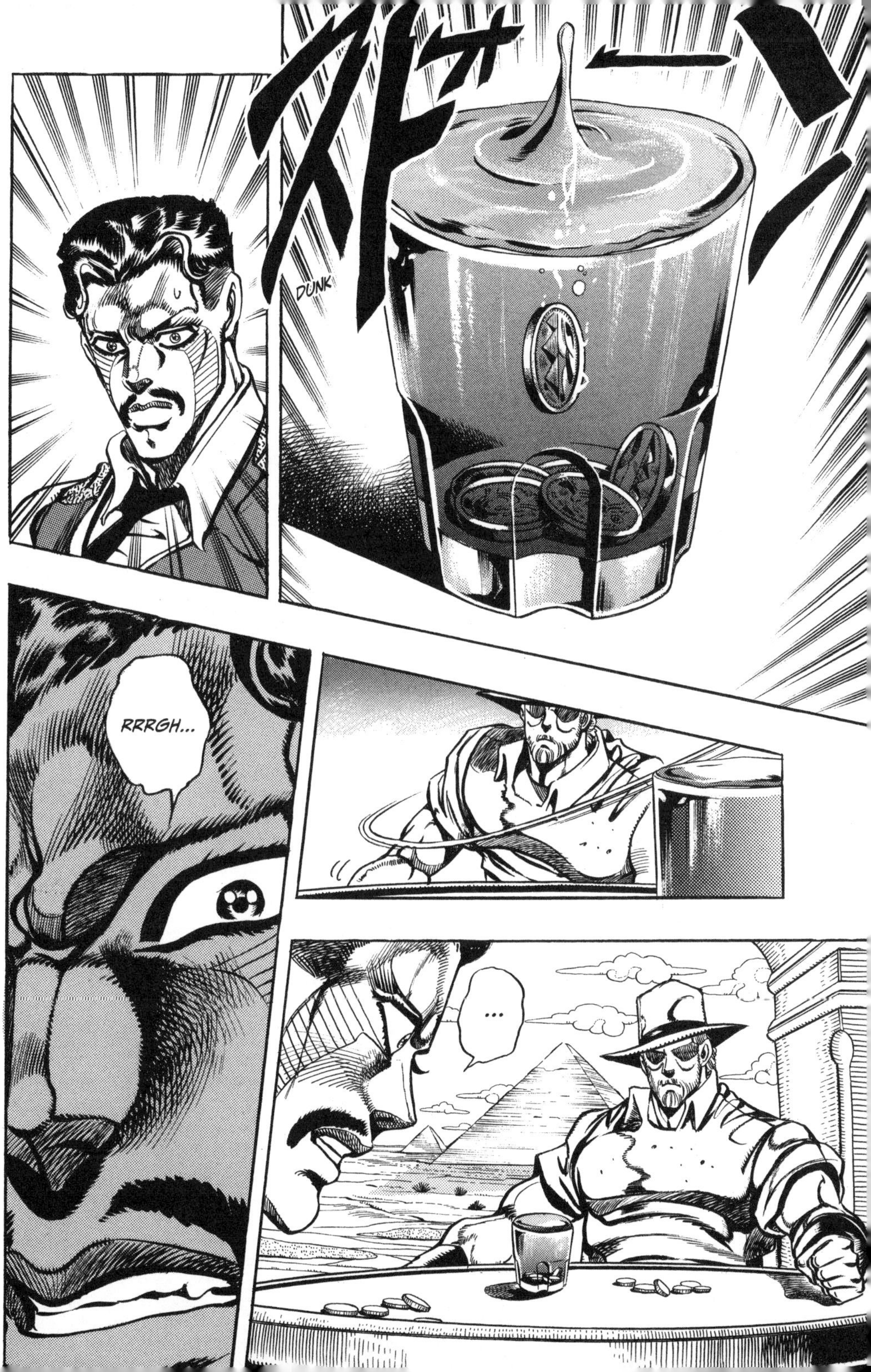
DUNK
...
RRRGH...

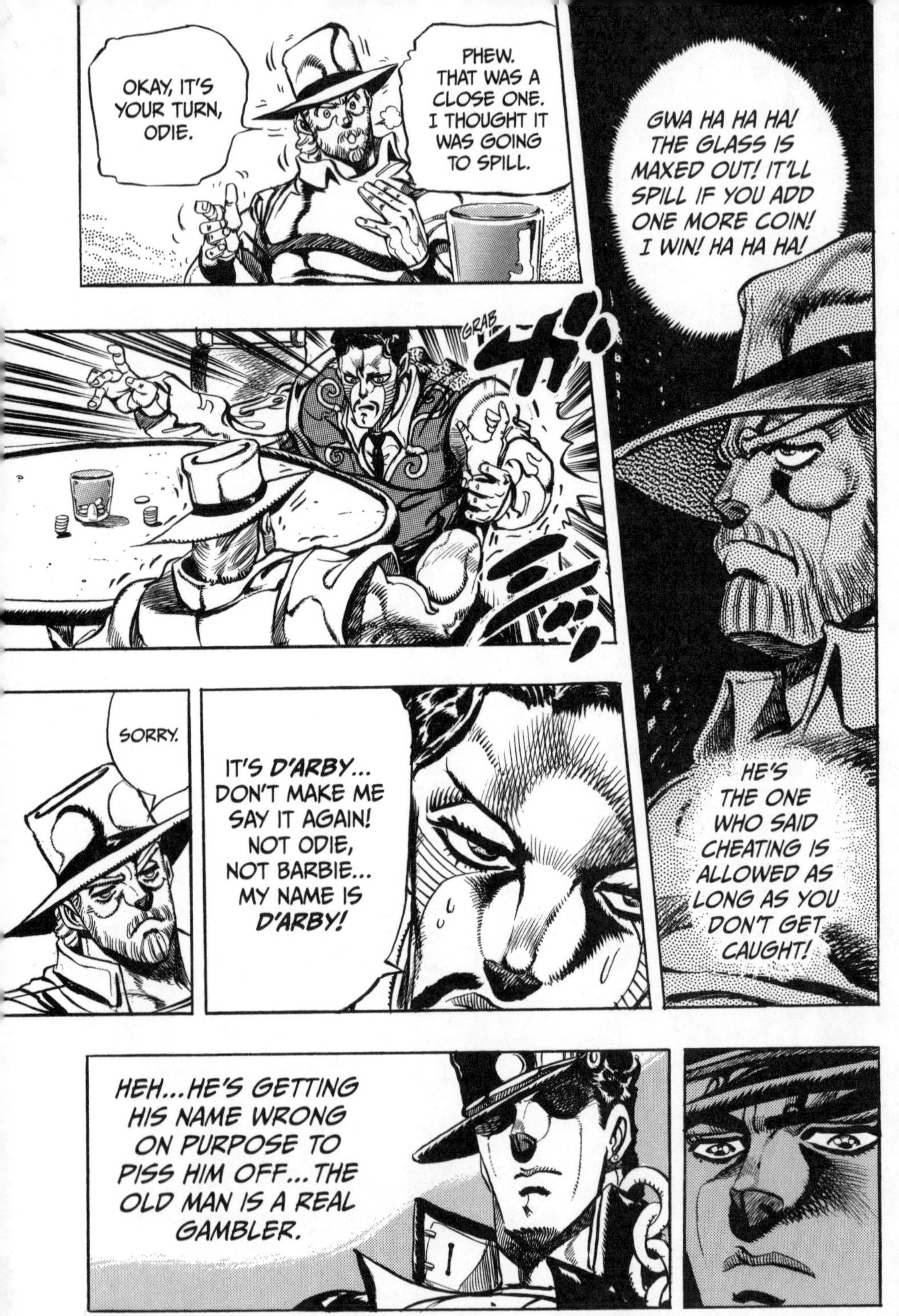
GWA HA HA HA! THE GLASS IS MAXED OUT! IT'LL SPILL IF YOU ADD ONE MORE COIN! I WIN! HA HA HA!
HE'S THE ONE WHO SAID CHEATING IS ALLOWED AS LONG AS YOU DON'T GET CAUGHT!
PHEW. THAT WAS A CLOSE ONE. I THOUGHT IT WAS GOING TO SPILL.
OKAY, IT'S YOUR TURN, ODIE.
GRAB
IT'S D'ARBY... DON'T MAKE ME SAY IT AGAIN! NOT ODIE, NOT BARBIE... MY NAME IS D'ARBY!
SORRY.
HEH...HE'S GETTING HIS NAME WRONG ON PURPOSE TO PISS HIM OFF...THE OLD MAN IS A REAL GAMBLER.

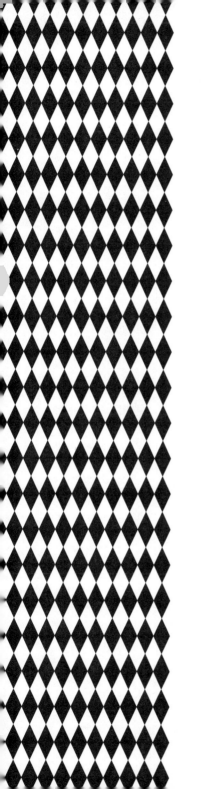
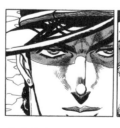
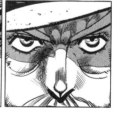
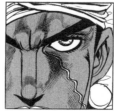
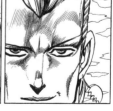

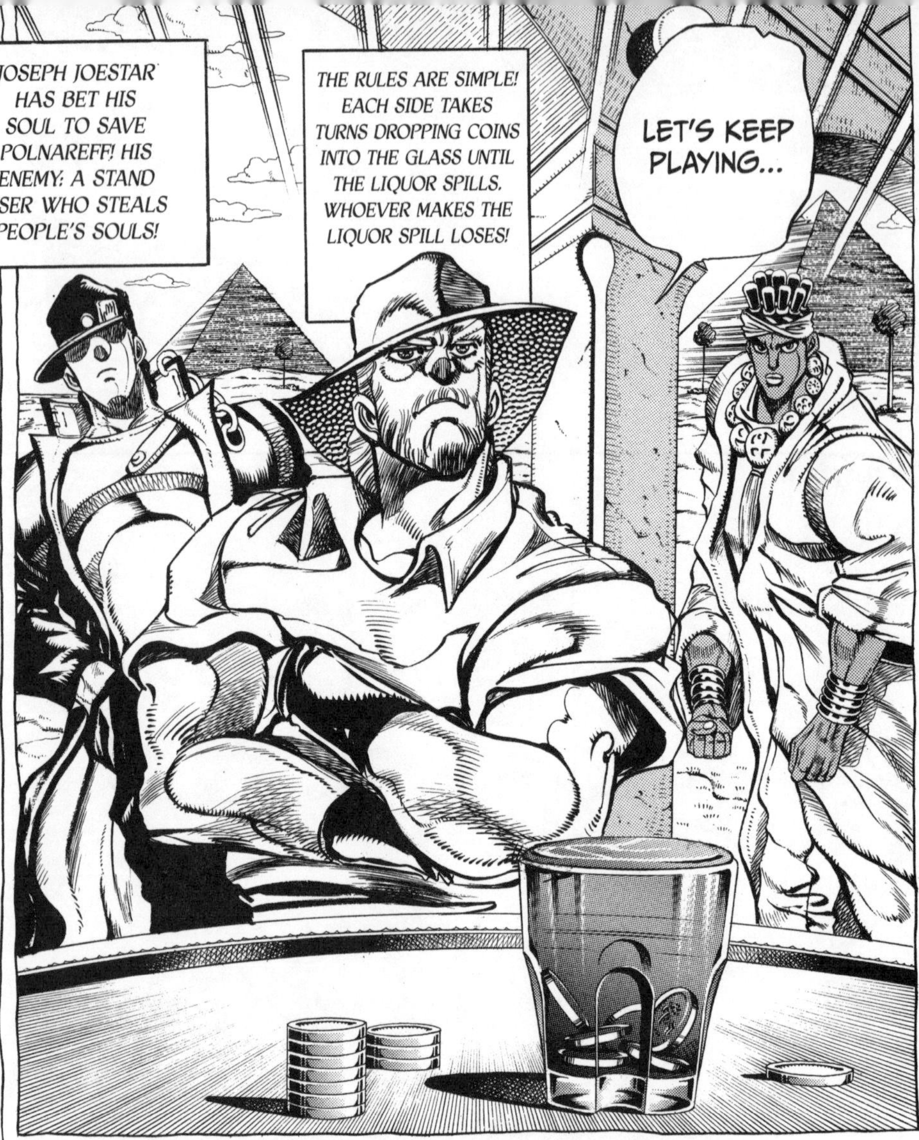
LET'S KEEP PLAYING...
THE RULES ARE SIMPLE! EACH SIDE TAKES TURNS DROPPING COINS INTO THE GLASS UNTIL THE LIQUOR SPILLS. WHOEVER MAKES THE LIQUOR SPILL LOSES!
JOSEPH JOESTAR HAS BET HIS SOUL TO SAVE POLNAREFF! HIS ENEMY: A STAND USER WHO STEALS PEOPLE'S SOULS!

CHAPTER 100: D'Arby the Gambler PART 3

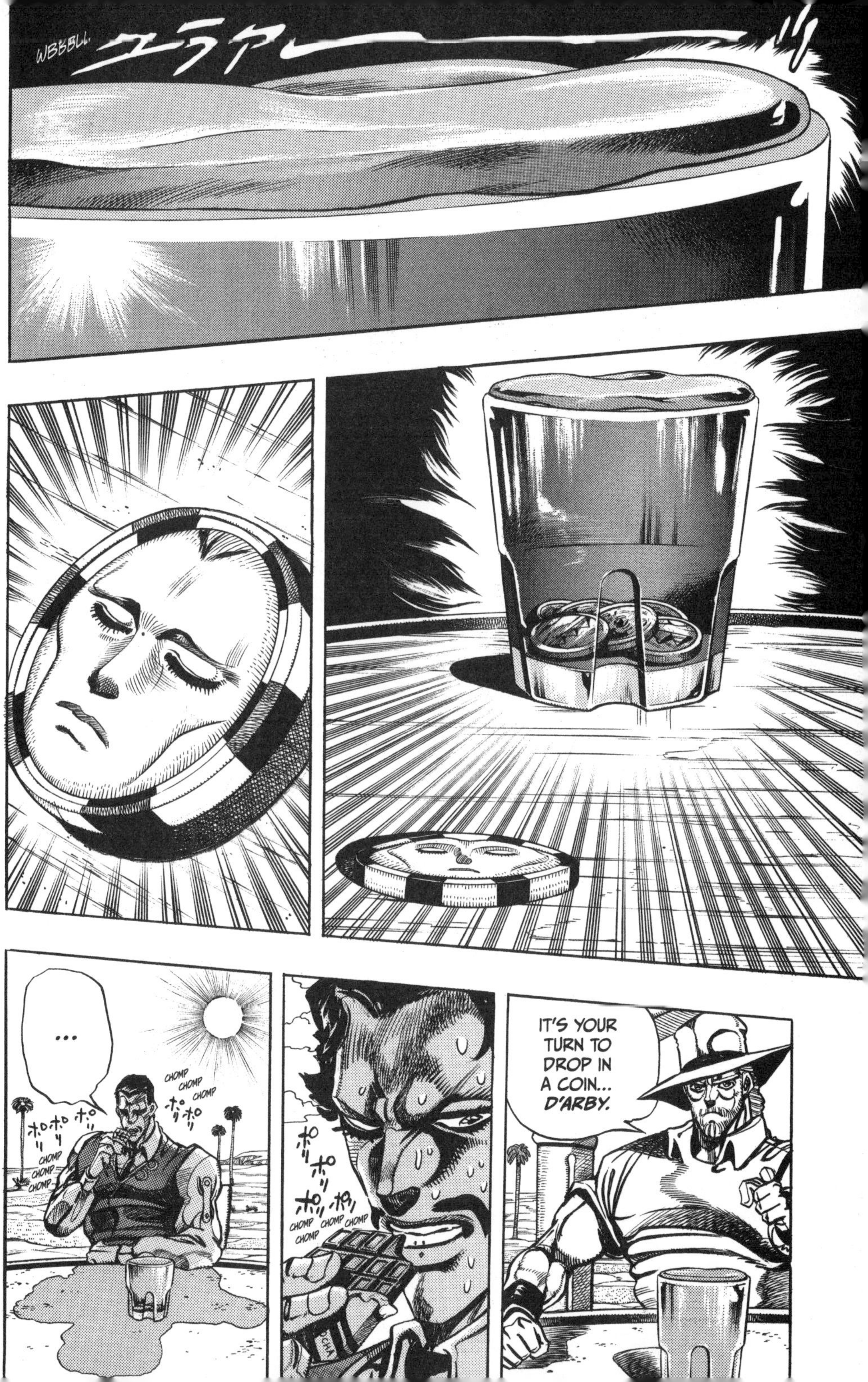
WBBBLL
ユラアー
IT'S YOUR TURN TO DROP IN A COIN... D'ARBY.
ポリポリポリポリ
CHOMP CHOMP CHOMP CHOMP
...
CHOMP CHOMP CHOMP
ポリポリ
ポリポリポリ
CHOMP CHOMP CHOMP

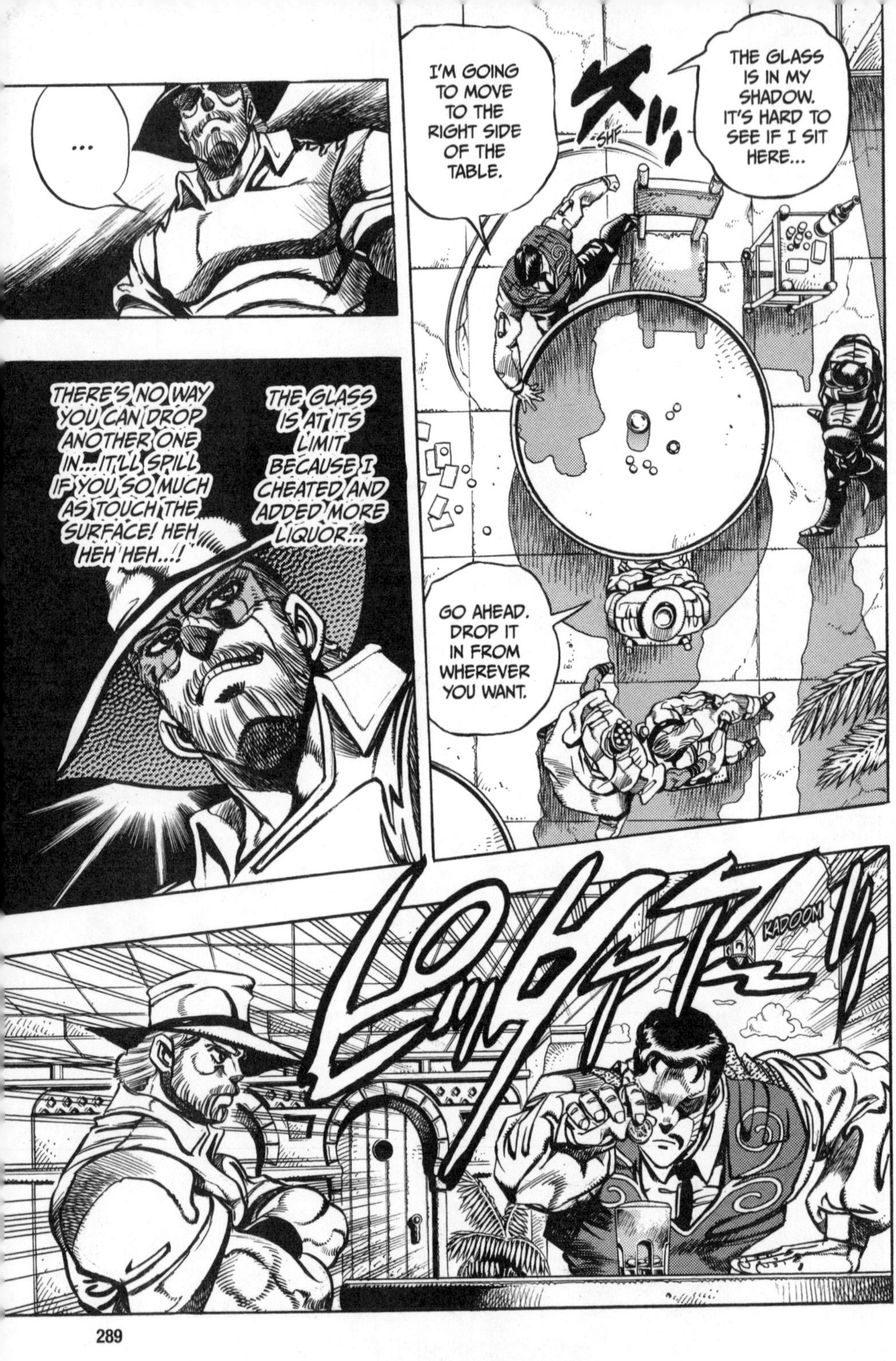
THE GLASS IS IN MY SHADOW. IT'S HARD TO SEE IF I SIT HERE...
SHF
I'M GOING TO MOVE TO THE RIGHT SIDE OF THE TABLE.
GO AHEAD. DROP IT IN FROM WHEREVER YOU WANT.
...
THE GLASS IS AT ITS LIMIT BECAUSE I CHEATED AND ADDED MORE LIQUOR...
THERE'S NO WAY YOU CAN DROP ANOTHER ONE IN...IT'LL SPILL IF YOU SO MUCH AS TOUCH THE SURFACE! HEH HEH HEH...!
KADOOM

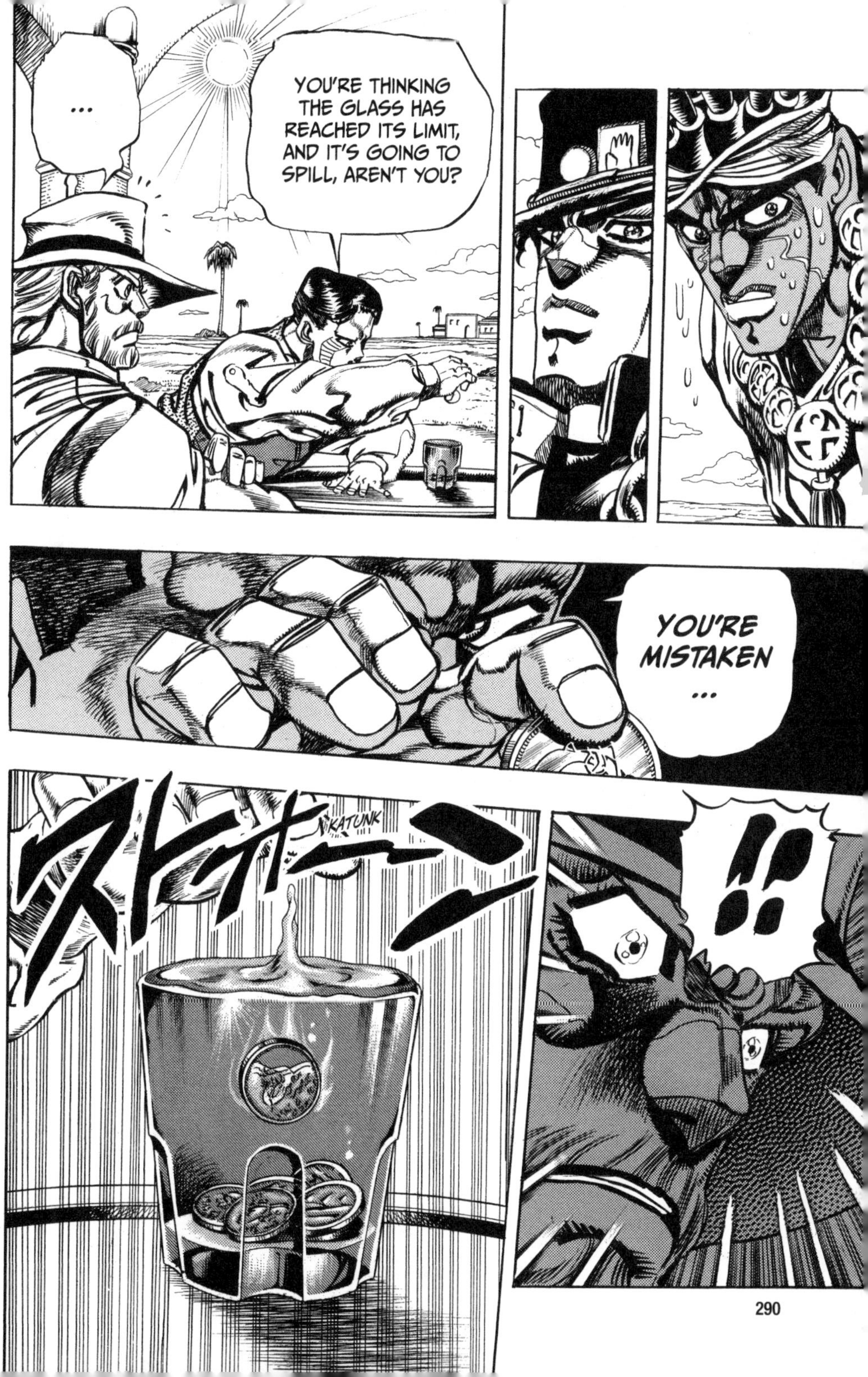
YOU'RE THINKING THE GLASS HAS REACHED ITS LIMIT, AND IT'S GOING TO SPILL, AREN'T YOU?
...
YOU'RE MISTAKEN ...
!?
KATUNK

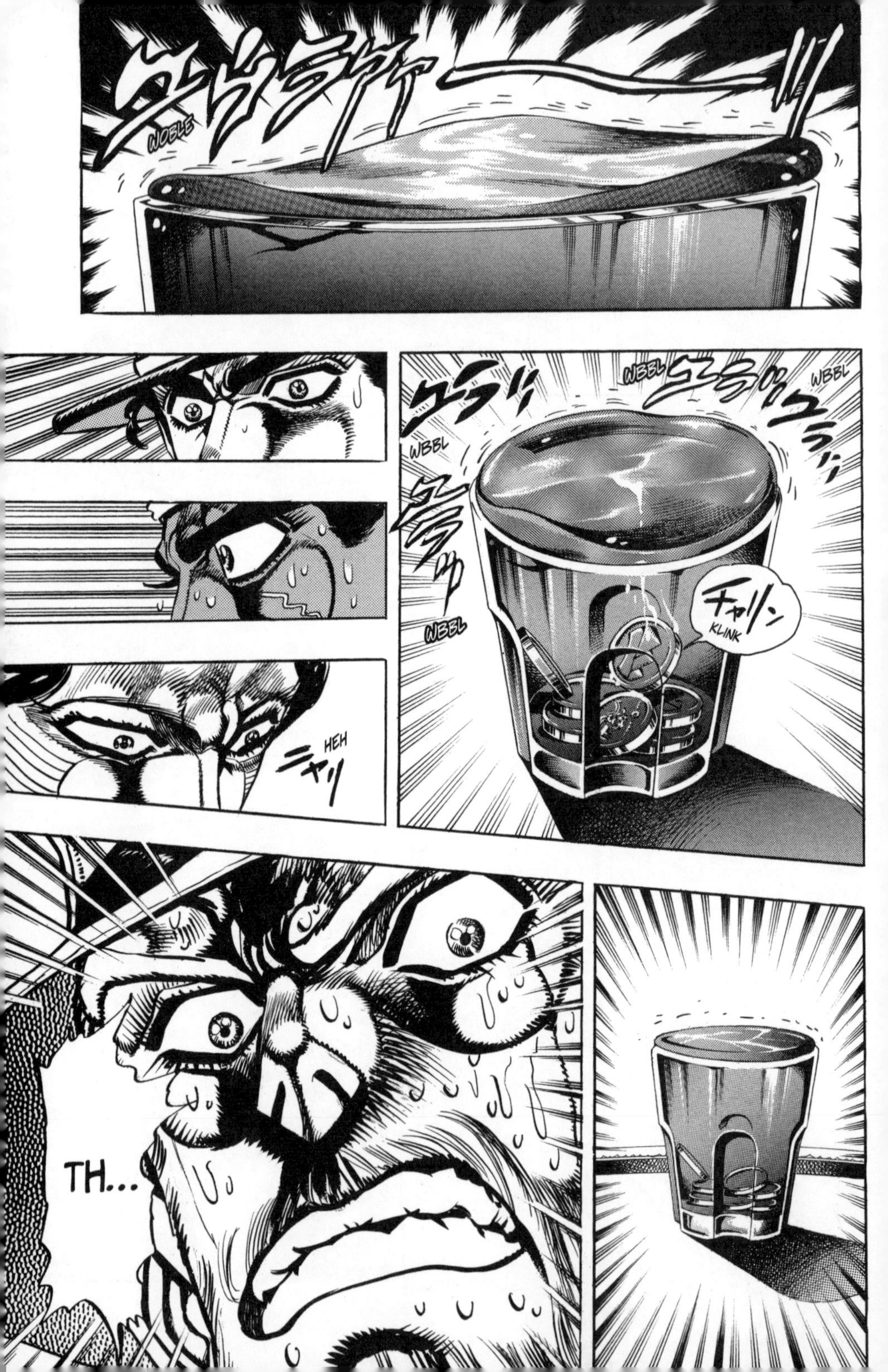
WOBLE
WBBL
WBBL
WBBL
WBBL
チャリン
KLINK
HEH
ニヤリ
TH...

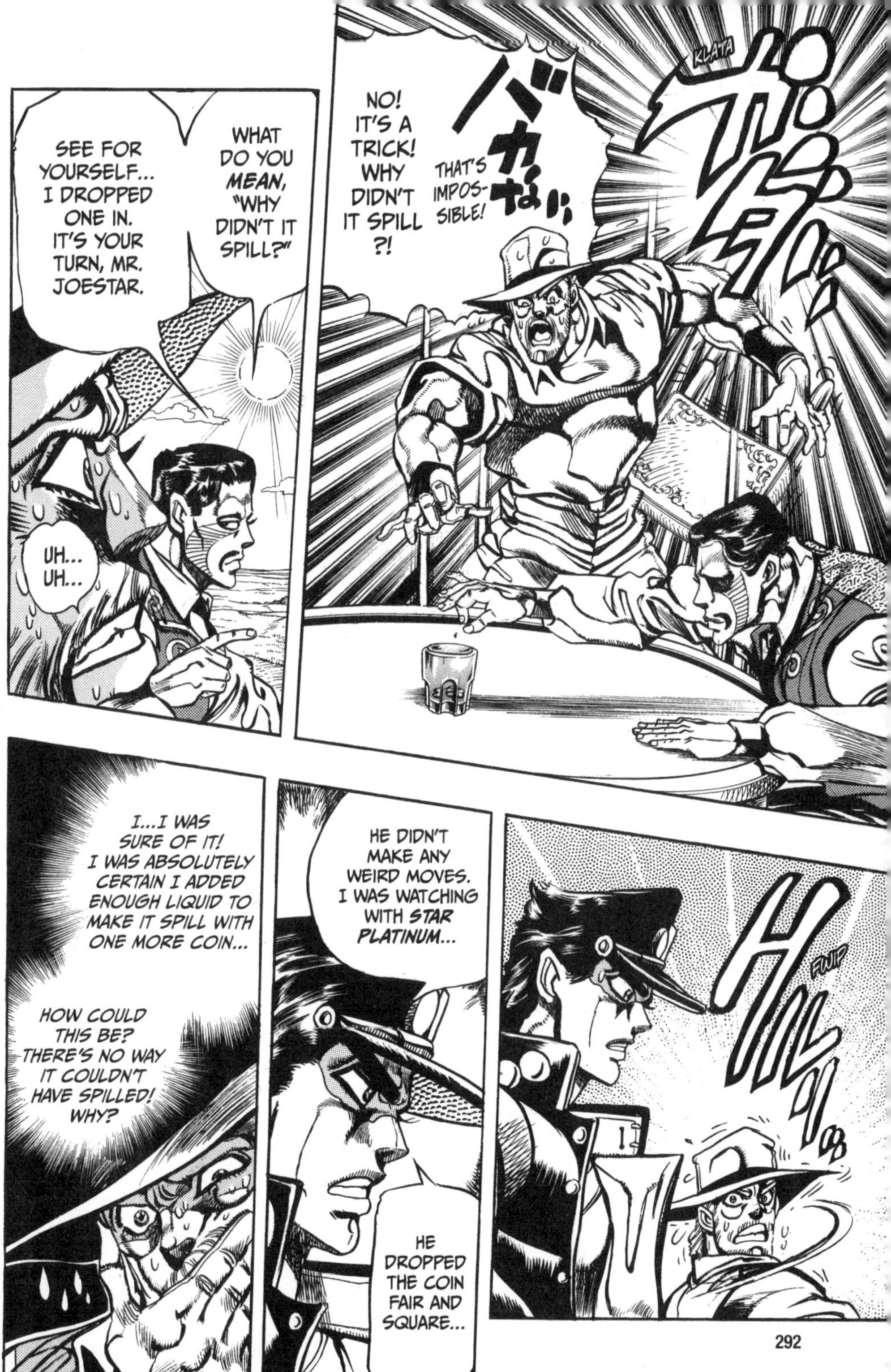
KLATA
THAT'S IMPOSSIBLE!
NO! IT'S A TRICK! WHY DIDN'T IT SPILL?!
WHAT DO YOU MEAN, "WHY DIDN'T IT SPILL?"
SEE FOR YOURSELF... I DROPPED ONE IN. IT'S YOUR TURN, MR. JOESTAR.
UH... UH...
FWIP
HE DIDN'T MAKE ANY WEIRD MOVES. I WAS WATCHING WITH **STAR PLATINUM**...
HE DROPPED THE COIN FAIR AND SQUARE...
I...I WAS SURE OF IT! I WAS ABSOLUTELY CERTAIN I ADDED ENOUGH LIQUID TO MAKE IT SPILL WITH ONE MORE COIN...
HOW COULD THIS BE? THERE'S NO WAY IT COULDN'T HAVE SPILLED! WHY?

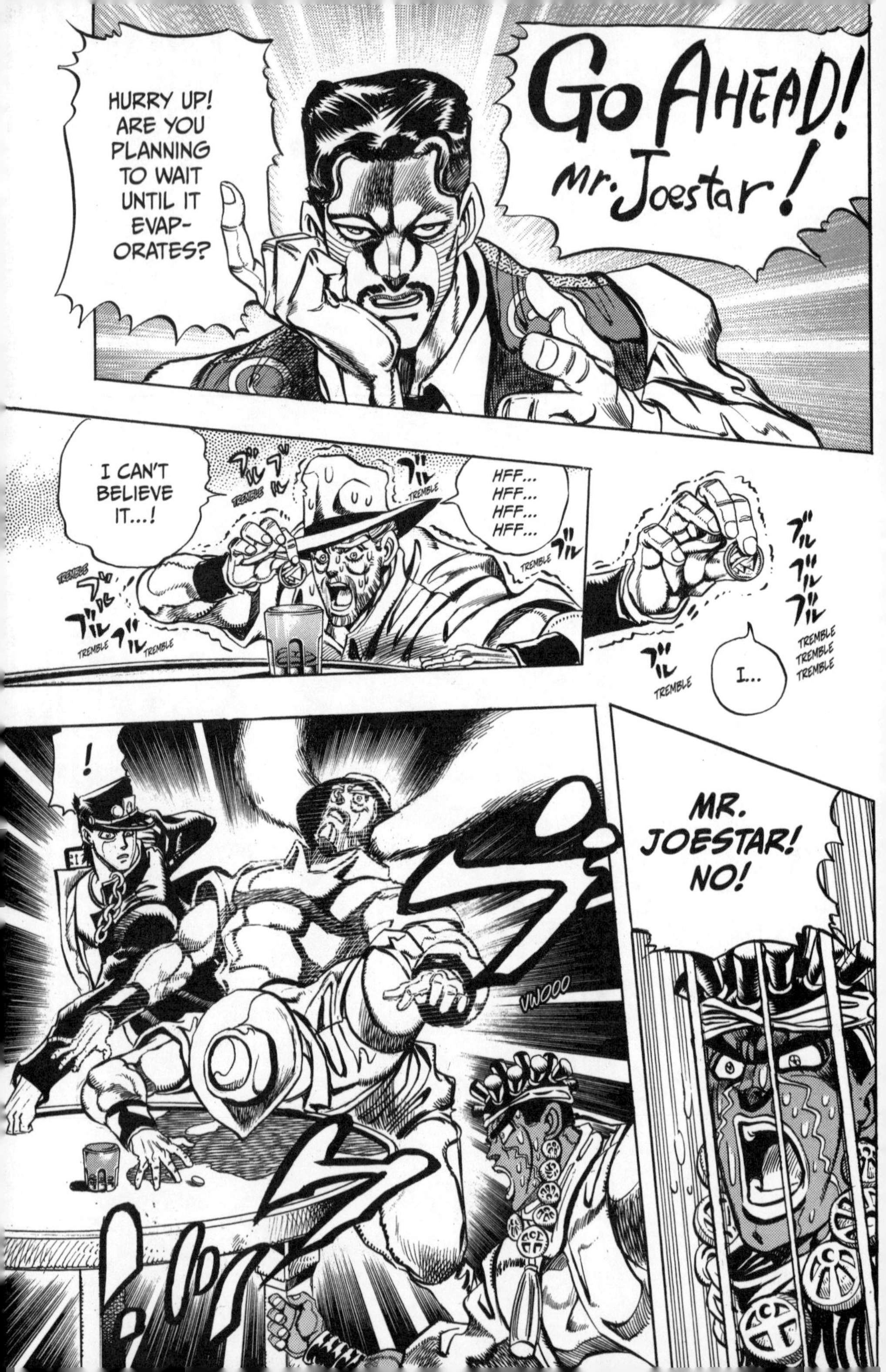
GO AHEAD! Mr. Joestar!
HURRY UP! ARE YOU PLANNING TO WAIT UNTIL IT EVAP-ORATES?
ブル ブル ブル
TREMBLE TREMBLE TREMBLE
ブル
TREMBLE
I...
HFF... HFF... HFF... HFF...
ブル
TREMBLE
ブル
TREMBLE
I CAN'T BELIEVE IT...!
ブル ブル ブル
TREMBLE TREMBLE TREMBLE
MR. JOESTAR! NO!
!
VWOOO

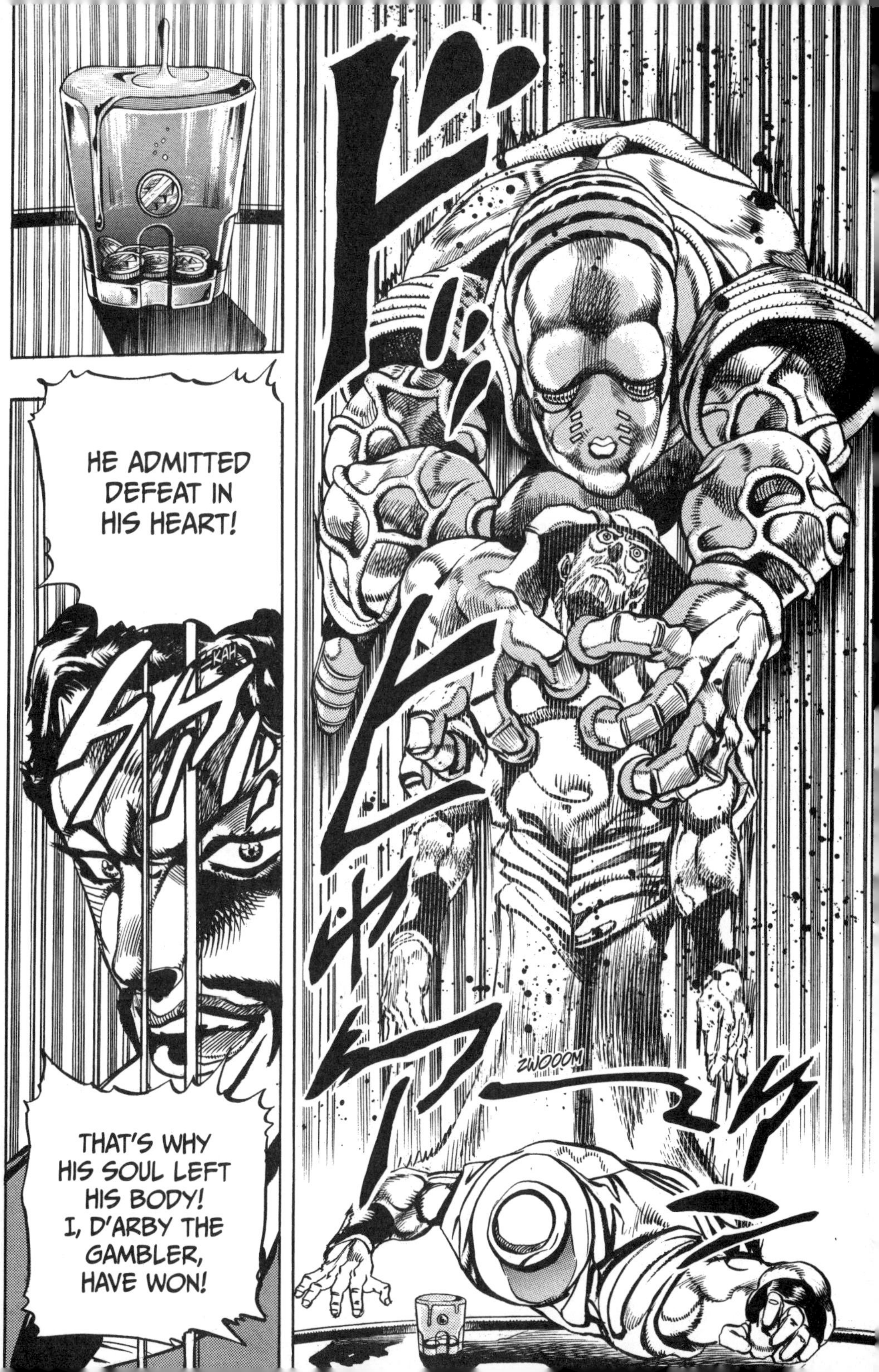
ZWOOOM
HE ADMITTED DEFEAT IN HIS HEART!
KAH
THAT'S WHY HIS SOUL LEFT HIS BODY! I, D'ARBY THE GAMBLER, HAVE WON!

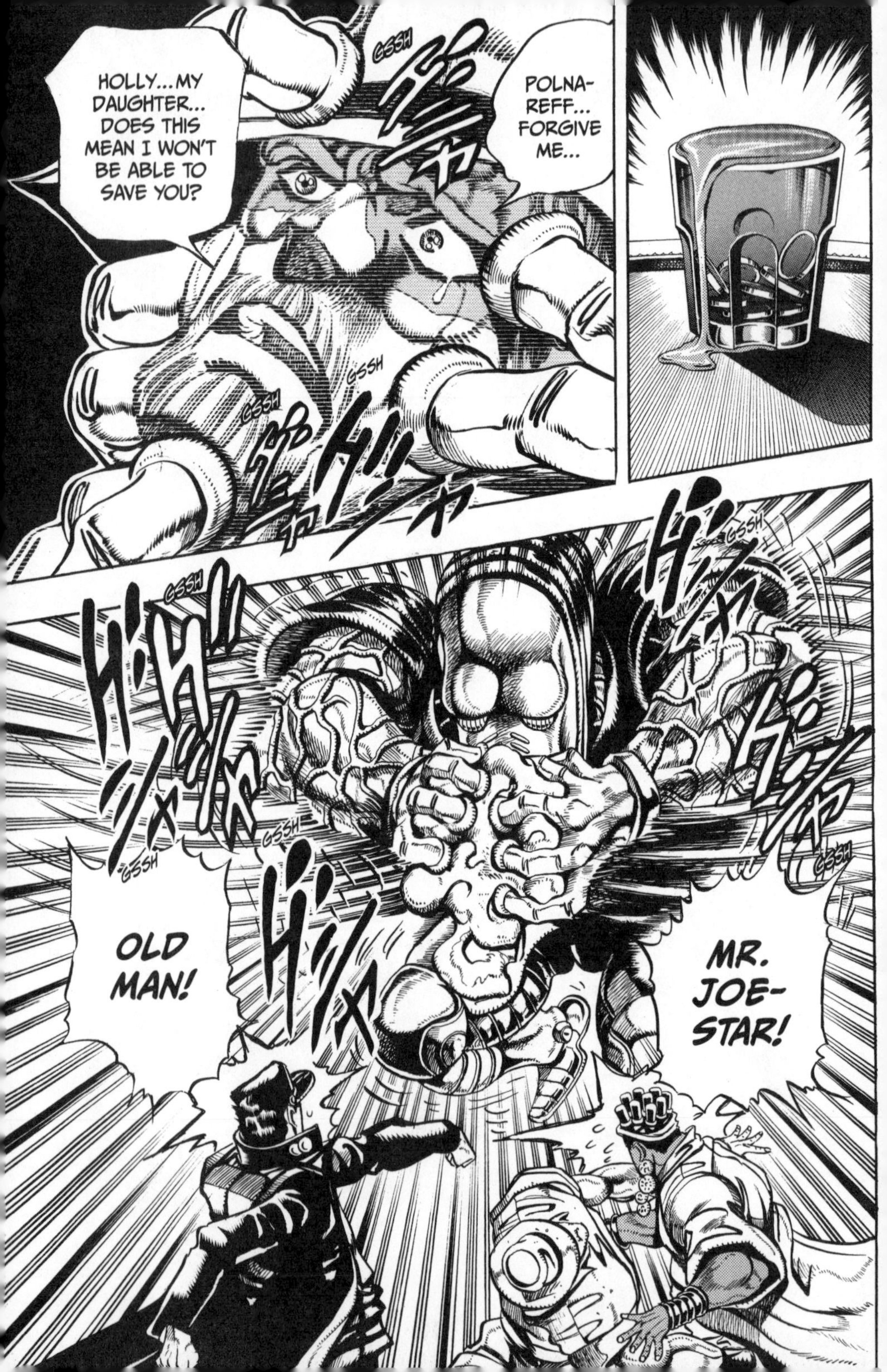
GSSH
POLNA-REFF... FORGIVE ME...
HOLLY... MY DAUGHTER... DOES THIS MEAN I WON'T BE ABLE TO SAVE YOU?
GSSH
GSSH
GSSH
GSSH
GSSH
MR. JOE-STAR!
GSSH
GSSH
OLD MAN!

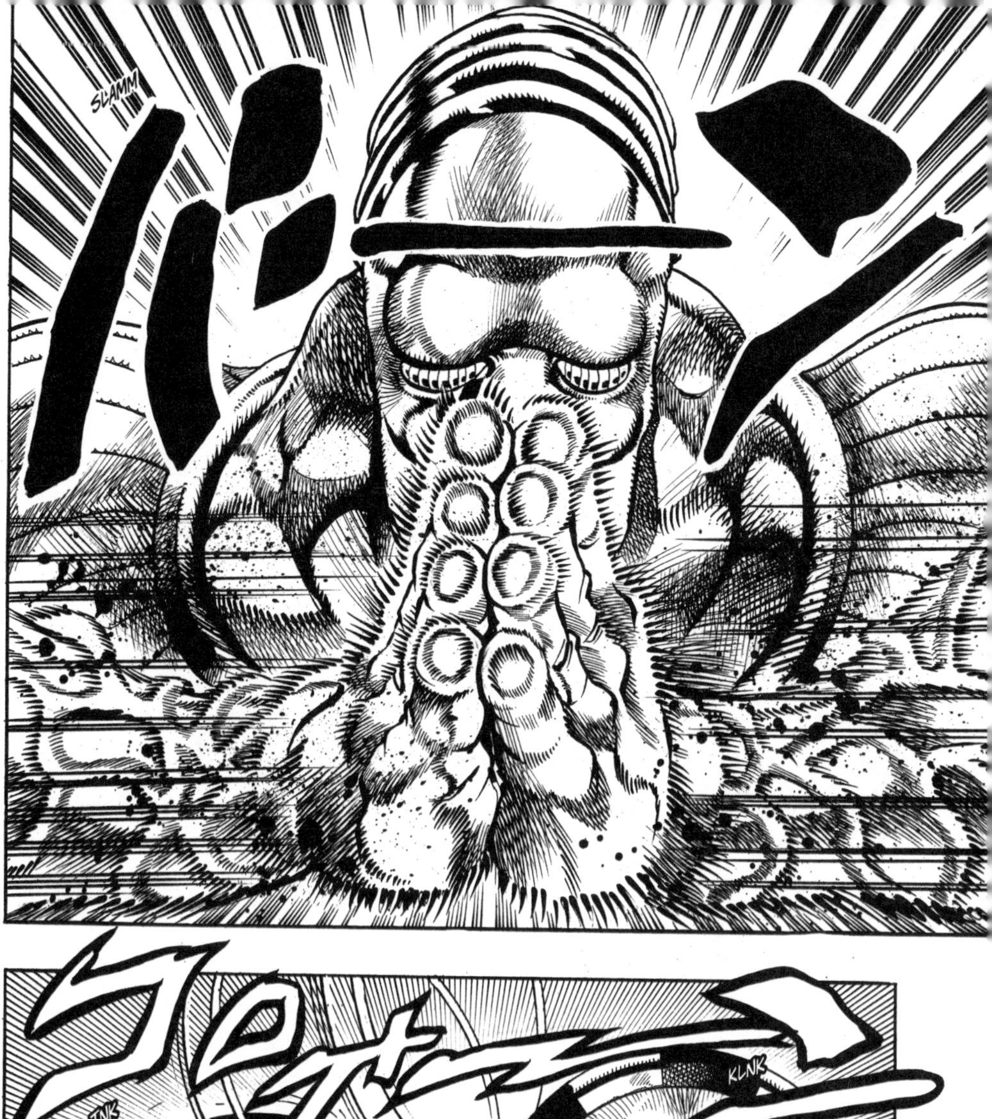
SLAMM
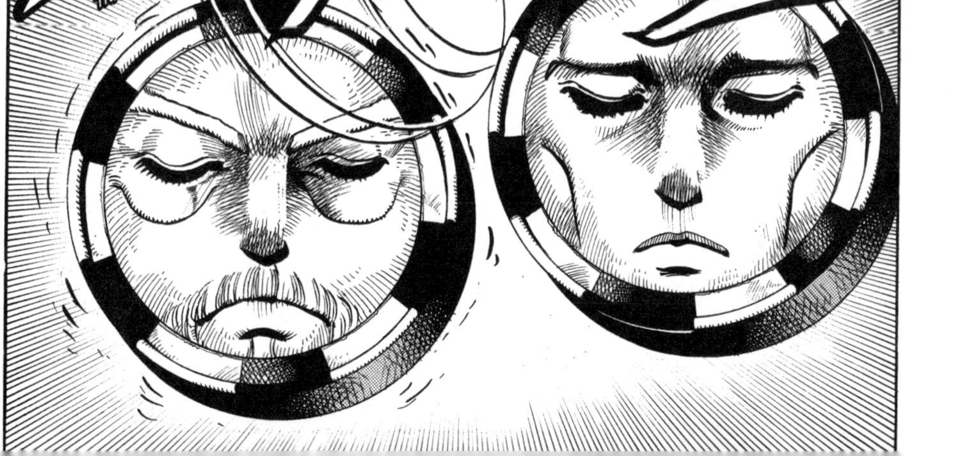
KLNK
TNK

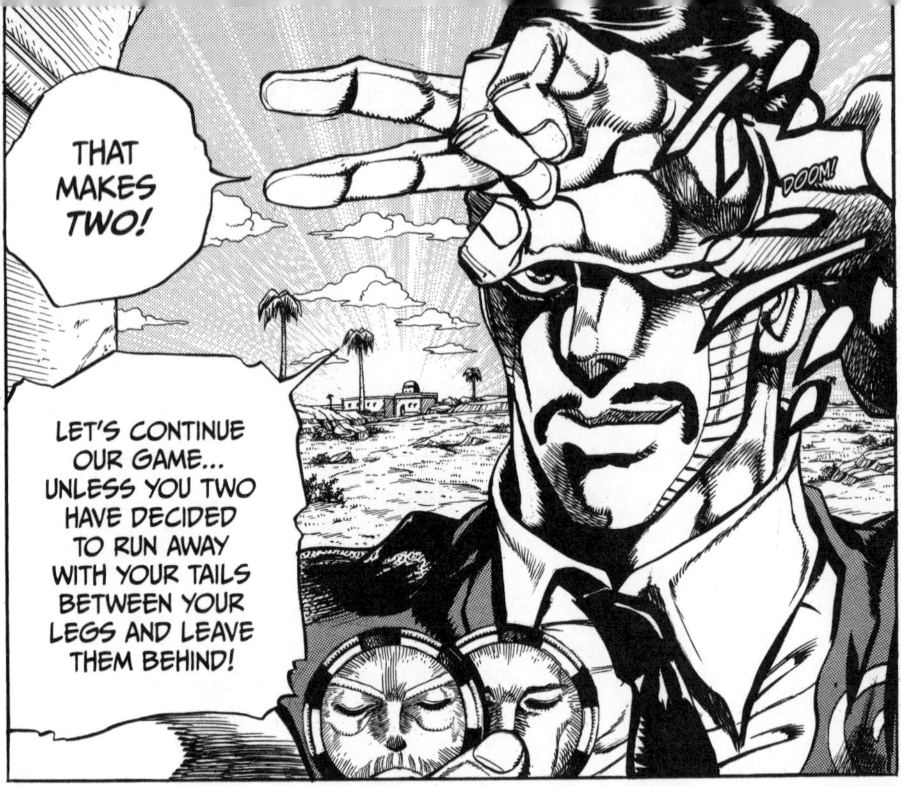
DOOM!
THAT MAKES TWO!
LET'S CONTINUE OUR GAME... UNLESS YOU TWO HAVE DECIDED TO RUN AWAY WITH YOUR TAILS BETWEEN YOUR LEGS AND LEAVE THEM BEHIND!
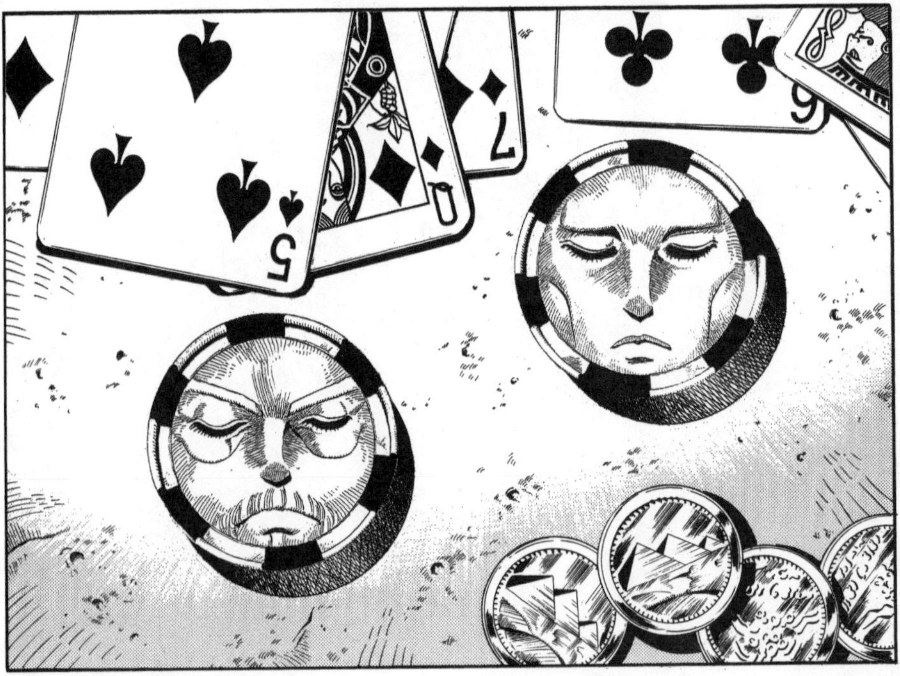

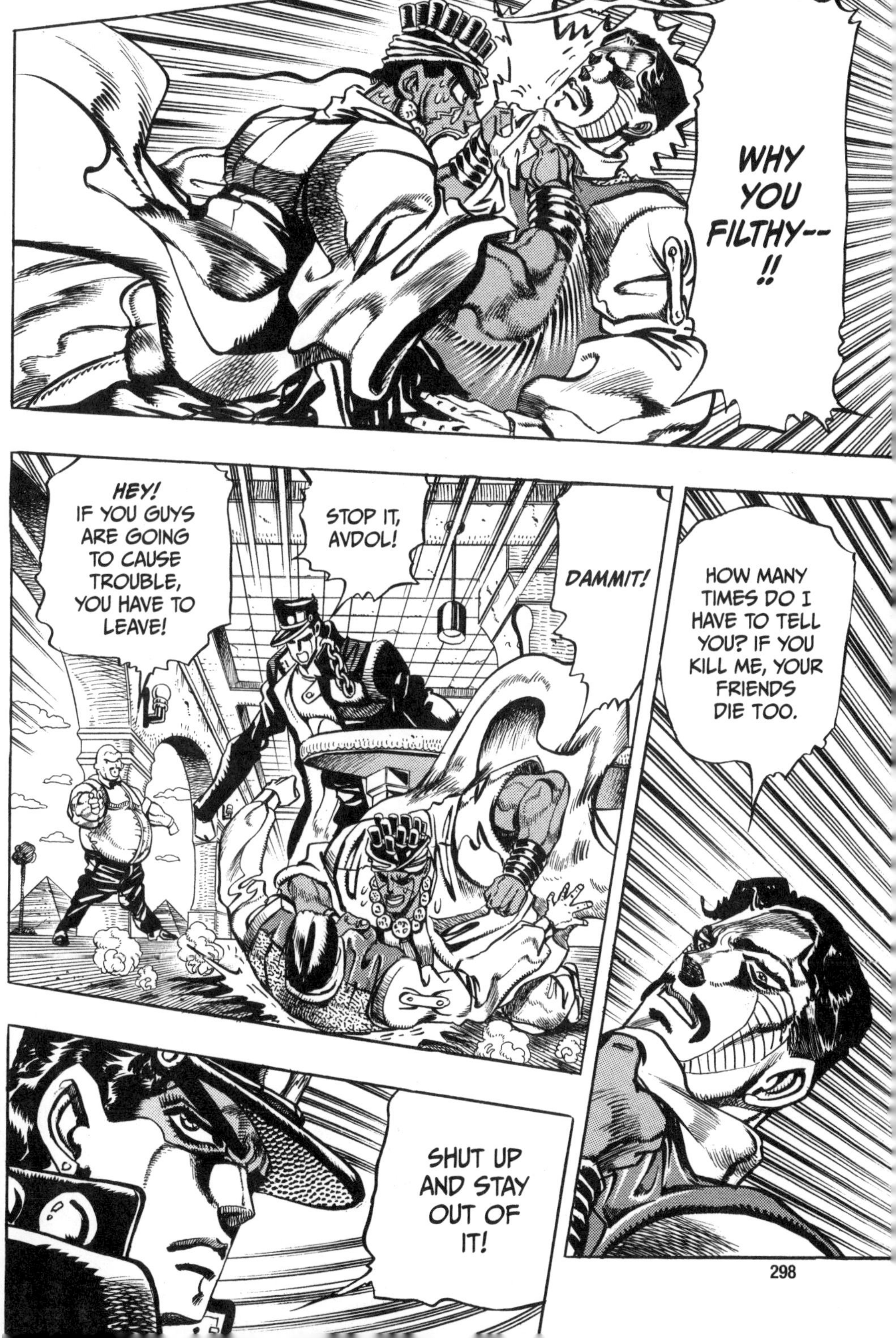
WHY YOU FILTHY-- !!
HOW MANY TIMES DO I HAVE TO TELL YOU? IF YOU KILL ME, YOUR FRIENDS DIE TOO.
DAMMIT!
STOP IT, AVDOL!
HEY! IF YOU GUYS ARE GOING TO CAUSE TROUBLE, YOU HAVE TO LEAVE!
SHUT UP AND STAY OUT OF IT!

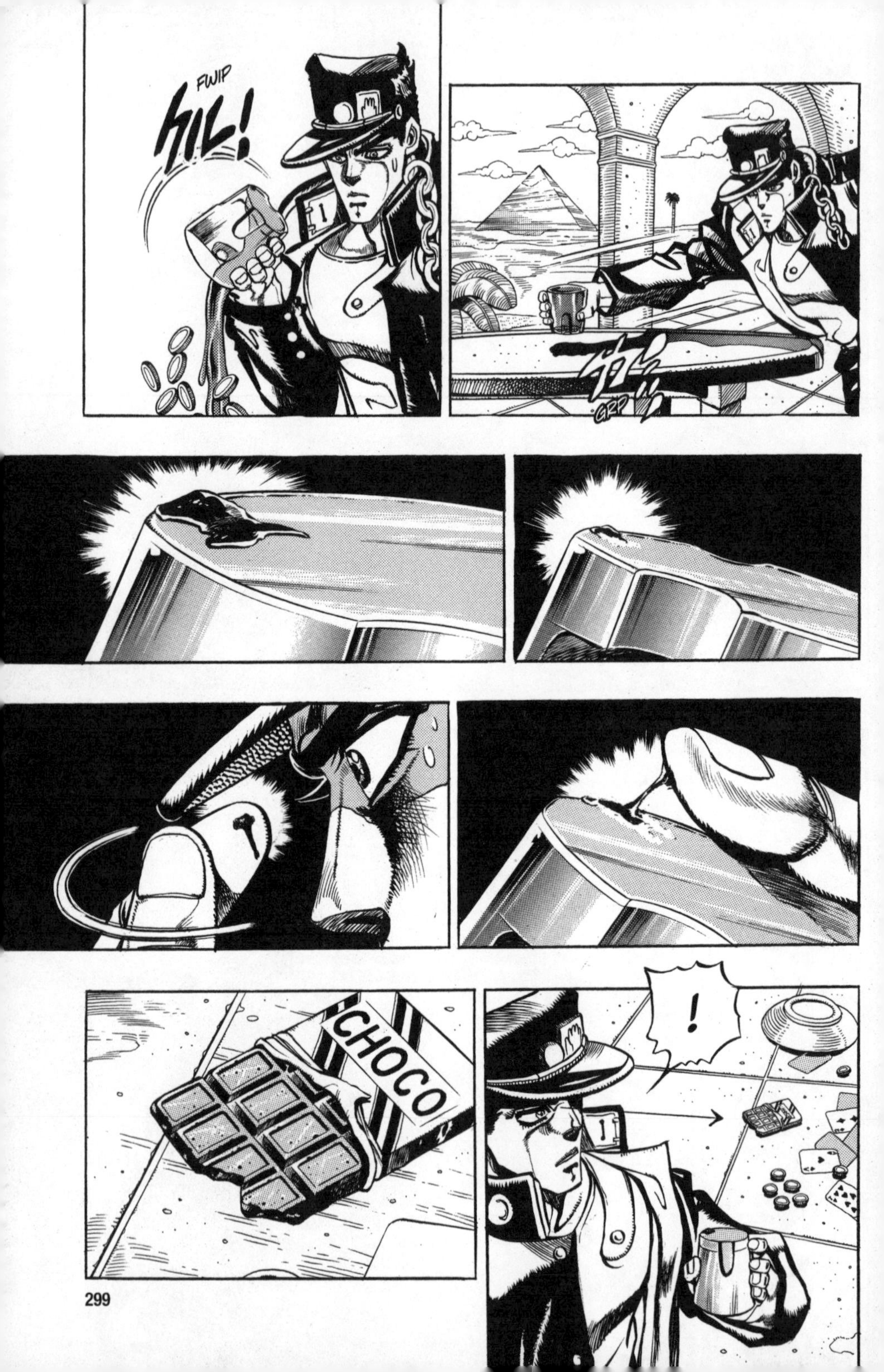
GRP
FWIP
!
CHOCO

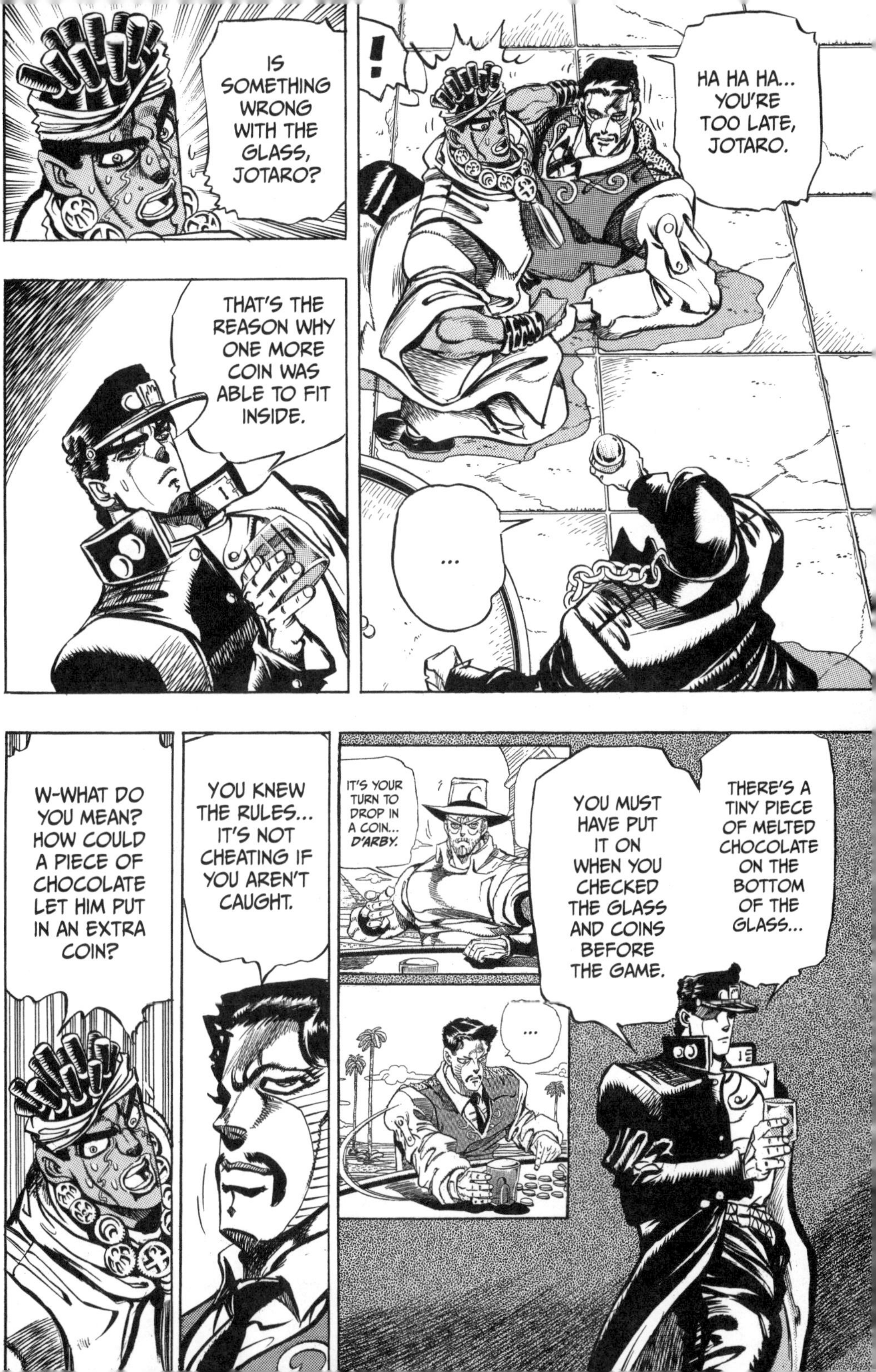
!
HA HA HA... YOU'RE TOO LATE, JOTARO.
...
IS SOMETHING WRONG WITH THE GLASS, JOTARO?
THAT'S THE REASON WHY ONE MORE COIN WAS ABLE TO FIT INSIDE.
THERE'S A TINY PIECE OF MELTED CHOCOLATE ON THE BOTTOM OF THE GLASS...
YOU MUST HAVE PUT IT ON WHEN YOU CHECKED THE GLASS AND COINS BEFORE THE GAME.
IT'S YOUR TURN TO DROP IN A COIN... D'ARBY.
...
YOU KNEW THE RULES... IT'S NOT CHEATING IF YOU AREN'T CAUGHT.
W-WHAT DO YOU MEAN? HOW COULD A PIECE OF CHOCOLATE LET HIM PUT IN AN EXTRA COIN?

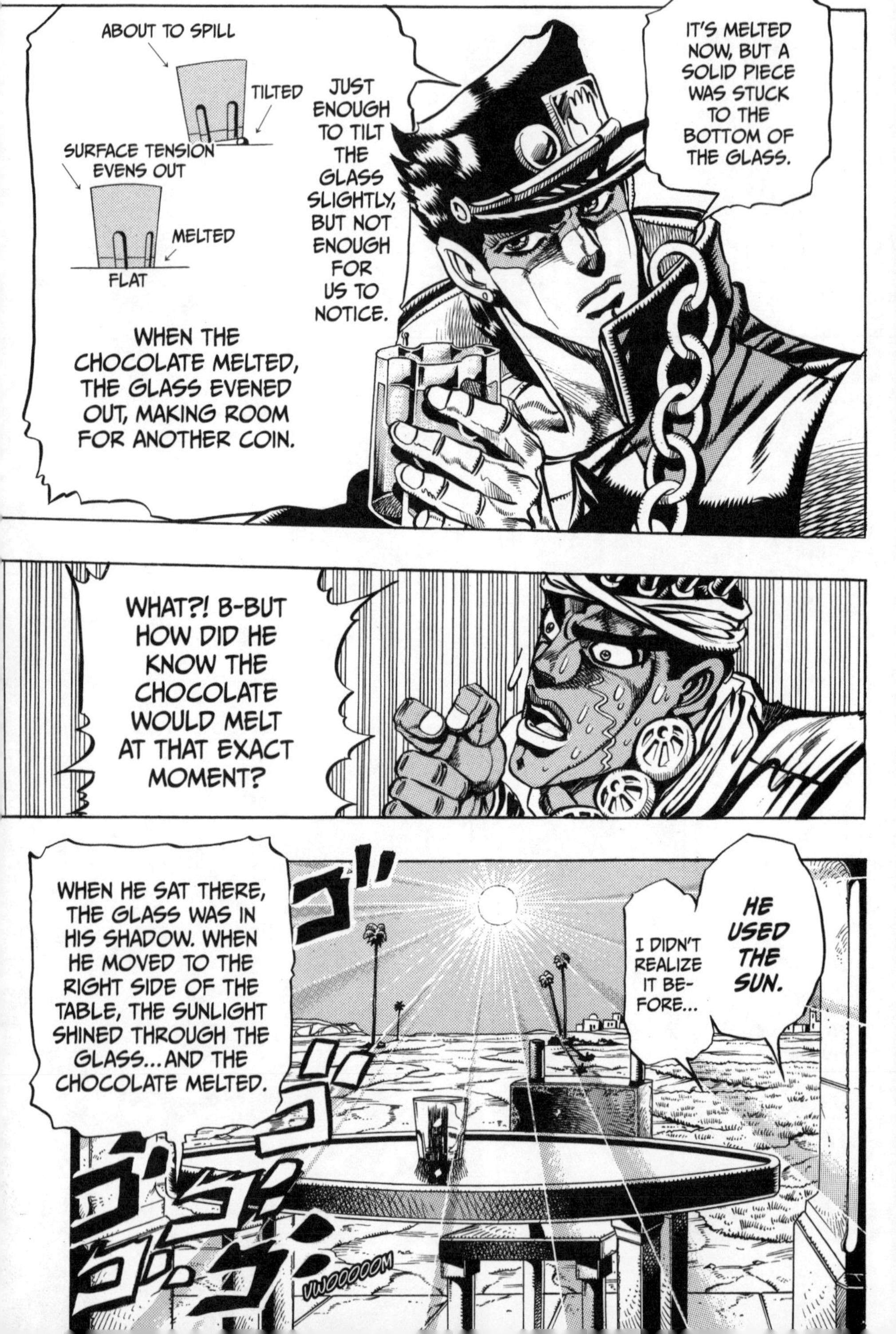
IT'S MELTED NOW, BUT A SOLID PIECE WAS STUCK TO THE BOTTOM OF THE GLASS.
JUST ENOUGH TO TILT THE GLASS SLIGHTLY, BUT NOT ENOUGH FOR US TO NOTICE.
ABOUT TO SPILL
TILTED
SURFACE TENSION EVENS OUT
MELTED
FLAT
WHEN THE CHOCOLATE MELTED, THE GLASS EVENED OUT, MAKING ROOM FOR ANOTHER COIN.
WHAT?! B-BUT HOW DID HE KNOW THE CHOCOLATE WOULD MELT AT THAT EXACT MOMENT?
HE USED THE SUN.
I DIDN'T REALIZE IT BE-FORE...
WHEN HE SAT THERE, THE GLASS WAS IN HIS SHADOW. WHEN HE MOVED TO THE RIGHT SIDE OF THE TABLE, THE SUNLIGHT SHINED THROUGH THE GLASS...AND THE CHOCOLATE MELTED.
VWOOOOOM

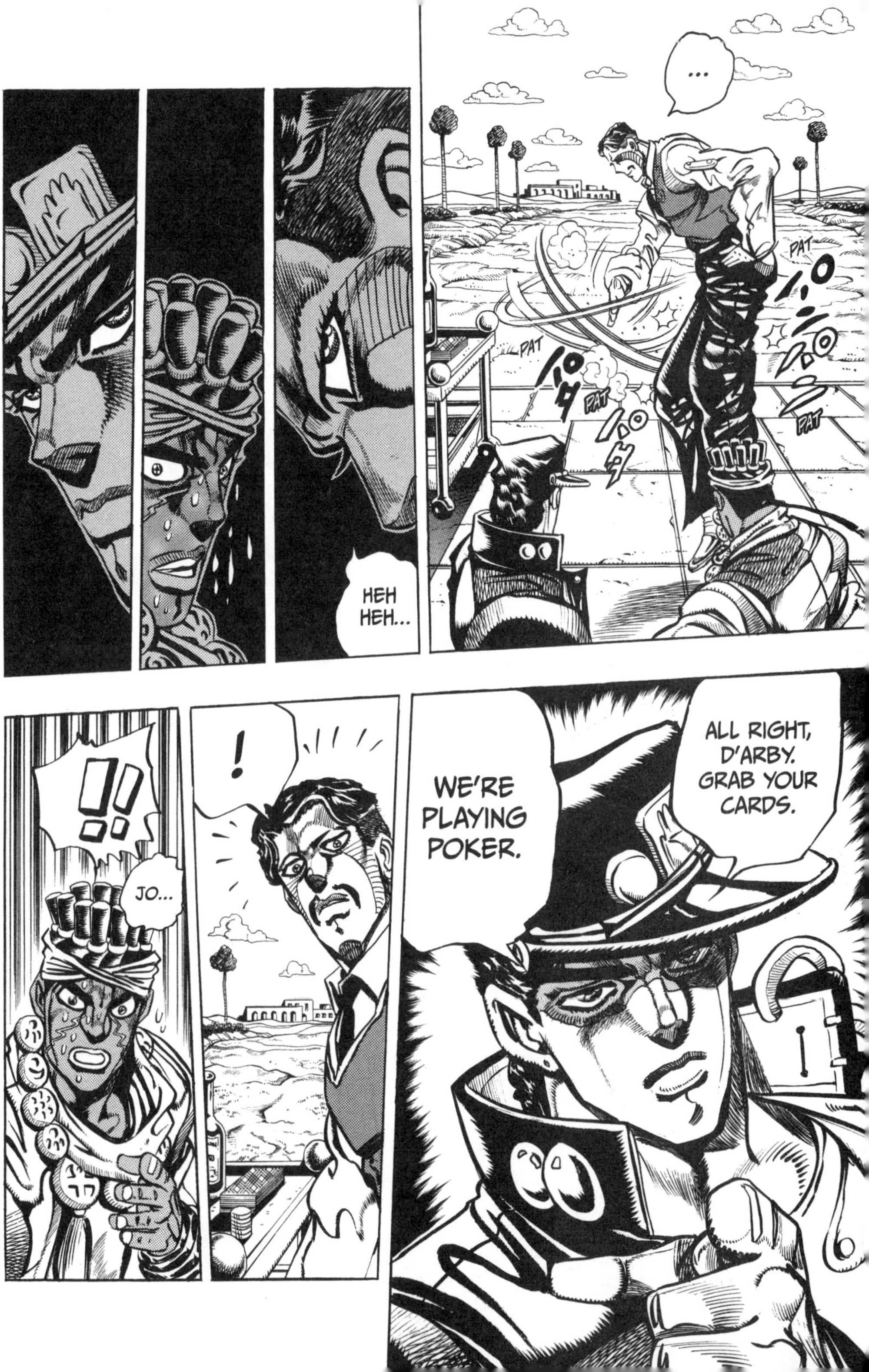
...
PAT
PAT
PAT
PAT
HEH HEH...
ALL RIGHT, D'ARBY. GRAB YOUR CARDS.
WE'RE PLAYING POKER.
!
!!
JO...

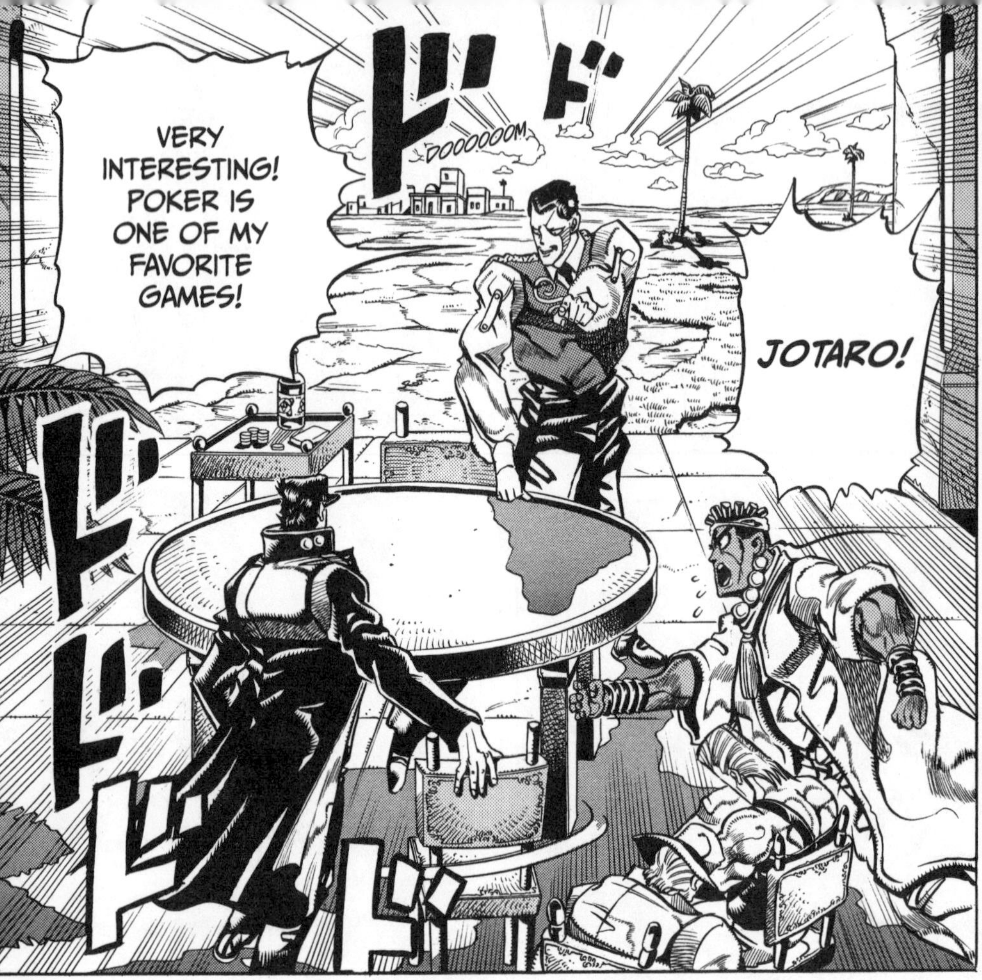
DOOOOOOM
VERY INTERESTING! POKER IS ONE OF MY FAVORITE GAMES!
JOTARO!

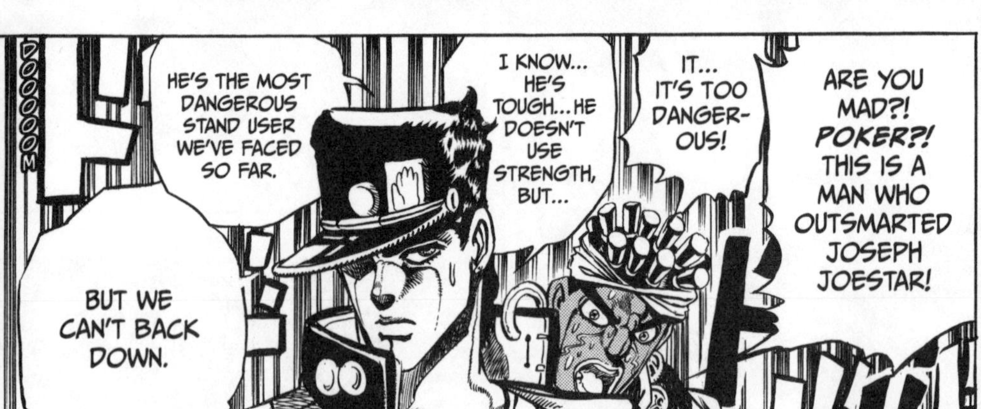
ARE YOU MAD?! *POKER?!* THIS IS A MAN WHO OUTSMARTED JOSEPH JOESTAR!
IT... IT'S TOO DANGER-OUS!
I KNOW... HE'S TOUGH... HE DOESN'T USE STRENGTH, BUT...
HE'S THE MOST DANGEROUS STAND USER WE'VE FACED SO FAR.
BUT WE CAN'T BACK DOWN.
DOOOOOOM

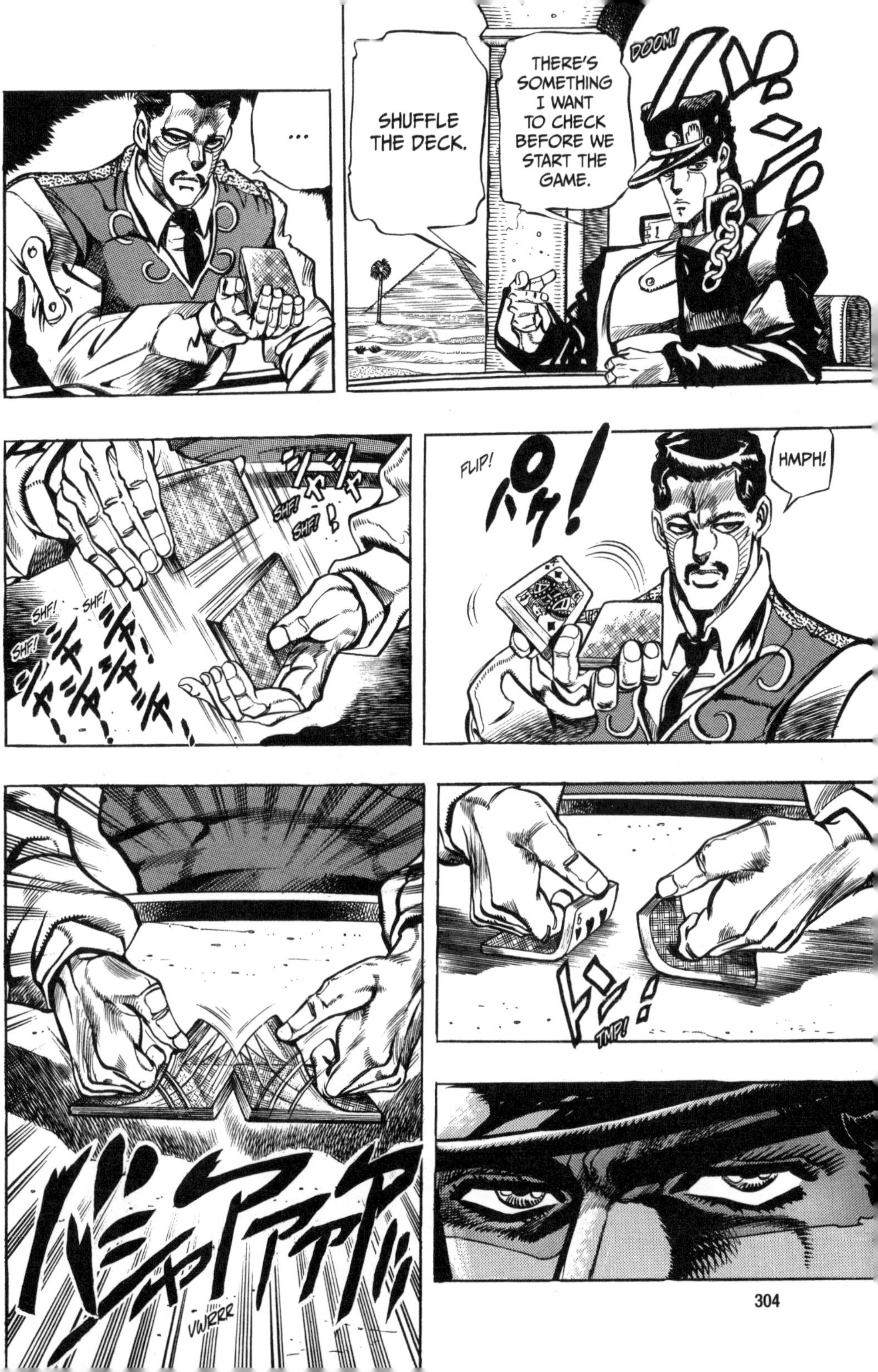
DOOM!
THERE'S SOMETHING I WANT TO CHECK BEFORE WE START THE GAME.
SHUFFLE THE DECK.
...
FLIP!
HMPH!
SHF!
SHF!
SHF!
SHF!
SHF!
TMP!
VWRRR

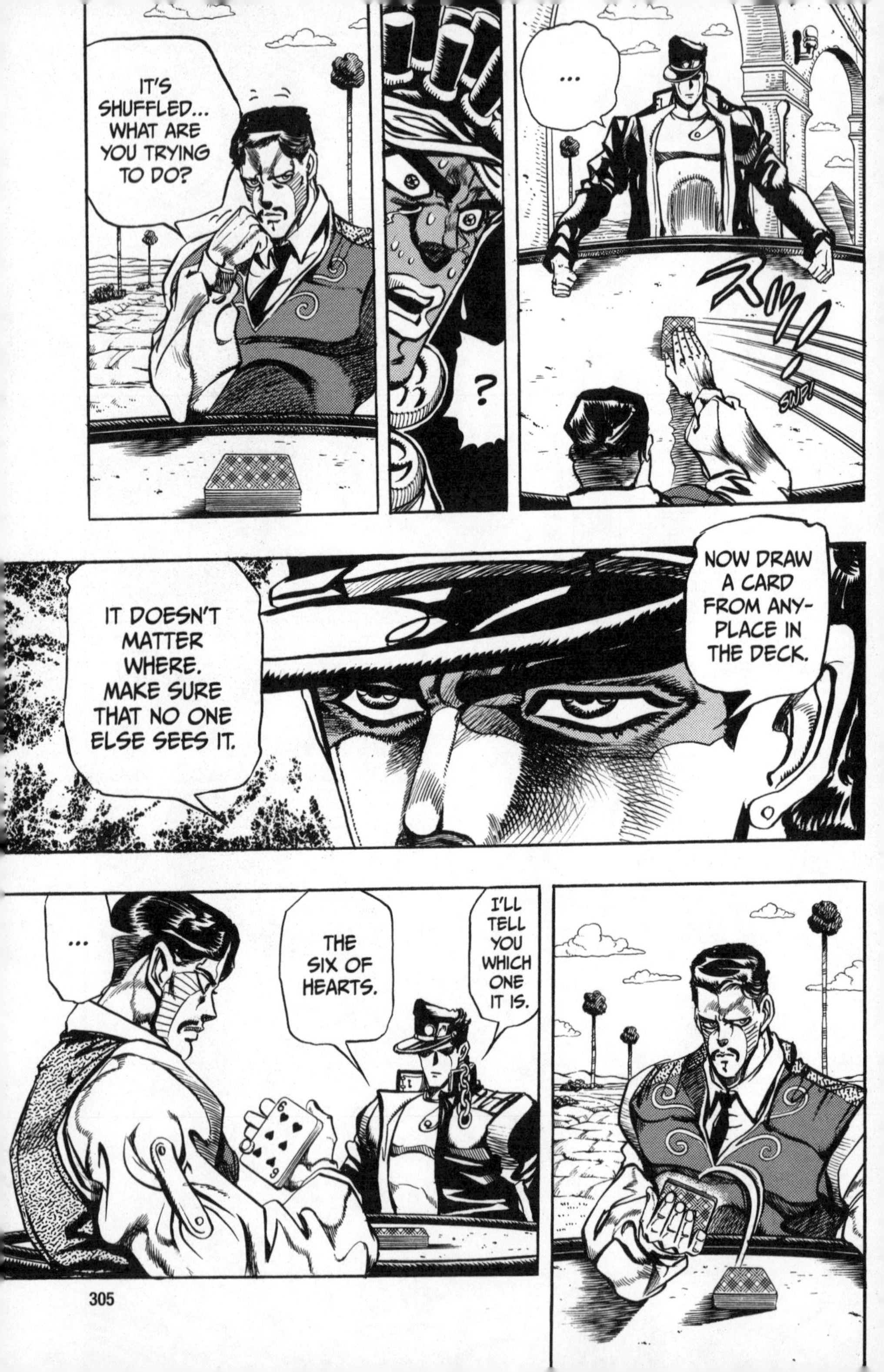
...
SWP!
?
IT'S SHUFFLED... WHAT ARE YOU TRYING TO DO?
NOW DRAW A CARD FROM ANY-PLACE IN THE DECK.
IT DOESN'T MATTER WHERE. MAKE SURE THAT NO ONE ELSE SEES IT.
I'LL TELL YOU WHICH ONE IT IS.
THE SIX OF HEARTS.
...

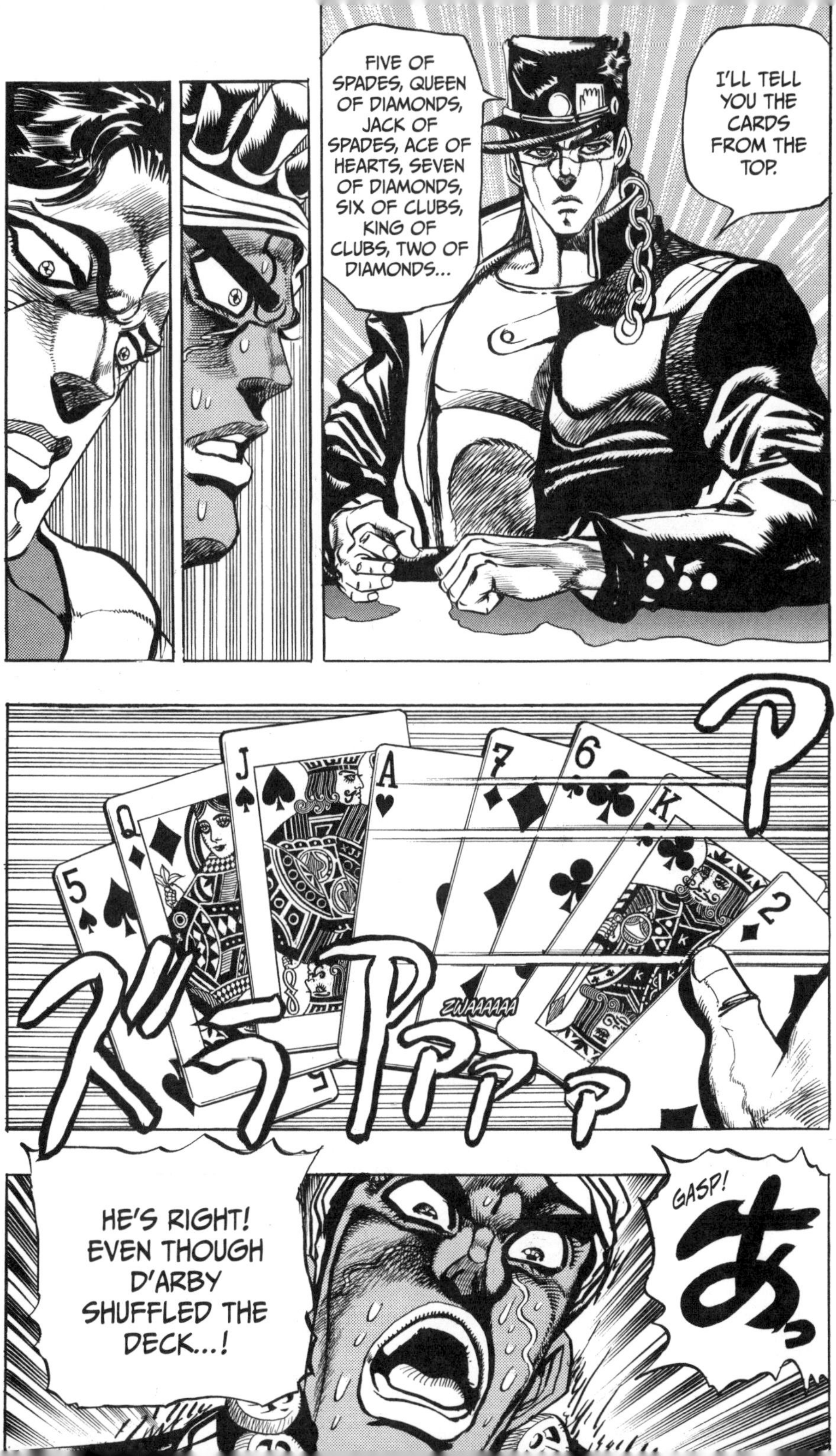
I'LL TELL YOU THE CARDS FROM THE TOP.
FIVE OF SPADES, QUEEN OF DIAMONDS, JACK OF SPADES, ACE OF HEARTS, SEVEN OF DIAMONDS, SIX OF CLUBS, KING OF CLUBS, TWO OF DIAMONDS...
ZWAAAAAA
GASP!
あっ
HE'S RIGHT! EVEN THOUGH D'ARBY SHUFFLED THE DECK...!

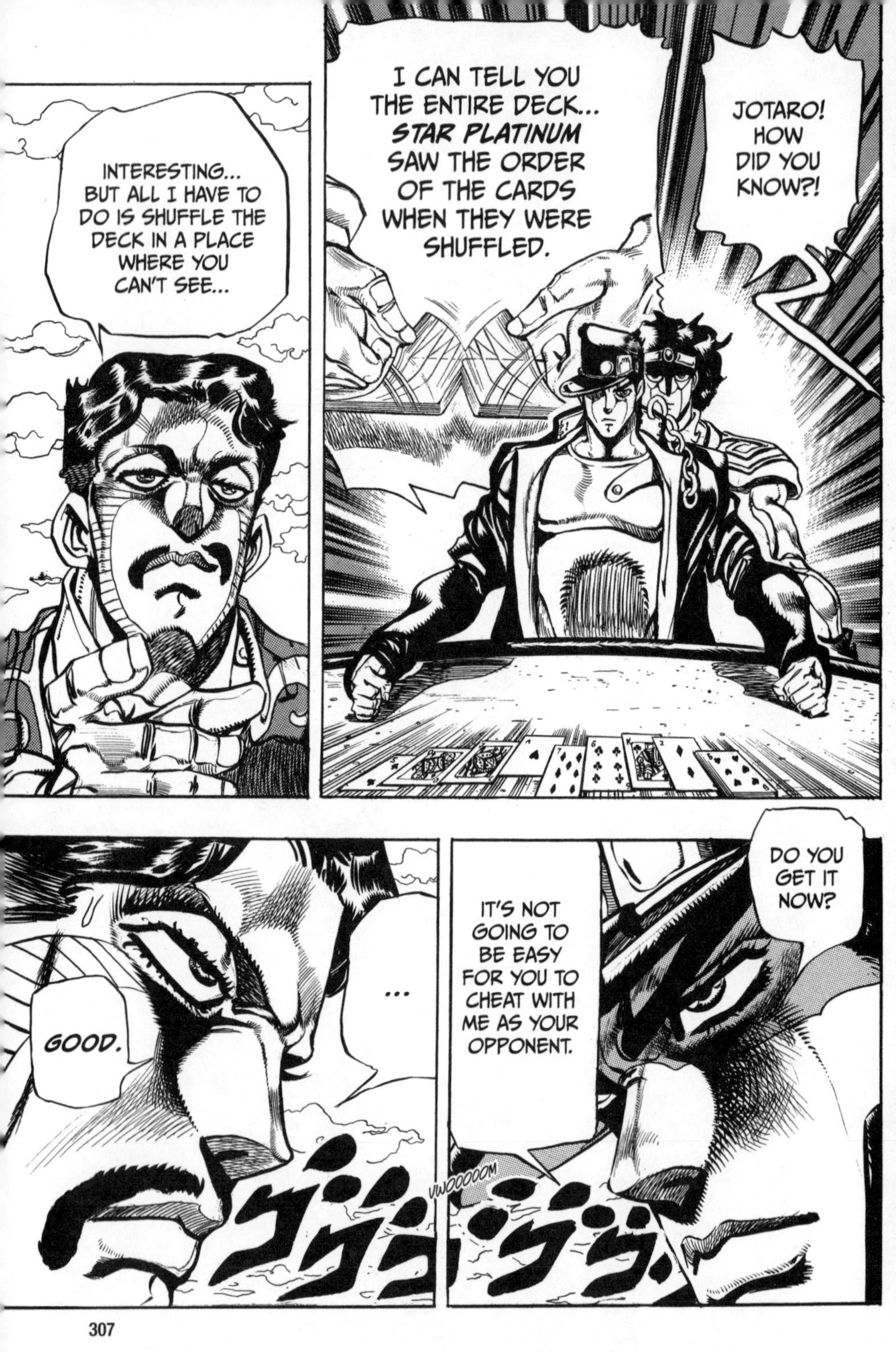
JOTARO! HOW DID YOU KNOW?!
I CAN TELL YOU THE ENTIRE DECK... STAR PLATINUM SAW THE ORDER OF THE CARDS WHEN THEY WERE SHUFFLED.
INTERESTING... BUT ALL I HAVE TO DO IS SHUFFLE THE DECK IN A PLACE WHERE YOU CAN'T SEE...
DO YOU GET IT NOW?
IT'S NOT GOING TO BE EASY FOR YOU TO CHEAT WITH ME AS YOUR OPPONENT.
VWOOOOOM
...
GOOD.

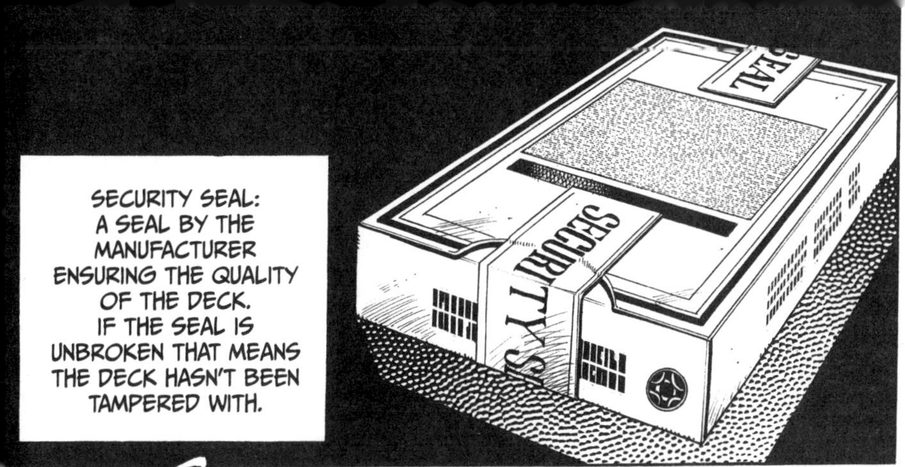
SECURITY SEAL:
A SEAL BY THE MANUFACTURER ENSURING THE QUALITY OF THE DECK.
IF THE SEAL IS UNBROKEN THAT MEANS THE DECK HASN'T BEEN TAMPERED WITH.
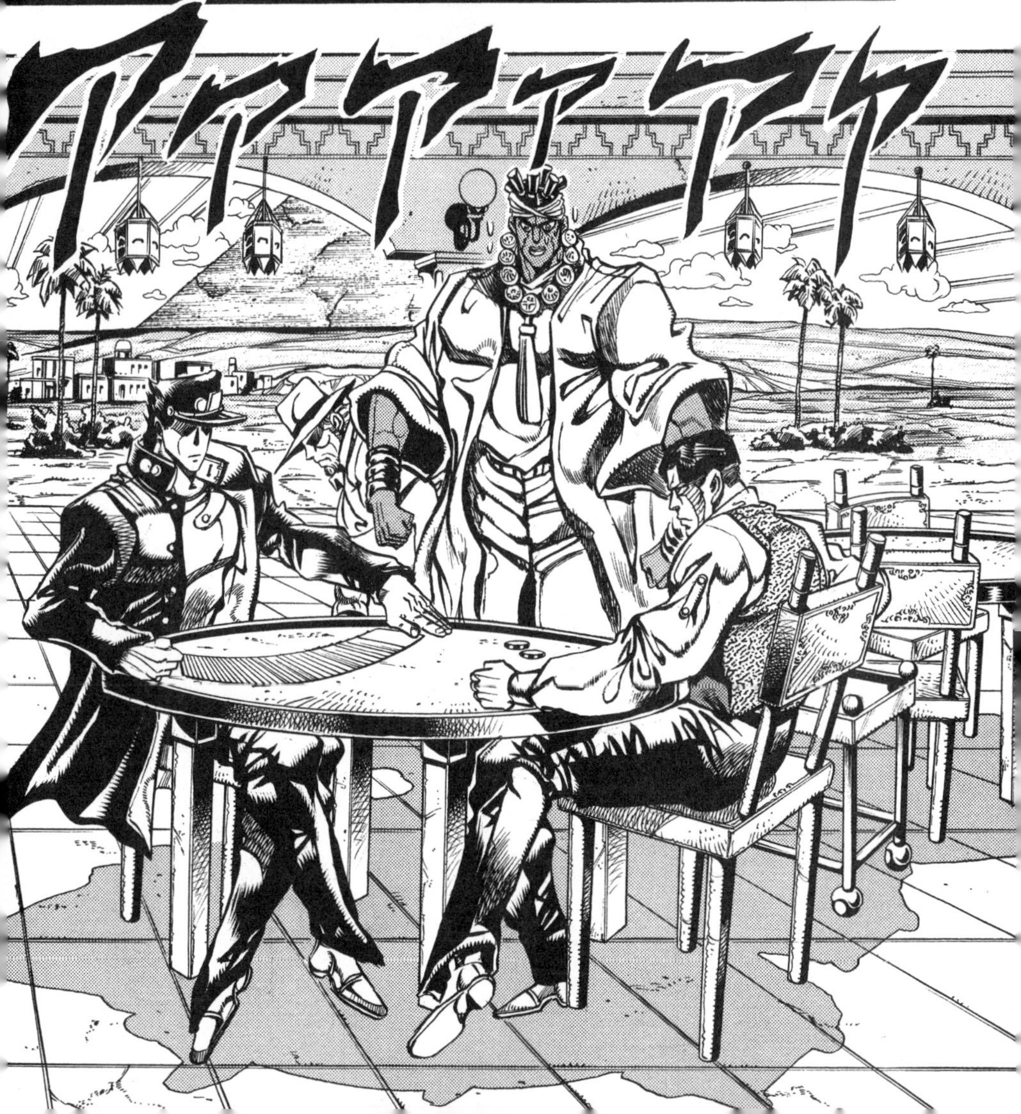

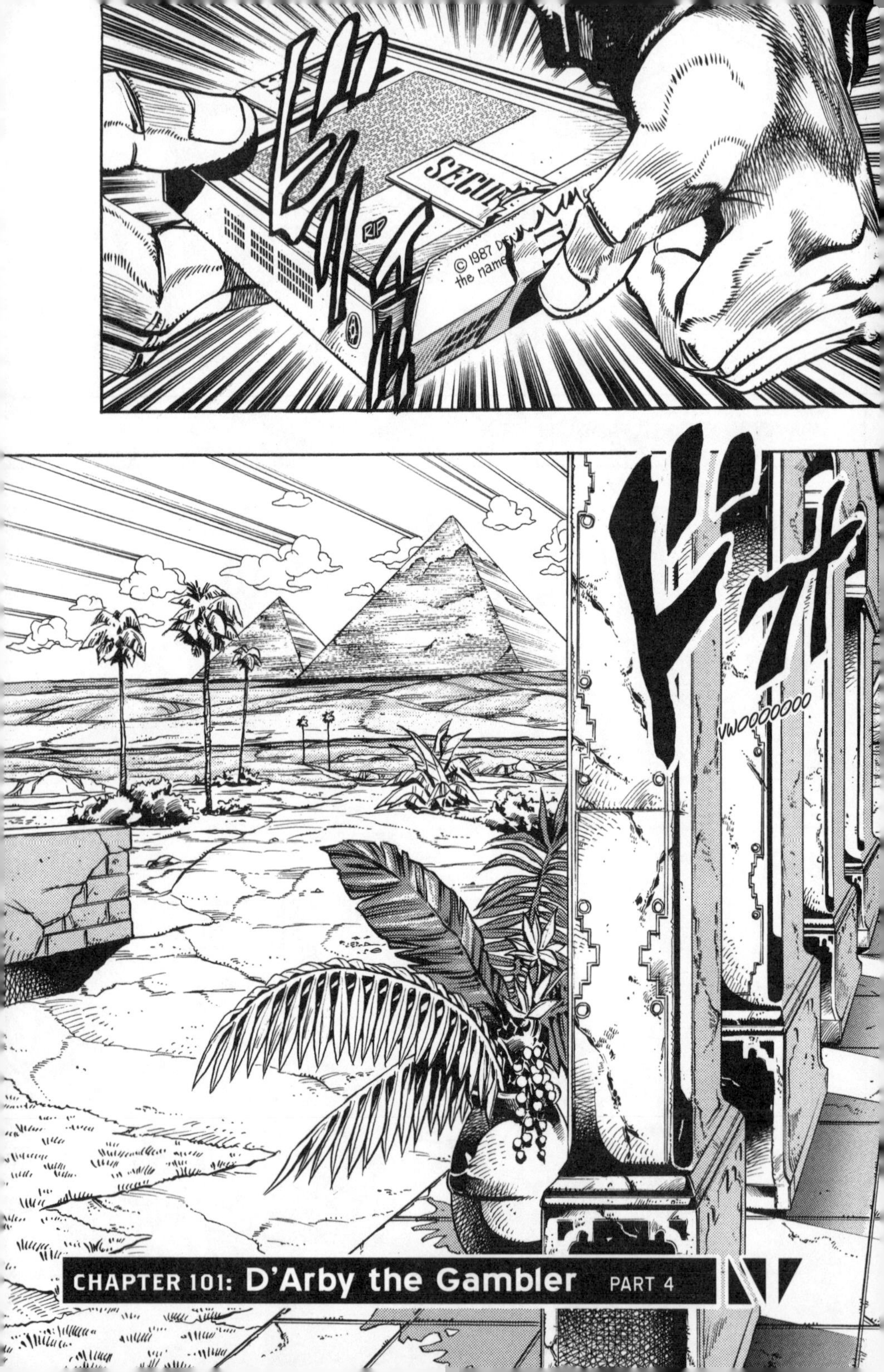
RIP
VWOOOOOOO

CHAPTER 101: D'Arby the Gambler PART 4

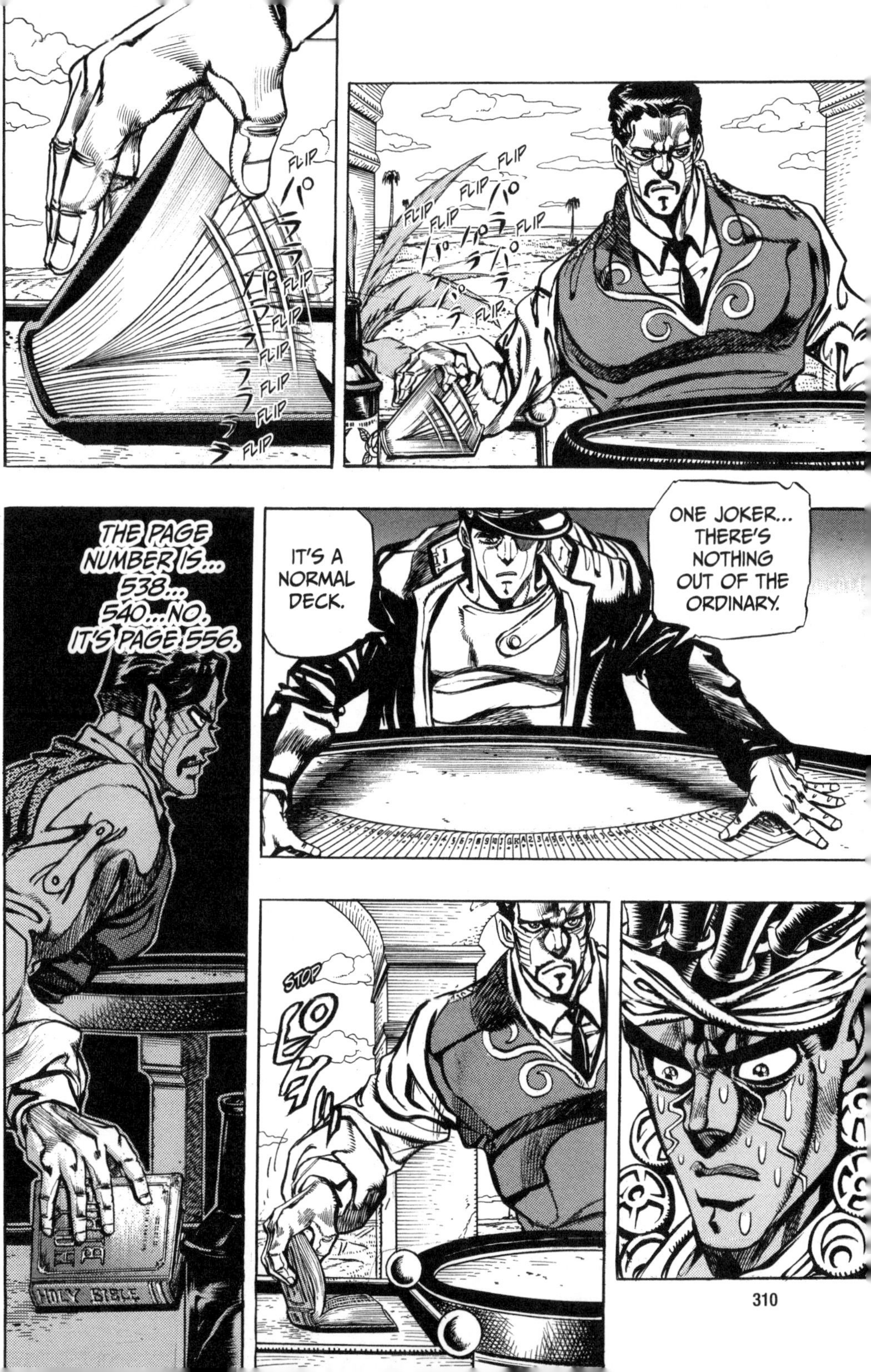
FLIP FLIP FLIP FLIP FLIP
FLIP FLIP FLIP FLIP FLIP FLIP FLIP
ONE JOKER... THERE'S NOTHING OUT OF THE ORDINARY.
IT'S A NORMAL DECK.
STOP
THE PAGE NUMBER IS... 538... 540...NO. IT'S PAGE 556.
HOLY BIBLE

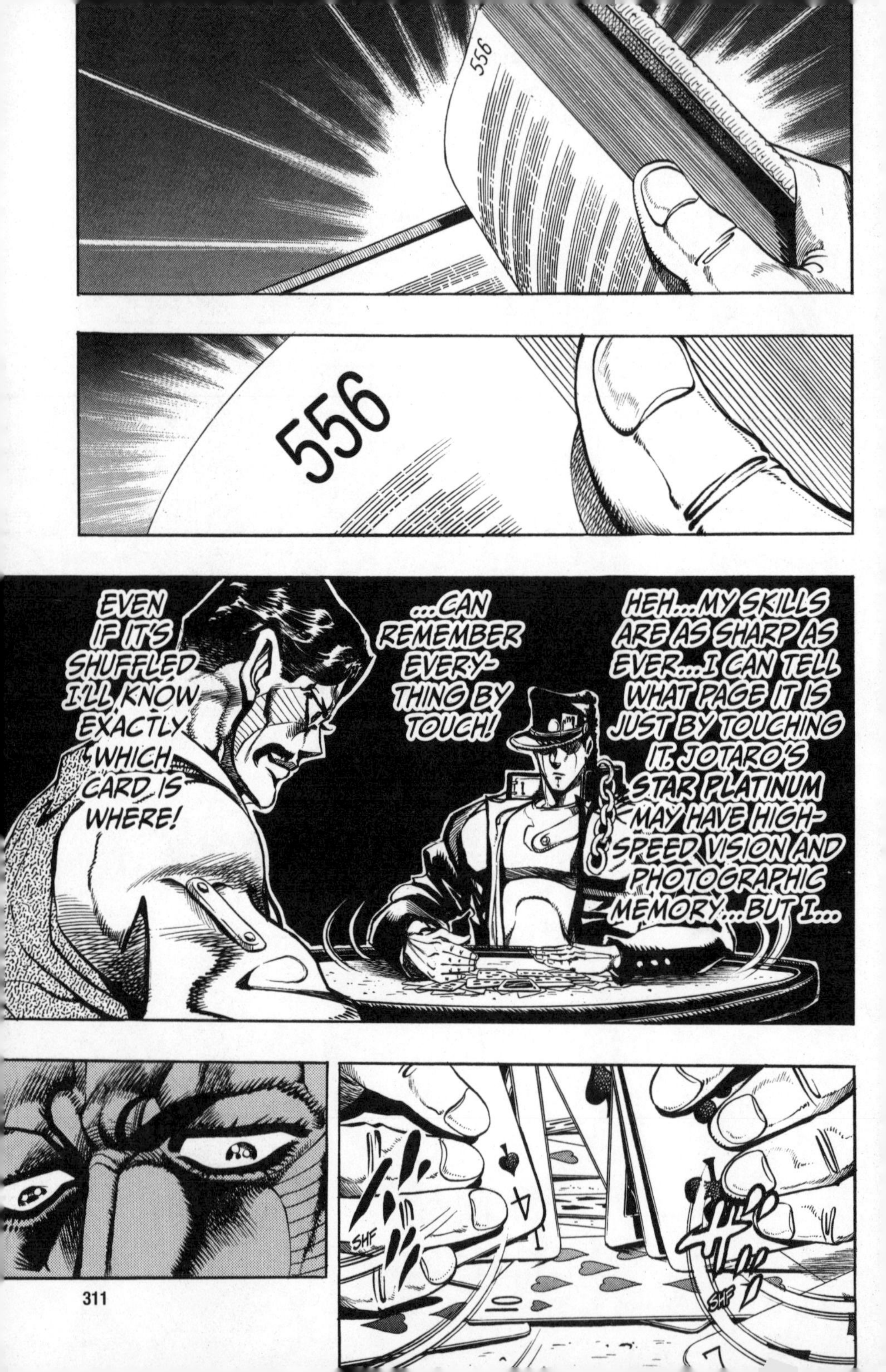
556
556
HEH...MY SKILLS ARE AS SHARP AS EVER...I CAN TELL WHAT PAGE IT IS JUST BY TOUCHING IT. JOTARO'S STAR PLATINUM MAY HAVE HIGH-SPEED VISION AND PHOTOGRAPHIC MEMORY...BUT I...
...CAN REMEMBER EVERY-THING BY TOUCH!
EVEN IF IT'S SHUFFLED I'LL KNOW EXACTLY WHICH CARD IS WHERE!
SHF
SHF

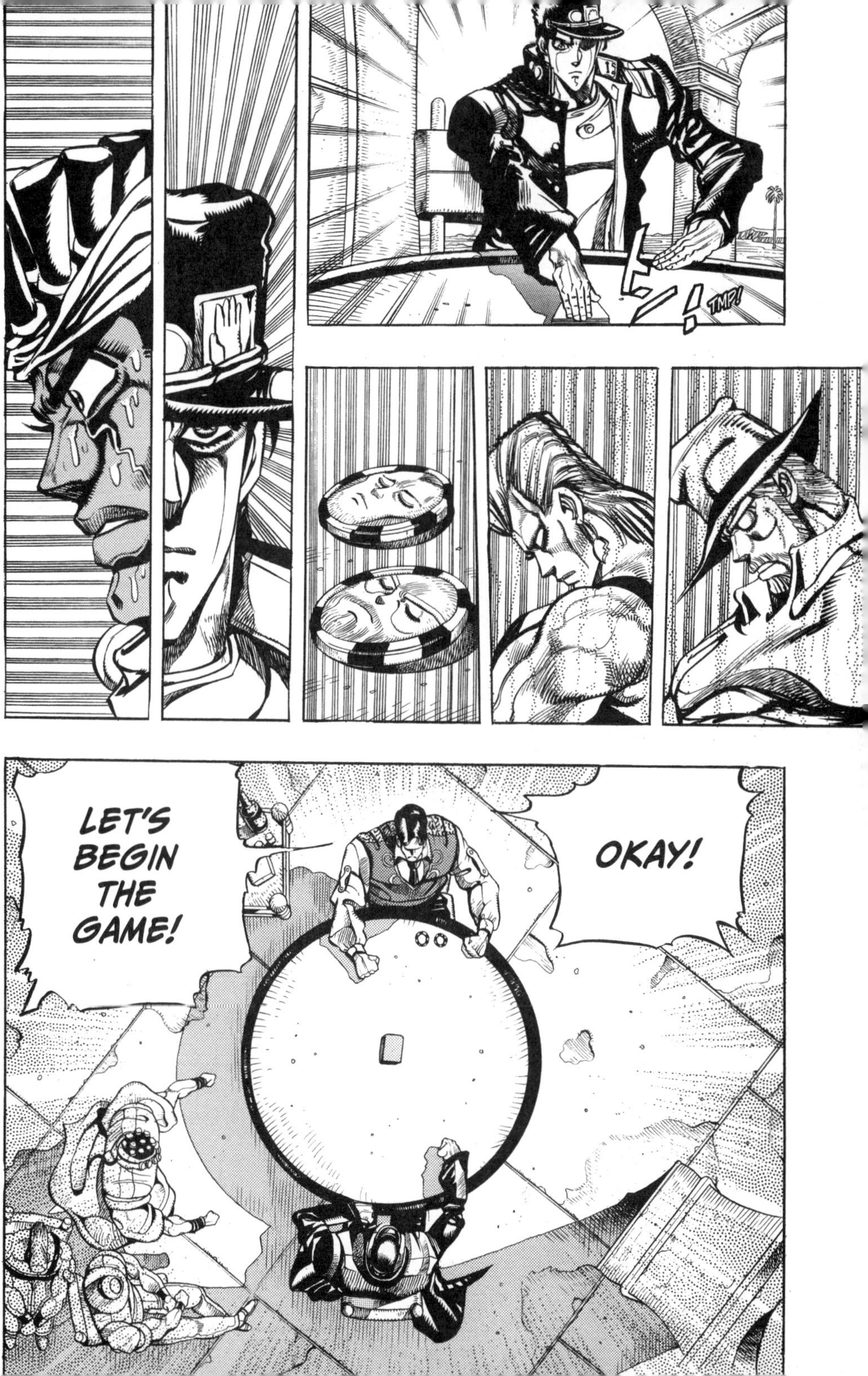
TMP!
LET'S BEGIN THE GAME!
OKAY!

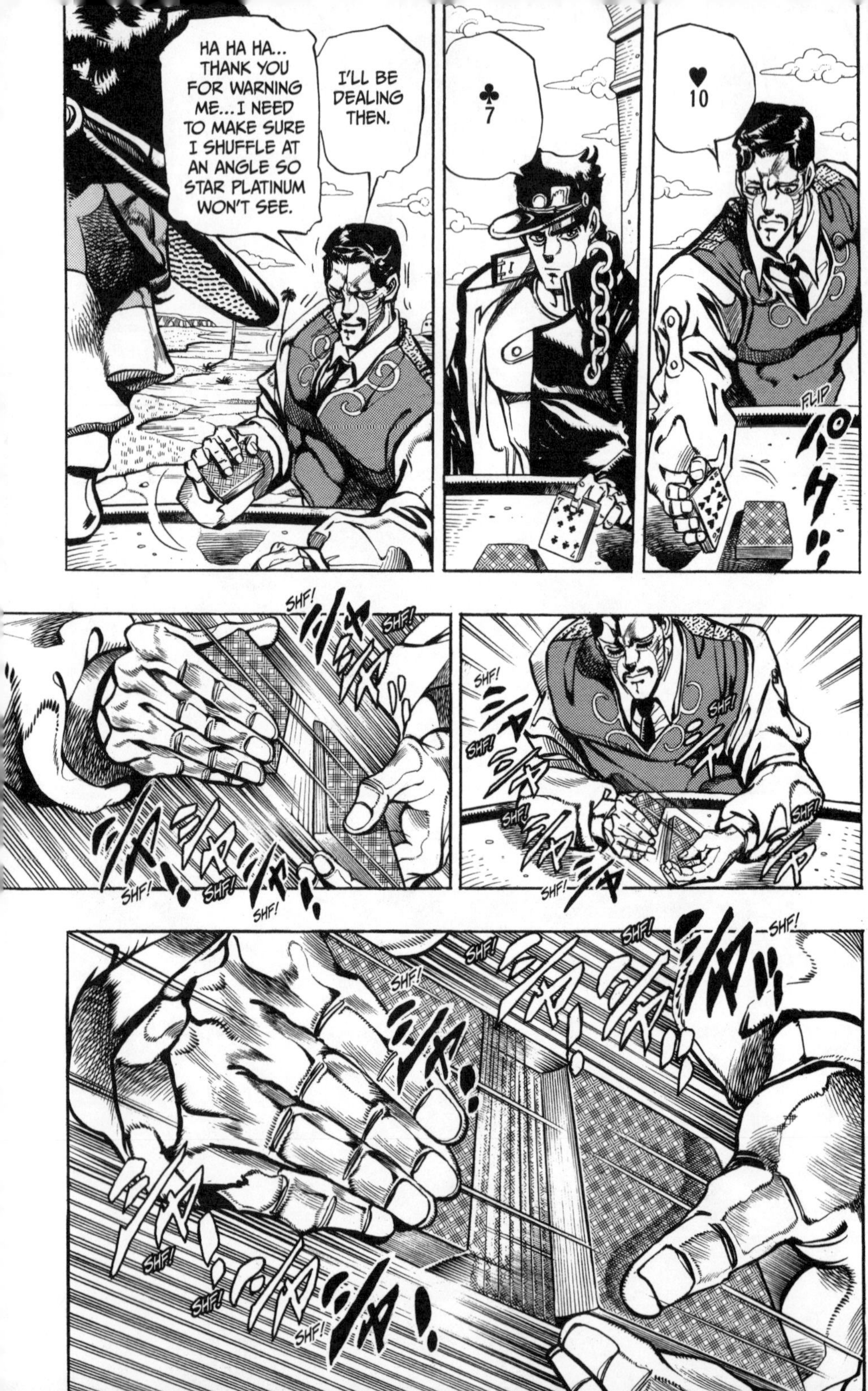
♥
10
FLIP
♣
7
I'LL BE DEALING THEN.
HA HA HA... THANK YOU FOR WARNING ME...I NEED TO MAKE SURE I SHUFFLE AT AN ANGLE SO STAR PLATINUM WON'T SEE.
SHF!
SHF!
SHF!
SHF!
SHF!
SHF!
SHF!
SHF!
SHF!
SHF!
SHF!
SHF!
SHF!
SHF!
SHF!
SHF!

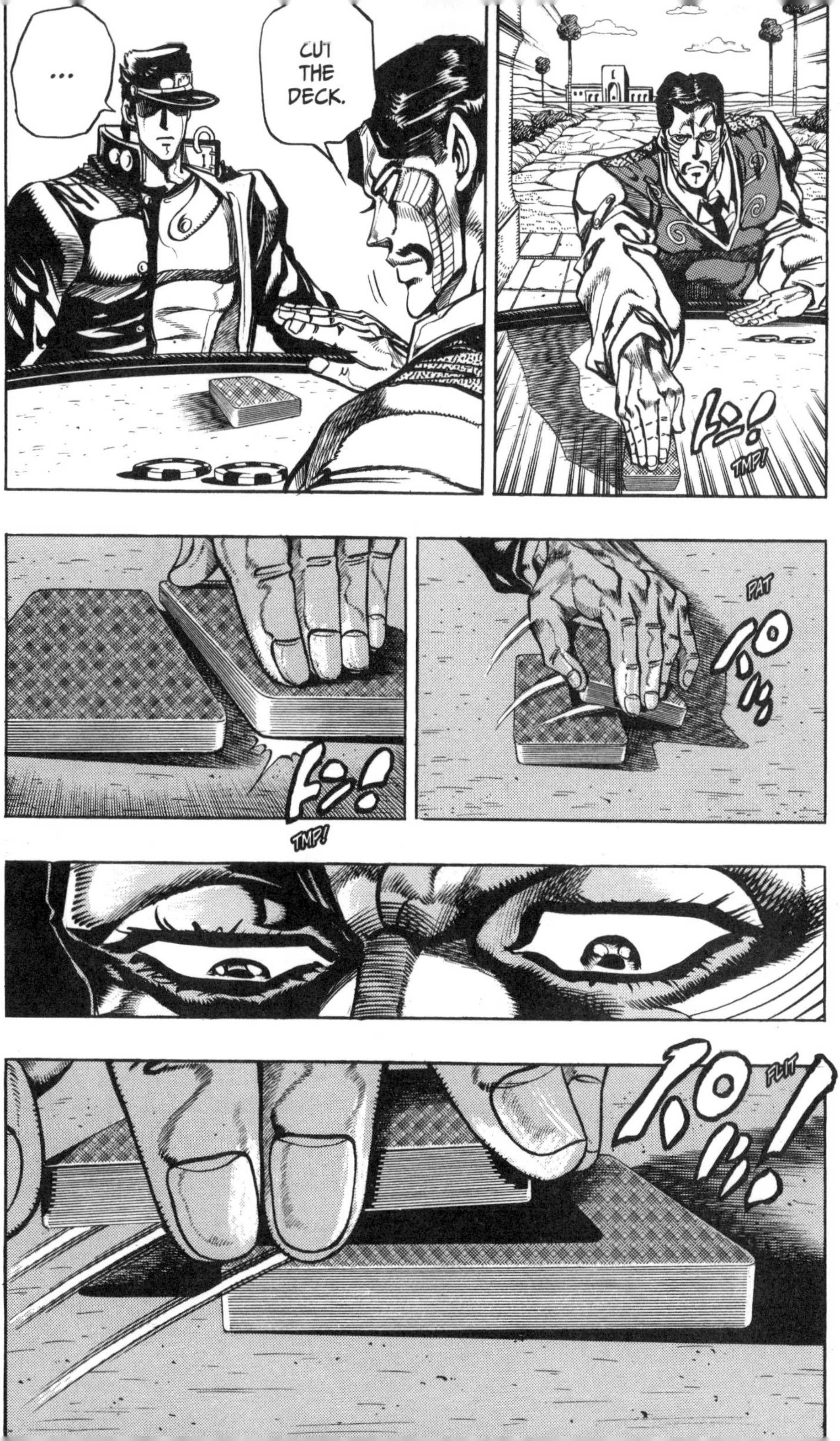
TMP!
CUT THE DECK.
...
PAT
TMP!
FLIT

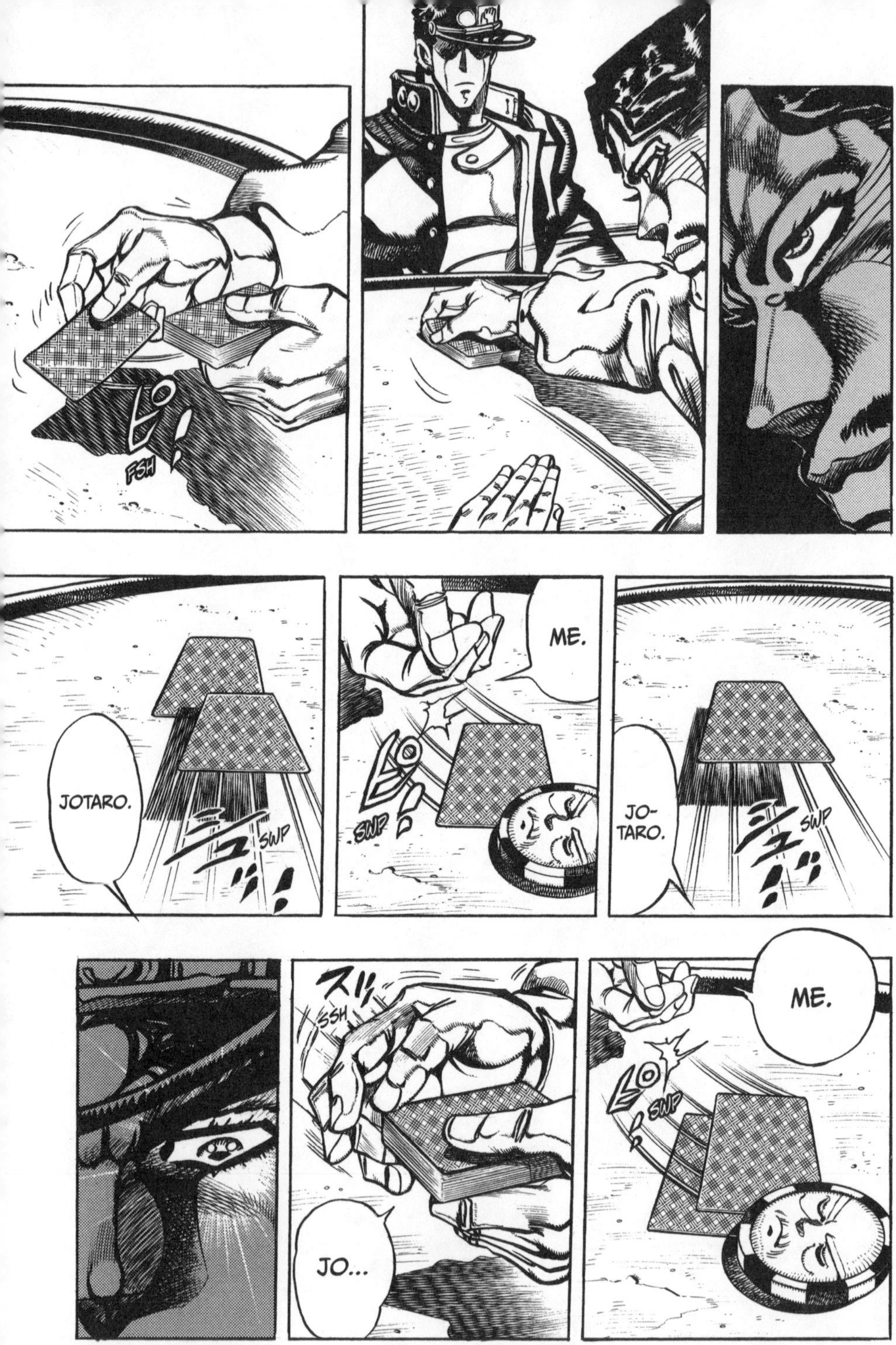
FSH
JO-
TARO.
SWP
ME.
SWP
JOTARO.
SWP
ME.
SWP
SSH
JO...

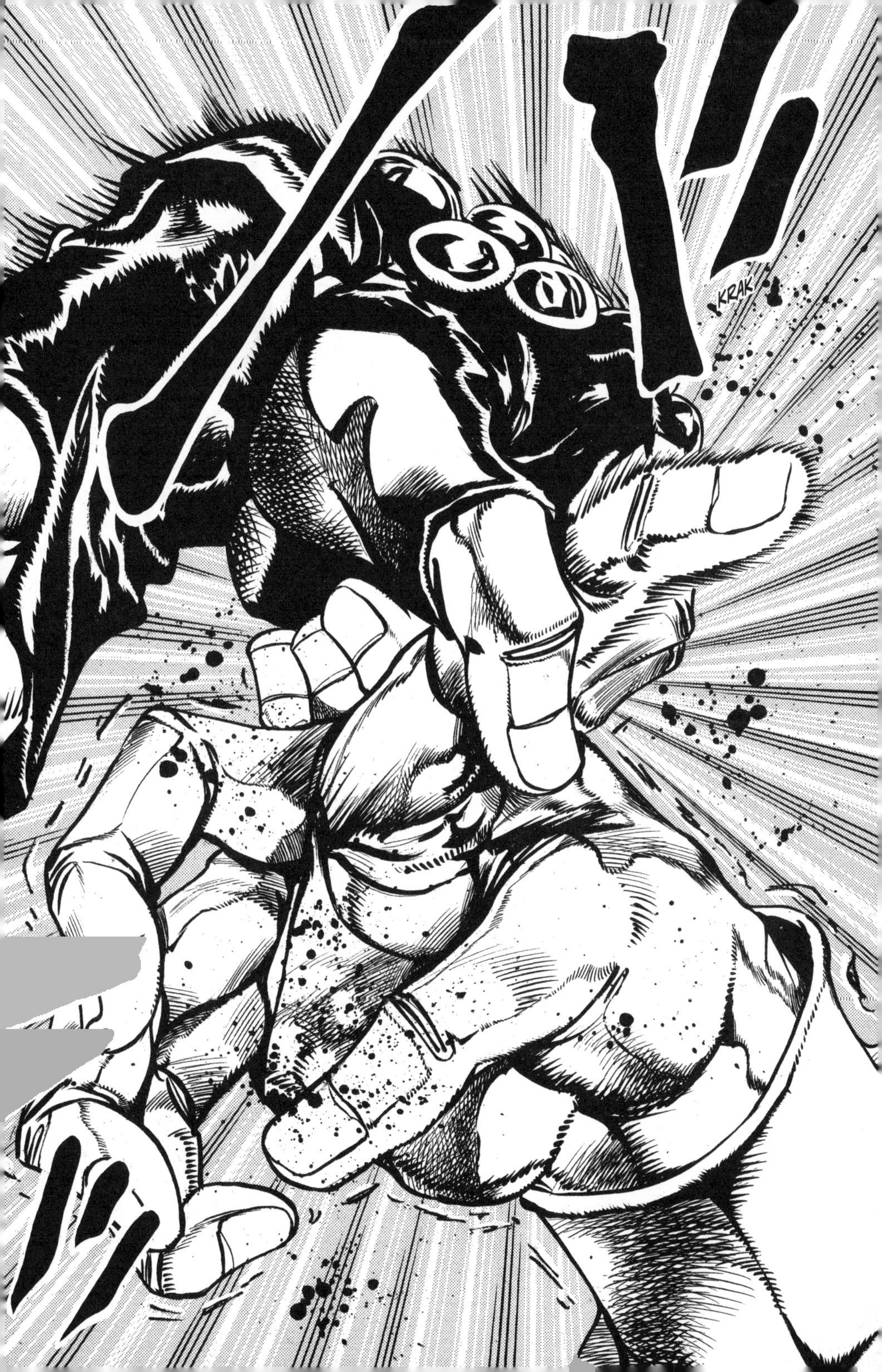
KRAK

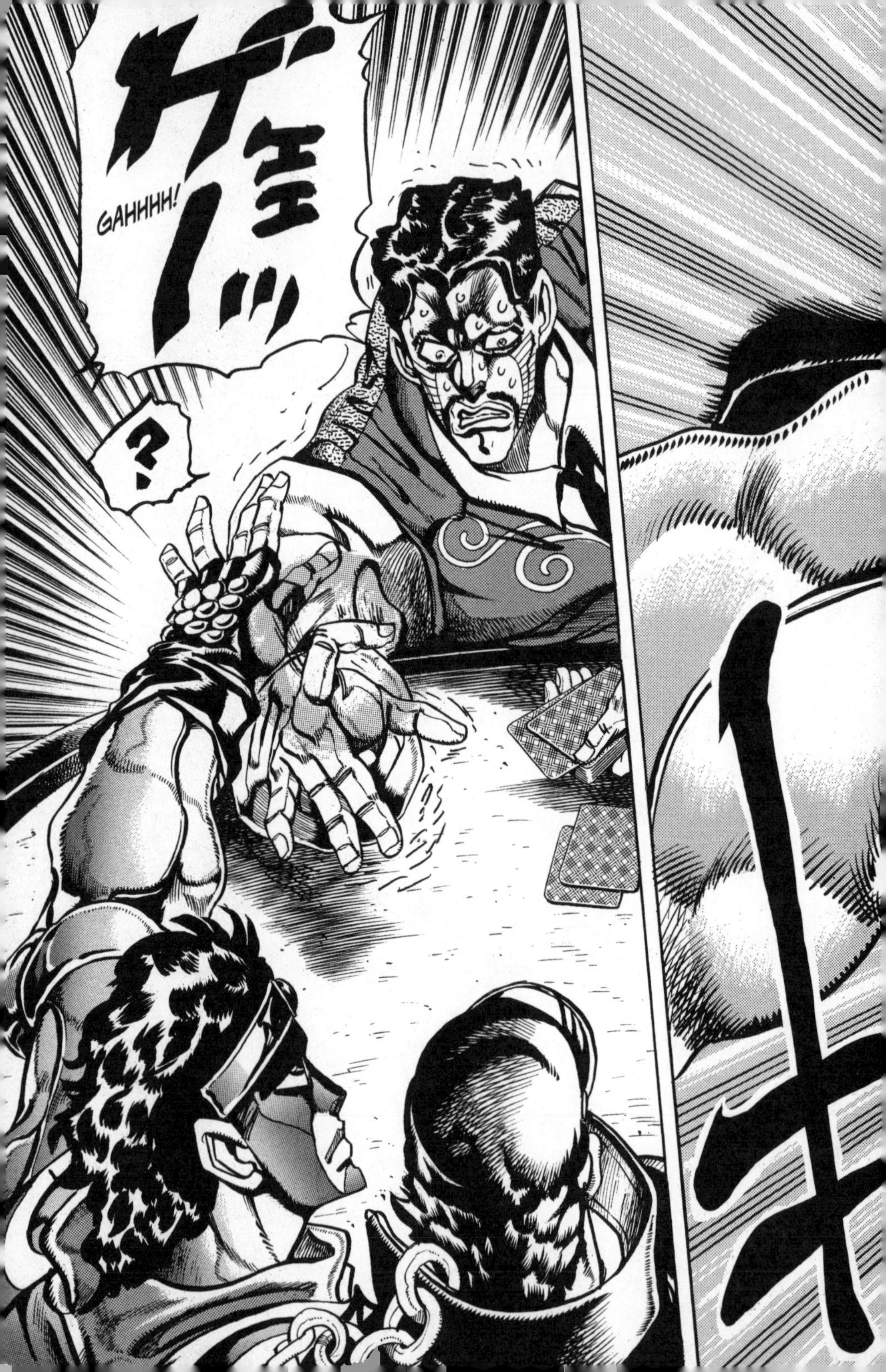
ゲェーッ
GAHHHH!
?

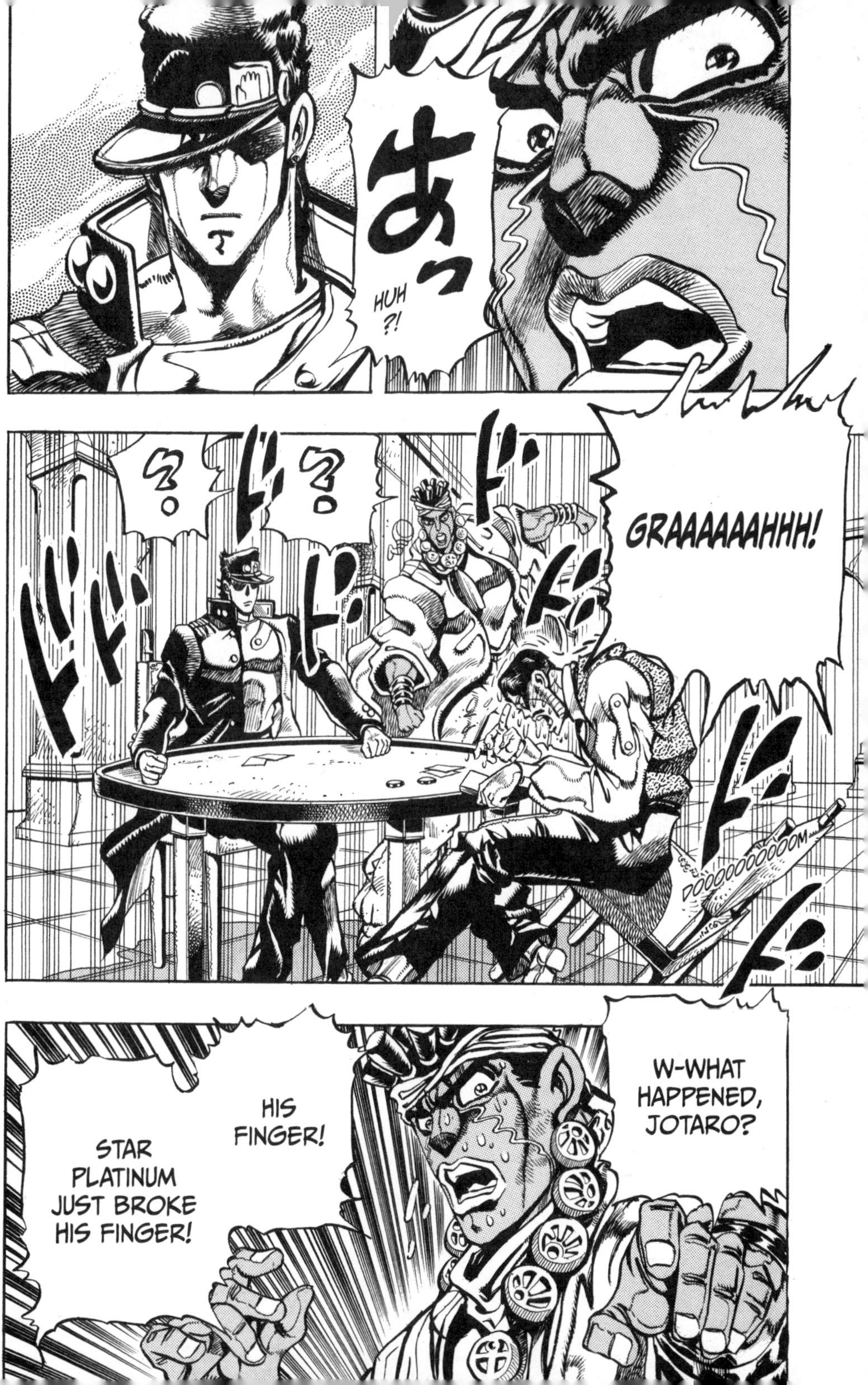

あっ
HUH ?!
GRAAAAAHHH!
？ ？
DOOOOOOOOOOM
W-WHAT HAPPENED, JOTARO?
HIS FINGER!
STAR PLATINUM JUST BROKE HIS FINGER!

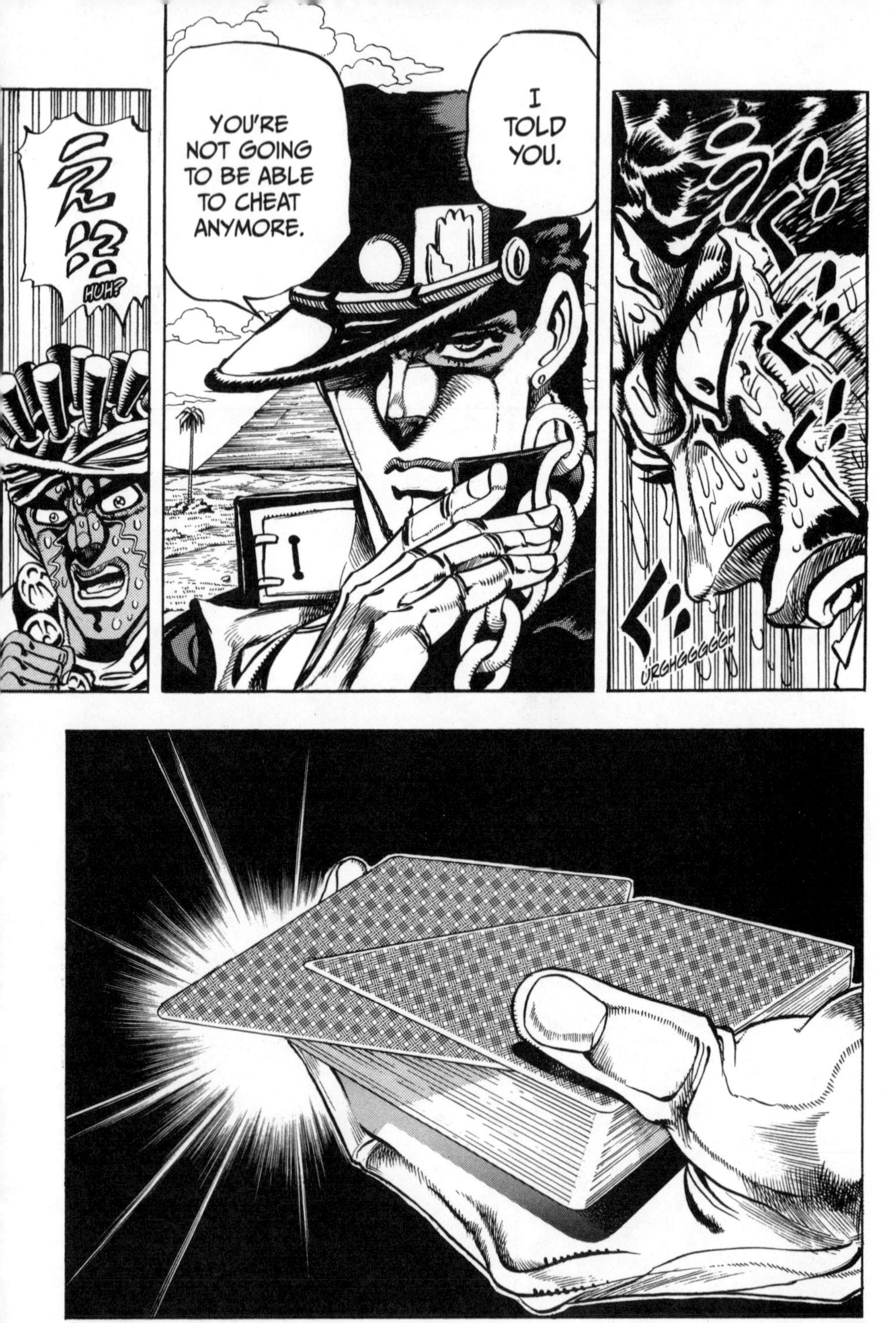
URGHGGGGGH
I TOLD YOU.
YOU'RE NOT GOING TO BE ABLE TO CHEAT ANYMORE.
HUH?

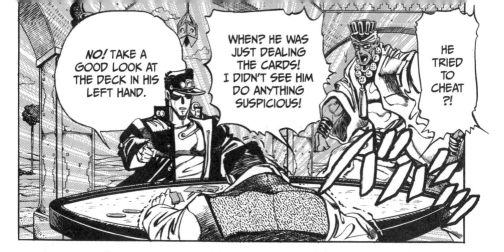

HE TRIED TO CHEAT?!
WHEN? HE WAS JUST DEALING THE CARDS! I DIDN'T SEE HIM DO ANYTHING SUSPICIOUS!
NO! TAKE A GOOD LOOK AT THE DECK IN HIS LEFT HAND.
!
THE SECOND CARD IS STICKING OUT...
IT'S THE CARD HE TRIED TO DEAL ME.
AT FIRST HE WAS DEALING FROM THE TOP OF THE DECK, BUT HE JUST TRIED DEALING ME THE SECOND CARD...
SO THE ONE ON TOP WOULD GO TO HIM.

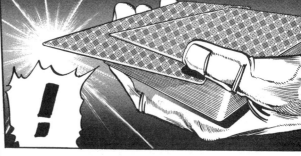

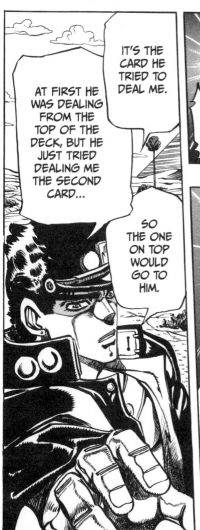

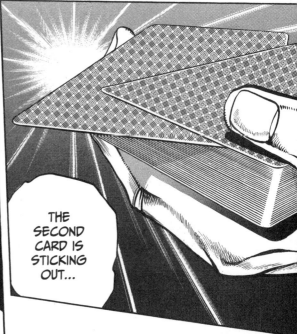

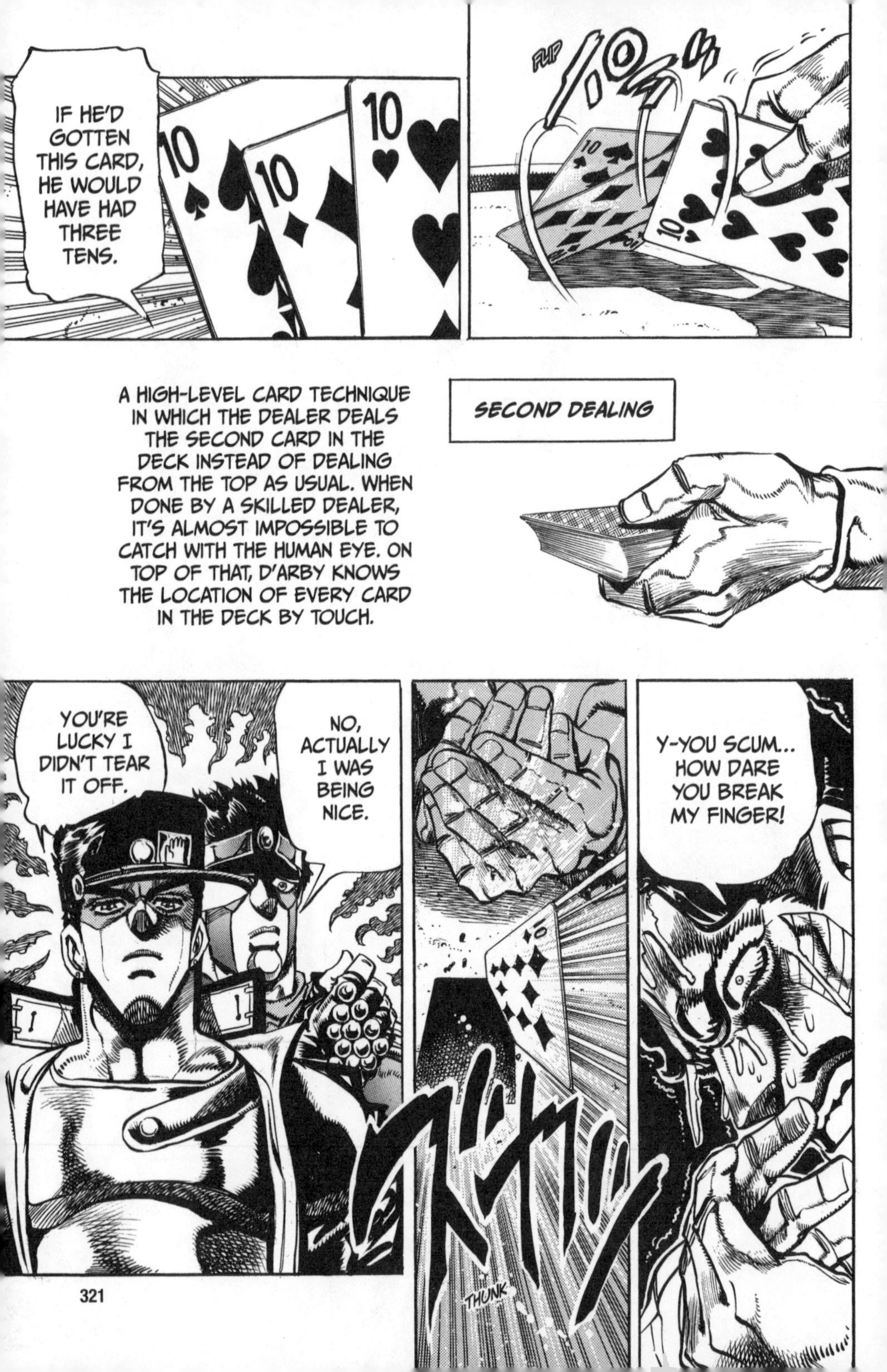
FLIP
IF HE'D GOTTEN THIS CARD, HE WOULD HAVE HAD THREE TENS.
SECOND DEALING
A HIGH-LEVEL CARD TECHNIQUE IN WHICH THE DEALER DEALS THE SECOND CARD IN THE DECK INSTEAD OF DEALING FROM THE TOP AS USUAL. WHEN DONE BY A SKILLED DEALER, IT'S ALMOST IMPOSSIBLE TO CATCH WITH THE HUMAN EYE. ON TOP OF THAT, D'ARBY KNOWS THE LOCATION OF EVERY CARD IN THE DECK BY TOUCH.
Y-YOU SCUM... HOW DARE YOU BREAK MY FINGER!
THUNK
YOU'RE LUCKY I DIDN'T TEAR IT OFF.
NO, ACTUALLY I WAS BEING NICE.

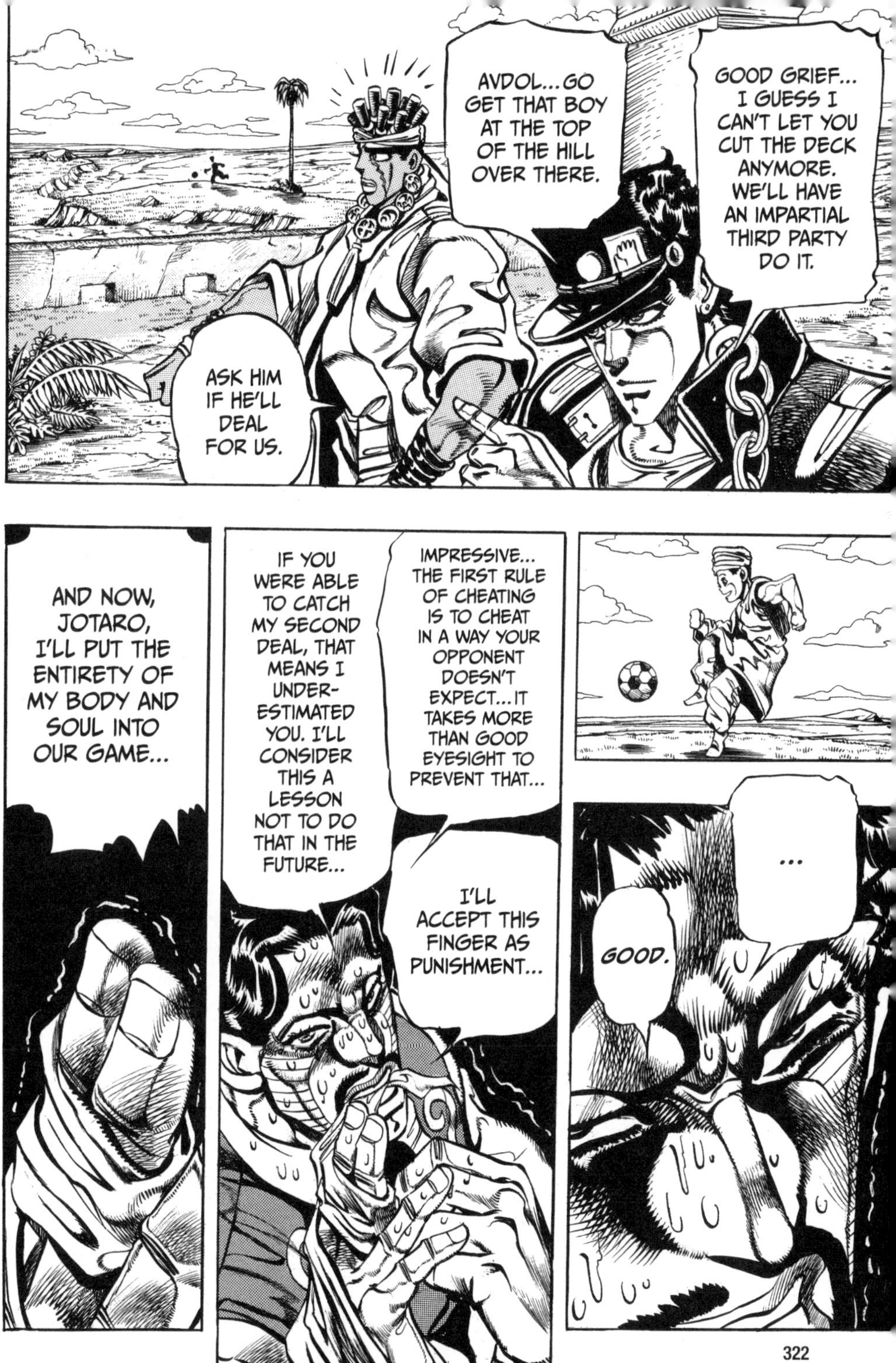
GOOD GRIEF... I GUESS I CAN'T LET YOU CUT THE DECK ANYMORE. WE'LL HAVE AN IMPARTIAL THIRD PARTY DO IT.
AVDOL...GO GET THAT BOY AT THE TOP OF THE HILL OVER THERE.
ASK HIM IF HE'LL DEAL FOR US.
...
GOOD.
IMPRESSIVE... THE FIRST RULE OF CHEATING IS TO CHEAT IN A WAY YOUR OPPONENT DOESN'T EXPECT...IT TAKES MORE THAN GOOD EYESIGHT TO PREVENT THAT...
IF YOU WERE ABLE TO CATCH MY SECOND DEAL, THAT MEANS I UNDER-ESTIMATED YOU. I'LL CONSIDER THIS A LESSON NOT TO DO THAT IN THE FUTURE...
I'LL ACCEPT THIS FINGER AS PUNISHMENT...
AND NOW, JOTARO, I'LL PUT THE ENTIRETY OF MY BODY AND SOUL INTO OUR GAME...

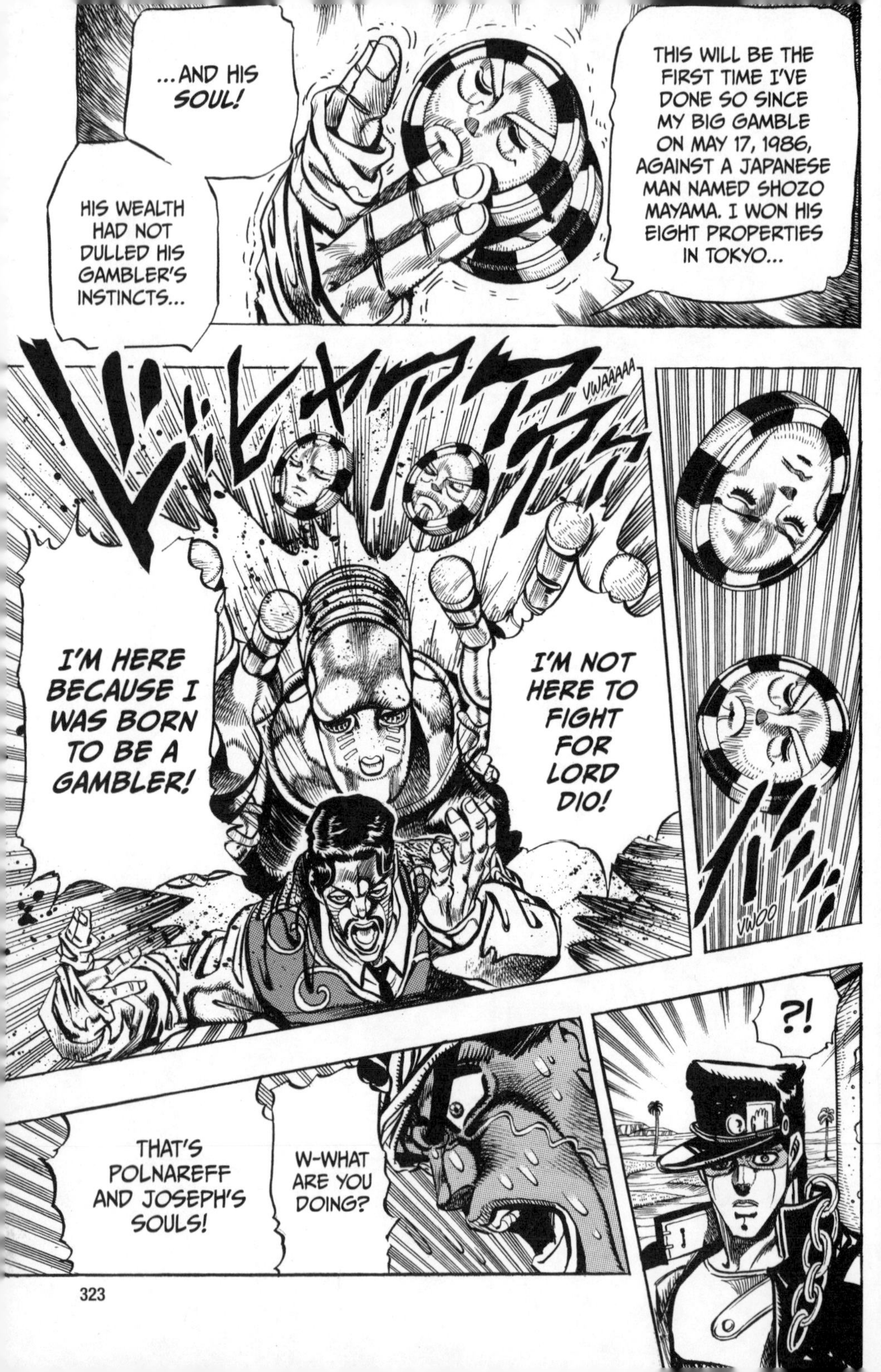
THIS WILL BE THE FIRST TIME I'VE DONE SO SINCE MY BIG GAMBLE ON MAY 17, 1986, AGAINST A JAPANESE MAN NAMED SHOZO MAYAMA. I WON HIS EIGHT PROPERTIES IN TOKYO...
...AND HIS SOUL!
HIS WEALTH HAD NOT DULLED HIS GAMBLER'S INSTINCTS...
VWOO
VWAAAAA
I'M NOT HERE TO FIGHT FOR LORD DIO!
I'M HERE BECAUSE I WAS BORN TO BE A GAMBLER!
?!
W-WHAT ARE YOU DOING?
THAT'S POLNAREFF AND JOSEPH'S SOULS!

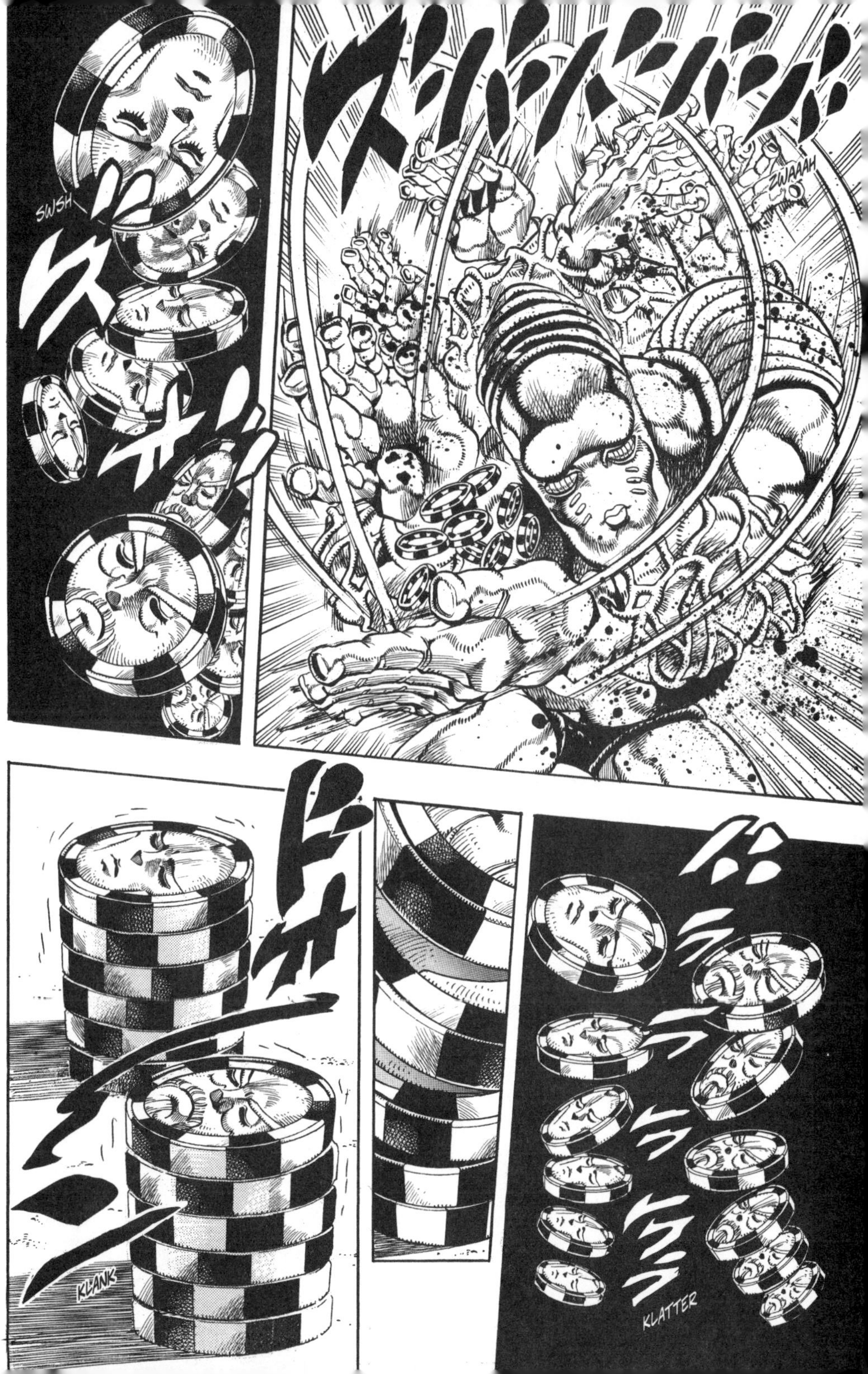
ZWAAAH
SWSH
KLATTER
KLANK

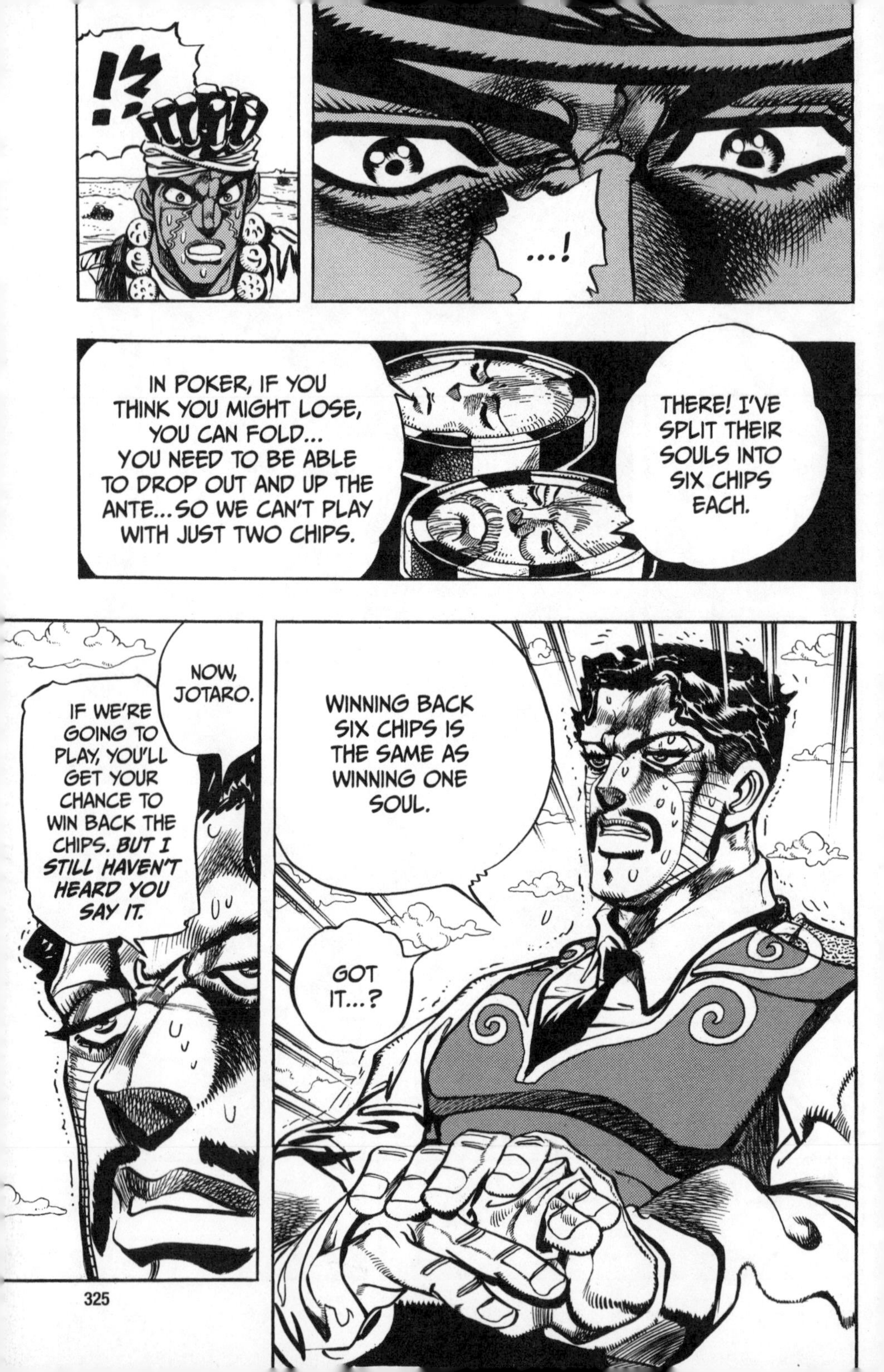
...!
!?
THERE! I'VE SPLIT THEIR SOULS INTO SIX CHIPS EACH.
IN POKER, IF YOU THINK YOU MIGHT LOSE, YOU CAN FOLD... YOU NEED TO BE ABLE TO DROP OUT AND UP THE ANTE...SO WE CAN'T PLAY WITH JUST TWO CHIPS.
WINNING BACK SIX CHIPS IS THE SAME AS WINNING ONE SOUL.
GOT IT...?
NOW, JOTARO.
IF WE'RE GOING TO PLAY, YOU'LL GET YOUR CHANCE TO WIN BACK THE CHIPS. *BUT I STILL HAVEN'T HEARD YOU SAY IT.*

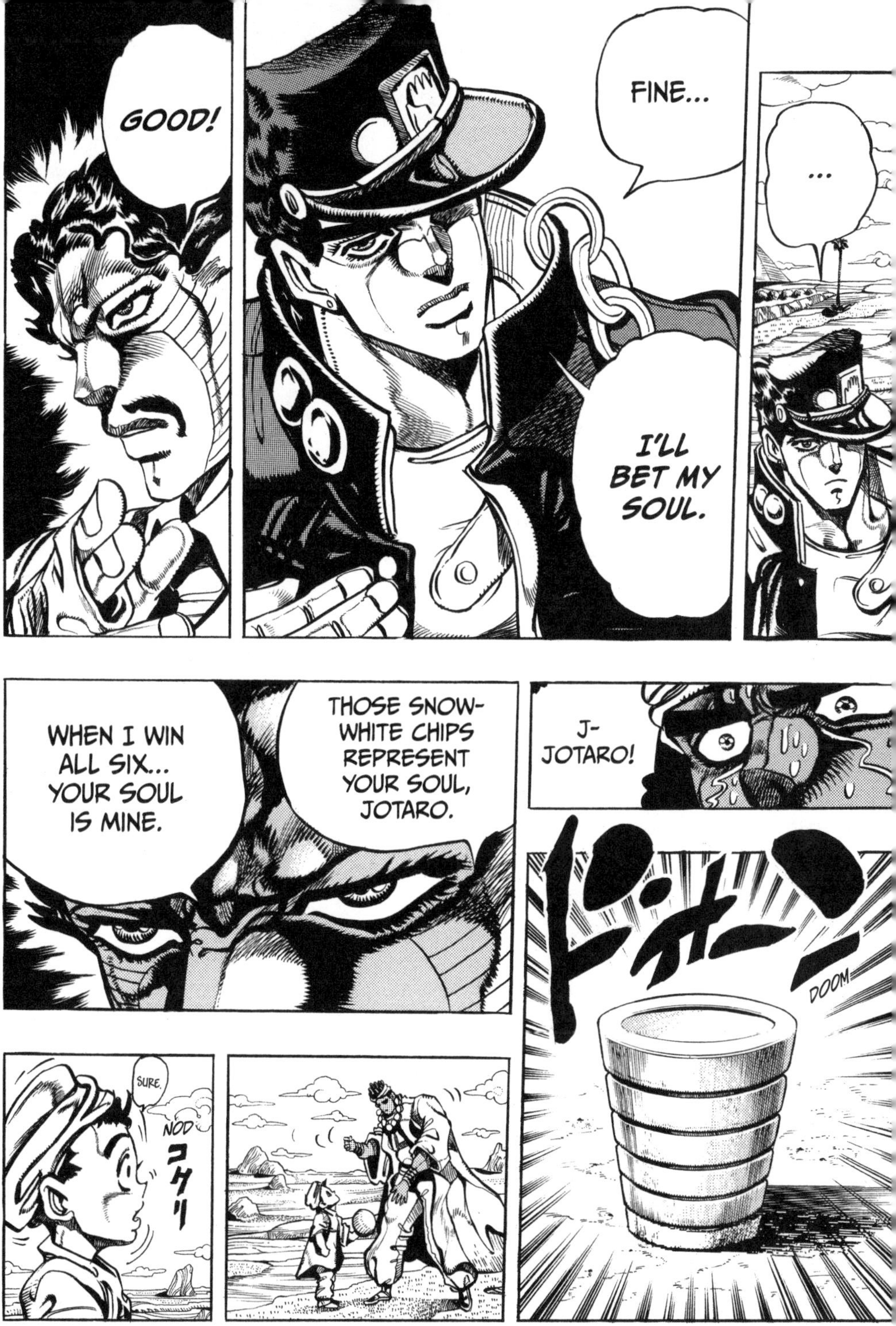
...
FINE...
I'LL BET MY SOUL.
GOOD!
J- JOTARO!
DOOM
THOSE SNOW-WHITE CHIPS REPRESENT YOUR SOUL, JOTARO.
WHEN I WIN ALL SIX... YOUR SOUL IS MINE.
SURE.
NOD

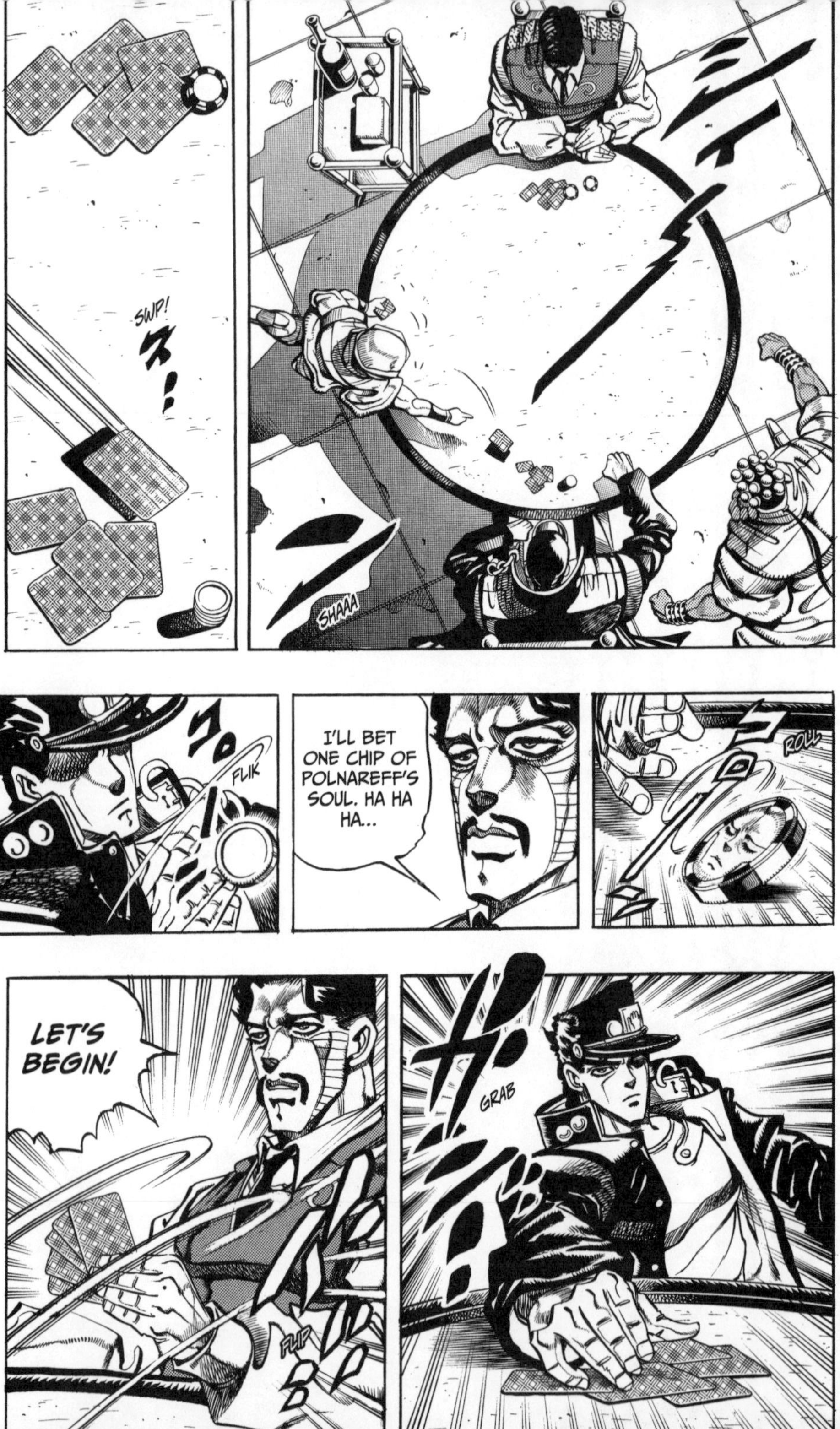
SHAAA
SWP!
ROLL
I'LL BET ONE CHIP OF POLNAREFF'S SOUL. HA HA HA...
FLIK
GRAB
LET'S BEGIN!
FLIP

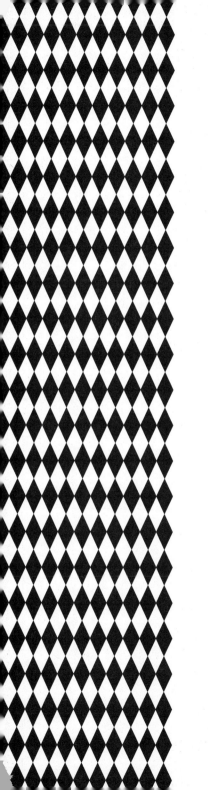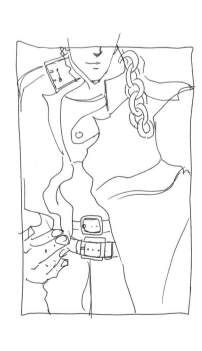

CHAPTER 102: D'Arby the Gambler PART 5

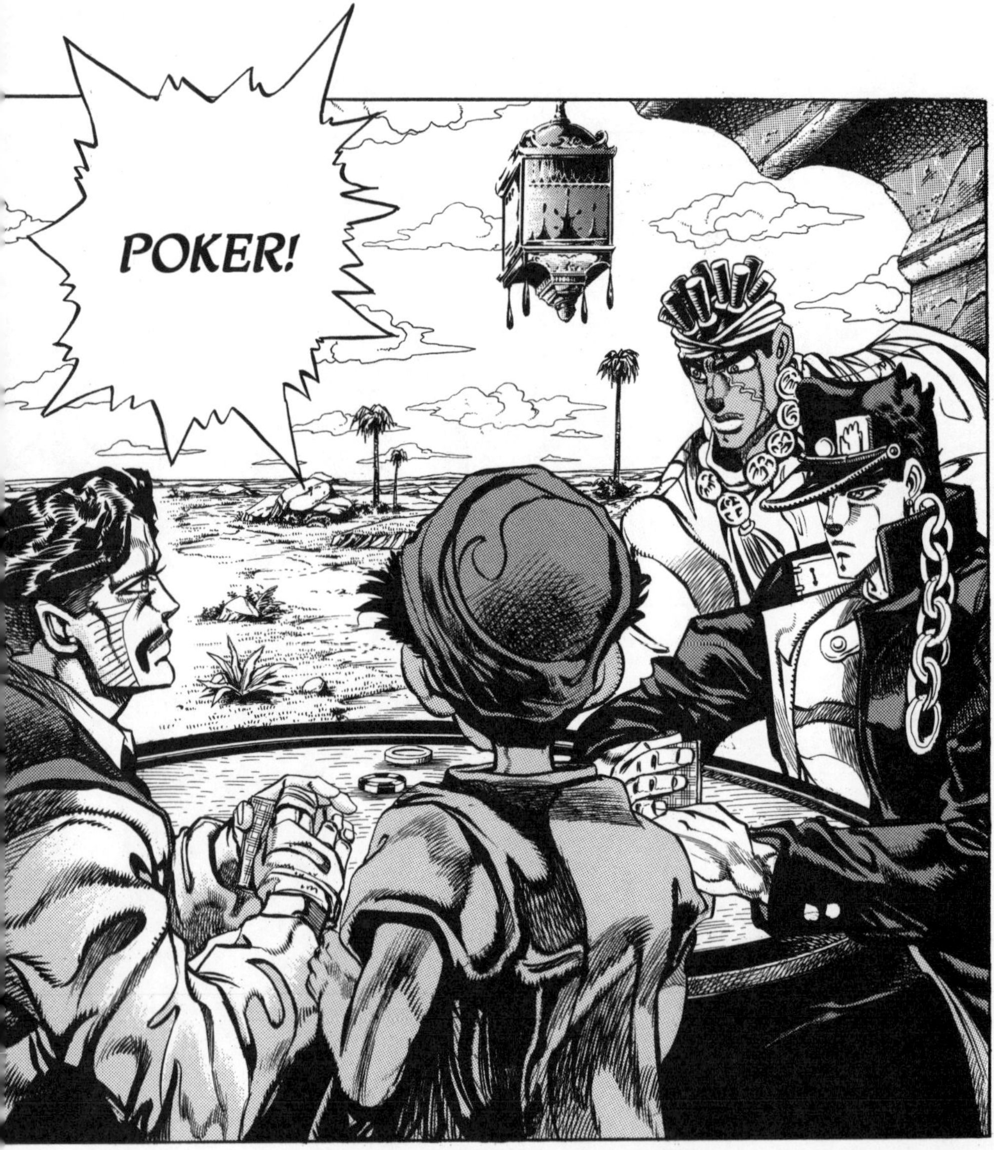
POKER!

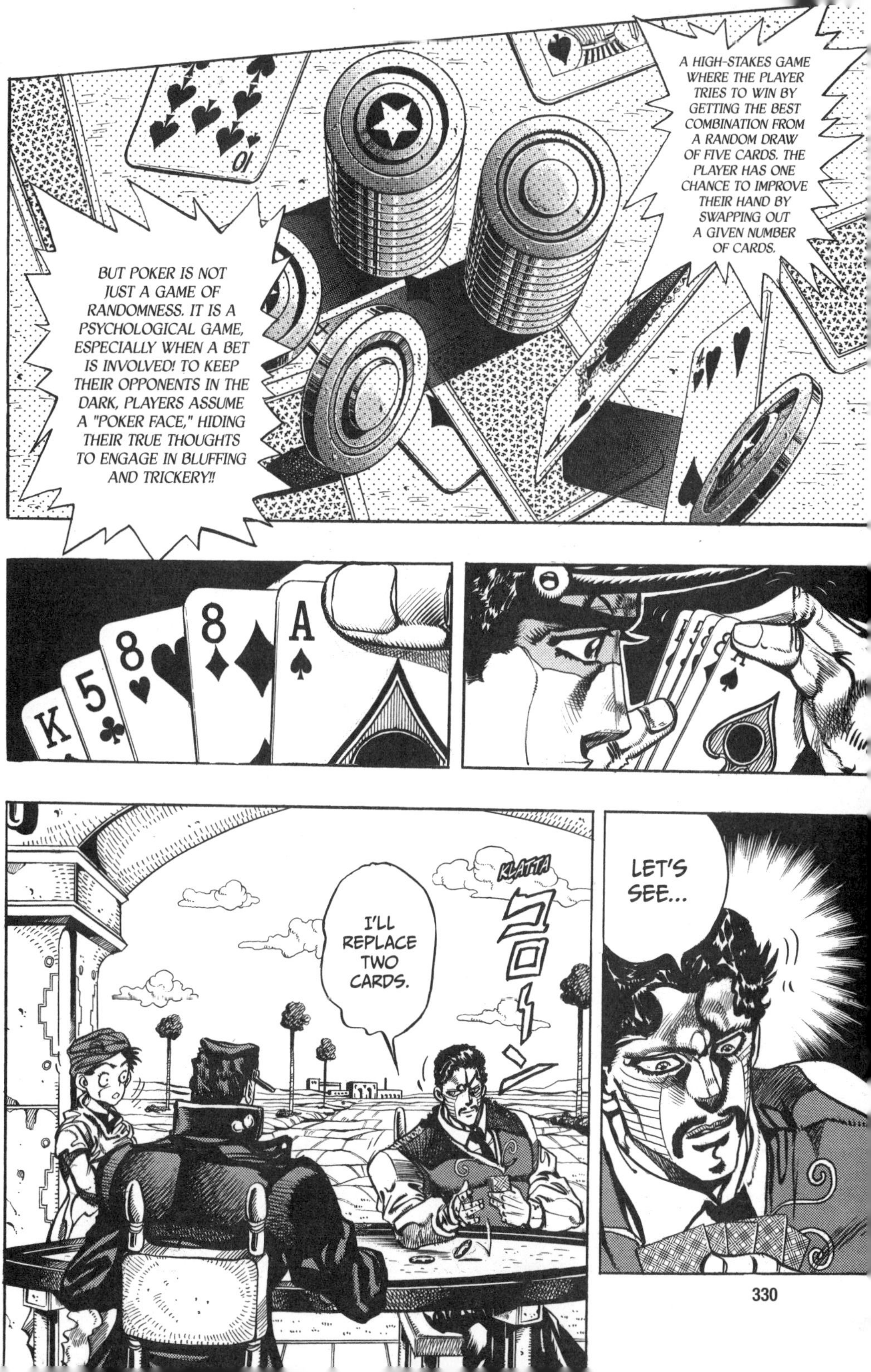
A HIGH-STAKES GAME WHERE THE PLAYER TRIES TO WIN BY GETTING THE BEST COMBINATION FROM A RANDOM DRAW OF FIVE CARDS. THE PLAYER HAS ONE CHANCE TO IMPROVE THEIR HAND BY SWAPPING OUT A GIVEN NUMBER OF CARDS.
BUT POKER IS NOT JUST A GAME OF RANDOMNESS. IT IS A PSYCHOLOGICAL GAME, ESPECIALLY WHEN A BET IS INVOLVED! TO KEEP THEIR OPPONENTS IN THE DARK, PLAYERS ASSUME A "POKER FACE," HIDING THEIR TRUE THOUGHTS TO ENGAGE IN BLUFFING AND TRICKERY!!
LET'S SEE...
KLATTA
I'LL REPLACE TWO CARDS.

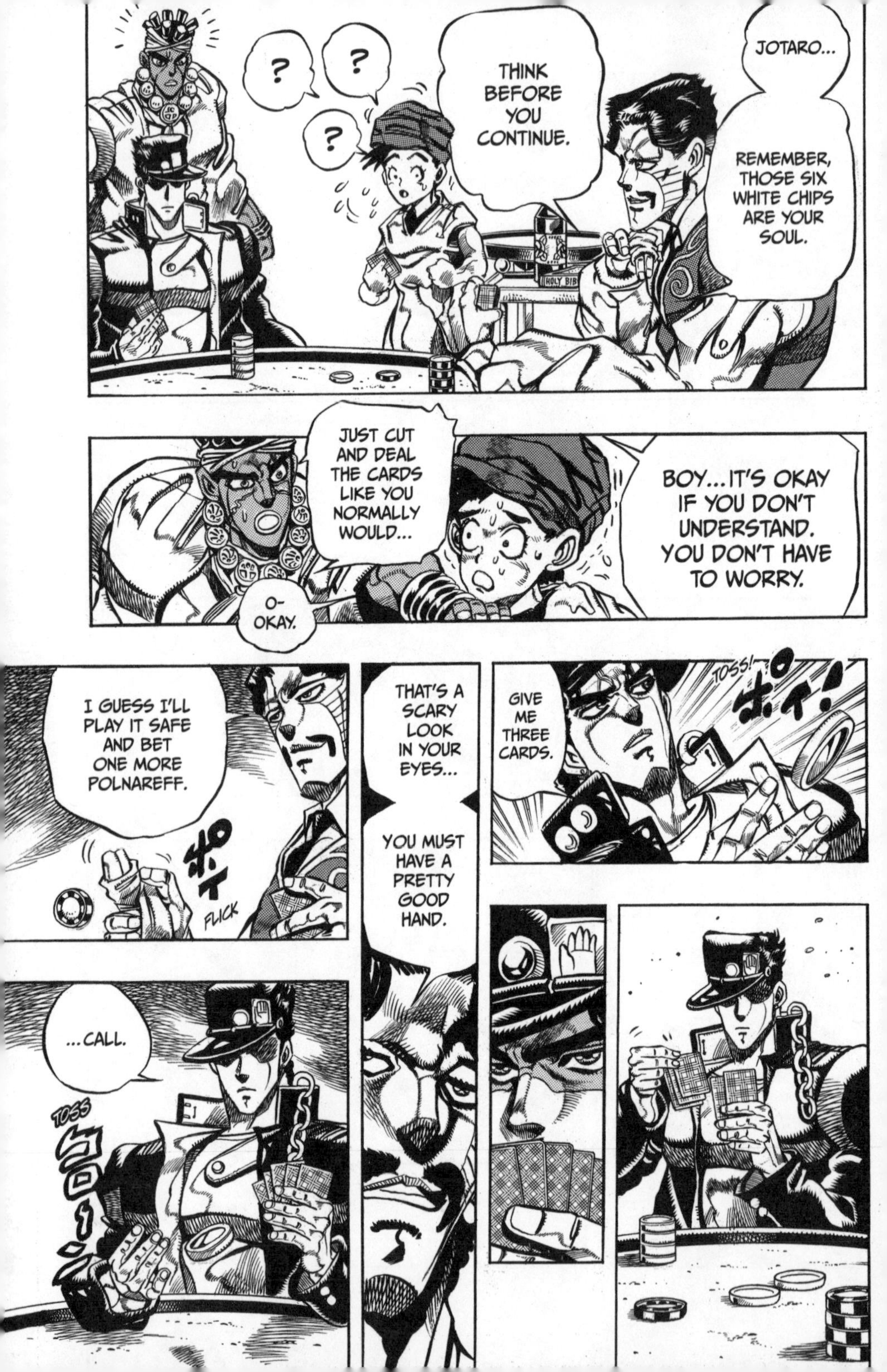
JOTARO...
REMEMBER, THOSE SIX WHITE CHIPS ARE YOUR SOUL.
THINK BEFORE YOU CONTINUE.
?
?
?
BOY...IT'S OKAY IF YOU DON'T UNDERSTAND. YOU DON'T HAVE TO WORRY.
JUST CUT AND DEAL THE CARDS LIKE YOU NORMALLY WOULD...
O- OKAY.
TOSS!
ポイ!
GIVE ME THREE CARDS.
THAT'S A SCARY LOOK IN YOUR EYES...
YOU MUST HAVE A PRETTY GOOD HAND.
I GUESS I'LL PLAY IT SAFE AND BET ONE MORE POLNAREFF.
ポイ
FLICK
...CALL.
TOSS

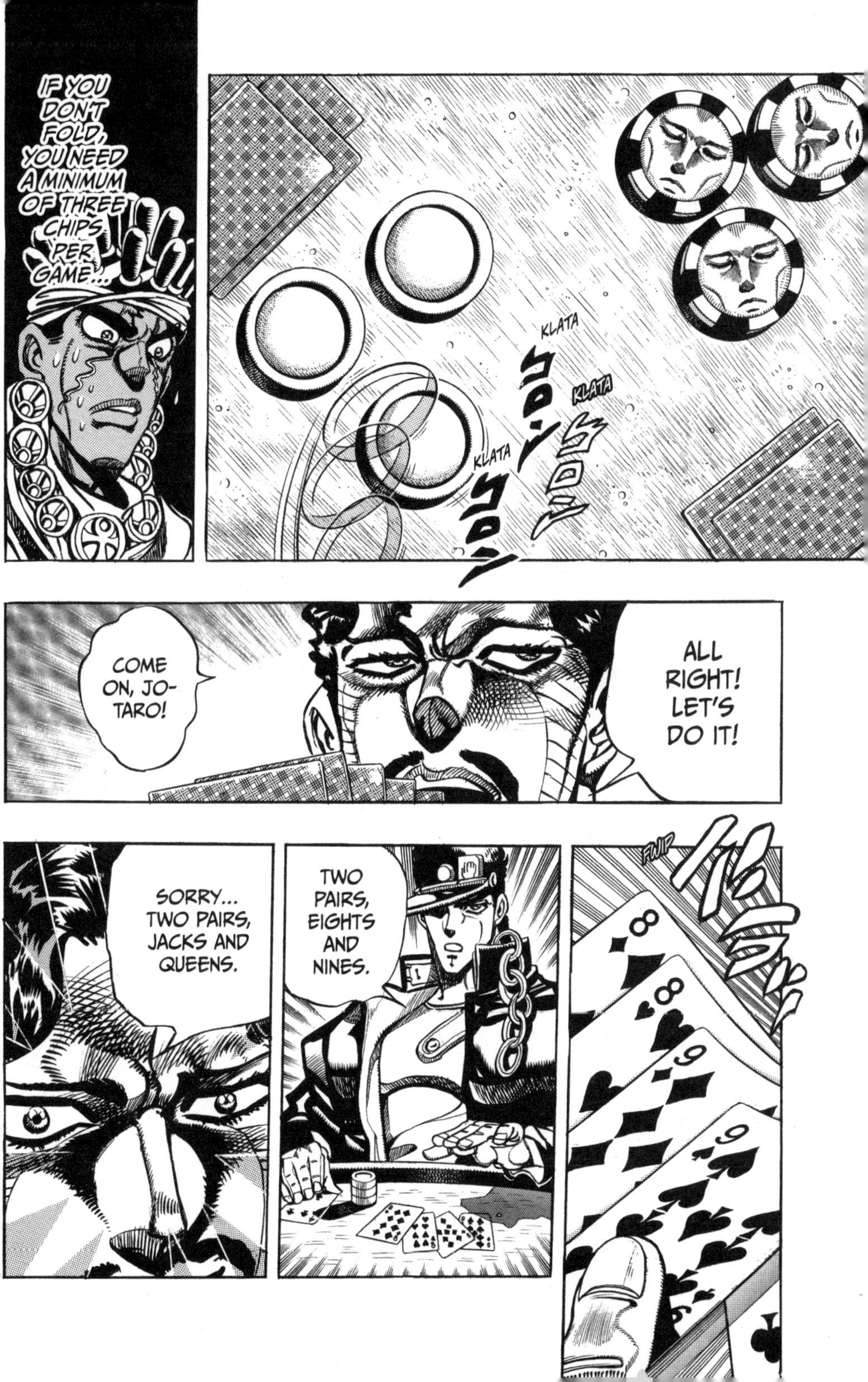
KLATA
KLATA
KLATA
IF YOU DON'T FOLD, YOU NEED A MINIMUM OF THREE CHIPS PER GAME...
ALL RIGHT! LET'S DO IT!
COME ON, JO-TARO!
FWIP
TWO PAIRS, EIGHTS AND NINES.
SORRY... TWO PAIRS, JACKS AND QUEENS.

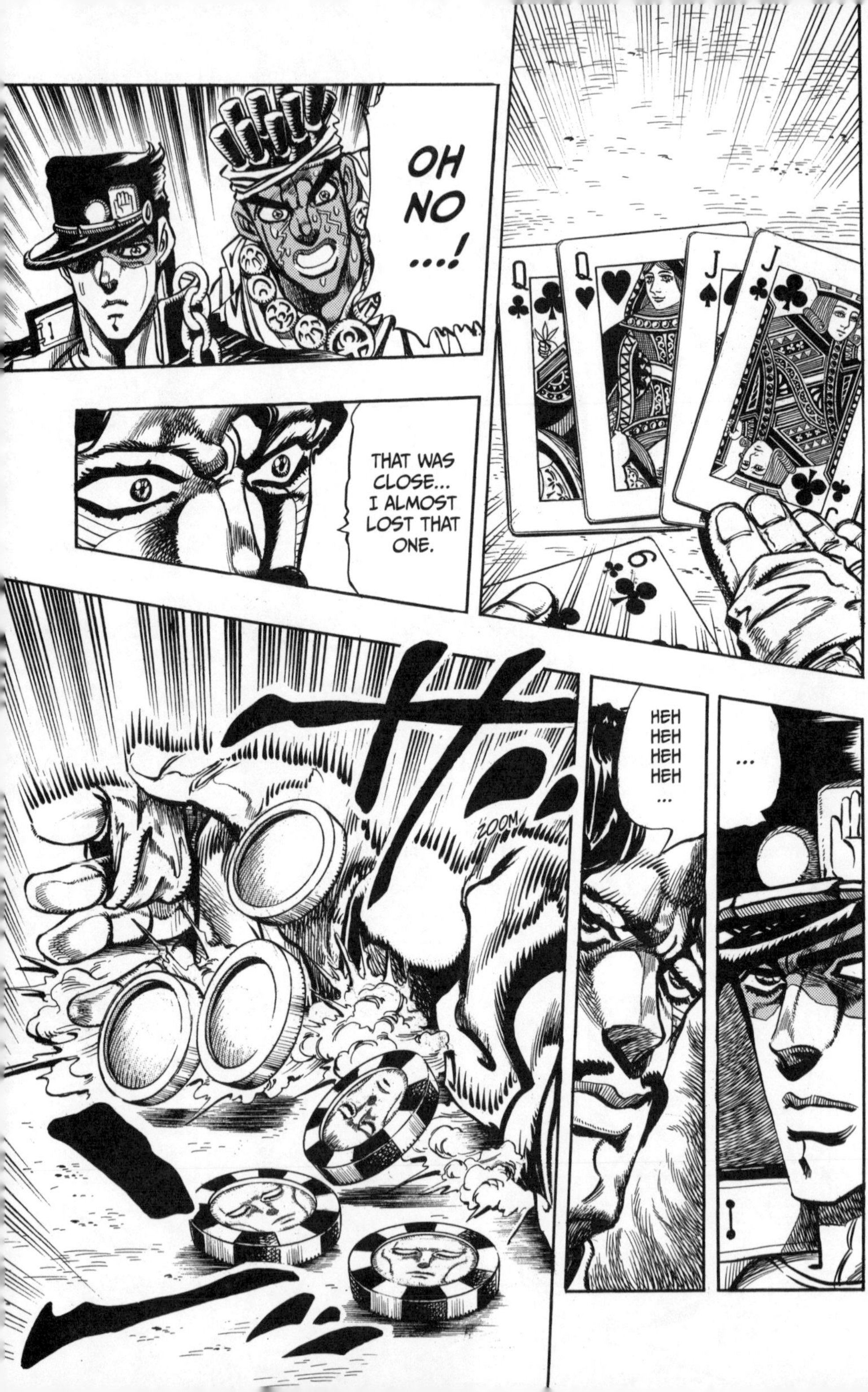
OH NO ...!
THAT WAS CLOSE... I ALMOST LOST THAT ONE.
...
HEH HEH HEH HEH ...
ZOOM

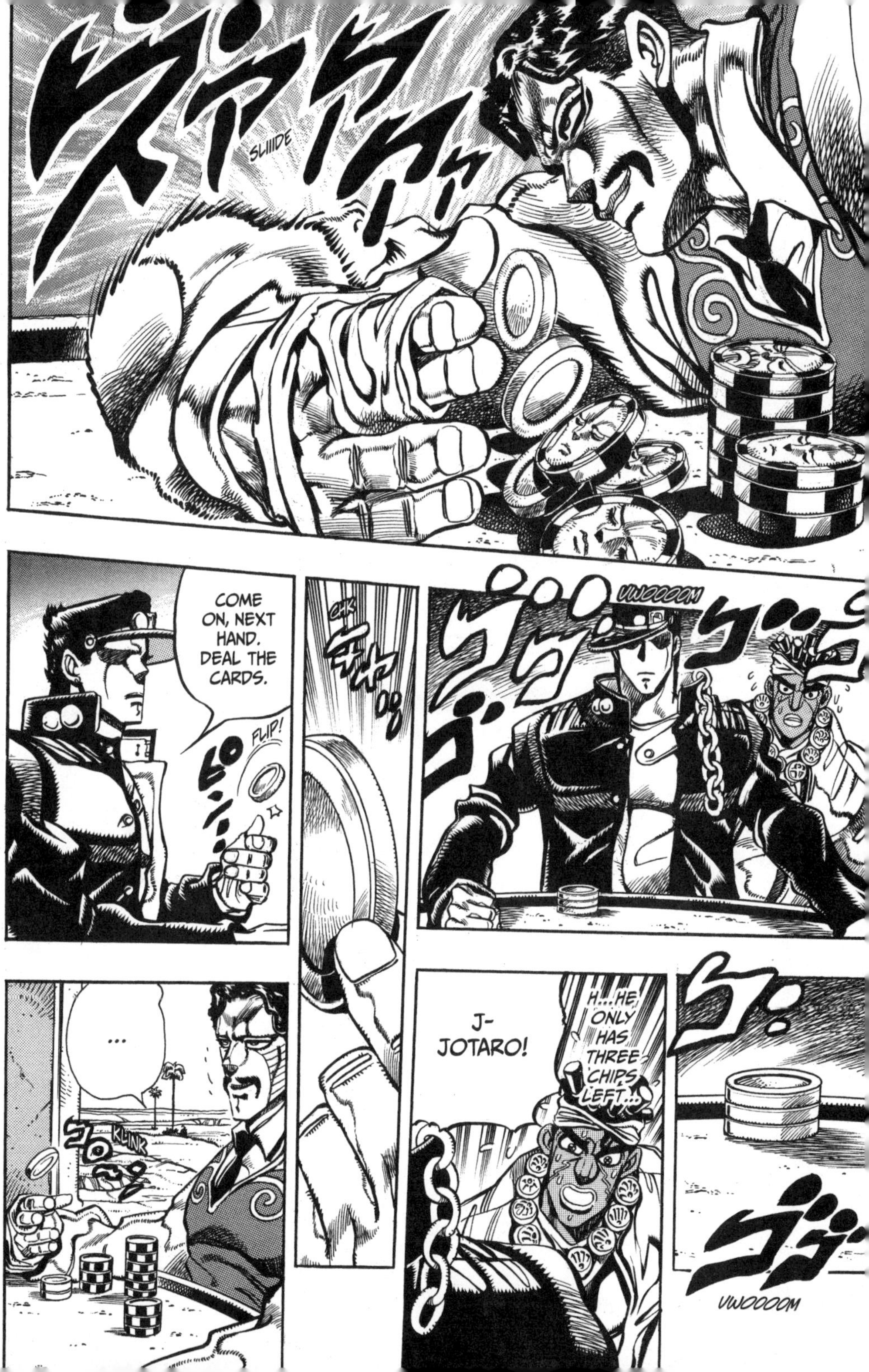
SLIIIDE
VWOOOOM
VWOOOOM
H...HE ONLY HAS THREE CHIPS LEFT...
J-JOTARO!
CHK
COME ON, NEXT HAND. DEAL THE CARDS.
FLIP!
...
KLINK

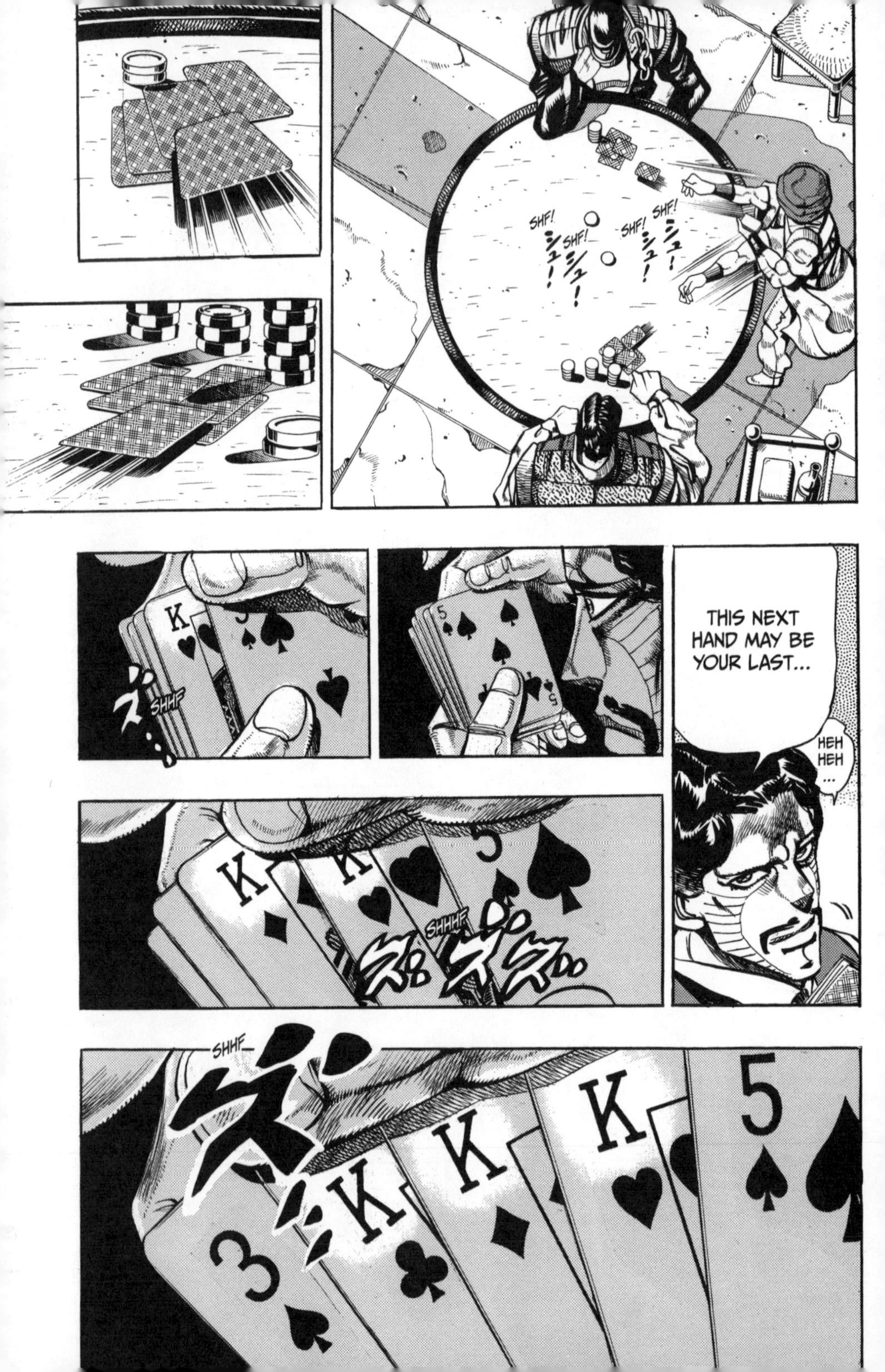
SHF!
シュ!
SHF!
シュ!
SHF!
シュ!
SHF!
シュ!
THIS NEXT HAND MAY BE YOUR LAST...
HEH HEH ...
SHHF
SHHHF
SHHF

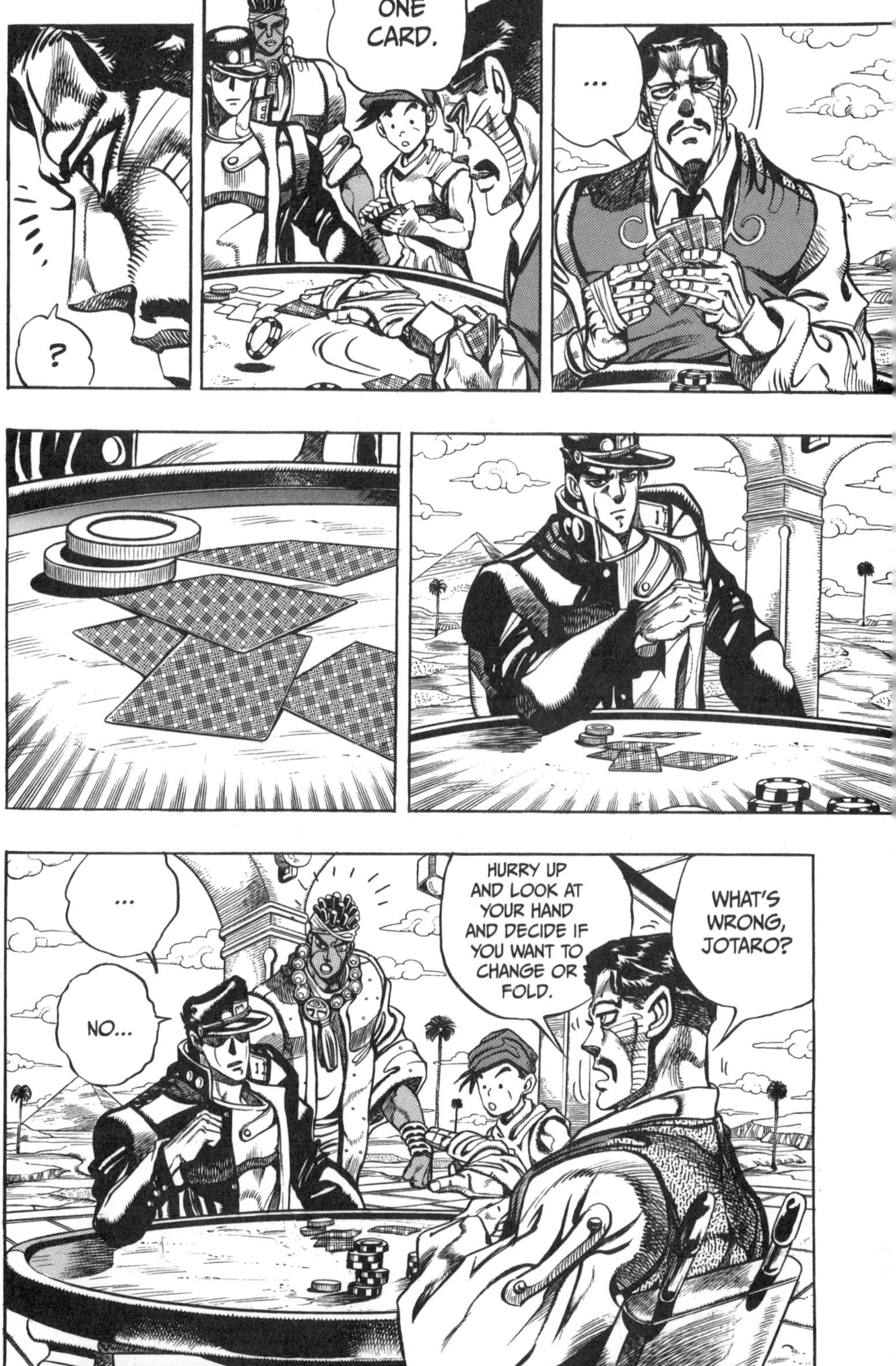
...
ONE CARD.
?
WHAT'S WRONG, JOTARO?
HURRY UP AND LOOK AT YOUR HAND AND DECIDE IF YOU WANT TO CHANGE OR FOLD.
...
NO...

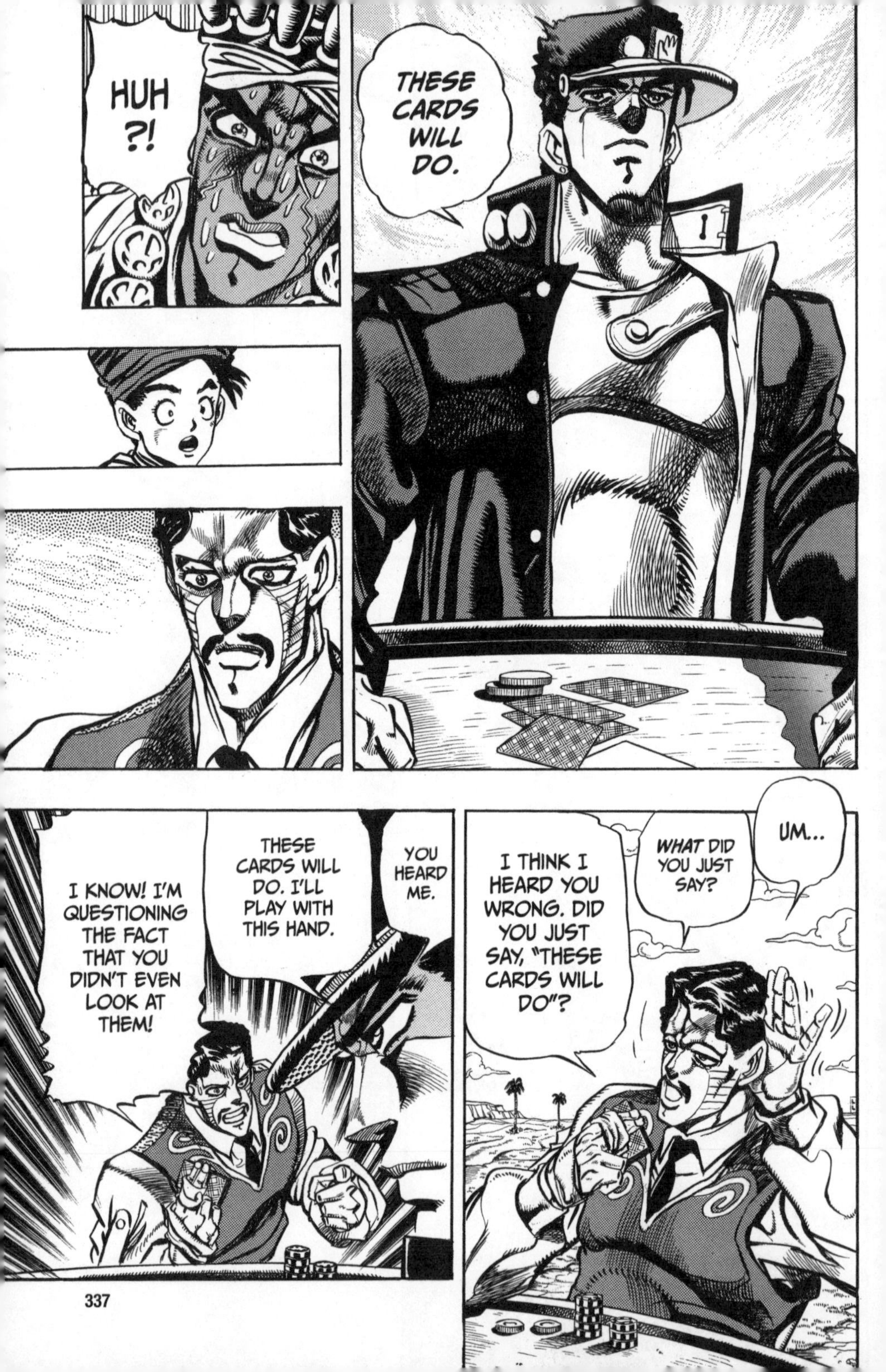
THESE CARDS WILL DO.
HUH ?!
UM...
WHAT DID YOU JUST SAY?
I THINK I HEARD YOU WRONG. DID YOU JUST SAY, "THESE CARDS WILL DO"?
YOU HEARD ME.
THESE CARDS WILL DO. I'LL PLAY WITH THIS HAND.
I KNOW! I'M QUESTIONING THE FACT THAT YOU DIDN'T EVEN LOOK AT THEM!

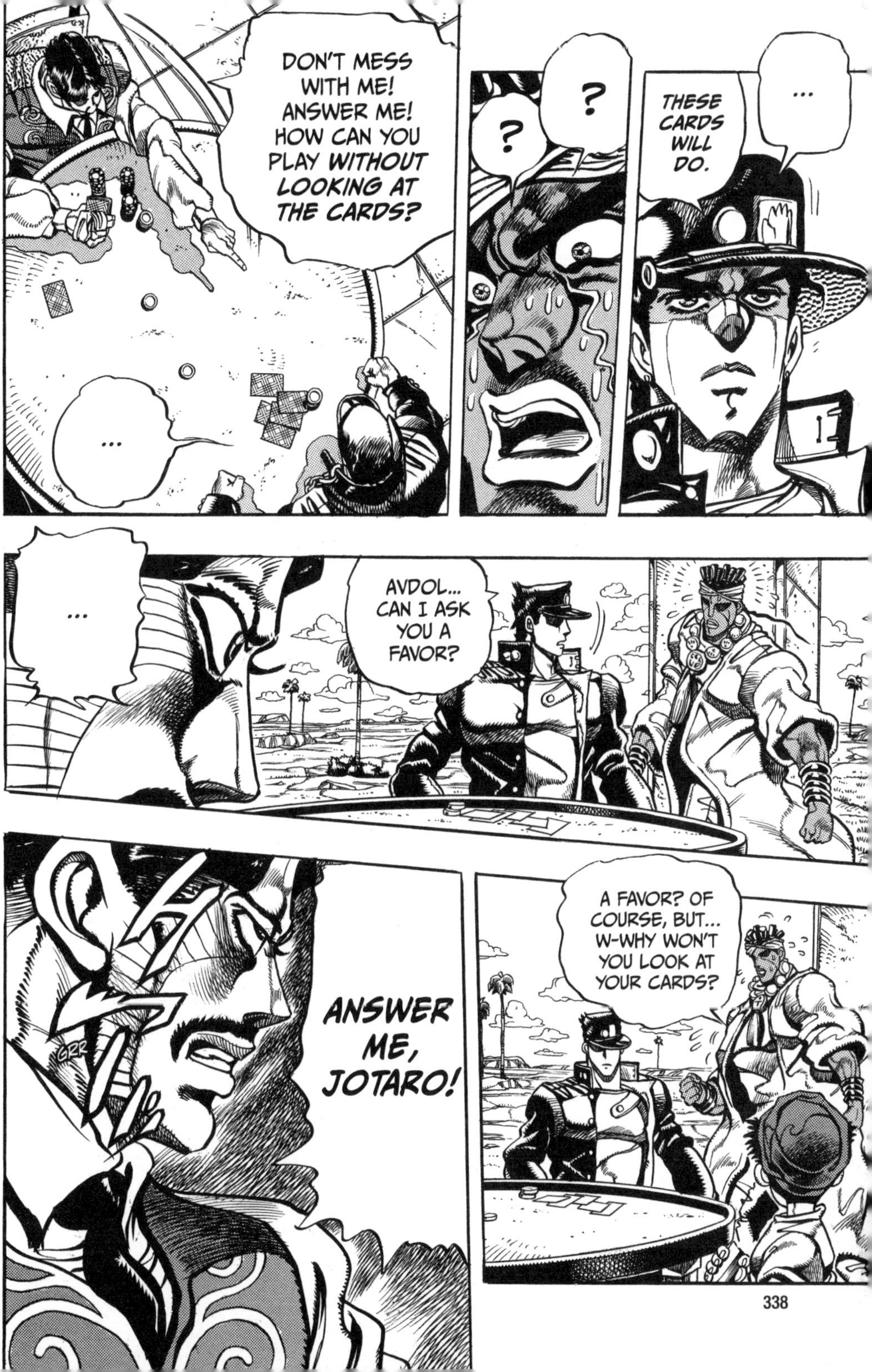
...
THESE CARDS WILL DO.
?
?
DON'T MESS WITH ME! ANSWER ME! HOW CAN YOU PLAY WITHOUT LOOKING AT THE CARDS?
...
AVDOL... CAN I ASK YOU A FAVOR?
...
A FAVOR? OF COURSE, BUT... W-WHY WON'T YOU LOOK AT YOUR CARDS?
ANSWER ME, JOTARO!
GRR

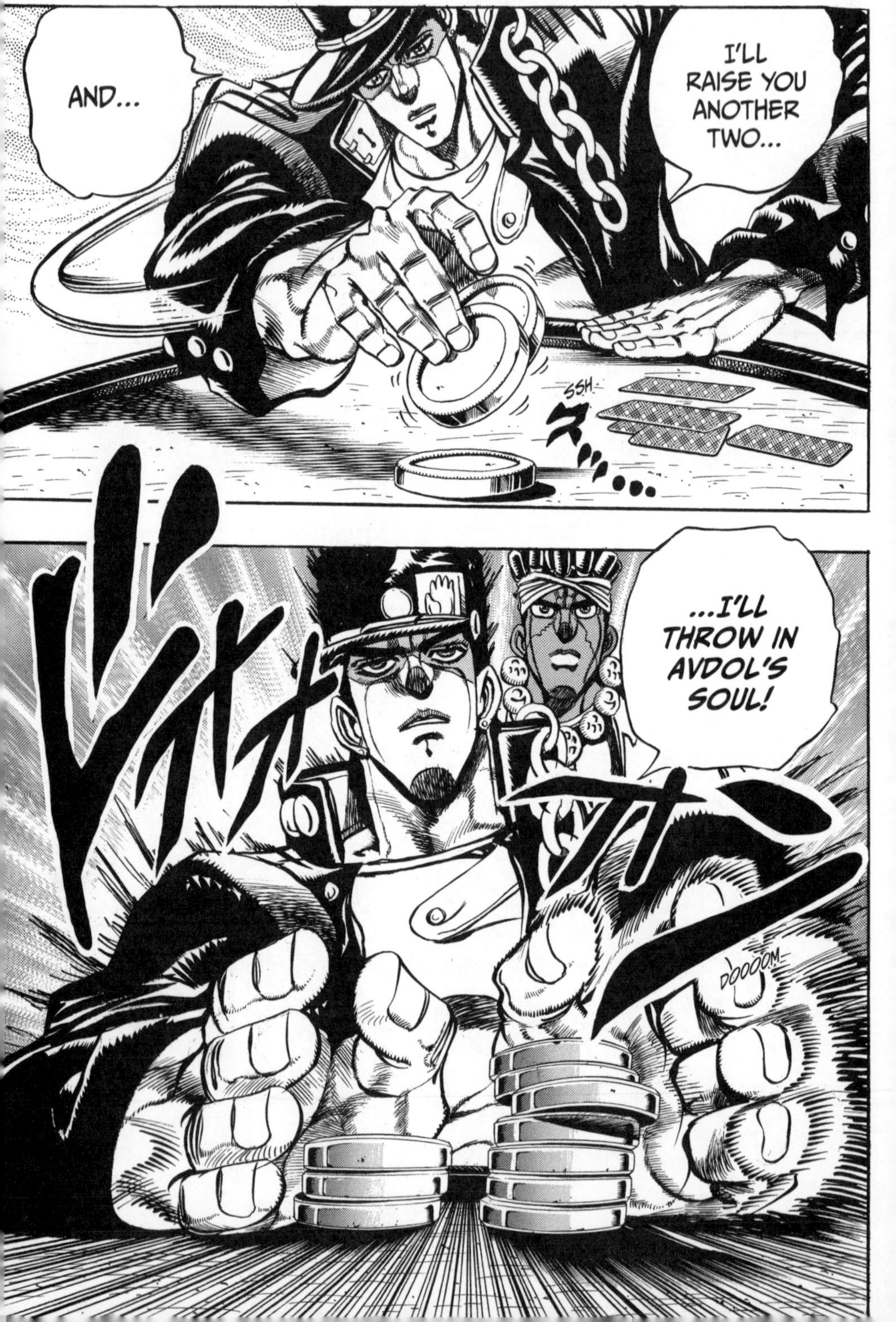
I'LL RAISE YOU ANOTHER TWO...
AND...
SSH
...I'LL THROW IN AVDOL'S SOUL!
DOOOOM

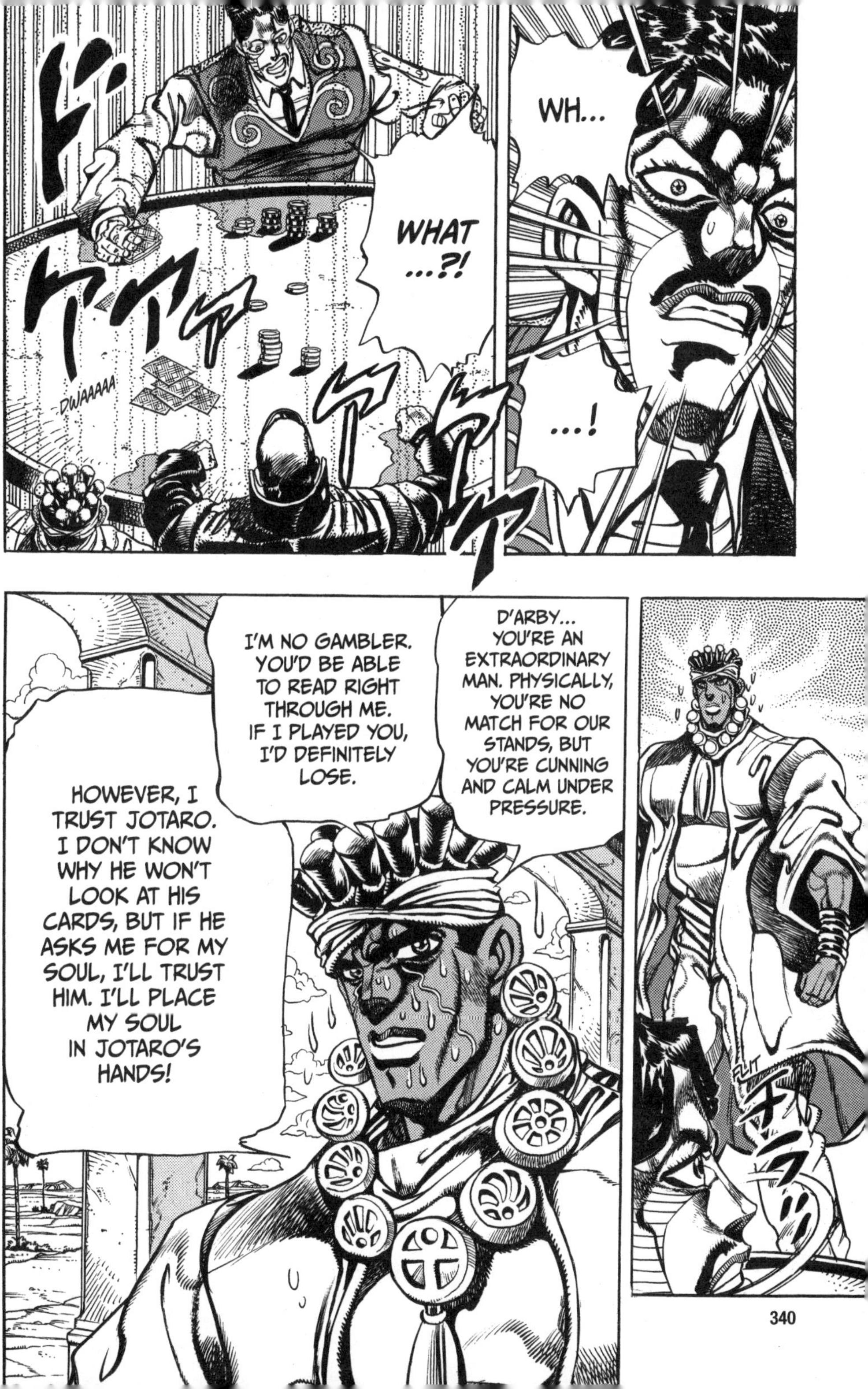
WH...
...!
WHAT ...?!
DWAAAAA
FLIT
D'ARBY... YOU'RE AN EXTRAORDINARY MAN. PHYSICALLY, YOU'RE NO MATCH FOR OUR STANDS, BUT YOU'RE CUNNING AND CALM UNDER PRESSURE.
I'M NO GAMBLER. YOU'D BE ABLE TO READ RIGHT THROUGH ME. IF I PLAYED YOU, I'D DEFINITELY LOSE.
HOWEVER, I TRUST JOTARO. I DON'T KNOW WHY HE WON'T LOOK AT HIS CARDS, BUT IF HE ASKS ME FOR MY SOUL, I'LL TRUST HIM. I'LL PLACE MY SOUL IN JOTARO'S HANDS!

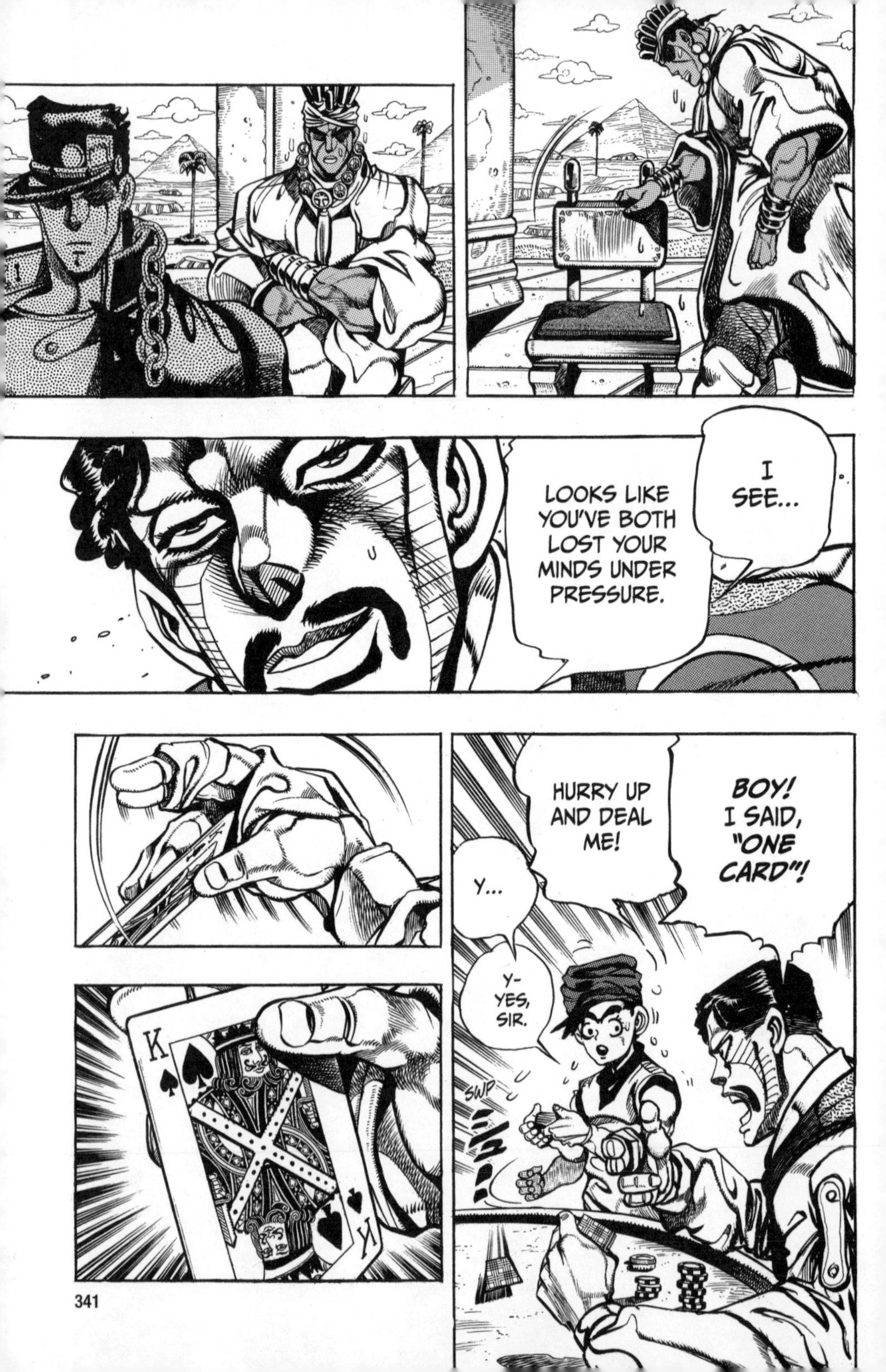
I SEE...
LOOKS LIKE YOU'VE BOTH LOST YOUR MINDS UNDER PRESSURE.
BOY! I SAID, "ONE CARD"!
HURRY UP AND DEAL ME!
Y...
Y-YES, SIR.
SWP

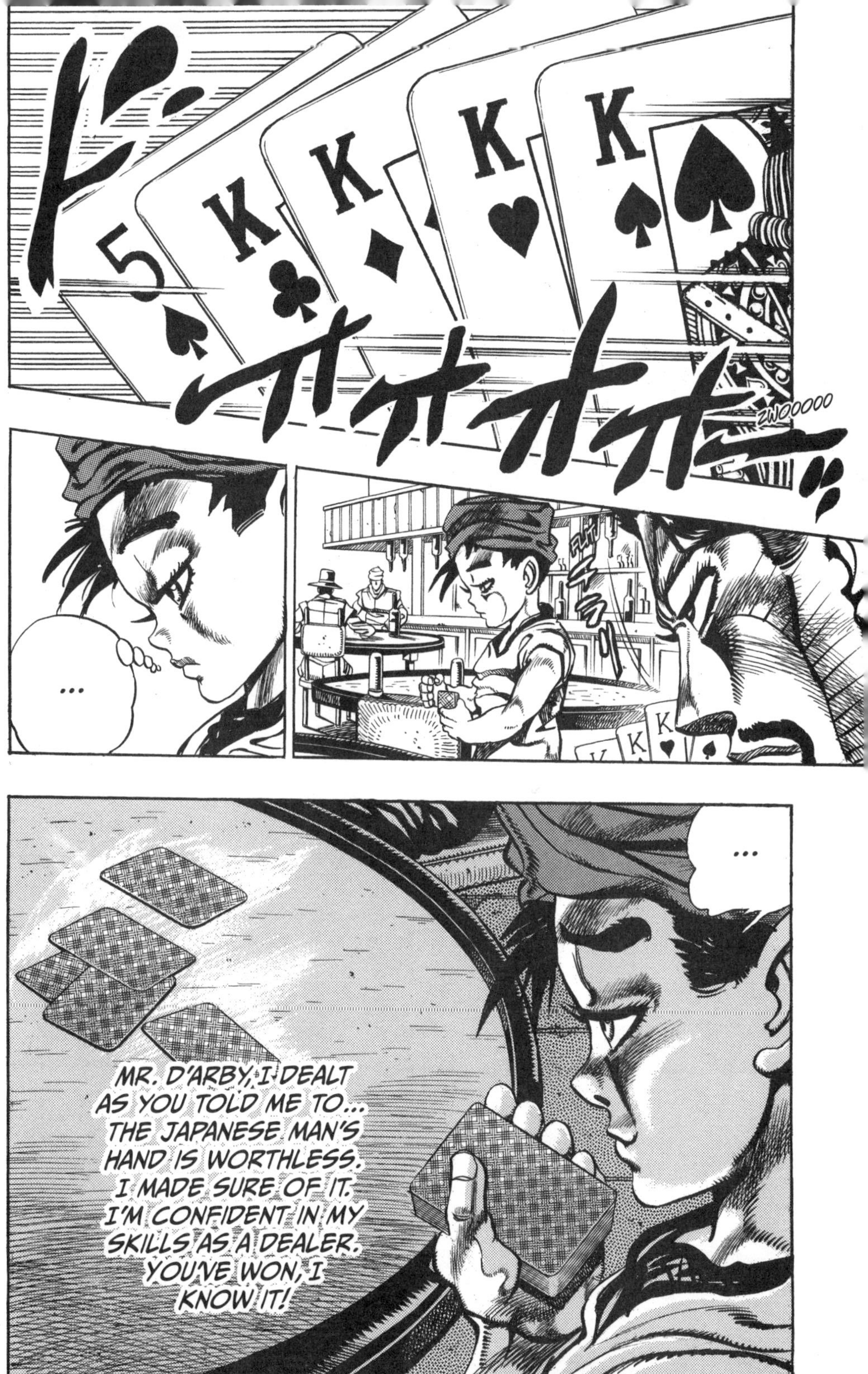
ZWOOOOO
FLIT
...
...
MR. D'ARBY, I DEALT AS YOU TOLD ME TO... THE JAPANESE MAN'S HAND IS WORTHLESS. I MADE SURE OF IT. I'M CONFIDENT IN MY SKILLS AS A DEALER. YOU'VE WON, I KNOW IT!

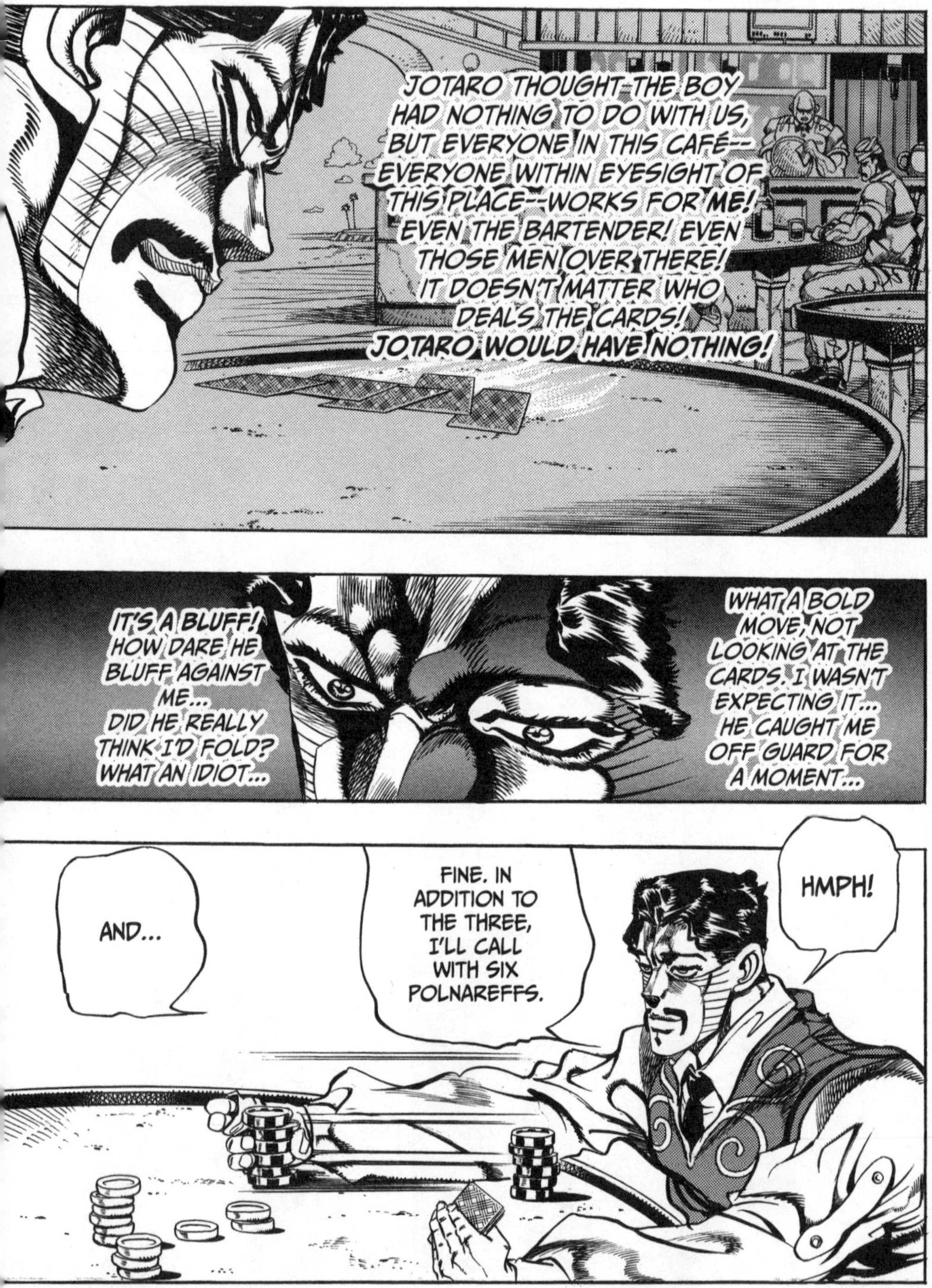
JOTARO THOUGHT THE BOY HAD NOTHING TO DO WITH US, BUT EVERYONE IN THIS CAFÉ-- EVERYONE WITHIN EYESIGHT OF THIS PLACE--WORKS FOR ME! EVEN THE BARTENDER! EVEN THOSE MEN OVER THERE! IT DOESN'T MATTER WHO DEALS THE CARDS! JOTARO WOULD HAVE NOTHING!
WHAT A BOLD MOVE, NOT LOOKING AT THE CARDS. I WASN'T EXPECTING IT... HE CAUGHT ME OFF GUARD FOR A MOMENT...
IT'S A BLUFF! HOW DARE HE BLUFF AGAINST ME... DID HE REALLY THINK I'D FOLD? WHAT AN IDIOT...
HMPH!
FINE. IN ADDITION TO THE THREE, I'LL CALL WITH SIX POLNAREFFS.
AND...

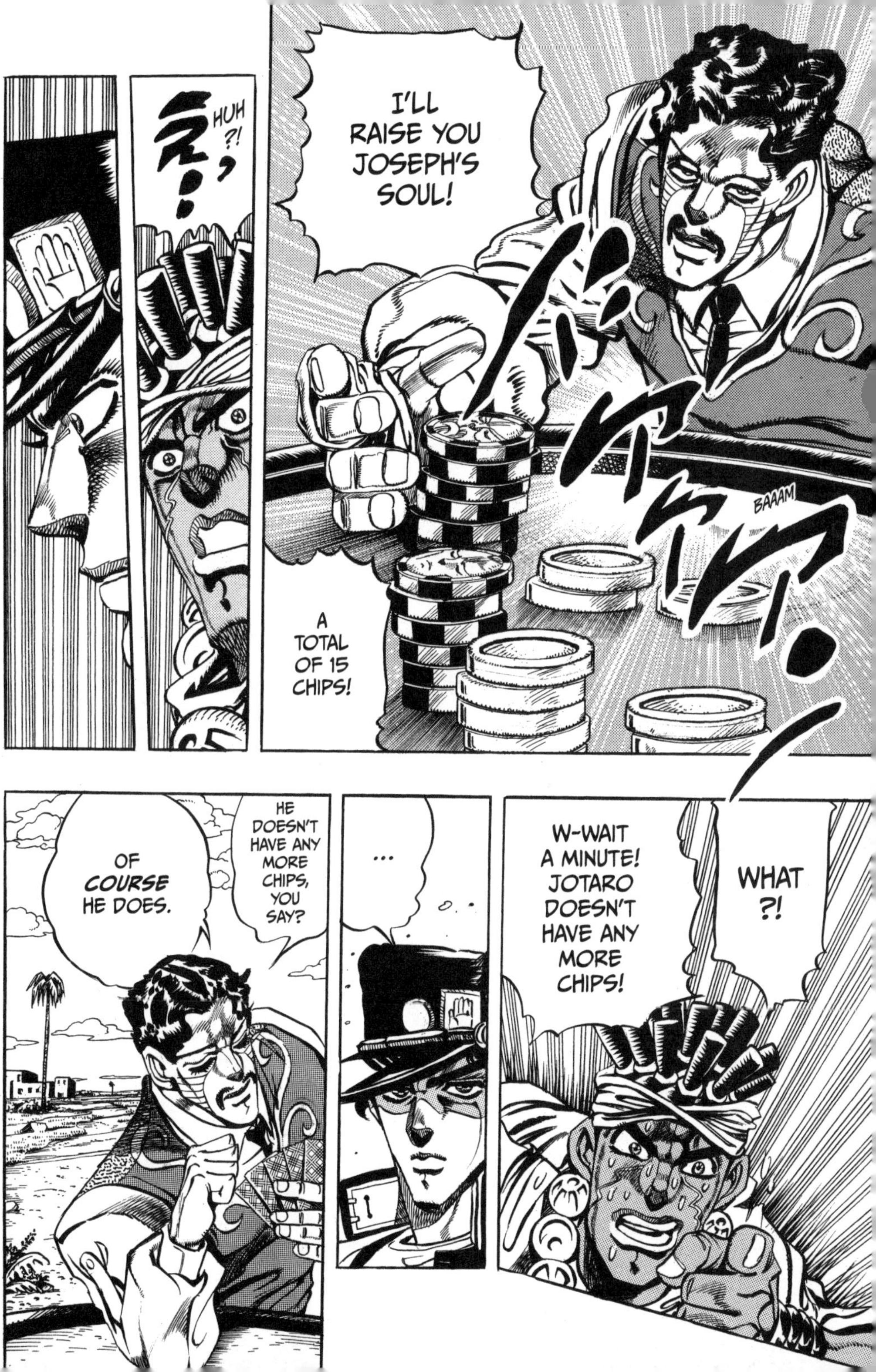
I'LL RAISE YOU JOSEPH'S SOUL!
BAAAM
A TOTAL OF 15 CHIPS!
HUH ?!
WHAT ?!
W-WAIT A MINUTE! JOTARO DOESN'T HAVE ANY MORE CHIPS!
...
HE DOESN'T HAVE ANY MORE CHIPS, YOU SAY?
OF *COURSE* HE DOES.

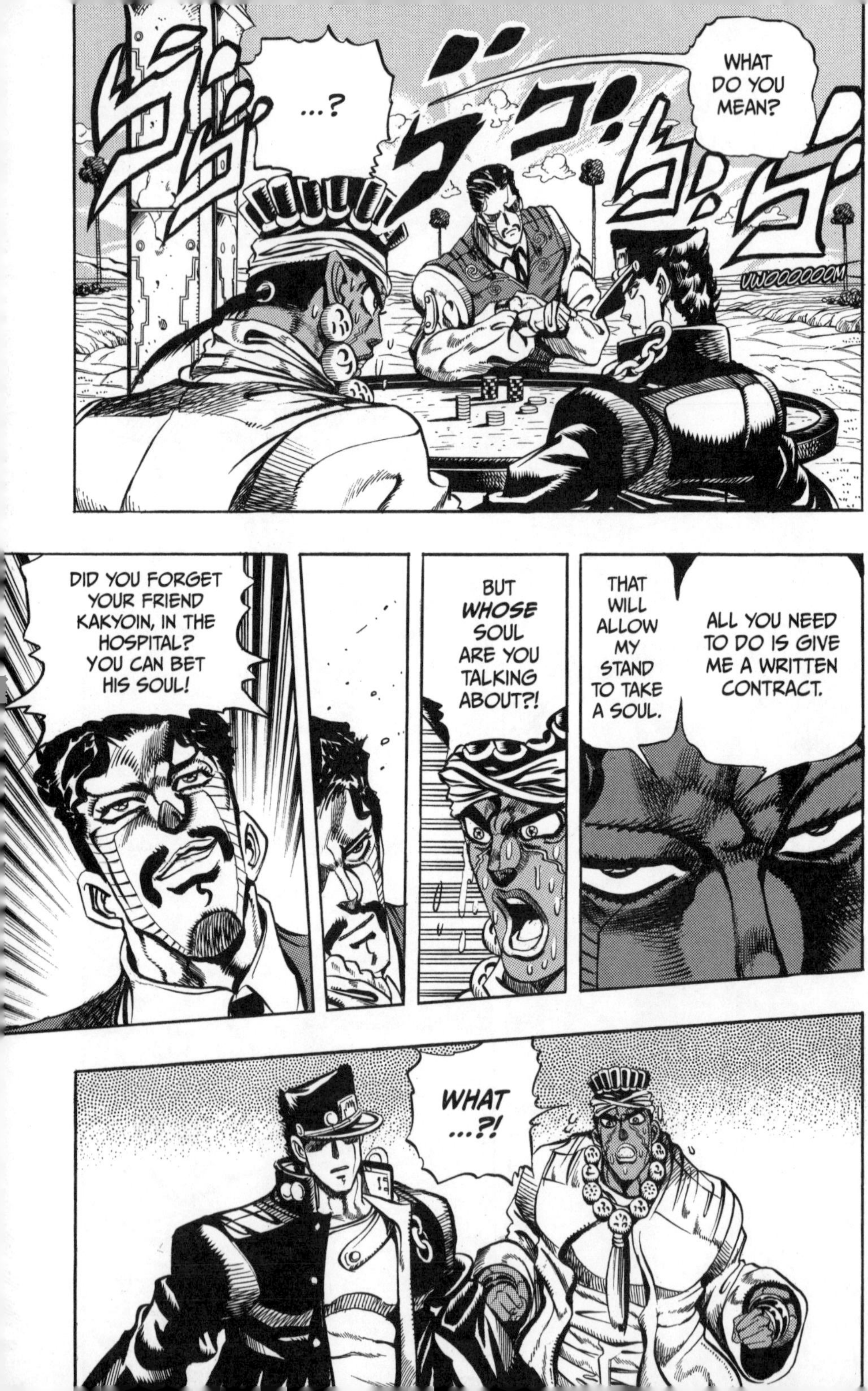

WHAT DO YOU MEAN?
UWOOOOOOM
...?
ALL YOU NEED TO DO IS GIVE ME A WRITTEN CONTRACT.
THAT WILL ALLOW MY STAND TO TAKE A SOUL.
BUT *WHOSE* SOUL ARE YOU TALKING ABOUT?!
DID YOU FORGET YOUR FRIEND KAKYOIN, IN THE HOSPITAL? YOU CAN BET HIS SOUL!
WHAT ...?!

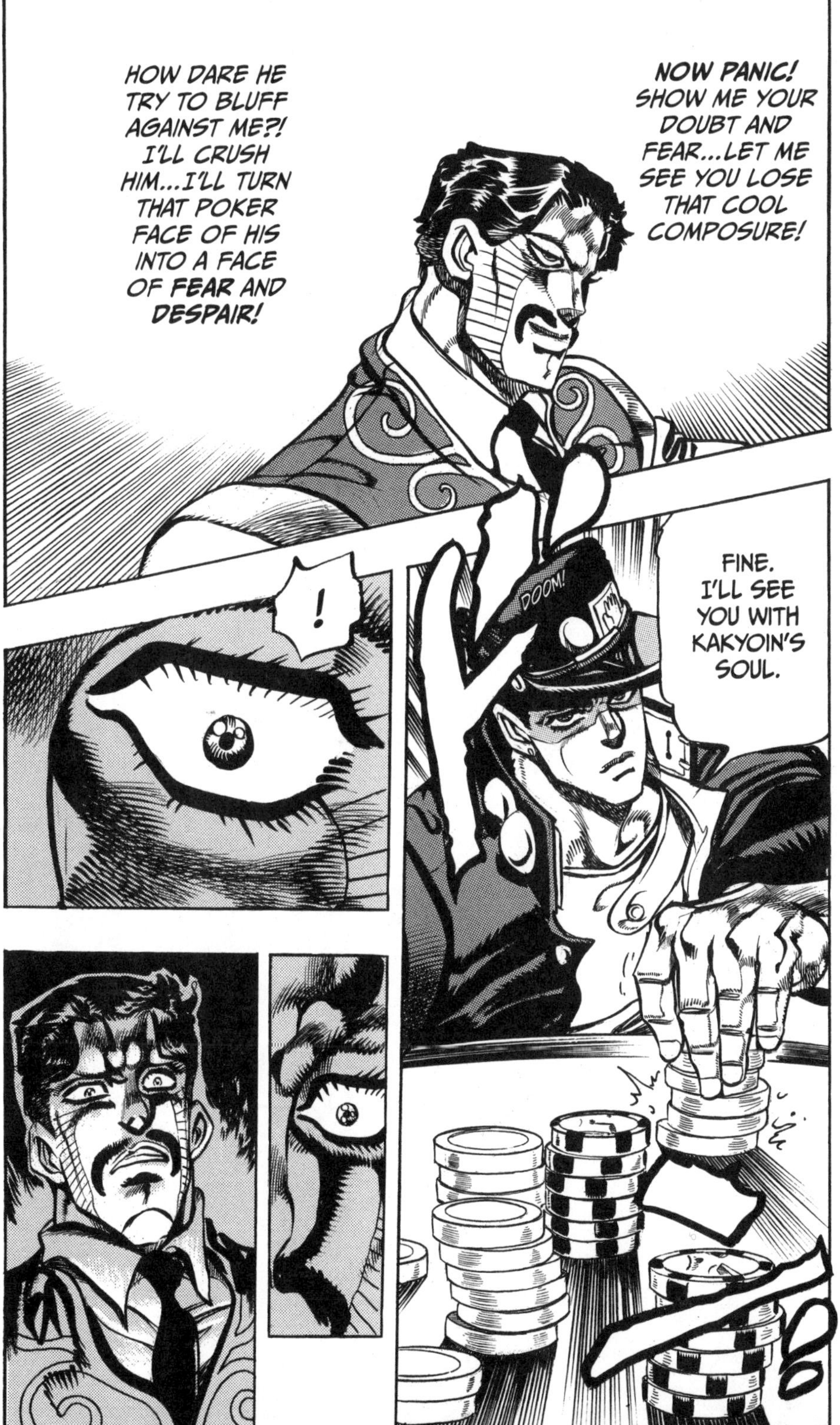
NOW PANIC! SHOW ME YOUR DOUBT AND FEAR...LET ME SEE YOU LOSE THAT COOL COMPOSURE!
HOW DARE HE TRY TO BLUFF AGAINST ME?! I'LL CRUSH HIM...I'LL TURN THAT POKER FACE OF HIS INTO A FACE OF FEAR AND DESPAIR!
FINE. I'LL SEE YOU WITH KAKYOIN'S SOUL.
DOOM!
!

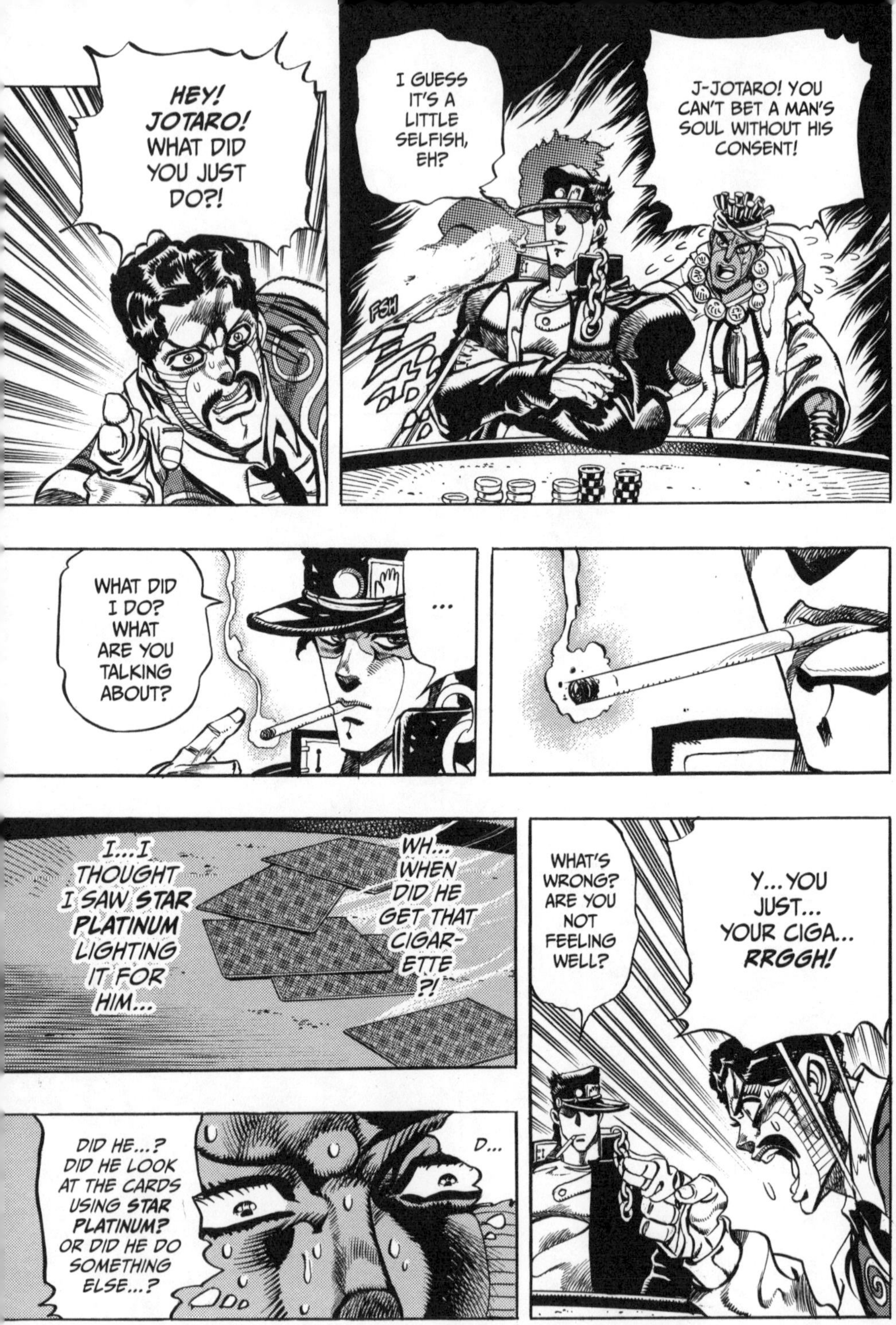
J-JOTARO! YOU CAN'T BET A MAN'S SOUL WITHOUT HIS CONSENT!
I GUESS IT'S A LITTLE SELFISH, EH?
FSH
HEY! JOTARO! WHAT DID YOU JUST DO?!
...
WHAT DID I DO? WHAT ARE YOU TALKING ABOUT?
Y...YOU JUST... YOUR CIGA... RRGGH!
WHAT'S WRONG? ARE YOU NOT FEELING WELL?
WH... WHEN DID HE GET THAT CIGARETTE?!
I...I THOUGHT I SAW STAR PLATINUM LIGHTING IT FOR HIM...
D...
DID HE...? DID HE LOOK AT THE CARDS USING STAR PLATINUM? OR DID HE DO SOMETHING ELSE...?

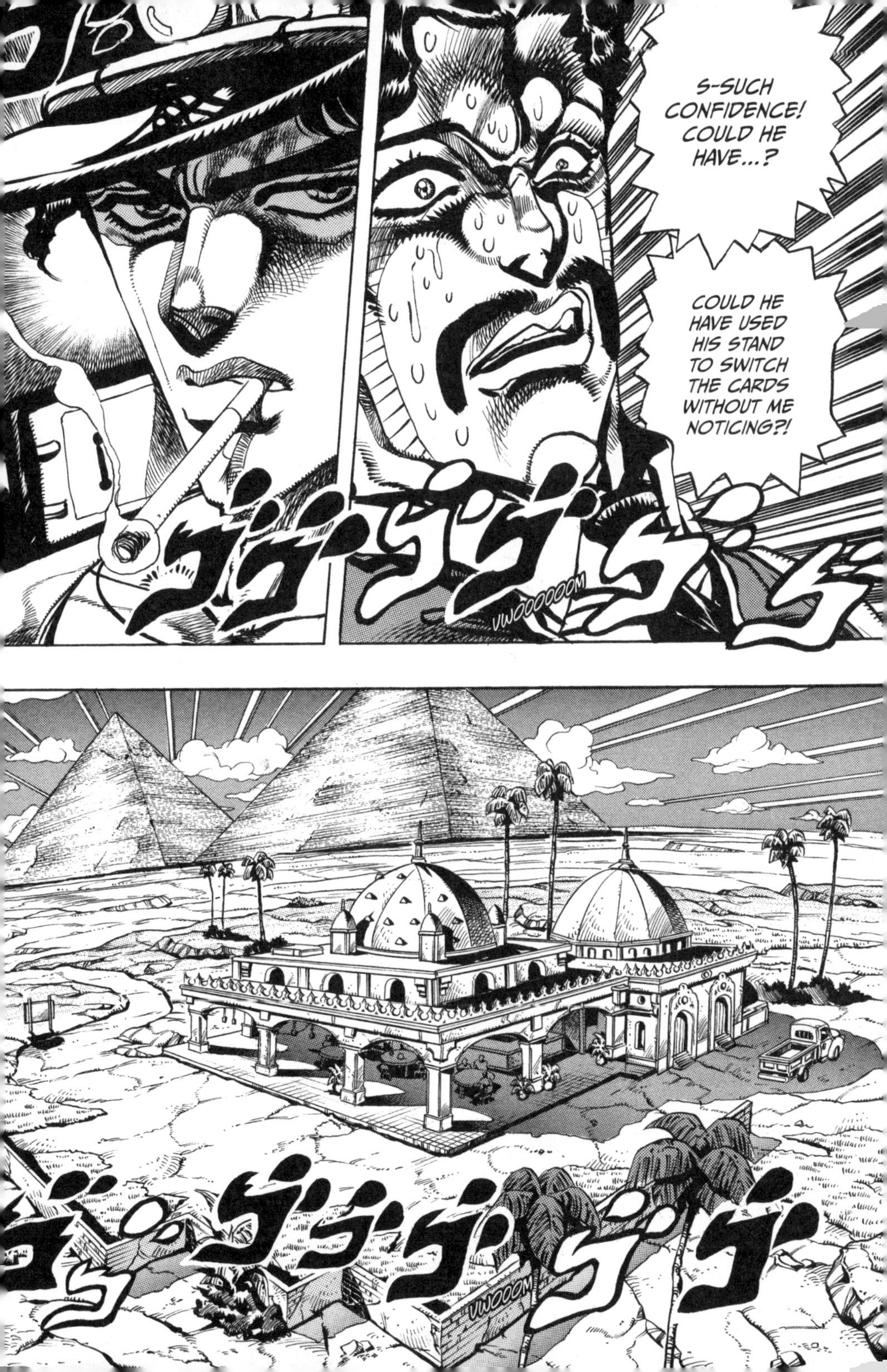
S-SUCH CONFIDENCE! COULD HE HAVE...?
COULD HE HAVE USED HIS STAND TO SWITCH THE CARDS WITHOUT ME NOTICING?!
VWOOOOOOM
VWOOOM

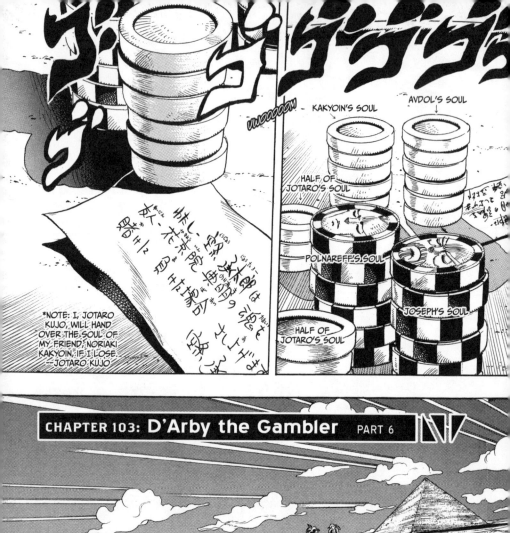

VWOOOOOM - KAKYOIN'S SOUL

AVDOL'S SOUL

HALF OF JOTARO'S SOUL

POLNAREFF'S SOUL

JOSEPH'S SOUL

HALF OF JOTARO'S SOUL

*NOTE: I, JOTARO KUJO, WILL HAND OVER THE SOUL OF MY FRIEND, NORIAKI KAKYOIN, IF I LOSE. —JOTARO KUJO

CHAPTER 103: D'Arby the Gambler PART 6

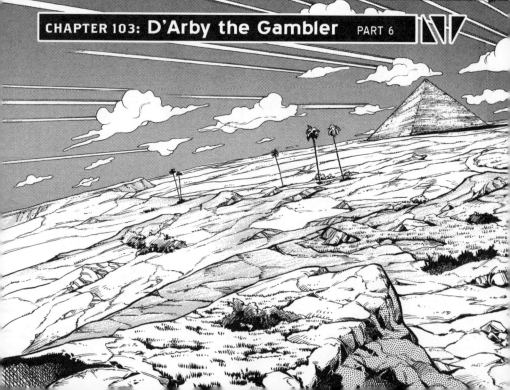

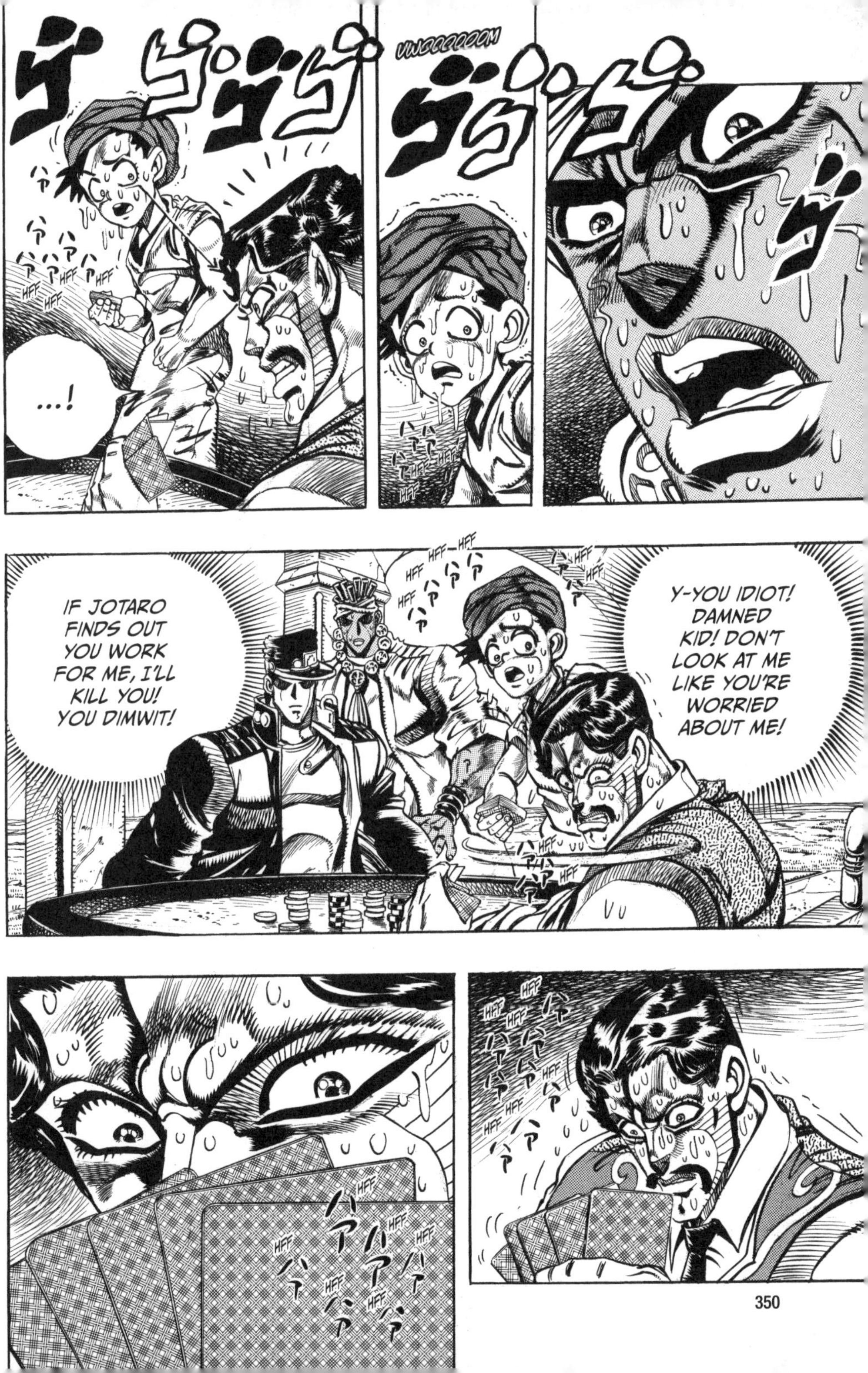
VWOOOOOOM
HFF HFF
...!
HFF HFF HFF HFF
Y-YOU IDIOT! DAMNED KID! DON'T LOOK AT ME LIKE YOU'RE WORRIED ABOUT ME!
IF JOTARO FINDS OUT YOU WORK FOR ME, I'LL KILL YOU! YOU DIMWIT!
HFF HFF HFF HFF HFF HFF HFF HFF
HFF HFF HFF HFF HFF HFF HFF HFF

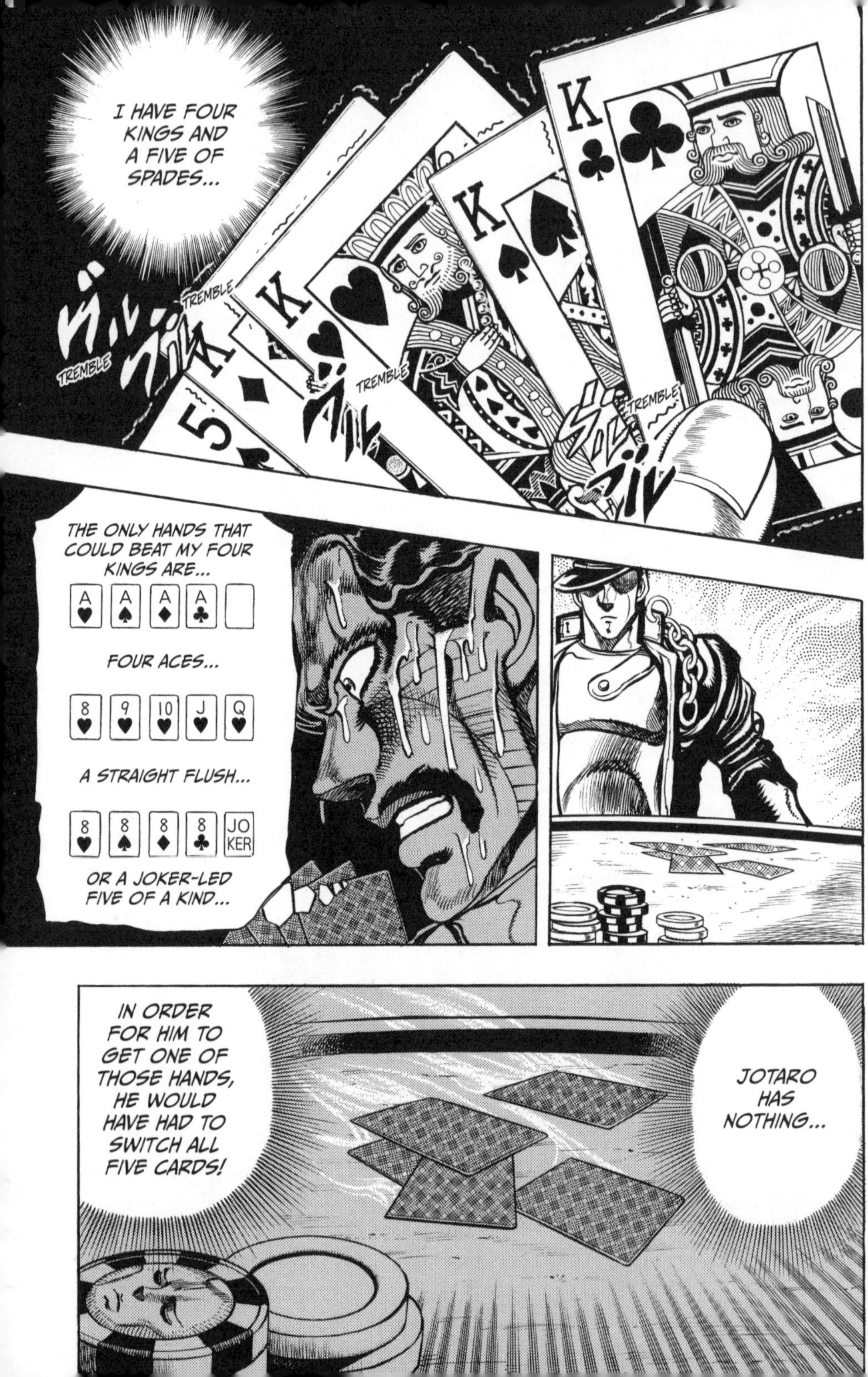
I HAVE FOUR KINGS AND A FIVE OF SPADES...
TREMBLE
TREMBLE
TREMBLE
TREMBLE
THE ONLY HANDS THAT COULD BEAT MY FOUR KINGS ARE...
A A A A
FOUR ACES...
8 9 10 J Q
A STRAIGHT FLUSH...
8 8 8 8 JOKER
OR A JOKER-LED FIVE OF A KIND...
JOTARO HAS NOTHING...
IN ORDER FOR HIM TO GET ONE OF THOSE HANDS, HE WOULD HAVE HAD TO SWITCH ALL FIVE CARDS!

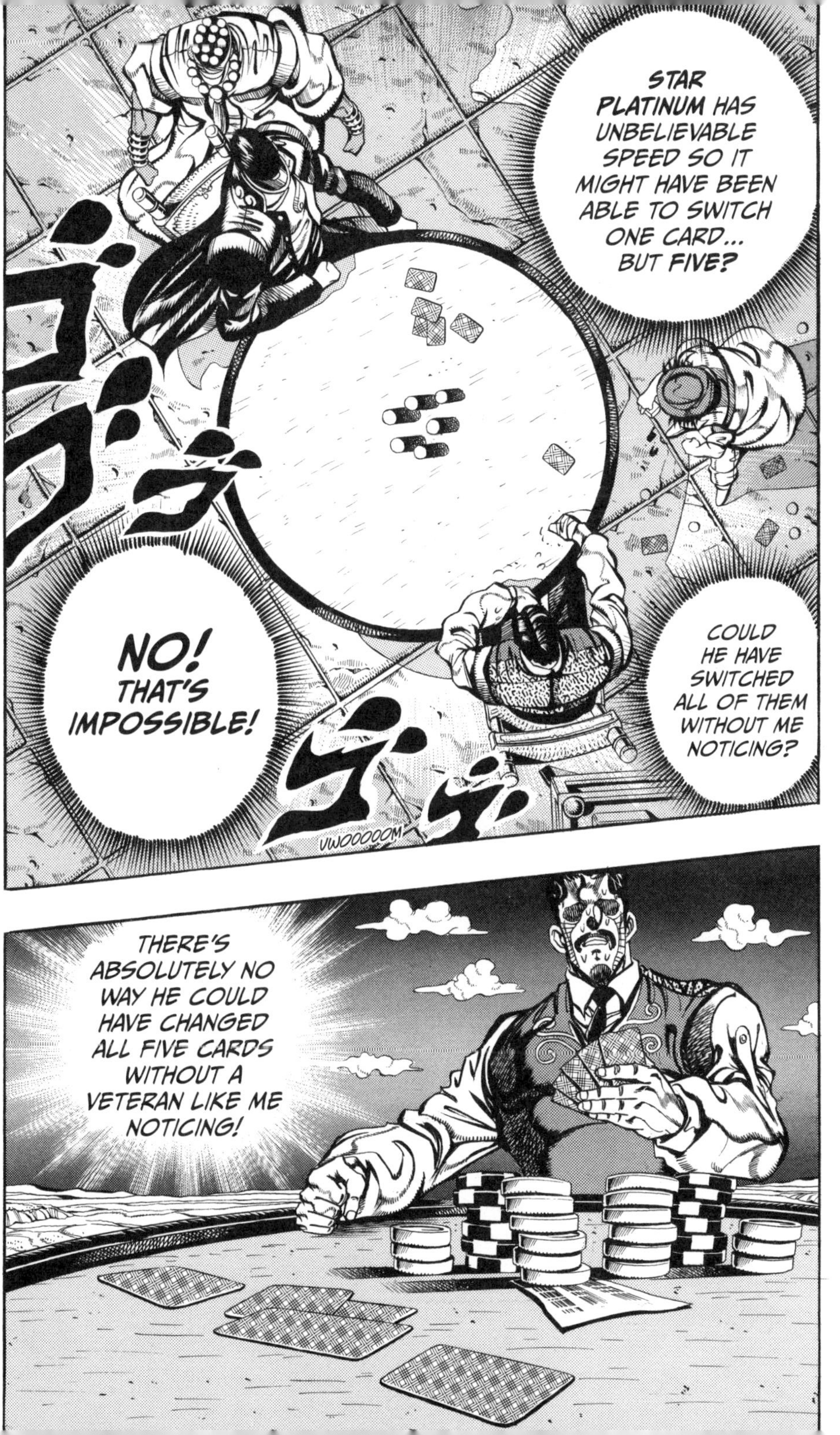
STAR PLATINUM HAS UNBELIEVABLE SPEED SO IT MIGHT HAVE BEEN ABLE TO SWITCH ONE CARD... BUT FIVE?
COULD HE HAVE SWITCHED ALL OF THEM WITHOUT ME NOTICING?
NO! THAT'S IMPOSSIBLE!
VWOOOOOM
THERE'S ABSOLUTELY NO WAY HE COULD HAVE CHANGED ALL FIVE CARDS WITHOUT A VETERAN LIKE ME NOTICING!

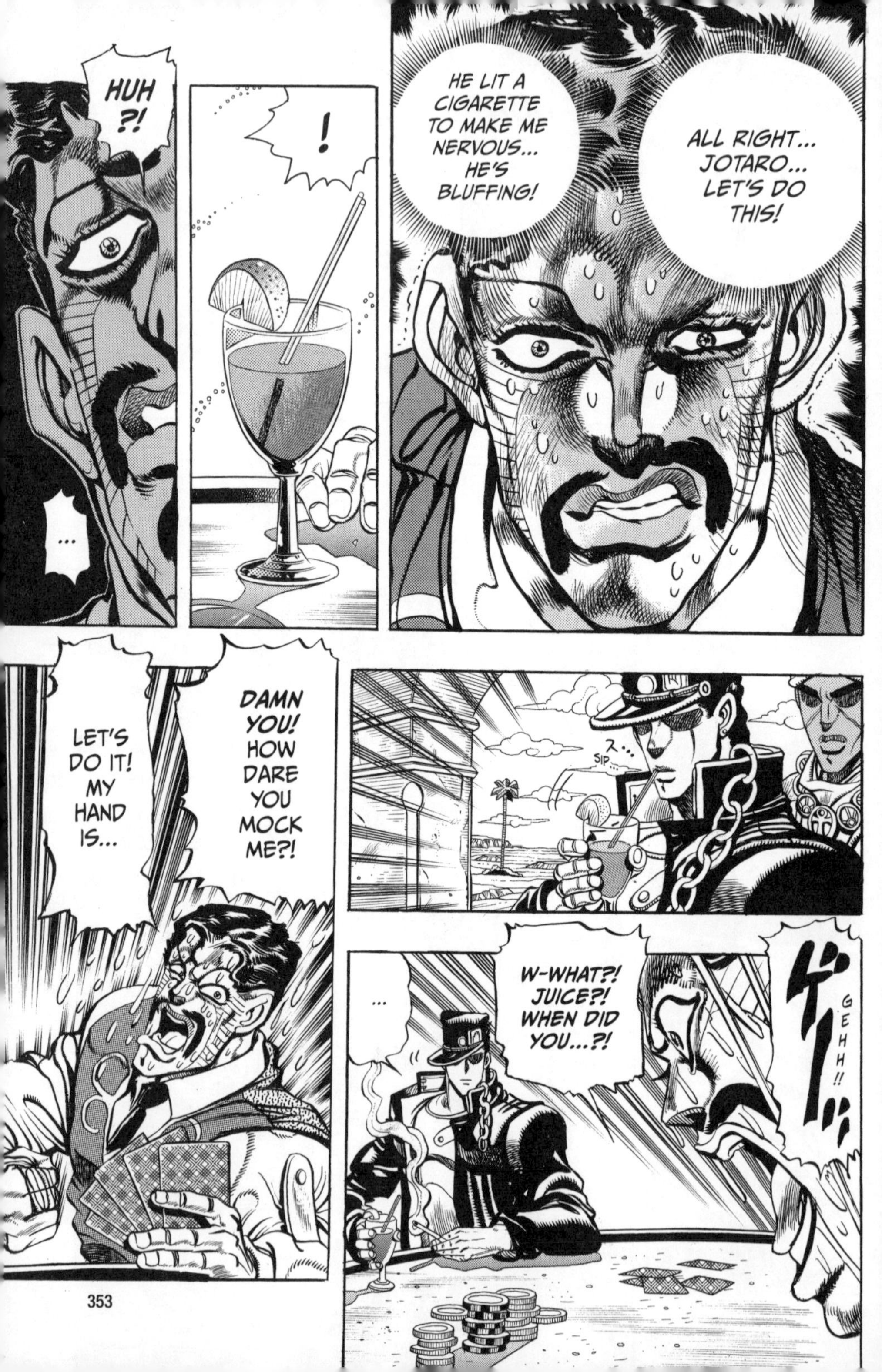
HE LIT A CIGARETTE TO MAKE ME NERVOUS... HE'S BLUFFING!
ALL RIGHT... JOTARO... LET'S DO THIS!
!
HUH ?!
...
SIP...
W-WHAT?! JUICE?! WHEN DID YOU...?!
GEHH!!
...
DAMN YOU! HOW DARE YOU MOCK ME?!
LET'S DO IT! MY HAND IS...

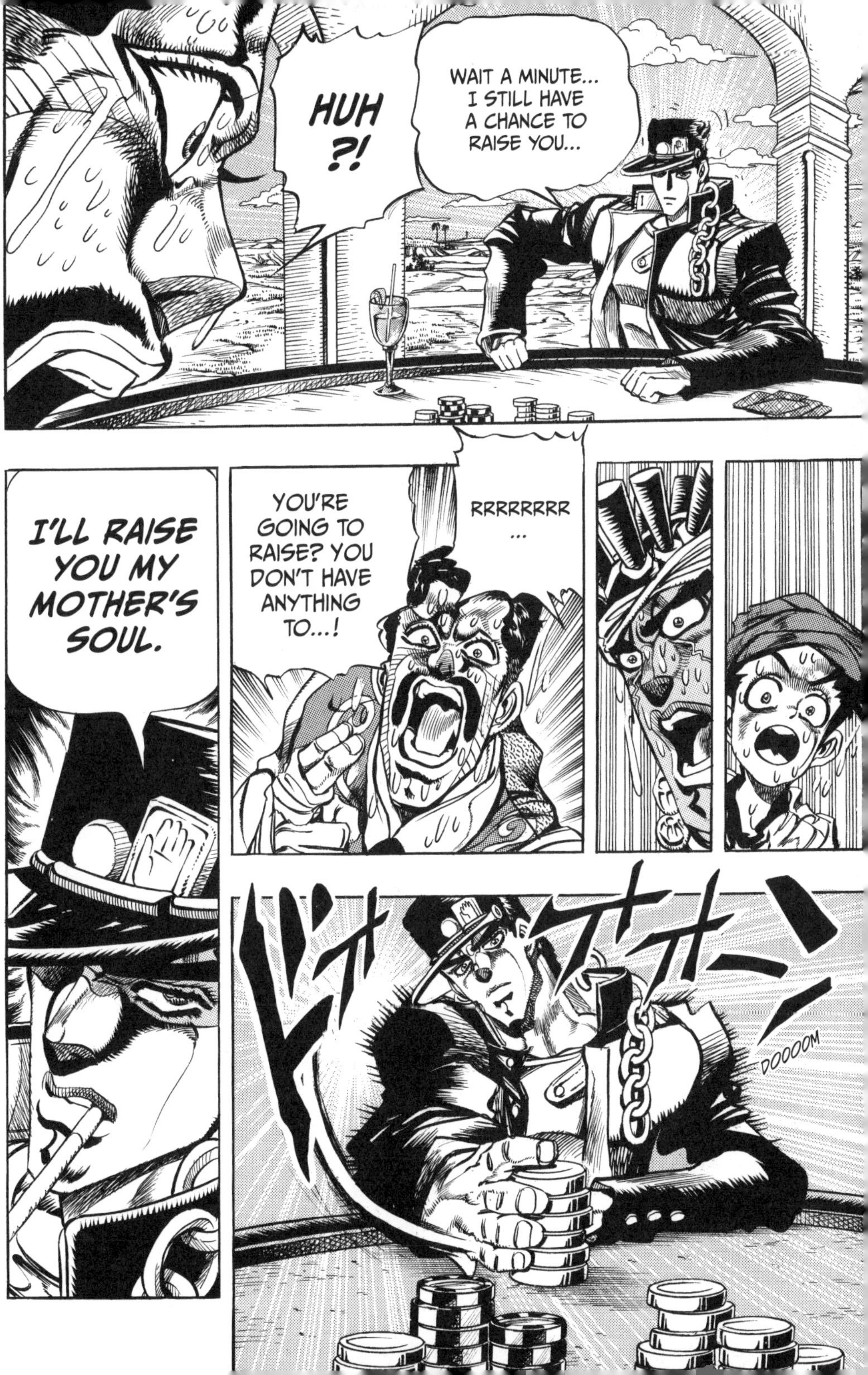
WAIT A MINUTE... I STILL HAVE A CHANCE TO RAISE YOU...
HUH ?!
RRRRRRRR ...
YOU'RE GOING TO RAISE? YOU DON'T HAVE ANYTHING TO...!
DOOOOM
I'LL RAISE YOU MY MOTHER'S SOUL.

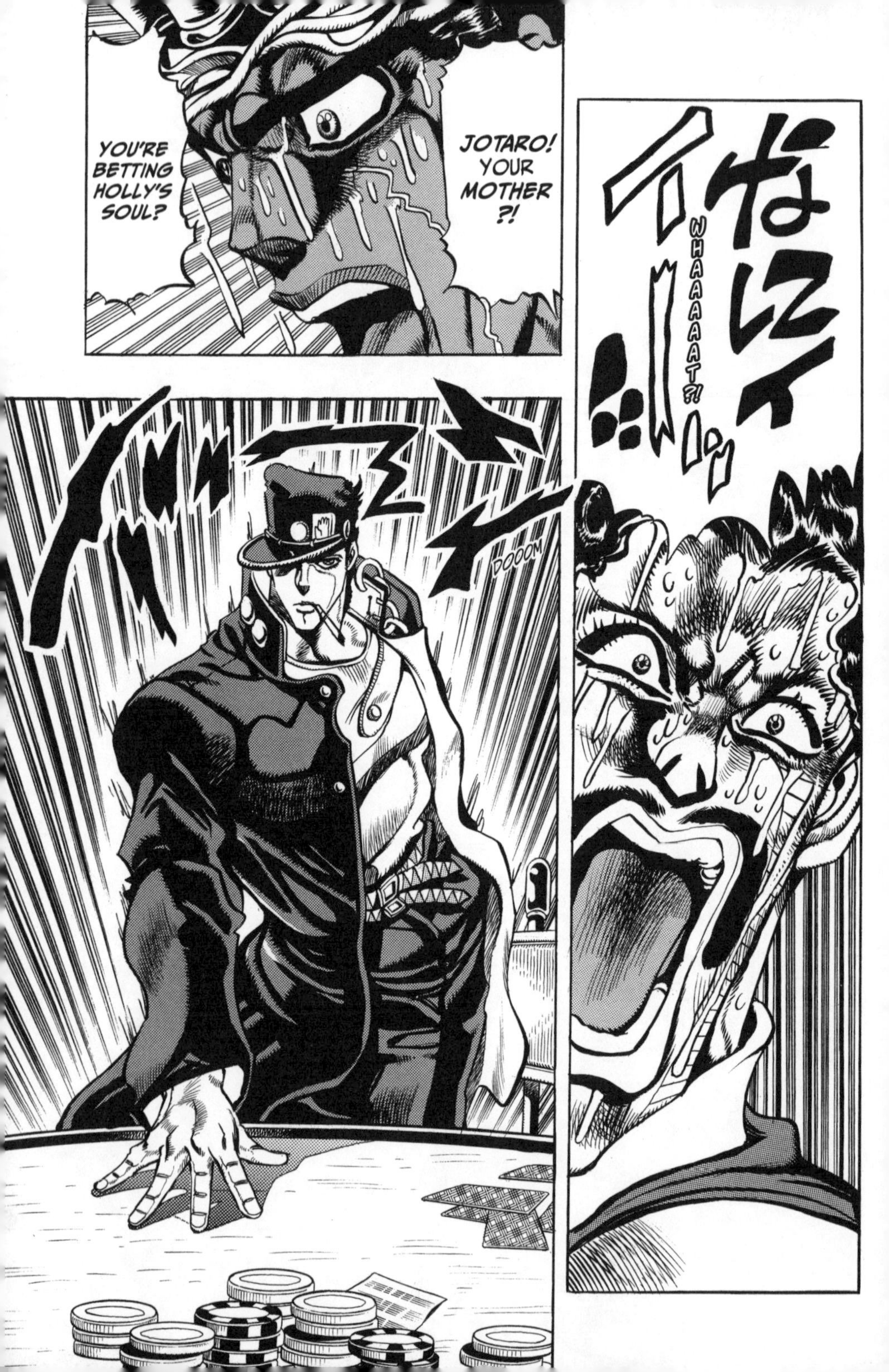
WHAAAAAAAT?!
JOTARO! YOUR MOTHER ?!
YOU'RE BETTING HOLLY'S SOUL?
DOOOM

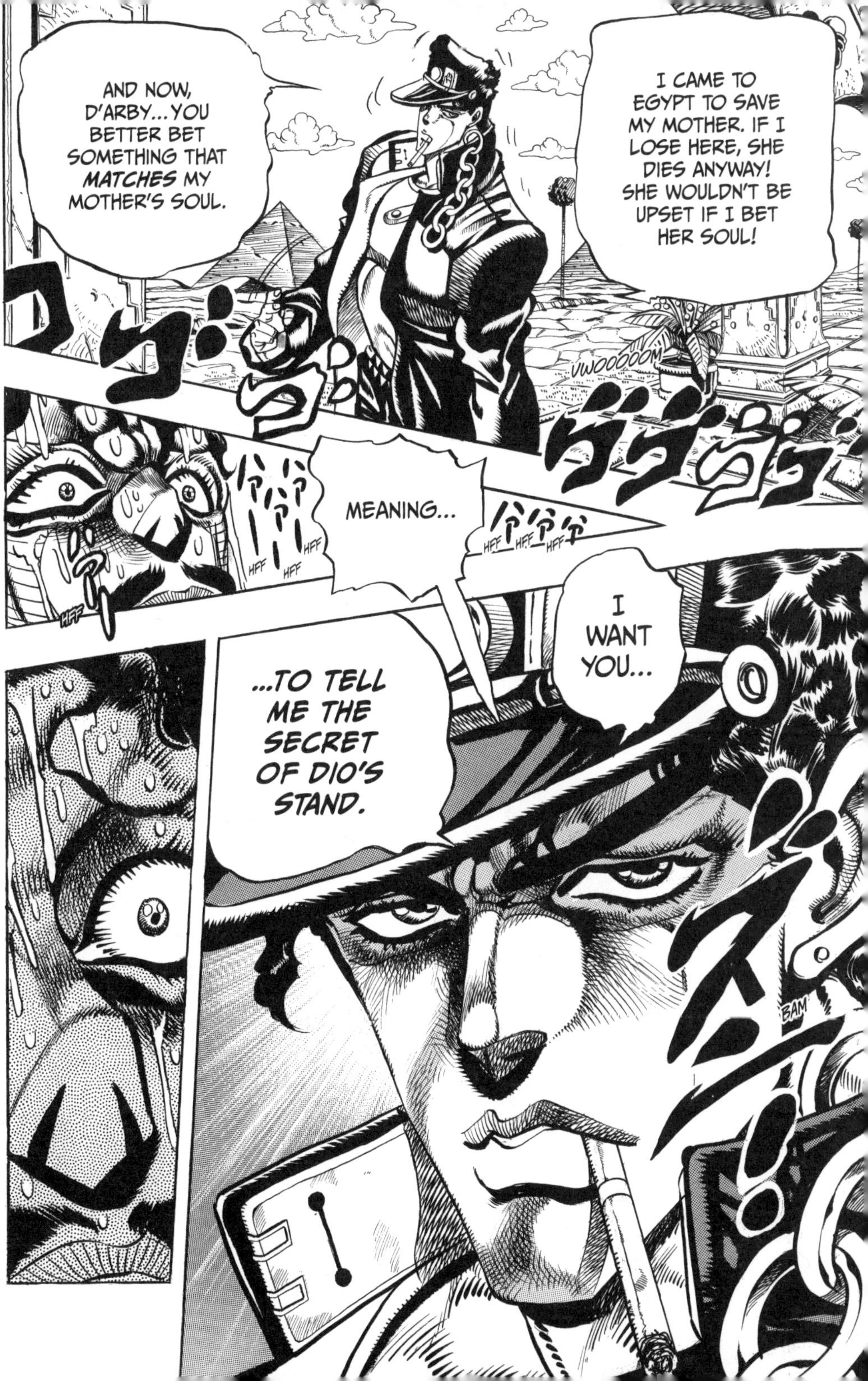

I CAME TO EGYPT TO SAVE MY MOTHER. IF I LOSE HERE, SHE DIES ANYWAY! SHE WOULDN'T BE UPSET IF I BET HER SOUL!
AND NOW, D'ARBY...YOU BETTER BET SOMETHING THAT *MATCHES* MY MOTHER'S SOUL.
VWOOOOOM
HFF HFF HFF
MEANING...
HFF HFF HFF HFF
I WANT YOU...
...TO TELL ME THE SECRET OF DIO'S STAND.
BAM

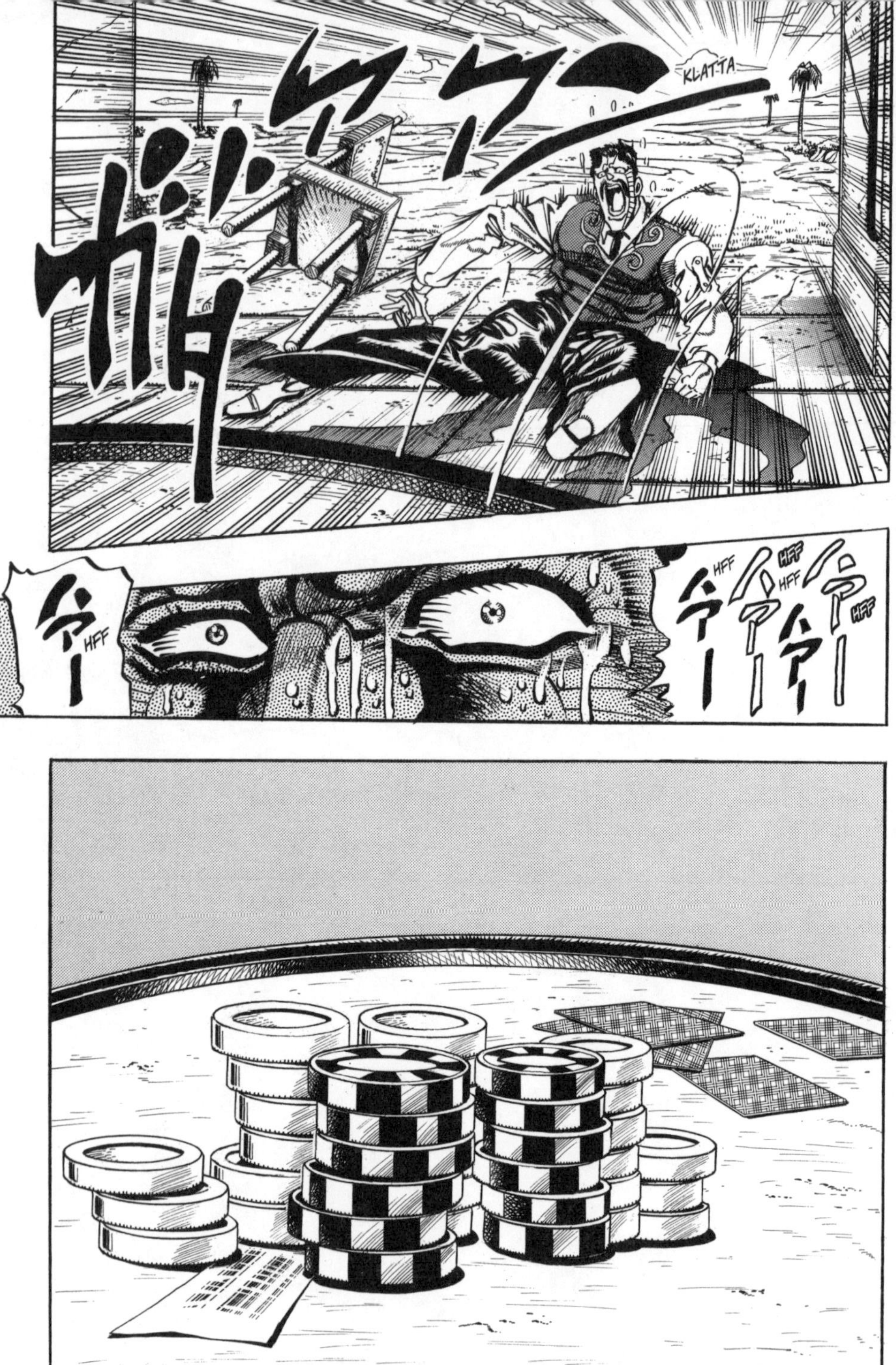
KLATTA
HFF
HFF
HFF
HFF
HFF

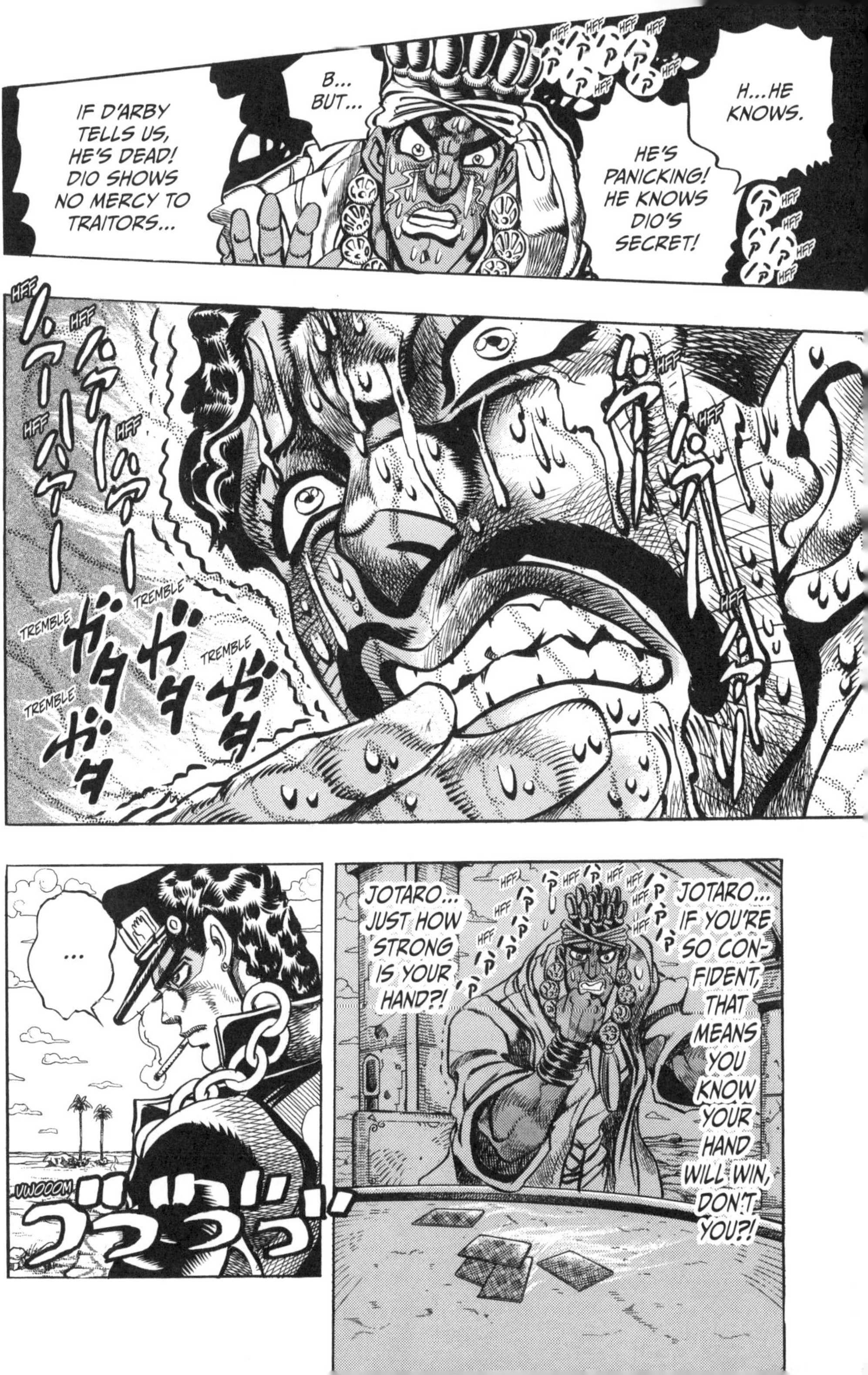
H...HE KNOWS.
HFF HFF HFF HFF HFF HFF
HE'S PANICKING! HE KNOWS DIO'S SECRET!
B... BUT...
IF D'ARBY TELLS US, HE'S DEAD! DIO SHOWS NO MERCY TO TRAITORS...
HFF HFF HFF HFF HFF
TREMBLE TREMBLE TREMBLE TREMBLE
JOTARO... IF YOU'RE SO CON-FIDENT, THAT MEANS YOU KNOW YOUR HAND WILL WIN, DON'T YOU?!
JOTARO... JUST HOW STRONG IS YOUR HAND?!
HFF HFF HFF HFF HFF HFF
...
VWOOOM

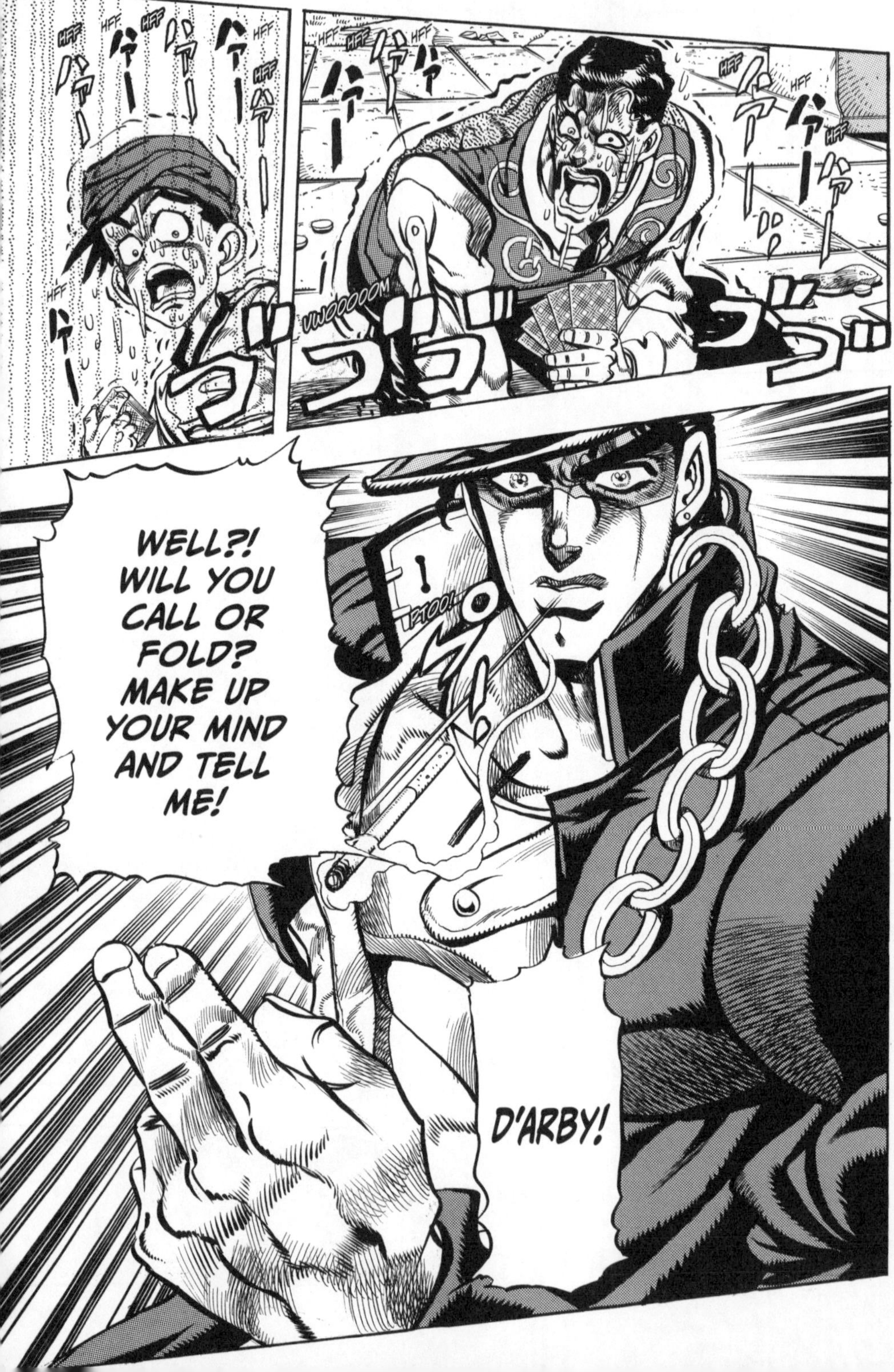
HFF
HFF
HFF
HFF
HFF
HFF
VWOOOOOM
HFF
HFF
HFF
HFF
HFF
WELL?! WILL YOU CALL OR FOLD? MAKE UP YOUR MIND AND TELL ME!
PTOO!
D'ARBY!

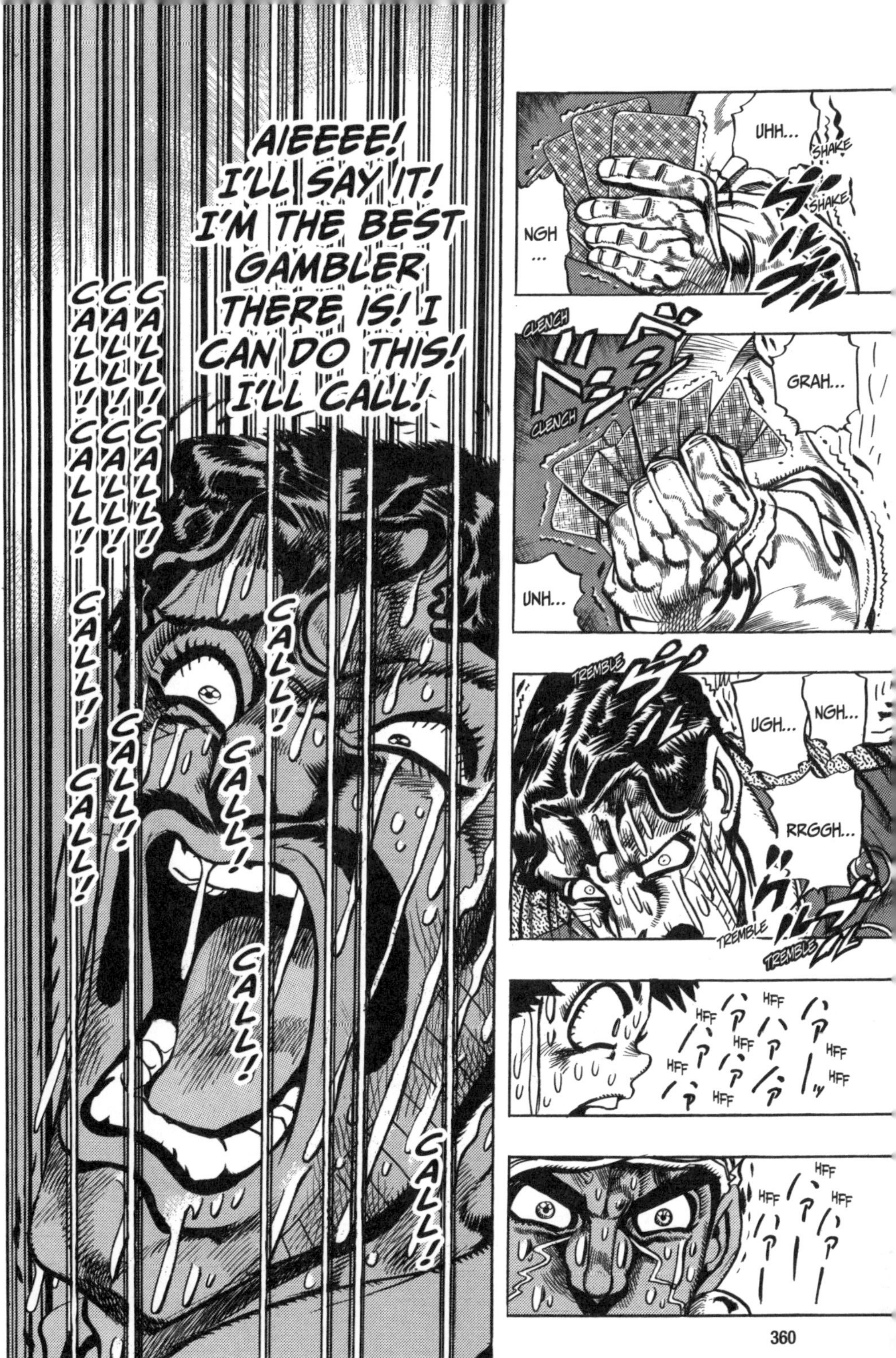

UHH...
SHAKE
SHAKE
NGH...
GRAH...
CLENCH
CLENCH
UNH...
NGH...
UGH...
TREMBLE
RRGGH...
TREMBLE
TREMBLE
HFF
HFF
HFF
HFF
HFF
HFF
HFF
HFF
HFF
HFF
HFF
AIEEEE! I'LL SAY IT! I'M THE BEST GAMBLER THERE IS! I CAN DO THIS! I'LL CALL!
CALL! CALL!
CALL! CALL!
CALL! CALL!
CALL!
CALL!
CALL!
CALL!
CALL!
CALL!
CALL!

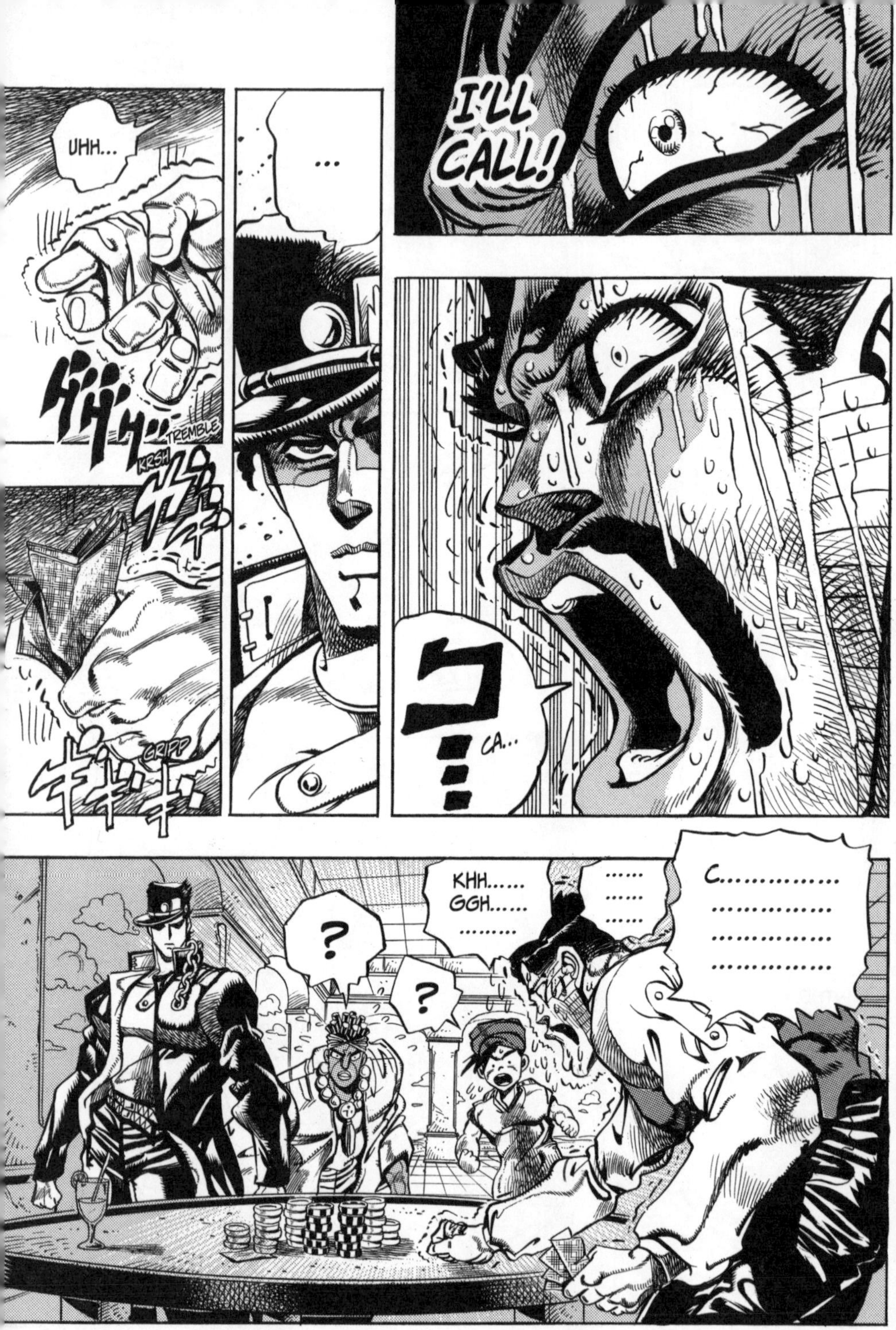
I'LL CALL!
CA...
...
UHH...
TREMBLE
KRSH
GRIPP
C........................
......
......
......
KHH......
GGH......
....
?
?

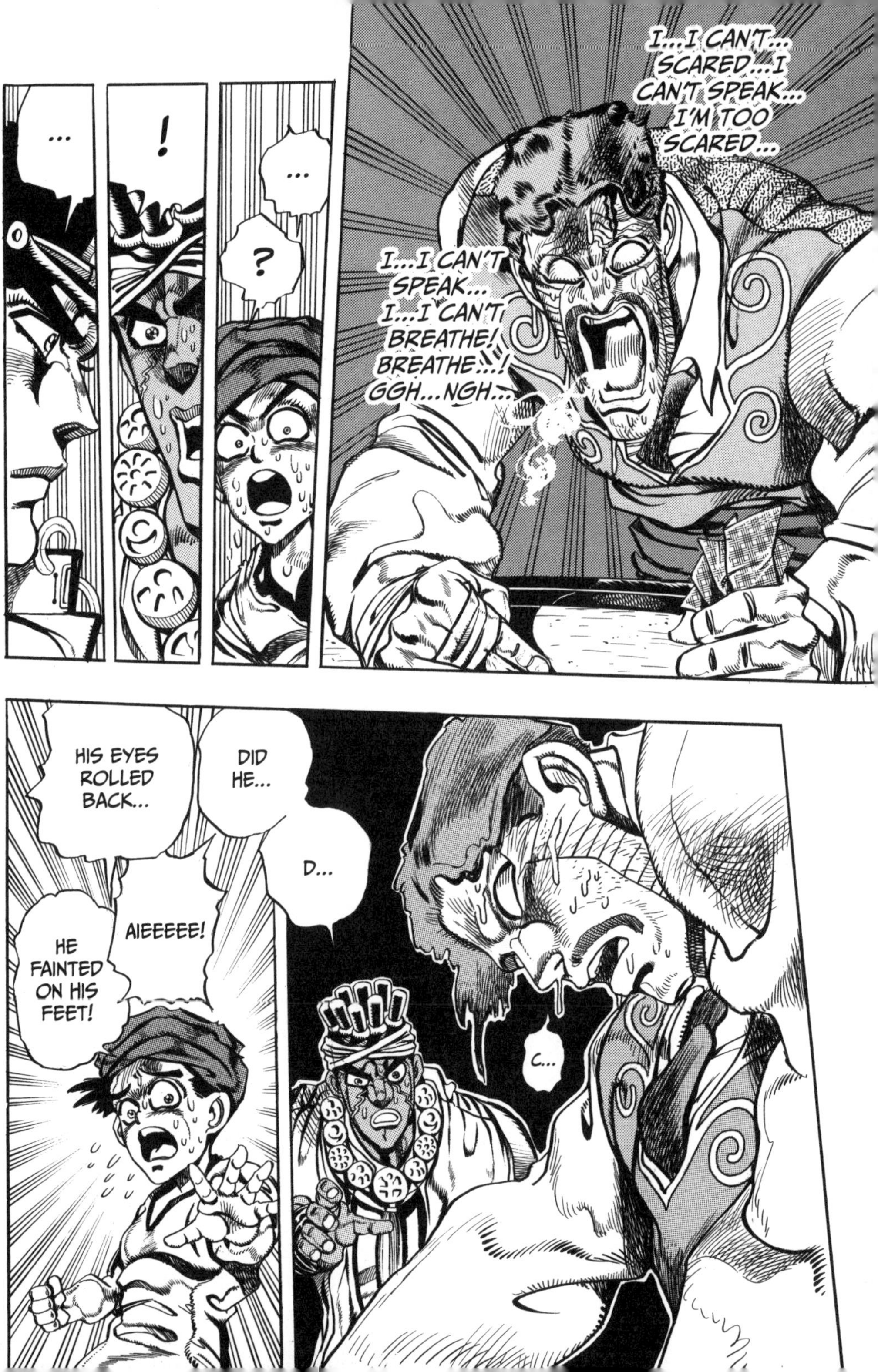
I...I CAN'T... SCARED...I CAN'T SPEAK... I'M TOO SCARED...
I...I CAN'T SPEAK... I...I CAN'T BREATHE! BREATHE...! GGH...NGH...
...
?
!
...
DID HE...
D...
C...
HIS EYES ROLLED BACK...
AIEEEEE!
HE FAINTED ON HIS FEET!

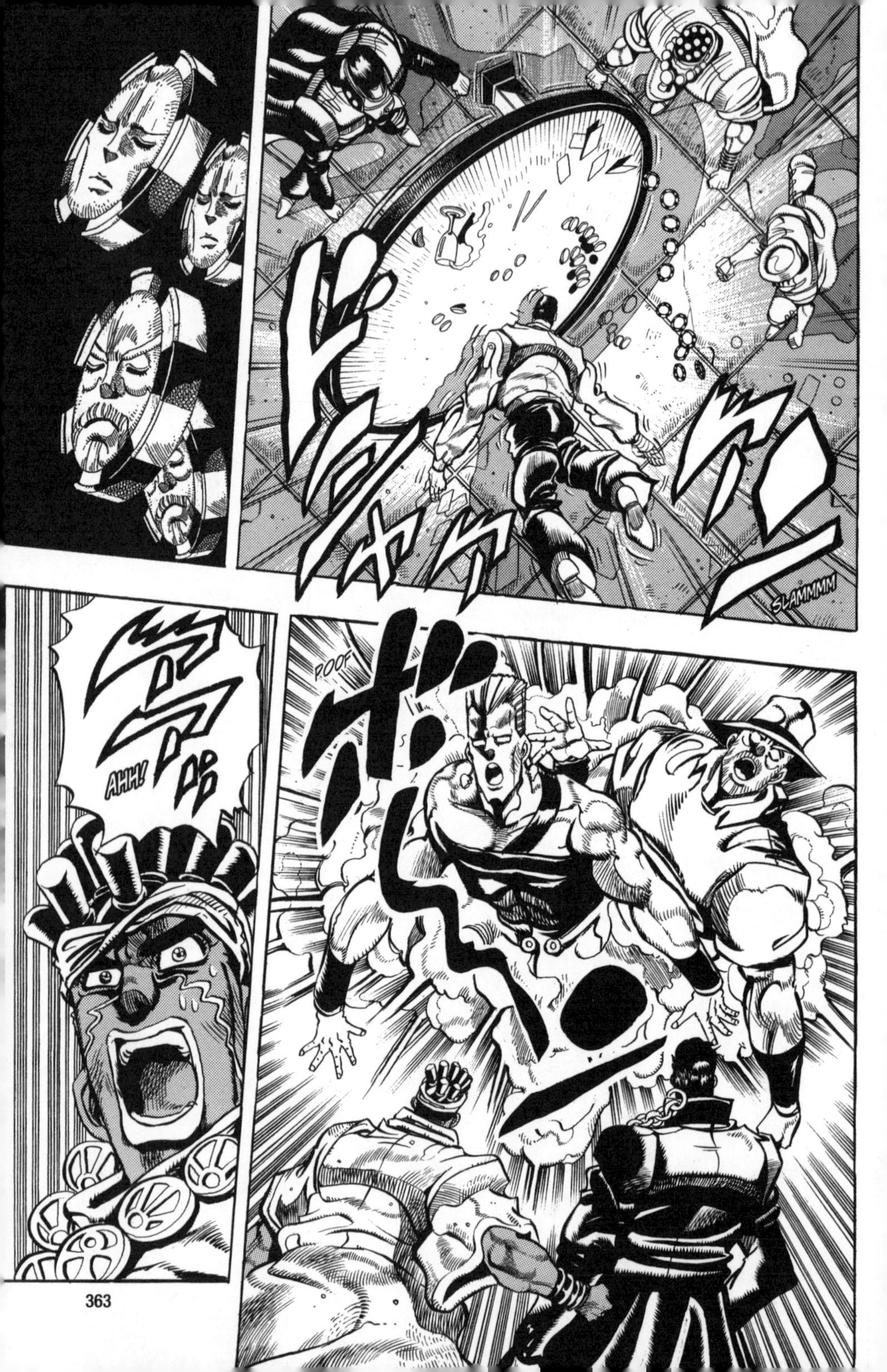
SLAMMMM
POOF
AHH!

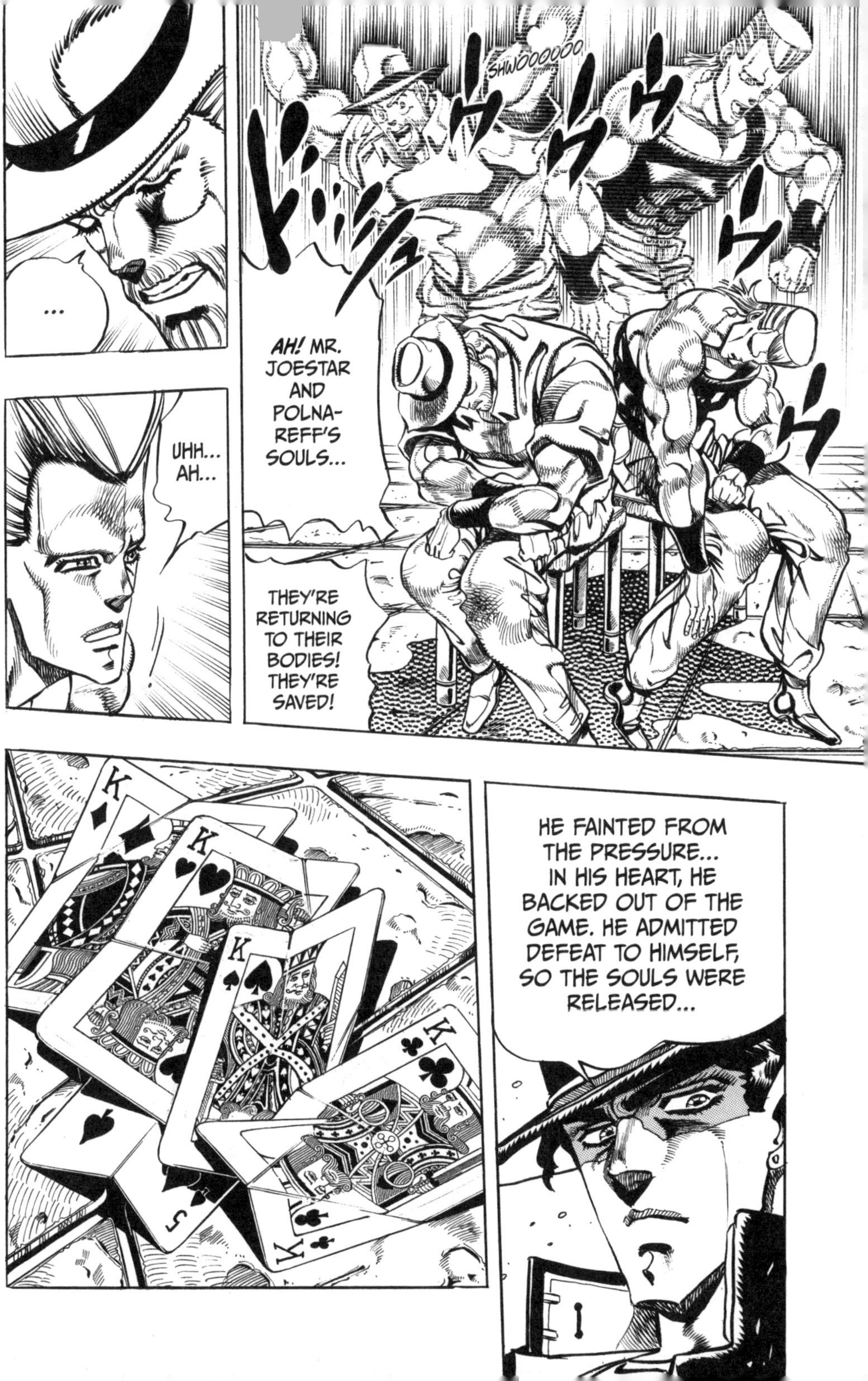
SHWOOOOOOO
AH! MR. JOESTAR AND POLNAREFF'S SOULS...
THEY'RE RETURNING TO THEIR BODIES! THEY'RE SAVED!
...
UHH... AH...
HE FAINTED FROM THE PRESSURE... IN HIS HEART, HE BACKED OUT OF THE GAME. HE ADMITTED DEFEAT TO HIMSELF, SO THE SOULS WERE RELEASED...

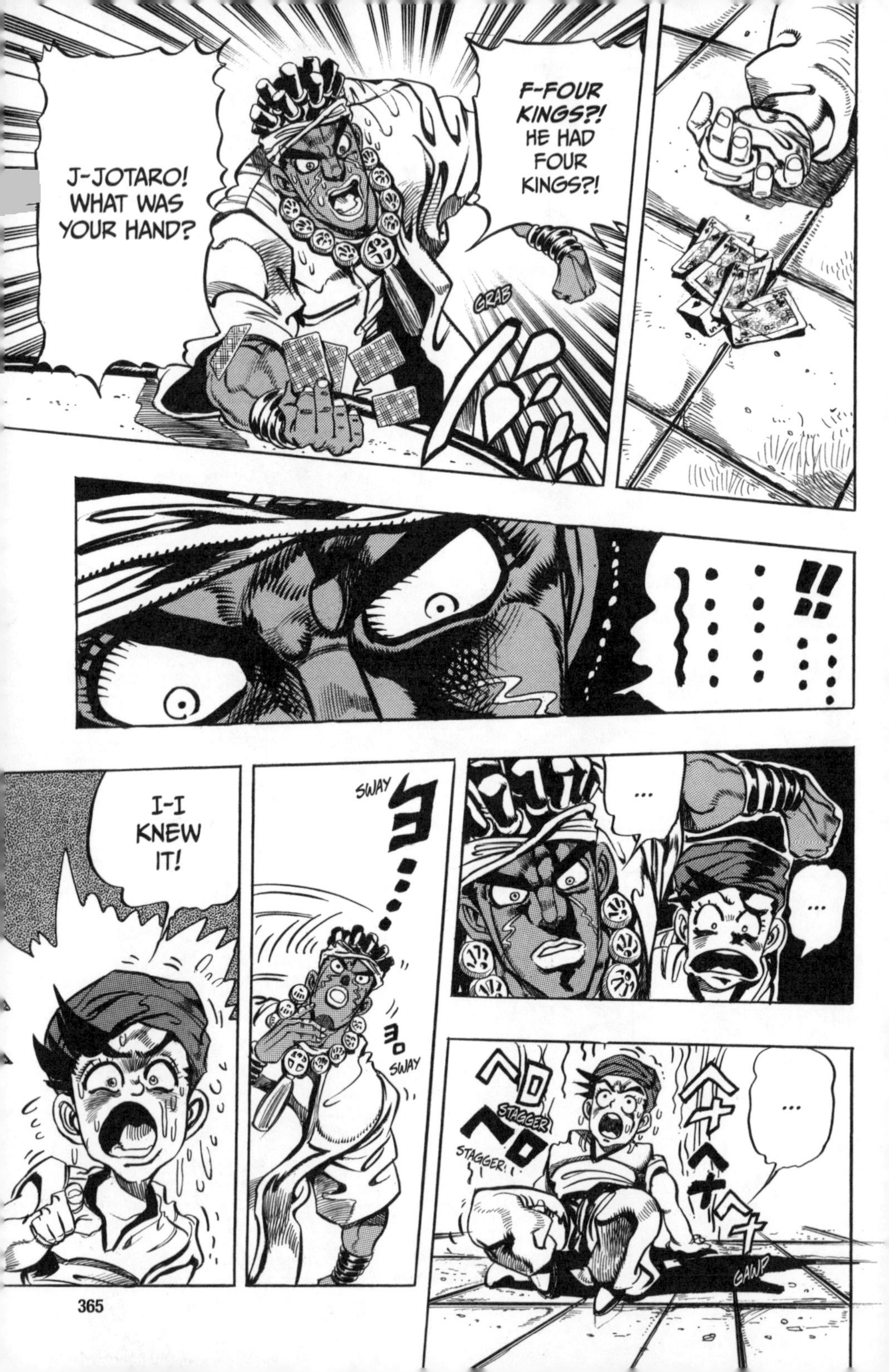

F-FOUR KINGS?! HE HAD FOUR KINGS?!
GRAB
J-JOTARO! WHAT WAS YOUR HAND?
...
...
...
STAGGER
STAGGER!
GAWP
SWAY
SWAY
I-I KNEW IT!

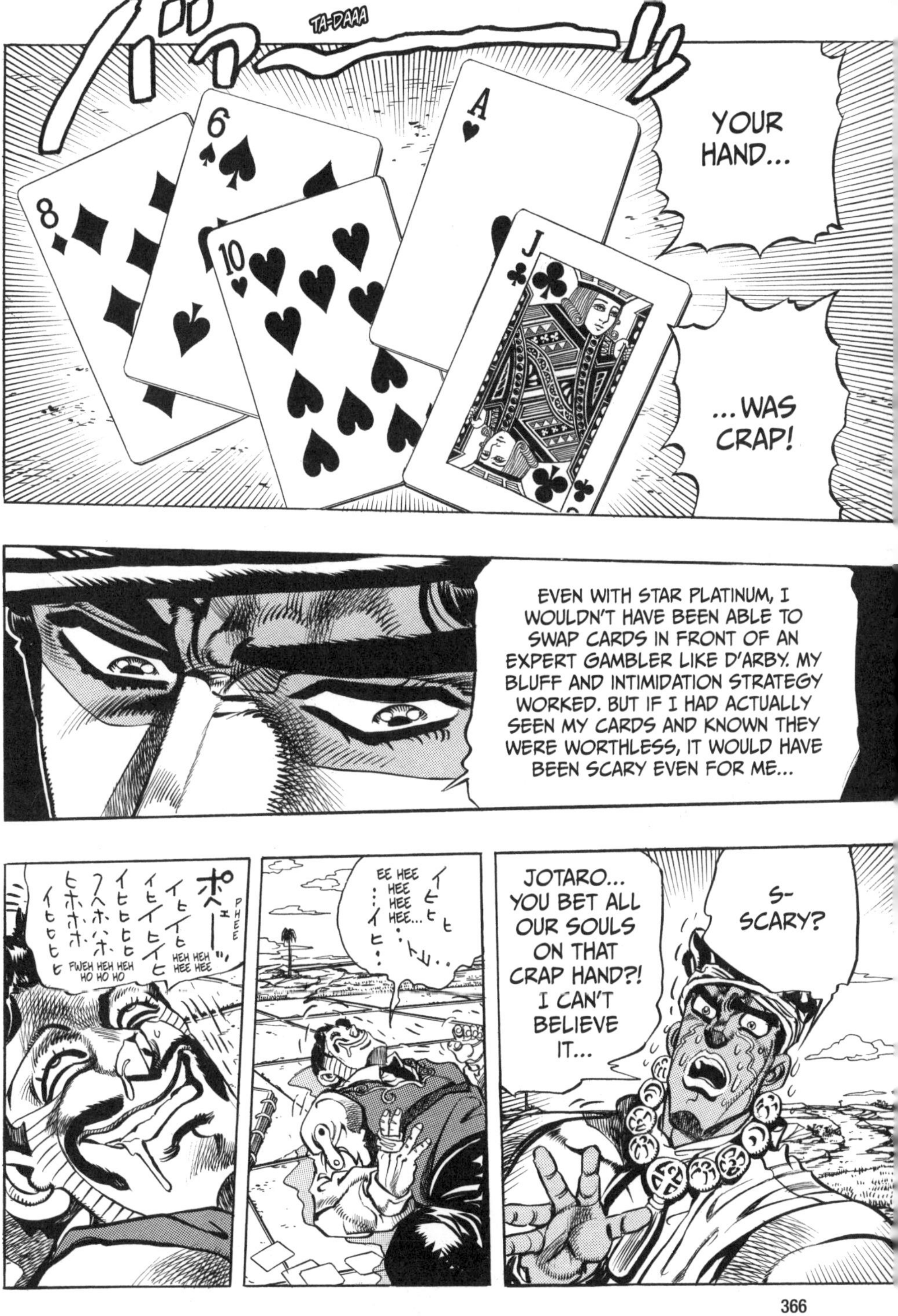
TA-DAAA
YOUR HAND...
...WAS CRAP!
EVEN WITH STAR PLATINUM, I WOULDN'T HAVE BEEN ABLE TO SWAP CARDS IN FRONT OF AN EXPERT GAMBLER LIKE D'ARBY. MY BLUFF AND INTIMIDATION STRATEGY WORKED. BUT IF I HAD ACTUALLY SEEN MY CARDS AND KNOWN THEY WERE WORTHLESS, IT WOULD HAVE BEEN SCARY EVEN FOR ME...
S-SCARY?
JOTARO... YOU BET ALL OUR SOULS ON THAT CRAP HAND?! I CAN'T BELIEVE IT...
EE HEE HEE HEE HEE...
PHEE
HEH HEH HEE HEE
FWEH HEH HEH HO HO HO

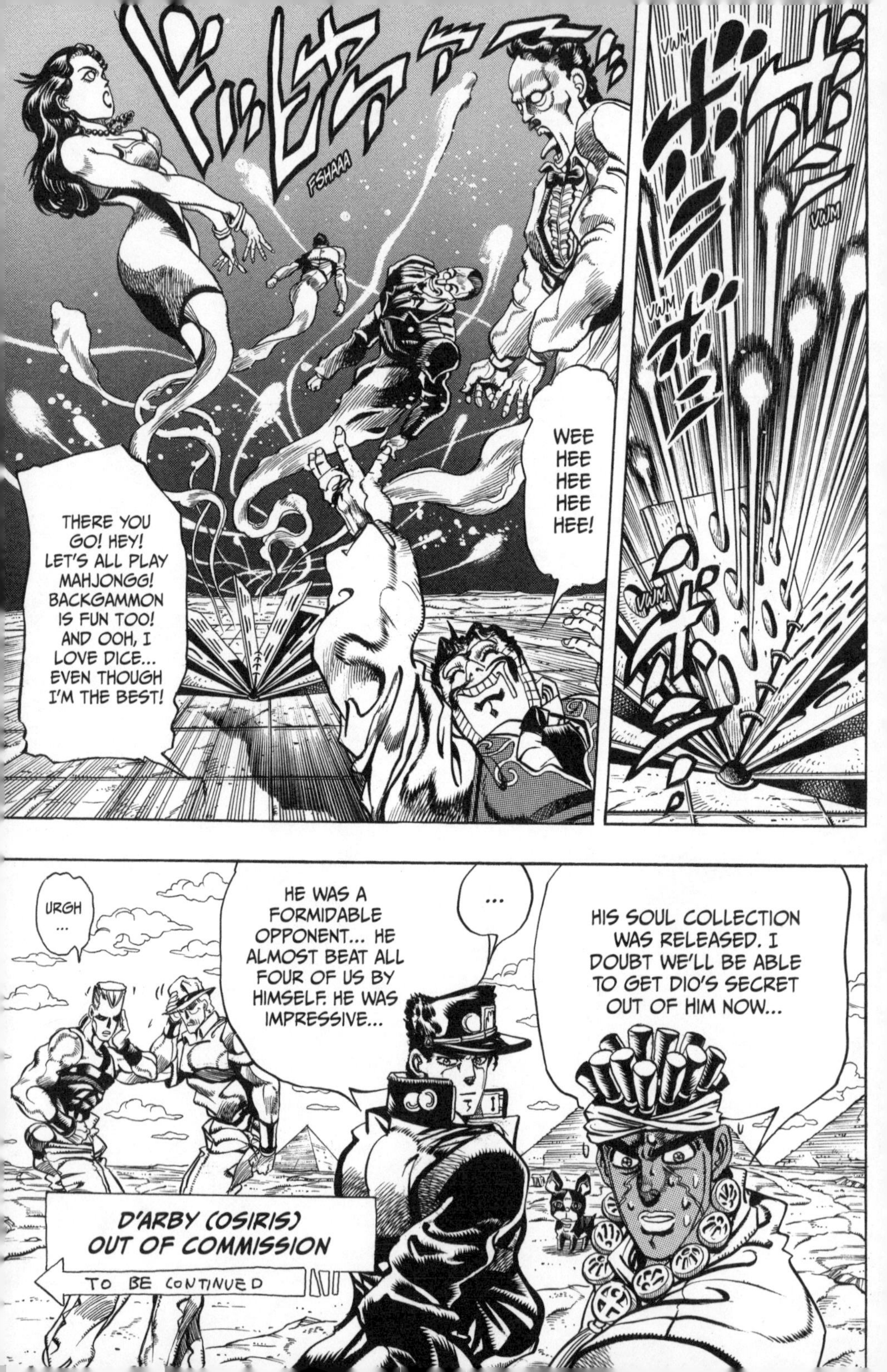
VWM
VWM
VWM
VWM
FSHAAA
WEE HEE HEE HEE HEE!
THERE YOU GO! HEY! LET'S ALL PLAY MAHJONGG! BACKGAMMON IS FUN TOO! AND OOH, I LOVE DICE... EVEN THOUGH I'M THE BEST!
HIS SOUL COLLECTION WAS RELEASED. I DOUBT WE'LL BE ABLE TO GET DIO'S SECRET OUT OF HIM NOW...
...
HE WAS A FORMIDABLE OPPONENT... HE ALMOST BEAT ALL FOUR OF US BY HIMSELF. HE WAS IMPRESSIVE...
URGH ...
D'ARBY (OSIRIS) OUT OF COMMISSION
TO BE CONTINUED

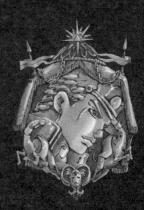

JoJo's
BIZARRE ADVENTURE

07

END

 To Be Continued

JoJo's BIZARRE ADVENTURE

07

Dd

荒木飛呂彦が
語る
キャラクター
誕生秘話

Hirohiko Araki talks about character creation!

JoJo's BIZARRE ADVENTURE
PART 3
STARDUST CRUSADERS

the Elder

07

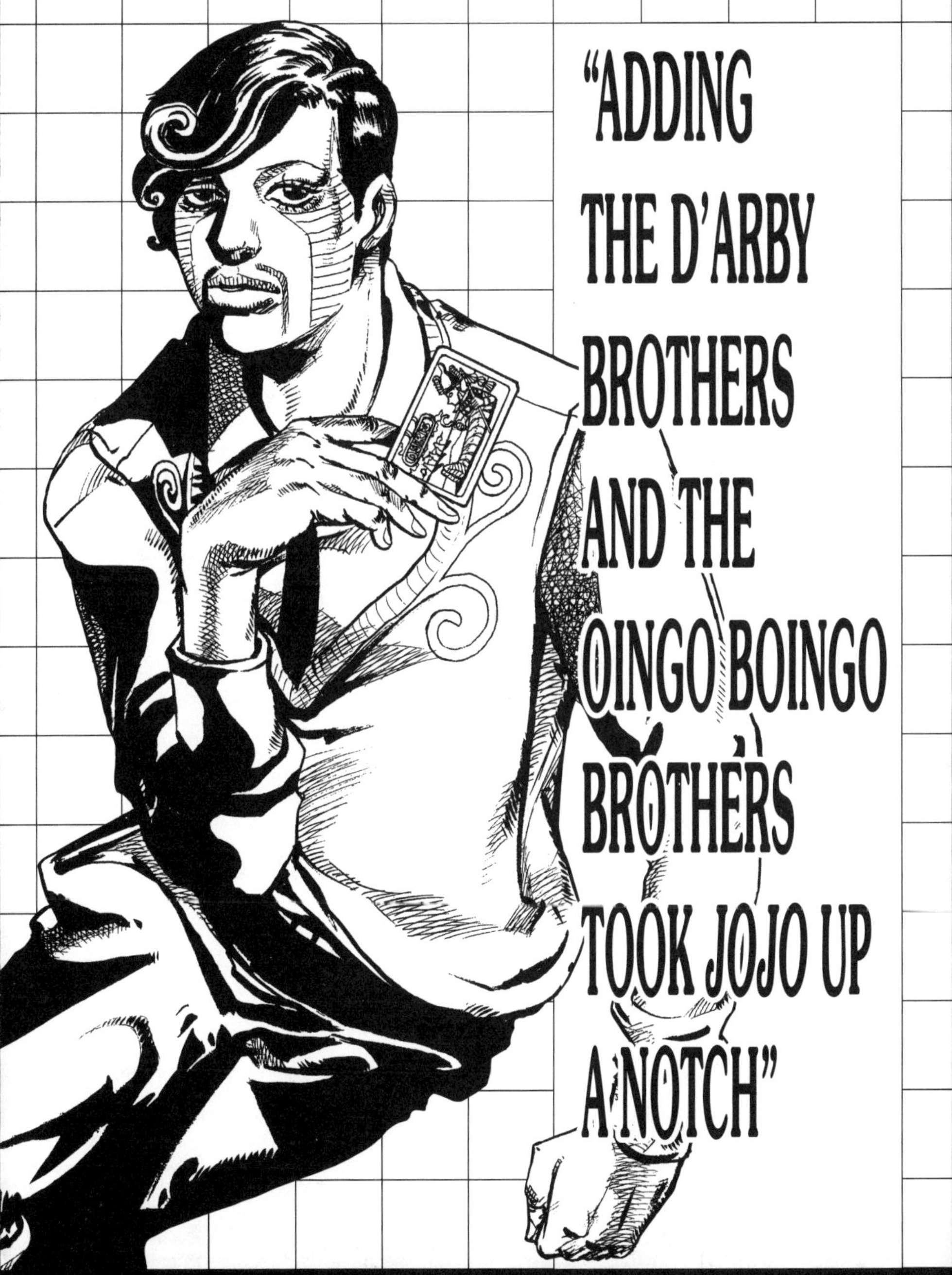
"ADDING THE D'ARBY BROTHERS AND THE OINGO BOINGO BROTHERS TOOK JOJO UP A NOTCH"

Dd

D'Arby

Given the evolution from the Hamon to Stands that came with *JoJo* entering Part 3, I wanted to include some battles that didn't just boil down to fistfights. I mentioned this in the Hol Horse retrospective, but I wanted to keep the face-offs between the Joestar party and DIO's minions fresh by switching back and forth between one-on-one battles and team battles, and as part of that, I needed to add some variance to the Stand abilities themselves as well. I actually did a "gambling battle" in *Cool Shock B.T.*, but I wanted to try doing it again differently as a Stand battle. D'Arby came from my desire to do that.

I think of gambling as something where you bet your own soul and pride as part of the process. To me, the money and chips you actually use at a real casino are just a representation of your soul. So it felt natural to have D'Arby take the souls from his opponents once they lost. Well, the fact that I can depict it the way I did is all thanks to the concept of Stands (*laughs*). As far as gambling is concerned, you can only win or lose--there is no in-between. With D'Arby as the sole challenger, I wanted to give him the mental fortitude and strategic cunning to give Jotaro a run for his money, as well as be able to instill some fear.

I had D'Arby face off with the Joestar party in a few different ways. I like coming up with ideas for gambling because you can turn almost anything into a bet. Bets involving animals are particularly interesting to me. It's hard to predict what they're going to do, so it works as a bet. I like situations where it doesn't seem possible to cheat, but maybe they actually are somehow. It's also important for the bet to feel like it fits *JoJo*. Poker is pretty mainstream, so I assume many of you have played it before, but the key point to winning at it is perfecting the "bluff." It's less of a surefire way to win the battle, and more of a battle of wits between you and your opponent, testing just how much you can fool them along with just how gutsy you are, so I think it was appropriate for the final face-off between Jotaro and D'Arby. I really enjoyed drawing the D'Arby battle, so I introduced his younger brother before the final showdown with DIO. I didn't want to give readers yet another poker match, so that time I had them play video games instead. Video games have all kinds of genres, like baseball or racing, so I had plenty of ideas to play around with, just like with the gambling theme.

Looking back on it now, I think introducing the D'Arby brothers and the Oingo Boingo brothers in Part 3 separated *JoJo* from other manga, because it allowed me to add just that much more variation to the battles. Jotaro and D'Arby's gambling battle led to Josuke and Rohan's dice battle in Part 4, and in *JoJolion*, which is being serialized right now, Josuke and Jobin's beetle fight. Battles in *JoJo* can be both fistfights and battles of wits. I think the D'Arby battle might have been the starting point for that.

The story behind the new illustration for JoJo Part 3 07!

Q. Who got turned into soul chips?!

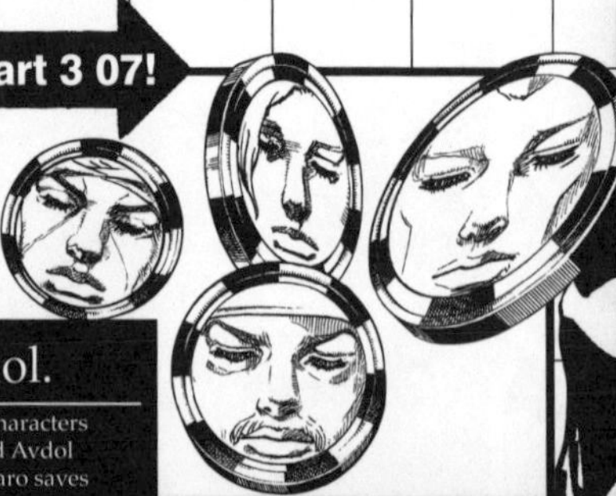

A. Polnareff, Joseph, Kakyoin and Avdol.

Only drawing two didn't seem like enough, and it wouldn't make sense to draw characters who didn't have anything to do with that part of the story, so I added Kakyoin and Avdol here as a special bonus. Looking at these, you can easily imagine a story where Jotaro saves

07

JoJo's Bizarre Adventure

Part 3 Stardust Crusaders

By

Hirohiko Araki

SHONEN JUMP ADVANCED EDITION
Translation ☆ Mayumi Kobayashi
Editor ☆ Jason Thompson

DELUXE HARDCOVER EDITION
Translation ☆ Evan Galloway
Touch-Up Art & Lettering ☆ Mark McMurray
Design ☆ Izumi Evers
Editor ☆ Urian Brown

Original Japanese cover design by
MITSURU KOBAYASHI (GENI A LÒIDE)

Printed in the U.S.A.

Published by VIZ Media, LLC
P.O. Box 77010
San Francisco, CA 94107

10 9 8 7 6 5 4 3 2 1
First printing, May 2018

RATED T+ FOR OLDER TEEN ratings.viz.com

PARENTAL ADVISORY
JOJO'S BIZARRE ADVENTURE PART THREE STARDUST CRUSADERS
is rated T+ for Older Teen and is recommended for ages 16 and up.
This volume contains graphic violence and some mature themes.

www.viz.com

SHONEN JUMP ADVANCED
www.shonenjump.com

Jo

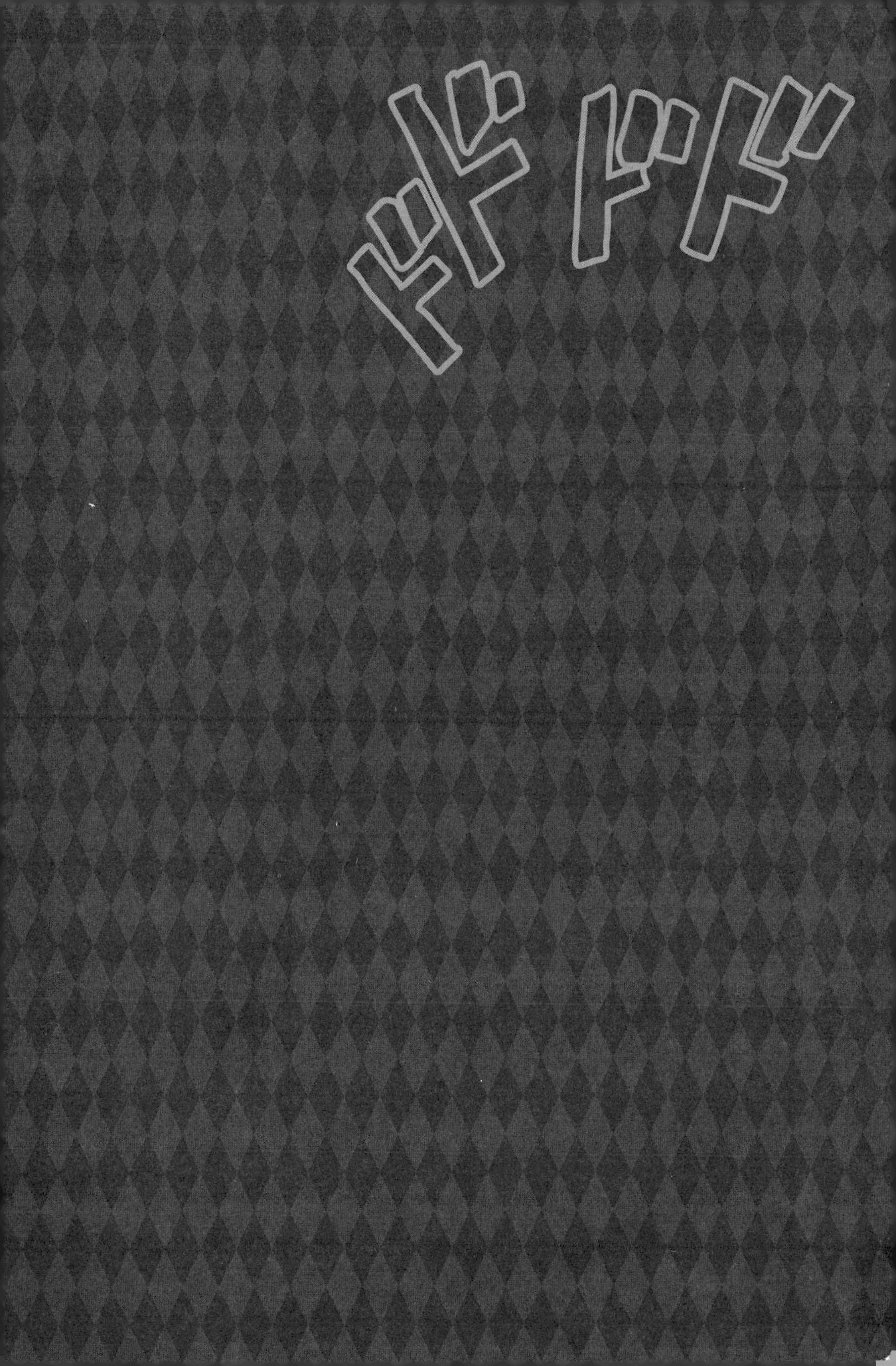
ドドドド

JO

JoJo's BIZARRE ADVENTURE

PART 3 STARDUST CRUSADERS

THIS IS THE LAST PAGE

ドドド

JoJo's Bizarre Adventure
has been printed in the original
Japanese format in order to
preserve the orientation of the
original artwork.

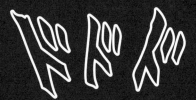

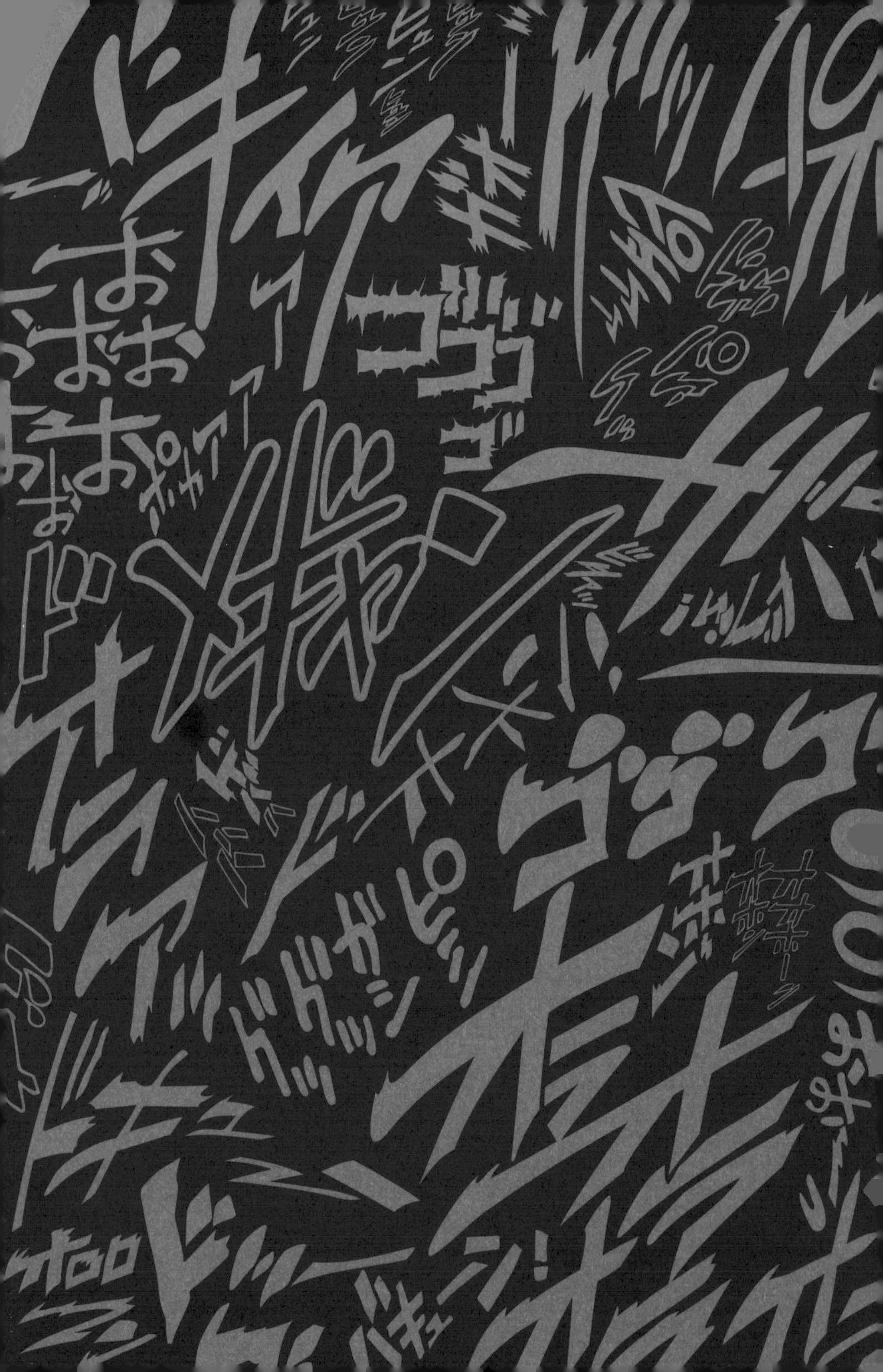
ゴゴゴゴ
ピッ
ホロロ